THE NEXT GENERATION WEB SOLUTION

To the reader

During the production stages of this book, international interest in Hyper-G has increased to such an extent that an international marketing and support company has been created. For trademark reasons, their commercial version of the Hyper-G software will be marketed under the name HyperWave. It will be available in May 1996. It will be identical to Hyper-G as described in this book but will have additional features in areas important for commercial applications: statistical packages, security and firewalls. For more information visit http://www.hyperwave.com.

The name Hyper-G will, for the time being, continue to be used in research and development.

HYPER-G now HYPERWAVE™
THE NEXT GENERATION WEB SOLUTION

Hermann Maurer

Institute for Information Processing and Computer Supported Media
Graz University of Technology

ADDISON-WESLEY PUBLISHING COMPANY

HARLOW, ENGLAND • READING, MASSACHUSETTS • MENLO PARK, CALIFORNIA • NEW YORK
DON MILLS, ONTARIO • AMSTERDAM • BONN • SYDNEY • SINGAPORE
TOKYO • MADRID • SAN JUAN • MILAN • MEXICO CITY • SEOUL • TAIPEI

Addison Wesley Longman Limited
Edinburgh Gate
Harlow
Essex
CM20 2JE
England

Cover designed by Designers & Partners, Oxford
Typeset by the author
Printed and bound in the United States of America

First printed 1996

ISBN 0–201–40346–3

British Library Cataloguing-in-Publication Data
A catalogue record for this book is available from the British Library.

Library of Congress Cataloging-in-Publication Data is available

Foreword

My first contact with Hyper-G was through the "Hacker's Jargon Dictionary" in 1990, when that collection of Internet jokes became available on the Web through the Hyper-G server in Graz. WWW was itself then in a start-up phase, and Tim (Berners-Lee) and I worked all the time at its implementation. Tim had a browser-editor running on NeXTStep (the original NeXT cube, now blissfully retired, still squats under my desk at CERN with the original computer center dust sticking to it). When Mosaic made the Web explode, we lost some of the original functions of that prototype browser, but it was clear even from 1990, that authors needed much more computing support at their server site than just wysiwyg HTML editing.

Our knowledge, as implemented by the Web, is grainy: there are things like servers, which hold collections of documents, and around those servers are, geographically located, groups of authors. And it is just as well that the Web is not smoothly distributed: we need some objects to focus on, such as the local school, the tourist info of Munich, the art collections of the Louvre, the frogs of Australia, the armor museum of Graz.

As Hyper-G matured (and how often have I witnessed the brilliant multimedia demonstration by Keith Andrews, until my neural network began to equate Hyper-G with fractal mountains and rock music) it became increasingly clear to me that it would make a very good authoring server: here were all the tools that we really wanted, but which the extremely distributed nature of WWW prevented us from even thinking about.

Hyper-G is the workbench of the Internet publishing workgroup: here we can author collections of documents, apply various transformations and semantics, experiment with multimedia documents. Yet at the end of the day, the community of users out there can use their ordinary Web browsers to look at what we have done. Anyone who has struggled with a flat set of HTML files in pure text will appreciate the structuring support that Hyper-G offers. Maintenance of structure in large numbers of documents becomes affordable. But there is much more: authors will find support for versions, multiple languages (a very European problem), cooperative work and so on.

This book is a tribute to the work of many dedicated developers, some I have met, some not, but I admire the efforts of all of them. It is my pleasure to recommend this volume to anyone who considers setting up "an Internet site." Enjoy reading this very informative and richly detailed description of the most advanced authoring server available!

Robert Cailliau
Geneva, CERN, Switzerland, December 1995

Preface

The Internet continues to expand dramatically. Wide-area multimedia information systems starting with Gopher achieved a breakthrough and a first climax with WWW, the World Wide Web. Developed by pioneers at CERN, WWW has changed the Internet to the extent that "the Web" has become almost synonymous with the modern use of the Internet. However, the tremendous success of WWW is also creating problems. WWW was never designed to handle so many and such large applications as numerous organizations are starting to use it for. An evolutionary step, to take us from "first-generation" Web systems to more powerful "second-generation" systems, is necessary and is now in the making. This is what this book is all about: describing the next evolutionary step beyond WWW and how you can profit from it.

This book is for everyone who intends to become a major player on the Internet, or "the Web" as we will keep calling it. Whether you provide a server to clients, offer services worldwide, offer services to a particular organization, or even if you are just a serious user who wants to be free of restrictions of earlier Web tools this book will probably help you. This book is also for those who feel that their current system is reaching the limits of manageability, yet want to preserve their investment by seamlessly being able to use their current database with increased functionality and better data management. Finally, this book is for all those who want to develop software based on Hyper-G. The Hyper-G Consortium (HGC) supports such activities (see Appendix C for details).

This book is for practitioners; but it is also for those who want to teach practitioners: be it in seminars, schools or universities. It is a good companion to the more theoretical and technical hypermedia books required for the in-depth understanding required for, say, advanced computer science courses or as the basis for research. It is not intended, however, as a survey or in-depth study of all issues concerning multimedia and hypermedia systems. It concentrates on what you can do now, and how to do it.

Depending on whether you read this book as a serious services provider, user or teacher, you will take slightly different paths through this book. After reading it, you will have a clear understanding of the power of second-generation hypermedia systems; you will know why they are necessary and why they will replace current systems wherever substantial amounts of data are involved; you will have learnt the important features of the first second-generation hypermedia system Hyper-G and you will be able to set it up and run it with the software that comes with this book. You will also have understood enough of the general issues to appreciate the design decisions of Hyper-G, to see it as a logical extension of both Gopher and WWW that preserves full interoperability with those systems. Finally, you will probably have learnt about possible applications that you have never dreamt of before. We also hope that after having read this book you will be a Hyper-G fan and that you will join us in the exciting effort of using second-generation hypermedia systems to their full potential.

Hermann Maurer
Graz, Austria, January 1996

Acknowledgments

In presenting the background and details of Hyper-G, this book describes the outcome of the efforts of a team of researchers and developers mainly at the Graz University of Technology. Hyper-G would not have been possible without the support of the Austrian Federal Ministry for Science, Research and Arts, the government of the province of Styria through JOANNEUM RESEARCH and a number of research grants too numerous to list here.

Above all, Hyper-G would not have been possible without the support of colleagues and organizations from all over the world. It is not possible to mention all, but it is fair to make an attempt to mention at least a few: Bruno Buchberger from Linz, for his support and for accepting the directorship of the Hyper-G Consortium; Dieter Fellner from Bonn for his work on computer graphics and digital libraries; Thomas Ottmann from Freiburg for his belief in Hyper-G's suitability for teleteaching; Martin Grötschel and his team from Berlin including Joachim Lügger, Wolfgang Dalitz and Gernot Heyer for their critical evaluation of Hyper-G, for writing the first book about Hyper-G (Dalitz and Heyer, 1995) and proposing it as the distributed information system for all activities of the German Mathematical Society; Richard Christ from the Austrian Ministry of Science and Research and Hubert Partl from Austria's agricultural university for endless hours of testing and valuable suggestions; Gerhard Triebnig from the European Space Agency for making it possible to adapt Hyper-G for ESA applications; Zavisa Bjelogrlic from Intecs in Italy as one of the first to use Hyper-G commercially; Hans Steiner from Siemens Austria as an early proponent of Hyper-G as both the basis of projects and a company-internal information system; Robert Cailliau from CERN, one of the fathers of WWW, for encouraging us to move beyond WWW; Mark McCahill, chief designer of Gopher, for his help and cooperation; Joseph Hardin from the NCSA for his cooperation on VRML and other aspects of Hyper-G; Cris Calude from Auckland and Arto Salomaa from Turku for suggesting Hyper-G as the basis for J.UCS, the *Journal of Universal Computer Science*; and Arnoud de Kemp from Springer who helped to make J.UCS a reality; the over 170 J.UCS editors who have contributed to establish Hyper-G as a basis for electronic publishing to the extent that a range of publishing companies including Springer, Academic Press, Addison-Wesley, Wiley, Meyer, Bibliographisches Institut, Langenscheidt and Oxford University Press are now using Hyper-G or Hyper-G spin-offs; the HyperMedia Unit of the University of Auckland for supporting Hyper-G from the beginning; MONZ, the Museum of New Zealand, with Channa Jayasinha as the first testbed of Hyper-G in the context of museums; Ed Fox from Virginia Tech, David Skillicorn from Queens University in Ontario, Dan Sutherland from Pittsburgh and Steve Poltrock from Boeing in Seattle as the first Hyper-G users and constructive critics in the USA and Canada; Ivan Tomek from Acadia University in Canada for important advice in the design phase; Peter Wegner from Brown University for continuing encouragement; Pat Hall from the Open University in the UK for a careful evaluation of Hyper-G for European projects; Gunter Schlageter from the Distance Education University of Hagen in Germany for getting Lufthansa interested in Hyper-G; Gerhard Barth from Daimler Benz for considering Hyper-G as a tool for storing corporate knowhow;

Udo Flohr for his very careful and positive evaluation of Hyper-G; Jakob Nielsen and Billy Barron for their early interest in Hyper-G as noticeable in their recent publications on hypertext/hypermedia (Nielsen, 1995) and the Internet (Barron *et al.*, 1995); Georg Stork from the European Commission for his interest in Hyper-G for digital library projects; our partners in a number of European research projects; Austrian organizations such as WIFI, Bundeswirtschaftskammer, the University of Klagenfurt and others who started with Hyper-G early on, and, above all, the large number of current Hyper-G users who have stuck with us through a long series of early problems, improvements and bug fixes. To all of them, and to many who have not been mentioned, a cordial thank-you: thank you for helping us in moving from first-generation success stories such as Gopher and WWW to the next generation of hypermedia systems in which we believe Hyper-G will have a significant role to play.

Finally, as editor of this book my special thanks go to the other authors as listed in the various chapter headings; to all other members of the Hyper-G team at Graz who have substantially contributed to Hyper-G yet do not appear as authors, such as Jörg Faschingbauer, Mansuet Gaisbauer, Bernhard Heidegger and Bernhard Marschall. My thanks also go to all our students who have worked with, tested, criticized and improved Hyper-G, to Robin Balean from Australia who helped polish our English and Achim Schneider from Germany who was instrumental in the final phase to get this manuscript out in a proper format; and finally to Addison-Wesley for helping us make this book project a reality.

Hermann Maurer
Graz, Austria, January 1996

Contents

1 Introduction

Hermann Maurer

In this chapter we explain why this book was written, for whom it is intended, how to use it and – most important of all – why you will benefit from reading it.

1.1 General

Computer networks have been around for a long time. Initially, they were mainly used for organization-internal matters. As they grew and became more and more widespread, other applications such as **Email** and file transfers (FTP) became increasingly important. The wide penetration of the **Internet** helped; however, it was the advent of **Gopher** that, for the first time, allowed the average computer user to see the Internet as an easy to use worldwide information repository. While Gopher started the first ripples, the big wave of change towards an information society came with **WWW**, the **World Wide Web**. We are now seeing the world of computer networks dominated by WWW. Intensive and often over-hyped media coverage seems to indicate that with current systems the future **information society** is about to be upon us and that it is only the speed of current communication links that is currently frustrating us: we all have seen messages such as "please wait" or "document being downloaded" more often than we care for.

But even if the problem of speed is neglected, sparks of unrest are brewing. Those more deeply involved in the modern Internet, or the **Web**, as it is now often called in deference to the tremendous success of WWW, have become increasingly aware that the Web will and must develop further. Gopher, easy to use databases and WWW have paved the way for the massive use of the Internet and other computer networks as **first-generation tools**, but are reaching their limits. In the explosively growing pool of information that is available worldwide, finding pertinent information is getting ever more difficult; administrating large amounts of data is equally frustrating with the tools now at hand; new applications – whether they be **teleshopping, teleteaching, telepublishing, networked discussions** or **network-based co-operation** (to name a few) require new techniques. The first generation of WWW tools has to and is about to evolve towards a second-generation set of tools. These will retain all that we have learned to like and appreciate about WWW but will alleviate some of the most evident shortcomings.

This is what this book is all about: a new second-generation hypermedia system called **Hyper-G** that extends WWW. In discussing Hyper-G in relation to other systems such as Gopher, **WAIS** and traditional WWW, you will understand the beauty of the simplicity of those early systems; you will see that for first fledgling steps on the Web and for small amounts of information those systems may be quite adequate. You will also learn to appreciate the limits of those systems that will force you, if you are a serious information provider or even just a sophisticated user, to go beyond first-generation systems to second-generation versions of WWW such as Hyper-G at some stage. To be able to compare what is explained to you in writing with the "real thing," a **CD-ROM** is provided with this book; you may want to use it on either a PC (Windows 3.1 or higher) or a UNIX workstation for hands-on experience with Hyper-G and the Web.

1.2   Audience of this book

This book is more or less self-contained. It only assumes a vague familiarity with Email, FTP, computer-based multimedia and WWW. It addresses a fairly broad audience:

(1) It is written for all those who are interested to learn (or to teach) the important issues involved in large networked multimedia systems. However, a word of caution is in place: as comprehensive as this book is, it is more directed towards practical aspects, rather than towards some of the theoretical underpinnings. To be concrete, selecting appropriate chapters of this book will, for example, provide a good basis for courses on multimedia at various levels in most disciplines; but the book should not be used on its own for advanced courses in computer science since we have not included deeper discussions of such things as standards, database theory, compression techniques, network protocols and so on. For such issues, the literature referred to in the further reading sections at the end of the chapters should be consulted.

(2) The book is further designed for all those who want to set up a substantial Web server, either for the general public on the Internet or for organization-internal applications (maybe behind **firewalls**), or for both. It contains enough information to set up and operate a Hyper-G server, to perform user and data administration, to provide the overall structure of information and services to be offered, to input data, to convert existing material (for example, in standard databases) to a format suitable for the Web and to design gateways to other information systems.

Hyper-G allows the seamless incorporation of WWW and Gopher databases (as described in Chapters 20 and 21) and thus allows for the concentration of otherwise dispersed material. Hyper-G software is free for educational institutions and is available to others very liberally (see Appendix C).

(3) This book is also written for all those who operate a substantial Gopher or WWW server and are having serious problems administrating the information as the data volume increases. Such people may wish to structure the data automatically in a semi-hierarchical fashion; they may want to add attributes to documents (such as creation or expiry date

and author) so that they will be better able to locate documents again at a later stage; they may need to define subsets of their data to be used in full text queries; they may desire to restrict access to certain parts of the database for specific groups of persons; they may need to support documents in more than one language or version; they may wish to provide users with better navigational tools; they may find it desirable to allow users to "customize" information to their needs; they may feel the necessity for automatic link maintenance or even generation; and so on. All these features and many more are routinely available in second-generation hypermedia systems such as Hyper-G.

Since simple procedures are available to "roll over" a Gopher or a WWW database into Hyper-G, providers of Web services will be confronted with the decision of when is the best time to upgrade their servers to Hyper-G. This book is intended to provide a solid foundation for this decision.

(4) This book should also satisfy those who do not want to install a Web server, but just use an existing one for offering their services to a wide public. Special tools (such as the **"gardening" and "linkage" facilities** of **Amadeus** and **Harmony,** and the scripting and conversion utilities for Hyper-G) are discussed in sufficient detail for practical applications.

(5) This book was also written for more sophisticated Web users: for those who are fed up with **"getting lost in hyperspace"** and hence want to employ **location feedback, local maps** and **information landscapes** for convenient navigation (**surfing the Web**); for those who not only want to use the Web for simple information retrieval but also for more advanced facilities like restructuring information for a **personalized view**, adding links and **annotations** to material of interest, participating in discussions and carrying out **transactions** beyond the simple ones usually associated with WWW.

(6) This book also explains how to use the Web for special applications such as **electronic publishing**, building **digital libraries**, supporting fancy **multimedia presentations**, offering **courseware** and teleteaching facilities on the Web, combining Web and CD-ROM publishing, organizing Web-based **computer conferencing**, or using the Web for preparing and supporting conventional symposia. The above list is by no means exhaustive but only indicative of the wide range of applications of second-generation hypermedia systems such as Hyper-G.

(7) Finally, this book contains enough information to extend Hyper-G to suit individual requirements an organization may have, particularly concerning the user interface or the integration of existing software.

1.3   How to use this book

As explained in Section 1.2 this book addresses quite a large and varied audience. Hence not all chapters are necessarily of importance to all readers. In every case, we suggest you start by superficially reading Chapters 1–10, returning for details later as may be necessary. To make the reading of independent parts of this book possible, we have deliberately provided some redundancy; in other words, essential information is sometimes discussed in more than one chapter from slightly different points of view. It is thus possible to some degree to read chapters independently of others, using the cross-references provided where necessary. For a systematic study of the book and following the classification of Section 1.2 we recommend the following chapters for each of the groups (1)–(7):

(1) Chapters 15, 17, 19–22

(2) Chapters 11–25

(3) Chapters 11–25

(4) Chapters 15–19 and 22–25

(5) Chapters 15, 17, 19 and 22

(6) Chapters 12–19, 22–30

(7) Chapters 11–31

In each of the above cases the remaining chapters will be of interest to some extent, depending on the individual situation.

1.4   Hyper-G: How does it differ from WWW and Gopher?

Hyper-G is an extension of WWW. Hyper-G servers provide WWW pages with lots of additional functionality: WWW can be considered as a "thin interface layer" that allows you to access and display multimedia documents; WWW as such does not support any data and link management, search facilities, authorization mechanisms and so on. Thus, as a WWW database grows, its administration gets very cumbersome and modules have to be continually added to "prop it up" and satisfy user needs. This leads to systems with a small WWW core and an assortment of modules added to it; different installations have a different assortment. This results in a system which is increasingly incompatible and nonuniform from a user's point of view. In contrast, Hyper-G integrates all the functionality of WWW with a clean set of tools, assuring much additional functionality yet complete compatibility across diverse user sites. This compatibility has far-reaching consequences as will be explained later. In particular, **link consistency** within servers and across server boundaries can be assured and **searches** in a combination of parts of even different Hyper-G databases become possible. To be concrete, consider the following example: how often have you clicked on a link in WWW and received a message such as "Object cannot be located"? It is this kind of "**link inconsistency**" that can be avoided with Hyper-G.

It has to be clearly understood that Hyper-G is really just a very powerful WWW server; it is not a new system, but the extension of an existing one. Thus, conventional WWW viewers such as **Mosaic**, **Netscape Navigator**, **Spyglass** or whatever your favorites are work great with Hyper-G; conversely, "native" Hyper-G viewers such as Harmony (Chapters 15, 16 and 23) and Amadeus (Chapters 17, 18 and 24) work fine with all conventional WWW servers. The native Hyper-G viewers (the term "client" will also be used synonymously with "viewer") exploit some specific features of Hyper-G servers a bit better than "generic" viewers but are, above all, powerful editing tools. However, if you prefer to use other tools for editing and you are satisfied with your current viewer, you may never want to touch a native Hyper-G viewer. Actually, this is oversimplifying matters: it is probably true if you are mainly interested in occasionally browsing the Web; but if you are using the Web professionally, you will miss out on a lot if you never use some of the functionality of native Hyper-G clients, particularly if you are an information provider!

Since Hyper-G allows you to incorporate WWW databases as they are, it is often worthwhile to move up from ordinary WWW servers to Hyper-G, providing database and structuring facilities desperately needed for large amounts of data. As a by-product, Hyper-G allows you to combine physically remote Hyper-G servers into one database (in other words, Hyper-G can act as a so-called "**distributed database**") with a single command. This allows you, for example, to search a large number of servers run by a university with a single query, rather than having to direct this query to all individual servers. If this sounds confusing right now, do not worry: we are trying to whet your appetite for Hyper-G but will discuss all of these features in detail later.

The relationship between Hyper-G and Gopher (or **Gopher⁺**) is somewhat similar: the structuring facilities of Gopher are a step towards those in Hyper-G. Hence Hyper-G can also be considered a "superset" of Gopher. Gopher and Hyper-G clients can both access Gopher and Hyper-G servers and a simple utility allows you to "roll over" a complete Gopher database into Hyper-G. WWW is currently much more widespread than Gopher, despite the fact that modern versions of Gopher really offer all of WWW, and more. Be that as it may, if you were to start with a WWW or Gopher database, it is good to know that moving up to a second-generation system such as Hyper-G is easy, whenever the need arises. Although some parts of Table 1.1 will not make much sense right now, it will show why upgrading from, say, ordinary WWW to Hyper-G servers will be advisable sooner or later.

1.5   Hyper-G: More than an information presentation system

Networked multimedia systems such as WWW are often seen as mainly information presentation systems.

This is a major misunderstanding: if the Web only allowed the presentation of information, it would have neither the potential to be a major step towards the information society, nor the potential to be a long-lasting commercial success.

Nice presentations on the Web are great, sure. Some information providers fall so much in love with pictures, movie clips and all kinds of gadgets that they force us to waste our time watching these gimmicks!

Table 1.1   Features of first-generation and second-generation WWW.

Feature	First-generation WWW	Second-generation WWW like Hyper-G
Bidirectional links	no	yes
Separate link database	no	yes
Hierarchical structure	no	yes
Document attributes	no	yes
Authorization facilities	limited	yes
Inherent multilingual support	no	yes
HTML support	yes	yes
PDF support	announced	announced
HTF support	no	yes
HM-Card support	yes	yes
Integrated search facilities	no	yes
Automated CD-ROM production	no	yes
Typed links	no	partial
Link authorization	no	partial
Form support	yes	yes
Clickable maps	yes	yes
Distributed database architecture	no	yes
Access control for billing	partial	partial
Annotations	partial	yes

However, information presented to us is only part of the picture. The feedback from users to the information providers is at least as important! Information providers, when asked about the most important feature of the Web, routinely answer: the **form feature**. That is, the possibility to let users fill out a form, as a questionnaire, as a registration or ordering form, for voting, or whatever.

In more general terms, the future of the Web depends not only on how well organized and up-to-date the information we find in it is (and we will return to this point shortly), but at least as much on how well it will support communication features, transactions and other special applications.

Forms that can be filled out on the Web are a rudimentary means of communication. Beyond this, the Web would have to allow structured discussions between groups of persons (such as the extension of Email facilities, which also needs to become more integrated) and support collaborative work, to mention two of the most important communicational components. Hyper-G with its general annotation facility and "scripting support" goes a long way in this direction ... its architecture is open to further improvements.

When we talk about transactions on the Web we usually mean things like registering for events and ordering items, or even tasks requiring very high security such as financial transactions. We will discuss those applications in detail in this book and will particularly show how electronic publishing and digital libraries can be readily supported by Hyper-G (see Chapters 26 and 28).

The Web should also provide other facilities. Again we can use Hyper-G to show where we are heading and how you can use Hyper-G to do things you may have always wanted to do: like teleteaching over the Web or distributing courseware specifically tailored for use on the Web (see Chapters 27 and 29); how to combine Web and CD-ROM publishing, how to use the Web for entertainment purposes, and how to tailor the Web by imposing your very personal view. Finally, let us back up completely and return to the question of providing information on the Web.

There is a German saying that it is easy to become a father, but difficult to be one. Well, it is also easy to put information onto the Web. But it is quite difficult to keep expanding it, to "put up" large quantities of information and to keep the information up-to-date. Experience has shown over and over again that substantial quantities of information can only be kept up-to-date, on any information system such as the Web, if two conditions are met: (a) if it is possible to automatically import information either from existing databases or as a by-product of other activities; (b) if the system supports consistency maintenance as much as possible.

Both issues are addressed in Hyper-G and in this book (see mainly Chapter 25). However, to give you the flavor of things, here are two typical examples:

Suppose a Web server contains a document announcing a seminar talk for 3 March 1996. What would an ordinary Web server do on 4 March 1996? Unfortunately nothing! It is up to the person responsible for the information in the server to manually do something with this now obsolete document. What does a more advanced Web server like Hyper-G do when properly used? When the document is entered this is done with "expiry date 4 March 1996" and the script "seminar collection." When 4 March 1996 rolls around, the Hyper-G server automatically moves the document from the collection "Upcoming events" to "Seminar talks of 1996." On 1 January 1997 the document is automatically dealt with again, copying it, say, into the collection "Seminar talks 1991–2000," to be available for a "Ten Year Report."

As a second example, suppose the document at issue is not the announcement of a seminar but the request for a donation with the same expiry date, and the document should be entirely deleted after the expiry date. If no script is associated with the document Hyper-G will delete the document ... and do more: if other documents have links to this call for a donation, all those links are automatically removed!

1.6   Should you continue reading this book?

Do not continue reading this book (and try to return it to the bookstore immediately!) if you thought the Web has something to do with spiders or weaving carpets. Also discontinue reading if you never intend to use a computer in a network. However, if you have been using the Internet (the "Web"), and you are not convinced that what you have seen there is easy to use and orderly, then you should continue reading. Likewise, if you are not entirely sure how you can use the Web to your maximum advantage.

1.7 Further reading

The classic introductory paper to Hypermedia (even though it is a bit dated) is Conklin (1987). A more modern survey is Tomek *et al.* (1991). An excellent general book on Hypermedia is Nielsen (1995), while Buford-Koegel (1994) is more dedicated to matters of standards and technical details. A modified version of the classic paper on Gopher is McCahill and Anklesaria (1995), on WWW Berners-Lee *et al.* (1992, 1994). The first major exposition of design issues of Hyper-G is Kappe (1991), while Andrews *et al.* (1994) is a short summary of why Hyper-G is a second-generation system. Some of the historically earliest and most influential contributions are Bush (1986) and Nelson (1987).

To keep up-to-date it is important to follow a number of pertinent international annual or biannual conferences, such as ACM Hypertext (USA), ECHT (Europe), ED-MEDIA (rotating between USA/Canada and Europe), WebNet, the Internet, WWW conferences and the yearly Gopher conference, just to mention a few. There are also a number of journals that deal regularly with hypermedia issues, such as *Hypermedia*, J.UCS (*Journal of Universal Computer Science*), *Multimedia Systems*, J.NCA (*Journal for Network and Computer Applications*, formerly J.MCA, *Journal for Micro Computer Applications*), again to list just a few examples.

2   Information systems and the Internet

Keith Andrews

The **Internet**, the worldwide computer network, now connects over 6.6 million individual computers (July 1995) with a growth rate of between 10 and 15% per month or around 100% per year. Estimates of the number of regular users of the Internet vary from 20 million to 50 million. If current growth rates were to continue, the whole of the world population would be connected by the year 2004!

Around 18 Terabytes of information (18 000 000 000 000 bytes) traversed the main US backbone of the network, the **NSFNET**, in the month of November 1994, a figure which was also double that of the previous year. In December 1994, NSFNET traffic began migrating to the new **NSF** network architecture, for which no comparable statistics are available. These statistics highlight the immense social and economic significance which the Internet is attaining. More and more businesses are realizing the enormous potential of the Internet: in the summer of 1994, the number of commercial sites in the United States overtook the number of educational sites.

Over the past couple of years, with increasingly powerful desktop computers and heavy investment in network bandwidth, attention has shifted significantly from traditional **Internet services** such as **electronic mail** and **file transfer** to more appealing, but resource-hungry, information systems and interactive services, which now account for more Internet traffic (in bytes) than any other Internet service.

2.1   The Internet

The Internet began life as a research project of the US Department of Defense's **Advanced Research Projects Agency** (ARPA). The original purpose was to build a communications system capable of withstanding partial fallout of nodes during a nuclear attack, through the use of automatic rerouting. The first remote terminal connection from the University of California at Los Angeles (UCLA) to the Stanford Research Institute (SRI) was demonstrated in November 1969. From these humble beginnings grew the **ARPANET**, a fully operational computer network, based on a host-to-host protocol called the **Network Control Protocol**

(NCP), and running services such as **remote login** (**Telnet**) and file transfer (FTP). Electronic mail was added as an afterthought, after two programmers decided to send each other messages as well as data.

By 1981 there were some 200 sites on the ARPANET. In order to link in other vendors' physical networks into one seamless network, a new standardized protocol, the **Transmission Control Protocol/Internet Protocol** (TCP/IP), was developed. On "flag day," 1 January, 1983, the whole ARPANET was switched from NCP to TCP/IP protocol and the foundation for the Internet was laid. The inclusion of the TCP/IP protocol suite into Berkeley UNIX around the same time and its subsequent adoption by the vendor community gave a major boost to the Internet.

In March 1986 the Internet had around 3000 sites, and the **US National Science Foundation** (NSF) initiated development of the NSFNET, connecting six NSF supercomputer centers, to provide a major backbone communication service for the Internet. By late 1989, the Internet had grown to over 150 000 sites in North America, Europe, South America, Australasia and beyond.

The **Internet Society** (ISOC) was founded in January 1992 as a non-profit, voluntary body to oversee development of the Internet. It appoints a council of elders, the **Internet Architecture Board** (IAB), which coordinates various sub-committees. The **Internet Engineering Task Force** (IETF) develops new standards and recommends them to the IAB for approval.

Table 2.1 summarizes the historical development of the Internet. Today, the Internet is a vast, self-regulating network of national, regional, campus and private networks based on the TCP/IP protocol suite and various connecting gateways. This "network of networks" (currently more than 60 000 individual networks) is funded bottom-up – everyone pays for their part. Although many governments currently finance Internet connectivity for their educational and research institutions, the sheer demands for connectivity mean this is now changing to more direct forms of accounting. Indeed, the Internet is becoming so pervasive that it is often referred to simply as **The Net**. The recent popularity and visibility of the World Wide Web on the Internet has introduced the term **The Web**, embracing the sum of Internet services and becoming more or less synonymous with "The Net" and the Internet.

Table 2.1   The development of the Internet.

Time	Stage of development
Early 1970s	ARPANET, US military network, designed to withstand partial fallouts
Early 1980s	TCP/IP introduced to connect diverse networks together; Ethernet LANs and workstations become popular, Berkeley UNIX supports TCP/IP
Late 1980s	NSFNET backbone
1992	Internet Society founded as ultimate authority
Today	"The Net", a network of networks

2.1.1   Internet protocols

The Internet is a **packet switched** network. The underlying protocol, the **Internet Protocol** (IP), provides **envelopes** or **packets** for up to 1500 bytes of data. Each packet is stamped with a unique **source** and **destination address**. Packets are passed through the Internet from **router** to router until they reach their destination, like letters through the postal system; they occasionally get damaged or lost or arrive in a different sequence.

The **Transmission Control Protocol** (TCP) builds on the basic service provided by the IP. TCP breaks messages larger than 1500 bytes into a sequence of small IP packets. On the receiving side, packets are collected, placed in order and their data extracted. Missing and corrupted packets are retransmitted. TCP creates the appearance of a dedicated link between sender and receiver, which Internet applications use to communicate and exchange data. To this end, TCP also defines the concept of contact **ports** to be used by individual applications or services. The more common services use permanently assigned, "well-known" port numbers by default (but usually can be configured to use an alternative port). Port numbers are assigned by another Internet body, the **IANA** (Internet Assigned Number Authority).

2.1.2   Internet addresses

Every computer (or host) on the Internet has a unique address; **Internet addresses** are 32-bit numbers, in four 8-bit parts, for example 129.27.153.10. They are split between the **network** and **host parts**: so-called **class A networks** have a 1-byte network and a 3-byte host part (providing for up to 16 777 214 hosts per network), **class B networks** a 2-byte network and a 2-byte host part (providing for up to 65 534 hosts per network), and **class C networks** a 3-byte network and a 1-byte host part (providing for up to 254 hosts per network). Computers connected to the same **physical network** generally all have the same network part plus their own unique host part.

Since human beings are notoriously inadequate when it comes to remembering sequences of numbers, a multi-level, hierarchical naming scheme, the **Domain Name System** (DNS), is available as an alternative way of specifying computers on the Internet. Each level is called a **domain** and there may be any number of domains in a name (although usually no more than five). Domains in a name are separated by periods and become successively smaller from right to left. For example, the computer named aw.com is the machine serving as the main access point to the Addison-Wesley Publishing Group and is in the commercial domain. The machine's Internet address is 192.207.117.2. The computer on which I do most of my work is fiicmds06.tu-graz.ac.at, a DECstation at Graz University of Technology in the academic domain in Austria. Its address is 129.27.153.10. There is a unique mapping from domain name to Internet address, but not vice versa. Several domain names (**aliases**) may, and often do, refer to the same physical machine. Aliases are particularly useful for naming services in a machine-independent fashion. For example, ftp.aw.com, Addison-Wesley's anonymous FTP archive, is in fact an alias for aw.com, but publicizing the alias rather than the real domain name or Internet address means that the FTP service can be moved to another machine simply by changing the address for the alias, without causing any disruption in service.

The top-level (rightmost) domains currently in use consist of the original six US domains: com (commercial), edu (educational), gov (government), mil (military), org (organizations), and net (network resources), plus around 150 of the 300 or so international two-letter country codes (such as uk for the United Kingdom or at for Austria). Responsibility for the registration of domain names at the second level has been delegated by the IANA to regional Network Information Centers: the **RIPE NCC** in Europe, the **AP-NIC** in the Asia-Pacific region and the **InterNIC** for the USA and the rest of the world. The name space at each lower level is controlled by the appropriate body, for example domains beneath tu-graz.ac.at are assigned by the Computer Center at Graz University of Technology.

A common misconception is that the parts of a domain name correspond directly to parts of the Internet address – they do not. **DNS name servers** are used to look up the address corresponding to a particular domain name: if the local DNS server does not know the address itself, it asks the DNS server of the top-level domain for the address of the DNS server responsible for the next lower domain, and so on down the domain hierarchy until the actual Internet address is found.

2.2 Basic Internet services: Remote login, file transfer, Email and Network News

Many Internet applications are two-part, **client–server** applications. **Client** programs are started by users on their local machines. The client establishes a connection across the Internet (usually via TCP) to a **server** on the remote host machine via a particular port. The host/port pair uniquely defines a particular server. If the server is not running, or is listening to another port, no connection can be made. Communication follows according to an agreed protocol for that application; often multiple implementations of a particular service are available.

The four traditionally most widely used Internet applications are remote login, file transfer, electronic mail, and Network News. The remote login tool **Telnet** is a client–server application used to log into another computer on the Internet. It provides a basic, terminal-style interface to the remote machine.

The file transfer tool **FTP** is another client–server application, used to retrieve files from a remote machine. Two kinds of access are possible: **identified** (with account and password) and **anonymous** (no account or password required). Most public archive sites operate **anonymous FTP servers**. Until early 1995, FTP data accounted for by far the largest amount of traffic on the Internet (about one third of the total traffic in bytes). A related service, **Archie** (discussed in Section 2.3), provides an indexing facility for anonymous FTP archives, making it easier to find FTP resources.

Electronic mail (Email) is arguably the most popular of all network services, and is not restricted to just the Internet but can be exchanged via gateways with other networks like **BITNET** and **UUCP**. Email is not an "**end to end**" **service** like the previous applications, but a "**store and forward**" **service**: mail is passed from one machine to another until it reaches its destination. There are many mail programs; most of them use the **Simple Mail Transfer Protocol** (SMTP). On the Internet, SMTP is implemented atop TCP. Commonly supported features include aliases, forwarding, carbon copies and automatic reply. **Mailing**

Table 2.2   The four basic Internet services.

Tool	Purpose	Protocol	Assigned port
Telnet	remote login	TELNET	23
FTP	file transfer	FTP	20 (data), 21 (control)
mail	electronic mail	SMTP	25
news	Network News	NNTP	119

lists allow mail to be automatically directed to particular user groups. The **MIME** (Multipurpose Internet Mail Extensions) specification defines how to include multimedia objects in pieces of Email, and FTP-to-Email gateways allow files to be retrieved from FTP servers by Email.

Network News is the Internet equivalent of a discussion group or **bulletin board**. News is organized hierarchically into broad topics called **newsgroups** dealing with particular themes, for example comp.lang.c++ for the C++ programming language. The **USENET** comprises a set of voluntary rules for passing and maintaining newsgroups in one of seven categories (comp being computer science). In addition, many "alternative," commercial, and local newsgroup hierarchies also exist. News is passed from **news server** to news server according to bilateral agreements between server administrators using the **Network News Transfer Protocol** (NNTP). The main problem with news is the overwhelming amount of material – a typical news server might carry several thousand newsgroups and receive hundreds of megabytes of news per day!

Table 2.2 summarizes the four basic Internet services. These tools are now in fact so common, they are almost taken for granted by most Internet users. In contrast, **Internet information systems** are currently enjoying an explosion of interest.

2.3 Archie

As increasing numbers of FTP archive sites came online in the late 1980s, it became increasingly difficult for Internet users to know which resources and information were available at which sites – word of mouth no longer sufficed. Archie was a first attempt to provide a comprehensive index to information resources on the Net. Developed at McGill University in Canada, it was made widely available in December 1990. Today, Archie tracks the contents of around 1300 (known) anonymous FTP archive sites by actively visiting each site about once a month and updating its index with the name of every file and directory in the archive. For a site to be indexed, Archie's maintainers have to be informed of the site's existence by Email.

Users can perform queries on one of the **public Archie servers** (there are about 25 publicly accessible Archie servers worldwide) in a number of ways: by Telnet, by Email, by using a native **Archie client** and more recently through a **WWW gateway to Archie**. In January 1992, the creators of Archie founded Bunyip Information Systems to market and develop Archie and the Archie server software became a commercial product, although Archie searches continue to be free of charge.

2.4 WAIS

WAIS, or Wide Area Information Servers, began in 1989 as a joint development of Thinking Machines Corp., Apple Computer and Dow Jones to provide online access to the *Wall Street Journal*. WAIS is a client–server system which supports content-based search of (previously) **indexed databases**.

WAIS clients provide users with the ability to query and retrieve information from remote databases anywhere on the Internet. A **WAIS query** is typically a simple list of words separated by spaces; WAIS supports **"natural language" queries** in the sense that a naturally phrased question can also be treated as a simple list of words. On receiving a query, the **WAIS server** (in WAIS terminology, servers are usually called "Sources" and queries "Questions") responds by looking up the search terms in its index, calculating a weighted score for each document containing the search terms, and returning a ranked list of documents to the client. Clients present the results to the user using a normalized score of 1000 for the best matching document. Users, through their client software, can then request that particular documents be sent in full.

WAIS is not restricted to text documents. Any body of documents which can be indexed (for example, by file name, associated attribute fields or descriptions) can be made available through WAIS, including images, PostScript files, video clips and so on.

A unique feature of WAIS is its support for **relevance feedback**: (parts of) text documents returned by a search which are deemed by the user to be particularly relevant can be used as input for a further search, in effect refining the search by asking WAIS to look for further similar documents. Newer versions of WAIS also support **stemming** (the automatic truncation of search terms), **Boolean expressions**, **partial word searches** and **stop-lists** (the automatic exclusion of non-productive filler words).

A problem for users of WAIS is to know which servers exist in the first place. The solution provided was the **directory-of-servers database** maintained (originally) by Thinking Machines, which contains entries describing all registered WAIS servers. This server can be searched to find other servers with appropriate databases, resulting in a two-level search strategy. Since manually recording server names or repeatedly searching the directory of servers would rapidly become tedious, most WAIS clients provide facilities for saving and reusing personal lists of servers. Most clients also support personal lists of queries, so that accurate and successful queries can be periodically restarted with minimal effort.

Most WAIS servers run on UNIX machines, although server software is also available for VAX/VMS. The **WAIS package** includes an indexing utility, `waisindex`, which extracts index terms from a body of documents and creates an inverted index structure (an alphabetical list of terms, each with an associated list of documents in which the term appears). A sophisticated data structure (a **two-level B-tree**) provides fast access to the index. The `waisindex` utility automatically recognizes and indexes a wide range of text formats. Other document types, such as images, can be indexed by file name or `waisindex` can be customized to index associated descriptions, attributes, and so on. For standard text documents the inverted index takes up approximately the same amount of disk space as the original data set. Once an inverted index has been created, `waisserver` is started to serve client requests.

WAIS clients and servers communicate using a binary protocol derived from the **Z39.50-88** (1988) **ANSI** Draft Standard for bibliographic retrieval and by default WAIS uses port 210, the port assigned to Z39.50. Communication is **stateless**, no state being retained by the server between transactions with a client. The Z39.50-88 standard was superseded in 1992 by the much improved, but incompatible, **Z39.50-92** protocol (which has now itself been superseded by **Z39.50-1995**). In the summer of 1992, **WAIS Inc.** was formed to develop WAIS commercially, and support and development of the public-domain WAIS (called **freeWAIS**) passed to **CNIDR** (the Clearing house for Networked Information Discovery and Retrieval). Both WAIS Inc. and CNIDR have now developed fully compliant Z39.50-92 servers. In deference to the popularity of the WWW, these WAIS servers are equipped with WWW gateways, allowing users of WWW browsers to search WAIS servers. Indicative of the commercial importance of powerful search engines, WAIS Inc. was acquired in May 1995 by the largest US online service provider, **America Online**.

WAIS is eminently suited to remote querying of individual, large databases for specific content. There are now (January 1996) approximately 540 registered WAIS servers worldwide. WAIS also lends itself to integration within other information systems. Gopher and World Wide Web servers generally do not provide their own integrated search facilities, but do provide mechanisms for querying WAIS servers or accessing WAIS's inverted index structure directly. WAIS itself is not a general-purpose information system, but purely a search engine – it provides no other means of structuring or navigation.

2.5   The Internet Gopher

The Internet **Gopher,** or Gopher for short, was started in 1991 as a **CWIS** (Campus-Wide Information System) at the University of Minnesota. It is a client–server TCP/IP application which provides seamless, menu-like access to information resources on multiple hosts. The name Gopher comes from the American nickname for natives of Minnesota: it is actually a burrowing rodent the size of a large rat. Since Gopher's purpose is to "go for" things across the Internet, its name was born!

A **Gopher client** provides the user with a view into **gopherspace** presented as a hierarchy of menus and document nodes, very much like a (virtual) file system of directories and files. Although the menu presentation gives the impression of a tree, gopherspace is in fact a graph containing many loops, since sub-menus can appear in multiple places. Typically, users begin navigation at the top of the tree for a particular server and traverse down to leaf nodes containing actual data, which may be texts, GIF images, audio files and so on.

Sub-spaces on remote Gopher servers can be seamlessly incorporated by simply including references to them. **Gopher servers** usually have a menu of other Gopher servers somewhere in their tree. Access to these remote servers is totally transparent to the user; the Gopher client simply fetches the next selected sub-menu from the appropriate server. Special nodes called **index nodes** provide the interface to search engines at particular levels of the tree. They prompt the user for a search string and then present a virtual menu containing the list of matching items. Other special leaf nodes include Telnet sessions and binary archives.

As with WAIS, a meta-level of access became necessary as the number of Gopher servers increased and users lost track of which servers provided which resources. A special set of Gopher servers, the so-called **Veronica** servers, provide a keyword search of all menu titles in gopherspace. The index used by Veronica servers is constructed by the Veronica Harvester, a robot which periodically (every 7–14 days) tree walks the whole of gopherspace collecting menu titles (similar to the way Archie indexes FTP servers).

Gopher clients are available for most common platforms. Most clients provide support for Telnet sessions, text and multimedia documents (images, audio, video and so on), the latter usually by starting external viewer programs. Clients also commonly provide a history list of nodes visited during the current session, and bookmarks (pointers left by the user) to return to in future sessions. Nowadays, multi-protocol Internet browsers such as Mosaic and Netscape which speak FTP, Gopher and WWW protocols are becoming increasingly popular.

The standard UNIX Gopher server gopherd is very straightforward to use. It exploits the hierarchical nature of the UNIX file system and implements a simple mapping from UNIX directories to Gopher menus and UNIX files to Gopher documents. Configuration files are used to specify the display names of Gopher entries and to represent entries pointing to other Gopher servers.

Gopher owes its popularity to the ease with which a server can be set up and populated with data, particularly under UNIX. The availability of both client and server software for all major platforms and Gopher's interoperability with WAIS and FTP (servers) and WWW (clients) have also contributed to its widespread penetration: there are currently (June 1995) around 5500 Gopher servers. Gopher's hierarchical menus make it easy both to structure and find information. However, Gopher is almost purely hierarchical in nature: it provides no inherent support for hypermedia links and search facilities require explicit configuration. The technique of serving HTML pages from a Gopher server does combine hierarchical structure with hyperlinks, but in a rather ad hoc fashion. The Internet Gopher is described in more detail in Chapter 6.

2.6   The World Wide Web

The **World Wide Web** project (**WWW** or **W3** for short) was initiated at CERN (European Laboratory for Particle Physics, the acronym originates from the former French name Conseil Européen pour la Recherche Nucléaire), Geneva (Switzerland), in 1989, originally as an information system for the particle physics community. WWW is a **distributed, heterogeneous, hypermedia information system**: hypertext links embedded in text documents can be followed to access related textual or multimedia (image, audio, video, . . .) information.

The World Wide Web is defined by three key specifications: **HTML**, **HTTP** and **URL**. HTML (the HyperText Markup Language) defines how text is marked up with tags to define certain constructs (such as emphasized text, an enumerated list or a hypertext link). HTML is an **SGML**-conformant mark-up language; the final presentation of a text document depends on how individual WWW clients render particular HTML constructs. HTTP (the Hypertext

Transfer Protocol), the WWW's client–server protocol, uses the MIME Internet Email conventions to encode header information associated with documents. Clients send a request message and servers reply with a response message, in a single stateless transaction. Through its URL (Uniform Resource Locator) mechanism, WWW cleverly encapsulates other Internet protocols: by enabling hypertext links to point to any document on any WWW, Gopher or FTP server worldwide, as well as network newsgroups or Telnet sessions, "The Web" has embraced and become almost synonymous with "The Net."

Although first made available in August 1991, WWW only really gained prominence in early 1993 after the release of NCSA's graphical **WWW client, Mosaic**. Mosaic's intuitive point-and-click interface and glitzy **inline images** made WWW accessible to a wide and diverse user community. This trend was accelerated with the release in October 1994 of the **Netscape Navigator** by a commercial company co-founded by the original author of Mosaic. Today, dozens of WWW browsers are available for all major computer platforms.

The publicly available CERN and NCSA WWW servers simply serve HTML files from the local file system, with only rudimentary access control, little or no information management and no integrated search facilities. However, the **common gateway interface** (CGI) allows WWW servers to start arbitrary application programs, for example linking into external databases or implementing complex search algorithms. More sophisticated, commercial servers are also becoming available, one common approach being to put a WWW front end onto an existing information or database system. With commercial servers, professional **HTML authoring tools** are also starting to appear.

As WWW growth exploded in 1994 and 1995, the problem of finding resources on the Net became particularly acute and was exacerbated by the WWW's reliance on hypertext links and its lack of meta-search facilities. Web crawlers, programs such as **Lycos** which relentlessly traverse the links of the Web to build centralized indexes of the contents of sites, and manually maintained catalogs of sites such as **Yahoo**, have alleviated the situation somewhat, but neither approach is able to keep up with exponential growth rates.

In October 1994, the **World Wide Web Consortium (W3C)** was formed to develop WWW standards and reference code; it currently (January 1996) has around 110 member organizations. The **Virtual Reality Modeling Language** (VRML), a 3D file format for modeling objects and worlds on the Web, was specified in June 1995 and is rapidly being extended. The introduction of **Java**, a secure language which executes on a "virtual machine", by Sun Microsystems promises to bring interactivity to the Web in the form of downloadable mini-applications, or "applets".

Despite its broad appeal, the World Wide Web has a number of limitations. It does not provide any information structuring facilities beyond hyperlinks; its links are **one-way** (there is no way of determining which other documents refer to a particular document, leading to inconsistencies when documents are moved or deleted, resulting frequently in "**dangling links**") and embedded within text documents (there are no links from other kinds of documents). Like Gopher, WWW has no native search facilities, but relies on external search engines such as WAIS, leading to patchy server-by-server provision of search facilities by individual sites and no real-time cross-server searches (searches in previously generated cross-server indexes are available). The flexibility provided by CGI is achieved at great cost: the uniformity of the interface disappears, different WWW servers behave differently – resulting in the "Balkanization" (to quote Ted Nelson) of the Web into independent "WWW Empires." Also, there is little support for the maintenance of large data sets, so it is not uncommon to see several WWW servers within a single organization, each with a fundamentally separate interactive context. The Web today is very much "read-only," in the sense that information providers prepare data sets in which information consumers can generally only browse. Finally, although its URL mechanism endows WWW with scalability in terms of number of servers, it is not scalable in terms of number of users. Extremely popular WWW servers such as Sun Microsystems' World Cup USA '94 site can often become overwhelmed by "flash crowds" of tens of thousands of users, necessitating their physical mirroring to many alternative sites. The World Wide Web is described in more detail in Chapter 7.

2.7   Hyper-G

The **Hyper-G** project at Graz University of Technology builds upon the WWW and tackles some of its main shortcomings: in particular the lack of composite and hierarchical structures, the embodiment of links within documents and the inadequate provision for cross-server and focused searches. This is why we refer to Hyper-G as a "second generation" Web system. You are, of course, reading the definitive guide to Hyper-G right now; detailed coverage of Hyper-G starts in Chapter 9.

2.8   Further reading

The number of books about the Internet, its services and applications seems to be growing faster than the Internet itself. Two popular general guides are *The Whole Internet* by Krol (1994) and *The Internet Unleashed* (Barron *et al.*, 1995). The Electronic Frontier Foundation's (extended) guide to the Internet is available free of charge on the Web (Internet Guide). For a comprehensive Internet bibliography consult the *Unofficial Internet Book List* by Savetz which lists 230 titles. Other online resources include the Internet Society's home page (Internet Society Home Page), the very extensive *Internet Tools Summary* by December, and for Internet statistics the *Internet Domain Survey* by the Network Wizards. There are also a number of magazines which cover the Internet, the Web and related topics. Most prominent among them are probably *Wired* (Wired Ventures) and *Internet World* (Mecklermedia Internet World).

3 Hypermedia systems

Keith Andrews

The body of human knowledge is so large and is growing so fast that no single human mind can possibly comprehend its entirety. The best we can hope to do is to provide mechanisms which help us locate, structure and compile useful information. One approach is hypermedia. The human mind operates by association, jumping from one item of thought to the next, almost instantaneously. The hypermedia paradigm attempts to model this process with associative links between chunks of information.

3.1 What is hypertext and hypermedia?

Unlike the typical printed book, which is read sequentially from beginning to end, **hypertext** is inherently nonlinear: it is comprised of many interlinked chunks of **self-contained text**. Readers are not bound to a particular sequence, but can browse through information intuitively by association, following their interests by following a highlighted keyword or phrase in one piece of text to bring up another, associated piece of text. Figure 3.1 illustrates this difference.

The word *self-contained* is important. Whereas in traditional, linear writing, a piece of text has a well-defined context and is embedded within the linear structure of the work, in a hypertext environment a particular piece of text may be reached from any number of contexts, that is, other chunks of text. Hence it becomes important to avoid assumptions of prior knowledge and keep individual pieces of text as self-contained as possible.

Hypermedia is the generalization of hypertext to include other kinds of media: images, audio clips and video clips are typically supported in addition to text. Individual chunks of information are usually referred to as **documents** or **nodes,** and the connections between them as **links** or **hyperlinks** – the so-called **node-link hypermedia model**. The entire set of nodes and links forms a graph network. A distinct set of nodes and links which constitutes a logical entity or work is called a **hyperdocument**; a distinct subset of hyperlinks is often called a **hyperweb**.

A **source anchor** is the starting point of a hyperlink and specifies the part of a document from which an outgoing link can be activated. Typically, the user is given visual cues as to where source anchors are located in a document (for example, a highlighted phrase in a text document). A **destination anchor** is the endpoint of a hyperlink and determines what part of

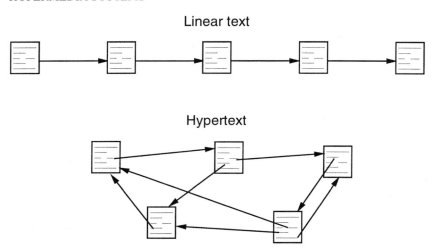

Figure 3.1   Linear text and hypertext.

a document should be on view upon arrival at that node (for example, a text might be scrolled to a specific paragraph). Often, an entire document is specified as the destination and viewing commences at some default location within the document (for example, the start of a text). Figure 3.2 illustrates these concepts graphically.

Some authors distinguish between **referential** and **organizational hyperlinks**. Referential links are the cross-references distinctive of hypermedia. Organizational links are special links which establish explicit structure by connecting a parent node with its children, forming a tree within the overall node-link graph.

The traditional definition of hypermedia as being "multimedia with links" belies many of the possibilities modern technology now offers. We like to define "real hypermedia" in a broader sense, with two additional components. Firstly, real hypermedia incorporates new technologies like interactive movies, panoramic images, navigable three-dimensional models and virtual reality. Secondly, real hypermedia involves more than read-only browsing: it possesses integral facilities for communication and collaboration such as annotations, structured discussion, user feedback, message passing and collaborative authoring.

3.2   The origins of hypermedia

Vannevar Bush, President Roosevelt's science adviser during the Second World War, is generally credited as being the first to propose a system similar to what we would now call hypertext. In his 1945 article, "As We May Think," he described a system called **Memex**, based on microfilm and mechanical projection equipment:

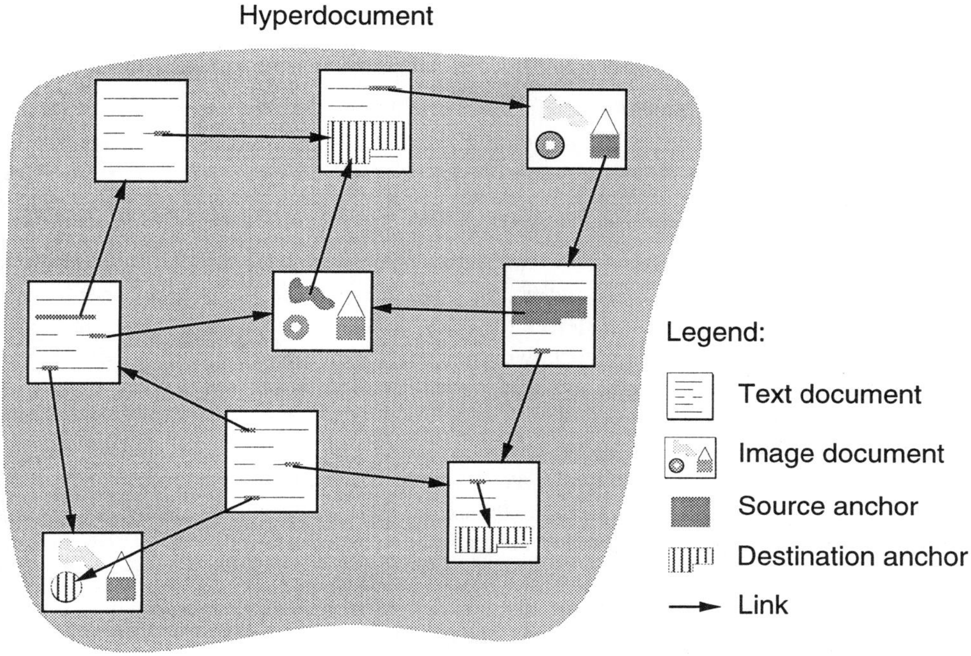

Hyperdocument

Legend:

⊞ Text document

⊡ Image document

▪ Source anchor

⫿⫿ Destination anchor

⟶ Link

Figure 3.2   Nodes, links and anchors.

Consider a future device for individual use, which is a sort of mechanized private file and library. It affords ... associative indexing, the basic idea of which is a provision whereby any item may be caused at will to select immediately and automatically another.

Bush also envisioned the provision of **"trails"**, sets of links relating information relevant to a specific purpose (that is, hyperwebs). Sadly, a functioning Memex was never built and the world had to wait another 20 years until computers became powerful enough to be applied to interactive tasks rather than pure scientific number crunching.

The term hypertext was coined by Ted Nelson in 1965. His (proposed) Xanadu system incorporated a **docuverse**, a universal repository for all the world's information and literature ever published. Nothing would ever be deleted, new versions of texts existing beside older versions. The system would be based on **transclusions** (virtual inclusions) as the fundamental structure, allowing the same material to appear in multiple contexts without being physically copied. This would also allow a business model where authors could be identified and paid pro-rata royalties on any portion of their works used elsewhere (by transclusion). Nelson has struggled for 30 years to implement Xanadu, so far without success. We are proud to say that, in Ted Nelson's opinion, Hyper-G comes closest to realizing Xanadu's ambitious dreams.

The first real working hypertext system was the **Hypertext Editing System** built at Brown University in 1967 under the leadership of Andries van Dam. It ran with 128 KB memory on an IBM/360 mainframe and most of the interface was text-based. Douglas Engelbart's **NLS** system (part of the **Augment** project), which had a number of hypertext features such as interlinked cross-references and a graphical mouse-based interface, was successfully demonstrated in 1968.

The first working hypermedia system was the **Aspen Movie Map** developed at the Massachusetts Institute of Technology by Andrew Lippman and his colleagues in 1978. The town of Aspen, Colorado, which has a very regular, rectangular street layout, was filmed by driving a truck through every street and taking front, rear, left and right view photographs every three meters. These were transferred to videodisc and linked to follow the street grid. Users sat in front of a vertical monitor showing the street view and a flat monitor showing an overview map and could navigate forwards, backwards and (at a junction) left and right with a joystick. Short video clips of many of the buildings in Aspen were also linked in, so users could stop and explore them.

Intermedia, developed at Brown University from 1985 to 1990, introduced the concept of **link anchors** and the use of a separate database for links (rather than storing them within documents), allowing links to be bidirectional and link webs to be maintained as distinct entities. Intermedia was a multi-user system based on the client–server architecture and combined hypermedia features with information retrieval facilities such as full text search and dictionary lookup. It aroused great interest in the research community and generated numerous academic publications, but only really saw use within Brown University. Promising though it was, Intermedia only ran on the Apple Macintosh under UNIX and died a slow death in 1990 due to lack of funding to upgrade to a new operating system version.

The first widely available commercial hypertext product was OWL's **Guide**, developed out of the University of Kent's original UNIX version and released in 1986 for the Macintosh and later for the IBM PC. This system marked the transition of hypertext from a plaything of the research community to a real-world technique for actual applications, and has now sold tens of thousands of copies.

The real breakthrough in popularity for hypermedia came in 1987, when Apple decided to bundle **HyperCard** free with every Macintosh. Within months, everyone seemed to be producing HyperCard "stacks," as HyperCard documents are called. HyperCard is a frame-based, standalone hypermedia system incorporating a simple, but powerful scripting language called **HyperTalk**. Links do not have to be hardwired, but can be programmed in HyperTalk and computed dynamically.

The same year also saw Jeff Conklin's hypertext survey article in *IEEE Computer* and the first conference dedicated exclusively to hypertext, ACM Hypertext'87 at the University of North Carolina. The conference proved so popular that only half of the 500 people wanting to attend could be accommodated and there were still so many people crammed into the two lecture theaters that some had to sit on the floor!

The following years saw much research and development effort put into hypermedia, with hypermedia systems and projects being announced almost monthly. The next major milestone was the dawn of the **World Wide Web** (WWW or W3), first demonstrated at the ACM Hypertext'91 conference in December 1991, but whose real breakthrough came in 1993 when the National Center for Supercomputing Applications (NCSA) released **Mosaic**, a point-and-

Table 3.1   Milestones in the history of hypermedia.

Year	System	Originator	Milestone
1945	Memex	Vannevar Bush	Microfilm-based device
1965	Xanadu	Ted Nelson	Term "hypertext"
1967	Hypertext Editing System	Andries van Dam, Brown University	First working hypertext system
1978	Aspen Movie Map	Andrew Lippman, MIT	First working hypermedia system
1985	Intermedia	Brown University	Anchors, webs
1986	Guide	OWL	First commercial product
1987	HyperCard	Apple Computer Corp.	Free with every Macintosh
1987	ACM Hypertext '87	University of North Carolina	First ACM conference on hypertext
1991	WWW	Tim Berners-Lee, CERN	Hypermedia across the Internet
1993	Mosaic	NCSA	Graphical browser for WWW
1994	Hyper-G	Graz University of Technology	Hypermedia information system

click graphical browser for the WWW. Chapter 7 is devoted exclusively to WWW.

The **Hyper-G** project at Graz University of Technology built upon the ideas of WWW, while overcoming some of its shortcomings. Hyper-G recognized the lessons learned from the Intermedia project and adopted the concepts of link anchors and of storing hyperlinks in a separate link database. Hence, Hyper-G supports bidirectional linking and **automatic link consistency**. Hyper-G also has orthogonal hierarchical structuring and composition facilities and integrated indexing and search facilities. In June 1994, a first prototype Hyper-G server was officially released, together with preliminary versions of authoring/browsing tools for XWindows and Windows (**Harmony** and **Amadeus**, respectively).

Table 3.1 summarizes some of the milestones in the history of hypermedia.

3.3   Types of hypermedia system

Hypermedia systems can be classified according to a number of criteria. An important criterion is how much control over a hyperdocument's look and feel an author should be allowed to exercise: the "form versus content" debate.

Many hypermedia systems have traditionally been **frame-based**, that is, documents must fit into a fixed-size frame (screen) and authors have full control over both content and presentation (form). Examples of frame-based systems include **KMS**, HyperCard, **ToolBook** and **HM-Card**. This notion of authoring, inherited from the field of Computer Aided

Instruction (CAI), has the advantage that individual authors can create very colorful, inter-active hyperdocuments. The HM-Card package, for example, supports vector graphics, animations and question–answer dialogs within reusable hypermedia chunks. The price of full layout control, however, is that it becomes nearly impossible to maintain interface consistency across a related set of hyperdocuments having multiple authors.

In **window-based** hypermedia systems, documents may be of any size, and each is displayed in its own (scrollable) window. Authors typically specify only the information content of documents, while style sheets control their presentation. Thus, authors are relegated to the role of **information suppliers**, supplying marked-up documents devoid of specific presentation attributes. A heterogeneous collection of information delivery tools can then present the information according to their own capabilities and users' preference configurations.

Modern hypermedia information systems like WWW and Hyper-G provide for both form-free and form-specific documents. An SGML text mark-up format like HTML supports information suppliers who are keen to avoid presentation-specific dependencies in their documents. Page description document formats like PostScript and PDF support authors who want full control over end-user presentation of their material (like marketing executives). The **Easy** viewer for Hyper-G, which is used for kiosk-like public display terminals, takes a hybrid approach. It interprets layout meta-information, such as size and position, which is associated with otherwise form-free documents.

Another distinction is that between standalone, single-author hypermedia systems and distributed, multi-author systems. In a collaborative, multi-author environment, support for document locking and atomic transactions becomes a necessity to prevent authors mutually overwriting one another's changes. Communication facilities between authors and the sharing of resources are also highly desirable in such an environment.

3.4   When to use hypermedia

Hypermedia is an enabling technology, from which an extremely wide variety of application domains profit. In his book *Multimedia and Hypertext*, Jakob Nielsen lists four golden rules for determining whether an application is suitable for hypermedia:

(1) A large body of information is organized into numerous fragments.

(2) The fragments relate to each other.

(3) The user only needs a small fraction at any time.

(4) The application is computer-based.

Given these requirements, current hypermedia application domains include:

- **Help and documentation**: Exemplified by the Help system provided as part of MS-Windows, this is a classic application of hypertext. Typically, the various command and function descriptions making up online documentation contain many cross-references, links to more detailed information, links to examples, and so forth.

- **Reference works**: Electronic dictionaries and encyclopedias are composed of fragmented chunks of material with a high degree of cross-referencing and are hence ideally suited to hypermedia.

- **Software engineering**: The software engineering development cycle generates a wealth of interrelated documents. Modern CASE tools are also increasingly offering hypermedia features within program code editors, for example to bring up more detailed information about a procedure or variable.

- **Organization of ideas**: Hypermedia has been used in systems such as **NoteCards** to support the personal organization of notes and ideas. The **gIBIS** system was used to support debate and argumentation amongst multiple participants: nodes of type Issue, Position and Argument can be manipulated and related.

- **Tourist information systems** provide tourists with information on accommodation, services, places of interest, and so on. These systems often combine text and images with location and overview maps.

- **Interactive fiction**: Writers and novelists are now exploring the use of hypertext for interactive, nonlinear fiction. Readers are allowed to explore an underlying fictional construction interactively.

- **Rapid prototyping**: An important part of interface design is the creation and evaluation of early mock-up designs. Since mock-ups often consist of interlinked screen designs, hypermedia systems can be used to rapidly generate such prototypes. **ToolBook** was used to generate and test early prototypes of a graphical interface to Hyper-G.

- **Online marketing**: In the World Wide Web, it is increasingly common to see glitzy sites offering a mix of advertising and information.

- **Teaching support**: Courseware has long been distributed in hypermedia form, typically with additional functionality for conditional branching and answer-judging. More recently, distance learning materials are proliferating on the Web.

- **Communication and collaboration**: Applications such as intelligent Email, interactive questionnaires, online order forms and academic reviewing can all benefit from the application of hypermedia technologies.

Chapter 4 contains a concise survey of potential applications of hypermedia systems, together with specific examples.

3.5   Navigating hyperspace

The primary advantage of hypertext and hypermedia systems over more traditional information systems based on databases is that users need not formulate queries to find information. Instead, graphical **point-and-click style interaction** is possible, which is easy and intuitive even for computer novices. This is what makes the hypermedia paradigm so attractive to millions of new Internet users.

Studies have shown that users employ a number of different **navigation strategies** when navigating through a complex information space:

- **Scanning**: covering a large area without depth.

- **Browsing**: following a path by association until one's interest is caught.

- **Searching**: striving to find an explicit goal.

- **Exploring**: finding out the extent of the information space.

- **Wandering**: ambling along in a purposeless, unstructured manner.

By its very nature, hypermedia is an ideal medium for associative browsing. However, the increased freedom offered by hypermedia brings with it increased complexity. Readers of a linear document have only two choices when looking for information: forwards or backwards. Readers of hyperdocuments, on the other hand, can rapidly become overwhelmed by the plethora of choices available to them. This problem is known as the "user disorientation" or "lost in hyperspace" problem (see Section 8.1).

To help users orient themselves in the information space, many hypermedia systems provide one or more of the following navigational aids in addition to hyperlinks.

3.5.1   Search facilities

Sophisticated search facilities from the field of information retrieval, such as keyword search, content search, fuzzy (inexact) search and similarity measures are indispensable for finding specific information once the size of the hyperweb exceeds browsable proportions (say many hundreds or thousands of nodes). As Halasz indicated in his reflections on NoteCards:

> For NoteCards to be useful in managing large heterogeneous networks, search and query needs to be elevated to a primary access mechanism on par with (browsing) navigation.

Hypermedia systems which provide information retrieval facilities in addition to hyperlinks are often called **hypermedia information systems** to emphasize this important distinction.

3.5.2   Hierarchical structure

NoteCards was notable among early hypermedia systems for its provision of **Fileboxes**, containers which may hold both Notecards (primitive nodes) and other Fileboxes. This proved to be extremely valuable, allowing users to employ hierarchical composition (inclusion relations) in addition to standard referential links when structuring and later navigating through their data.

However, the NoteCards implementation was fundamentally flawed: composite nodes were implemented using standard referential links and not as a separate concept. This caused considerable confusion and led Halasz to conclude:

> *Inclusion should be implemented within, as opposed to on top of, all hypermedia systems. Moreover, all aspects of hypermedia should support inclusion (or part-of) relations as a construct distinct from standard (reference) links.*

Fully integrated **hierarchical structuring**, such as that found in Hyper-G, is not only useful for hierarchical navigation: documents devoid of links can be inserted (and retrieved!), composite nodes can be assigned (searchable) attributes, and perhaps most importantly, the scope of searches can be focused on particular subsets of the database.

3.5.3   Guided tours

Guided tours were foreseen by Vannevar Bush in 1945 as "trails" through the available material. In essence, a guided tour is a predefined path through a subset of hyperspace, generally with no or only a few branches. They are particularly useful for introducing new readers to a hypermedia data set. As long as readers stay on the tour, they can navigate using simple "next" and "previous" commands. The advantage over tourist guided tours is that the reader, unlike the tourist, can leave the tour to explore and return to it at will.

3.5.4   Overview documents

Overview documents are "hand-crafted" to illustrate the structure of (part of) a hyperweb; they typically provide direct links to documents within the web. Examples include texts containing a list of links to other documents, an annotated diagram, map, photograph or a 3D model of a spatial layout.

Such manually edited overviews are only really of use in hyperdocuments which are not expected to change much during their lifetime, since changes to the hyperdocument often necessitate manually changing the overview. They also do not scale very well: drawing an overview of a 20 or 30 node hyperdocument is both manageable and often very helpful to users, drawing an overview of a 1000 or 10 000 node hyperdocument by hand is a thankless and futile task. For this reason, overview documents tend to be used for small, stable subsets of hyperspace and standalone, read-only hypermedia systems.

3.5.5   Graphical browsers

In contrast to overview documents, **graphical browsers** rely on dynamically generated structure maps. Graphical browsers come in many flavors:

- **Hierarchical browsers** display hierarchical structures (or organizational links) and allow navigation in a hierarchical fashion.

- **Global maps** attempt to map the entire hyperspace, but usually run up against problems of sheer scale.

- **Local maps** show the "vicinity" of the current node in terms of hyperlinks to and from other related nodes.

- **Fish-eye views** are employed to focus attention on important nodes by deliberately distorting the view (like using a wide-angle "fish-eye" lens).

- **Automatic clustering** techniques combine similar nodes into larger composites, thus reducing the overall amount of clutter in the structure map.

3.5.6   Backtracking

Backtracking allows users to return to previously visited nodes. This facility is an important confidence builder, since users are encouraged to experiment if they know they can always backtrack. Within the course of a single session, backtracking usually takes the form of a **history list** of visited nodes, with backwards and forwards functions available to navigate within the list. A more general facility is the history tree which can also visualize backing up and branching into other directions. The Intermedia Web View in fact combines a history list with a local map in one diagram. Being able to save and edit history lists is an elegant way of finding information again and preparing guided tours.

Bookmarks are pointers to specific nodes in hyperspace which persist between sessions. Users can thus build up a set of direct jumps to their favorite places in hyperspace. Good examples of this are Mosaic's hotlist and Netscape's bookmarks. These, however, have the major disadvantage that they are maintained locally by the client. Changing your client software necessitates converting your bookmark list. Access the Web from any computer other than your regular computer (say at a conference) and you must have remembered to take your bookmarks with you. For these reasons, Hyper-G users have a personal **home collection** or area of the Hyper-G server, within which they can both organize pointers to Web resources (bookmarks) and keep personal or unreleased documents. The personal home collection is accessible through any WWW, Gopher or Hyper-G client from any location, and can be structured arbitrarily like any other Hyper-G collection.

3.6   Further reading

For a good overall introductory text on hypertext and hypermedia, *Multimedia and Hypertext: The Internet and Beyond* by Nielsen (1995) is highly recommended. Nielsen also includes a valuable annotated bibliography with pointers to many of the systems mentioned in Section 3.2. Vannevar Bush's 1945 *As We May Think* article was reprinted in 1986 (Bush, 1986). Ted Nelson's definitions of hypertext and hypermedia are described in *Computer Lib/Dream Machines* (Nelson, 1987), his vision of Xanadu in *Literary Machines* (Nelson, 1993). The *Hypertext/Hypermedia Handbook* (Berk and Devlin, 1991) is an excellent, though somewhat outdated, collection of introductory papers; the glossary at the end of the book should be especially useful to newcomers. Conklin's 1987 survey article gives a good introduction to basic principles and an enlightening overview of early systems. A good online starting point is SIGLINK, the ACM Special Interest Group on Hypertext/Hypermedia (ACM SIGLINK Home Page).

4 Applications of hypermedia systems

Hermann Maurer

In this chapter we discuss some of the most important applications of hypermedia systems. We do not try to list all of the hundreds of existing and potential applications, but you will probably find many of them anyway when browsing on the Web. We also explain some of the pitfalls you have to watch out for when you are developing your own applications and point out in some places how Hyper-G can help you. This will prepare for the more detailed discussion of Hyper-G and other Web systems that follows in Chapters 5–10.

4.1 Information presentation

The presentation of multimedia information is certainly *the* leading application of hypermedia systems on the Web. As we will argue in Section 4.2 this is likely to change in the future. However, most substantial organizations today are operating a Web server and the majority are just using the Web much like a glossy printed brochure for general information. Universities, university institutes or even individuals explain their programs and areas of expertise; museums try to "whet the appetite for the real thing"; tourist organizations inform about the facilities of a place or a region much as a flyer would do (see for example Figure 4.1); companies present themselves and their products; societies praise their services; and so on. As cute as some such presentations may be, they are – from a wider perspective – fairly useless. What does it matter that most organizations have "some presence" on the Web when the contents, reliability and level of detail differ vastly from organization to organization. You are likely to be disappointed whenever you look for something fairly specific!

Much as the invention of the printing press initially created a flood of pamphlets until publishing and newspaper companies started to concentrate, filter and package information, the Web also has to go from its current "pamphlet" stage through a shakedown to larger, well-structured pools of information. Organizations that collect, unify, filter and package information for various tastes will become more and more commonplace and will guarantee a certain level of reliability and uniformity of material offered on the Web.

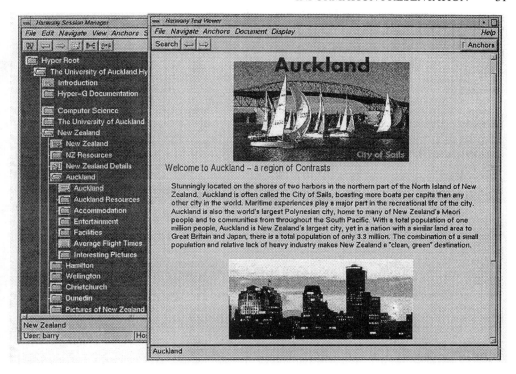

Figure 4.1   Typical tourist page on a server in Auckland.

Till then, the Web will remain hard to use as a general information system. To be concrete, let us mention a few specific examples. It would be nice if the major cities of each country were present on the Web, but if each city were to do its own thing with no coordination, users could get quite frustrated; the information they might find for one city may be there in a completely different form, or not there at all for another. Similarly, information on museums or theaters in a certain region presented on the Web can be extremely useful, particularly if all museums or theaters use the same approach and an index covers a region as large as possible. Descriptions of university departments within a university (or even within a state or country) can be very useful, but only if all departments cooperate and present what they wish to present according to a similar scheme. Airline connections are great to have on the Web: if no coordination between airlines exists such efforts are, however, doubtful. This list can be extended arbitrarily.

The Web today can be compared to a huge library where most books contain only moderately useful information, and books are structured very differently, confusing the reader.

The essence of the above is that all organizations and persons providing information on the Web should try to do so under as large an umbrella with as uniform and consistent a structure as possible. Thus, the concept of combining many small Web servers, at least logically (but not necessarily physically), into a single larger one while retaining a reasonable degree of "local" autonomy is crucial for the success of the Web. This amounts to moving from many individual small servers to one or more larger distributed databases of hypermedia servers such as Hyper-G.

The above statements may be surprising for some. The Web has often been seen as the big liberator that makes everyone a publisher. Unfortunately, if everyone publishes something without coordination, the result is not richness of information but a cacophony of data, close to unusable chaos. Far too much time is wasted today – and this is particularly true of university environments that started the big Web wave, after all – by individuals doing their own cute stuff on their own little server, a server that probably is down a good portion of the time for whatever reason. Information that is to be available on a seven days a week, 24 hours a day basis has to be served by computers that are run professionally, with appropriate maintenance and backup procedures.

One other aspect should not be overlooked: Web servers are often seen as serving the entire world. This may be so in the future; at the moment they are usually accessible only within a certain region at sufficient speed to be seriously usable. However, Web servers that are basically designed to serve a particular constituency belong to the most successful ones: they may be installed for a university, a school district, a company, an administrative unit, a certain city, and so on, where users have access via reasonably fast networks. Such servers may still make use of the Web as a global network, by importing large chunks of information, "caching" them, so to speak, locally. We will return to this later and in particular detail in Chapter 28. For the time being it is enough to realize that (a) small individual servers have to merge into substantial conglomerates to be useful and (b) servers can be set up to serve the world ... or just a small part of it; and the latter variety should not be underestimated.

4.1.1   Display issues

Let us now turn our attention to other aspects of multimedia information presentation on the Web. Typically such multimedia information consists of text and pictures, the pictures often fitted into the text as "inline images" as shown in Figure 4.2. This figure shows a typical "home page" on a Hyper-G server. Parts of the text or pictures are highlighted (in some viewers in a special color, in others by showing buttons); clicking on such highlighted areas leads to additional information; this is after all the link concept explained in Chapter 3.

The multimedia information available can also include audio and video clips, and even 3D objects and 3D scenes (this will be discussed in more detail in Chapter 15). For example, Figure 4.3 shows an example taken from the Hyper-G server of the University of Auckland; the 3D model of part of the campus can be viewed from any point desired. However, on the Web as it currently presents itself, text and raster images (that is, pictures made up of a large number of colored "pixels") dominate, and are often indeed intermixed. Although this gives a pleasing appearance, such inline images do not provide the flexibility of other applications; most importantly, they are fixed in size and cannot be moved. We are now used to being able to scale images to whatever size we like (including the whole screen) but this cannot be done with inline images. Often by clicking on a highlighted "stamp sized" inline image, you may think you are being given a rescaled enlargement, though it should be emphasized that this is

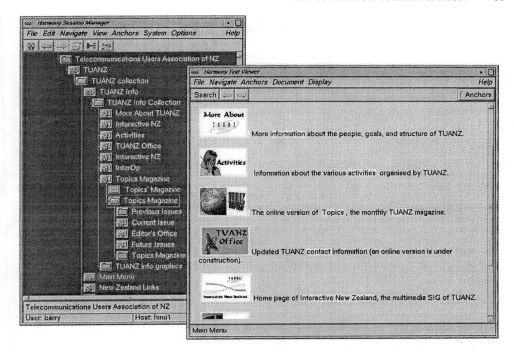

Figure 4.2   Typical "home page" with inline images on a server "Down Under".

really just a trick: the image is not being rescaled, but instead a whole new image is loaded. In some situations it is preferable to be able to manipulate pictures independent of the text: changing their size may be one reason, iconizing a number of them (so that they can later be reactivated instantaneously with a single click) is another and arranging pictures side by side for comparison a third. This additional facility to deal with pictures separately is not provided by all Web systems, but is provided by Hyper-G.

Pictures in Web pages are not only beautiful but also a problem: a reasonable quality raster image (640×480 pixels and with "3 byte deep" color information – that is, about 17 million colors) requires (without compression) about 900 KB. Using the best standardized compression technique (JPEG) can cut this to about 40 KB, an impressive reduction. However, the Internet often does not effectively deliver more than some 2–5 KBps. Hence the loading of such a picture can take up to 20 seconds, an eternity if you just want to take a quick look at the image!

Loading time can be reduced by using smaller images; local area networks (if not overloaded) are often much faster; and most viewers now have the option to display inline images only on demand. Yet the fact remains: pages with (unwanted) pictures are often more a nuisance than a pleasure for the serious user! To put it bluntly: if you insist on having a large picture in your home page it is unlikely that many people will revisit the site.

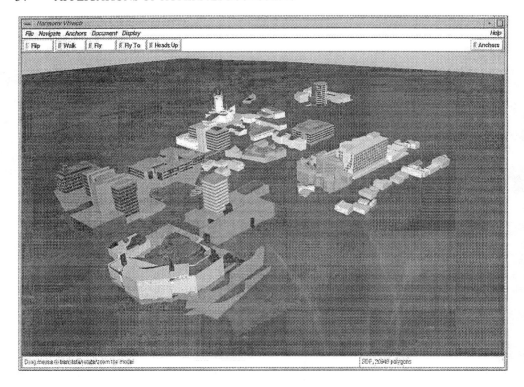

Figure 4.3   3D model of the University of Auckland campus.

In summary, do not use pictures, audio and video clips, and other features as gimmicks, but only where they are needed to convey serious information; and only when explicitly wanted by the user.

The right mix of textual and other information is just one of the critical issues when using the Web for information dissemination. Another probably still more important aspect is the right way to organize information so users find what they want.

4.1.2   Navigational issues

Much has been written about the "lost in hyperspace" phenomenon mentioned already in Chapter 3. To avoid getting lost, a clear and simple structure of the material is of crucial importance to users: although we all talk about the Web of interconnected computers it is not wise to structure information within a server as a web. It is preferable to follow something like the structure of a book, which has a table of contents leading to chapters, each having a table of contents showing its subchapters, these in turn may show a number of sections, and so on.

Within a section you may go from screen to screen (or you may back up to a previous screen). You may have links to footnotes, to supporting material, or **"cross-reference"** links to other chapters. But it should be clear to users that following such a "footnote link" indeed leads to a footnote; that another link supplies supporting information (maybe a picture or movie clip) and that still another link leads to related material but maybe in a completely different chapter. When using such a "book paradigm" (more technically called a menu or hierarchical structure) one can not only browse dynamically forward and backward (akin to turning book pages) but can also go back to the table of contents at the beginning of a section, a chapter, at the start of a book and so on.

It is this kind of explicit structure that makes it easier to classify and find information. It is amusing to note that the original Gopher system relied only on such hierarchical structures (ignoring the flexibility offered by links); that WWW went to the other extreme by only using links with no explicit support for hierarchical structuring; and that it took second-generation hypermedia systems such as Hyper-G to marry both concepts: a powerful link mechanism and a general structuring facility going a bit beyond hierarchical structures. On the one hand, each document or collection of documents can have more than one "parent" in the hierarchical structure; on the other, the same document set can be structured in an arbitrary number of different ways hierarchically. For more theoretically minded readers the first aspect means that data is structured in Hyper-G not as tree, but as a **DAG** (Directed Acyclic Graph) and the second means that a database can be given arbitrarily many different "views." We will return to these properties of Hyper-G later, particularly in Chapters 8 and 9, but it is important to understand why such structuring facilities are needed when dealing with more than very modest amounts of information.

4.1.3   Maintenance issues

Whenever a Web server with substantial amounts of information is built, a number of important issues arise that are often initially overlooked:

(1) How do you ensure that the information remains up-to-date and consistent?

(2) How do you import existing information into the server?

(3) How do you ensure that a steady flow of information keeps pouring into the server after the first enthusiasm has evaporated?

We will see that most Web servers do not provide help concerning the crucial point (1), but Hyper-G does. By providing all documents with expiry dates (which can be used to trigger actions automatically) the obsolescence problem can be all but solved; and the general link concept (providing a separate database of bidirectional links) is not only a tremendous help with the consistency problem, but actually provides new and more elegant ways to browse information. This will be explained in detail in Chapters 8–10. We mention it here to give assurance to all those who have desperately tried to maintain a Web database that Hyper-G technology, at last, makes life much easier.

The second point (2) has three completely different solutions: you can provide "gateways" to existing databases or information systems (as will be discussed in Chapter 12); you can automatically "import" data using scripting (see Chapter 25); or you can convert material initially prepared for other electronic publishing purposes (see Chapters 26–28). Most Web servers will support some form of gateway and scripting, but few except for Hyper-G allow you to make good use of material prepared for other purposes.

The third point (3), to ensure a steady flow of information, is probably the one posing the greatest challenge. It is our credo that large hypermedia systems will only contain all the information desired if the information enters the system "automatically," as a by-product of other activities. Within an organization, this can normally only be achieved by restructuring information processing activities. This can be quite a challenge in itself and we will return to this in Chapter 29.

Summarizing this section we have emphasized that hypermedia systems that only provide information fall into two broad categories: those mainly used for organization-internal purposes (that is, for a well-defined constituency) and those intended for a worldwide audience. Due to network limitations, the media content beyond simple pictures has to be kept to a minimum in the second category. In both categories, the concentration of information in a well-structured uniform database is essential, and the initial creation of a database is often easier than its constant maintenance.

We conclude this section with a remark on providing information on CD-ROM versus on the Web. It is a fact that for some time yet if you just want to sell information at a profit, you would be better off using CD-ROM than the Web. On the other hand, CD-ROMs do not allow the feedback possibilities that you have on the Web. The beauty of second-generation hypermedia systems like Hyper-G is that you need not make difficult decisions: you can prepare material for CD-ROM distribution yet also integrate it into a Web server (see Chapters 26–28) and conversely, you can prepare information on a Web server using Hyper-G and automatically produce a CD-ROM of all or part of the material (see Chapter 13). Thus, you can "go digital" without having to make a choice between CD-ROM and Hyper-G, as long as you use the right tools.

4.2   Beyond information presentation

Although information presentation is, at the moment, the most important Web application this will change rapidly over the next year or two. In this section we mention applications that go beyond information presentation and how Hyper-G supports some of them better than most other Web systems.

The most widely used application currently on the Web that goes beyond mere information presentation is "**information feedback.**" This is almost always done with a **form** that can be filled out by the user, the information gathered being passed on to the operator of a particular Web server. The information gathered can be used for a tremendous variety of purposes such as:

(1) to register for some event (like a conference);

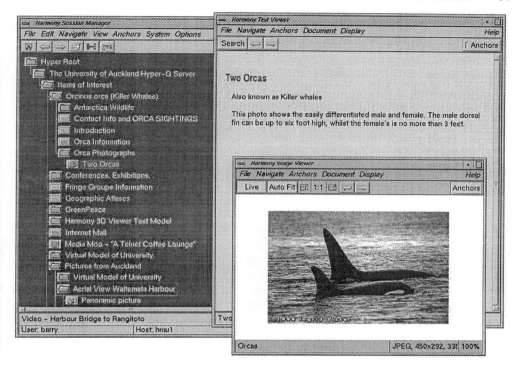

Figure 4.4   Collecting information on whale sightings with Hyper-G.

(2) to order some information material (like a leaflet on some tourist resort, or email or fax concerning a particular topic);

(3) to supply information for a questionnaire (say for statistical purposes) or some other reason (as shown in Figure 4.4, where Hyper-G is used to collect information on whale sightings);

(4) to collect names supporting some cause (like collecting protests against French nuclear tests during the second half of 1995);

(5) to sign up for some service (like the subscription to a journal – electronic or otherwise – or ordering books, tickets, flowers, and so on).

Note that in case (5) some payment may be involved. One usual form of payment is to specify a credit card and the card number. It has often been said that the Web is not "secure," hence sending a credit card number over the Web should not be done. We cannot follow this argument: transactions over the Web are indeed vulnerable to "**eavesdropping.**" However, finding out the number of a credit card is not finding out a secret. Whenever you pay with a credit card and you leave your payment slip, the salesperson, merchant, waiter or whoever you are paying now knows your number. Hence sending your credit card number does not represent any additional risk; whenever you use your credit card number without signature (like making a reservation on the phone, or ordering over the Web) it is not you who run a risk, but the parties accepting your credit card as payment.

Observe that we do not claim that credit cards are safe. They are not always safe even with signature, let alone without. But sending your credit card number over the Web does not give away anything that you are not already giving away every time you use your card.

The only reason why payment by credit card on the basis of a card number works at all is because the beneficiary of the transaction is the owner of the credit card. Thus, if you register with your credit card number for a conference for yourself, send flowers to yourself, and so on, the risk that some one else is impersonating you is small. The use of a credit card number without signature, benefiting someone other than the card owner, should be made illegal everywhere: after all, a waiter to whom you have paid your restaurant bill by credit card could otherwise easily order airline tickets for someone else!

Summarizing, putting your credit card number on a Web form is not really increasing the risks of using a credit card. That credit cards are, however, a fairly unsafe mechanism of payment (or better, that you run a certain risk by just owning a credit card) should be clear to you. Note, however, that you should never put your credit card number and your **PIN** (Personal Identification Number) or even a **TAN** (Transaction Number) on a Web form.

Those of you familiar with TANs which were (and still are) used for certain telebanking applications might be surprised to hear that even the use of a once-only TAN is not safe on the Web; without wanting to go into details it may suffice to say that transactions can be intercepted on the Web and can be changed, using a valid TAN for the modified transaction.

Thus, although some ordering and paying (using credit cards) is possible on the Web there are limits. Secure ways of carrying out highly volatile monetary transactions over the Web using techniques involving so-called public-key cryptography are emerging and should soon permit perfectly safe transactions. Similar techniques can also be used for ensuring the privacy and authenticity of information on the Web: privacy to make sure that only the intended recipients of information can receive this information; and authenticity to ensure that you know that some information was not supplied by an imposter or manipulated by someone else. We will return to security aspects in Chapter 31.

Forms can be used for many other purposes. They are a way to send information to a server that incorporates this information into its database, effectively providing a simple editing tool or creating server-internal news groups. Even full-fledged electronic discussions with links to other documents can be implemented in this way. The basic idea is to allow users to fill out forms (or send files possibly including pictures by Email to a server). The server extracts the relevant information from the forms or the Emails and stores contributions consecutively numbered in the server; by adding in the text something like ⟨see n⟩ (where n is the number of a contribution) the server can even create a link to contribution n automatically.

Carrying out discussions using forms works moderately well, but is also typical for the world of conventional Web servers and Web viewers: a feature for which those tools were not designed is added in a moderately clumsy fashion for the lack of better facilities.

Such better facilities are available in Hyper-G: you can link an arbitrary document y that you have created to a document x created by someone else, although you have no editing privileges for x. This is possible due to the general link concept of Hyper-G; it also ensures that y points to x. And if you choose the "annotation" facility all links are created automatically. Thus, by using Hyper-G and one of its native viewers, electronic discussions involving all media types and arbitrary links (for instance, to background material in a "digital library," see below for more details) can be carried out in a natural fashion. Since links in Hyper-G can have "types," a discussion system that displays a discussion with its structure is a natural extension of current facilities (this feature is not available at the time of writing; it is currently under development and likely to be released in 1996). The authorization facilities available in Hyper-G make it possible to define who can see what of any information, including a discussion as described.

Future hypermedia systems will have to support more than just "asynchronous" computer conferences as discussed above. They will also have to provide the basis for synchronous cooperation including the provision of a "shared workspace." We will return to this in Chapter 30. However, it is important to realize the broad applicability of the variety of discussions that can be carried out Web-based. Here are just a few samples:

- help in the decision making process by discussing important matters electronically (for example, for preparing a meeting, a vote, an election, ...);

- joint preparation of material of any kind (for example, a contract, technical report, specification, ...);

- coordination of project activities (for example, between parties in sites spread all over the world: a number of large European projects have already been managed this way);

- support of teaching and learning (for example, by discussions among students, or students and tutors);

- support of communication (for example, by multimedia multi-person Email).

Note that a special discipline, **CSCW** (Computer Supported Cooperative Work), has been spawned due to the recognition of the importance of cooperative tools. A good hypermedia system must support such tools: either as such, or by providing an architecture that allows them to be integrated.

The Web is often also mentioned in connection with electronic publishing of newspapers, journals, conference proceedings and books: large collections of such material make up so-called "digital libraries."

The electronic publication of material on the Web raises a number of issues including the following particularly important ones:

(1) What is the right data format?

(2) How can users find the desired information?

(3) How can one charge for such publications?

(4) How can one personalize publications?

(5) How can one incorporate advertisements?

(6) What kind of material should be published and how should it be used?

We will not fully go into details here but refer to Chapter 28. It is, however, important to understand that electronic publishing requires a number of features that are not available in ordinary Web servers, yet can be found in Hyper-G.

As for point (1), there is probably no "right data format." A good hypermedia system must surely support the "standard" hypertext data format HTML. However, HTML does break down for certain types of scientific publications (consider formulae in chemistry) and is lacking some layout features required by professional publishers. Hyper-G was thus designed not only to support all kinds of data formats (and is entirely open-ended in this respect), but it also supports both "**logical markup languages**" (SGML, the Standard General Markup Language and its DTD – Document Type Definition – facilities) for describing the logical structure of documents without fixing the (display-dependent) form the user will see, and "**page description languages**" (PostScript and its younger cousin PDF – the Portable Document Format) for the exact specification of what the display of a document should look like.

Concerning point (2), it is clear that powerful search facilities have to be provided to find the desired information. The main problem is not to incorporate such facilities in a Web server (all servers can be more or less elegantly supported by a number of "search engines"), but rather that you have to be able to define the "scope" of the search; in other words, you have to be able to limit the part of the database you are currently interested in. A search of the whole server will usually be an "overkill" by producing too many irrelevant documents. On the other hand, if the scope of the search is limited too much, the "right one" may be missing. Since structuring facilities do not exist on WWW servers it is only systems like Gopher (with its hierarchical structure) and Hyper-G (with its **DAG structure**, a generalization of the notion of hierarchical structure) that allow flexible scope definitions.

Point (3) was the aspect of charging for publications. One of the most useful charging strategies for electronic publishing is the local "**at most n user(s) at a time**" license and is built into all Hyper-G servers (see Section 11.3).

The basic idea is that organizations who want to provide their staff with access to some publication install their own server and buy the publication with an "at most n user(s) at a time" license (downloading the publication from the Web, or even receiving it on a CD-ROM). Now everyone in the organization has access to the material, but only n users at a time. In some cases one license (n equals 1) may be sufficient; it will not be sufficient for popular publications in a large organization, however! This charging strategy has, for example, been used successfully for a German ten-volume encyclopedia and for J.UCS, the *Journal of Universal Computer Science* published by Springer Publishing Co. Note that this charging mechanism, although well suited to organizations, is not appropriate for private individuals. Analogously, if you are a member of a library, you can borrow a book, but if you are not a member you have to buy it!

People who wish to make use of such services but are not members of organizations can be dealt with in other ways, though. Typical approaches include (a) page, volume, time or (b) subscription charges. These all require some username/password combination.

In case (a), users have an account. If someone finds out somebody else's username/password, they can access information at the expense of somebody else. Within the low security environment of the Web this is unacceptable. To overcome this problem we recommend prepaid accounts of moderate size (say US$ 10 or 25) with costs charged against such accounts until they are depleted, in which case they can be reactivated by again prepaying a certain sum. This technique reduces risks for both users and publishers to very acceptable levels. Both techniques have been used in connection with Hyper-G. For instance, the proceedings of the ED-MEDIA '95 conference was accessible to all registrants (and only to registrants) for up to three times per document on a username/password basis. After the conference, the proceedings are now freely available to the public at `http://hyperg.iicm.tu-graz.ac.at/edmedia`.

In case (b), the problem is that the publisher who has received payment from one customer cannot be assured that the customer does not give the username/password to friends who can then also peruse the information without having paid for it. To overcome this problem we recommend that a "subscription" just means that a customer can read each document at most (say) three times. This is no serious restriction for the user, yet prevents uncontrolled spread of passwords.

All of the above charging issues will be addressed more fully in Chapter 28 on the subject of electronic publishing.

An important issue that is often overlooked is the one addressed in point (4): if one uses a "digital library," there is a need for personalization. At each point in time you may want to have certain material "active," in the sense that all searches are carried out in this active material but nowhere else. That is, you may wish to be able to define a "scope." Another way you may wish to personalize your library is to add comments to any document, either for yourself or a group of persons (for example, your students or fellow workers). In other words, you may wish to be able to make "annotations" to documents. A third example of personalization is that you may want to prepare your own material by combining pieces from various sources with some of your own ideas. Both scope definitions and annotations are available in Hyper-G, and the concept of private "home collections" and the general link concept go a long way towards defining your "own view" of the library. This will all be discussed in more detail in Chapters 8–10.

Point (5), advertisements in electronic publications, is one that is very important to publishers since they usually derive much of their revenue from such advertisements. A number of questions come up with advertisements in Web publications. Since downloading advertisements costs users both time and money, it is considered unethical on the Web to "molest" users with long or picture-intensive advertisements; at most, a short "pointer" (which when clicked yields more information) is considered acceptable. There have been attempts to offer entertaining materials on the Web (like collections of regularly changing jokes or cartoons) which are only put on the Web to attract users. Embedded in this material are pointers to advertisements and the insertion of such a pointer is sold like an advertisement in a printed publication! This kind of advertisement on the Web is still fairly close to traditional printed media techniques. However, totally new ways are also emerging. One is called **selling ads**, the other **sponsoring**.

In "selling ads," the idea is that users should not be showered with unwanted ads in the way it is done on TV, where only a fraction is of interest at any one time, but they should instead be able to actually look for information (that is, advertisements) when they are interested in something, for instance a new gardening tool, a vacation package, new car or what have you. Such "collected ads" are a convenience for the user and hence they may be willing to pay for them ... almost like people are often willing to pay a small amount for a substantial catalog.

A still different approach is "sponsoring" books or journals. To be specific, suppose a university is interested in installing an "up to ten users license" for some book on their hypermedia server. Rather than paying for the license, they get it free since the material is sponsored by one or more companies. Whenever the book is accessed by staff or by students of the university, a message advertising the sponsor is displayed. This approach thus permits universities either to buy books on the Web without advertisements, or to use them free of charge but with advertisements, in other words, with messages from the "sponsors." Note that this puts publishers in a new role: they basically have to sell the product not to potential readers (readers will have free access) but to potential advertising sponsors!

Clearly, the above techniques can be combined and variants are possible. The ideas outlined just show that Web publishing also introduces new and surprising aspects to advertising strategies.

The last point (6) mentioned above concerns the kind of material that should be published in a digital library and how it should be used. Certainly the material can and should go beyond what we know from printed media. It can and should include large numbers of pictures, diagrams, audio and video clips, and more. Note first that digital libraries, although they may receive material through the Web from far away, are often run in local area networks and hence speed-bottlenecks are not such a problem; and second, there is much more to multimedia than mentioned above: there are also animations, simulations, movies allowing "interaction" in a variety of ways, panoramic images, 3D objects that can be manipulated, 3D scenes ("virtual reality") in which users can move and look around and so on. Above all, the material incorporated can contain "**courseware**": material that is used for the support of teaching, be it for in-class use (for example, sets of prepared "transparencies" that are projected in a class or seminar) or in the form of standalone teaching units with question/answer dialogs to control the flow of material and to test students as to their level of understanding. We will return to these issues in Chapters 27 and 29 but it should be clear that teaching material can be used together with much of what has already been hinted at in an impressive fashion:

- Teaching material is available for specific tasks and can be perused by students; question/answer dialogs control the level of understanding; and all aspects of multimedia are used for optimal presentation.

- Help through synchronous or asynchronous discussions is provided; some problems and topics are discovered in a cooperative mode supported by the system.

- Background material is available in the "digital library" to dig deeper, or to find additional information where necessary.

It is the last comment that also explains where we see the overriding value of a digital library: not only that it is "always available at your fingertips," that material is hopefully easier to find than in printed collections and that new modes of multimedia information presentation are possible; but, above all, that while you are working (reading, writing, thinking, arguing, ...) part of the library relevant to your needs is available in the background as a silent assistant whenever needed. We believe that this kind of integration of library and teaching material with communicational aspects and everyday activities is one of the most important issues that can be addressed and solved with suitable hypermedia technology.

In this chapter we have discussed some of the major applications of hypermedia systems. It should have become clear that for many of the applications mentioned fairly sophisticated tools going beyond multimedia presentation on the Web are needed. After showing a few examples in the next chapter we will systematically explain how first-generation systems like Gopher and WWW need to and can evolve to second-generation systems such as Hyper-G.

4.3   Further reading

A description of many specific applications of hypermedia systems is contained in Lennon and Maurer (1994a). A good technical description of compression techniques for pictures and other media is found in Buford-Koegel (1994). The standard book on text compression is Witten *et al.* (1994). A very readable survey of CSCW work is Dewan (1993). For an electronic discussion on Hyper-G facilities, browse the site `http://hgiicm.tu-graz.-ac.at`. For digital libraries and their applications to teaching see, for example, Marchionini and Maurer (1995) and Maurer and Lennon (1995) and the special issue on digital libraries of the *Communications of the ACM* (1995). J.UCS can be found at `http://hyperg.-iicm.tu-graz.ac.at/jucs` and the server of the ED-MEDIA 95 conference is at `http://hyperg.iicm.tu-graz.ac.at/edmedia`. Security aspects of hypermedia systems are, for example, dealt with in Posch (1995) and public-key cryptography is explained in Schneier (1995).

For more information on multimedia document formats refer to Berners-Lee and Conolly (1993) for HTML, Wallace (1991) for JPEG, Adobe Systems Inc. (1990) for PostScript, Adobe Systems Inc. (1993) for PDF and ISO (1986) for SGML.

5   Introducing Hyper-G

Frank Kappe

The purpose of this chapter is to give the reader a quick first impression of what is possible with Hyper-G, in terms of both typical applications and features of the Hyper-G software. Instead of lengthy explanations we will use a set of screen shots from actual Hyper-G applications to show most of the features as well. The in-depth description of the concepts behind Hyper-G, the goodies found in the software, and how they can be used to create interesting applications are, of course, contained in the remaining chapters of this book.

5.1   Hyper-G as Web server

Most users will access Hyper-G using a standard Web browser such as Mosaic or Netscape. In this case, Hyper-G behaves like a "standard" Web server with some special features. In fact, if you have surfed the Web a lot already, chances are good that you have retrieved information from a Hyper-G server without even noticing it.

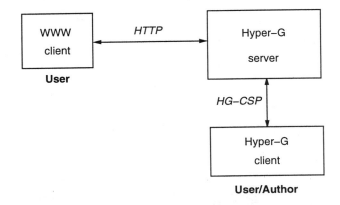

Figure 5.1   Providing information to the Web with Hyper-G.

Figure 5.1 shows how Hyper-G serves information to the Web. Users (that is, people wishing to retrieve information) will most likely use a WWW client (or browser) and WWW's HTTP protocol to access the server. The information providers (or authors) on the other hand will use a Hyper-G client, which is also an authoring tool, for maintenance of the server's content and structure. Since Hyper-G clients can be used over the Internet as well (using **HG-CSP**, the Hyper-G Client–Server Protocol, see also Appendix F), there may also be some "power users" using a remote Hyper-G client for browsing because of its rich navigational functions, or even for contribution to, or maintenance of (parts of), the information on the server. Of course, Hyper-G supports a powerful access control scheme for this purpose.

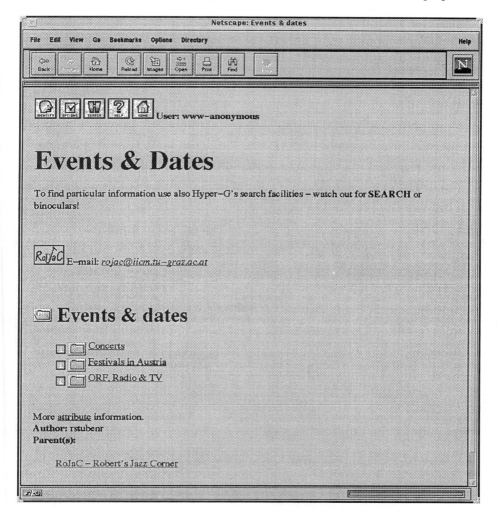

Figure 5.2   Hyper-G collection seen through Netscape.

In Figure 5.2 we see what a small **Hyper-G collection** looks like when accessed with a WWW browser like Netscape. The collection concept is described in detail in Section 9.2. In short, collections are hierarchical structuring mechanisms that greatly reduce authoring and maintenance effort and facilitate user orientation. The user interface seen through WWW browsers is highly configurable, and not part of the contents (see Section 8.2.6 for a discussion on this topic). In Figure 5.2, only the text from Events & Dates up to and including the Email address is written in HTML. Everything else is generated by the Hyper-G server on the fly.

In particular, the icon bar near the top leads to Hyper-G-specific functions (identification, display options, language preferences, searching and so on), while the section at the bottom may contain attribute information. All this is configurable and may be switched off altogether. In Figure 5.3 we see the collection ERS-1/ERS-2 Images on the Hyper-G server (of the European Space Agency). Please notice the different icon bar and the different set of meta-information about the collection near the bottom. Again, only the "Remote Sensing Images" part is content authored by somebody. The collection listing below reflects the collection hierarchy in the Hyper-G database. The meta-information below tells us that user hgsystem is responsible for collection ERS-1/ERS-2 Images, when it was created and last modified, and how many documents it contains.

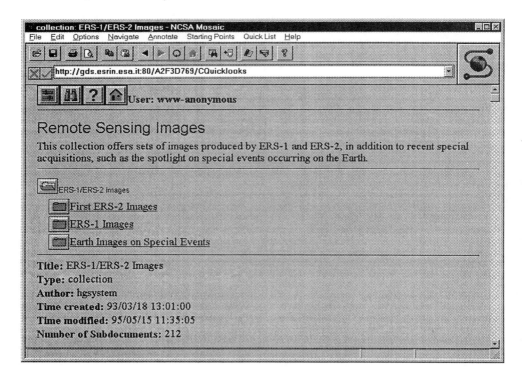

Figure 5.3   Another collection from ESA's Hyper-G server.

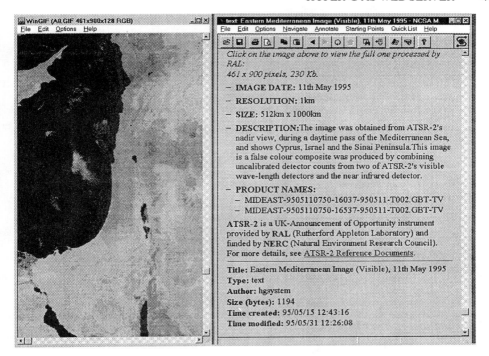

Figure 5.4   Multimedia cluster (seen through Mosaic for Windows).

Figure 5.4 shows a multimedia **cluster**, again from ESA's server. Clusters are composite documents comprised of other documents (see Section 9.2). In the example, it contains a text document (shown on the right, with a link to `ATSR-2 Reference Documents` and meta-information at the bottom), and a GIF image shown to the left. Because the image is displayed in its own window, it may be interactively resized, zoomed and so on. Still, the two documents can be treated as one (logical) document in Hyper-G, which means they are always visualized together and hyperlinks may point to the cluster rather than an individual document.

Figure 5.5 shows a search dialog of the University of Klagenfurt's CWIS. Hyper-G supports a variety of search facilities through document attributes and the contents of text documents. All documents inserted are automatically searchable, without the author having to worry about it. Users may decide to restrict the search scope to certain collections, rather than always having to search through everything. Searches may also span server boundaries (see Section 9.3). The dialogs for WWW access are configurable by the server provider (in our example, the collections `Courses`, `Persons` and so on have been hardwired into the search dialog).

Detailed information on all aspects of using Hyper-G with WWW clients is found in Chapter 20.

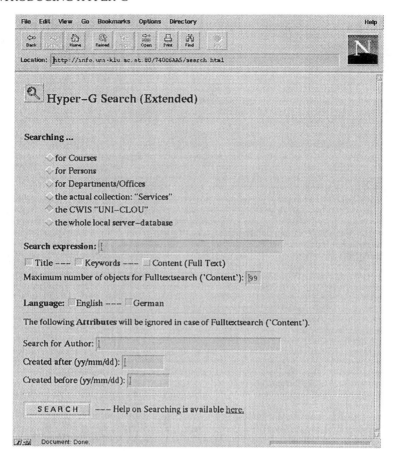

Figure 5.5 CWIS of the University Klagenfurt (extended search dialog).

5.2 Hyper-G clients

When accessing a Hyper-G server with a "native" Hyper-G client, users are offered additional navigation aids and other features, and may also modify the information on the server (provided that they have been granted appropriate access permissions). Of course, Hyper-G clients are also compatible with "standard" Web servers, that is, users may choose to use Hyper-G clients for Web browsing. However, advanced features are only available when talking to a Hyper-G server.

Currently there are four native Hyper-G clients available: **Harmony** (see Chapters 15 and 16) is the client for UNIX/XWindows, and supports a variety of navigational tools,

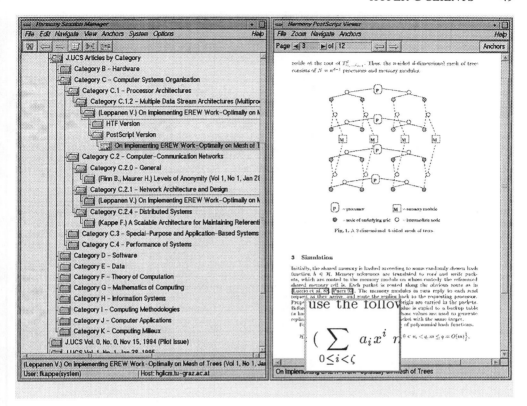

Figure 5.6   J.UCS seen through Harmony.

browsers for various document types and authoring capabilities. **Amadeus** (Chapters 17 and 18) is the client for MS-Windows (3.1, 95 and NT) and offers about the same functionality. **Easy** (Section 19.2) is another MS-Windows client, but with much less functionality and a very easy user interface (intended for information kiosks and pure information presentation purposes). **HGTV** (Section 19.1) is the Hyper-G Terminal Viewer, and can be used with any VT100-type terminal. A Macintosh client is in preparation.

Figure 5.6 shows J.UCS (the *Journal of Universal Computer Science*) using Harmony. On the left we see Harmony's **Collection Browser** visualizing the classification of J.UCS articles by category. Users may click on the collection icons to open and close the corresponding collection views. We see that an item may appear in more than one place in the hierarchy (look at the highlighted Leppanen V.: On Implementing ... item). The right side shows Harmony's PostScript Viewer which lets users view high-quality documents. Near the bottom we see a magnifying glass, and above it two hyperlinks (Luccio et al. 88, Pucci 93) emanating from the PostScript document (links in Hyper-G are not restricted to

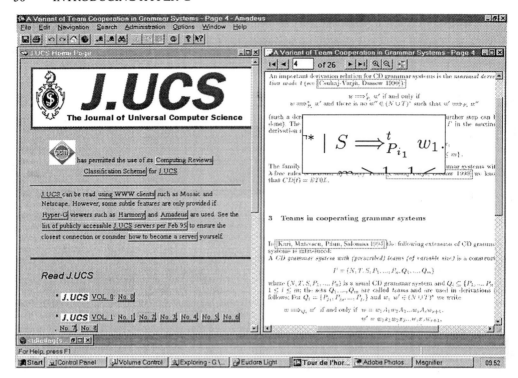

Figure 5.7   J.UCS seen through Amadeus.

HTML documents). Figure 5.7 shows the PostScript Viewer of Amadeus, which has the same features, alongside the Amadeus Text Viewer.

In Figure 5.8 we see another visualization of the relationships between documents: Harmony's **Local Map** gives a graphical overview of the link structure around the current document. In this example, the current document is the wizard entry in the *Hacker's Dictionary*. We see not only links that emanate from wizard, but also links pointing to wizard in other documents (links in Hyper-G are bidirectional, see Section 9.4). This is most useful for authoring hyperdocuments: let us assume we would like to modify or even delete the wizard entry. The local map shows which other documents might be affected (because they contain a link to wizard, or are reachable from wizard).

The local map is active, that is, you may navigate by clicking on the surrounding document. It can be configured to display only links of certain types, including the collection-member relation shown in the collection browser (Figure 5.6). You may also note that the little check-marks indicate already visited documents.

Figure 5.9 shows J.UCS as seen in Harmony's **Information Landscape**, which is a 3D representation of the collection hierarchy. Users may "fly" around, looking for interesting

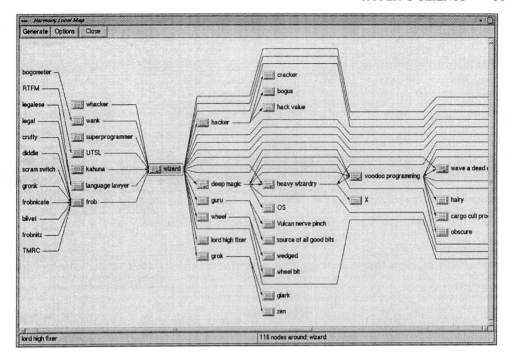

Figure 5.8   Link structure of the "Hacker's Dictionary".

objects. Hyper-G's rich data model (see Section 11.1) lends itself nicely to **information visualization**. This is a new and rapidly evolving field of research, so you may expect to see more and improved 3D navigation aids in the future.

Among the other notable features of Hyper-G clients is the ability for **interactive link editing** in arbitrary document types. We have already seen links in PostScript documents (Figures 5.6 and 5.7). Figure 5.10 shows a "virtual museum" type application – a tour through the Austrian National Library – with links in 3D scenes (in the scene shown in the bottom-left window, the hand of the statue is highlighted by a different color, which unfortunately cannot be seen easily in the black and white print), films (in the film being played in the bottom-right window, the rectangle around the statue actually moves while the film is being played back), and texts (as seen in the top-left window). The links may be interactively placed without editing the documents themselves. This is made possible by Hyper-G's separate link database (see Section 9.4).

In Figure 5.11 we see the definition of an elliptical anchor around the clocktower in Amadeus.

Hyper-G documents carry attributes (**meta-information**). Some of them are searchable (for instance, `Title`, `Name`, `Keyword`, `Author` and `ModificationTime`). Some of them can be edited (for instance, `Title`), some are set by the server (for instance,

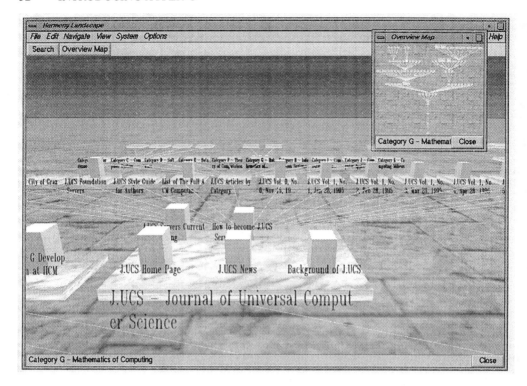

Figure 5.9   Fancy "virtual reality" style view of a collection hierarchy.

ModificationTime). Figure 5.11 shows the Images of Austria collection. We are looking at a cluster containing an image and a number of text documents in different languages. The preferred language has been set to French in this example, so we see the French text. The author is just modifying the French title of the cluster. The attribute information shows that it also contains titles in English, German, Italian and Spanish. Depending on the user's preferences, the appropriate title is shown in the collection hierarchy (in our case, French).

Hyper-G clients connect to their server using a connection-oriented protocol (see Section 8.3.6 and Appendix F). The protocol is asynchronous and bidirectional, which means it is possible to send messages from servers to clients, without the clients having to ask for them. Figure 5.12 shows a nice application: in the background we see Harmony's Status Browser which lets you see who else is currently connected to the same server as you. You may send and receive messages to (and from) other users.

The material presented in this chapter represents only a small subset of Hyper-G's features and possible applications. A more detailed discussion of what was presented here, along with many other ideas, awaits you in the forthcoming chapters.

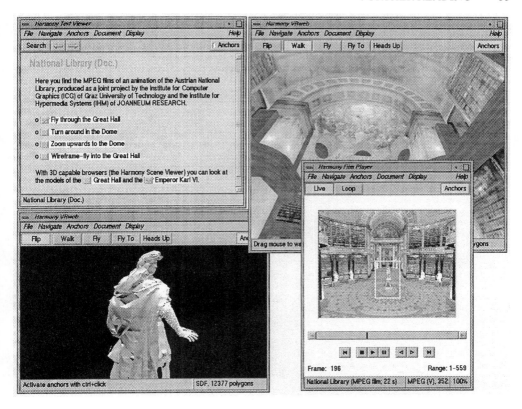

Figure 5.10   Interactive link editing in arbitrary document types.

5.3   Further reading

More information on Hyper-G is, of course, contained in the other chapters of this book. A good overview article on Hyper-G appeared in the November 1995 issue of *Byte* magazine (Flohr, 1995).

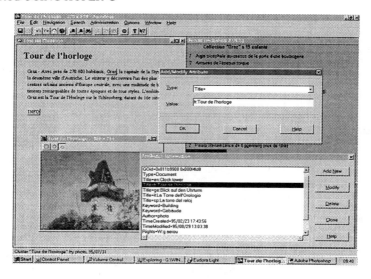

Figure 5.11   Images of Austria (editing meta-information, multilingual).

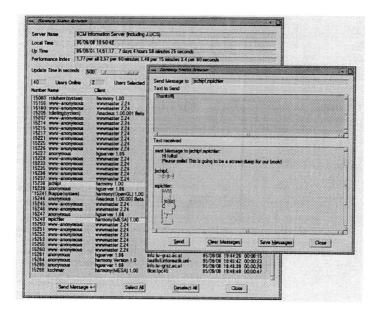

Figure 5.12   Synchronous communication between users.

6 Gopher: The first revolution

Mark McCahill

The **Internet Gopher** was the first popular client–server distributed information system on the Internet to include both browsing and full text searching of collections of documents.

6.1 Background

In late 1990 and early 1991, staff at the **University of Minnesota** computer center began studying how to build a campus-wide information system to make information more accessible to the university community. By late spring of 1991, a first release of the Internet Gopher software was available, and over the next year and a half, Gopher was rapidly adopted as both a **campus-wide information system** and as a basic Internet tool for locating and publishing information.

Because Gopher was designed so that users could seamlessly navigate through information published on servers located anywhere on the Internet, it quickly evolved from a local campus-wide information system into a global information mesh. As of 1995, there are approximately 7500 Gopher servers on the Internet containing around 2.5 million documents. What drove this growth and why was Gopher different from previous Internet applications? The best way to understand what made Gopher part of the first revolution in Internet information systems is to look at the original design goals of Gopher and trace how Gopher has evolved during the past four years.

Studying the aims and evolution of the Internet Gopher system can also tell us a lot about the characteristics that are desirable in a modern information system, and this chapter will discuss these issues as well.

6.2 Early CWISs and Gopher

In 1990 and 1991, many university computer centers were either considering or deploying some form of CWIS. The typical CWIS was a mainframe application that users accessed by running terminal emulation software from a Macintosh or PC. The motivation for running a CWIS was to show how making information available online could benefit a university or other institution. Since the people running the CWIS were generally the same people that ran the campus mainframe, another (usually) unspoken part of the agenda was to show that the campus mainframe had an important role to play in the brave new world of online information access. Given the central computing/mainframe heritage of most early CWISs it is not surprising that there was an implicit assumption that a campus would have exactly one CWIS that would run on the mainframe and that all users would access the CWIS by starting from the same centrally controlled menu. Gopher's design was a reaction to the problems inherent in a mainframe-oriented, centralized CWIS system such as those prevalent in 1990.

6.3   Problems with CWISs

There are several serious problems with the typical early 1990s CWIS. First, because there is only one server and one entry point to the server, there are inevitable and cataclysmic battles over whose information is located at the top (or most visible part) of the information hierarchy.

Veterans of the political struggles to decide names and location of information on a centralized CWIS still bear the scars of these struggles. These disagreements over information organization are nearly impossible to resolve because, for instance, people from the chemistry department might have one view of what is most important to them, but this view is unlikely to coincide with the views held by the athletics department. Since each group has a different view of what is important, reconciling these views in a single system is a recipe for never-ending struggle. People naturally form groups based on common interests, and information system architectures that do not accommodate this reality create ongoing organizational struggles.

A second problem is that early CWISs generally ignored the possibility that information of interest might be published at other institutions (or even on other computers at the home institution). These systems were designed as inward-looking, self-contained systems. An inward-looking self-contained system requires that information available elsewhere is duplicated inside the system to be accessible. This can be a waste of resources and will certainly limit the scope of the information that is available.

A third problem is that the searching capabilities of the CWISs were usually quite limited. The sort of full text searches we take for granted in WAIS, Gopher, WWW or Hyper-G today were not widely known or deployed in 1990. While browsing through collections of information can be a pleasant pastime, any large information system requires a fast search capability to be really useful. Beyond the ability to submit queries to a search engine, it is also important to be able to select the scope of the search so that the user can control what portion of the information space is searched.

Finally, the early CWISs were generally terminal-based mainframe applications, so all users were reduced to interacting with VT100 or 3270 dumb-terminal sessions. This prospect did not please anyone who was used to a user interface experience better than a VT100 terminal. However, because the systems were not client–server systems, everyone was reduced to the lowest common denominator (dumb-terminal) user interface.

6.4   Gopher's design goals

6.4.1   Client–server architecture

Gopher was designed with the idea of avoiding the problems inherent in a centralized single-server information system. Gopher has a client–server architecture so the user interface on a Macintosh can look like a Macintosh, a PC's interface can look like a PC, and so on. In addition to providing for a better user interface, the client–server architecture also made it possible for Gopher servers to run on inexpensive desktop systems.

Gopher servers are fundamentally simple programs that accept a connection from a client and either return documents, collections of documents (directories), or references to objects on other servers (links) or perform searches of document collections. By keeping the demands on the server low and having the user's client software do most of the work of displaying the information, a Gopher server does not have to be a mainframe-class machine to handle large numbers of users. To simplify server administration, Gopher servers are generally configured to publish a part of the server's file hierarchy, and this information space is presented to the user as a browsable collection of documents and directories. The simplicity of the protocol and architecture was intentional so that publishing information could be handled by nearly anyone, from a network connected desktop personal computer. Given this goal, it should be clear that Gopher was intended from the beginning to become a mesh of interconnected servers.

6.4.2   Distributed servers

Rather than requiring users to connect to a single central system, Gopher has a distributed server architecture. This means that there are many servers and further that users are not all expected to start from the same point in the information system. Instead of a single, centrally managed server, information producers run their own servers. This helps minimize struggles over finding an optimum organization of information on a single institution-wide server. Anyone is free to run their own servers and organize them to meet their needs. Users are free to connect to any server they like, so the information that appears to be at the "top" of the information system depends on which server the user contacts first. This trend of offering users the ability to create their own collections and content and then the ability to publish them appears to be a key to the acceptance of not only Gopher but also WWW and Hyper-G.

6.4.3   Links between servers

Once the idea that a single server will hold all information is abandoned, it is crucial to be able to make navigating from one server to another as painless as possible. The Gopher architecture would not work without the concept of links (or references) to objects located on other servers. A Gopher link contains enough information that a Gopher client software knows which server to contact and how to ask the server to retrieve the information to which the link refers (see Table 6.1).

Table 6.1   Gopher link information.

Gopher link information
Server name
Port on which the server process listens
Type of object (document, directory, sound, picture...)
Selector string to send server to request object

By making information referred to by links automatically retrievable by the client software, users do not need to worry about exactly which server holds the information they are accessing. In the process of exploring information available in Gopher, a user may traverse many servers without noticing that information came from different ones in different locations managed by different groups. Because navigation through the Gopher information space (**gopherspace**) is seamless, Gopher servers on the Internet quickly moved from being a few islands of information (a campus-centric system) to being a global information system with cross-references between servers.

6.5   Searching in gopherspace

While browsing is a popular way of interacting with an information collection, it is not a very efficient way to locate specific information. Being able to submit queries to a search engine is an important part of being able to make efficient use of an information system to actually locate items of interest. Besides making distributed servers appear as one seamless system, when Gopher was released, it was a revolutionary Internet information system because it popularized combining the browsing of hierarchical collections of documents with a full text search capability. Combining a structured information hierarchy with search engines at several levels in the hierarchy gives users an intuitive method for controlling the scope of their search. If the organization of the information hierarchy is well designed, the user can easily traverse the collections to find the appropriate scope (for instance, today's news or last month's news) before submitting a query.

Because a Gopher server can return either references to objects that reside on that server or links to objects stored elsewhere in gopherspace, a search engine does not need to be on the same machine as the documents it searches for. As long as the search engine returns valid references or links to Gopher objects, the user's client software can automatically resolve these references. By allowing the search function to be independent of the document storage location, it is possible for a search engine to return results for a collection of Gopher servers (perhaps for an entire organization) or even all of gopherspace as in the case of the **Veronica** database.

So, Gopher also became popular because it combined some explicit organization of the information space (the Gopher directories) with advanced searching capabilities. Browsing through an unorganized mass of information is frustrating, but most Gopher server administrators tended to structure their information hierarchy reasonably well. By browsing, the user could get to the right general area of a server and then use a search engine to quickly locate items of interest. This concept (an explicit organization of the information space external to documents combined with searching) is carried further in Hyper-G where there is more consistency to the availability of search engines than in Gopher. In Gopher, the user has to depend on the server administrator to set up a search engine for a given section of gopherspace; in Hyper-G search engines for a given area of the information space are more readily available.

6.6   Veronica

It would not be very efficient to visit 7500 Gopher servers and to look through 2.5 million documents if you were only interested in finding recipes for salmon. How can a search engine efficiently allow for searching through all of gopherspace? Keep in mind that the Gopher servers are located all over the Internet and are not run by a single organization.

A specialized searchable database called Veronica has a searchable index of all titles of objects in gopherspace. This searchable index is built automatically by a process that connects to Gopher servers and walks through their information hierarchy. As it passes through, it collects the names of objects and links pointing to other Gopher objects on other servers. By adding the objects' names to a searchable index and keeping track of links that point to servers that have not yet been visited by this harvesting process, it is possible to build a searchable database even though there is no central organization of the Gopher servers and the servers are run independently. To the user, the Veronica search engine looks like any other search engine in Gopher; when you select it you are prompted to enter the words to search for and the results of the search are returned as a Gopher directory containing the objects (documents and directories) that match the search criteria. Again, because Gopher servers can return references to objects that are stored on other servers, there is a great deal of flexibility about where the search is submitted and where the actual documents reside.

6.7   Putting Gopher into perspective

So far, we have looked at how Gopher was a break from traditional centralized mainframe-oriented information systems in the early 1990s. To quickly summarize: Gopher is a distributed server system. Gopher client software can automatically use the information from a Gopher link to fetch items on servers elsewhere on the network. Gopher combined browsing a structured collection of documents with full text search engines, and extended the search engines across server (and organizational) boundaries. People publishing information might not necessarily write new documents; instead their contribution might be to collect and organize links to documents published by others, so the Gopher architecture supports an editorial/cataloging function.

Gopher became a popular framework for organizing and publishing information on the Internet, partly because it is very easy to use Gopher to publish a portion of your hard disk or file system. Since Gopher was designed to be a distributed framework, Gopher did not require that documents be in any particular page description language or data types. While text is the most common format, other formats are also popular, and Gopher can accommodate a variety of formats and data types (video, graphics, sound and so on). As WWW became popular, it became common practice to serve HTML documents from Gopher servers so that Gopher could be used to combine a searchable, structured information space with hypertext documents. This idea is again similar to what the Hyper-G system provides in a more advanced form.

Although the initial system design for Gopher was a real success, it became clear that there were limitations to the system that needed to be addressed. The major issues were meta-information, alternate data formats and electronic forms.

6.8   Evolution to Gopher+

After it had been in use for about a year or so, it became painfully obvious that Gopher had a number of severe limitations. To address these limitations, **Gopher+** was created as a

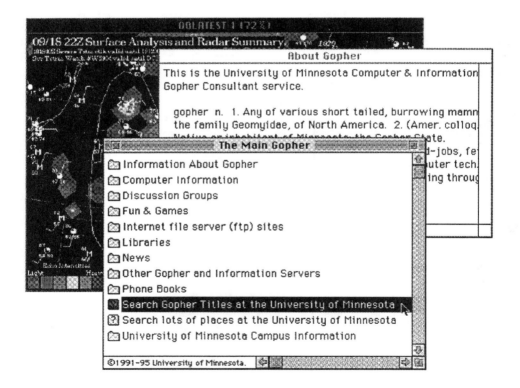

Figure 6.1   Typical Gopher client.

backward-compatible set of extensions to the original Gopher system. The most important addition to the base Gopher system was Gopher$^+$meta-information. The Gopher system needed a place to store arbitrary information about documents/directories such as owner, creation date, size, abstract and so on. It was also clear that this information ought to be stored separately from the document's actual content so that it could reliably be retrieved in a standard format, independent of the document content. Providing space for meta-information made it possible to handle issues such as determining how large an object was before starting to fetch it over a slow connection, finding out who owned the document, and being able to read an abstract of a document before fetching the document itself.

With a place to store arbitrary meta-information, Gopher$^+$ had provisions for solving another problem. The lowest common denominator for document formats is ASCII text, but there are a large number of other data formats. By using an "alternate view" block of data stored as meta-information, it was possible to advise users that a given document was available in more than one data format so that they could pick the format that best suited their needs.

The idea of alternate views is even carried over to directories; some Gopher$^+$ servers can automatically provide HTML-formatted alternate views of a Gopher directory, as seen in Figures 6.1 and 6.2. Note that the meta-information also contains an abstract.

The Gopher$^+$ meta-information block was also pressed into service to hold definitions for Gopher electronic forms. By making provisions for clients to fetch electronic form descriptions from Gopher$^+$ servers it became easier to interface Gopher clients to more complex search engines and SQL databases, as well as to solicit credit card numbers, shoe sizes, and any other information that might be requested in a paper form.

Figure 6.2   Gopher$^+$ meta-information.

6.9   User interface metaphors

Gopher is intended to be a framework into which documents in a variety of formats can be placed. The Gopher+ extensions continue this philosophy by keeping meta-information separate from document content so that the Gopher system can handle any sort of document. Given this orientation, it is not surprising that most Gopher clients display the Gopher information space as a hierarchical set of menus that the user navigates through. For most client software, this is displayed in a similar fashion to the way a file system directory structure is displayed.

While a hierarchical menu interface is fast to view and navigate, there are limitations to this sort of interface. Menus are fundamentally one-dimensional lists, so it is difficult to show complex relationships. To explore more advanced user interface metaphors for showing relationships between documents, a 3D version of the familiar Gopher clients (**GopherVR**) has been developed during the past two years (see Figure 6.3).

GopherVR-aware servers can return Gopher+ meta-information to specify the location of Gopher objects in a 3D virtual reality information landscape. Once again, this is similar to what is possible in some of the advanced Hyper-G clients. Note that because Gopher and Hyper-G have an explicit organization of information objects (documents and directories), which is stored separately from the document content, it is straightforward to employ a 3D scene as a user interface to a collection that can also be viewed as a menu. This is in sharp contrast to WWW.

Figure 6.3   GopherVR scene.

Note that a key difference between Gopher and the WWW system is the user interface metaphor for how information and relationships between documents are displayed. Gopher has a clear distinction between document content, meta-information and directories. In contrast, the WWW system treats everything as some sort of page; it displays all information as a page containing hypertext links. When everything is a page, it is difficult to extract information to create reasonable 3D scenes from the pages because it is unclear what to call objects. It is also hard to determine how much of the text that surrounds a hypertext link should go with it.

If 3D virtual reality is a valid way to visualize relationships between documents (perhaps to show how documents semantically cluster), then the architecture used by Gopher and Hyper-G for separating information space structure from content is important for enabling these 3D interfaces.

6.10   Problems with current information systems

While Gopher and WWW have enjoyed great success on the Internet, both Gopher and WWW suffer from a fundamental architectural problem as systems grow large. Since all references to objects on servers are in terms of locations (a specific object on a specific server), if a server's name changes, or the location of an object on the server changes, any links to that object break. This problem with dangling links can be illustrated by thinking about what happens if someone tells you to grab the fifth book from the fourth bookshelf at the University of Minnesota bookstore. This reference to a specific location works well until the bookstore rearranges its shelves. Another problem with this reference by location is that it might not be convenient to visit the University of Minnesota if you live in Austria. The problems with referencing by location are, then, that we can get into trouble if we rearrange servers and that even if we do not, we do not necessarily retrieve information from the most convenient place. In our bookstore analogy, if we refer to books by name, the problems with reference by location go away. By addressing these problems, Hyper-G provides a logical next step from systems such as Gopher and WWW. However, this next step carries with it some costs in terms of complexity of server and authoring, so it is likely that for small collections of information, less robust and simpler systems such as Gopher and WWW will continue to be adequate solutions.

6.11   Conclusions

Gopher was designed as an information system that is easy to use and easy to publish with and has been successful in achieving this goal. Some of Gopher's strengths turn into liabilities if the information being published is very large, since maintaining consistency of the links between servers becomes problematic as information and servers move. This makes Hyper-G a logical next step for Gopher administrators who wish to publish large collections of information since Hyper-G retains the user-visible strengths of the Gopher system (browsable/searchable hierarchy, possibility of advanced user interfaces) with a system that can avoid the problem of dangling or broken links.

6.12   Further reading

For further details about Gopher please refer to McCahill and Anklesaria (1995), for Gopher+ to Anklesaria *et al.* (1993a) and for GopherVR to McCahill and Erickson (1995). If you want general information about Internet information services see Liu *et al.* (1994).

7 World Wide Web: A first plateau

Christian Huber

In this chapter we give a brief overview of the **World Wide Web** (WWW). Beginning with the history of WWW, we describe the three elements of which WWW is comprised: **HTML**, **HTTP** and **URL**. In the last part of this chapter we introduce some WWW servers, WWW browsers and WWW editors. With **CGI** (the Common Gateway Interface), it is possible to improve WWW. How this can be done and what drawbacks remain are discussed at the end of this chapter.

7.1 World Wide Web history

In 1989, Tim Berners-Lee and Robert Cailliau started to think independently about the possibility of using a hypertext system for international cooperation, an idea proposed already by Ted Nelson in his Xanadu project in 1965. Researchers in high energy physics at **CERN** wanted to share information with each other, but previous attempts had met with many problems due to a range of different network information retrieval protocols. Another problem was the variety of different workstations with widely varying display capabilities.

The first technical breakthrough concerning WWW was achieved by Nicola Pellow, a technical student at CERN. He developed a **line mode browser**, a character-grid oriented client, in 1991. A year later, the incorporation into the WWW browser of the most important Internet protocols, such as Gopher, Telnet and FTP, was also completed. In 1993, ripples of excitement went through the UNIX world: the first XWindows WWW browser was born. Developed by the National Center for Supercomputing Applications (**NCSA**), it was a graphical browser called **Mosaic** and was the first one able to show color images and proportional type fonts. Then, in 1994, perhaps "The year of the Web," the first WWW conference took place at CERN. From this moment on, the WWW spread from the high energy physics community into all areas of academia and then into commercial enterprises and to the general public.

7.2   The main concepts behind WWW

WWW is officially described as an Internet-wide distributed hypermedia information retrieval system which provides access to a large universe of documents. It began as a set of simple protocols and formats and was originally seen as a testbed for various sophisticated hypermedia and information retrieval concepts. WWW, like many other applications on global networks, uses a client–server model. These clients (called Web browsers if they are intended for interactive use) are nothing more than collections of fairly simple programs which can send requests for documents to WWW servers. On the other hand, WWW servers are programs that, after they receive requests, send back the appropriate answers – either documents or error messages.

To make this flow of information possible, three major "standards" and conventions were defined. First, a consistent address system using a compact syntax for a **Uniform Resource Locator** (URL) was defined. In addition to other protocols which may be used with WWW a new protocol, the **Hypertext Transfer Protocol** (HTTP) was defined, giving performance and features not otherwise available. A set of data formats can be used in which data can be transferred. One of them was a new data format, the **HyperText Markup Language** (HTML), which has become the main format for transmitting hypertext. These three most important elements of WWW are explained in the following subsections.

7.2.1   HyperText Transfer Protocol (HTTP)

The purpose of the HyperText Transfer Protocol is to provide a fast and flexible mechanism for following references between units of information which are distributed at different locations across the Internet. Its name may be misinterpreted. It is not only a protocol for transferring hypertext, but for transferring all sorts of information with the efficiency that is needed for following links in a hypertext system. The protocol is stateless and object-oriented. Eight-bit transfer is always used. It provides several commands for retrieval, manipulation and searching of data in a distributed collaborative hypermedia information system. One of its properties is that the set of HTTP commands can be extended easily. The process of retrieving or manipulating information using this stateless protocol always consists of two operations. A request is sent from the client to the information source, the server. This request contains the type of operation (retrieval, searching and so on) which the client wants the server to perform and secondly, some sort of identifier for the object on which this operation is to be performed. The type of operation is specified by the command called the "method" of the HTTP request. The problem of referencing a certain object is solved by using the concept of a Uniform Resource Locator (URL). In addition to this, for some types of operation the client can send additional data to the server within the request. The server, after trying to fulfill the request, sends a response to the client. This response depends on the request and on whether or not the request has been processed successfully. The server establishes a connection between client and server. Normally, when TCP/IP is used, the default port for HTTP transaction is the reserved number 80. Other port numbers may be used if they are specified in the URL of the request. After setting up a connection, the client sends the request and waits for the response from the server. After that, the connection is closed by either or both parties. In other words, a connection between client and server is only set up for one transaction.

7.2.2 The Uniform Resource Locator (URL)

A URL is a Uniform Resource Locator, a standard way developed to specify the location of a resource available electronically. URLs make it possible to direct both people and software applications to a variety of information, available from a number of different Internet protocols. You are bound to encounter URLs when using a WWW client, since URLs link WWW pages together. In your WWW browser's "location" box, the item that generally starts with `http` is a URL. Files available over protocols besides HTTP, such as FTP and Gopher, can be referenced by URLs, too. Even Telnet sessions to remote hosts on the Internet and someone's Internet Email address can be referred to by a URL.

URLs have a very specific syntax. They consist of a number of elements which are delimited by colon, slash and hash. They follow the following format:

`protocol://domain:port/full-path-of-file/#internalanchor`

The first element of a URL, `protocol`, is a naming scheme specifier which refers to Internet protocols. Then an Internet domain name of the desired host follows (it is also possible to use the IP address as a set of four decimal digits but usually names are simpler to remember). After the Internet domain name it is possible to request a port number after a colon. The rest of the URL points to a full-path-of-file on a WWW server and `internalanchor` refers to a fragment of the node. Examples of the naming scheme specifiers are:

`http`	HyperText Transfer Protocol
`hyperg`	Hyper-G Protocol
`gopher`	The Gopher Protocol
`mailto`	Electronic Mail Address
`ftp`	File Transfer Protocol
`news`	Usenet News
`wais`	Wide Area Information Servers

As an exercise, let us look at the following URL:

`http://www.w3.org/hypertext/Conferences/WWW4/`

The protocol defined by URL is `http` for the HyperText Transfer Protocol. The Internet address of the machine is `www.w3.org`, and the path to the file is `hypertext/Confe-rences/WWW4`. When working with WWW, most URLs will be very similar to this one in their overall structure.

In this example the "full-path-of-file" ends in a slash. This indicates that the URL is pointing not to a specific file, but to a directory. In this case, the server generally returns the "default index" of that directory. This might be just a listing of the files available within that directory, or a default file that the server automatically looks for in the directory. With HTTP servers, this default index file is generally called `index.html`, but is frequently seen as `homepage.html`, `home.html`, `welcome.html` or `default.html`.

7.2.3   HyperText Markup Language (HTML)

The most important document format in WWW is HTML, or HyperText Markup Language. HTML is an application of SGML (Structured Generalized Markup Language). It is a simple markup language used to create hypertext documents that are portable from one platform to another. The document is divided into parts like headings, paragraphs, footnotes and so on. It is the aim of HTML, and this is typical for SGML, to describe the logical structure of the document and not the actual layout of the screen. The appearance of a text depends on the capabilities of the WWW browser and the display used. Browsers decide what headings should look like, what kind of font should be used and so on.

HTML serves for the representation of:

- Hypertext/hypermedia

- Simple text with inline images

- Queries to databases

- Menus

- Email and News.

The specification of HTML can be divided into three levels.

HTML level 1 This specifies a set of HTML properties which is understood by almost all WWW browsers at this moment. In addition to the HTML of the initial clients, it defines the use of inline images. HTML level 1 is often called HTML 1.0.

HTML level 2 This specification includes additional properties like forms for user input. Some of its features are already in use by various clients, for instance Mosaic and Netscape, although the specification is still being refined. This level is also called HTML 2.0.

HTML level 3 This specification is also referred to as HTML 3.0. It defines more sophisticated features for HTML such as tables, figures and mathematical formulae. HTML 3.0 builds upon HTML 2.0 and provides full backwards compatibility.

General syntax

An HTML document consists of simple text, except that parts of the text are interpreted as markup. For this purpose, a number of elements are defined. All elements are surrounded by left and right angle brackets. Most of them mark blocks of the document for the particular purpose of formatting. Tags delimit elements such as headings, paragraphs, lists, character highlighting and links. Most HTML elements are identified in a document as a start-tag, which gives the element name and attributes, followed by the content, followed by the end-tag. Start-tags are delimited by < and >; end-tags are delimited by </ and >. The name of the element is case-insensitive and has to follow immediately after the tag open delimiter. Some elements only have a start-tag without an end-tag. For example, to create a line break, you use the

`<BR>` tag. Additionally, the end-tags of some other elements, such as Paragraph (`</P>`), List Item (`</LI>`), Definition Term (`</DT>`) and Definition Description (`</DD>`), may be omitted. In all these cases, the browser knows that there must be an implied end-tag in order to end all previous blocks. In a start-tag, white space and attributes are allowed between the element name and the closing delimiter. An attribute specification typically consists of an attribute name, an equals sign and a value, though some attribute specifications may be just a name token. White space is allowed around the equals sign. The value of the attribute may be either:

- a string literal, delimited by single or double quotes and not containing any occurrences of the delimiting character.

- a name token (a sequence of letters, digits, periods, or hyphens). Name tokens are not case-sensitive.

In this example, `IMG` is the element name, `SRC` is the attribute name, and `http://myhost/ images/file.gif` is the attribute value:

```
<IMG SRC="http://myhost/images/file.gif">
```

A typical example of an HTML text could be:

```
<HTML>
<HEAD>
<TITLE> My first HTML document.  </TITLE>
</HEAD>
<BODY>
Any text
</BODY>
</HTML>
```

Basically, HTML documents should contain an initial HEAD element followed by a BODY element, although this is not obligatory. The HEAD element contains all the information about the properties of the whole document, but it does not contain any text which is part of the document. All the information that belongs to the document is in the BODY element. Some elements that can appear in the HEAD element are listed in the following.

Basic markup tags

Title Every HTML document should have a title. A title is generally displayed separately from the document and is used primarily for document identification in other contexts (for example, a WAIS search). Choose about half a dozen words that describe the document's purpose, for example:

```
<TITLE>The Hyper-G Home Page</TITLE>
```

Headings The HTML elements for headings are called H1, H2, H3, H4, H5 and H6. The H1 element is the most prominent heading. Once more, how the rendering is done is decided by the browser. This includes the generation of vertical white space before and after such heading elements. Therefore, it is not required to put a paragraph mark after the heading element. The syntax of the heading tag is:

```
<Hy>Text of heading</Hy>
```

where y is a number between 1 and 6 specifying the level of the heading. For example, the coding for this section about HTML is

```
<H3>7.2.3 HyperText Markup Language (HTML)</H3>
```

Title versus first heading In many documents, the first heading is identical to the title. For multi-part documents, the text of the first heading should be suitable for a reader who is already browsing related information (for example, a chapter title), while the title tag should identify the document in a wider context. For instance, the title tag could include both the book title and the chapter title, although this can sometimes become overly long.

Paragraphs Unlike documents in most word processors, carriage returns in HTML files are not significant. Word wrapping can occur at any point in the document and multiple spaces are collapsed into a single space. There are some exceptions: for instance, spaces following one of the heading elements or the <P> element are ignored. The line break in the next example will be ignored by every HTML client. It starts a new paragraph only when it reaches a <P> tag. This is very important because the browsers ignore any indentations or blank lines in the source text. HTML relies almost entirely on tags for formatting instructions and without the <P> tags the document becomes one large piece of text with no breaks.

```
<H3> Paragraph example:   </H3>
<P>
Welcome to Hyper-G.<P>
We are glad to see you.
</P>
```

Links to other documents The main power of HTML derives from the ability to link regions of text and images to another document. The browser highlights such regions to indicate that they are hypertext links. The text between the anchor start-tag <A> and the anchor end-tag </A> is expected to specify a source or a destination anchor according to the optional attributes included in the start-tag. The attribute HREF specifies a source anchor. The value of this attribute is either the address (usually the URL) of the destination document or the identifier of a destination anchor within the same document prefixed by the hash sign #, or the URL plus an identifier which refers to a certain destination anchor in a different document (see below). The text of the anchor is "sensitive"; for instance, it can be displayed "clickable" by the browser.

Here is a sample hypertext reference:

```
Go to the <A>
HREF='http://hyperg.tu-graz.ac.at/homepage.html'>Hyper-G
</A> homepage
```

This entry makes the word `Hyper-G` the hyperlink to the document `homepage.html`, which is in the root directory of the Hyper-G home server.

Anchors can also be used to move to a particular section in a document. Suppose you wish to set a link from document A to a specific section in document B. (Call this file `documentB.html`.) First you need to set up a named anchor in document B. For example, to set up an anchor named "Austria" in document B, enter

```
Here is <A NAME="Austria">my destination.</A>
```

Now when you create the link in document A, include not only the filename, but also the named anchor, separated by a hash mark (#).

```
This is my <A HREF="documentB.html#Austria">link</A>to
document B.
```

Now clicking on the word `link` in document A sends the reader directly to the words "my destination" in document B. Links to specific sections within the current document are reached with the same technique except that the filename is omitted.

Additional markup tags

The preceding is sufficient to produce simple HTML documents. For more complex documents, HTML has tags for several types of character formatting, lists, forms, tables, extended quotations, and other items.

Character formatting

It is possible to code individual words or sentences with special styles. There are two typical styles: logical and physical. The first style tags text according to its meaning, while the second one specifies the specific appearance of a section. Whenever possible, logical styles should be used.

- Logical styles

`<DFN>`	Used for definitions, typically displayed in italics.
`<EM>`	For emphasis, typically displayed in italics.
`<CITE>`	A citation, for titles of books, films and so on. Displayed in italics
`<CODE>`	Used for computer code, typically displayed in a fixed-width font.
`<KBD>`	For user keyboard entry, typically displayed in a fixed-width font.
`<SAMP>`	A sequence of literal characters, displayed in a fixed-width font.
`<STRONG>`	Strong emphasis, typically displayed in boldface.
`<VAR>`	a Variable name; typically displayed in italics.

- Physical styles

`<B>`	Bold text.
`<I>`	Italic text.
`<TT>`	Typewriter text, that is, fixed-width font.

Lists

Lists provide a very useful way to focus a user's attention on a series of items. HTML supports three kinds of lists: unnumbered, numbered and definition lists. A simple list can be composed by putting a number of list items between a list start-tag and a list end-tag. Each list item starts with the list item tag LI, which has no end-tag. Two different list tags are possible. UL starts an unnumbered list. The list items are often displayed with bullets. An ordered list starts with OL, where each item is numbered in some way.

Example of an unnumbered list:

```
<UL>
<LI>This is the first entry.
<LI>This is the second entry.
</UL>
```

produces the following formatted output:

Example of an unnumbered list:

- This is the first entry.
- This is the second entry.

A definition list is similar to a glossary and consists of a list of terms with corresponding explications or definitions. This list starts with the DL tag and contains term elements marked with DT. The corresponding definition elements are marked with DD. Term and definition must appear in pairs.

Example of a definition list:

```
<dl>
<dt>Hyper-G</dt><dd>Hyper-G is a second-generation
distributed hypermedia system</dd>
<dt>Hypertext</dt><dd>Pieces of text with interactive
links between (parts of) them</dd>
</dl>
```

produces the following formatted output:

Example of a definition list:

Hyper–G
    Hyper–G is a second–generation distributed hypermedia system
Hypertext
    Pieces of text with interactive links between (parts of) them

Lists can be arbitrarily nested, although it is better to limit the nesting to three levels. It is also possible to have a number of paragraphs, each containing a nested list, in a single list item.

An example nested list:

```
<H3>A nested list:</H3>
<UL>
<LI>Dark colors
<UL>
    <LI>Black
    <LI>Brown
</UL>
<LI>Bright colors
<UL>
    <LI>White
    <LI>Yellow
</UL>
</UL>
```

outputs as follows:

Inline images

An HTML document can contain embedded images. They are specified within the text using the IMG tag. Each image takes time to process and slows down the initial display of the document, so it is generally better not to include too many or overly large images. The attribute SRC in the IMG tag is needed by the browser in order to retrieve the image data. The value of SRC is the URL of the image document. The difference from a normal link is that the image is not displayed as a separate document, but embedded within the text at the location of the IMG tag. By default the bottom of an image is aligned with the text in the document. If we add the ALIGN=TOP attribute, the browser will align adjacent text with the top of the image. ALIGN=MIDDLE aligns the text with the center of the image.

Preformatted text

Use the PRE tag (which stands for "preformatted") to generate text in a fixed-width font and cause spaces, new lines and tabs to be significant (that is, multiple spaces are displayed as multiple spaces, and lines break in the same locations as in the source HTML file). This is useful for displaying program listings, for example.

Forms

HTML fill-out forms can be used for questionnaires, hotel reservations, order forms, data entry and a wide variety of other applications. The form is specified as part of an HTML document. The user fills in the form and then submits it. The user agent then sends the form's contents as designated by the FORM element. Typically, this is to an HTTP server, but you can also Email form contents for asynchronous processing.

Forms are created by placing input fields within paragraphs, preformatted text, lists and tables. This gives considerable flexibility in designing the layout of forms.

The following field types are supported:

- simple text fields

- multi-line text fields

- radio buttons

- checkboxes

- range controls (sliders, or knobs)

- single/multiple choice menus

- scribble on image

- file widgets for attaching files to forms

- submit buttons for sending form contents

- reset buttons for resetting fields to their initial values

- hidden fields for bookkeeping information.

It is expected that future revisions to HTML will add support for audio fields, multi-row entry of database tables and extended multi-line text fields to support a range of other data types, in addition to plain text. Client-side scripts will provide the means to constrain field values and to add new field types.

Tags in a form and an example of a simple form

There are a variety of tags that can be used within a form to provide interfaces for user response. In the following we will explain the most important tags in a form.

The INPUT tag

The input tag is the basic way to get input from the user. Here is an example input tag that queries the user for a name:

```
<INPUT TYPE="TEXT" SIZE=40 NAME="NAME">
```

An input tag can have many values for TYPE, including the following:

- TEXT (shown previously) is used for alphanumeric string entry.

- NUMBER causes the input to be read as a number.

- PASSWORD causes the text to be read as an alphanumeric string, but the characters are displayed as stars when entered.

- CHECKBOX enables the user to toggle a single button on or off.

- RADIO enables the user to choose to toggle on exactly one button out of a set of buttons.

- SUBMIT and RESET are two pushbuttons. The first causes the current form to be submitted to the query program. The second clears all values that a user might have entered in the form and sets them to their default settings.

- The SIZE portion of the INPUT tag determines how wide a box or input area is displayed.

- The NAME portion of the INPUT tag designates the variable name that will be used in the data structure sent to the query program. This name is then used to pull the value of the user's response from the data structure.

- The VALUE field is used to specify default values.

The TEXTAREA tag

This tag is used to allow the user to enter several lines of text. An example TEXTAREA tag is:

```
<TEXTAREA NAME="comments" ROWS=4 COLS=30> </TEXTAREA>
```

The attributes of the TEXTAREA tag are NAME, ROWS and COLS. NAME is used to identify the text in the data structure sent to the query program. ROWS is the number of vertical rows displayed for the user entry. COLS is the number of horizontal columns displayed for the user entry.

Forms used as a questionnaire

The following example is a questionnaire. It uses the INPUT element for simple text fields, radio buttons, checkboxes, and the submit and reset buttons. The TEXTAREA field is used for a multi-line text entry field. The form fields are laid out with several paragraph elements and an unordered list. Notice the use of the NAME attribute to name each field:

```
<TITLE>Questionnaire</TITLE>
<H1>A very simple questionnaire </H1>
<P>Please fill out this questionnaire:
<FORM METHOD=post ACTION="http://www.hal.com/sample"><P>
Your name:   <INPUT NAME="name" SIZE="48"><P>
<INPUT NAME="male" TYPE=RADIO>Male
```

```
<INPUT NAME="female" TYPE=RADIO>Female
<P>How many employees are working in your firm:
<UL PLAIN>
<LI><INPUT NAME="numbers" TYPE=CHECKBOX VALUE="fifty">
up to 50
<LI><INPUT NAME="numbers" TYPE=CHECKBOX VALUE="hundred">
between 50 and 100
</UL>
<P>Do you have any suggestions:<P>
<TEXTAREA NAME="other" COLS=48 ROWS=4></TEXTAREA><P>
Thank you for responding to this questionnaire.<P>
<INPUT TYPE=SUBMIT> <INPUT TYPE=RESET>
</FORM>
```

The Netscape Web browser produces the formatted output shown below:

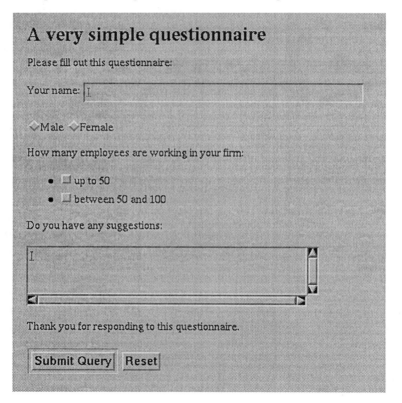

Tables

The HTML table model was chosen for its simplicity and flexibility. By default, tables are automatically sized according to the cell contents and the current window size. The COLSPEC attribute can be used when needed to exert control over column widths, either by setting explicit widths or by specifying relative widths. You can also specify the table width explicitly or as a fraction of the current margins.

A table starts with an optional caption followed by one or more rows. Each row is formed by one or more cells, which are differentiated into header and data cells. Cells can be merged across rows and columns and include attributes assisting rendering to speech and Braille, or for exporting table data into databases. The model provides little direct support for control over appearance, for example border styles and margins, as these can be handled via subclassing and associated style sheets.

Tables can contain a wide range of content, such as headers, lists, paragraphs, forms, figures, preformatted text and even nested tables. When the table is flush left or right, subsequent elements flow around the table if there is sufficient room. This behavior is disabled when the noflow attribute is given or the table align attribute is center (the default) or justify. There are several points to note:

- By default, header cells are centered while data cells are flush left.

- Cells may be empty.

- Cells spanning rows contribute to the column count on each of the spanned rows, but only appear in the markup once (in the first row spanned).

- If the column count for the table is greater than the number of cells for a given row (after including cells for spanned rows), the missing cells are treated as occurring on the right hand side of the table and rendered as empty cells.

- The row count is determined by the TR elements – any rows implied by cells spanning rows beyond this should be ignored.

- The user agent should be able to recover from a missing <TR> tag prior to the first row as the TH and TC elements can only occur within the TR element.

- Cells are not allowed to overlap. In such cases, the rendering is implementation dependent.

7.2.4 HTML editors

Several HTML editors are available at the moment. We only want to briefly mention a few of them.

HTML Assistant

One of the most popular editors for Microsoft Windows is the HTML Assistant. There are two different versions: a commercial version called HTML Assistant Pro and a free version HTML Assistant. HTML Assistant is a hypertext editor for creating and editing documents for the WWW. It permits you to validate and test your work with the browsers of your choice without leaving the editor. In addition to its editing facilities, HTML Assistant incorporates features which can help you to organize and keep track of the Web resources that you use. The HTML documents created with HTML Assistant can be displayed on any computer for which browser software exists, including PCs, Apple Macintosh, UNIX and simple terminal-based systems.

HTML Assistant has additional features including:

- an automatic HTML page creator plus pushbutton templates for forms and tables to get you up and running quickly;

- the ability to edit files of any size;

- toolbar support for HTML level 2 and HTML level 3 tags including forms, tables and background designs;

- formatting filters that make it easy to create readable documents from HTML files;

- timesaving file and URL search features;

- a printed manual.

Easy HTML

Easy HTML, written by Mike Gebis at NCSA, is an HTML editing system that uses your browser as a display. As you add sections to your document, Easy HTML gives you feedback as to how your document will look. Easy HTML is not for everyone; some of the complexity of HTML has been omitted. However, if you do not want to learn HTML, or do not need some of the more exotic features, or just need a simple document, Easy HTML might be your solution.

Internet Assistant

Internet Assistant for Microsoft Word is a free add-on to Microsoft Word that lets users create, share and explore information on the Internet right from within Microsoft Word. It is a template package for Microsoft Word that provides an impressive WYSIWYG environment for creating HTML documents. But not only editing or creating Web pages is possible with the Internet Assistant, you can also use it as a Web browser. Buttons like History, Open/Add favorites, URL and Home show that it is a small browser tool. Clicking on a link is also possible. The Internet Assistant loads the document from the Web and uses Microsoft Word to display the document, even with all images. The only disadvantage of the Internet Assistant is its performance. Loading and displaying a document with the help of Microsoft Word macros is not as fast as with an ordinary browser tool.

SoftQuad's HoTMetaL Pro 2.0

HoTMetaL Pro is a commercial product, but a free version, HoTMetaL, is also available for free via FTP. The commercial version, HoTMetaL Pro, has more features and comes as a standalone program, so it does not require a word processor. With HoTMetaL it is very easy to create hypertext linked, multimedia Web documents for Mosaic, Netscape or any other WWW browser. HoTMetaL Pro helps you to publish home pages, order forms, data sheets, any type of Web document you want. Creating a new document is easy, just open a template and start typing. Next, choose HTML tags from a list of currently valid elements. Adding a hypertext link is just a matter of copying and pasting the URLs for the document to which you want to point. Or use HoTMetaL Pro's URL Editor to insert URLs.

HoTMetaL Pro displays HTML tags and URLs, making it easy to distinguish them from the rest of your document. Hide the tags, change the formatting, and display graphics inline for a WYSIWYG view of your document. Or click on `Preview` to fire up your favorite Web browser for a view of your document as it will appear on the Web.

Some features of HoTMetaL Pro 2.0:

- A new user interface with redesigned dialogs, toolbars, floating windows and so on.

- HTML elements can be added from a toolbar. Common operations also done from the toolbar. Toolbars are also tear-away palettes.

- Supports most Netscape and HTML 3.0 extensions, such as "Background" and "HTML 3.0 Tables."

- Keyboard and toolbar interface to inserting markup: simplified interface to creating HTML documents which more closely matches the operation of traditional word processors.

- Import and conversion of files from other applications, including popular word processing applications such as Word and WordPerfect (not available for the Macintosh version).

- Enhanced URL support: hotlists and pasting of URLs is supported.

- Find and replace of elements and attribute values using regular expressions.

7.3   WWW servers

In this and the next section we will discuss some commercial and non-commercial WWW browsers and WWW servers. From Mosaic, to Netscape, to Website or Spyglass, each software package has features which are worth mentioning. Of course, we cannot describe all software existing on the Web, but we think we present a good cross-section. The two WWW browsers Amadeus and Harmony are tools especially made for Hyper-G. More than just normal browsing tools, they are also powerful authoring tools. We will deal with them in two separate chapters (see Chapters 24 and 23).

7.3.1   The Mosaic WWW browser from NCSA

The National Center for Supercomputing Applications (NCSA) began a project to create an interface to WWW shortly after the group at CERN proposed their WWW. Some graphical browsers were developed for XWindows and NeXT systems. Like Viola or Midas, hyperlinks were represented through underlining or by using different colors. With a mouse or other pointing device you could follow links by just clicking on them. Then in 1993 NCSA developed a versatile, multi-platform interface to the World Wide Web and called it Mosaic.

Here are the main features of Mosaic:

- allows the display of hypertext and hypermedia documents;

- users use a mouse-driven graphical interface;

- uses many different fonts and displays text in bold, italics or strike-through styles;

- layout elements such as paragraphs, lists, numbered and bulleted lists and quoted paragraphs can also be displayed easily;

- supports sounds and movies (MPEG-1 and QuickTime);

- shows layout elements such as lists, paragraphs, numbered and bulleted lists and quoted paragraphs;

- allows you to create and follow hyperlinks;

- understands the most important Internet protocols such as FTP, Gopher, Telnet, WAIS, NNTP;

- supports current standards of HTTP and HTML;

- can store and retrieve a list of documents viewed for future use;

- can keep a history of traversed hyperlinks.

7.3.2   HotJava browser

HotJava is a dynamic, extensible WWW browser that shows many of the capabilities of the **Java** language. Java is a new object-oriented programming language developed at Sun Microsystems to solve a number of problems in modern programming practice. The Java and HotJava products are currently in the alpha stage of development. The primary goal of the alpha release is to demonstrate the concept of executable content and enable WWW software developers to use the Java language to create compelling Web pages.

HotJava is a WWW browser that makes the Internet "come alive." It builds on the Internet browsing techniques currently implemented in Mosaic or Netscape and expands them by including the capability to add arbitrary behavior, which transforms static data into dynamic applications. Using HotJava, you can add applications that range from interactive science experiments in educational material, to games and specialized shopping applications. You can implement advertising and customized newspapers. There are many possibilities. Another advantage of HotJava is that software transparently migrates across the network. Installation of software is not required. Developers of WWW do not have to worry about whether or not a special piece of software is installed in a user's system. It gets there automatically.

Java programs, called **applets**, can be included in any HTML pages, much like an image can be included. When you use the HotJava browser to view a page that contains an applet, the applet's code is transferred to your system and executed by the HotJava browser.

The further reading section provides further material on the WWW browser HotJava and the programming language Java.

7.3.3   Netscape Communications Corp.

Netscape Communications is a founding member of the WWW Consortium, a group devoted to establishing international WWW protocols and standards. Future security standards supported by the Consortium will be implemented in Netscape Communications' products.

Netscape Communications Corp. produces **Netscape Navigator**, **Netsite Communications Server** and **Netsite Commerce Server**, the online hypermedia document navigation system. The Netscape Navigator and Netsite server software make commerce and information exchange on the Internet and other TCP/IP-based networks as simple as point-and-click.

The Netscape Navigator and the Netsite servers bring secure communications, performance and point-and-click simplicity to companies and individuals who want to create or access information services on global networks. The Netscape Navigator and Netsite servers offer easy to use interfaces for serving and accessing multimedia and hypermedia information on the net, including formatted text, graphics, audio and video.

The products are fully compatible with other HTTP-based clients and servers, while offering integrated security and good levels of performance.

Netsite network server software

Netsite is a commercial Internet server software that is compatible with the NCSA httpd server. Netsite software allows organizations to "serve" or post information, including formatted text, graphical images, audio and video and to conduct transactions on the Internet and other global networks using the Internet protocol.

The Netsite product line includes two products available for UNIX-based platforms:

- Netsite Communications Server

- Netsite Commerce Server

The Netsite Communications Server is designed for applications that do not require the security features contained in the Netsite Commerce Server. Such applications include the delivery of online marketing materials and customer support information to customers, and communications to employees.

The Netsite Commerce Server makes electronic commerce a reality, allowing transactions and the exchange of sensitive data on the Internet. This server provides security based on public-key cryptographic technology from RSA Data Security Inc. Security features include data encryption to ensure the privacy of client–server communications and server authentication, which uses certification and a digital signature to verify the legitimacy of the server.

Netscape Navigator

The Netscape Navigator is a graphical WWW browser. It has a very simple, easy to learn and use interface. Of course, transactions carried out over the net demand that your personal information is protected; the Netscape Navigator provides a secure Internet interface (see also Chapter 30 for security features). The Netscape Navigator is available – and is functionally identical – on Windows, Macintosh and UNIX XWindows systems (LAN edition only). This common look, feel, and behavior is a major advantage in mixed computing environments.

Following are the main features of the Netscape Navigator:

- multiple, simultaneous image download;

- continuous document streaming;

- document and image caching;

- native JPEG image decompression;

- interoperates with multi-protocol Web clients and servers;

- native support for HTTP, FTP and NNTP means FTP and news reader/posting utilities are no longer necessary;

- multiple search technologies are supported through Web page instant links – no UNIX commands or separate utilities to learn or use;

- data encryption ensures unwelcome eyes will not have access to private information;

- server authentication provides assurance your information is going where you planned;

- Netscape Communications' **Secure Socket Layer** (SSL) technology provides application-independent secure connectivity to all S-HTTPS server sites; for alternatives see Chapter 30;

- toolbar for frequently used commands;

- bookmark facility allows maintenance, index and search of a hierarchical list of favorite Internet sites;

- network transfer progress indicator makes wait time predictable.

7.3.4   WebFORCE from Silicon Graphics

WebFORCE is a line of solutions from Silicon Graphics Inc. for media-rich Web authoring and high-performance Web serving. The WebFORCE family consists of three different products: WebFORCE Indy provides a complete solution for authoring and serving on the Web; WebFORCE Challenge S is designed for dedicated serving; WebFORCE Indigo 2 Extreme is designed for high-end, 3D-intensive dedicated authoring.

The WebFORCE authoring solutions combine hardware specifically designed to handle all types of digital media with advanced Digital Media Tools that allow you to easily capture and edit video, audio and images. In addition, every WebFORCE authoring system comes with Adobe Photoshop and Illustrator pre-installed. Finally, WebMagic Author – a WYSIWYG HTML editor – completes the cycle by letting you seamlessly incorporate digital media directly into your Web site.

The Club WebFORCE is a resource offered by SGI to WebFORCE customers, giving them late-breaking news about the WebFORCE products and applications, a chance to interact with other WebFORCE users, automatic rendering software to develop customized buttons and much more. Any customer who has purchased a WebFORCE system or software upgrade can register for Club WebFORCE.

7.3.5   Spyglass Inc.

Spyglass Inc. was formed in January 1990 by scientists and software engineers from the National Center for Supercomputing Applications (NCSA) at the University of Illinois.

A very well-known product developed at NCSA is the WWW browser Mosaic. This is a tool that provides point-and-click access to the WWW. Spyglass develops and distributes its **Enhanced Mosaic** for Windows, Macintosh and XWindows system computers, under a multi-million dollar joint development and master licensing agreement with the University of Illinois. Since forging its Mosaic agreement with the university in May 1994, Spyglass has licensed its technology to 36 companies that incorporate it into over 80 products.

By creating robust, commercially enhanced versions of Mosaic and a broad distribution channel, Spyglass is supporting electronic commerce on the Internet for millions more businesses and individuals.

The Spyglass browser: Enhanced Mosaic 2.0

Enhanced Mosaic 2.0 from Spyglass is a WWW browser that offers high performance and additional features. Its open, standards-based architecture makes Enhanced Mosaic adaptable to the varied requirements of electronic commerce and publishing. It also ensures that Enhanced Mosaic will continue to push the advancement of WWW technology.

Some features of this browser are:

- High performance
  No matter what kind of connection you have, Enhanced Mosaic provides the best possible performance by letting you interact with documents during downloads. Text is

displayed instantaneously, and it is possible to follow hyperlinks to new locations without waiting for the entire document to arrive.

- Client-side image mapping
  Image maps or graphical "maps" that follow different hyperlinks according to where you click can be used. Enhanced Mosaic uses an image-mapping technique that does not require server intervention, making image maps useful for CD-ROM and other non-Web applications.

- Built-in JPEG and GIF viewer
  View, print, and save standalone JPEG and GIF images; Enhanced Mosaic automatically recognizes and displays both image file types.

- Built-in audio
  Listen to AU and AIFF sound files with Enhanced Mosaic's built-in sound players.

- Style sheets
  Customize how you view the different text elements you encounter on the Web with Enhanced Mosaic's selection of style sheets.

- Easy to use toolbar
  A toolbar provides quick access to the most frequently used menu commands.

- History list
  Return to previous destinations on the fly with Enhanced Mosaic's comprehensive history list of recently visited URLs.

- Hotlist
  Add favorite Web site URLs to Enhanced Mosaic's hotlist – once the location is selected from the hotlist, Enhanced Mosaic accesses the URL immediately.

Spyglass WWW server

The **Spyglass WWW Server** is a high-performance HTTP engine designed to handle a minimum of 100 simultaneous hits. It is built on an open architecture and conforms to all relevant industry standards. It includes an open interface for security, CGI 1.1 scripts, and high-performance application interfaces for database and commercial transaction processing. This server will be available for Microsoft Windows NT 3.5, Sun Solaris, DEC OSF/1 and IBM AIX, but Spyglass will not offer the server to end users. Like the Enhanced Mosaic browser, Spyglass licenses the server in large volumes to other companies who add value and integrate the technology in a variety of products. Those products will range from heavy-duty commercial servers to easy to use personal servers.

7.3.6   WebSite – The Web publishing solution

WebSite is an elegant, easy solution for Windows NT 3.5 users who want to start publishing on the Internet. WebSite is a 32-bit WWW server that combines the power and flexibility of a

UNIX server with the ease of use of a Windows application. Its intuitive graphical interface is natural for Windows NT users. WebSite provides a tree-like display of all the documents and links on your server, with a simple solution for finding and fixing broken links. You can run a desktop application like Excel or Visual Basic from within a Web document on WebSite. Its access authentication lets you control which users have access to different parts of your Web server. In addition to NT 3.5, WebSite runs on the current version of Windows 95. WebSite is a product of O'Reilly & Associates Inc. It was created in cooperation with Bob Denny and Enterprise Integration Technology.

In the software package there will be a 32-bit HTTP server that lets you maintain a set of Web documents, control access, index your desktop directories and use a CGI (Common Gateway Interface) program to run Excel, Visual Basic and other programs from within a Web document. The WebView program provides a tree-like display of the documents and links on your server, icons for file type, access state and broken links, a graphical editor for enhancing images in Web documents, wizards that automatically create common Web documents, a search button, an indexing tool that allows users to search for terms on your server, and multiple windows to view several Web sites simultaneously. And finally, Enhanced Mosaic 2.0 with progressive display of documents, a toolbar, support for sound and external viewers, display of inline JPEG and other graphical files and support for DDE is also included.

7.3.7   Where does Hyper-G fit into the above?

Note that all WWW editors and browsers can be used for Hyper-G. Some of the WWW servers available offer great features, yet none of them sufficiently support data management. Hyper-G is the only feasible hypermedia solution for handling large amounts of multimedia data at the time of writing.

7.4   CGI scripts: A way to improve WWW

The **Common Gateway Interface** (CGI) is a standard for interfacing external applications with information servers, such as HTTP or Web servers. A plain HTML document that the Web daemon retrieves is static, which means it exists in a constant state: a text file that does not change. A CGI program, on the other hand, is executed in real time, so that it can output dynamic information.

Let us suppose that you want to "hook up" your favorite database to WWW, so that people from all over the world can access it. Basically, you need to write a CGI program which will be executed by the Web daemon. The program should transmit information to the database engine, receive the results back again and display them to the client. This is an example of a gateway and is how CGI started.

The database example is a simple idea, but most of the time rather difficult to implement. There is really no limit to what you can hook up to the Web. The only thing you need to remember is that whatever the CGI program does, it should not take too long to process. Otherwise, the users have to stare too long at their browsers waiting for something to happen.

Since a CGI program is executable, it is basically the equivalent of letting the world run a program on your system, which is not the safest thing to do. Therefore, there are some security precautions that need to be implemented when it comes to using CGI programs. Probably the one that will affect the typical Web user the most is the fact that CGI programs need to reside in a special directory, so that the Web server knows to execute the program rather than just display it to the browser. This directory is usually under direct control of the webmaster, prohibiting the average user from creating CGI programs. There are other ways to allow access to CGI scripts, but it is up to your webmaster to set these up for you. This directory is called `cgi-bin`. A CGI program can be written in any language that allows it to be executed on the system, such as:

- any UNIX shell

- Perl

- Visual Basic

- AppleScript

- C/C++.

It just depends what you have available on your system. If you use a programming language like C or Fortran, you know that you must compile the program before it will run. If you look in the `cgi-src` directory that came with the server distribution, you will find the source code for some of the CGI programs in the `cgi-bin` directory. If, however, you use one of the scripting languages instead, such as Perl, TCL or a UNIX shell, the script itself only needs to reside in the `cgi-bin` directory since there is no associated source code. Many people prefer to write CGI scripts instead of programs, since they are easier to debug, modify and maintain than a typical compiled program.

7.5 Further reading

An excellent WWW text is December and Randall (1994). Virtually all topics relating to the World Wide Web are treated here. This book was designed to cater for readers of all levels. Beginners as well as advanced readers will find many interesting topics.

Another reference is Maxwell and Grycz (1994). This book is like a phone book full of different URLs. An A–Z will help you find many HTTP URLs, links to different newsgroups and so forth. This book is interesting for everyone who likes surfing on the Internet.

Liu *et al.* (1994) and Krol (1994) are two books which give good background information about the Internet. You will find interesting topics about HTTP, HTML, WWW, Email, news and more. Both are recommended for readers who want to know more about the technical side of the Internet. Some experience with the Internet is assumed.

All WWW browsers or WWW servers mentioned in the previous sections have nice home pages. Here are the URLs:

- Silicon Graphics is reachable in WWW at:

  `http://www.sgi.com`

- NetScape is home at:

  `http://www.netscape.com.`

- The Microsoft server is at:

  `http://www.microsoft.com.`

- SoftQuad is at:

  `http://www.softquad.com.`

- Information on Java and the HotJava browser can be obtained at:

  `http://www.javasoft.com.`

- For more information about HoTMetaL look at:

  `http://www.sq.com/products/hotmetal/hmp-org.htm`

8 The need for second-generation hypermedia systems

Frank Kappe

It turns out that the application of hypermedia technology to small, self-contained material (say, about a hundred documents and links typically) is a manageable task and produces good, that is, usable results. With a growing number of documents and links (thousands or even millions), however, a number of problems arise that do not manifest themselves in small-scale environments. The **WWW** described in the previous chapter is no exception in this respect.

In this chapter, we will look at these problems – and possible solutions – in detail, as a preparation for the next chapter, in which we explain how these issues have been addressed in the design of **Hyper-G**. The problems associated with **first-generation hypermedia systems** can roughly be divided into three groups: those that are faced primarily by the consumer of information (the *user*), those that involve the information provider (the *author*), and weaknesses in the system architecture of first-generation systems. We will henceforth use the terms *user* and *author* to refer to the *roles* of consuming and providing information, respectively, rather than referring to different sets of people. Of course, an author is also a user and users may easily become authors.

8.1 Getting lost in hyperspace

The typical problem reported by users of large-scale hypermedia systems is that one can get lost quite easily. This phenomenon is usually described as the "**lost in hyperspace**" syndrome. Looking at it more closely, we may distinguish a number of symptoms, which we will discuss below, together with possible treatments.

8.1.1 How to get an overview?

In most popular hypermedia systems (for example, WWW), users see only one document at a time (the so-called "**current document**"). Outgoing links are visualized and may be activated. However, it is unclear how the current document is related to other documents. In particular, one cannot find out which links from other documents lead to the current document. The user is like a stranger in an unknown city who can only look in one direction as far as the next crossing. Looking backwards or using a map is not possible.

Of course, a map would help. Unfortunately, in a large hyperdocument, a complete **global map** of all the documents and links is too complex to be useful. A hand-crafted map drawn by the author of the information content is more organized than an automatically created map, but because of the manual labor involved, this seems only possible for relatively small and static material.

It only really seems feasible to use **local maps** instead of global ones. A local map shows only the vicinity of the current document. Local maps were first implemented in the Intermedia System and are now being used in Hyper-G as well (see Figure 5.8). In our city analogy, a local map is like a radar screen with limited range.

A variant of local maps are the so-called **fish-eye views**. These behave like extreme wide-angle lenses that enlarge everything in the vicinity and reduce the size of things far away. In analogy, fish-eye views emphasize more important documents by enlarging their visual appearance and distorting the graph accordingly. Automatic clustering algorithms can be used to identify closely related documents. Such **clusters** can then be visualized as one object, thus reducing the number of cross-references and the complexity of the resulting map.

A different method tries to group together related material in advance ("a priori") in so-called **collections**, which behave like directories in file systems. By recursion, a **collection hierarchy** is defined. This structural information may be contained in links of a special type ("is-a-member-of"), sometimes called **structure-representing** or **organizational** hyperlinks, as opposed to the usual **referential** hyperlinks. This concept has already been used in Engelbart's Augment system and KMS. The NoteCards system had the concept of "Fileboxes" which could contain files or other file boxes, but did not use a separate link type for them, which often led to significant confusion. It is possible – with restrictions – to separate organizational and referential hyperlinks subsequently ("a posteriori"), but classification by the author is of course more exact.

This distinction may reduce the number of referential links significantly, since the local map may be configured to show only links of a particular type, which in turn reduces the complexity of the local map. Alternatively, the collection hierarchy may be browsed by a different mechanism, as we will see in Chapter 15. An important means of reducing the "lost in hyperspace" effect is **location feedback**, in other words, showing the current position in the (global) collection hierarchy.

In our city analogy, the collection hierarchy is equivalent to a hierarchy of overview maps of different scales (world, continent, country, region, city, district and so on), with the current position highlighted on all maps (for example, using a satellite navigation system). In conjunction with a local map, we now have a pretty good means of navigation.

8.1.2 How do you avoid seeing the same information again and again?

To reduce the possibility of wandering around in circles, most hypermedia systems offer a **footprint feature** (sometimes also called **breadcrumbs**): links that point to documents already visited are marked in a special way, often with a check mark or in a different color. This requires that the system remembers what documents have already been visited, either within the current session or in all sessions. However, this is not sufficient: if a document that you have visited is subsequently modified (for instance, new information is added), it should no longer be marked as having been seen. This means that the system needs to take version numbers or modification time stamps of documents into account.

8.1.3   How much information exists (on a certain topic)?

Let us assume you would like to go on a trip to New Zealand, and would like to get some information about the country before you physically go there. Suppose that you find some references to hypermedia information on New Zealand. How can you find out, before following a particular reference, if it will lead you to substantial information (say, with 500 documents) or not (say, only 3 documents)?

Again, the collection hierarchy can help a little bit if it can tell you how much information (such as how many documents, how many megabytes) exist within a certain collection (recursively down the tree).

8.1.4   How much of it has been seen already?

A significant advantage of linear text (for example, a book) over hypertext is the following: when you start reading on page one and continue to the end, you can always tell how much you have already read and how much further you still have to go. In particular, when you are at the end, you can be sure that you have seen everything.

In a hypertext, this is not at all trivial. Let us assume that you start to read the hyperdocument shown in Figure 8.1 at document A and continue by following the link to document C, and then documents D, E, F, G and H. Should you meanwhile have forgotten that you still need to follow the link from A to B, you will never see documents B and I. Observe also that document J cannot be reached from A at all! A lot depends on your entry point.

Of course, the more complex the hyperdocument gets, the more difficult it is to see everything. We discovered this problem when we assigned students to read hypertext lessons as part of preparation for an exam. They found it very difficult to make sure that they had seen and learned everything that was contained in the lesson.

A hierarchical structure of the material, by organizing it into a collection hierarchy, in conjunction with the "already seen" marks, can solve this problem: the hierarchy implicitly defines a linear sequence of documents (for instance, by depth-first traversal), so that it becomes possible to read it in linear order. Even if one does not want to navigate in hierarchical fashion but would rather follow the (referential) links in the documents, it is possible to verify at the end whether everything has been seen and to access documents that are not reachable from the entry point just by following referential hyperlinks.

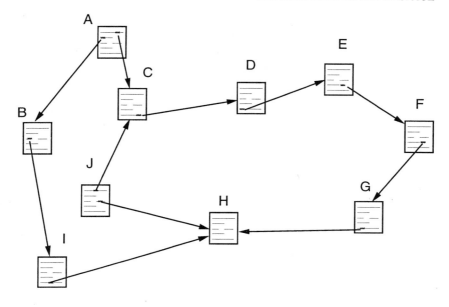

Figure 8.1   Hyperdocument.

8.1.5   How do you find specific information?

If we do not only want to browse the information in random ways ("surfing the Web"), but also need to perform more serious, goal-directed work, we have to have a search function. A **full text search** is nice, but sometimes not sufficient. In addition, we would like to have searchable attributes (**meta-information**) attached to each document, such as title, author, keywords, type, modification time and so on.

In a large system, it is imperative that the search scope can be reduced to part of the information space. Otherwise, we would always have to search globally, and almost certainly find too much. Again, the collection hierarchy can be used nicely to restrict the search scope to a set of collections.

While there are search engines for the Web (for example, **InfoSeek**, **Lycos** and **WebCrawler**), they all have scalability problems (they try to index an exponentially growing Web in one place), are always outdated and know only about a small part of the Web (because indexing cannot keep up with the growth), and do not allow the user to narrow the search scope.

8.1.6   How do you find information which you have already seen?

Sometimes you remember a certain document that you looked at some time ago and want to look at it again, but cannot remember where it was and how you got there, that is, which entry point you used and which links you followed from there.

So-called **bookmarks** allow you to save a list of documents and to access them directly later on. In fact, these bookmark documents become new entry points. The obvious disadvantage is that you have to know in advance that you will later want to find a specific document again. Also, if you save too many bookmarks, you will get lost in the bookmarks.

Conversely, the **history** is a trace of your way through the hyperspace and allows you to find and access documents again based on the time you accessed them the first time. Some systems keep the history only within a session, some support saving and loading of the history of previous sessions. Most systems offer only a linear list of previously accessed documents which can be navigated by functions like "back" and "forward." A more general approach is to visualize the history as a tree, showing also documents that were accessed after stepping back in the history.

8.1.7   What's new?

Let us assume you have already found some interesting sources of information for your particular interests in a distributed hypermedia information system like the World Wide Web. It would be a tedious exercise to keep monitoring these resources (for example, servers) every day to find out if something has changed or something new has been added. "**Monitoring**" essentially means retraversing everything. Of course, the information providers could be kind enough to maintain a what's new document with links to updated or new documents, but because of the human efforts involved, this solution is not very satisfying.

If the system supported searches by modification or creation date, you could simply search for new things. Even more elegant would be an information system that performed these searches itself (for example, once per day) by launching a set of predefined queries and mailing you the results. Such a system can be called an **active information system**.

A similar idea involves so-called **intelligent agents**: programs that are constantly seeking useful information on behalf of the user. Efficient agents require the use of artificial intelligence, and are sometimes also called **knowbots** ("knowledge robots") and **softbots** ("software robots").

8.1.8   How do you recognize outdated information?

In a way, this is the inverse problem of finding new information, but much more difficult. The information system usually cannot work out for itself which information is now out of date, unless the author attached an expiry date when it was inserted (which can only be done for some types of information).

A special problem with hypertexts is **version control**. From the user's perspective, it should be possible to recognize whether the user is currently looking at an old version of a document, and if so, to directly get the new version of it. This can be implemented using a special "new-version-of" link type. A more advanced system would also highlight parts that have been changed in the new version.

8.2   Authoring in the large

Of course, information providers (authors) of large-scale systems face the same problems as every other user, plus some additional ones.

8.2.1   The "essay problem"

Today's authors have undergone significant training on writing linear texts. We were all taught for years in school how to write essays. First, there is an introduction, then the main part and then a conclusion. The same is true for newspaper stories, books, reports, scientific papers, theses and so on. They are always designed to be linear texts: it is assumed that they will be read in the order defined by the author.

Hypertext, however, is completely different. The *user* decides when to read what. This has some significant consequences on the rhetoric of hypertexts:

- Every node should be **self-contained**, without implicit assumptions on what has been read before. Whenever a term is used that is defined elsewhere, a link to the definition should be placed. In a linear text, it is sufficient to place the definition only at the point where the term is first used. Similarly, titles of nodes should be self-contained (not "Introduction" but "Introduction to Hyper-G").

- The size of a node should not exceed a few **screenfuls**. Otherwise, access to specific portions requires reading and scrolling, and slows down as it becomes linear text again. In addition, usability studies show that users do not like using scrollbars. If it is not on the first page, it is likely to be overlooked.

- The structure of the hypertext should be simple, so that users can evolve a mental model of the hypertext as they navigate. A good example is a hierarchical structure with linear sequences of documents and only a few cross-references. Of course, the availability of different link types eases the structuring.

- Therefore, a good transformation of linear text to hypertext is not at all trivial.

8.2.2   Linking considered harmful

It was Laura DeYoung who presented a paper entitled "**Linking Considered Harmful**" at the ECHT'90 conference (DeYoung, 1990), which in turn was a reference to the famous 1967 article of Edsger Dijkstra, entitled "Goto Statement Considered Harmful." In her paper, she emphasized the analogy between the node-link model and the GOTO statement in programming languages, and consequently advocated the use of high-level structuring in hypermedia. Comparing the node-link model to data types, we could as well draw an analogy between links and pointers, and structured hypermedia and abstract data types or classes in object-oriented programming languages.

One of the most important advantages of structured programming is that it becomes easier to reuse parts of the program (subroutines, functions, classes and so on). Similarly, additional structuring mechanisms could help to reuse hypertext components. To ensure consistency, it is necessary to restrict links to and from such modules to certain points within that module (in the same way that you may not jump into the middle of a procedure or loop, or access private variables of an object). However, to our knowledge, the only system that manages to systematically avoid arbitrary hyperlinks is **HM-Card** (see Chapter 27). In principle, hypermedia systems without any links are conceivable.

8.2.3   Link creation

Large hypermedia systems cannot be maintained by just one author and there are usually quite a number of them. Since it is impossible for one author to know about all the documents in the system, it is difficult to apply meaningful links between documents. In addition, attaching links manually is a tedious and time-consuming task.

It is thus highly desirable, in large-scale systems, to have some support for automatic or at least semi-automatic generation of hyperlinks. By automatic, we mean that the system automatically inserts links and by semi-automatic, we mean that the system suggests and the author confirms. For some types of document, relatively simple heuristics can lead to satisfying results:

- So-called **glossary links** which point to a previously inserted glossary can be created by looking for keywords of the glossary in the newly inserted text document and suggesting a link if found. The user has to direct the system which glossary to point at, and to confirm the generated hyperlinks.

- An **encyclopedia** is a special case of glossary links, where the collection that holds the link destinations and the collection that holds the texts to be searched for the destination are identical. The same is also true for the glossary itself and similar types of collections (for example, dictionaries, thesauri) where terms are explained by other terms.

- So-called **vocative links** contain an implicit link within the text. Examples are text fragments like "see Appendix A," "(Figure 2)," or just "[22]." In such cases, a table-driven hyperlink generator can be used, with tables of regular expressions that are adapted to specific document types.

The above-mentioned mechanisms are currently being implemented in Harmony (see Chapter 15), as part of a document management project for the European Space Agency (ESA) (see Chapter 31).

8.2.4   Version control

When (part of) a hyperdocument is to be replaced by a new version, we have the problem of what to do with links pointing to the old one. The old version cannot just be replaced by the new one. We have to move the old links to their corresponding place in the new version. Unfortunately, this requires finding out what parts of the document have been replaced or deleted or inserted. Sometimes a part of the old document cannot be found in the new version, so this process cannot be made fully automatic.

Another possibility is to leave the old document unchanged, including the links pointing to it, and to insert the new version in addition to it. In this case it is reasonable to attach links of a certain link type ("new-version-of") between corresponding parts of the hyperdocument, so that the browser can recognize this and let the user navigate between the two or more versions. Again, finding corresponding locations in the documents is difficult.

8.2.5   Authentication and access control

In a multi-author scenario the system must offer convenient methods for the definition of access rights, in particular for operations which modify data. Again, the collection hierarchy provides a means to define the scope of such permissions.

The collection hierarchy also solves a related problem: in an ordinary hypertext system without collections, it is the author's responsibility to ensure that every document inserted is reachable from at least one other document via a link. This means that when inserting a document at least one other document has to be edited as well. This is not only time-consuming, but also requires write access permissions to the other document. In contrast, all that is needed in a collection-based system is to insert the document into one of the collections which are writable for the author.

It is also wise to separate the right to attach links to documents from the right to modify documents. This way, users who are not allowed to modify a document can still attach links to or from it. A link to an annotation is a good example of this. It is also possible to control the visibility of links to certain user groups if the links carry access rights themselves. Of course, this requires that links are objects with their own access control and – at least logically – separated from the documents.

8.2.6   Separating content and presentation

Many first-generation systems give the author control over the visual appearance (the **presentation**) of the information. For example, the WWW allows you to completely define the user interface using clickable inline images. While it may be tempting for the author to do so (and in fact the Web is full of such pages), it is a step back to the old frame-based systems (see Section 3.3) and has some severe drawbacks:

- The interface for the end user becomes inconsistent. For example, different authors will have different ideas of what a "back" icon should look like, where it should be placed, and where it actually leads to. This is a nightmare for the users who are, after all, primarily interested in the contents, and not in exploring user interfaces.

- Documents that are in fact pictures are difficult to maintain and to transfer to other (future) formats and systems. They are **dead documents** (Robert Cailliau) and tomorrow's legacy data.

- Since it is not possible to effectively search in pictures, such documents do not lend themselves to goal-directed searching.

- Because the user interface is built right into the content, the content is only browsable using the interface it was designed for. A page designed for point-and-click interfaces relying heavily on graphics is difficult to convert to text for transmission over slow lines, or for reading to a blind user. Likewise, it will not be suitable for tomorrow's 3D information visualization user interfaces.

Therefore, features like inline images should be handled with care. Well-designed systems support a clean separation between form and content. For example, the SGML standard for text representation nicely supports this concept: text documents are written in a **semantic markup** ("this is a heading"), the **layout information** is contained outside the document in a so-called style sheet ("headings should be rendered in 18 point Times Roman, boldface, centered"). The author is only responsible for supplying the semantic markup; the layout is defined by others. The semantic markup makes it easy to convert the document to other formats.

8.3   Architectural considerations

The early "resource discovery and retrieval systems" of the Web, as they were called, were designed to be simple and easy to deploy. It is no surprise that their architecture is sometimes over-simplistic, sometimes non-scalable, and sometimes simply flawed.

8.3.1   Object naming

In the design of any distributed system, it is important to find a good scheme for naming its objects (like files, documents, links, users, servers). In this context, we should distinguish clearly between an object's **name**, its **address (location)** and its **route (access procedure)**:

- The *name* uniquely identifies an object. Books, for example, are identified by their title, author and publisher (or better still, their ISBN number). It is important that no name describes more than one object, but note there may be many copies of the same object (for example, book) around.

- The *address* describes the physical *location* of an instance of an object. For example, a book may be described by a certain position on a certain shelf on a certain floor of a certain library in a certain city. For a file on an Internet computer, this may be the Internet address of that computer plus the file name.

- The *route* finally describes how to access a certain object at a certain address, just as to access a book at a certain library, you may have to physically go there. The route describes how. For a file on an Internet computer, the route would describe what packets need to be sent and received (most easily by naming a well-known protocol that can be used to access the file).

Unfortunately, the first-generation systems do not use names to identify documents. Instead, **URLs** (Uniform Resource Locators) are used, which are a mixture of address and route information (see Chapter 7). This is of course easy to implement, but *fundamentally wrong*, and has severe disadvantages:

- URLs cannot describe multiple instances of the same document. In the book analogy, this means there exists exactly one copy of the book at exactly one location. Everybody reading the book has to go there and try to grab it. Caching servers enable us to produce temporary copies of it, but there is no way of locating the nearest copy.

- Documents are tied to their physical location. When they move (either within a computer or between computers), their URL changes. At this time, all references to the document become invalid.

Obviously, URLs should be replaced by **URNs** (Uniform Resource Names), which are persistent names independent of the document's location. This would allow for moving documents around and having multiple copies of them (this is known as **location transparency**). While Hyper-G's Object IDs (see Section 10.1) are very similar to URNs, at the time of writing it is unlikely that the transition from URLs to URNs throughout the Web will happen soon.

Other problems with names include whether the reuse of names should be allowed (like reusing ISBN numbers) and whether or not new versions of a document should be given the same name.

8.3.2   Link consistency

The problem is quite familiar to all net surfers: every now and then you activate a link (in the case of WWW) or menu item (in the case of Gopher), but the document the link or menu item refers to cannot be fetched. This may be a temporary problem of the network or the server, but it may also indicate that the document has been permanently removed. Since the systems mentioned above rely on URLs for accessing information, it may also mean that the document has only been moved to a new location (see discussion on URLs above). It may also happen that a document is eventually replaced by a different one under the same URL.

The net effect of this is that a certain percentage of references are invalid. We may expect that this percentage will rise as time goes by, as more and more documents become outdated and are eventually removed, services are shut down or moved to different servers, URLs get reused and so on. Obviously, it would be desirable to have some support for automatically removing such dangling references to a document when it is deleted, or at least to inform the maintainers of those documents. However, this requires a **link database** that keeps track of all incoming and outgoing links of a document.

In the WWW data model, links are stored directly inside the documents, which has the advantage of a simple server implementation. On the other hand, the absence of a separate link database not only limits the set of linkable document types and prohibits advanced user interfaces (overview maps, 3D-navigation and so on), it also makes it hard, if not impossible, to ensure the integrity of the Web. When a document is removed, all other documents should really be parsed to find the links pointing to that document. This way, they could also be removed, or at least the owners of these links could be informed that they are now invalid. While such a tool is conceivable for the local server, it is simply impossible to scan all WWW documents on all Web servers in the world, without the aid of pre-indexed link databases. The consequence is that there is no referential integrity in today's Web, not even between documents stored on the same server.

Interestingly, the more "primitive" Gopher system does maintain referential integrity in the local case. When a document (which is an ordinary file on the server's file system) is deleted (or moved or modified), the menu item that refers to it (which is a directory entry) is updated as well. This is automatically taken care of by the underlying operating system (unless you try really hard to break it and use the symbolic links of UNIX). References to remote servers remain insecure, however.

8.3.3 Scalability

An important issue that needs to be addressed when dealing with distributed systems is that of **scalability**. Ideally, the behavior of a scalable system should not – or "almost not" – depend on variables like the number of servers, documents, links or concurrent users of the system. In the Web, scalability is a very important aspect of system design, since the values of these variables are already high and are continuing to grow extremely fast. Looking more closely at the issue with respect to distributed Internet information systems, we may distinguish four kinds of scalability:

- **Scalable performance:** The performance (measured by the response time perceived by the user) should not depend on the number of concurrent users or documents. This requirement cannot be met in a centralized system, and therefore implies the use of a distributed system, where users and documents are more or less evenly distributed over a number of servers which are connected by a network.

  Unfortunately, it may still happen that for some reason a large number of users access a small set of documents residing on a single server. Under such circumstances, the distributed system performs like a centralized system, with all the load placed on a single computer and on a certain part of the network. Obviously, one has to avoid such situations, for instance through the use of **replication** (placing copies of that scarce resource on a number of servers) and caching. A good example of a scalable system which relies heavily on replication is the Network News service. When you read news, you are connected to your local news server which holds copies of the news articles that have been posted lately. When accessing a certain article, it does not need to be fetched from the originating site and so the response time does not depend on how many other Internet users access the same article at the same time (it does depend on the number of users connected to your local news server, though).

- **Scalable traffic:** While replication and caching can be used to reduce traffic, replication may require some additional traffic to be sent over the network. Obviously, every news article has to be sent to every news server so that it can be read locally. However, it may well be that most of the articles that have been sent to your local news server are never read by anyone there. Care has to be taken that total traffic increases not more than linearly with the number of servers.

- **Scalable robustness:** By robustness we mean that the system should not rely on a single server or a single network connection to work at all times, nor should it assume that all servers of a given set are available at a given time.

- **Scalable management:** The functioning of the system should not rely on a single management entity. For example, the Internet's Domain Name Service works because its management is distributed. With the current Internet growth rate of about 3 million hosts per year (about 10 000 per work day) centralized registration is infeasible. This requirement also suggests that configuration and reconfiguration of server–server communication paths should be automatic, as opposed to managed by a central service.

8.3.4 Performance and network load

While both Gopher and WWW scale quite well with respect to the number of servers, documents and links, there is a scalability problem with respect to the number of users. When a large number of users for some reason decide to access the same document at the same time, the URL "naming" scheme demands that they access the same server. The affected server and the network region around it become overloaded. This phenomenon (Jakob Nielsen calls it a **"flash crowd"** after a 1973 science fiction story by Larry Niven) was observed during the 1994 Winter Olympics in Lillehammer, where Oslonett (a Norwegian Internet provider) put the latest results and event photographs on the Web and drowned in information requests. Similar but smaller flash crowds appear when a new service is announced on the NCSA "What's New" page or in popular newsgroups.

This problem may be alleviated by the use of **cache servers**, which keep local copies of information which has been recently requested, and give users requesting the same information again the local copy instead of fetching it from the originating site. This strategy does not work, however, in two cases:

(1) When users access many different documents from a large data set (for instance, an encyclopedia or a reference database). Replication of the whole data set would help, but this would in general require moving from URLs to URNs (see above).

(2) When the information is updated frequently. In this case, some **update protocol** would be required that ensures that caches are updated so that the latest version of the document is delivered.

8.3.5 Searching

The first-generation systems do not support searching very well. Searching is not defined in the protocol, but is an add-on implemented by individual information providers. Consequently, the search functionality and the user interface are inconsistent and not available everywhere. It is not the user's decision what should be searched. Rather, the information provider has to anticipate the user's needs and implement searching for certain parts of the information space.

A number of global search engines (such as Archie for FTP, Veronica for Gopher and Lycos for the WWW) have been implemented. They are all similar in that they gather information about documents on other servers in a central index, which can then be searched and yields pointers to the original document. Consequently, they all suffer from the same problems:

- Since all users access a central index (or a small number of indexes distributed over the world), performance is poor.

- With an exponentially growing number of users and documents, there are obvious scalability problems.

- It is not possible to narrow the **scope** of the query (say, to find all references to "Harmony" that are not in the field of Music). Searches are always global and usually return too much.

- Since it takes a lot of time to gather the information and build the index, the index is always outdated and inconsistent with the documents themselves.

WAIS uses a two-stage search process. First, you have to search through a database of all servers to find a suitable subset of servers. The query itself is then sent to these servers. The problem with WAIS is that the directory of all servers only indexes the server descriptions and not their contents. Server descriptions have to be formulated very cleverly so that users have a chance to find what they need.

Harvest is a new Internet-based resource discovery system which supports an efficient distributed "information gathering" architecture. So-called "**Gatherers**" collect indexing information from a resource, while the so-called "**Brokers**" provide an indexed query interface to the gathered information. Brokers retrieve information from one or more Gatherers or other Brokers and incrementally update their indexes. The idea is that Gatherers should be located close to the resources they index, while Brokers are located close to the users. Harvest relies heavily on replication to achieve good performance. The indexes created by the Gatherers are periodically replicated to the Brokers. Since the indexes tend to be large, this has to be done efficiently. Like Hyper-G, Harvest uses a flooding technique to update indexes.

8.3.6 Protocol and server architecture

All of today's Internet information systems are similar in that they are client–server systems. The client (or browser) is what the user interacts with and executes on the user's machine, while the server is located at the information provider, stores the documents and performs the searching.

The clients typically communicate with the servers using a certain protocol on top of TCP (see Section 2.1.1). We may distinguish between **connectionless** and **connection-oriented** (also **session-oriented**) protocols.

In a connectionless protocol, clients open a new TCP connection to the server on every request. After the request has been handled, the connection is closed again. This has the advantage of a simple implementation of servers and clients, in particular, when clients connect to a number of servers in a session (and do not make use of proxy servers or firewalls).

However, opening and closing TCP connections is costly. TCP requires three packets to be exchanged when opening a connection, and four for closing it. In addition, TCP has a built-in "slow start" mechanism to avoid congestion of routers, which effectively means that on a new connection, data can be transmitted rather slowly. The HTTP protocol of WWW and the Gopher protocol are both connectionless. On every access to a server a new connection is opened, and worse, one additional connection for every inline image. It has been shown that HTTP typically utilizes only about 10% of the available bandwidth!

Connection-oriented protocols are used by FTP, WAIS and Hyper-G, and are in general more efficient (for example, FTP can use almost 100% of the bandwidth), but require a more complex server architecture. We may distinguish between two commonly used server architectures:

- The server handles every request in a separate subprocess. This allows the server to handle several requests in parallel. Such an architecture is suitable for implementing **stateless** servers, since information from one request is lost when the request is finished (because the subprocess terminates).

  A stateless server is simple to understand and implement, but it requires that information about the client (for example, protocol version, acceptable data formats, authentication data) be passed and evaluated at every request. Typical WWW clients send more than about 1 KB of such data on every request and thus waste up to 1 second per request on a 14.4 Kbps modem line. HTTP and Gopher protocols are stateless. Most WWW and Gopher servers use this architecture.

- Servers for connection-oriented protocols typically fork one subprocess per client connection, and keep the connection and process alive for the duration of the session. This allows **stateful** servers. In other words, variables set in one request are available in the next request on the same connection.

  This server architecture is more complex and uses slightly more table resources from the server (the process table and the TCP connection table), but is in general faster, because it saves costly **fork** operations on the server side, and because format negotiations and authentication have to be performed only at the beginning of the session. FTP, WAIS and Hyper-G use this server architecture.

It is also possible to use a stateful server for connectionless protocols. This is done by Hyper-G's WWW gateway (see Chapter 20), and even NCSA's latest WWW server reuses subprocesses for requests because it saves fork operations and makes the server faster.

Protocols may be human-readable or in binary format. Of course the binary format is more efficient, but more difficult to debug. HTTP, Gopher, and FTP are human-readable, while WAIS uses a binary protocol. Hyper-G supports both formats (subject to a negotiation at the beginning; see Appendix F).

The proposed new version of HTTP, HTTP-NG (for "next-generation") will – like the Hyper-G protocol – be an efficient binary, connection-oriented and stateful protocol (should it ever be implemented).

8.4 Further reading

The "lost in hyperspace" syndrome was described by Bernstein (1991) and Gay and Mazur (1991). You may also wish to look at previous hypermedia systems like Intermedia (Haan *et al.*, 1992; Utting and Yankelovich, 1989) NoteCards (Halasz, 1988), Engelbart's Augment system (Engelbart, 1963) and KMS (Akscyn *et al.*, 1987). For more about local maps and clustering see Noik (1993), Sarkar and Brown (1994), Feiner (1988) and Botafogo (1993).

References on active information systems, agents, knowbots and softbots include Kappe and Maurer (1994), Crowston and Malone (1988), Maes (1994) and Etzioni and Weld (1994).

The problem of automatic hyperlink generation is covered partially in Chang (1993), Mülner (1989) and DeRose (1989).

Thoughts on the separation of presentation and context in large hypermedia systems can be found in Andrews and Kappe (1993), Stubenrauch *et al.* (1993) and Maurer *et al.* (1994a).

The proposed next-generation HTTP is described in *Progress in HTTP-NG* (Spero), which also contains an analysis of current HTTP's performance problems.

9 The design of Hyper-G

Frank Kappe

In the previous chapter we discussed the problems encountered in first-generation distributed hypermedia systems. This chapter describes how the problems identified have influenced design decisions taken in the Hyper-G project. We start with a brief review of the history of Hyper-G.

9.1 The history of the Hyper-G project

The **Institute for Information Processing and Computer Supported New Media** (IICM) of the **Graz University of Technology**, where Hyper-G was conceived, has had long experience in design, implementation and operation of large online hypertext services for fairly large user communities. In particular, the institute (which was then called IIG, Institute for Information Processing Graz) played a significant role in the introduction of videotex systems in Austria and parts of Europe starting in 1982. Later, there were activities and developments of systems for computer aided instruction (**CAI**) called **COSTOC**: sophisticated but basically standalone, frame-based hypermedia systems.

Around 1989, the idea emerged to combine the expertise in the two fields, and to design a completely new system, based on past experiences and avoiding the design problems of both videotex and frame-based hypermedia systems (for instance, the confusion of form and content, the lack of a search function, inconsistent links, difficult information provision, user disorientation and so on). A small team consisting of Hermann Maurer, Ivan Tomek (now at Acadia University in Canada) and Fritz Huber (now with Anderson Consulting) gathered some requirements for "the optimal large-scale hypermedia system," code-named Hyper-G. Of course, the designs of other similar systems were also taken into account, most notably Intermedia, NoteCards and Xanadu (see Chapter 3).

After the **Austrian Ministry of Science** agreed to fund a prototype development phase of Hyper-G in January 1990, Frank Kappe began to consolidate the requirements and came up with an architectural design for Hyper-G in his PhD thesis in 1991. A very small group of two (!) programmers implemented the first generation of the server (Gerald Pani) and the VT100 client (Frank Kappe) now known as **HGTV** (see Section 19.1). During that time loose contacts with the Gopher group at the University of Minnesota and the WWW designers at

CERN were established, so that the first prototype of Hyper-G could already speak to Gopher and WWW servers and clients.

In January 1992, the system was put into real use as the **University Information System** (TUGinfo) of the Graz University of Technology, one of the first such systems worldwide (it has been up and running for four years now). The success of this system, together with the increasing popularity of the Internet and simple Internet-based information systems, made it evident that Hyper-G could really be useful for a wide range of applications. This made it possible to acquire funding from various sources for a second phase, in which the prototype was to be transformed into a real product, including graphical user interfaces for MS-Windows and UNIX/XWindows.

Phase 2 began in the summer of 1992. Since then the project has been carried out by IICM in cooperation with the **Institute for Hypermedia Systems** (HMS) of **JOANNEUM RESEARCH**, an Austrian nonprofit research institution. An important milestone was the adoption of Hyper-G by the **European Space Agency** (ESA) for its "Guide and Directory" system in late 1992. An early version of **Amadeus** was released in June 1993 and a year later version 0.84 of **Harmony** appeared. In summer 1995, both products reached version 1.0. Meanwhile, Hyper-G has been demonstrated at a number of conferences and exhibitions and is in operational use at a number of institutions and projects (some of them are mentioned in Chapters 5, 28 and 29). During that time, the Hyper-G project team has grown by 3150%, from 2 (1991) to 65 (August 1995)!

9.2   Structured hypermedia

Early in the Hyper-G design process it was decided that the Hyper-G Data Model must contain structuring elements beyond the primitive node-link model (see also Sections 8.2.2 and 3.5.2). While this can in principle be realized by specialized link types, we chose to extend the node-link data model by introducing a particular object class, the **collection** (see also Section 11.1).

A collection is a composite (container) object. It contains documents or other collections. It may be helpful to think of collections as directories in a file system, which may contain files or other directories. This – recursive – definition leads to the concept of a **collection hierarchy** (see Figure 9.1). Two restrictions apply:

(1) Every document or collection must be a member of (at least) one collection (its so-called **parent collection**), with the exception of the server's **root collection**.

(2) While a document or collection may be a member of more than one collection (see Figure 9.1), the collection hierarchy must be cycle-free. The hierarchy is a **directed acyclic graph** (DAG), a generalization of tree structures.

The above rules apply on a per-server level only and are enforced by the Hyper-G server. For example, it is not possible to insert a document or collection without specifying a parent collection (the root collection always exists). Likewise, it is not possible to remove a nonempty collection without removing its children first. This ensures that every document is accessible through the collection hierarchy, while the cycle-free nature is required to make

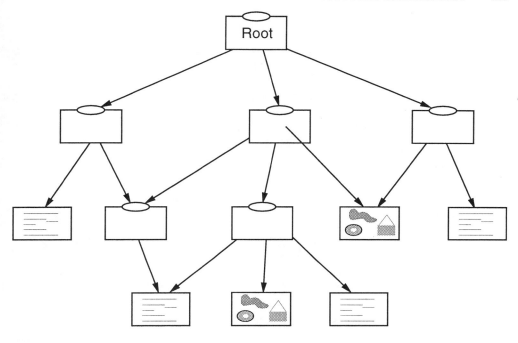

Figure 9.1   The collection hierarchy – a directed acyclic graph.

certain algorithms work (like counting the number of documents recursively contained within a collection, and recursive searching of parts of the hierarchy). It is possible, however, to insert a collection or document into a collection on a remote server, even if this creates a cycle in the cross-server hierarchy.

The collection hierarchy is useful for a number of purposes:

- It can be used for navigating. Depending on the user interface possibilities, the user may be able to choose from a sequence of menus (like in the **Easy** browser and the WWW and Gopher interfaces to Hyper-G), or more sophisticated visualizations of the collection hierarchy may be offered (like the collection browsers of Harmony and Amadeus and Harmony's 3D information landscape). In each case, the logical structure of the information as defined by the author is made explicit to the user. This makes it easier to grasp a mental model of the information space than with the ordinary node-link model, where organizational and referential links are indistinguishable. Also, the number of documents recursively contained within a collection is made available by the Hyper-G server; this gives users a feeling of the size and importance of collections (see Section 8.1.3).

- A collection may contain a special document called the **collection head** (see the PresentationHints attribute in Section E.1). The collection head is visualized (additionally) whenever the collection is visualized (navigated to). The idea is that the collection head contains a short text or image describing the contents of the collection, possibly with links to its elements (document, sub-collections), so that the user is presented with a graphically appealing description of the collection's contents and is given the choice of navigating by clicking, following links from the collection head or in the collection hierarchy. A **full collection head** is like a collection head, but it is assumed to contain links to *all* of the collection's elements, so that it is sufficient to visualize the full collection head when visualizing the collection. It is the author's responsibility to ensure that the full collection head really contains all necessary links.

- Even when the collection hierarchy is not directly used for navigation, the system is always able to show the position of the current document (which may also have been reached by a search or following a hyperlink) with respect to the collection hierarchy. We call this technique **location feedback**. In our experience, location feedback is the most important weapon in the battle against the "lost in hyperspace" syndrome. It answers the "where am I?" question and lets users explore the "logical neighborhood" of the current document; this is particularly useful after a search operation.

- The collection hierarchy can be used to define the **search scope** (see Section 9.3), even across server boundaries.

- Since collections are derived from documents in the Hyper-G Data Model, they contain attributes which may be searched for (see Section E.1). In other words, a search may return not only individual documents, but also composite documents, that is, collections.

- It greatly reduces the **maintenance** effort of the information provider. In the node-link model, the insertion of a new node always requires editing of at least one other node, in order to create a link to the newly inserted document (otherwise it would not be reachable at all). Likewise, deletion of a node requires finding and editing all nodes containing links to it (otherwise dangling links would occur).

  Since collections are managed by the Hyper-G server database which enforces rule (1) above, a newly inserted document is automatically accessible through the collection hierarchy (and through searching), without creating any links or editing any document by hand. To a WWW user it would appear as if a new menu item had been edited in the collection listing, but it is really generated on the fly. The SortOrder attribute of collections defines where the new document should appear in the listing of a collection's members. It is possible to define the position manually (with the Sequence attribute) or to let the system sort the members according to title, author, creation time, expiry time, document type and so on (see the description of SortOrder in Section E.1).

- **Access permissions** can be attached to collections (and documents), in particular the ability to define individual write permissions to certain collections. This means that items may only be inserted into the collection by certain users or user groups. The result is that a single Hyper-G server can be used by a number of authors without interfering with one another. For example, in the information system of the Graz University of Technology, every department has its own collection where it inputs relevant information (descriptions of research projects, people, courses, images and so on). The advantages over an individual WWW server per department are, of course, reduced maintenance effort, consistency and the ability to perform searches over all (or a subset of) departments. Hyper-G also supports accounting and collection-level licensing (see Section 11.3).

- Identified users may be given a **home collection,** where they can construct their own view of the information space and where private documents are stored (for example, annotations). This feature is similar to the "hotlist" or "bookmarks" in the WWW, but more general and powerful. Also, the home collection is stored on the server side, which means that it can be accessed independently of the user's physical location and browser software.

From the user's perspective, a collection may be perceived as an ordered set of elements to choose from during the navigation process. This concept is extended by two subclasses of a collection, **clusters** and **sequences**.

A cluster is a composite document comprised of other documents. Rather than letting the user choose from a list (like in the case of collections), the semantics of clusters imply that the members of the cluster are visualized together. Clusters can be used for a number of purposes:

- For the creation of **compound documents**. For example, an audio document may be grouped together with a text document and an image in a cluster. A well-behaved client would try to display the text and the image simultaneously, while playing the audio stream.

- A very well-behaved client would also interpret **layout** and **synchronization** information attached to the cluster, for instance "display the image, scaling it to full screen, play the audio stream, and after it has finished replace the image with the text." This enables Hyper-G to be used for true multimedia presentations. Currently, the only client interpreting this information is Easy (see Section 19.2).

- Clusters can be used to realize **multilingual documents**. The client may choose one of a number of documents which only differ in their language, based on the user's language preferences. The exact rule for visualizing a cluster is as follows:

  (1) All language-independent members of the cluster are visualized. Language-independent objects are defined as those which have more than one Title attribute (in different languages).

  (2) From the remaining language-dependent members, one per document type is chosen (based on the user's language preferences) and visualized.

On some (rare) occasions it may be necessary to visualize a number of language-dependent documents of the same document type in a cluster (for example, two language-sensitive images in two languages each). To achieve this effect, the author can group related documents in different languages into language-independent subclusters.

An interesting application is to define "synthetic" languages (for example, technical English vs plain English), and let users choose between them. This has already been done in a Hyper-G-based museum application (Chapter 29).

- The Hyper-G server knows about clusters on search operations. When a query matches a document's attributes, and this document is a member of one or more clusters, the cluster(s) are returned instead of the document. This ensures that compound documents as described above are always displayed correctly (that is, all components together, possibly with layout and synchronization taken into account), even when only one member has matched the query, and it also ensures that the preferred language rules (see above) can be applied. The described behavior does not apply to full text searches, so the client will not be confused when displaying the matched word in the text.

A sequence is similar to a collection in that it is an ordered list of sub-collections or documents. However, instead of letting the user choose from a list of alternatives (like with ordinary collections) or visualizing them all together (like in a cluster), the members are visualized one after the other in the sequence defined by the SortOrder attribute of the sequence and possibly the Sequence numbers of the members (see Section E.1).

The user perceives the members of the sequence as nodes connected by "next" and "previous" links. However, these links are generated dynamically ("on the fly") during browsing, which again greatly reduces the maintenance effort on the author's side. For example, when

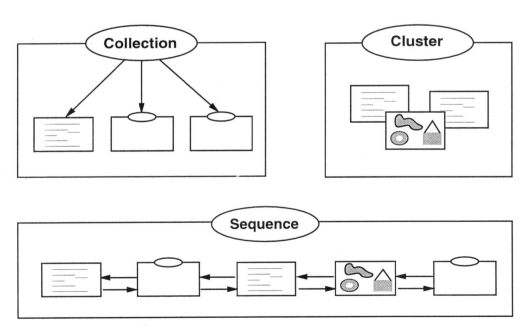

Figure 9.2   Hyper-G structuring elements (collection types).

deleting a node, the node's predecessor and successor are automatically connected. Similarly, a new member can easily be inserted into the sequence, either at a position defined by its Sequence attribute or by sorting on another attribute (for example, by CreationTime or alphabetically by Title). No further editing is necessary. Note also that the (virtual) links are always consistent.

So far, sequences have only been implemented in the Easy client and the WWW interface of Hyper-G. Other clients show them as collections.

Figure 9.2 summarizes the three kinds of structuring elements of the Hyper-G Data Model, which may be combined to form other structures. Some combinations are useful (sequences of collections or clusters or sequences, collections of collections or clusters or sequences, clusters of clusters), others are not (clusters of collections or sequences) and may lead to unexpected results.

The structure elements can be seen as self-contained, reusable hypermedia components, similar to procedures in programming languages (compare Section 8.2.2). For example, it is possible to use the same document in two different sequences, without having to worry about the link structure at all. Since a good deal of the user interface for navigation is generated on the fly by the client (for example, "next" and "previous" links in sequences, menus for collections), they also contribute to separation of content and presentation (see Section 8.2.6). It should be noted that the Hyper-G data model just described is a subset of the HM Data Model (see Chapter 27).

9.3   Searching

Experience with previous large-scale hypermedia systems (our own experience with Videotex, but see also Frank Halasz's words regarding NoteCards in Section 3.5.1) strongly suggested that **searching** was a key feature of any large-scale system. Consequently, it was decided that searching would have to be built right into Hyper-G (as opposed to first-generation systems like Gopher and WWW where searching is merely an add-on that has to be provided by the server administrator).

The Hyper-G server is thus built on top of a powerful object-oriented database engine, and not just a simple file system (see next chapter). *Every* Hyper-G object (including documents, links, collections) can be searched for. Moreover, searching is **seamlessly integrated** with browsing. For example, a user may first navigate the collection hierarchy until a set of interesting collections is found, then issue a query with the search scope limited to these collections, then use location feedback to see the positions of the hits in the collection hierarchy, look at some of the documents returned, display a local map showing the links around the document (including links pointing to the document), follow a few hyperlinks, then return to the collection hierarchy and explore the "neighborhood," refocus the query to a different set of collections or search terms, and so forth.

Every Hyper-G object has a set of attributes (meta-information) attached to it, some of which is indexed so it can be searched for very fast (these include: title, keywords, author, creation/modification time; see also Section E.1). Boolean combinations (AND, OR, AND NOT), prefix searches and range searches (greater than, smaller than) are supported. Nonindexed attributes can only be used in conjunction with index searches to further reduce the set of matches, but allow regular expression searches also.

In addition to the search on meta-information, every text document inserted into the Hyper-G server is accessible by a full text search. The Hyper-G full text engine supports weighted Boolean searches, nearest-neighbor searches, prefix searches, stemming and stop-words, and returns a scored list of matches.

Both kinds of searches can be performed either on the whole server or restricted to a subset of the collection hierarchy. In the latter case, any set of collections can be specified, and only hits that are members (recursively) of at least one of them are returned. The searched set of collections may also reside on different servers, which means that consistent cross-server searches can be performed. It is possible to construct collections (for example, in one's personal home collection) that contain as members a set of collections on different servers, and query them all in one request.

9.4   Links separated from documents

Like the Intermedia system (see Section 3.2), and unlike WWW, Hyper-G stores links that are separated from the documents themselves in a database (details can be found in Section 11.1), which has the following advantages over storing the link directly in the source document (like in WWW):

- Links are **bidirectional**. This means it is possible to find the source from the destination and so you can navigate backwards from destination to source. What is perhaps even more interesting is that you can generate link maps that show both incoming and outgoing links around a certain document (like Harmony's Local Map).

- The bidirectional links allow you to guarantee **link consistency**. For example, if a document is removed, links pointing to it are removed as well (in Hyper-G, they are really flagged as "open," which makes them invisible to the ordinary user, but they can still be maintained by their owners; if the document removed is reinserted, the links become visible again). A server–server protocol even allows for maintenance integrity of the link database across server boundaries (see Section 10.6).

- Links are realized as Hyper-G objects (for details see Section 11.1), which contain attributes (most importantly, the anchor's `Position` and the `LinkType`). They may also be assigned keywords and are searchable ("give me all links with keyword A attached which can be modified and remove all links created by author B after date C") using the operations of the Hyper-G server.

- Links may be assigned individual access permissions, meaning that certain links in a document may only be visible (accessible) to certain users or user groups.

- It is possible to link all types of documents with each other, because the anchor positions are stored separately from the document itself. For example, Hyper-G can deal with links in MPEG video streams, without a need to modify or extend the MPEG standard.

When showing the movie, the movie player receives both the MPEG stream and the associated anchor objects, and shows both.

- Creating and manipulating links does not require modification of the documents the link is attached to. This simplifies interactive link creation, but it also means that creating a link to or from a document does not require write permission for the document. This is useful for annotations (which are realized as a link type in Hyper-G), where the person annotating is not necessarily the owner of the object. It is also necessary in order to attach links to read-only documents (for example, data on CD-ROMs or other servers to which the Hyper-G server cannot write). A further advantage is that it simplifies automatic link generation.

A link in Hyper-G is modeled by a source anchor, attached to the source document on one side and to a destination anchor or a whole destination document on the other. The destination anchors allow the making of links to selected portions of a document (for instance, a paragraph of a text document, a fraction of a large map, a few bars of a piece of music). It is the client's responsibility to visualize anchors (both source and destination) accordingly. Details of the relationships between anchors and documents can be found in Section 11.1.

9.5   Multi-user, multi-author system

Most hypermedia systems are designed as one-way streets: authors provide (information), users browse. Authors and users use different tools. In contrast, Hyper-G is designed as a two-way system: users may also contribute material (for example, annotations, personal home collections) to the information base, using their standard Hyper-G client. This has some implications for system design:

- The **Hyper-G Client–Server Protocol** (HG-CSP, see Appendix F) is capable of manipulating the server database (insertion, deletion and modification of objects and relations). This means that clients can be built which are, in fact, authoring systems.

- The Hyper-G server (see next chapter) is a multi-user, multi-author database that must allow concurrent updates (including indexing, object locking) by different authors, while the system continues to serve information to users.

- To distinguish and protect different identified users (authors) from each other, a powerful, hierarchical scheme of users and user groups and access permissions is implemented (see Section 22.1).

- Of course, we do not want to allow everybody to modify the server's contents. Therefore we distinguish between four identification modes:

    (1) In **identified mode** users identify themselves to their Hyper-G server by username and password. Identified users can create, modify and delete Hyper-G objects, subject to access permissions.

(2) The **semi-identified mode** also allows you to perform write operations on objects. The difference to identified mode is that the real identity of the user is known to the system, but to nobody else. This ensures that users are prevented from making slanderous comments, contributions violating pornography laws and so on (since they can be identified by the law, if necessary), yet their real identity is shielded from other users: they can choose an arbitrary pen name. This mode has proven to be particularly valuable for discussions in groups to ensure that the usual barriers of job hierarchy or such are broken down, thus stimulating free discussion.

(3) The **anonymously identified mode** is similar to the semi-identified one except that the real identity of the user is not known even to the system. Users can select any still available pen name and password, and this combination can be used whenever they access the system. The purpose of this mode is that user preferences, bookmarks and so on can be stored across session boundaries.

(4) The **anonymous mode** can be used most of the time to avoid the "big brother syndrome." Of course, anonymous users are not allowed to enter or modify information.

In all modes, with the exception of anonymous mode, the user has write access to a private home collection, where user interface preferences, history, bookmarks and so on are stored.

The anonymously identified mode is not yet implemented in Hyper-G. All identified users are in fact semi-identified, as their identity (represented by the `Descr` attribute in their user record) is not revealed to other users (with the exception of system users).

9.6 Client–server architecture

Figure 9.3 shows the "simple" client–server architecture found in most Internet information systems (WWW, Gopher, WAIS). The client may access information on different servers by directly connecting to them. Most of the time, however, users will access a series of objects (text documents, inline images and so on) from the same server. As already explained in Section 8.3.6, this introduces extra overhead by opening and closing TCP connections, and also makes clients more complex if they want to talk to a variety of server types.

In contrast, Hyper-G uses the **"proxy" architecture** shown in Figure 9.4. Clients are supposed to connect to their "nearest" (in terms of network bandwidth) server, which is called the **local server** or **proxy server**. Should objects from remote servers be required, the local server fetches them for the client. This architecture offers the following advantages over the "simple" model:

- The local server can cache remote objects, or even keep permanent **replicas**, which can increase the perceived performance dramatically.

- Since the client talks to the same server all the time, there is no point in opening and closing the connection for every request. As already explained in Section 8.3.6, a

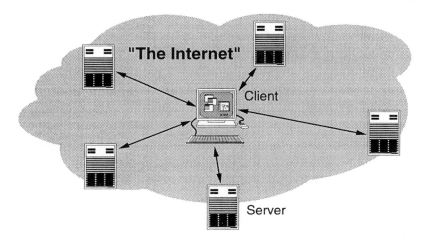

Figure 9.3   "Simple" client–server architecture.

connection-oriented protocol like Hyper-G's client–server protocol uses the available bandwidth more efficiently.

- The connection-oriented protocol makes it possible to use a stateful server architecture, which further reduces the overhead for format negotiation, authentication and so on.

- The server can not only cache remote documents, but also convert protocols and document formats for the client. This makes the server more complex, but simplifies clients. Since the server is implemented only once, but clients exist for various platforms, this is a reduction of overall system complexity.

- The local server keeps the user's access control list, passwords, account balance, home collection and annotations. Subject to their access permissions, users may insert or modify data on the local server, but not on remote servers (unless they have an account on a remote server also). However, this does not imply that they cannot annotate documents on remote servers!

- The proxy architecture allows organizations behind firewalls to publish information to the outside without breaching security on their site. The local (proxy) server needs to be run on the firewall computer.

- This setup is also ideal for online service providers offering phone access to their server which keeps a lot of information locally, but on request fetches information from remote servers. Since every call passes through the local server billing can be performed here.

It should be noted that other WWW servers (the CERN http server) also now support the proxy architecture. The proposed **HTTP-NG** (for "next-generation") will also be a connection-

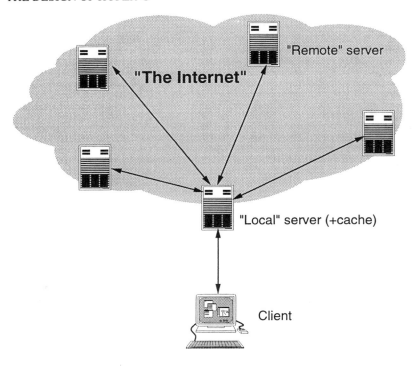

Figure 9.4   "Proxy" client–server architecture.

oriented protocol, much like the HG-CSP (see Appendix F). It fills us with pride to see that many ideas implemented in Hyper-G are also being slowly incorporated into other systems.

9.7   Further reading

The consolidated requirements for Hyper-G and the original architectural design of Hyper-G are found in Kappe's (1991) PhD thesis. HTTP-NG is outlined in *Progress in HTTP-NG* (Spero).

10 The Hyper-G server

Frank Kappe

After an introduction to the terminology and concepts regarding Hyper-G's object naming and addressing, this section contains a high-level description of the Hyper-G server. The server description is sufficient to understand *how the server works*. More detailed information on certain aspects of the server is contained in Chapters 11, 12, 14, 20 and 21.

10.1 Object IDs, objects and documents

As discussed in detail in Section 8.3.1 under "Object Naming," network documents should not be accessed using their (location-dependent) *address* (that is, URL). Rather, a (location-independent) *name* or *identifier* should be used to refer to the document.

The Hyper-G server stores not only documents, but also anchors, collections, users, user groups and server descriptions, and derived classes thereof. Hence we will use the term **object** to refer to all of these entities, including – but not restricted to – documents.

All Hyper-G objects are assigned a unique **object ID** (OID). The OID is a 32-bit number that is unique within a server, also called the **local OID** (LOID). The server starts numbering objects from 1 upwards. By convention, the object with OID 1 is always the user record for the "super-user" user, OID 2 is the server's root collection. These two objects are automatically generated when the server is started for the first time and cannot be deleted. When a new object is created, it is assigned a new OID by the server. OIDs are never reused. Since there are 2^{32} OIDs per server, you can continue creating a million objects per day for almost 12 years, before you need to open a second server.

By concatenating the 32-bit OID to a 32-bit **birthplace ID** we get a 64-bit **global object ID** (GOID), which is globally unique. The birthplace ID is the **server ID** (SID) of the server that created the object, which is not necessarily the one that stores it now, or the only one that stores it now. When a server is first started, its 32-bit Internet address is used as its server ID. There is a server-to-server protocol (more on that in Section 10.6) that ensures servers know each other. The same protocol is used to broadcast changes in the server's address, in case it moves later on. When an object moves to a new server, the birthplace server stores its new GOID.

There may also be more than one copy of the same object. Important and heavily used resources (documents, collections) can be **replicated** at other Hyper-G servers. At the moment, this has to be decided manually, and is not feasible for resources that are updated frequently. For instance, replication is used for electronic journals like J.UCS, where material is only added and not modified or deleted. In addition, objects may be temporarily **cached**. This is similar to replication, but cached objects have a limited lifetime. In each case, the server will first check whether a local copy exists before trying to access a remote object. In principle any Hyper-G server can be contacted for a certain object. However, as described in the previous chapter (see Figure 9.4), clients should connect to their "nearest" server to make replication and caching a performance win.

Figure 10.1 summarizes the name resolution process just described. It allows retrieval of an *object* for a given *object ID*. An object is returned as a set of attribute–value pairs (see Section E.1 for a list of possible object attributes). One of the attributes is the `Rights` attribute which determines the access permissions for the object. The object retrieval will fail if the user does not have permission to access the object. In case of a document, the object contains a `Path` attribute, which may subsequently be used to access the document itself (Figure 10.2).

To complicate things further, a server may be accessed in local mode, in which case only local objects can be accessed. In both modes (distributed and local), clients deal with 32-bit OIDs only. In local mode, these are the "real" OIDs of the local server; in distributed mode, these are "virtual" OIDs generated on the fly by the server (like virtual addresses or handles), which are valid only within the current session. The client should not make any assumptions based on the values of such "small" IDs, nor save them for use in other sessions.

10.2   The server architecture

The Hyper-G server is not a monolithic block of software. Rather, it consists of a number of modules organized in a three-layer architecture (see Figure 10.3).

The modules are realized as concurrent UNIX processes (the Hyper-G server runs on most UNIX flavors, and a version for Windows NT is planned) communicating with each other using Internet sockets. This contributes to the flexibility of Hyper-G, as modules may be added or replaced by others. For instance, one could add a new protocol conversion module and replace the free full text server by a commercial package for the same purpose. It also means that the server modules may run on different computers (although this is normally not the case) to increase performance or for debugging purposes. Of course, the concurrent processes also take advantage of multi-processor hardware platforms.

The individual processes are started, monitored and restarted if necessary by a control process (`dbserver.control`, not shown in Figure 10.3); some of them are optional (a minimal Hyper-G server requires only `hgserver`, `dbserver` and `dcserver`).

The **protocol conversion layer** makes the Hyper-G server a multi-protocol server. A set of gateways transforms other protocols to Hyper-G's client–server protocol (HG-CSP), see Appendix F), so that lower layers need to deal only with a single protocol. Currently,

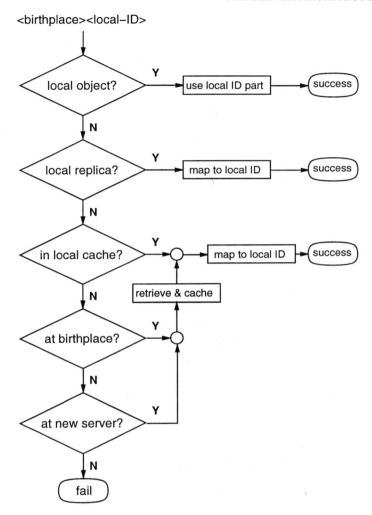

Figure 10.1   Object name resolution in Hyper-G.

gateways for HTTP, Gopher and SNMP are available (see below). It is relatively easy to write and plug in new gateways (for example, a Z39.50 or FTP gateway).

The **session layer** communicates with the database layer and other (remote) servers on behalf of the client, and of course with the client (sometimes indirectly via a gateway). An instance is created for every client connection, to retain state information and to parallelize client requests.

The **database layer** stores the server's information and meta-information. It is organized as three parallel processes: the **object server** creates, modifies and deletes objects and

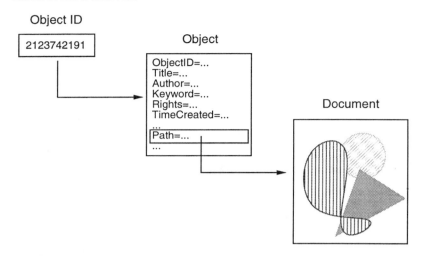

Figure 10.2   Document addressing from OID to object to document.

their relationships (for example, links), indexes them for searching, and manages users and access permissions. The **full text server** maintains an inverted index of all text documents for searching. The **document cache server** stores the local documents of the server, as well as cached documents from remote servers.

The following sections give a functional description of the individual server components, with pointers to more detailed information found elsewhere in this book.

10.3   Protocol conversion layer

10.3.1   WWW gateway (wwwmaster)

The **WWW gateway** (for historical reasons, the program is known as wwwmaster) is a very important part of the Hyper-G server, because it resembles the system's "front end," that is, it defines the visual appearance for the user. Its task is to enable users with WWW clients (like Netscape or Mosaic) to access information on a Hyper-G server (compare Figure 5.1).

This is not as simple and straightforward as it sounds. The gateway must not only transform the protocols (from connectionless and stateless HTTP to connection-oriented and stateful HG-CSP) and map Hyper-G's separated links to HTML's embedded links, but also, because the separation of content and presentation is less strict in WWW than in Hyper-G, define the presentation details of collections, clusters, search forms and buttons for navigation – things that are usually left to the client in the Hyper-G model.

Figure 5.2 shows a typical user interface when looking at a (small) collection through the WWW gateway. The collection itself, its collection head, and all user interface and navigation elements are assembled into a single HTML document, which is then visualized in a

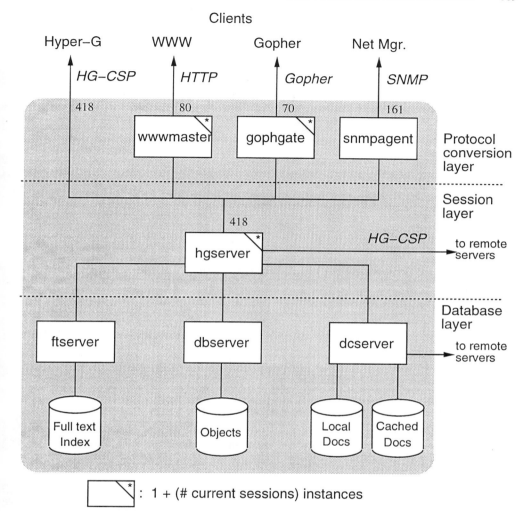

Figure 10.3   The architecture of the Hyper-G server.

single window by the WWW client (in our case, Netscape). The top section (before the first horizontal separator in the text window) contains icons for user identification, setting options (for example, preferred language), searching, help and returning to the home collection. Below, we see the collection head (which could of course contain inline images), followed by the collection listing itself. The bottom section contains selected meta-information about the collection (in our case, the author) and links to the parent collection(s).

A key feature of wwwmaster is its flexibility. The headers, footers, icons, forms, help pages and so on are all ordinary HTML code that can be modified by the server administrator (compare Figures 5.2 and 5.3). In this respect, the contents and the user interface are still separated. Certain aspects (for example, user interface language, amount of meta-information in collection listings) can even be configured by the client, that is, the user. It is possible to forget about Hyper-G's additional features, configure the WWW gateway to use empty headers and footers, use text documents and full collection heads where possible, even switch off the session-oriented behavior of wwwmaster, to make Hyper-G look like any other WWW server – but why would you want to do that?

More detailed information on the WWW gateway is contained in Chapter 20.

10.3.2   Gopher gateway (gophgate)

Similar to the WWW gateway, the **Gopher gateway** allows Hyper-G servers to be accessed by Gopher clients. Gopher supports hierarchical menus and various visualizations thereof (see Chapter 6), which can naturally map Hyper-G's collections. In fact, the Gopher gateway is much simpler than the WWW gateway. Nevertheless, the current version called gophgate is a bit outdated (for example, it does not speak the Gopher$^+$ protocol), but a new one is in the works (see Chapter 21).

10.3.3   SNMP agent (snmpagent)

The **Simple Network Management Protocol** (SNMP) has become the *de facto* standard for network management in the Internet. SNMP allows not only monitoring of low-level network components (for example, routers), but can be extended by application-specific **MIBs** (Management Information Bases) to just about anything. The protocol itself is based on ISO's **ASN.1** ("Abstract Syntax Notation One") encoding standard.

As part of a contract for the European Space Agency (ESA), the Hyper-G team defined a Hyper-G MIB for remotely monitoring a Hyper-G server. The idea is that a single network manager can easily manage a reasonably large number of Hyper-G servers at different sites.

The Hyper-G **SNMP agent** can be used to poll (in SNMP terminology: get) performance statistics of a running Hyper-G server. Typically, an SNMP **management station** would gather this information from a number of SNMP agents (installed at Hyper-G servers) and use it to display a screen with a graphical representation of, for example, the load over time. The Hyper-G agent also monitors the other components of a Hyper-G server (see Figure 10.3) and generates an SNMP trap (or alarm) when some other component fails and sends it to the management station. Although SNMP supports sending commands to the agent (SNMP terminology: set), for example to switch it on and off, this function was not implemented for security reasons.

The SNMP agent is rarely used and is not part of the standard Hyper-G distribution, but is available on request.

10.4 Session layer (`hgserver`)

The session layer talks to the client using the Hyper-G client–server protocol (HG-CSP) described in detail in Appendix F. The client may be a native Hyper-G client, or a gateway of the protocol conversion layer (see Figure 10.3). To the session layer, they look the same.

As discussed in Section 8.3.6, the connection-oriented HG-CSP protocol naturally supports an efficient server architecture, where one server process is forked per client connection only at the beginning of a session. In our case, this process is `hgserver`, a lightweight process (that is, it uses almost no memory) that is created by a master copy listening on port 418 (the well-known port number reserved for Hyper-G), whenever a client connects. The child process is terminated when the client connection is closed, or when no client requests have been received for a certain timeout interval (by default 12 hours).

At the beginning of the session, the `hgserver` negotiates communication parameters with the client, and remembers them for the remaining session, that is, it keeps some state information, including user identification data.

The `hgserver` process has no direct access to persistent data. Rather, it is itself a client of the servers in the database layer, most importantly the object server (`dbserver`). Because the low-level databases process transactions serially (that is, one after the other) it is important that the `hgserver` splits operations that might take a long time into a number of small (fast) transactions for the database servers. In this way, requests from one client do not block execution of requests from other clients, as they are processed in parallel. The `hgserver` also employs a small cache of often-used objects (for example, the current user record) to further speed things up.

When accessing objects from remote Hyper-G servers, `hgserver` opens connections to the other servers (using HG-CSP, that is, looking like a client to the other server), forwards the requests to the other servers, assembles the results and passes them on to the client. The number of parallel connections to other servers is limited to 10 (if more would be needed, the connection least recently used would be closed to open the new one). As already explained in Section 10.1, the client is always given 32-bit "virtual" OIDs. To map them to "real" 64-bit OIDs, `hgserver` maintains a translation table in memory for the duration of the session. In essence, the session layer makes the (local) databases of the database layers of various servers appear as one distributed database.

As an example of a fairly complex request, let us consider the deletion of a text document from a certain collection, which is a special case of the `MVCPDOCSCOLL` command that can delete, move and copy documents from and to collections (see Appendix F). The client specifies the (virtual) OIDs of the document and the collection.

(1) First, `hgserver` needs to check access permissions by looking at the user record and possibly the `Rights` attribute of the collection object (see Section 11.2). In other words, it has to retrieve the collection object from the `dbserver`. Let us assume access permissions are granted.

(2) A quick look at the document–collection relation (again something for `dbserver`) tells `hgserver` whether the document is also a member of other collections or resides on a remote server (which implies that there is another parent collection on the remote server). If so, `dbserver` is instructed just to remove the document from the collection

as requested (by removing the corresponding entry in the document–collection relation), and the client request is finished. If the document was on a remote server, this server is informed by the mechanism described in Section 10.6, so that it can update its document–collection relation, too.

(3) If, however, the collection is the only parent of the document, the document has to be physically removed.

    (a) In order to do that, the document object is retrieved from `dbserver`. The `DocumentType` attribute (see Section E.1) reveals that it is a text document. The `Path` attribute contains a handle for the actual document in the `dcserver`.

    (b) Because it is a text document, the `ftserver` is instructed to remove the words occurring in the document from its indices. Since these indices are organized to find the OIDs a given word occurs in, and not the words of a given OID, `hgserver` has to retrieve the document from `dcserver` and pass it on to `ftserver`.

    (c) Next, `dcserver` is told to physically remove the document, freeing up the space it used to occupy.

    (d) Finally, `dbserver` is instructed to remove the document object. In an atomic transaction, it also removes the entry in the document–collection relation as well as all the anchor objects (source and destination) attached to the document. Anchors pointing to the document are flagged as "open" (see Section 11.1).

We may notice that although the whole operation is fairly complex and may take some time (up to a few seconds, depending on the size of the document), the individual requests in particular for `dbserver` are rather small, so they do not block parallel operations of other clients for an undue amount of time (a few milliseconds). In the case of a server crash in the middle of the operation (for example, as the result of a power failure), we could theoretically end up with the document removed from `ftserver` or `dcserver`, but now from `dbserver`. However, the special transaction logging performed by `hgserver` makes sure that the whole operation can be completed as part of the recovery process taking place when the server is restarted, so that the server databases are always in a consistent state.

10.5 Database layer

10.5.1 Object server (`dbserver`)

The Hyper-G object server (`dbserver`) is a multi-user, read-write database. As such, it has to cope with the classical problems of concurrency control and recovery of atomic transactions. While a number of solutions exist for both concurrency control (various kinds of locks, optimistic concurrency control, time stamps) and the recovery problem (intentions lists, file versions), they are all relatively complex to implement and not particularly fast.

The approach taken in the design of the Hyper-G server is much simpler and very effective. It works under the assumption that the individual transactions of the `dbserver` can be completed fast (in the order of 10 milliseconds), and are processed serially. The session layer (see Section 10.4), which consists of one process per client running in parallel, can then divide longer operations into a sequence of dbserver requests, so that requests of different simultaneous client operations are interleaved. The effect is that a long client operation does not block other clients, even though the low-level database transactions are processed serially. Because of that, no conflicts can occur (such as two transactions modifying the same object at the same time).

Measurements show that the average transaction time is in fact about 10 milliseconds. Write operations (that is, those that modify the object database) can take longer though, since a number of objects and relationships may have to be modified in one atomic transaction. For longer atomic write operations dbserver supports explicit object locking (that is, the hgserver may lock an object on behalf of the client when it intends to write to it later, so that no other hgserver process can write to the object until it is unlocked again). The IICM Hyper-G server currently processes about 1 million dbserver transactions per week. While on average this is less than two transactions per second, peak load is significantly higher (up to 100 transactions/sec).

The dbserver stores a database of objects (in the file Object.db) and relations of objects (in the files *.rel). The other files in the server directory are indices derived from these files for faster access and searching, and log files. Write operations always append to the database files. Deleted records are not removed physically until the next **database reorganization**.

The objects include documents, collections, anchors, users, user groups and server descriptions. The relations define collection membership and links. In fact, the link information of all documents is contained completely in dbserver, hence dbserver has historically been called the "link server," even though it contains much more. The dbserver is also responsible for generating unique local OIDs for new objects.

Normally, the dbserver keeps a connection open to every hgserver attached (that is, one connection per client). When you issue a status command in a client, you can see what other clients are currently connected to dbserver. This requires an open UNIX file descriptor for each connection, in addition to the file descriptors needed for the data and index files. Unfortunately, the underlying operating systems impose a hard limit on the number of open file descriptors per process, and thus the number of simultaneous users connected to dbserver. For example, this limit is 1024 on SUNs, 4096 on DEC Alphas, but only 256 under Linux, and can be changed only by recompiling the kernel.

Therefore, dbserver may disconnect the hgserver with the longest idle time when running out of file descriptors. This does not disconnect the client, however, since it remains connected to its hgserver process. Should the client issue a request again, the hgserver reconnects to dbserver (and the connection to some other idle hgserver is closed). Since dbserver is completely stateless, the client will not notice. In fact, one can stop and restart dbserver – thus disconnecting all hgserver processes at once – without affecting the clients if the server is restarted again soon. The hgserver will reconnect to the new dbserver process on the next request.

This is most useful for upgrading the software while the server is running. The other server components (Figure 10.3) share this feature with dbserver, so that all components may be upgraded to new versions without interrupting service (this is done by the hginstserver script; see Chapter 14).

10.5.2   Full text server (ftserver)

The full text server (ftserver) is capable of storing inverted indexes of word lists. Whenever a new text document is inserted, it is sent to ftserver by hgserver, and its words are inserted into the index data structure. Likewise, when the document is deleted, its words are removed from the index. Unlike in many other systems, indexing is performed immediately.

One index per language is available. A language-specific, configurable list of stop-words contains very frequent words that are not indexed. A stemmer – also language-dependent – cuts off common suffixes (so that, for example, "computer" also matches "computers"), and words are converted to lower case before indexing.

Querying ftserver with a list of words ("terms") results in a ranked list of OIDs and scores. The list of terms can be a whole document, or even several documents, in which case we speak about "nearest-neighbor" search. The query language supports weighted searches (terms may have different importance), Boolean *AND* and *OR*, and *fuzzy AND* (see "Further reading" at the end of this chapter for more information on the features of ftserver).

It would be possible in principle to replace ftserver by a different full text indexer without affecting the rest of the system.

10.5.3   Document cache server (dcserver)

The document cache server (dcserver) is the part of the Hyper-G server that behaves most like a conventional Web server. Its tasks are:

- to serve local documents (that is, the documents on the local server) to the client;

- to accept documents from the client and store them;

- to fetch documents from remote servers (Hyper-G servers, but also WWW, Gopher, FTP and SQL servers), pass them on to the client and store them in a local cache;

- to serve previously cached documents to the client;

- to run CGI scripts (see Section 7.4), and send their output to the client.

Among the things that are specifically *not* the task of dcserver is checking access permissions. Small documents can be sent to the client via hgserver (see the GETTEXT command in Appendix F), but clients may also request to receive the document over a separate, direct connection between dcserver and the client (this connection is not shown in Figure 10.3 so as not to overload the picture). This is useful to prevent blocking the main HG-CSP connection while sending large documents (so that the user may continue to interact with the server while receiving a large document), and to receive documents in parallel (for example, an audio and a video document). In the case of a separate connection, the client may again choose between two options:

- The client may open a socket on its side and listen to incoming connections (documents) on this port (for example, Harmony opens a socket per document viewer). To request a document, the client sends a PIPEDOCUMENT or PIPEREMOTE command over the HG-CSP connection (see Appendix F), specifying the host and port of the listening socket. The hgserver retrieves the document's meta-information, checks access permissions, and in case access is granted, instructs the dcserver to directly deliver the document specified in the Path attribute to the specified client socket (see also Figure 10.2). This "callback" behavior allows separation of access permission aspects from actual document delivery in the server, that is, the dcserver does not need to know the identity of the client, nor the access rights of the document to deliver.

  Note that the document may be delivered to a different process (potentially even on a different machine) than the one that holds the HG-CSP connection. This allows the design of clients like Harmony (see Section 16.1), which are composed of a session manager and independent viewer processes.

- The "callback" behavior has problems, however, if the client is behind a firewall. In this case, it may not be possible to connect from the outside to the incoming port of the client. Therefore, it is also possible to specify no socket in the PIPEDOCUMENT/ PIPEREMOTE command. In this case, the dcserver will open a socket on its side. The client receives its port number and a key as return parameter of the PIPE-DOCUMENT/PIPEREMOTE command. With these values, it may actively connect to the dcserver and retrieve the document. Should it not connect within a certain time, the dcserver closes the socket again.

The behavior just described also works in the opposite direction, in other words, it also works when sending documents to the server with the PUTDOCUMENT command. Small documents (typically, text documents) are preferably sent over the main connection, to avoid the overhead associated with opening and closing TCP connections (compare Section 8.3.6).

To avoid costly fork() system calls for every document retrieved, the dcserver is realized as a single process. It uses nonblocking I/O for retrieving, sending, reading, storing and caching many documents in parallel and as fast as possible. The number of simultaneously open connections to clients and remote servers is limited by the number of open file descriptors per process (as discussed in Section 10.5.1). If all are used, new document requests have to wait until an old request is finished. A connection is closed after a period of inactivity (by default, 120 seconds; see Chapter 14), to avoid the blocking of file descriptors by inactive clients.

Many applications (for example, encyclopedias, bibliographies) need to store a large number of small documents. Because the UNIX file systems are not very efficient in this respect (many small files), the dcserver stores small documents (<8 KB) packed together in so-called **page files**. To reduce fragmentation, page files with a maximum document size of 128 bytes, 256 bytes, 512 bytes, 1 KB, 2 KB, 4 KB and 8 KB are used. For example, a document of 1500 bytes would be stored in the "2 KB" page file. Obviously, the average utilization of disk space in the page files is 75%. Documents larger than 8 KB are stored as individual UNIX files.

The dcserver employs its own database (the "map") which tells it where to look for a document. Documents are assigned a **Local Resource Number** (LRN), which is what is stored in the `Path` attribute of documents. LRNs are unique within a `dcserver`, and do not contain the position of the document in the page files. This allows reorganization of the page files and documents to be moved around without any effect on the remaining components of the server. For example, when a document is deleted, a temporary "hole" in the corresponding page file appears. It is filled by moving the last document in the page file to the hole, truncating the page file, and reflecting this change in the "map." Currently, this operation is performed immediately when a document is deleted. This policy has the advantage that page files are compact and no disk space is wasted for already deleted documents, but means that documents deleted by mistake cannot be "undeleted." Therefore, the policy might be changed to physically remove the documents only at a "database reorganization," as is the case with the `dbserver`. The page files are organized so that the map can be reconstructed at server restart time.

The `dcserver` is also capable of retrieving remote documents from a Hyper-G server, but also from WWW, Gopher, FTP and SQL servers (see Chapter 12). In this case, it not only delivers them to the client, but also writes them into a cache area that has been reserved on the disk (see Chapter 14). The cache uses the same mechanisms (page file, map) as the local document store.

It is also the responsibility of the `dcserver` to run CGI scripts, which result in dynamically generated documents or remote objects (usually, however, an HTML document will be generated). See Chapter 12 for more information on CGI scripts and the SQL gateway for access to SQL databases without CGI scripts.

10.6   Maintaining referential integrity

By now, it should be apparent that **referential integrity** (consistency of the links and collection hierarchy) is guaranteed by the Hyper-G server in the local case, that is, both endpoints of a link are on the same server, or both the collection and child object are on the same server. This section presents a scalable architecture for automatic maintenance of referential integrity in large (thousands of servers) distributed information systems.

A central feature of the proposed architecture is the **p-flood** algorithm, which is a scalable, robust, prioritizable, probabilistic server–server protocol for efficient distribution of update information to a large collection of servers. We give only a short overview (see "Further reading" at the end of this chapter).

Figure 10.4 illustrates this situation. The hyperweb is partitioned by server boundaries (the servers are labeled A, B and C in the figure). Links which span server boundaries are shown as thicker edges. We will call these links **surface links**, and documents connected to other servers by such links shall be called **surface documents** (the others are called **core links** and **core documents**, respectively). Although not apparent from Figure 10.4, a server's surface will typically be small compared to its core.

In order to keep the useful property of bidirectional links, the link information of surface links must be stored in both affected servers. For increased performance, the servers also keep replicas of the other surface documents' meta-information. In Figure 10.4, server A stores document 1 plus a replica of document 2's meta-information and the link between them, while server B stores document 2 plus replicas of the meta-information from documents 1 and 3 and the links from 1 to 2 and from 2 to 3.

In this setup, documents on different servers are interconnected as tightly as the documents on a single server. The bidirectional links enable more advanced navigation techniques (such as Harmony's local map, collection browser and information landscape), but also simplifies maintenance of the hyperweb.

The problem which remains is how to inform the other servers that document 2 has been removed. An earlier implementation of Hyper-G used the knowledge about what documents are affected to directly engage the other servers in a multi-server transaction, in order to remove document 2 and all links to and from it. However, this approach has scalability problems when many servers must participate in the transaction (because many links point to the document).

Therefore, it was decided to adopt a **weak consistency approach,** whereby it is accepted that the hyperweb may be inconsistent for a certain period of time, but is guaranteed to converge to a consistent state eventually. Of course, we would like to keep the duration of the inconsistency as short as possible.

Updates may only take place at a well-defined server. This server is not the same for all

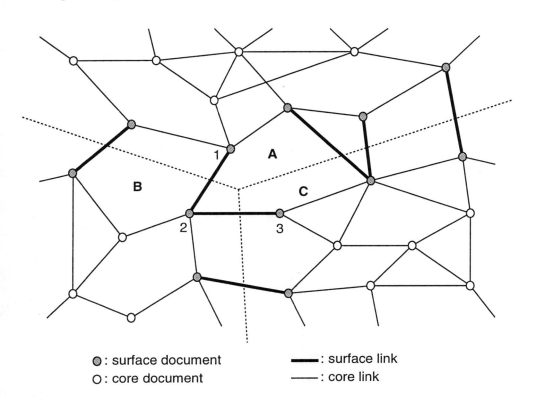

⊚ : surface document   ━━━ : surface link
○ : core document   ─── : core link

Figure 10.4   Partitioning the Web among servers.

operations, but depends on the document or link being modified (or removed or inserted): for documents, it is the server which holds the document; for links, it is the server which holds the document where the link emanates (in our example, server B would be responsible for updates of document 2, while the link from 1 to 2 would be updated by server A). This eliminates the problem of conflicting updates (they are handled one after the other). Of course, the server must be available at update time. However, since for security reasons users wishing to update document 2 must have write permission for document 2 (this is checked by server B which holds document 2), this fact is inevitable and we have to live with it, anyway.

Updates of core documents or core links require no further action (integrity is maintained by the dbserver). However, other servers need to be notified of updates happening at a server's surface (that is, updates of surface documents or surface links). We chose to use a flood algorithm to propagate updates from the master to the slaves (that is, all other servers), because of its scalability (the traffic generated does not depend on the number of references to the object in question), because it does not require that the recipients are available at update time, and because it can be used for other purposes as well (like distributing server addresses and statistics, and maintaining the consistency of replicas and caches).

10.6.1   The p-flood algorithm

Our application – sending update notifications – sends only small messages ("document 2 removed" can be encoded in a few bytes), and has the following requirements:

- **Speed:** Messages should propagate fast in order to minimize the duration of inconsistencies.

- **Robustness:** The protocol should *guarantee* eventual delivery of every message to every server, even when some servers are down. When a server that has been unavailable comes up again, it should receive all the messages it has missed in between.

- **Scalability:** The time it takes to inform all servers should not depend heavily on the number of servers. Likewise, the amount of traffic generated should not depend heavily on the number of servers. Of course, since every message must be sent to every server at least once, $O(n)$ is a lower bound for the total traffic generated.

- **Automatic:** We do not want to configure flood paths manually (like in the News service).

- **Priority:** Since we intend to use the protocol for other purposes as well, it would be nice to have a priority parameter attached to every message that determines its acceptable propagation delay and bandwidth consumption.

The **p-flood algorithm** is a probabilistic algorithm which fulfills the above requirements. Figure 10.5 illustrates its behavior. The servers are arranged in a circle (for example, by sorting them according to their Internet address). Every server knows all other servers (updates of the server list will of course be transported by the algorithm itself).

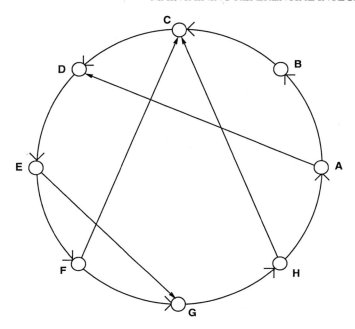

Figure 10.5   One step of the p-flood algorithm ($p = 1.5$).

Servers accumulate **update messages** which are either generated by the server itself (as a result of modification of a surface document or surface link), or received from other servers, in their **update list**. Once in a while (every few minutes) the update list is sent to p other servers ($p \geq 1$). We will call this time period a *step* of the algorithm. For $p = 1$, updates are sent only to the immediate successor, otherwise they are also sent to $p - 1$ other servers that are chosen at random. If p is fractional, they are sent to other servers only with probability $p - 1$. For example, $p = 1.3$ means that one message is sent to the successor, and another one with probability 0.3 to a random server; $p = 3.2$ means that it is sent to the successor, two other random servers plus one other random server with probability 0.2.

Figure 10.5 shows one step of the p-flood algorithm with $p = 1.5$. Note that at every step the operations described above are performed by all servers in parallel, that is, within the step time period every server performs one step (the clocks of the servers do not have to be synchronized). We may observe that at every step $p \cdot n$ update lists are sent (n being the number of servers).

The higher the value of p, the shorter the time it takes to reach all servers, but the higher the amount of traffic generated (it happens that the same message is received more than once by some servers). The algorithm in principle allows the assignment of different values of p to individual messages, so we may call p the *priority* of the message.

After a message has successfully been transmitted to a server's immediate successor, it is removed from the sending server's update list and not sent again to any server in future steps. This ensures that messages are removed after they have been received by all servers and keeps the update lists relatively short. Messages are time-stamped using a per-server sequence number, so that duplicates can be discarded and messages can be processed in the correct order by the receiver.

What happens when a server is down or unreachable? Since a message must not be discarded from the update list until it has successfully been sent to the successor (we assume that a reliable transport protocol like TCP is used and that receipt is acknowledged), the message will effectively wait there until the successor comes up again. Almost immediately after that, the accumulated update messages will be sent. In a way, every server is responsible for delivering messages to its successor. The penalty is that when a server is down for a long period of time, its predecessor's update list grows.

Setting the priority $p = 1$ (send messages only to the successor) will effectively block update messages in case of an unreachable server and is therefore not feasible. A higher value of p not only speeds up the propagation of the messages significantly, but also contributes to the robustness of the algorithm. In the example of Figure 10.5, a crash of server B would not inhibit update messages from server A being propagated to the other servers.

10.6.2 Simulation results

This section presents data gathered by running extensive simulations of p-flood. We will only concentrate on "perfect world" simulations here (see "Further reading" at the end of this chapter). First we want to find out exactly how weak our weak consistency is, in other words, how long it takes to arrive at a consistent state after updates have stopped, how this time depends on the number of servers and the priority factor p, and how much traffic is generated over time.

Figure 10.6 gives us a feeling of how p-flood performs. It is assumed that m update messages have been generated at the n different servers before the simulation starts, and we watch their propagation to the other servers, in particular how long it takes until they arrive there. It turns out that it does not matter whether all m updates are made on a single server or whether they are distributed randomly over the n servers, but the random placements give smoother curves, so this method was chosen for producing the graphs.

The top graph shows how the update information is propagated to the 1000 servers, using different values of p. A higher value of p gives faster propagation, for example at $p = 2$ and $n = 1000$, 50% of the servers are reached after about 4 steps, 99% after 7 steps, and the last one is typically updated after 10–13 steps. The price for faster propagation is a higher load on the servers and networks: the middle graph shows the average size of the update list held at each server, and the bottom graph shows the traffic in messages that is sent at each step.

Since every message has to be sent to every server at least once, every algorithm that delivers every message to every server will need to transmit at least $m \cdot n$ messages, so we will call this number the *optimum* traffic. Under perfect-world conditions, the total traffic sent by p-flood is $p \cdot n \cdot m$ messages, or $p \cdot optimum$. The point is that the flood algorithm distributes this traffic nicely over time and over the whole network, as opposed to the trivial solution where every server simply sends all its updates to all other servers (which requires only *optimum* messages to be sent). The lower the value of p, the more network-friendly the update.

Clearly, there is a trade-off between fast propagation and peak network load. Figure 10.6 suggests that a good setting of p is somewhere between 1 and 2.

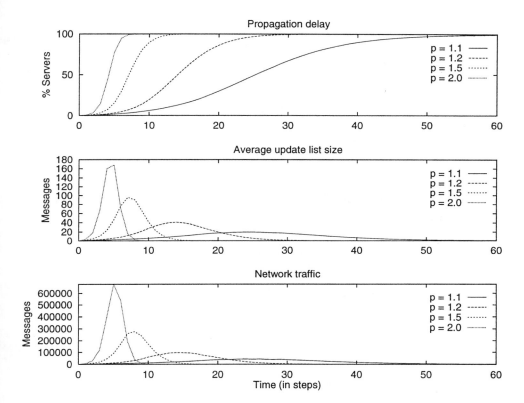

Figure 10.6   Performance of p-flood at different values of p ($n = 1000, m = 1000$).

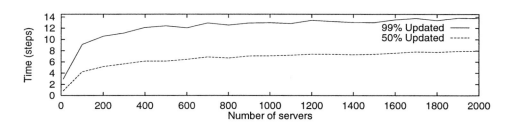

Figure 10.7   Time to update 50% (99%) of the servers ($p = 1.5$) by n.

Figure 10.7 demonstrates the remarkable scalability of p-flood with respect to the number of servers. The time to reach 50% and 99% of the servers is plotted against the number of servers. The logarithmic performance of p-flood is clearly visible, meaning that p-flood is well suited for use in the context of very large server groups.

Figure 10.8 plots the propagation delay (again, reaching 50% and 99% of the servers) versus the priority p for a constant number of servers ($n = 1000$).

10.6.3 The p-flood daemon

A daemon process (pflood) runs at every Hyper-G server. An instance of hgserver is logged into dbserver with system privileges and acts as a client of pflood. This instance reads the transaction logs of dbserver, looking for modifications of surface objects. When such a modification is found, an appropriate message is generated and sent to pflood. This results in eventual distribution of the message to all other Hyper-G servers. When pflood receives a message, it is passed to the hgserver acting as client. The hgserver instance analyzes the message and – should local objects or relations be affected – performs the necessary modifications of the local database.

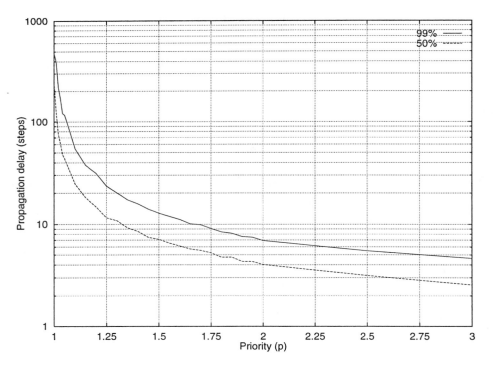

Figure 10.8   Time to update 50% (99%) of the servers, by p ($n = 1000$).

10.7   Performance issues

Although no "hard data" is available on the performance of Hyper-G servers, we may look at some existing installations to find some indications. For example, the Hyper-G server at IICM currently (September 1995) stores about 188 000 documents, organized in 34 800 collections (including clusters), with 170 000 hyperlinks, and 810 user accounts organized in 22 user groups. About half of the documents (90 000) are visible for anonymous users. In August 1995, the server processed about 69 000 user sessions resulting in 4.2 million `dbserver` transactions, or about 3000 sessions per working day. There are Hyper-G servers with more documents (about 300 000 are currently stored in a bibliographic database jointly maintained by the three universities of Graz), and there are servers that see more sessions (for example, the Graz University of Technology server gets about 6000 sessions per working day).

A SUN 10/40 (single processor) with 64 MB (the machine used by the Graz University of Technology) can cope with about 200 simultaneous users with its CPU load factor still below 1. Of course, "simultaneous" means they are connected to the Hyper-G server, not that they are performing searches or the like simultaneously. In our experience, a connected user only issues about two requests per minute. Also, users seem to prefer point-and-click navigation over searching: the `dbserver` processes about 800 times as many requests as the `ftserver`.

It was a design decision to optimize the Hyper-G server for fast retrieval, rather than fast update. Therefore, inserting documents is relatively slow, because indexes are updated immediately (including the full text index), though recent optimizations in the server code have increased updating significantly. For example, in inserting the above-mentioned bibliographic database, about 3500 small documents could be inserted per hour (or about one per second) on a DEC 3000 (Alpha processor at 100 MHz, 128 MB RAM), including network transfer over Ethernet.

10.8   Further reading

SNMP is defined in the Internet RFC 1157 (Case *et al.*, 1990), a standardized MIB (MIB-II) is in RFC 1213 (McCloghrie and Rose, 1991). ASN.1 is defined in ISO standards 8824 (ISO, 1987a) and 8825 (ISO, 1987b).

Derler's (1995) master's thesis contains an in-depth description of `wwwmaster`, Faschingbauer's (1993) master's thesis describes the `ftserver`.

A good introduction to the problems associated with concurrency control, recovery, replication and caching in distributed databases is in the book by Coulouris and Dollimore (1988). Flood algorithms are described in Danzig *et al.* (1994). Papers on p-flood, including more detailed simulation results, have appeared in Kappe (1995a) and Kappe (1995b).

11   Inside Hyper-G

Frank Kappe

This chapter contains some more technical yet generic details of Hyper-G which do not fit into other more specialized chapters, since they apply to the whole system. In particular, we discuss the Hyper-G data model and class hierarchy, as well as issues of access permissions, licensing of resources, accounting, billing, and replication.

11.1   The Hyper-G data model

The Hyper-G object server (see Section 10.5.1) maintains a database of **objects** (as discussed in Section 10.1) and certain **relations** between them. The objects are instances of certain **classes** (for example, the `TextDocument` class) with certain semantics, and have a number of attributes attached (for example, the `Title` attribute). As in object-oriented programming, more specialized classes are derived from more general ones (for example, class `TextDocument` is derived from class `Document`). The resulting class hierarchy is described in Section 11.1.2, but we will first look at the relations between objects.

11.1.1   Relations

Let us first explain how links are realized. Hyper-G links are not stored inside the documents, nor is there a link object (although there was one in earlier versions of Hyper-G). Rather, links are defined by **source** and **destination anchors**. The source anchor is the starting point of a hyperlink and specifies the part of a document from which an outgoing link can be activated. Typically, the user is given visual cues as to where source anchors are located in a document (for example, a highlighted phrase in a text document). A destination anchor is the endpoint of a hyperlink and determines what part of a document should be on view upon arrival at that node (for example, a text might be scrolled to a specific paragraph).

Figure 11.1 illustrates the general case and shows the relevant objects and relations as they are realized in the object server. Any number of anchors may be attached to a document, some of them source anchors, others destination anchors. This "attachment" relation is implemented as an **anchor–document relation** in the `dbserver` database. It may be

134

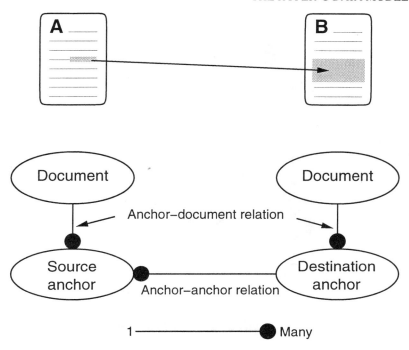

Figure 11.1   Anchor–anchor and anchor–document relations.

searched in both directions by the client, that is, it is possible to find the document an anchor is attached to (there may be only one), and all the anchors of a given document (using
the GETDOCBYANCHOR and GETANCHORS commands of HG-CSP, respectively; see Appendix F). In a similar way the source and destination anchors are connected by the **anchor–
anchor relation**, which constitutes the actual link. The same destination anchor may be
pointed to by a number of source anchors, but a given source anchor resembles exactly one
link.

Often, an entire document is specified to be the destination and viewing commences at
some default location within the document (for example, the start of a text). In this frequent
case, no destination anchor is created. Rather, the anchor–anchor relation points directly to the
destination document instead of the destination anchor. Figure 11.2 illustrates this situation.

As well as links to documents and regions of documents, Hyper-G also supports links
to groups of documents, that is, collections, clusters and sequences (described in Section 9.2).
Since the class collection is derived from class Document (see Section 11.1.2), and cluster
and sequence are in turn specialized collections, this case is the same as links to a whole
document, at least as far as the implementation is concerned (see Figure 11.3).

The anchor–anchor relation is also bidirectional, that is, it is possible to find the destination anchor (or document) for a given source anchor (by retrieving the anchor object and
looking at the **Dest** and **GDest** attributes supplied by the server on the fly from the anchor–

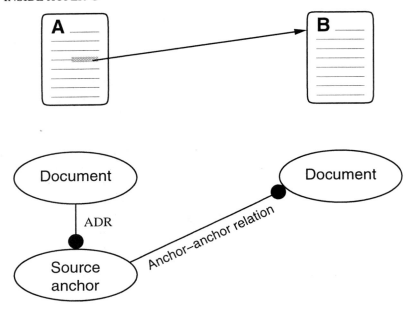

Figure 11.2   Link from source anchor to a whole document.

anchor relation), and vice versa (using the GETSRCSBYDEST commands of HG-CSP; see Appendix F).

The attributes of the link are stored with the source anchor, in particular the link type (the LinkType attribute) and its access permissions (the Rights attribute).

Although in principle we want to guarantee link consistency, it is sometimes useful to relax this requirement a little bit: for example, when inserting a hyperdocument consisting of interrelated documents (such as an encyclopedia), there are likely to be circular references of documents. When we insert these documents automatically, in alphabetical order of their title, we could not create any links to documents inserted later if complete consistency at all times was required. Likewise, when we replace a document by a new version by deleting the old one and inserting the new one afterwards, links pointing to the document as a whole would be destroyed when the old document is removed, and are not propagated to the new document.

In order to overcome this problem, Hyper-G introduces the concept of **open links**. An open link is a link whose destination has not yet been inserted into the object database. In this case, the source anchor keeps information about the anticipated destination in its DHint attribute. This information comprises the name of the collection the destination is supposed to appear under (recursively), and the title of the destination document. If the title is not unique within the specified collection, one can also choose a (unique) keyword that is known to be attached to the target document. If the link should point to a destination anchor, this anchor needs to be assigned a title or keyword as well. If the link should point to a collection, only its name would need to be specified (see Section 25.2.2 for examples).

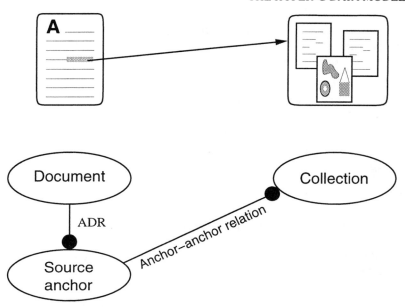

Figure 11.3   Link from source anchor to a collection (cluster, sequence).

Whenever a new document, destination anchor or collection is inserted, the Hyper-G server checks all open links (the DHint is indexed, of course) and closes them if possible. When a document is deleted, links pointing to it are flagged as *open*, that is, the DHint attribute of the source anchors are set to the document's parent collection and title. Likewise, links pointing to destination anchors with a title or keyword attached are flagged open by copying the title or keyword to the source anchor's DHint attribute. However, links to destination anchors without titles have to be removed! It is therefore good practice to assign a title to a destination anchor, if it is of some importance. This not only allows searching for the anchor, it also enables temporarily "opening" and "closing" it as just described, and attaching multiple links to the same destination anchor.

You may have noticed that the data model as described above does support links from a single source anchor to a single destination (**1-to-1 links**), as well as links from many sources to a single destination (**n-to-1 links**). It does not directly support links from one source anchor to multiple destinations (**1-to-n links** or **n-to-n links**). However, there are two possibilities to overcome this asymmetry:

- You can define overlapping anchors, in other words, a number of source anchors on the same position. Although Hyper-G clients support this feature for all document types (including text), it is feasible only for a small number of destinations (n), because with increasing n it becomes increasingly difficult for the user to step through the possible anchors. Also, the WWW data model does not support overlapping anchors, so it is not possible to get this functionality over the WWW gateway.

- You can put the destinations into a collection, and point a single link to that collection. Since it is possible to insert any document, collection, and even destination anchor into any number of parent collections, and the number of children of a collection is unlimited, there are no restrictions for this method.

The effect for the users is that they are presented with an intermediate menu (a collection listing, depending on the client), from which they may choose a destination.

We may note that the WWW data model supported by first-generation systems has no mechanism for links to multiple destinations at all.

Collections

Although it is possible in principle to realize the collection–membership relation through special link types, for performance reasons this is implemented differently in the dbserver. Two dedicated relations define collection membership of documents and collections, respectively (Figure 11.4).

The **collection–collection relation** defines what parent collections a collection belongs to. Every collection belongs to at least one parent collection (with the only exception being the root collection). Vice versa, a collection may contain a number of sub-collections, so it is a many-to-many relation. Again, the relation may be searched in both directions (commands GETCHILDCOLL and GETPARENTS of HG-CSP). Similarly, there is a **document–collection relation** for sub-documents of collections (commands GETCHILDCOLL and GETPARENTS). They have been separated to make certain algorithms (for instance, counting the documents recursively down a collection tree, limiting the search scope to certain collections) run faster in the server. The client usually uses the command GETCHILDREN to get both sub-documents and sub-collections of a given collection in one transaction. The GETPARENTS command works for both collections and documents (it looks at the object's type to figure out what relation to look at).

Collection–collection relation

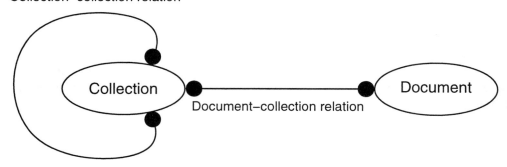

Figure 11.4   Collection–membership relations for collections and documents.

The relations may span server boundaries, with the exception of the anchor–anchor relation (see also Section 10.6). More precisely, the relation is stored on both servers (since we have only binary relations, there are at most two different servers involved), and a "dummy object" (a copy of the other endpoint) is maintained in each server for increased performance.

11.1.2 Class hierarchy

Figure 11.5 shows the class hierarchy of Hyper-G objects (classes marked with an asterisk are abstract base classes, that is, no instances of such classes can be created).

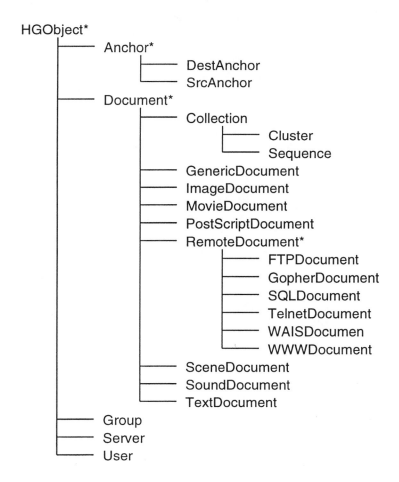

Figure 11.5   Class hierarchy of Hyper-G objects.

We will now discuss the individual classes in detail, but without detailed description of the object's attributes (they are listed in Section E.1). The class hierarchy shows the view of a Hyper-G client; the server maintains a slightly different hierarchy, as it only needs to know about some of the classes (for example, it does not distinguish between ImageDocument and MovieDocument), and stores some object attributes in a slightly different fashion and converts them to the client representation. Some attributes are not stored at all, but generated on the fly for the client.

HGObject

The class HGObject is an abstract base class and so instances of this class cannot be created. Its sole purpose is to let derived classes inherit its attribute definitions. All Hyper-G document classes are derived from HGObject. The attributes which may be found in all object types are listed in the following table. "User" means the attribute can be set by users with write access (see Section 11.2), "System" means the attribute can be set by the system user only. "Server" means the attribute is generated and stored by the server itself, while "Synthetic" means that the attribute is not directly stored but set by the server on the fly.

Name	User	System	Server	Synthetic
Author		√		
GOID				√
Keyword	√			
Layout	√			
ObjectID			√	
Parents				√
Repl			√	
Rights	√			
Score				√
Sequence	√			
Serv				√
Title	√			
TimeCreated			√	
TimeExpire	√			
TimeModified			√	
TimeOpen	√			
Type	cannot be modified after creation			

Detailed attribute descriptions in alphabetic order are found in Section E.1. In reality, many of the attributes listed above are not applicable in User, Group, and Server objects; however, it has been found convenient to derive all classes from a common base class.

The following sub-classes are derived from HGObject:

- Anchor

- Document.

Anchor

The object class Anchor is derived from class HGObject. Anchors are objects that describe a portion of a document. In Hyper-G there are two types of anchor:

- A *source anchor* is the visible representation of a link, that is, a clickable area of a document that should be highlighted somehow. When a user activates the anchor (for example, by clicking on it with a mouse), the corresponding link to the destination document is followed (that is, the destination document should be displayed). In addition, the source anchor carries information about the link, such as the link type. When retrieving a source anchor, the server also supplies information about the link's destination, which is generated on the fly.

- A *destination anchor* also specifies an area of a document. Its purpose is to specify only a part of a document as the destination of a link. The client should also try to highlight a destination anchor that has just been "jumped to," but would normally ignore destination anchors (except when editing documents). Destination anchors often have their Title or Keyword attribute set, so that they can be searched for during the link creation process.

The following attributes are applicable (in addition to the attributes inherited from class HGObject):

Name	User	System	Server	Synthetic
Cost				√
Dest				√
GDest				√
DHint			√	
LinkType	√			
Position	√			
Price	√			
TAnchor	cannot be modified after creation			

The following classes are derived from class Anchor, without additional attributes:

- DestAnchor (TAnchor=Dest)

- SrcAnchor (TAnchor=Src).

Document

The object class Document is derived from class HGObject. Documents are objects that can be viewed by a client. It is an abstract base class, and so only derived classes have to be created. The attributes common to all documents are (in addition to the ones inherited from class HGObject):

Name	User	System	Server	Synthetic
DocumentType	cannot be modified after creation			
MimeType	√			
Name	√	√		
Path			√	
PresentationHints	√			

The DocumentType attribute specifies the type of the document and determines which of the derived classes is created in the client (the MimeType attribute may contain additional encoding information). The following classes are derived from class Document, but have no additional attributes. They are only used to distinguish between different document types (and therefore not discussed any further):

- CGIDocument (DocumentType=CGI; a script to be executed by the server, see Section 7.4);

- ImageDocument (DocumentType=Image; a raster image in any of the popular formats, for example GIF, TIFF, JPEG);

- MovieDocument (DocumentType=Movie; a movie in MPEG format);

- PostScriptDocument (DocumentType=PostScript);

- ProgramDocument (DocumentType=Program; a program to be executed by the client, for example a Java applet);

- SceneDocument (DocumentType=Scene; a 3D scene description in VRML or SDF format);

- SoundDocument (DocumentType=Sound; a sound in SUN .au format);

- TextDocument (DocumentType=Text; a text, for example, in HTML).

The following classes are also derived from class Document and have additional attributes:

- Collection (DocumentType=collection);

- GenericDocument (DocumentType=Generic);

- RemoteDocument (DocumentType=Remote).

Collection

The object class Collection is derived from class Document, and therefore inherits all its attributes. A collection is a group of documents (and because every collection is a document, this includes collections!). This recursive definition yields a collection hierarchy similar to a tree, but with the property that a document (and hence also collection) may be a sub-document of many collections (see Section 9.2). The semantics of a collection are that the client should present a menu of the sub-documents (and/or sub-collections) when it displays a collection document. This default behavior is changed in the derived classes `Cluster` and `Sequence`. The following attributes are applicable to collections:

Name	User	System	Server	Synthetic
CollectionType	√			
Description	√			
License	√			
SortOrder	√			
Subdocs				√

The following classes are derived from class `Collection`, but have no additional attributes. They are distinguished by the value of the `CollectionType` attribute, and their semantics are described in Section 9.2:

- `Cluster` (`CollectionType=Cluster`; a compound document);
- `Sequence` (`CollectionType=Sequence`; a linear sequence of elements).

GenericDocument

The object class `GenericDocument` is derived from class `Document`, and is for storing arbitrary documents – in addition to those listed under Section 11.1.2 – in a Hyper-G server. Two additional attributes are used by the clients to select an appropriate helper application for handling the document and optionally pass parameters to that application:

Name	User	System	Server	Synthetic
Arguments	√			
SubType	√			

RemoteDocument

The `RemoteDocument` class, derived from `Document`, is an abstract base class, that is, no instances of this class can be created. Its purpose is to describe common attributes of objects not stored on a Hyper-G server, that is, "pointers" to such foreign objects. The following attributes are applicable to all `RemoteDocuments` (in addition to those of class `Document`):

Name	User	System	Server	Synthetic
Host	√			
Path	√[a]			
Port	√			
Protocol	√			

[a] `Path` is an attribute of class `Document`. However, the `Path` of a `RemoteObject` may be edited, while it is otherwise set by the server.

The `Path` attribute of class `Document` is reused and the `Protocol` attribute specifies the type of the remote document and determines which of the derived classes is created in the client. The following classes are derived from class `Document`, but have no additional attributes, and are not discussed any further:

- `FTPDocument` (`Protocol=ftp`);
- `TelnetDocument` (`Protocol=telnet`; a Telnet session);
- `WWWDocument` (`Protocol=http`; a remote WWW document on a non-Hyper-G server).

The following classes are also derived from class `Document` and have additional attributes:

- `GopherDocument` (`Protocol=gopher`);
- `SQLDocument` (`Protocol=sql`);
- `WAISDocument` (`Protocol=wais`).

GopherDocument

Class `GopherDocument` is derived from class `RemoteDocument`. It is a reference to a Gopher document on a (remote) Gopher server (see Chapter 6 for information on Gopher). The *GopherType* attribute defines the document type, according to the Gopher protocol specification (for example, "1" is a Gopher directory).

Name	User	System	Server	Synthetic
GopherType	✓			✓[a]

[a] The server generates `Gopher` objects on the fly when accessing a Gopher directory or Gopher index.

SQLDocument

Class `SQLDocument` is derived from class `RemoteDocument`. It is a reference to a synthetic document (or collection) generated on the fly by accessing an SQL database (see Chapter 12 for information on the Hyper-G SQL gateway). The following attributes are applicable, in addition to those inherited from `RemoteDocument`:

Name	User	System	Server	Synthetic
Database	✓			
Pwd	✓			
SQLStmt	✓			✓
Uid	✓			

The server generates `SQLDocuments` on the fly as a result of SQL queries. The `MimeType` field contains the type of the document in MIME format.

WAISDocument

Class WAISDocument is derived from class RemoteDocument. It is a reference to a WAIS document on a (remote) WAIS server, or to a whole WAIS server. The WAISType attribute defines the WAIS document type (for example, "WSRC" is a WAIS source, that is, a server).

Name	User	System	Server	Synthetic
Size				√
WaisDocID				√
WAISType	√			√[a]

[a] The server generates WAIS objects on the fly for results of WAIS searches.

Group

The class Group describes a user group (see also Section 11.2). Although it is formally derived from the abstract base class HGObject, no attributes of HGObject except ObjectID are applicable. Objects of type Group can only be read and written by system users. The following attributes are defined:

Name	User	System	Server	Synthetic
Descr		√		
UGroup		√		

Server

The class Server describes other servers (a Hyper-G server knows about all other Hyper-G servers). Although it is formally derived from the abstract base class HGObject, no attributes of HGObject except ObjectID are applicable. The following attributes are defined for Server objects:

Name	User	System	Server	Synthetic
Dead			√	
DocCount			√	
Modified			√	
OHName			√	
SString			√	
UServer			√	

User

The class User describes users of the Hyper-G server (see also Section 11.2). Although it is formally derived from the abstract base class HGObject, no attributes of HGObject except ObjectID are applicable. Only the corresponding user and system users may read the user record, and so the user's real identity (represented by the Descr attribute in his or her user record) is not revealed to other users (compare the identification modes discussed in Section 9.5). With the exception of the Passwd attribute, attributes of a User object may only be set by system users.

Name	User	System	Server	Synthetic
Account		√	√	
Descr		√		
Group		√		
Home		√		
Host		√		
Passwd	√			
UName		√		

11.2 Access permissions

Access rights are specified in the Rights attribute of a Hyper-G object (that includes documents, collections and anchors). The attribute value is composed of read (R:), write (W:) and unlink (U:) permission fields, separated by semicolons. For each field, the value a means that the author of the object has access, u users means that the specified users (user names separated by blanks) have access, and g groups means that the members of the specified user groups (group names separated by blanks) have access. While each field may appear only once, colons may be used to combine field values (for example, R:a,u users,g groups).

The Rights attribute can only be modified by the author of the object or system users (that is, members of user group system).

By default (that is, when no Rights attribute is present or a field is empty or missing) only the author of the object and members of the "system" group have write and unlink permissions while all users (including anonymous users) have read permission. In principle, the Rights attribute allows you to reduce the set of users having read access, to enlarge the set of users having write access, and to reduce the write access set to a set of users with unlink access.

Write access implies read access. Unlink permissions are only meaningful for collections, as they control the right to unlink (remove) something from that collection. By default (that is, if the unlink field is not present) users with write permission have unlink permission.

If the write field is present and the unlink field is not, the users specified by the write field also have unlink permission and can thus delete the object from the collection. Specifying the unlink field allows you to have collections where a (large) group of users may write documents into them, but only a (small) group of users may remove documents from them (this can be used for hypertext discussion).

In addition to the `Rights` attribute, access is controlled by the `TimeOpen` and `TimeExpire` attributes. After the date specified by `TimeExpire` the object becomes invisible to users not having write access to the object (the object is not physically removed from the database, however). Similarly, an object is invisible before the date specified by `TimeOpen` to users without write access to the object. See Section 22.3.1 for possible applications of the `TimeOpen` and `TimeExpire` attribute.

Summarizing, write access is granted, if:

(1) the user has system privileges (that is, is a member of user group "system"), or

(2) the user is the author (owner) of the object, or

(3) the user is a member of the users or user groups specified in the write field (`W:`) of the object's `Rights` attribute.

Read access is granted, if:

(1) the user has write access (see above), or

(2) the time constraints are met (`TimeOpen`, `TimeExpire`), and

(a) The read field (`R:`) of the object's `Rights` attribute is not present or empty (that is, unlimited read access granted), or

(b) the user is a member of the users or user groups specified in the read field of the object's `Rights` attribute.

Unlink access is granted, if:

(1) the user has system privileges (that is, is a member of user group "system"), or

(2) the user is the author (owner) of the collection to unlink from, or

(3) the user has write access to the collection to unlink from (see above), and

(a) the unlink field (`U:`) of this collection is not present or empty, or

(b) the user is a member of the users or user groups specified in this field.

As a special case, `U:a` refers to the author of the object to be deleted (not the author of the collection), so authors are allowed to delete their own objects only, even if they have write access to the collection.

Write (unlink) access for a document implies write (unlink) access for all anchors attached (that is, even for private anchors of other users). The access permissions contained in the `Rights` attributes are checked when the object (document, collection, anchor) is requested. In other words, if you do not have read permission for a document, you will not even be able to access its meta-data, let alone the document itself. But even if you have access permissions, you may not be allowed to fetch the document for other reasons (see Section 11.3).

Two more permission fields are allowed in the `Rights` attribute, although they do not directly control access to the object record. The `I:` field can be used to control the inheritance of a collection's access rights to its children. It is meaningful only for collections, and should be interpreted by a client wishing to insert something into the collection (it is not interpreted by the server), and suggested to the user as default `Rights` attribute. The `I:` is followed by a combination of the letters R, W, U, L and I. For example, `I:R` means that *only* the R: portion of the collection's `Rights` attribute should be copied to the client's `Rights` attribute. By default (that is, when the `I:` field is missing), clients should copy (inherit) all fields (equivalent to `I:RWULI`).

The `L:` field is meaningful for documents only, and used to limit simultaneous access to resources. It is described in detail in Section 11.3.

11.2.1 Examples

`Rights=R:g abcd,u xyz` Members of user group `abcd` and user `xyz` have read permission, only the author of the object has write and unlink permissions (the write field is not present and thus the defaults are used).

`Rights=R:g a1 a2;W:g a1` User groups `a1` and `a2` have read permission, but only group `a1` has write and unlink permissions.

`Rights=W:g b1 b2;U:g b1` All users have read permission (default; read field is empty), and groups `b1` and `b2` are granted write permission, but only the members of `b1` may also remove objects from this collection (the unlink field is ignored for non-collections).

`Rights=R:a` Only the author has read (and by default write and unlink) permission.

`Rights=W:a` This is the default setting that is used when the `Rights` attribute is not present: everybody can read, but only the author may write and unlink.

`Rights=I:R;R:g abc xyz;W:g xyz;U:a` This setting of a collection is useful in situations like electronic discussions, where only members of groups `abc` and `xyz` are allowed to read the contributions contained in the collection, only members of `xyz` are allowed to write contributions, but no user should be allowed to unlink the contributions of others (`U:a` means that authors can unlink only their own documents from this collection). The `I:R` prevents unwanted copying of the `W:` field to documents inserted into this collection, so that write access for documents in the collection remains with the authors only.

Attributes may be changed and added interactively using any Hyper-G client. If you have to change a number of objects in a similar fashion, you may use the `hgmodify` command, either by itself or in a script.

11.3 Accounting, billing and licensing

Hyper-G allows you to attach a "price tag" to individual documents. Identified users may be given an account with virtual money, from which the price of a document is deducted when the document is transferred to the client. When there is not enough virtual money left in the user's account, the document is not transferred and the server sends an error code (INSUFF_FUNDS). Note that the amount is not deducted when transferring the object's meta-information. Thus, searching and collection listings are free, only looking at documents themselves may cost. Of course, anonymous users cannot access priced documents. Also, clients are expected to inform users of the document's price before attempting to load it, unless the user has chosen to accept documents priced below a certain threshold.

As in real life, the price of an object may depend on who wants to buy it. It is always accessible for free for users with write permissions (including its author and system users). It is possible to define different prices for members of specific user groups or specific users. The price itself is specified as a currency-independent, integral number (relationships to real currencies, if any, have to be defined by the server administrator). Negative prices are not possible, and the balance on user accounts is always positive (or zero).

Authors specify the price in the document's Price attribute. Loosely speaking, the syntax is as follows: an unsigned 32-bit integer (the price), optionally followed by a colon and a specification of users and user groups (like in the Rights attribute). This may be repeated a number of times (different prices for different user groups) separated by semi-colons. For example, Price = 0x00000064;0x00000050:g websoc,u wonko; 0x00000000:u fkappe specifies that the document should be worth 100 units (64 in hexadecimal), but members of user group websoc and user wonko get a rebate of 20% and pay only 80 units (50 in hexadecimal), while user fkappe would have to pay nothing. The hexadecimal notation is a bit unwieldy for the user, but fast for the server. Clients should therefore translate it to decimal notation.

When a user accesses the document, the server uses the information in the Price attribute to dynamically generate a Cost attribute, taking the user's identity and group memberships into account (offering the smallest possible price, of course). In our example, Cost = 0x00000050 would be generated for wonko and members of websoc and Cost = 0x00000064 would be generated for others, including anonymous users. Since anonymous users have no Hyper-G account, the document is inaccessible to them. No Cost attribute would be generated for the user fkappe, the author of the document, the users with write permission, and system users (members of user group system). They can access the document even without a Hyper-G account.

Only the system administrator can set the balance of user accounts (for example, with haradmin; see Sections 14.8.1 and E.1.1). The idea is that users can fill up their Hyper-G accounts by transferring real money to the corresponding system administrator.

The actual transfer of "real" money (billing) is outside the scope of the system. What is important is that there are ways to transport it anonymously, either electronically (for example, with *ecash* from *DigiCash*; see Section 30.4.2) or the old-fashioned way. This means that the anonymously identified users mentioned in Section 9.5 can buy documents anonymously. No credit card information and the like is transferred over the Web. Users prepay, so the risk (in case someone stole your username and password) is limited to the amount paid.

Another interesting application of the accounting feature is to involve no real money at all, but to use it to protect issued passwords. For example, in the ED-MEDIA 95 Online Support system outlined in Chapter 29, usernames and password were sent to the participants before the conference, so that they could already browse through the papers before going to the event. The papers were assigned a certain price, and the participants were each given an account with a balance that lasted for a limited number of document downloads. In this way, participants were deterred from giving away their passwords to others.

In a different business model also supported by Hyper-G, users do not "pay per view." Rather, a Hyper-G system administrator may buy "licenses" for certain collections of information (such as electronic books, journals, newspapers, databases) from the owner of the information (for example, a publisher), similar to how a library would buy a book or a CD-ROM. The idea is that if n copies of the book (licenses of the collection) have been bought, the book (collection) can only be read by n persons simultaneously. Hyper-G supports this model (see also Section 22.3.2) by the `License` attribute of a collection and the "L:" field of the `Rights` attribute of individual documents of that collection. When a user retrieves a document from the licensed collection for the first time, one license is assigned to that user, and thus locked for others. The user may continue reading other documents from that collection. If no retrieval of documents by that user happens for a certain *timeout period* the license is unlocked (like the book would be returned to the shelf).

For example, the `License` attribute of Meyer's 10-volume Encyclopedia on IICM's Hyper-G server looks like this:

```
License = 0x0000012C 0x00000003 0x00000014
```

The first of the three hexadecimal numbers specifies the *timeout period* – in our example 5 minutes (hexadecimal 12C is 300 seconds). This represents the length of time that a user can lock the collection without retrieving documents. A timeout value too large blocks the collection unnecessarily, while a timeout value too small effectively circumvents the license restrictions. The second hexadecimal number specifies the number of licenses or simultaneous accesses to the collection – in our example, 3. The fourth user would be denied access (the server would generate an LC_NO_MORE_USERS error). The last hexadecimal number specifies the number of documents a user is allowed to retrieve in a single "grab" of the license. This is a measure against somebody trying to download the whole collection (of possibly copyrighted material) and blocking it for a long time for others. In our example, a user may look at 20 encyclopedia entries before having to return it. Thus, the maximum time a single user can keep the encyclopedia is $5 \times 20 = 100$ minutes. Also, the time to download the whole encyclopedia (43 820 documents) is significantly increased (left as an exercise for the reader!).

Every document of the encyclopedia must contain a reference to the collection (named `ref.m10`) to which it belongs in the "L:" field of the `Rights` attribute:

```
Rights=L:ref.m10
```

so that every access to a document of the collection is taken into account, regardless of how it was found (including searching and link following). It is not necessary to directly access the collection with the `License` attribute to enable the license mechanism.

11.4   Replication

As mentioned in Section 10.1, Hyper-G supports replication of objects, to overcome WWW's scalability problems when many users want to access the same object (see Section 8.3.4). A replica is a local copy of a remote document. The idea is that users access remote documents through their local server (see Section 9.6). When the user tries to access a remote object, the local server first checks whether there is a local replica available. If this is the case, the user is given the local object instead of the remote object, and no interaction with the remote server is required.

This is implemented using the `Repl` attribute of a `HGObject`. If present, the `Repl` attribute stores the GOID of the remote object of which this object is a replica. The `Repl` attribute is indexed, so that the `dbserver` can decide very fast whether a local instance of a remote object (referred to by its GOID) exists.

Replication is intended for important and heavily used hyperdocuments that are modified infrequently (encyclopedias, bibliographies, electronic journals and so on). At the moment, replication has to be managed manually.

Replication should not be confused with document caching. The latter is done by the `dcserver` independently and automatically, but leaves the objects untouched. Following links or giving location feedback from a cached document still requires contact with the original server, while doing the same for a replicated server does not bother the remote server at all, since all objects (including anchors and collections) can be replicated.

This is important for creating local databases which work independently of network connectivity (for example, from a CD-ROM), with copies of objects from real Hyper-G servers. It is also possible to put the most important or long-to-load documents on a local database (provided that they are not changed too frequently), in addition to accessing information over the network, for example in an "information kiosk" installation.

11.5   Further reading

Information on *ecash* can be found at `http://www.digicash.com`. The MIME (Multipurpose Internet Mail Extensions) Internet standard is defined in RFC 1341 (Borenstein and Freed, 1992).

12   Hyper-G and gateways to external databases

Srinivasan Parthasarathy

The previous chapters have dealt with the dissemination of hypermedia information on the Web and the role of Hyper-G. Chapter 10 has dealt with the intrinsic details of Hyper-G's server architecture. This chapter primarily focuses on the architecture of gateways to third-party servers, including **SQL servers** and other online systems such as **Videotex**. This chapter assumes at least some familiarity with **SQL queries and databases**.

12.1   Importance of gateways

The extensive usage of the Web as a medium for information supply has increased both the bulk of information and the variety of information available today. In order to provide the user better access to a cacophony of information systems, it is of paramount importance to provide so-called **gateways**. A gateway acts as a sort of interpreter which converts design-specific protocols, information structures and presentation-specific details of one system into corresponding counterparts of the other system. Gateways allow you to view the whole complexity of information contents of different representations in a unified way as one single information system. Much interesting data, such as online telephone directories, railway time-tables and many other collections of information are of a very dynamic nature that require robust distributed database management systems. The problems that information providers are commonly confronted with are the following:

- provision of adequate end-user training;

- necessity of a standard graphical user interface (GUI) to access the information content;

- standardization of the format for representation.

Let us briefly elaborate on these issues. The access mechanisms and the presentation capabilities of distributed database systems and other third-party information systems are often complicated and specified for a single hardware platform, requiring extensive end-user training. Traditionally, access to such databases has been mostly textually or menu driven.

Application programmers usually had the possibility of enhancing the interfaces based on an Application Programmers' Interface (**API**) in C or Fortran. The fourth-generation programming languages (often called **4GLs**) like SQL reduced the effort involved in developing interfaces to the databases considerably. However, the resulting systems were rather cumbersome, single-purpose solutions requiring periodic redesign of the architecture.

The emergence of information systems like Gopher, WWW and Hyper-G marked a new phase in the standardization of data formats. ASCII text and HTML became the *de facto* standard for providing information on the Web. Therefore, it became desirable to use these new emerging "standards" by translating the results of usual database queries into those formats. This way Web users can browse through the information contents of servers of heterogeneous nature and functionality using their favorite Web browser. However, worldwide dissemination of the information via the Web cannot be achieved by simply converting the results into the above-mentioned formats. It is necessary to implement robust coupling mechanisms between the servers involved: this is the main functionality of a gateway.

12.1.1   Gateway design considerations

In contrast to other Web systems like Gopher and WWW, Hyper-G offers a complete working environment to the user. In other words, Hyper-G handles not only common Web facilities like Email, News, FTP and so on, but also provides reciprocal seamless interoperability with other information systems.

By "reciprocal," we emphasize the fact that a Hyper-G server can transform information contents and formats of foreign servers so that native Hyper-G clients can handle them. On the other hand, third-party clients (for instance, WWW clients like Netscape, Mosaic and others) are supplied with information in the corresponding formats (HTML documents in the case of WWW).

12.1.2   Common approaches to gateway design

Before going into details of the gateway mechanism let us take a brief look at how other information systems like WWW or Gopher tackle this issue. As discussed in Section 7.2.3, WWW operates basically with HTML documents. The other formats are handled via the so-called Common Gateway Interface (CGI) (see Section 7.4). The http daemon essentially executes an external program and additionally passes on the arguments from the client. The output of the program is channeled back directly to the client. The CGI binaries (the common term for such programs) usually produce the output in HTML format or in the conventional MIME format. For a more detailed description of CGI refer to Section 7.4.

The advantages of this approach are:

- Complicated user input analysis mechanisms can be implemented independent of the server architecture.

- It enables server-side scripting, thereby providing a certain degree of customization of the server functionality.

- CGI programs can be enhanced to take over the task of connecting to other third-party servers.

The disadvantages of this approach are:

- The whole mechanism is stateless; in other words, the Web server is unaware of the activities of the CGI scripts.

- In case of gateways to databases, every transaction initiates a new connection, thereby increasing the network overhead enormously.

- Security leaks are possible, as the information transferred from the client to the scripts is very vulnerable. You might often have encountered the warning messages in submitting forms in WWW clients.

- Every user action initiates a new connection to the SQL server which could be time-consuming.

12.2   SQL gateway to databases in Hyper-G

In Hyper-G, as discussed earlier, hypermedia information is stored in the form of objects (text objects, image objects, movie objects and so on) and the meta-information is represented by collections, clusters and sequence objects (for more details, we refer to Sections 9.2 and 11.1). Beginning in the mid-1980s, most commercial databases started supplying a so-called SQL interface. However, it is quite complicated to develop a generic interface for accessing information via the SQL interface: most commercial vendors unfortunately deviate from the ANSI SQL standard (see Section 12.4); also such a generic interface only provides very limited capabilities.

12.2.1   General considerations

One of the main design considerations of Hyper-G was to provide a "program-free" interface to databases. In CGI (see Section 7.4), authors have to write a CGI script that corresponds to the HTML document. For instance, if the user wants to perform an SQL query from a database containing information on employees, an SQL query of the type `select empname, salary from emp` would return the names and salaries of all employees from the relation `emp`.

The CGI bin directory should contain a script that connects to the corresponding SQL server, waits for the result and finally formats the result and outputs it.

The SQL gateway (which is in turn a server) can be optionally installed with every Hyper-G server either at installation time or patched onto an existing Hyper-G server. The SQL gateway performs the following functions:

- parses the SQL statement;

- extracts details about the SQL server;

- connects to the SQL server;

- formats the result.

It is quite common to present the result of the query in the form of a table. However, if the result consists of several lines, then displaying the results in the form of a table decreases readability. In Hyper-G, the author of a query specifies the type of presentation (see the attribute `MimeType` of the SQL object below). If the query generates a large number of hits, then the SQL gateway can dynamically create SQL objects, where each object corresponds to a single row. The SQL objects are presented to the user in the form of a collection hierarchy, thereby providing a better overview of the contents. The user can browse this dynamically generated collection and choose the appropriate object (where every object contains a dynamically generated SQL statement that corresponds to a single row). These objects can contain the value of a single tuple, an indication of the contents of the object. In the example mentioned above, every object might display the name of the employee in the title as helpful information. In this way, user interface consistency is maintained, assuming that a native Hyper-G client like Harmony or Amadeus is used. The connection to the database and the corresponding **Logon Definition Area** (LDA) are kept open. This improves the performance when different SQL queries are performed on the same database, as only the **Cursor Definition Area** (CDA) has to be newly generated each time. Obviously, the connection is closed when a "Timeout" occurs, that is, when there is no request from the `DocCache` Server for a particular amount of time.

The `DocCache` Server communicates with the SQL gateway module. Figure 12.1 shows the communication process. When the user clicks on such an SQL object during

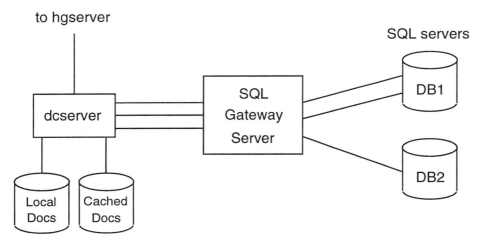

Figure 12.1   SQL gateway in Hyper-G.

navigation, the `DocCache Receiver` redirects the request to the SQL gateway server. In contrast to the CGI, the SQL gateway in Hyper-G is a full-fledged server. Users wishing to create Remote SQL objects do not have to bother about writing scripts or installing drivers.

12.2.2   Creating remote SQL objects

In order to perform an SQL query in Hyper-G, the author generally creates a Hyper-G remote object; refer to Chapter 22 for more details on remote objects, or Chapters 23, 24 and 25 which explain how to create remote objects. This section will focus mainly on the attributes that are of importance to authors (the information providers) who wish to create SQL documents.

Firstly, consider the following Hyper-G remote object of subtype SQL:

```
ObjectID      = 0x000001a
Type          = Document
DocumentType  = Remote
Author        = hgsystem
TimeCreated   = 95/08/10 12:25:36
TimeModified  = 95/09/10 18:21:11
Protocol      = SQL
Title         = en:List of Employees and their Salary
Uid           = scott
Pwd           = tiger
Host          = fstghp37
Port          = 1470
Database      = oracle:t:edvz
SQLStmt       = select ename,sal from emp
MimeType      = text/html
```

The SQL object has `ObjectID`, `Type`, `DocumentType`, `Author` and the attributes `TimeCreated` and `TimeModified`. For a description of the meaning of these attributes see Chapter 11. Chapters 23 and 24 contain details concerning the creation and insertion of Hyper-G objects. This section will focus on the object attributes that are important for the SQL object.

Protocol

The attribute `Protocol` should be set to `SQL`. The value `SQL` is used internally by the server to determine the type of remote object.

Uid and Pwd

The attributes `Uid` and `Pwd` are required for the authentication process of the SQL server. `Uid` stands for the username and `Pwd` for the password.

- The author of the SQL query can fill in the values for the attributes `Uid` and `Pwd`. These preset values are used for connecting to the SQL server. This is useful when the author wishes to provide anonymous (or public) access. Of course, public access must be used with caution. The author can additionally set the access rights to the SQL object – see Section 11.2 – and thereby suitably adjust the access to the SQL server.

- Both attributes can be left empty. In this case, the user would have to supply the necessary authentication information during the session, in order to obtain data from the remote database. Web clients display a dialog box for the user to type in username and password.

Host and Port

The attributes `Host` and `Port` contain the hostname and the port number of the SQL server. For example, `fstgshp20.tu-graz.ac.at` stands for the hostname. The author can also write the IP address instead of the canonical hostname or the DNS alias. The `Port` attribute denotes the port number of the SQL listener daemon.

Database

The SQL gateway can connect to different types of SQL server. For commercial SQL servers like Sybase, Oracle or Ingres, it is often necessary to use a vendor-specific protocol. The syntax for this attribute is `database:type:databasename`. For example, this attribute can have the value `oracle:t:edvz`. The first word `oracle` specifies that the remote SQL server is an Oracle database. The second word (in this case, the letter `t`) is specific to the type of Oracle installation. The `t` stands for transparent network substrate. This information can be obtained from the system administrator or the database administrator. Finally, the third component `edvz` stands for the name of the database.

SQLStmt

The attribute `SQLStmt` contains the actual SQL statement which is to be executed at the SQL server end in order to retrieve data. The author can specify any number of SQL statements. The purpose of supplying several SQL statements is rather specific to Hyper-G, particularly to the structural organization of information. The author can determine how the information content is to be organized and presented to the user (see Section 22.2).

The simplest case is that the attribute `SQLStmt` contains only a single SQL statement. In this case, the attribute `MimeType` specifies how the result of the query is to be formatted.

The author can define several SQL statements. Consider the following value for the attribute `SQLStmt`:

```
SQLStmt=[1=]select col1, col2 from table1;1
SQLStmt=[2=]select col3, col4 from table1
    where col1=!col1 and col3 = '5';2
SQLStmt=[3=]select col5, col6 from table2
    where col3=!col3;1,2
```

At first glance, the search predicate and the trailing semicolons with digits at the end of the SQL statement may appear to deviate from the proposed ANSI SQL standard. Actually, as will be explained and demonstrated later by the example in Section 12.2.3, this is not the case.

When such an SQL document is accessed for the first time, the first statement is executed and a "virtual" collection with dynamically generated child collections is created, where each child collection corresponds to a single row of the query result. These child collections are also SQL documents that are created on the fly by the SQL gateway. Each child collection contains the following value in the attribute SQLStmt:

```
SQLStmt=[2=]select col3, col4 from table1
    where col1=<<values>> and col3 = '5';2
SQLStmt=[3=]select col5, col6 from table2
    where col3=!co3
```

Notice that the value of the column col1 has been substituted. The search predicate expression col1=!col1 is simply a placeholder, where the right-hand side is substituted by the value of the corresponding column from the previous SQL statement for each row of the query result.

As will be demonstrated later in Section 12.2.3, this illustrates the possibility for the user to navigate through the database using the Hyper-G navigational paradigm.

The term ;1 at the end of the first SQL statement indicates to the SQL gateway what title should be assigned to the child collections. In this case, the value of the first column in the SQL statement is set as the title of the dynamically generated child collections.

Analogously, if the user selects a child collection, then SQL generates child collections corresponding to the rows of the query result. Once again the placeholders and titles are set appropriately as specified by the third SQL statement.

For the last SQL statement in the attribute SQLStmt, by default, the results are formatted as an HTML document. If the SQL statement returns binary data, then the author should specify this explicitly in the MimeType attribute.

Theoretically, the author can supply any number of SQL statements.

MimeType

The value of this attribute defines how the result of the query is to be displayed, whether as HTML text, image or whatever. If the SQL statement retrieves binary data (for instance, a picture), then the author should specify this in this attribute. The possible values conform to the MIME standard. If the SQLStmt attribute contains several SQL statements, then the value is effective only for the last SQL statement. By default, the attribute is set to text/HTML.

12.2.3   An example

The purpose of this section is to illustrate the functionality of the SQL gateway using a concrete example. We shall examine a practical application which permits students to obtain information about courses and the examination schedules at the Graz University of Technology. Courses, lecturers, lecture times, examination schedules, location of the lecture halls and so on are stored in an Oracle database. The information is publicly accessible. The example demonstrates how the user navigates through the relational database using the Hyper-G SQL object in order to obtain the necessary information.

```
ObjectID        = 0x000001b
Type            = Document
DocumentType    = Remote
Author          = hgsystem
TimeCreated     = 95/09/10 10:25:24
TimeModified    = 95/09/10 16:32:56
Protocol        = SQL
Title           = en:Courses at the Graz University
Uid             = scott
Pwd             = tiger
Host            = fstghp37
Port            = 1470
Database        = oracle:t:edvz
SQLStmt         =1= select distinct key, name from
                  inst_eng where key in (select distinct
                  instnr from ects);1;2
SQLStmt         =2= select coursenr, title from
                  inst_courses where instnr=!key;1;2
SQLStmt         =3= select coursenr, title, type,
                  week_hrs, sem, lecturer,syllabus from
                  ects where coursenr=!coursenr
MimeType        = text/html
```

First of all, a few words about the three SQL statements in the SQLStmt attribute. The first SQL statement retrieves all the institutes of the Graz University of Technology. The SQL statement contains only two columns, key and name, which are both automatically used as the title for the Hyper-G collections generated on the fly. The placeholders, crssem =! key, in the second SQL statement are replaced by the corresponding values of the variable key as a result of execution of the first statement.

A virtual collection containing all the institutes is created. For instance, the first child collection corresponds to the "Institute for Architectural Design and Architectural Science" and the dynamically generated SQL statement may contain the following value:

```
Title      = en:  Institute for Architectural
             Design and Architectural Science, 1410
SQLStmt    =2= select course,title from
             inst_courses where instnr==1410;2;1
SQLStmt    =3= select course,title,type,week_hrs,sem,
             lecturer,syllabus from inst_courses
             where coursenr=!coursenr;1,2;
```

Figure 12.2 shows the screen shot taken from the Web browser Netscape when the user selects the SQL document. It displays a list of institutes that offer courses for the students.

Assuming that the user selects the collection "Institute for Architectural Science and Architectural Design" at this level, the SQL gateway generates a list of collections corresponding to all the courses offered by this institute and a virtual collection is generated. Now, at the third level, the placeholders `coursenr != coursenr` are replaced by their respective values. Notice that the SQL statement has a prefix `;1;2;`. This tells the SQL gateway to assign the values of columns 1 and 2 from the SQL statement to the titles of dynamically generated collections, that is, the reference number of the course in the syllabus book and the name of the course are displayed as the title of the collection.

The attributes `Title`, `SQLStmt` and `MimeType` of the SQL document look as follows:

```
Title      = en:  Basic Principles of
             Design, 141002
SQLStmt    =3= select course, title, type,
             week_hrs,sem, lecturer, syllabus
             from ects where coursenr=141002
MimeType   = text/html
```

Figure 12.3 shows the screen shot of child collections representing the courses offered by the "Institute for Architectural Science and Architectural Design."

If the user opens the collection on "Basic Principles of Design" then an HTML formatted text is retrieved and displayed to the user.

The obvious advantage of this approach is that the user need not have any prior knowledge about the contents of the database. The SQL document allows the user to navigate the database in the same way as the Hyper-G server.

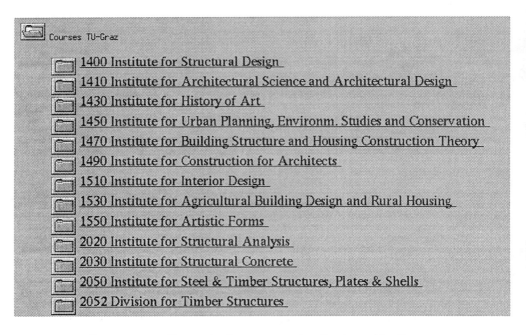

Courses TU-Graz

1400 Institute for Structural Design
1410 Institute for Architectural Science and Architectural Design
1430 Institute for History of Art
1450 Institute for Urban Planning, Environm. Studies and Conservation
1470 Institute for Building Structure and Housing Construction Theory
1490 Institute for Construction for Architects
1510 Institute for Interior Design
1530 Institute for Agricultural Building Design and Rural Housing
1550 Institute for Artistic Forms
2020 Institute for Structural Analysis
2030 Institute for Structural Concrete
2050 Institute for Steel & Timber Structures, Plates & Shells
2052 Division for Timber Structures

Figure 12.2   Dynamically generated collection of institutes.

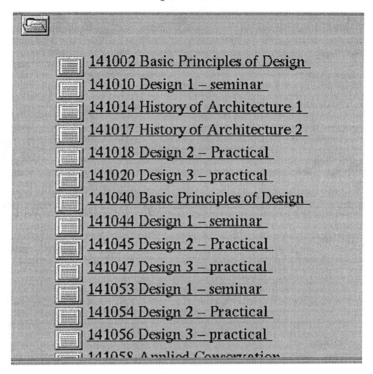

Figure 12.3   Collection showing the courses offered by the institute.

From the author's point of view, it allows greater flexibility. The author can add another intermediate level to the above SQL statement in order to differentiate between the courses offered during the spring and fall. For instance, consider the following SQL statement:

```
SQLStmt   =1= select distinct key,name from
           inst_eng where key in (select distinct
           instnr from ects);1;2
SQLStmt   =2= select distinct crssem from inst_eng
           where instnr=!key
SQLStmt   =2= select lecturer,degree,lectnr
           from inst_report where (instnr=!key &&
           crssem=!crssem);1
SQLStmt   =3= select coursenr,title,type,week_hrs,sem,
           syllabus from inst_report where
           lectnr=!lectnr
```

At the first level all the institutes are displayed as collections. The second level of the dynamic collections contains only two child collections corresponding to the fall and spring semesters. The third level displays the child collections corresponding to all lecturers who offer courses for the chosen semester and finally, the fourth level displays the information about the course.

12.2.4   SQL interface via CGI

Hyper-G supports the HTML 3.0 format (see Section 7.2.3) and CGI (see Section 7.4). This means that external scripts can be executed. There are a variety of interface kits to databases for WWW. However, in order to use them, authors must understand HTML and know how to write CGI scripts. The results of the scripts can be displayed as HTML forms or as tables.

If the interface to the database is realized using forms, then users should fill in the name of the courses (ideally, these would be chosen from a list of possible values) in order to obtain the details. However, this implies that the user must have prior knowledge about the curriculum in order to obtain results with a reasonable order of relevance. To fill out the forms, the user must be aware of the possible values. Currently several software CGI packages offer advanced solutions to this problem, and simplify the process of creating forms and writing scripts by automating these procedures to a considerable extent.

Thus, Hyper-G supports the already existing interfacing techniques of WWW. It additionally introduces an innovative approach for retrieving the necessary information from databases. Although native Hyper-G clients are ideally suitable for browsing SQL documents, WWW clients can also be used, see Chapter 20. The author is given the option to choose the desired interfacing technique for optimally accomplishing the task.

12.2.5   Summary

This chapter provides information about interfaces to databases, in particular to SQL servers from Hyper-G. The interface is fully compatible with what is already available for other WWW servers. Additionally, Hyper-G introduces a new mechanism for navigating through relational databases.

The approach taken has the following advantages:

- The connection to the database remains open and the results are cached.

- No knowledge about the contents of the database is necessary.

- The user navigates through the database without any change in the navigational paradigm.

- The mechanism is practically error-free as the SQL statements are always valid and the user does not have to type in the values.

The SQL gateway in Hyper-G is program-free. The author is not forced to write scripts or programs. On the other hand, the access and navigation through the contents of the database at the user end is consistent. The SQL gateway attempts to cache the results and keeps the connection between the Hyper-G server and the SQL server open in order to reduce network traffic and improve efficiency.

By supporting HTML and CGI, it is also possible to write CGI scripts in Hyper-G similar to WWW. Supporting the CGI interface is very essential because the existing interfaces to SQL servers on WWW can be reused without any change. The authors of the SQL objects can also create forms and write corresponding scripts, as is the case with WWW.

12.3 Gateway to videotex systems

In the early 1980s, the availability of microcomputers and modems initiated the development of so-called videotex systems. Videotex systems can be considered as the forerunners of today's networked information systems. The Austrian videotex system called PAN (which stands for Public Access Network) provides several online services ranging from weather reports and traffic schedules to online shopping, entertainment, mailing and faxing facilities. Users simply need a modem and a telephone account in order to connect to the videotex system. Hyper-G provides a gateway to PAN. The PAN is connected to videotex systems of other countries including Germany, France, Switzerland, Slovenia and Slovakia. Graphical interfaces are presently under development. At the moment, the information content of videotex systems is predominantly textual. The interface from Hyper-G to videotex systems is an emulation of an ASCII VT100 terminal; the connection is established using Telnet. Users of the Austrian videotex PAN can use Hyper-G. Videotex users who do not have a Hyper-G account log on to the Hyper-G server as anonymous users. The multimedia data available within Hyper-G can only be processed offline, that is, users must download the data and use external viewers in order to view it.

12.4 Further reading

The book by Van der Lans (1988) provides a good introduction to SQL. For more details on SQL, refer to *SQL – Structured Query Language* (Sayles, 1989). Date (1989) can be used as a reference to the SQL standard.

The URL `http://speckle.ncsl.nist.gov/flater/policy.html` contains information about obtaining the electronic version of the ANSI SQL Standard. The URL `http://www.contrib.andrew.cmu.edu/shadow/sql.html` can be used as an online SQL reference.

For more information on the MIME standard refer to Borenstein and Freed (1993). An introduction to writing CGI scripts can be found at `http://hoohoo.ncsa.uiuc.edu/cgi`.

Refer to `http://dozer.us.oracle.com:8080` for a list of Oracle interface kits. The FTP site `ftp://ftp.demon.co.uk/pub/DB` contains a large collection of interface kits written in Perl.

The URL `http://WWW.stars.com/Vlib/Providers/Database.htm` provides a comprehensive listing of interfaces to databases for the WWW. The URL `http://dozer.us.oracle.com:8080` contains demos and source codes of interfaces to Oracle databases.

13 Hyper-G as a standalone server

Steven Mitter

In June 1995, the ED-MEDIA 95 conference took place in Graz, Austria. A few months earlier the decision was made to publish the proceedings not only as a book but also on a **CD-ROM**. The system of choice for this task was Hyper-G. This CD-ROM was the motivation for the development of what is now called the **standalone server**. The goal was to have a software package to view Hyper-G data without the need for a connection to a Hyper-G server. In the second stage, the ability to edit documents offline was also implemented. It turns out that the standalone server can be used for a variety of important functions: to act as software for viewing Hyper-G data on a CD-ROM, as a basis for integrating local and remote functions and as an editing device, just to name the most important ones.

13.1 The standalone server: An introduction

The standalone server is an integrated part of some of the Hyper-G clients. At the moment, these are the clients Amadeus (see Chapters 17 and 18) and Easy (see Section 19.2) for MS-Windows and Harmony (see Chapters 15 and 16) for UNIX/XWindows environments. This new feature allows clients to work without a connection to the Web. In essence, the standalone server is a small and fairly simple database that can handle a subset of the features provided by a Hyper-G server. For a list of features that are not supported, or that are different for the time being, see Section 13.4. Most common features work as you would expect them to, like searching in titles, attributes and full text or following relationships like **is-parent**, **is-child** and of course all types of links. Since the standalone server complements or replaces a Hyper-G server the viewers for different data types are not affected by the use of the standalone server. This implies that all data types can be viewed regardless of the server used.

With the simple tools described in Section 13.5, databases that afterwards reside locally on a computer can be created from a collection in a Hyper-G server. This is also the reason why these databases are called **local databases**. You can create and use several local databases on a single computer. Clients also support the simultaneous use of several local databases and a Hyper-G server that is accessed as usual.

This is indeed one of the main achievements of the standalone server: to hold data locally on a computer for viewing with one of the Hyper-G clients. The other important point is the ability to create and edit data in the local database. Such material can be either left there to be used as is or transferred to a Hyper-G server.

To summarize the above, the standalone server has the following main features:

- It extends Hyper-G clients (either Amadeus, Harmony or Easy) for use with local databases.

- Different databases on a single computer can be used separately or simultaneously.

- The additional software in the clients is small and fairly simple.

- It includes a large subset of the features of a Hyper-G server.

13.2   Applications of local databases

This section gives some examples of the variety of possible uses for the standalone server. These examples are just meant to be illustrations and do not claim to be exhaustive.

13.2.1   Use without a connection to the Web

Let us assume you have a connection to the Web at work. At home you do not want to be connected: you might not want your children to be able to get certain data from the Web; or you might simply be reluctant to pay for the costs. Once you have made the decision not to have a connection at home, you would normally have no opportunity to use the hypermedia data that you can get from the Web at work. But with the standalone server, all you have to do is create a local database, take a copy of the database files home and use it with the appropriate client. This scenario would also apply, for example, if you had friends who wanted to share some information with you that they found on the Web, or if you want to give a Web presentation at a meeting where you do not want to rely on a connection to the Web.

13.2.2   Offline reading and authoring

As has been explained, it is sometimes desirable to read Web data offline. In fact almost the same arguments that apply for reading also apply for editing.

Another example of the need for offline clients is the growing number of people who use notebooks on a regular basis. Imagine you are on a long-distance flight that takes you from one continent to another to speak at a conference. You also want to do some final editing of your presentation, for which you will use Amadeus. You might even have a cellular phone and a modem so that you can connect to a Hyper-G server. But unfortunately your airline does not permit the use of cellular phones during the flight, or even worse, your phone does not work any more when you leave a certain geographic area.

Don't worry! All you have to do is use the standalone server. It offers the capability to insert, edit and delete data in a local database. This of course includes all types of data, like hypertext, video clips, audio and so on. The clients only offer the capability to create a Hyper-G database from existing documents, and to edit text documents. Data types such as video clips, audio or 3D scenes have to be edited with other software. However, when you have any data in a format that is supported by the client you can insert it into the local database. Relationships and links can also be edited just like you would do if you were connected to a Hyper-G server.

After you have arrived at the conference you connect your notebook to the Web and update the contents of your presentation on your Hyper-G server if you want to. As we all know, it sometimes happens that connections to the Web break down or are frustratingly slow. Anyway, by the time you give your talk you do not have to worry about such things, since you can use the data stored on your notebook for your presentation.

13.2.3   Catalogs, proceedings and presentations

As you know from reading this book, Hyper-G can manage all kinds of data in a structured and hyperlinked manner. This allows interesting applications to electronic catalogs, proceedings and presentations, since a hypermedia approach is useful in presenting large amounts of information.

Imagine, for example, an electronic catalog that is managed concurrently by several people. In this scenario, the Hyper-G server would be a clearing house that allows everybody to access the most recent version of every document. This makes it easy to refer to new documents, since once they have been incorporated into the server, they can be used immediately. If you want the public to be able to access the catalog, you might give everybody read access to your server, or offer public terminals. Through the identification mechanism of Hyper-G, you could also define groups of people who are allowed to access the catalog either in whole or only in part.

However, once you have the catalog in the Hyper-G server, you can also simply create a local database and use it to produce a CD-ROM. This makes it possible to distribute large amounts of data to your customers or your audience. On the other hand, you can update critical data, for example price-lists, using other media such as a floppy or even through the Web. Using CD-ROM also gives you the ability to use types of data that consume a lot of space, like video clips, audio or images; they would be a burden if you had to rely entirely on the Web, because of unacceptable demands on network traffic.

13.2.4   Information kiosks

The last example presented has its origins in a real project that is currently being undertaken. This project is part of a networked multimedia presentation using public kiosks that will feature interesting and economic new approaches. One problem that occurs when using kiosks to distribute information is the high bandwidth necessary if multimedia data is presented. The solution implemented includes kiosks that are equipped with very large hard disks, say five gigabytes or more. These hard disks hold local databases, which in turn store most of the large data-objects such as video or audio clips. Smaller objects, like the text portion of a

Figure 13.1   Presentation using Easy.

presentation and objects that are expected to change, reside in a remote Hyper-G server. This abolishes the need for a sophisticated high bandwidth network.

As in the example in Section 13.2.3, you might consider using the Hyper-G client Easy in such a kiosk situation since it allows you to create a particularly easy-to-use user interface (see Section 19.2). Figure 13.1 is a screenshot of a presentation of the city of Graz using Easy.

13.3   Accessing a local database

The file structure of a local database is defined in a `*.ld` file that can also be used to access the database. This can be done either by specifying the name of the `*.ld` file as a parameter when starting the client, or using the `Goto` command if it is available in the client. In any case the filename has to be preceded by the string `hglocal://`. Instead of using a `*.ld` file to access one local database you can also use a `*.ml` file to open multiple local databases. This file simply contains a list of `*.ld` files that will be loaded.

For example, let us assume you want to use a local database that is described by the file `edmedia.ld`. Amadeus would be started as follows:

```
amadeus -hghost hglocal://edmedia.ld
```

and Harmony like this:

`harmony -hghost hglocal://edmedia.ld`

   Whenever a local database is opened a set of paths is used to find the `*.ld` or `*.ml` file. First the current directory, then a path that optionally can be set for each client and finally the directory containing the clients is checked. The way in which the optional path is set depends on the client. Amadeus uses the entry `LocalDataPath` in the section `Amadeus` in its ini-file `amadeus.ini`. Harmony uses the environment variable `HARMONY_DATA_PATH`.

   The path in which the file is finally found is used as a basis for all relative paths that are used by the database. Usually, when you create your own local databases, all paths should be relative. Absolute paths mainly play a role when the database resides on a CD-ROM; normally you will not have to worry about this since the paths will be set during the installation of the CD-ROM.

   The file `localdb.ml` has a special function. If the client is started without a parameter specifying a local database and `localdb.ml` is found in the search path for local databases, this file is used to open all the databases it lists.

   When you are using an MS-Windows client it does not matter if you specify the file in lower case or upper case, but if you are using a UNIX client the case is significant. Normally you do not have to worry about this once you have specified the `*.ld` file correctly. If you intend to produce CD-ROMs for UNIX, you should use the script on the CD-ROM that comes with this book (see Section 13.8).

13.4   How the standalone server differs from the Hyper-G server

If you want to know more about the features common to both the standalone server and the Hyper-G server, consult the chapters that describe the Hyper-G server (for example, Chapter 10). In this section, only the differences between the two servers are described. Due to the complexity of both servers, some minor or irrelevant differences may not be listed here.

13.4.1   Direct access to database files

As has been pointed out previously, the main difference between the two servers is that the standalone server does not use the Web to manage data. Instead it uses the file system to access databases. In fact, when you open a local database, you specify a file that describes the database.

13.4.2   User management

The standalone server supports user management on a marginal level. You can still identify yourself with an arbitrary username and password, but if you are not connected to a Hyper-G server, the password is not checked. Rights are also not checked in the standalone server.

Everyone has full access to everything. When you create or modify an object in a local database your current username is inserted in the object. If you import the local database into a Hyper-G server at a later time, either your currently identified username replaces all entries in the Author attributes, or if you wish and you have system administrator privileges, you can keep the authors as they were in the local database.

13.4.3 Full text search

The algorithm used for matching queries during full text searches and for creating the necessary full text indexes is implemented slightly differently in the two servers. The Hyper-G server performs stemming on all words that are inserted into the full text indexes. It also uses a stop-list to eliminate frequently used terms like "the," "and," "it" and so on. When the Hyper-G server performs a full text query, it stems the words in the query except when the words are abbreviated. The returned results are sorted by a calculated weight. For more information see Section 10.5.2.

In contrast the standalone server inserts every word after using the same normalizing algorithm that is applied to keywords, titles and other attributes. It does not use a stop-list and the results after a query are not sorted by weight.

13.5 Creation of a local database

The easiest way to create and manage local databases is by means of the built-in features of the clients. These features may vary and change over time. Amadeus, for example, supports drag-and-drop of collections and documents between Hyper-G servers and local databases. Since not all features were implemented at the time this book was written, please check the client you are using for more details. Figure 13.2 shows the dialog box in Amadeus that is used to create new local databases.

The other way to create local databases is to use a series of tools. At the end you will have a local database and some protocol files. These protocol files contain information about possible and real errors that occurred during the process. This is explained in the following subsection.

13.5.1 Tools for creating local databases

The tools for creating a local database are hifexport for UNIX or hifexprt for MS-Windows (create HIF-files), hif2ldp, ldp2ldb, ldbkey and ldbfull. There is also a batch-file called makeldb that makes it easier as soon as you have a HIF-file. The batch-file cleanldb removes all protocol files. If you want to experiment with these tools you can use one of the HIF-files in the directory data on the CD-ROM distributed with this book.

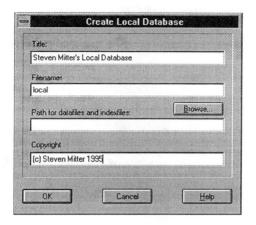

Figure 13.2   Creating a new local database with Amadeus.

Because these tools are likely to be changed in the near future, please check the specific readme files for more information. The tools and the readme files can be found on the CD-ROM in the directory `tools/ldbtools` in one of the subdirectories depending on the platform you use.

The result of creating a local database for the standalone server consists of several files that are distinguished by their filename extension:

`*.ld` description file for the local database;

`*.sik` index file for searchable attributes like title, name, author and others;

`*.sif` index file for full text searches;

`*.sdo` data file for objects like text-objects, collection-objects, anchor-objects and others;

`*.sdb` data file for binary data like pictures, movies, sounds, 3D scenes and others;

`*.sdt` data file for text data in HTF-format or HTML-format.

13.6   Limitations

Local databases are limited in the sizes of their files. The index files `*.sik` and `*.sif` cannot be larger than 65 MB. The data files `*.sdo` and `*.sdt` may not be larger than 1 GB and `*.sdb` than 2 GB. These restrictions arise from the internal structure of index files. They may be eased in the future. Since all of these files are managed by either the standalone server in the clients or the creation tools, these limits are checked automatically. If you ever

encounter problems because of these limits, split your database into several parts and use a
`*.ml` file to merge them again. This is easier said than done, of course, because you really
need to split your database at the top level.

13.7   Future plans

Some of the features described in this chapter had not been implemented when this book was
written but are scheduled to be complete in early 1996. If you find something that does not
work, it may be due to the fact that it is not implemented yet. In this case check if you are
working with the latest releases and check announcements for new ones!

There are also further plans for the future that will be realized according to demand and
available sometime in 1996.

- All Hyper-G clients and tools (if applicable) will support the standalone server.

- The limitations for file sizes will be increased to 4 gigabytes for each file of the local
  database.

- Results after a full text query will be sorted by a calculated weight.

- Simple user management and support for access rights will be implemented.

13.8   CD-ROM production: Hints and pitfalls

The biggest problems we encountered producing CD-ROMs were the case-sensitive file system and long filenames in UNIX environments. When you mount a CD-ROM in UNIX, it
depends on the device driver whether the filenames appear in lower case or upper case. The
solution was to create scripts that detect the case that is used by the device driver. The scripts
also use filenames that adhere to the rule that filenames may be no longer than eight characters
plus three characters for an optional extension. You should also keep this rule in mind when
you create your own local databases.

If you want to produce CD-ROMs with your own local databases you should use the
script `makecd` on the CD-ROM that comes with this book in the directory `tools/cdtools`.
Check the readme file carefully.

You will have to specify for which platforms (MS-Windows, UNIX version) you need
the clients (Amadeus, Harmony or Easy) and the local database. You must also specify a
directory where a copy of the CD-ROM will be created. You can use this directory for testing.
When you are satisfied with the result, you can burn the contents of this directory on a CD-
ROM.

If the CD-ROM is not intended for commercial use, all you have to do is make sure that
the copyright file that the `makecd` script created is present in the root of the CD-ROM. You
may add your own copyright notice in this file but you may not change the part that is already
there.

If you want to create and distribute a CD-ROM for commercial purposes please contact the Hyper-G Consortium at HGC@HGC.org or http://info.hgc.org.

13.9   Further reading

Much information on the ED-MEDIA 95 conference including technical papers can be found at http://hgiicm.tu-graz.ac.at/edmedia.

If you want to know more about how to create local databases consult the readme files on the CD-ROM that comes with this book in the directories tools/ldbtools and tools/-cdtools. The collection StandAloneServer in the IICM Hyper-G server hyperg:-//hgiicm.tu-graz.ac.at will be updated regularly when there are new versions of the tools or changes in the clients that affect the standalone server. You may also check the above collection in the local database that is supplied on the CD-ROM.

Ropiequet (1986) gives a broad and profound overview of things to consider when you produce your own CD-ROMs, but it does not cover the problems that occur when you produce CD-ROMs for UNIX. Additional information can be found in Buddine and Young (1987). ISO (1989) describes the ISO 9660 standard for CD-ROMs.

Blunden and Blunden (1994) is a compilation of case studies about electronic publishing. It also includes statistical data that can be useful in assessing profitability.

14 Hyper-G server installation, maintenance and administration

Gerald Pani, Klaus Schmaranz

Up to now you have read quite a bit about the philosophy and special features of Hyper-G which have hopefully made you seriously interested. In this chapter you will find the answer to the final question – *"How can I try it out?"* Please note that this is the most technical chapter so far and is only of interest to you when you are ready to install your own Hyper-G server. You will not need to read this chapter if you are only interested in browsing through information on a Hyper-G server or even if you wish to insert data into a Hyper-G server. This chapter assumes a basic knowledge of UNIX.

14.1 System requirements

To operate a Hyper-G server you need a UNIX PC or workstation connected to the Internet. Supported platforms at the moment are (ports to other platforms will follow):

- SUN Sparc (under SunOS 4.1.3 or Solaris 2.2 or above);

- HP 700 series (under HP-UX 9.01 or above);

- DECstation (under Ultrix 4.2 or above);

- SGI (under IRIX 3.0 or above);

- DEC Alpha (under OSF/1);

- IBM PC compatibles (under Linux).

To operate a serious Hyper-G server we suggest at least 64 MB of RAM for HPs, DEC-stations, DEC Alphas, SGIs and IBM workstations and at least 32 MB of RAM for SUNs and Linux PCs. The amount of memory needed is highly dependent on the expected number of simultaneous users browsing the Hyper-G server.

14.1.1   Space requirements

The Hyper-G server software itself consumes about 50 MB of disk space, depending on your platform. The installation also includes all offline data manipulation and administration tools (see Chapter 25) and a VT100 Hyper-G terminal viewer. In addition, you will need enough space for the documents you are planning to serve. The amount of disk space needed can be estimated using the following rules:

- Text: double the space for text documents (required for the full text index), and add an extra 500 bytes overhead per document.

- Multimedia: add an extra 500 bytes overhead per document.

- Hyperlinks: independent of the document type, hyperlinks need approximately 200 bytes each.

For example, if you are going to serve 50 000 text documents of 2 KB each, with an average of 10 hyperlinks per document plus 10 000 images of 50 KB each, with an average of 2 hyperlinks per image plus 2000 other multimedia documents such as 3D scenes, movies or sounds, with an average of 100 KB and 2 hyperlinks per document, this adds up to:

	Document	Overhead	Hyperlinks	Total
Text	50 000×2 KB	50 000×0.5 KB	50 000×10×0.2 KB	225 MB
Images	10 000×50 KB	10 000×0.5 KB	10 000×2×0.2 KB	509 MB
Multimedia	2 000×100 KB	2 000×0.5 KB	2 000×2×0.2 KB	202 MB
Total				936 MB

In addition, you will need some free disk space for logfiles, temporary files and so on, depending on how you have configured your server. See Section 14.4 below for more details on configuration issues.

14.2   Server installation

You have a choice between two different methods to install Hyper-G on your system:

- **automatic download, installation and update** using the Hyper-G installation script;

- **installation from a tar file**.

You can get the latest online information on the installation of a Hyper-G server by anonymous FTP from `ftp.iicm.tu-graz.ac.at`, directory `/pub/Hyper-G/-Server`, filename `HOWTO`.

You will also find the `HOWTO` file and the tar files for installation of a Hyper-G server on the CD-ROM that comes with this book. Please refer to Appendix B for further details of where the files are located on the CD-ROM.

14.2.1   General installation instructions

Independent of the method you choose to install your Hyper-G server, perform the following steps to prepare your machine for Hyper-G. You need `root` privileges to do this:

- Create a new UNIX user under which the Hyper-G server software will run, for example `hgsystem`. Optionally you can also create a new user group, for example `hyperg`. Put the home directory of this user on a file system that has enough free disk space. See Section 14.1.1 for how to calculate the space needed and also Section 14.5.3 for details of how to distribute the document store over a number of file systems. Give the user a standard C-shell (normally `/bin/csh`) or an enhanced version of the C-shell (normally `/bin/tcsh`). Please make sure that the shell start script is also `.cshrc` for `/bin/tcsh` and not `.tcshrc`.

- Create a directory (for example, `/usr/local/Hyper-G`) with owner `hgsystem`, group `hyperg` (optionally) and `0755` mode. This is the system-wide place for Hyper-G configuration files, documentation and so on. You do not need much room on the file system of this directory, as only symbolic links to the actual places will be generated and no files will be stored there. If you do not want to have a directory `/usr/local/Hyper-G` on your machine for whatever reasons, you can also create a directory with a different path and then set the environment variable HYPERG_HOME to point to this subdirectory in `hgsystem`'s `.cshrc` file.

- Install Perl (a popular script language) on the machine (your system administrator should have done this anyway). The Perl interpreter must either be in the standard place (`/usr/local/bin/perl`), or its actual location must be in the path variable of the user `hgsystem`. If you do not have Perl yet, it can be downloaded by anonymous FTP from `prep.ai.mit.edu` (and many other sites) in `/pub/gnu/perl-4.036.-tar.gz` or `/pub/gnu/perl5.000.tar.gz`.

14.2.2   Using the Hyper-G installation script

Using the **Hyper-G installation script**, the installation of the server software is automated to the greatest extent possible. Installation and software updates are done under control of the **Hyper-G Update Server**.

You can get the Hyper-G installation script by anonymous FTP from `ftp.iicm.-tu-graz.ac.at`, directory `/pub/Hyper-G/Server`, filename `hginstserver`.

Make sure you are identified as user `hgsystem` and your current working directory is `hgsystem`'s home directory (`~hgsystem`) and start `hginstserver`. The first time you start `hginstserver` the script asks you a series of questions needed to get the correct binaries for your platform and to configure the server appropriately. The script then connects to the Hyper-G Update Server, automatically copies all necessary files over the Internet (either compressed, or if gzip is in your path, gzipped), creates a file `.hgrc` in `hgsystem`'s home directory and modifies `.cshrc` so that `.hgrc` is included at the end of it. In `.hgrc` defaults like an extended path are defined.

hginstserver can be used not only for the first installation of the Hyper-G server but also for software updates. In order to keep your Hyper-G server up to date, just start hginstserver once in a while. The script will then connect to the Hyper-G Update Server to check whether pieces of the Hyper-G software have been replaced by new versions and install them if necessary. It is not necessary to stop the server while updating! As a result, you can start this script periodically (for example, by cron) to ensure you always run the latest software release.

When updating with hginstserver the only parts of the server that are installed are those that need to be replaced. The changes come into effect the next time you restart the server. The exit code of hginstserver is 0 if successful and nonzero if not, for instance due to an interrupted connection to the Hyper-G Update Server. If hginstserver was successful you can restart the server by executing the command dbstop; dbstart to let the changes come into effect. hginstserver also takes parameters controlling the way the updates are installed:

-h Print online help information.

-confirm Confirm installation of updated files. In this case the script will ask for confirmation for all files that need updating. Answers to these questions can be y (yes) or n (no) or c (only get changelog for this file but do not install).

-changelog Create a changelog file named hginstserver.clog showing all changes of the updated version compared to the previously installed version.

-nochanges Do not update the installation – only useful with option -changelog.

During installation hginstserver will also install a new version of itself in ~hg-system/bin/scripts if necessary. To avoid confusion, the old version in hgsystem's home directory that you got via FTP should be deleted after the first installation.

14.2.3   Installation from a tar file

The Hyper-G server can also be installed from a tar file that you can get by anonymous FTP from ftp.iicm.tu-graz.ac.at, directory /pub/Hyper-G/Server. This directory contains several tar files for different platforms and a description of which one you need for your appropriate platform.

We provide this special installation variant for people that cannot use our installation script; for instance, the server machine may be behind a firewall and only FTP to the outside world is allowed. Although Hyper-G can be installed from a tar file we strongly recommend the use of the Hyper-G install script if possible, especially for updating the server.

After having downloaded the tar file, make sure you are identified as user hgsystem and your current working directory is hgsystem's home directory (~hgsystem). Since the archive is in compressed form, untar it by executing the command:

```
gzip -dc <archive file name> | tar xvpf -
```

Having unpacked the archive start the installation script named `hginsttar` in `˜hg-system`. The script asks you a series of questions needed to configure the server appropriately. It creates a file `.hgrc` in hgsystem's home directory and modifies `.cshrc` so that `.hgrc` is included at the end of it. In `.hgrc` defaults like an extended path are defined.

14.3   Finishing the installation and starting the server

To finish installation, identify as user `root` and compile the program `˜hgsystem/-samples/hgbindport.c`. Copy the executable to `˜hgsystem/bin/$CPU/hgbind-port`. `$CPU` is an environment variable denoting your platform and is automatically set in `.hgrc`. Give ownership of `hgbindport` to `root` with the setuid bit set (mode `04755`).

This little program is used to obtain the privileged port numbers `418` for Hyper-G, `70` for Gopher and `80` for WWW, and pass the open file descriptors to another program that does not have `root` privileges. The program is delivered in source form so that the system administrator can check that it does not do nasty things as `root`. `hgbindport` opens a (system) port as file descriptor 3, changes its user id to `hgsystem` (the user who has invoked this command), and then executes the appropriate program (for example, `goph-gate`). `gophgate` recognizes the open file descriptor and uses it automatically, instead of opening a port of its own.

The effect of this is that (after the installation of `hgbindport`) you do not need `root` privileges to start the Gopher and WWW gateways, or the Hyper-G server. It therefore makes the system more secure; people do not have to rely on the gateways, they are started as ordinary users.

Now installation of the Hyper-G server is complete and you can start it. For this purpose identify as user `hgsystem` and execute the command `dbstart` (located in `˜hgsystem/-bin/scripts`).

If you want to stop the Hyper-G server execute the command `dbstop` (located in `˜hg-system/bin/scripts`).

However, in order to keep the Hyper-G server running all the time you should add the following lines to your local boot script (for example, `/etc/rc.local`):

```
# Start Hyper-G Server

if [-f /usr/local/Hyper-G/bin/scripts/dbstart]; then
    echo 'Starting Hyper-G Server' >/dev/console
    su - hgsystem /usr/local/Hyper-G/bin/scripts/dbstart
fi
```

14.4   Server configuration

Defaults of a Hyper-G server such as port numbers, gateways, caching and logging are freely configurable by editing `.db.contr.rc`, located in hgsystem's home directory.

Environment variables like HYPERG_HOME that are used by the tools that come with the server are set in .cshrc. All other configurations should be done by editing .db.contr.rc as described below.

Since the configuration files may contain more entries than are described here when new versions of Hyper-G are released, please also read the comments in the files themselves for last-minute information.

14.4.1 System defaults

System defaults that are not only needed by the Hyper-G server but also by other tools are set in the file .hgrc which is included in .cshrc and contains also variables like path. If you want to change the values of the environment variables make sure you are identified as user hgsystem. After you have finished editing, don't forget to execute the command source .cshrc from hgsystem's home directory. Then stop the server and restart it again to let the changes come into effect by invoking the command dbstop; dbstart.
Environment variables:

HYPERG_HOME The system-wide location for configuration files, documentation and so on. Only symbolic links to the actual location are stored in this directory, therefore it consumes nearly no disk space. The default is /usr/local/Hyper-G.

HGHOST Name of the machine where the Hyper-G server runs. The default is localhost.

14.4.2 Behavioral control

The file .db.contr.rc in hgsystem's home directory controls the behavior of the Hyper-G server like port numbers, gateways and cache size. If you want to change the settings in .db.contr.rc make sure you are identified as hgsystem. After having finished editing, stop and restart the server to let the changes come into effect by invoking the command dbstop; dbstart.

Please note that .db.contr.rc also contains explanation and last-minute information on new settings as comments.

The syntax for settings is <variable> value.

Configurable settings are:

<MAILTO> EmailAddress Mail critical errors to EmailAddress. The default is hgmgr@iicm.tu-graz.ac.at.

<WWWPORT> PortNumber Start the WWW gateway on port PortNumber. If PortNumber is 0 the WWW gateway is not started. It is highly recommended that you set PortNumber to 80, the default port number of WWW Servers.

<GOPHPORT> PortNumber Start the Gopher gateway on port PortNumber. If PortNumber is 0 the Gopher gateway is not started. It is highly recommended that you set PortNumber to 70, the default port number of Gopher Servers.

<SENV> EnvVar Set environment variable EnvVar (see Section 14.5 for supported environment variables).

<SENV> EnvVar value[value ...] Set environment variable EnvVar to value(s).

<USENV> EnvVar Unset environment variable EnvVar.

<WWWtimeout> Minutes Set the timeout for the WWW gateway to Minutes. The Hyper-G session of WWW users is then closed after Minutes minutes of inactivity. The default is 30 minutes.

<WWW_errors[remove_old | no_rename]> FileName Log WWW errors to FileName. The default is $HOME/wwwerrors ($HOME matches the home directory). FileName can be any valid UNIX filename, for example /dev/null if you do not want WWW error logging, or /dev/console if you want to see the error messages on your system console.

With the optional parameter remove_old only the last logfile is kept on disk. With the optional parameter no_rename logging produces one big file. If no optional parameter is given the logfile is renamed to FileName.timestamp after each program restart and kept on disk.

<WWW_log[remove_old | no_rename]> FileName Log WWW access to FileName. The default is $HOME/wwwlog.

<GOPH_log[remove_old | no_rename]> FileName Log Gopher access to FileName. The default is $HOME/gopherlog.

<GOPH_errors[remove_old | no_rename]> FileName Log Gopher errors to FileName. The default is $HOME/gopherrors.

<DB_log[remove_old | no_rename]> FileName Log object database server (db-server) access to FileName. The default is $HOME/server/db.log.

<DC_log[remove_old | no_rename]> FileName Log document cache server (dc-server) access to FileName. The default is $HOME/dcserver/dc.log.

<FT_log[remove_old | no_rename]> FileName Log full text server (ftserver) access to FileName. The default is $HOME/ftserver/ft.log.

<HG_log[remove_old | no_rename]> FileName Log Hyper-G session server (hg-server) access to FileName. The default is $HOME/hgserver/hg.log.

<MAIN_log[remove_old | no_rename]> FileName Log server main control (db-server.control) activity information to FileName. The default is $HOME/-server.log.

14.4.3   Changing the server start and stop scripts

The server start script ˜hgsystem/bin/scripts/dbstart is used to start the server control script ˜hgsystem/bin/scripts/dbserver.control which itself starts the different server modules and restarts them again, if they have accidentally crashed or been killed.

The server stop script ˜hgsystem/bin/scripts/dbstop is used to stop the server control script properly which itself stops all the different server modules.

If you really want to change the way the server is started (for example, you may wish to start an additional process that does logfile evaluation and statistics), you can copy the scripts dbstart and dbstop, include the start/stop of your special processes in the copies and use the copies for starting and stopping the server. It is important to copy the scripts first because the next server update could overwrite them.

Be careful! Editing dbstart and dbstop should only be done by specialists!

14.5   Environment variables

There are some special environment variables used to control the behavior of the different server modules. They should be set by a <SENV> entry in .db.contr.rc rather than in .cshrc, because they are only needed for the Hyper-G server and not by the tools or other programs that are started directly from the shell.

Online information on environment variables and corresponding command line parameters can be found in the man pages that come with the Hyper-G server (˜hgsystem/man/-man1/*.1).

14.5.1   General server environment variables

DIRdbs The directory containing all files needed by the object database server (db-server). Anchor, collection and object information database files, as well as transaction and error logfiles, are stored in this directory. The default is $HOME/dbserver.

DIRhgs The directory containing all files needed by the Hyper-G session server module (hgserver). The default is $HOME/hgserver.

DIRfts The directory containing all files needed by the full text server (ftserver). The full text index and special configurations like stop-lists are stored in this directory. For more information on stop-lists see Section 14.5.2. The default is $HOME/ftserver.

DIRdcs The directory containing all files needed by the document cache server (dc-server). The document database files as well as cached documents and error logfiles are stored in this directory (see Section 14.5.3). The default is $HOME/dcserver.

`DBHost` The name of the machine where the low-level database engine runs (that is, `db-server`, `dcserver` and `ftserver`). This variable is needed by `hgserver`, the main Hyper-G server module, because it can run on a different machine than the low-level database engine. The default is `localhost`.

`HGServerString` A string describing the server (for example, "University of Somewhere, SomeCity, SomeState"). Please use a reasonable name since this is how your Hyper-G server will be known to the world. If you enter an empty string your Hyper-G server will not be listed in Hyper Root on other servers. The default is what was entered when the installation script asked for it.

`OFFHOSTNAME` The fully qualified official domain name of the server machine, that is, the name under which your machine is addressable from the outside. This is used by Gopher and WWW gateways when they are sending out Gopher menus and URLs. This variable can also contain the IP address of the server instead of a domain name, but it is highly recommended to use the domain name. The default is what was entered when the installation script asked for it.

14.5.2 Full text server environment variables and configuration files

`FT_CACHESIZE NumBlocks` The maximum number `NumBlocks` of cached index blocks (4 KB per block) in memory. The default is 200 blocks. If you have enough RAM you may increase this value to speed up full text operations.

In addition to the behavioral configuration, the full text server has special configuration files that control the contents of the full text index. They can be found in the directory `~hg-system/ftserver/configuration`:

`stoplist.LANG`: these are stop-lists for full text searches in different languages. The extension `.LANG` must be replaced by the extension for the specific language, for example the stop-list for English is named `stoplist.en` and the stop-list for German `stoplist.de`.

The stop-list controls which words should not be considered in a full text search and therefore not be included in the full text index because they normally appear in every document (for example, *and*, *by*, *or*).

The file format of the stop-list is simply one forbidden word per line. Comments start with the special sequence `~=` or `/^#/` in the first column.

After you change the `stoplist.LANG` files it is necessary to generate a new full text index. To do so send `ftserver` a SIGHUP (`kill -1`).

14.5.3 Document cache server environment variables

`DC_CACHESIZE NumBytes` Maximum document cache size `NumBytes`. `NumBytes` can be given either as a number of bytes or in kilobytes by appending a `k` (for example, 512k), or also in megabytes by appending an M (for example, 64M). Data is cached in the directory ˜hgsystem/dcserver/cache. The default is 10M.

DC_STOREPATHnn Path The path for part nn of the document store. nn must be replaced by a number; these numbers must be consecutive starting with 0. For example, you could have DC_STOREPATH0, DC_STOREPATH1, DC_STOREPATH2 and so on. This allows you to use multiple file systems for storing documents.

DC_STORESIZEnn NumBytes Number of bytes for part nn of the document store. NumBytes can be given either as a number of bytes or in kilobytes by appending a k (for example, 512k), or also in megabytes by appending an M (for example, 64M). Each DC_STORESIZEnn entry must match a DC_STOREPATHnn entry. If no size is given for a certain path a new path is only taken if the file system is full.

DC_CONNTIMEOUT Seconds Timeout for unestablished TCP connections to remote servers in seconds. The default is 20 seconds.

DC_FROMTIMEOUT Seconds Timeout for interrupted TCP client to server transmissions in seconds. The default is 120 seconds.

DC_TOTIMEOUT Seconds Timeout for interrupted TCP server to client transmissions in seconds. The default is 120 seconds.

DC_ATTACHTIMEOUT Seconds Timeout for interrupted TCP server to server transmissions in seconds. The default is 50 seconds.

DC_CORE Bytes Maximum size of core dump that is written by the system in case of a dcserver crash in bytes. The default is according to the actual UNIX system limits.

14.6   WWW gateway environment variables

WWW_LOG_ICON Turns logging of successfully processed requests for inline icons used by the WWW gateway on or off. The default is off.

WWW_COLLHEAD Sets the default setting for displaying the collection-head document. Can be on or off. The default is on.

WWW_DATE_SIZE Sets the default setting for displaying the date and size of objects in collection lists. Can be on or off. The default is off.

WWW_AUTHOR Sets whether or not the author of objects in collection lists is displayed. Can be on or off. The default is off.

WWW_INFO_BUTTON Switches display of the info-button in collection lists on or off. The default is on.

WWW_COUNTRY Specifies the preferred language at session start. Can be en for English, de for German or detect for country detection. For example, when accessing the gateway from Austria or Germany, the default language is automatically set to German. The default is en.

WWW_ENTRY Specifies if an entry page is sent at session start or starts wwwmaster in no-session mode. entry can be always, never, home or no_session. always displays an entry page at every new session and does not use redirection. never uses http status code 302 for redirection. home sends an entry page if the path part of the URL at session start is either /, home, home.html or ROOT and uses redirection otherwise. no_session starts wwwmaster in the no-session mode. No session key is assigned, no entry page is sent, and the child process of wwwmaster that maintains the session exits immediately after every transaction. No session-dependent features (language setting and so on) are available in this mode.

WWW_USER A user name can be specified as default user at session start. If such a user has an account on the Hyper-G server and a home collection is defined, the entry point at session start will be the user's home collection.

WWW_PORT The port on which the WWW gateway listens for http-requests (default 80). Since this is a system port number, only the superuser can run wwwmaster listening on the default port. To overcome this limitation Hyper-G uses the hgbindport program (see Section 14.3).

WWW_ERRORS The filename of the error file. All error output generated by the WWW gateway is written to this file. The default is standard error.

14.7   Server maintenance

14.7.1   Backup and restore

Since the Hyper-G server stores relations, meta-information and documents in different files, a simple tar of the database files without denying write access first could lead to inconsistencies between the different database files. In order to do a file system-level backup of a Hyper-G server there is a special backup and restore program to avoid inconsistencies.

The special backup program is named hgbackup and uses tar to archive the contents of the Hyper-G server. As well as calling tar, it performs some additional actions that guarantee consistency of the backup. Using this script the server can be active even during the backup operation.

The special restore program is named hgrestore and also uses tar to restore the files from tape. While restoring the server is stopped and after reorganizing the database contents it is started again.

Both hgbackup and hgrestore can be configured by editing a file named .hgbackup.rc in hgsystem's home directory. Refer to the comments in this file for further explanation of how to configure the backup operation.

If you do not want to back up the entire server but only some collections, or if users want to back up their home collections themselves, the programs hifexport (for backing up) and hifimport (for restoring) are very useful. See Section 25.3 for details on these two programs.

14.8   Server administration

The central components of Hyper-G are user accounts, user groups, personal home collections for users and user access rights.

For setting up user accounts and user groups and for several other administrative purposes two tools are available:

hgadmin A VT100-based administration tool that is automatically installed with the server software.

haradmin An XWindows-based administration tool. It is not automatically installed with the server software but is part of Harmony and available by anonymous FTP from ftp.iicm.tu-graz.ac.at, directory /pub/Hyper-G/Harmony and from several mirror sites.

Both administration tools have the same basic functionality, only their user interface is different. In the following haradmin, the XWindows tool, is used in our examples where necessary, but everything is applicable to hgadmin as well.

14.8.1   User accounts

Hyper-G servers have their own user and group accounts which are completely independent of UNIX accounts. Hyper-G users can have their account in a Hyper-G server without having a UNIX account. The only thing Hyper-G servers can do is associate UNIX user accounts with Hyper-G server accounts to identify users automatically as we shall describe later.

When a Hyper-G server is started for the first time, it automatically creates a user hg-system, or whatever the user account is under which the server is started, and gives that user the same password as is used for the UNIX account.

To set up a new Hyper-G user account or to delete an existing one you must be identified as Hyper-G user hgsystem or any other user of user group system to have system rights on the Hyper-G server. If attributes of an already existing user are to be altered (for example, password), most of these can be changed if you are identified as this user.

A user account in Hyper-G is made up of at least the following parts:

- A username: The username on a Hyper-G server is completely independent of the account name a user may have under UNIX.

- One or more passwords: Hyper-G allows having more than one password for each user. Allowing more than one password is important for automatic user identification. Automatic identification is explained in more detail later in this chapter.

- A personal home collection: every Hyper-G user may have a personal home collection, comparable to a home directory under UNIX. Users have write access to this collection and can customize it according to their needs.

The personal home collection of a user must be created using one of the native Hyper-G clients Harmony, Amadeus or HGTV, but everything else is done from within one of the administration tools.

In creating a user's home collection do not forget to change the `Author` attribute of the collection to the user's account name and set the appropriate access rights, normally to `R:a` (only readable by author). See also Chapter 22 for a proposal of how to structure personal home collections and publicly accessible information about a user and how to give users reasonable access rights.

A new user must be given a unique account name and a password, which can be entered in two different ways:

- The password can be entered and confirmed as is normally done under UNIX.

- The password can be entered in encrypted form. In this case the encrypted password UNIX stores in `/etc/passwd` can be taken. This method has the advantage that a system administrator can set up a user with the same password this user has under UNIX without knowing the password itself. Additionally this feature is used for automatic user identification as will be described later.

The last step to create a fully featured user account is to enter the user's home collection name.

In most cases it is desirable to add the user to one or more user groups, especially if Hyper-G is also used for cooperative work. Managing user groups makes administration much easier for the operator. For more detailed information on user groups see Section 14.8.2 below.

For user accounts with only username, password, home collection and group, users have to identify themselves manually at the beginning of every Hyper-G session which can be annoying, especially while working with offline tools. There is a mechanism in Hyper-G allowing automatic user identification when accessing the Hyper-G server with known accounts from trusted machines. These account and machine names and the matching encrypted passwords can be added to the user attributes.

If you normally work on the machine `desktop.office.somewhere` under user account `user1`, add `user1-desktop.office.somewhere` to your user@host list and also add the encrypted password of your UNIX account to the list of encrypted passwords. The UNIX account name need not be the same as the Hyper-G account name, allowing automatic identification of a user working under different accounts on different machines.

Since Hyper-G supports billing and documents can have a price, a user can be given a certain amount of virtual money to access charged documents. Naturally only `hgsystem` is allowed to change the corresponding `Account` attribute for a certain user.

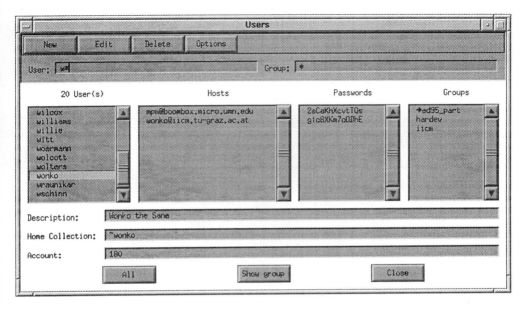

Figure 14.1   Browsing user accounts with `haradmin`.

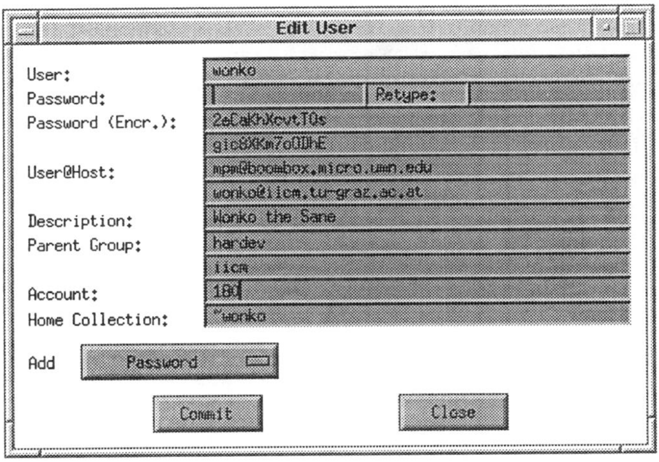

Figure 14.2   Editing a user account with `haradmin`.

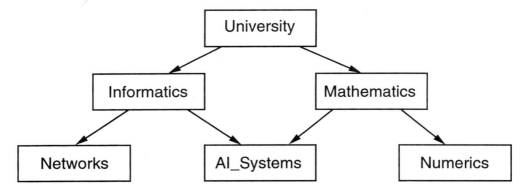

Figure 14.3   Example group structure.

14.8.2 User groups

Hyper-G supports the concept of having hierarchically structured user groups with inheritance. To set up a new group you must be identified as user hgsystem or any other user in group system.

A group in Hyper-G is defined by a group name and arbitrarily many parent groups. How the group structure on a Hyper-G server is made up is highly dependent on the organization operating the server. An example of a typical structure on a Hyper-G server operated by a university is shown in Figure 14.3.

A user that is a member of the groups numerics and informatics has all the rights that are given to the groups university, mathematics, informatics and numerics, but does not have the access rights of networks and AI_systems.

There is one special group of users on every Hyper-G server, named system. Members of this group, for example hgsystem or other users, have the right to read and write everything on a Hyper-G server analogous to the superuser concept in UNIX.

Users and user groups in Hyper-G are held in the server using the same mechanism as is used for storing document meta-information in Hyper-G objects. This makes it possible to insert, manipulate and delete users and groups with the Hyper-G offline tools. The user objects support the attributes:

UName The account name of the user.

Group A group the user is member of. There can be more than one Group entry if a user belongs to more than one group.

Passwd The password in encrypted form. There can be more than one Passwd entry for a user.

Host An entry in the form user@host used for automatic identification.

Home The name of the home collection of the user.

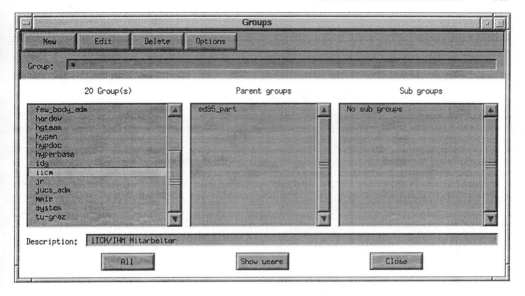

Figure 14.4   Browsing groups with `haradmin`.

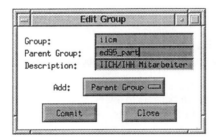

Figure 14.5   Editing a group with `haradmin`.

`Account` The amount of virtual money that is left for charged documents. If `Account` reaches zero, charged documents can no longer be opened. Post-billing is not allowed in Hyper-G.

`Descr` The description of this user, for example the full name.

Not all attributes need to be present for a certain user, only `UName` and `Passwd` are necessary for a user object.

Group objects support the attributes:

`UGroup` The group name.

Group A parent group of this user group. There can be more than one Group entry since a group can be inherited from more than one parent group.

Descr The description of the user group.

The attribute UGroup is mandatory, the other two attributes are only used where required and can be omitted.

For example, if you want to see a list of all user accounts on your Hyper-G server you could use the command (see also Chapter 25):

```
hginfo -key 'UName=*' -formatted -attr UName -mult -identify
```

Identify as user hgsystem, otherwise you will not get the desired information since only hgsystem has access to all user objects.

14.9 Troubleshooting

This section describes some common problems and their solution. If you do not find your particular problem here please refer to our FAQ list (http://hyperg.iicm.-tu-graz.ac.at/hginfo). If you are still unsuccessful, feel free to write an Email to hgsupport@iicm.tu-graz.ac.at. The Hyper-G support team will then answer your questions.

- **Problem** The server has not been stopped properly, for example due to a machine crash. Now the server has been started again, but accepts no connections from clients.

  Solution Wait a while. After not having been stopped properly the server is reorganizing its database. This is comparable to a UNIX file system check after a crash and makes sure that the database is in a stable state. After reorganizing has finished the server accepts connections again. You can see when the individual server modules have finished reorganizing their database by having a look at the file ˜hgsystem/server.log.

- **Problem** You accidentally deleted your Hyper-G (not UNIX!) user account hgsystem or whatever you called your Hyper-G account and there is no longer a system administrator's account in Hyper-G.

  Solution Log in locally on your server machine as user hgsystem and use either hgadmin or haradmin (see Section 14.8) to create the user hgsystem again. By locally logging in on your server machine as hgsystem the server can identify you automatically as a system administrator, even if the account is missing.

- **Problem** Full text search does not find anything in some documents.

  Solution Build a new full text index by simply sending ftserver a SIGHUP (kill -1). It is very likely that the full text server crashed while inserting those documents and therefore there is no full text index for them.

- **Problem** The server cannot be started by calling `dbstart`.

  Reason First have a look at `˜hgsystem/server.log`. In this file you will find the error messages telling you why the server could not be started.

  Solution 1 The logfile tells you that one of the gateways (WWW or Gopher) could not be started. If you are operating a WWW or Gopher server on the same machine make sure the Hyper-G Gopher and WWW gateways do not use the same port numbers as those servers (see Section 14.4.2 for details of how to configure different port numbers).

  Solution 2 The logfile tells you that one of the server modules could not be started. In this case the server has not been stopped properly (for example, by `kill -9` of `dbserver.control`) and at least one of the server modules is still running and still uses a port that is needed. Do a `ps` to find out if there are still server processes running (possible processes: `dbserver`, `dcserver`, `hgserver`, `ftserver`, `wwwmaster`, `gophgate`) and kill them (use a simple `kill` or `kill -15` to make them terminate properly; only if absolutely necessary use `kill -9`!).

- **Problem** The server cannot be accessed with Gopher or WWW clients.

  Solution Make sure the WWW gateway (`wwwmaster`) and the Gopher gateway (`gophgate`) are running and are configured to use the correct port numbers. Also make sure that your `OFFHOSTNAME` environment variable is set to the correct hostname that is known to the outside world (not a local alias!). Port numbers and environment variables are configured in `.db.contr.rc` (see Section 14.4.2 for details).

- **Problem** The file system where the database files are stored is full.

  Solution The database files need not reside in one file system. Arbitrarily many subdirectories on different file systems and their maximum capacity can be defined by setting the `DC_STOREPATHnn` and `DC_STORESIZEnn` environment variables. See Section 14.5 for details.

- **Problem** You are operating a master mirror server and are using `hifimport` with the `-replicate` option to mirror your documents to the mirror slaves (see Chapter 10 for a detailed description of replicas). Replicated documents automatically get the `Repl` attribute with the `GOID` (Global Object ID, see Chapter 10 for an explanation) of the original document as *Replica ID*. Now your master server crashes and you have a backup copy of the documents in a *HIF* file (see Section 25.3 for details of how to create a *HIF* file). Simply importing the data from the HIF file gives all the documents new Object IDs instead of the ones they had before and therefore neither replication nor incremental mirroring to the mirror sites works any more.

- **Solution** Completely erase the whole mirrored collection hierarchy on the mirror sites, `hifexport` the newly inserted master collection hierarchy and import this HIF file to the mirror servers. This makes sure that the Replica IDs are pointing to the new documents.

14.10   Further reading

Since this chapter is very UNIX oriented, you might need some reference literature on UNIX. Good overviews are given in the books by Gilly (1992) and Bourne (1982). A description of the script language Perl which is used for the install scripts can be found in Wall and Schwartz (1991).

15 Using Harmony

Keith Andrews

Harmony is the Hyper-G client and authoring tool for UNIX platforms under XWindows and is the most fully featured of the Hyper-G **authoring tools**. In this chapter we concentrate on using Harmony for searching and browsing through information on a Hyper-G server, communicating with other users and browsing resources on the wider Web. Chapter 16 describes how to install and configure Harmony and Chapter 23 discusses how to use Harmony's extensive authoring and annotation facilities.

Figure 15.1 shows Harmony as it is typically configured. On the left-hand side is the **Harmony Session Manager**, the main Harmony window, which is chiefly used for navigation. On the right-hand side is the **Harmony Text Viewer**, the window where text documents are displayed. Here we see an anonymous user, without any special access privileges, who has entered the main collection of the IICM Information Server in Graz.

Two broad principles govern the use of the mouse in Harmony. The left mouse button is the one most generally used for navigation: single-left-clicks *select* things, double-left-clicks actually *do* things. In the document viewers, the right mouse button is often used to mark regions of interest, for example to define link anchors.

The Hyper-G server facilitates three orthogonal means of organizing information so that it is easy to find: hierarchical structures, associative hyperlinks and sophisticated search mechanisms. The Harmony client provides fully featured interfaces to each of these facilities and goes one step further: tightly coupling them to give location feedback. In addition, Harmony provides backtracking facilities and a novel three-dimensional interface to the information space.

15.1 Browsing collections, clusters and documents

The Harmony Session Manager embodies most of Harmony's navigational facilities. From top to bottom, the Session Manager is composed of four distinct regions, as is illustrated in Figure 15.2: menu bar, tool bar, collection browser and a two-line status area. The collection browser is the main window of the Harmony Session Manager: it provides intuitive hierarchical navigation through Hyper-G collection structures. Icons are used to indicate collections, clusters, documents and anchors. Table 15.1 shows icons typically used to represent Hyper-G

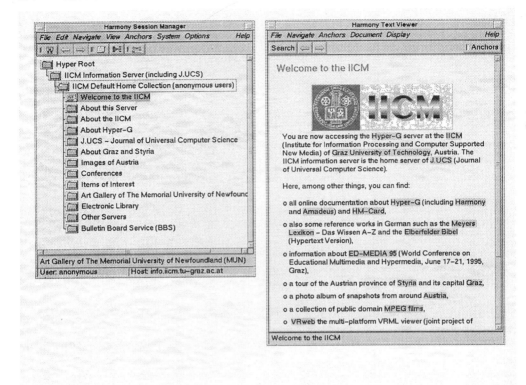

Figure 15.1   The Harmony client and authoring tool for Hyper-G.

objects in the Session Manager. A red tick overlaid in the bottom right corner of a document or cluster icon indicates that this object has been visited already during the current session. Ticks may appear in conjunction with any cluster or document icon, not only text documents. A green arrow overlaid in the bottom left of a document icon indicates an anchor object (either source or destination) in a document of the specified type. Anchor objects are not currently represented in the collection browser; they can, however, be assigned searchable attributes and thus appear in the search result list.

Hierarchical navigation through Hyper-G collection structures is extremely intuitive, since users are presented with a limited set of visible choices at each level. One popular way of finding information on a Hyper-G server is to start at the top collection and open up sub-collections until the desired information is found.

Collections may be opened and closed and documents retrieved in a number of alternative ways: by double-left-clicking, by selecting and using menu commands and via extensive keyboard shortcuts. The *currently selected object* (collection, cluster or document) is framed in a thin box. Objects may be selected by single-left-clicking with the mouse, or by using the

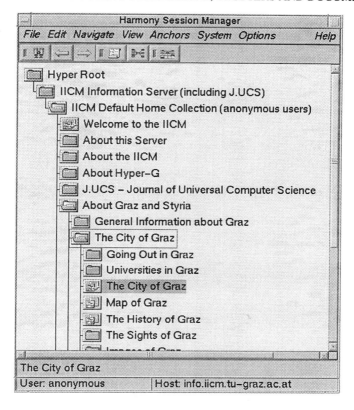

Figure 15.2   The Harmony Session Manager.

arrow keys to move the current selection focus. The currently selected object is the target of a number of commands and operations. To provide visual feedback, the most recently displayed document or cluster is underlaid with a solid bar (it is not necessarily the same object as the current selection).

15.1.1   Navigational functions

The Harmony Session Manager's **navigational functions** include:

- **Open**
  The Open operation lists a collection's members in the collection browser, displays the collection head (if present) and moves the selection focus to the first object in the collection. Opening a cluster displays the cluster (in the appropriate document viewers), but does not list its members in the collection browser. Cluster members whose

Table 15.1   Typical icons used for Hyper-G objects in Harmony.

Icon	Meaning	Icon	Meaning
	Collection (closed)		Image document
	Collection (open)		Film document
	Cluster		Audio document
	Cluster (visited)		PostScript document
	Text document		Scene document
	Text document (visited)		Generic document
	Anchor in text document		Telnet session
	Anchor in text (visited)		

`PresentationHints` attribute contains the word `Hidden` are not displayed (this is useful for keeping inline images and textures in the same cluster as the documents in which they are used, without have them also displayed in separate viewers). Clusters may contain a mix of language-dependent and language-independent documents. In this case the rules for presentation are:

(1) All language-independent members of the cluster are visualized. Language-independent objects are those having multiple `Title` attributes in different languages.

(2) From the remaining language-dependent members of the cluster, one member of each document type is chosen (based on the user's language preferences) and visualized.

Opening a document simply displays the document.

- **Close**
  When a collection or cluster is closed, its members are no longer listed in the collection browser (they are not removed from the document viewers, however). The Session Manager's `close` operation has no effect on document objects.

- **Children**
  The children (members) of the currently selected collection or cluster can be explicitly listed (or hidden) in the collection browser with the `Children` command. No documents (even a collection head) are displayed by the `Children` command.

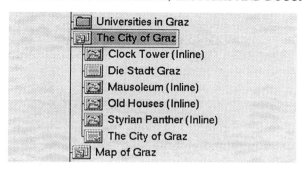

This command is often used to look inside clusters, which are normally considered atomic units as far as display is concerned, to see which documents they really contain. In the example above, looking inside the "City of Graz" cluster reveals an English text, a German text and four images used as inlines. Assuming that the user's first choice of language is English and that the inline images have PresentationHint hidden, then activating this cluster would actually only display the English text "The City of Graz" in the Text Viewer.

- **Home**
  With the Home command it is possible to jump to (and open if necessary) your home collection. Anonymous users share a single default home collection, which is the standard point of access to the particular Hyper-G server.

- **Go To**
  The Go To operation allows a specific Hyper-G object or any arbitrary URL to be accessed explicitly. A Hyper-G object can be specified through its object ID, name or Hyper-G URL. In the example below, the user wants to jump directly to the Hyper-G collection named graz.

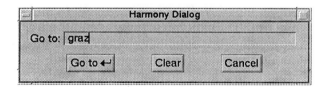

Other supported URLs include http, Gopher and FTP. For example, to access Addison-Wesley's WWW welcome page, http://aw.com/ could be entered into the Go to field. Harmony will then retrieve this WWW page through the Hyper-G server it is connected to.

- **Close All**
  After extensive navigation, the collection browser can become cluttered. The Close All operation tidies up by closing all open collections in the collection browser. This function is often followed by a Home command.

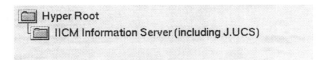

The example shows just the root collection of the IICM Information Server after issuing a `Close All`.

- **Hold**
  The most recently displayed document or cluster (the one underlaid with a solid bar) can be held on screen with the `Hold` function. The corresponding document viewer or viewers are frozen and fresh viewers are started for subsequent documents of the same type.

15.1.2   Informational functions

Informational functions provide additional information about Hyper-G objects. These include:

- **Attributes**
  The `Attributes` operation displays the Hyper-G attributes (meta-data) of an object in Harmony's Attributes window. The function is also available by right-clicking on any object in the collection browser, local map or search result list. Figure 15.3 shows the attributes for the collection "The City of Graz."

- **Show Host**
  `Show Host` displays the host on which the currently selected Hyper-G object resides. This is useful for determining whether an object is located on the local Hyper-G server (the one to which Harmony is connected), or on a remote Hyper-G server. Note that a host's name corresponds to its Internet address, which is incorporated as the first four bytes of the `GOid` attribute.

- **Show Count**
  `Show Count` turns on (or off) display of the document count for collections in the collection browser.

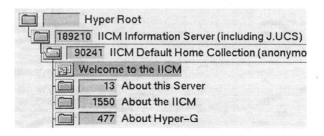

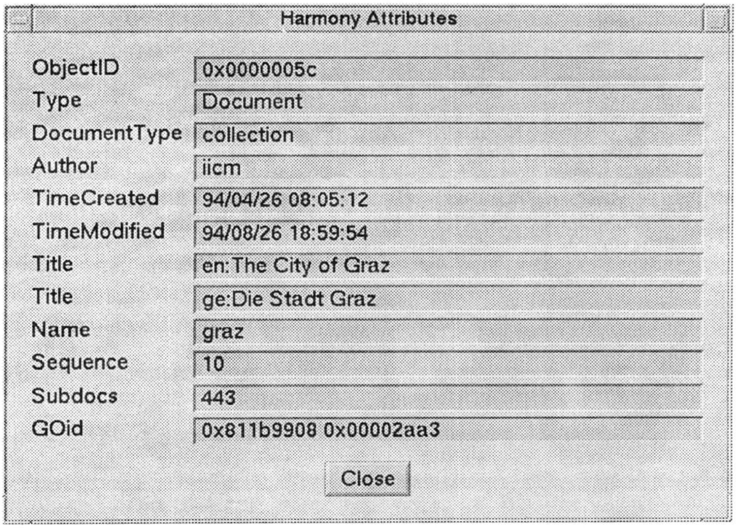

Harmony Attributes	
ObjectID	0x0000005c
Type	Document
DocumentType	collection
Author	iicm
TimeCreated	94/04/26 08:05:12
TimeModified	94/08/26 18:59:54
Title	en:The City of Graz
Title	ge:Die Stadt Graz
Name	graz
Sequence	10
Subdocs	443
GOid	0x811b9908 0x00002aa3

Close

Figure 15.3   The Harmony Attributes window.

The document count corresponds to the Subdocs attribute of a collection and gives the number of documents contained in the collection and all of its sub-collections (recursively), which are located on the local Hyper-G server. Member documents residing on remote servers are *not* included in the count.

15.1.3   The toolbar

The **Harmony Session Manager toolbar** provides direct access to the most frequently used Harmony functions. The Back and Forward buttons are disabled (grayed out) if the end of the history list in either direction has been reached. Table 15.2 explains the icons typicallly visible in the Session Manager's toolbar.

15.1.4   Keyboard support

The Harmony Session Manager has extensive keyboard support. The up arrow (↑) and down arrow (↓) keys move the current selection in the collection browser up and down as you would expect. The left arrow (←) key jumps the current selection back one level in the collection hierarchy to the current selection's parent. The Return key opens the current selection if

Table 15.2   Typical icons used in the Harmony Session Manager's toolbar.

Icon	Name	Meaning
	Search	Map/unmap Search window
	Back	Move back in history list
	Forward	Move forward in history list
	History	Map/unmap History window
	Local Map	Map/unmap Local Map window
	Landscape	Map/unmap Landscape window

it is a collection, or retrieves and displays the current selection if it is a cluster or document. The right arrow ($\rightarrow$) and the plus ($+$) keys do the same as the Return key, except that they also advance the selection into any collection which is opened. The minus ($-$) key closes the current selection if it is a collection or cluster. The Page Up and Page Down keys scroll the collection browser display by one page, Ctrl-l centers the display around the current selection, Ctrl-↑ and Ctrl-↓ scroll the display by one line up or down.

Table 15.3 gives a list of typical keyboard shortcuts in the Harmony Session Manager.

15.2   Harmony's document viewers and hyperlink navigation

Harmony has native document viewers for six kinds of media: text, image, film, audio, PostScript and 3D scenes. Many of the viewers recognize several document encoding formats. Harmony can also be configured to start external viewers for other document types (see Chapter 16), but external viewers do not generally possess the hyperlink facilities of Harmony's native document viewers.

Associative browsing through hyperlinks is the second main means of navigation in Hyper-G. Users often explore the information space by associative link browsing, either having started out directly from an introductory document with further links, or after having found an interesting document by hierarchical navigation or by searching and beginning from there. Hyperlinks in Hyper-G lead from part of one document to (part of) another associated document or to an associated cluster or collection. The source of a link is typically represented

Table 15.3 Keyboard support in the Harmony Session Manager.

Key	Function
x	Exit program (confirmation dialog)
Ctrl-x	Exit program (no confirmation dialog)
Tab	Next focus (used in dialogs and search)
Return	Open/close collection, display document
+ →	Open collection, goto first child, display document
−	Close collection/cluster
c	Show/hide children of collection/cluster, do not display collection head
Space, n	Next. Display next/current unvisited object
p	Previous. Display current/previous unvisited object
Ctrl-c	Close all collections, open path to root of local server
Ctrl-l	Recenter currently selected object
↑, ↓	Select previous/next object
Ctrl-↑, Ctrl-↓	Scroll one line up/down
Shift-↑, Shift-↓	Select previous/next object, including objects with no title
Page Down, Ctrl-v	Scroll one page down
Page Up, Alt-v	Scroll one page up
←	Select parent collection
a	Show object attributes
e	Edit object attributes
i	Map identify dialog
s	Map/unmap search dialog
b	One step back in history
f	One step forward in history
l	Generate local map
L	Unmap local map
R	Show references
A	Show annotations
P	Show parents
Ctrl-a	Annotate object
h	Map/unmap history window
H	Goto home collection
g	Goto dialog
Ctrl-d, Delete	Remove object from collection
Ctrl-i, Insert	Insert object into collection
Ctrl-s	Display system status
M	Move object
C	Copy object
Alt-s	Display server where the object resides

visually as a "clickable" hot region of a document. Since any kind of media may contain hyperlinks in Hyper-G, Harmony provides hyperlink facilities in each of its six document viewers.

In addition to a button to turn link anchor display on and off, all native Harmony document viewers share a number of common navigational facilities such as *hold* (to hold the current document on screen), *attributes* (to show the attributes of the current document), *shortcuts* to *history* functionality such as *back* and *forward* and shortcuts to Local Map functionality such as *references*, *annotations* and *parents*.

15.2.1   The Harmony Text Viewer

The **Harmony Text Viewer** displays documents in both HTML and Hyper-G's original HTF format. Inline images in GIF, JPEG, TIFF and PNG formats are supported. Figure 15.4 shows the Text Viewer displaying a text concerning the Graz Arsenal.

In the Text Viewer, a hyperlink is represented by default as a solid area underlying the extent of the source anchor, such as "Graz" or "Provincial Parliament" in Figure 15.4. A common technique is to create an itemized list in the text document and link members of the list to associated documents, as has been done for the main exhibits in the Arsenal. Anchors are selected by a single-left-click and activated by double-left-click. The Tab key can be used to cycle through the anchors and the Return key to activate the currently selected anchor.

Up to six levels of overlapping link anchors (overlapping links are possible in HTF, but not currently in HTML) are displayed as separate horizontal layers within the solid anchor area. In the example below, links emanate both from the word "Graz" and from the phrase "Graz University of Technology":

> You are now accessing the Hyper-G server at the IICM (Institute for Information Processing and Computer Supported New Media) of Graz University of Technology, Austria. The IICM information server is the home server of J.UCS (Journal of Universal Computer Science).

- **Search in Text**
  It is possible to search for regular expressions within a text document. The regular expression syntax is similar to that of the UNIX commands awk and egrep. For example, searching for [Aa]rsenal:

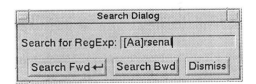

finds both capitalized and non-capitalized occurrences of the word:

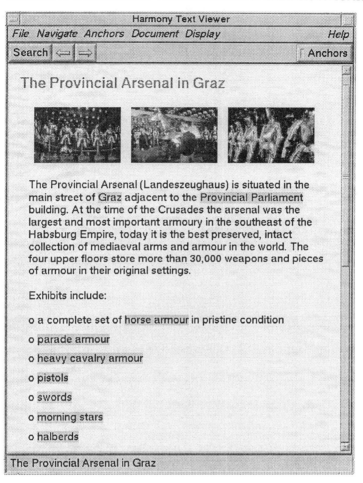

Figure 15.4   The Harmony Text Viewer.

The Provincial Arsenal (Landeszeughaus) is situated in the main street of Graz adjacent to the Provincial Parliament building. At the time of the Crusades the arsenal was the largest and most important armoury in the southeast of the Habsburg Empire, today it is the best preserved, intact collection of mediaeval arms and armour in the world. The four upper floors store more than 30,000 weapons and pieces of armour in their original settings.

The regular expression [0-9]+ matches one or more adjacent numeric digits:

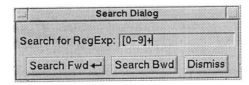

finding the digits 30 in the example below:

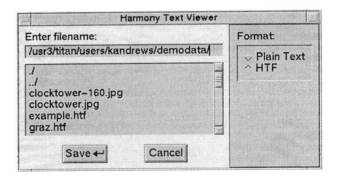

- **Save As**
  The current text document can be saved to your local UNIX file system, either as plain ASCII text or in marked-up hypertext format.

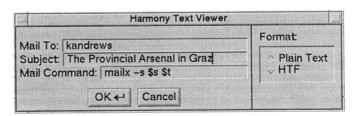

- **Mail To**
  The current text document can be sent as Email, either as plain ASCII or in marked-up hypertext format.

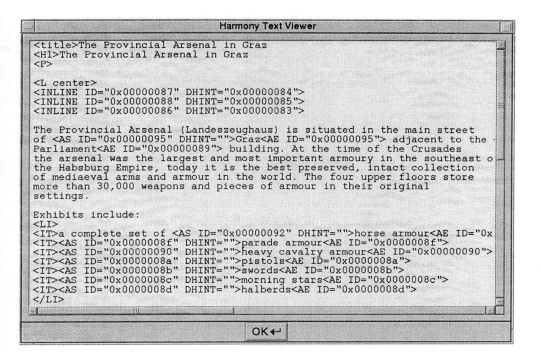

Figure 15.5   The Harmony Text Viewer Source Browser.

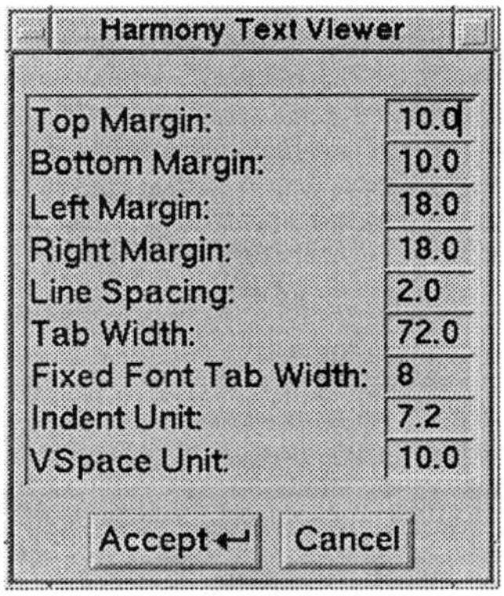

Figure 15.6   The Text Viewer Settings Panel.

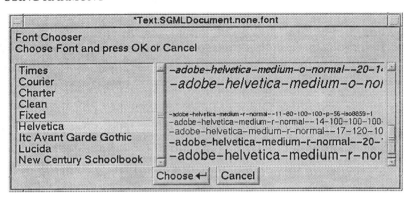

Figure 15.7   The Text Viewer Font Chooser.

- **View Source**
  The original marked-up source text can be viewed in Harmony's Source Browser. The example in Figure 15.5 shows the source of the text about the Graz Arsenal displayed in Figure 15.4.

Various Text Viewer settings such as margin sizes and spacing can be configured interactively in the Settings Panel shown in Figure 15.6. The fonts used to display various kinds of text can be configured in the viewer's font chooser. The example in Figure 15.7 shows a user selecting a Helvetica font for standard text. Similarly, the colors of text, link anchors and the background can be specified using a color chooser.

15.2.2   The Harmony Image Viewer

The **Harmony Image Viewer** displays images in a number of common formats, including GIF, JPEG, TIFF and PNG. Figure 15.8 shows the Image Viewer displaying a JPEG image of the castle hill in Graz city center. The status line at the bottom of the viewer indicates the image's title, format/resolution/size and current magnification.

Link anchors in image documents may be rectangular, circular, elliptical or polygonal in shape (this applies to both source and destination anchors). The image of Graz Arsenal in Figure 15.9 has two source anchors: a polygonal anchor enclosing the horse armor to the left and a circular anchor enclosing the heavy cavalry armor to the right. Anchors are selected by a single-left-click and activated by double-left-click. The Tab key can be used to cycle through the anchors and the Return key to activate the currently selected anchor (this is useful for overlapping link anchors). The colors used to represent link anchors can be configured using the Color Dialog shown in Figure 15.10.

The Live button determines whether or not images are displayed progressively as they are received. AutoFit causes images to be scaled (larger or smaller) so that they fit the

Figure 15.8   The Harmony Image Viewer.

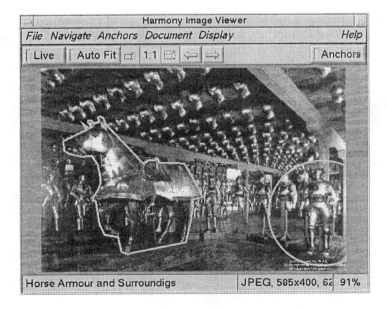

Figure 15.9   Links in image documents.

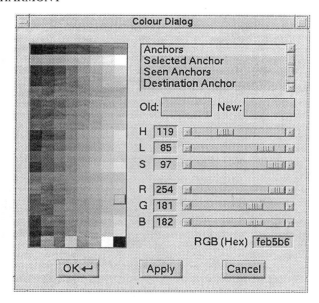

Figure 15.10   Image Viewer color configuration.

current image display area. Turning ShrinkOnly on will only scale images down and not enlarge them if autofitting is enabled. When AutoFit is disabled, the smaller ▣ (−25%), original size **1:1** (100%) and larger ▣ (+33%) buttons and menu items for zooming in and zooming out become accessible.

15.2.3   The Harmony Film Player

The **Harmony Film Player** displays film clips in MPEG-1 format. Figures 15.11 and 15.12 show the Film Player displaying a video clip taken from the Graz Arsenal. Analogous to the Image Viewer, the status line at the bottom of the Film Player indicates the film clip's title, format/resolution/size and current magnification. VCR style control buttons are provided for playing, pausing, rewinding and single-stepping through the film. The Live button determines whether or not films are played back as they are received. Loop causes the film to be played continuously.

Link anchors in films may be rectangular, circular or elliptical in shape (this applies to both source and destination anchors). Their position and size are defined for specific key frames and are interpolated in between. Source anchors may be activated even during playback. The image in Figure 15.11 shows a circular source anchor around the cavalry helmet in the first part of the film. The image in Figure 15.12 illustrates a destination anchor covering the last segment of the clip which deals with horse armor.

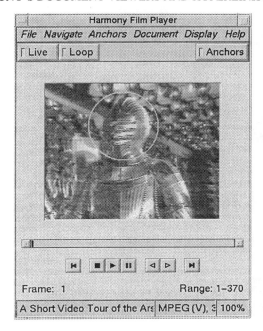

Figure 15.11   The Harmony Film Player.

The Film Player's Settings Panel, depicted in Figure 15.13, allows various settings to be configured interactively. Particularly useful are the brightness and the frame rate. By default frames are drawn as fast as possible; the frame rate is only synchronized upon specific request. The colors used to represent link anchors in the Film Player are configurable interactively using a Color Dialog similar to that of the Image Viewer.

15.2.4   The Harmony Audio Player

The **Harmony Audio Player** plays audio clips. The supported audio formats depend on the underlying platform and on the Audio Player's configuration. By default, the Audio Player does not look into the audio stream itself, but simply passes it on to the client machine's native audio play command. In this mode, illustrated in Figure 15.14, it is not possible for the Audio Player to resolve link anchors and the supported audio formats are exactly those supported by the client platform.

If the **Network Audio System** (NAS) is installed on your system or on another local machine, the Audio Player can be configured to use NAS. In this case, illustrated in Figure 15.15, the Audio Player examines the audio stream and performs audio output itself; it also supports link anchors. The status line at the bottom of the player indicates the audio clip's title and format/resolution/sampling rate/size.

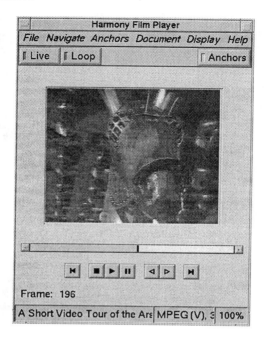

Figure 15.12   Destination region in a film clip.

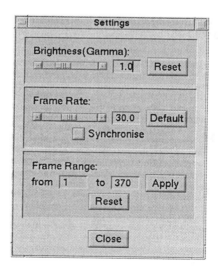

Figure 15.13   The Film Player Settings Panel.

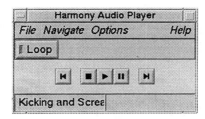

Figure 15.14   The Harmony Audio Player.

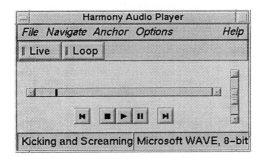

Figure 15.15   The Harmony Audio Player in NAS mode.

15.2.5   The Harmony PostScript Viewer

The **Harmony PostScript Viewer** displays documents described in the PostScript page description language. Documents compressed with GNU `gzip` are automatically decompressed and `ghostscript` is used to generate the individual page images (note that `gzip` and `gs` (GhostScript) should both be installed on your system and be in your path). Figure 15.16 shows the PostScript Viewer displaying an 18-page article which appeared in the *Journal of Universal Computer Science*.

Link anchors in PostScript documents are rectangular areas overlaid on the page, such as the four links to references later in the article in Figure 15.16. A destination anchor is highlighted (or rather the rest of the page is "low"lighted) as shown in Figure 15.17. Links can, of course, point to arbitrary objects; they are not restricted to being within a single document.

The page images are calculated once at 300 dpi (corresponding to 300% in the Zoom menu) and are scaled down appropriately to the current zooming factor, which is typically set at 100% or 75%. The document can be saved and printed directly from the viewer. The middle mouse button of the PostScript Viewer acts as a magnifying glass, magnifying the area immediately beneath the cursor.

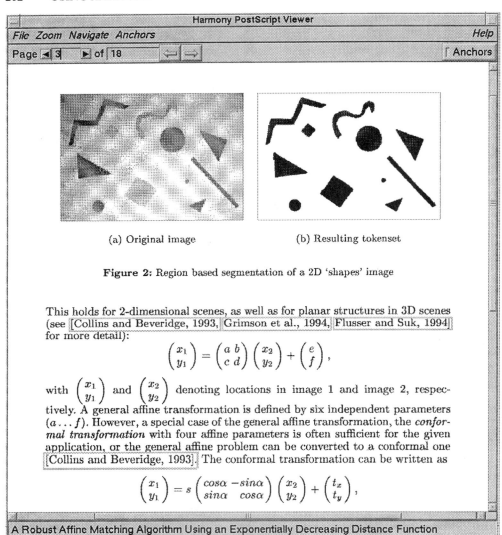

Figure 15.16   The Harmony PostScript Viewer.

15.2.6   The Harmony VRweb 3D Viewer

VRweb is Harmony's 3D viewer, which can display 3D models in VRML and SDF formats. VRML is the 3D model description format being standardized by the WWW community. SDF is a format derived from Wavefront's Advanced Visualizer and used by Hyper-G prior to the emergence of VRML. Figure 15.18 shows Harmony VRweb displaying a VRML model of a

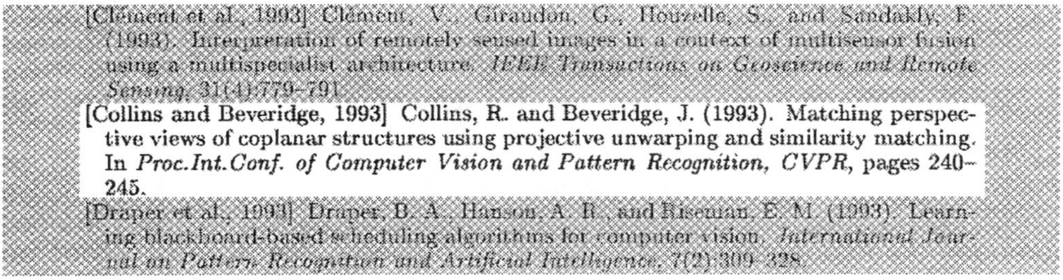

[Clement et al., 1993] Clement, V., Giraudon, G., Houzelle, S., and Sandakly, F. (1993). Interpretation of remotely sensed images in a context of multisensor fusion using a multispecialist architecture. *IEEE Transactions on Geoscience and Remote Sensing*, 31(4):779–791.

[Collins and Beveridge, 1993] Collins, R. and Beveridge, J. (1993). Matching perspective views of coplanar structures using projective unwarping and similarity matching. In *Proc.Int.Conf. of Computer Vision and Pattern Recognition, CVPR*, pages 240–245.

[Draper et al., 1993] Draper, B. A., Hanson, A. R., and Riseman, E. M. (1993). Learning blackboard-based scheduling algorithms for computer vision. *International Journal on Pattern Recognition and Artificial Intelligence*, 7(2):309–328.

Figure 15.17   Destination anchor in the Harmony PostScript Viewer.

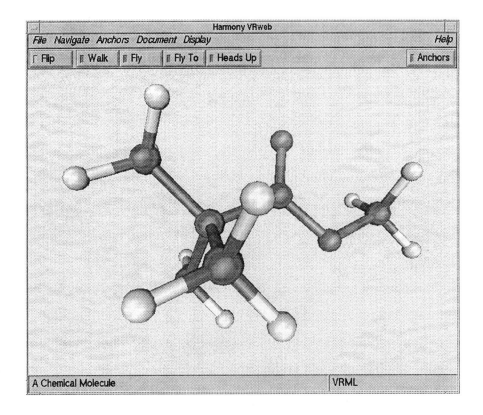

Figure 15.18   The Harmony VRweb 3D viewer.

chemical molecule. Flip navigation mode, active here, enables the model itself to be moved and rotated, without changing the user's position. VRweb's other four navigation modes (Walk, Fly, Fly To and Heads Up) all involve the user moving through the model.

Harmony VRweb is available in both OpenGL and Mesa versions. OpenGL is a cross-platform, industry-standard, 3D graphics API and library. The number of companies providing OpenGL on their machines is steadily increasing. The OpenGL version of VRweb can utilize OpenGL graphics hardware acceleration, if it is available on the displaying machine (note that under XWindows, the Harmony client might be running on one machine with its display set to a different machine). Mesa is a software-only graphics library which maps directly to XWindows. It neither requires nor benefits from 3D graphics hardware; hence it runs on any UNIX platform, albeit somewhat more slowly. In terms of interface and functionality, the Mesa and OpenGL versions of VRweb are identical.

Figure 15.19 shows the Mesa version of VRweb displaying an unusually tidy model of my office. In this figure, we see Heads Up navigation mode with its four icons overlaid atop the viewing area: looking, walking, vertical/sideways motion and point-of-interest motion.

Figure 15.20 shows VRweb in Fly navigation mode through a textured model of the

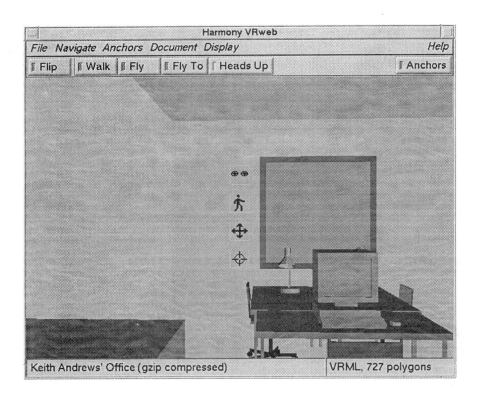

Figure 15.19   VRweb displaying a model of an office.

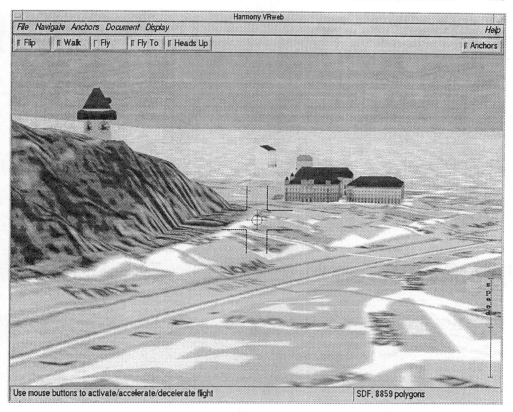

Figure 15.20   VRweb displaying a model of the city of Graz.

city of Graz. Source anchors can be attached to arbitrary parts of a 3D model. In the Graz model shown here, links lead from major sights to more detailed information about them. Destination anchors in 3D models are specified as camera positions, that is, views of the model from a particular position and orientation. Figure 15.20 also illustrates Fly navigation mode. The speed of flight is determined by mouse clicks to accelerate and decelerate, the direction of flight by the position of the cursor relative to the central cross-hairs.

VRweb has numerous display options. The display mode can be set independently during navigation and when stationary, to one of: wireframe, hidden line, flat shading, smooth shading and texturing. On a slower machine, wireframe might typically be used during navigation, since it is the least compute-intensive, and flat shading or smooth shading used when stationary. All polygons in a model can be explicitly rendered as two-sided polygons; generally, single-sided polygons are used in 3D models to reduce the polygon count, but these are transparent when viewed from behind. The frame rate can be overlaid in the status line. A viewing light or headlight can be turned on if desired, which is useful for simple models

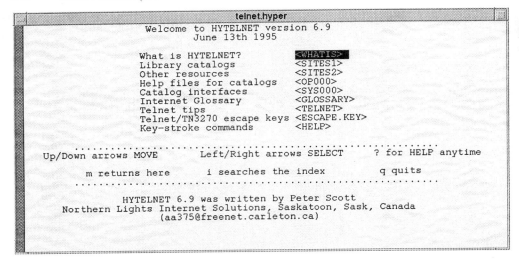

```
                              telnet.hyper
                   Welcome to HYTELNET version 6.9
                           June 13th 1995

              What is HYTELNET?              <WHATIS>
              Library catalogs              <SITES1>
              Other resources               <SITES2>
              Help files for catalogs       <OP000>
              Catalog interfaces            <SYS000>
              Internet Glossary             <GLOSSARY>
              Telnet tips                   <TELNET>
              Telnet/TN3270 escape keys  <ESCAPE.KEY>
              Key-stroke commands           <HELP>


    ..................................................................
  Up/Down arrows MOVE      Left/Right arrows SELECT      ? for HELP anytime

    m returns here         i searches the index         q quits
    ..................................................................

             HYTELNET 6.9 was written by Peter Scott
   Northern Lights Internet Solutions, Saskatoon, Sask, Canada
                  (aa375@freenet.carleton.ca)
```

Figure 15.21   A Harmony Telnet session to HYTELNET.

containing no light source definitions. Anchor highlighting modes include brightness (anchors are light, the rest of the model is dark), color code (anchors are one color, the rest of the model another color) and color edges (anchor polygons are outlined).

15.2.7 Harmony Telnet sessions

Telnet sessions can be started from within Harmony by activating a Telnet object. Figure 15.21 shows a Telnet session to HYTELNET. Upon activation, the Harmony Session Manager opens a new XTerminal (xterm) and starts the program `telnet.hyper`, a modified Telnet program which accepts login names and passwords as command line parameters. The Hyper-G object representing this particular Telnet service is a document of `DocumentType Remote` and `Protocol telnet`, as can be seen in Figure 15.22.

15.3 The Harmony Local Map

Harmony's Local Map is a graphical visualization of relationships between objects in Hyper-G. By default, the Local Map generates a visualization of a document's (referential) hyperlink relationships, but it can also visualize annotations and inline image, texture and parent–child (collection membership) relationships.

Figure 15.23 shows a local map of the hyperlink vicinity of the cluster "The Provincial Arsenal in Graz." Objects one hyperlink away in either direction are displayed – Hyper-G's

Harmony Attributes	
ObjectID	0x000000a4
Type	Document
DocumentType	Remote
Author	kandrews
TimeCreated	95/11/02 18:09:45
TimeModified	95/11/02 18:10:41
Title	en:HYTELNET
Protocol	telnet
Host	rsl.ox.ac.uk
Port	23
Path	hytelnet
GOid	0x811b9908 0x00187a9a

Edit   Close

Figure 15.22   A Hyper-G Telnet object.

links are stored in a separate database and hence can be followed both forwards and back-wards. Note that hyperlinks always emanate from documents, but may point to either documents, collections or clusters. Since collections and clusters do not themselves have hyperlinks, the links of the collection head and the cluster members are visualized in the local map. Multiple links between the same objects are collapsed down to a single edge in the local map. The map can be regenerated around any object by selecting (single-left-clicking) the object and issuing a `Generate` command, providing an alternate form of link navigation. Double-left-clicking an object activates that object, for example retrieving and displaying a document in the appropriate viewer.

The Local Map is closely coupled with the Session Manager's collection browser. When an object is selected in the Local Map and is not already visible in the collection browser, a path to that object is opened up automatically. This is called *location feedback*: users can gain an understanding of the context in which the object is embedded through its location in Hyper-G's collection structure, *prior* to any decision to view it. For example, selecting "Styrian Coat of Arms" in Figure 15.23 opens up the following path in the collection browser:

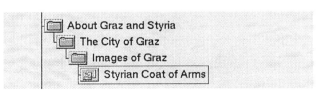

The Local Map can also be used to visualize other kinds of relationships. Figure 15.24

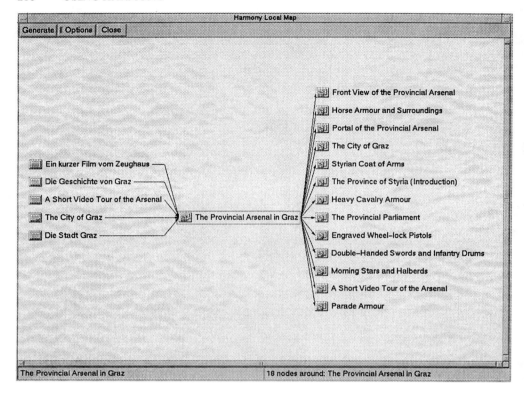

Figure 15.23   The Harmony Local Map.

shows a map of the inline images used in the cluster about the Graz Arsenal (see Figure 15.4). Imagine you were considering editing the image "Armour 1" or replacing the image with a newer photograph, but wanted to know whether "Armour 1" is used elsewhere. Selecting "Armour 1" and regenerating the Local Map shows the places where the image is used as an inline, in this case only in the English and German versions of the Arsenal text:

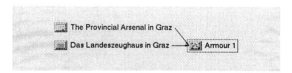

The Harmony Local Map has numerous options and settings, which can be configured in the **Options panel**. These include the number and kind of incoming and outgoing relationships to be visualized, the maximum number of objects in the map and the spacing to be used in the layout. Figure 15.25 shows the Options panel with settings to display parent–child membership relationships.

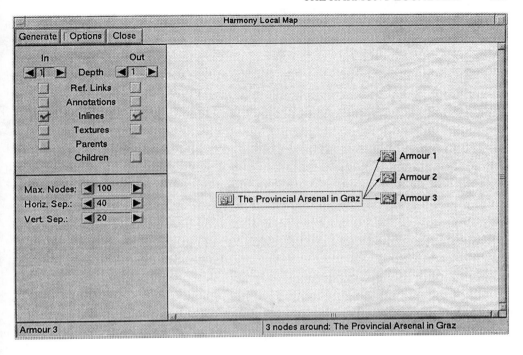

Figure 15.24   Local map of inline image relationships.

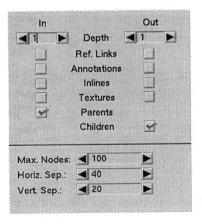

Figure 15.25   Options Panel for parent/child relationships.

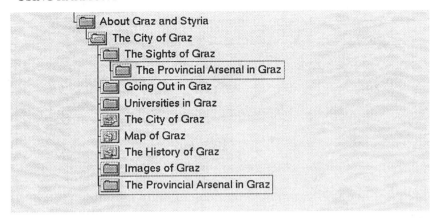

Figure 15.26   Multiple paths in the Collection Browser.

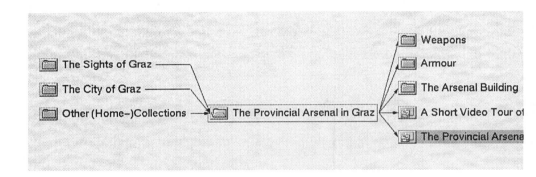

Figure 15.27   Local map of parent–child relationships.

Since Hyper-G collections, clusters and documents may belong to multiple parent collections, the collection browser's hierarchical display is sometimes confusing, as multiple paths have to be opened up to objects which belong to multiple parents. For example, in Figure 15.26, the collection "The Provincial Arsenal in Graz" belongs to both the collection "the City of Graz" and to its child "The Sights of Graz." In such cases, the Local Map can be used effectively to display parent–child membership relationships, in this case generating the map shown in Figure 15.27.

Both the Harmony Session Manager and the various document viewers have in-built shortcuts for generating local maps. For example, the document viewers have menu items to generate References, Annotations, and Parents local maps for the currently displayed document, the Harmony Text Viewer has a menu item to generate a map of the text's inline images and so on.

15.4   Searching in Harmony

The third main means of navigation in Hyper-G, in addition to hierarchical browsing of the collection structure and following hyperlinks, are Hyper-G's sophisticated **search facilities**. In contrast to WWW or Gopher, Hyper-G has *fully integrated* attribute and content search mechanisms.

Attribute search provides for searching in those attribute fields of Hyper-G which are indexed by the Hyper-G server. These typically include `Title`, `Keywords`, `Author` and `TimeModified`. Content search utilizes the Hyper-G server's full text inverted index to search for words or phrases contained in the content of a text document. Every text document's content is automatically indexed upon insertion into the server and the index is updated when a document is edited or deleted.

Harmony's interface to Hyper-G search facilities is the **Harmony Search Dialog**, shown in Figure 15.28. In this example, the user has searched for the word "grep" in the

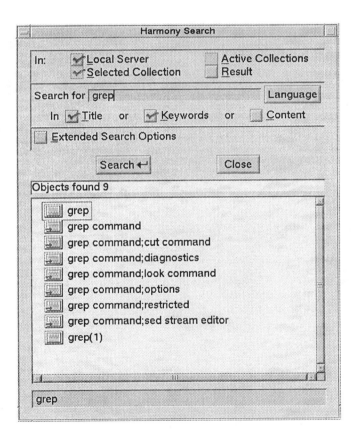

Figure 15.28   The Harmony Search Dialog.

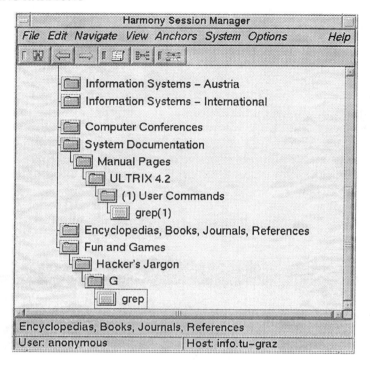

Figure 15.29   Location feedback from search results.

Title and Keywords attributes of all objects (collections, clusters, documents and anchors) on the local Hyper-G server. The languages in which to search can be specified in a separate dialog. The result here is a list of nine matching objects; the first and last in the list are text documents, the remaining seven objects are link anchors.

Single-left-clicking an object in the search result list selects the object and activates location feedback (as it does in the Local Map). The value of location feedback is illustrated in Figure 15.29. Here we see from the collection context that the first grep text document in the result list belongs to the collection "G" in the "Hacker's Jargon" and the second belongs to "(1) User Commands" in the "ULTRIX 4.2" manual pages. Assuming that the user was looking for a description of the UNIX grep command, it is now possible to make an educated choice between the two documents, before having retrieved either of them. Right-clicking an object in the search result list brings up the attributes of that object (as it does in the Collection Browser and Local Map) and double-left-clicking retrieves or activates an object.

Harmony's **Extended Search Options** allow a search to be further constrained to a particular author (owner) and to particular (ranges of) modification times. In the example in Figure 15.30, a search is being made for documents on the local server about Harmony or VRweb, authored by kandrews, after 1 July, 1995.

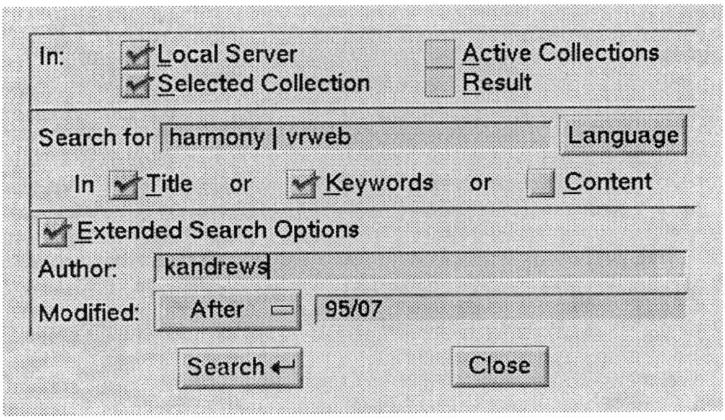

Figure 15.30   Harmony's extended search options.

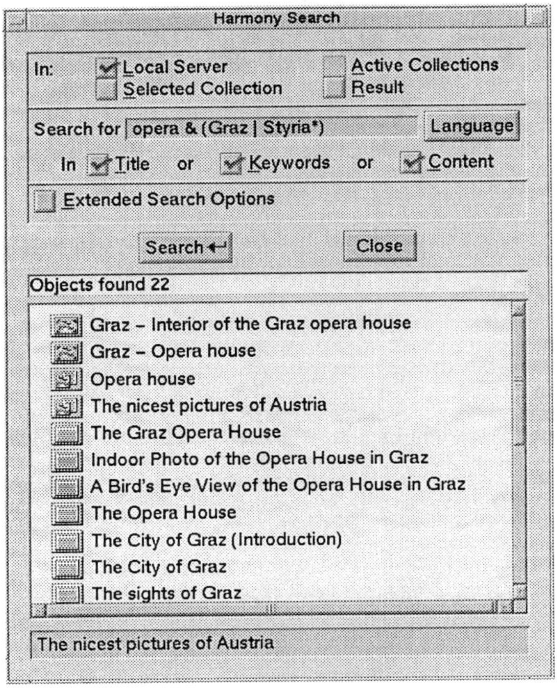

Figure 15.31   Combined content and attribute search.

Figure 15.31 illustrates the effect of combining content search with attribute search. An initial search in the `Title` and `Keywords` only resulted in four matching objects, whereas turning on content search as well found a further 18 documents.

The example in Figure 15.31 also illustrates the syntax of search expressions with the example `opera & (Graz | Styria*)`. Multiple search terms are implicitly ANDed together; an ampersand (&) can be used to explicitly express an AND operator. A vertical bar (|) represents the OR operator, which has lower precedence than AND. Terms may be grouped using parentheses. There is no NOT operator. Prefix search is supported using a trailing asterisk. Note that search terms in Hyper-G are principally case-insensitive.

A major strength of Hyper-G is the ability to control the scope of searches. As can be seen in Figure 15.31, searches may be restricted to objects residing on the local server, members of the current set of active collections or only members of the currently selected collection. A powerful additional feature is to search in the current search result list, which allows users to successively refine their searches. The Harmony Session Manager's **Active Collections window** displays the current set of active collections. The currently selected collection can be added to or removed from the active set in the Session Manager. The example in Figure 15.32 shows three active collections from the part of the IICM Information Server collection structure shown in Figure 15.33.

Searches are not restricted to objects on the local Hyper-G server. Collection members are sometimes located on remote servers; including such collections in the scope of a search initiates simultaneous searching on multiple servers. This is the case in the example, where the two bibliographic collections in fact reside on a remote Hyper-G server.

15.5   Harmony's History Browser

The **Harmony History Browser** (see 15.34) maintains a time-line of past interactive waypoints during browsing. Collections, clusters and documents visited are time-stamped and entered into the history list. Search queries are also entered into the history, enabling users to modify and reissue previous searches. Users can step backward and forward through the history list using the `Back` and `Forward` arrow buttons available in the Session Manager and in the document viewers. Within the History Browser, single-left-clicking an entry initiates location feedback, double-left-clicking activates an object and single-right-clicking displays an object's attributes.

15.6   Harmony for WWW and Gopher sites

Documents residing on WWW servers can be referred to as remote WWW documents on a Hyper-G server. They are then displayed with an icon appropriate to their type in Harmony and can be accessed transparently as if they were local documents. Figure 15.35 shows the WWW Project page at W3C as seen in Harmony. The attributes of the corresponding remote object are shown in Figure 15.36.

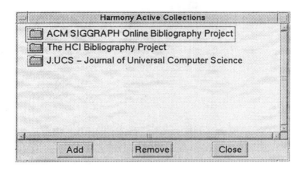

Figure 15.32   Set of collections activated for search.

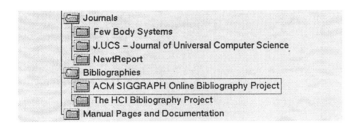

Figure 15.33   Activating local and remote collections for search.

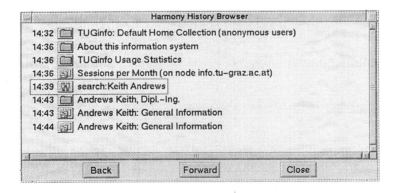

Figure 15.34   The Harmony History Browser.

In a similar fashion, remote Gopher menus and documents can be referred to using a remote Gopher object on a Hyper-G server. Figure 15.37 shows the remote Gopher object corresponding to the University of Minnesota's Gopher Server. Figure 15.38 shows the Minnesota server, as seen in Harmony. Note that Gopher menus are mapped transparently to Hyper-G collections. Gopher documents are mapped to documents of the same type in Hyper-G.

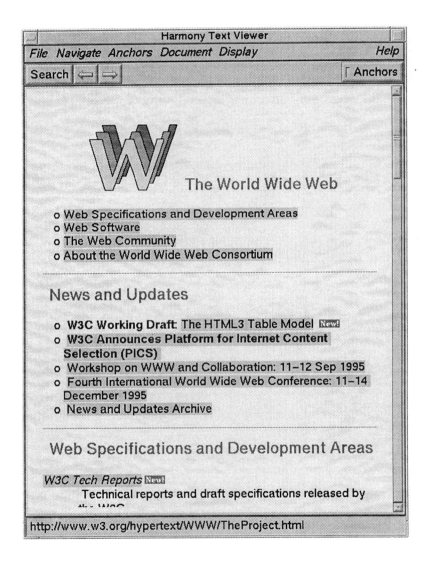

Figure 15.35   The WWW project page in Harmony.

15.7   Harmony system functions

Harmony's **system-oriented functions** include user identification, changing passwords and explicitly clearing Harmony's cache. The Harmony Identify dialog allows anonymous users to identify themselves to the server by entering their Hyper-G username and password.

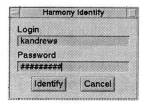

Identified users can make themselves anonymous by entering `anon` in the `Login` field. Identified users with system rights can identify themselves as any other user simply by entering the username in the `Login` field, without being required to enter a password.

The **Harmony Change Password** dialog allows identified users to change their password.

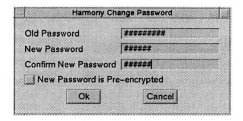

The new password is entered twice to guard against typing errors. For simplicity, a new password can also be entered in pre-encrypted form, for example when cutting and pasting from the UNIX password file.

Harmony maintains its own client-side cache, which may be explicitly cleared. Clearing the cache forces Harmony to (re-)fetch subsequently accessed documents from the server, rather than relying on cached copies.

15.8   Harmony options and preferences

Harmony **options and preferences** include language settings and the default sort order for members of a collection. Harmony's **Language Preference dialog** allows users to specify a prioritized list of preferred languages.

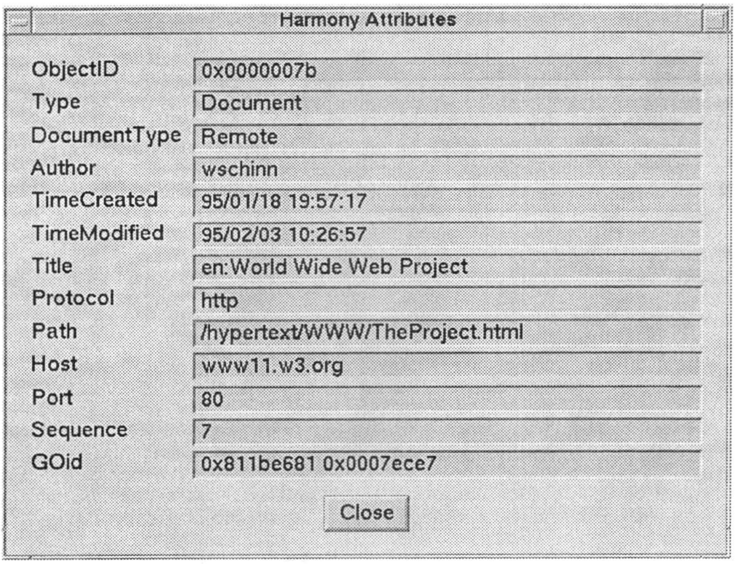

Figure 15.36   A WWW remote object.

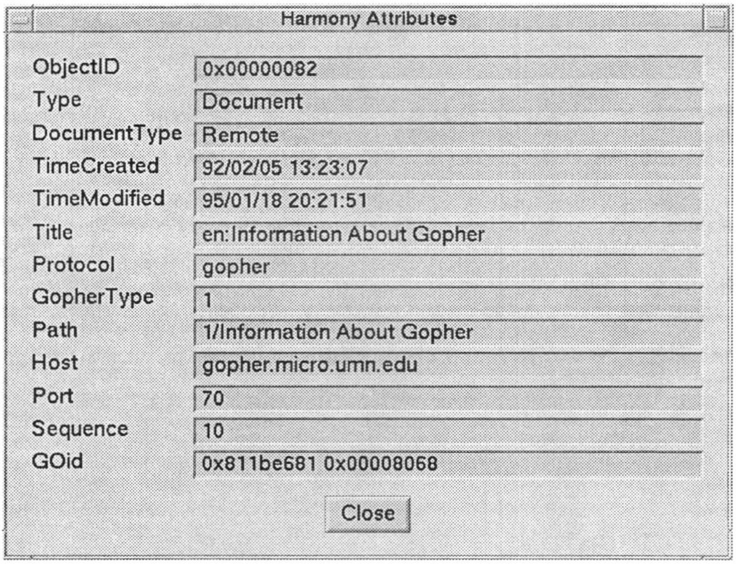

Figure 15.37   A Gopher remote object.

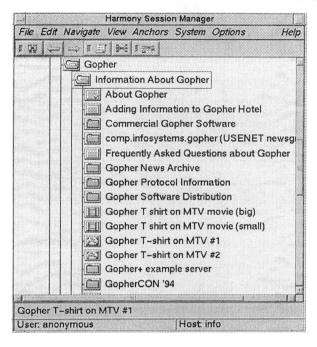

Figure 15.38   The University of Minnesota Gopher server in Harmony.

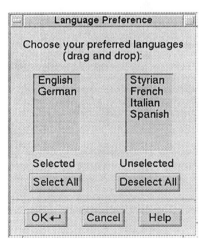

In the example above, English is currently the first choice language, followed by German. The language preference determines both Harmony's user interface and the selection of documents available in multiple languages. Languages can be selected and deselected by double-clicking and by dragging and dropping between the boxes. The preference order of selected languages can be changed by dragging and dropping inside the Selected box.

The **Default Sort Order dialog** allows users to specify the sort order used by default when listing members of a collection in the collection browser. The actual sort order can be overridden by setting a collection's SortOrder attribute. Hence the default sort order determines the order in which members of a collection are listed, *only* insofar as no particular sort order has been specified by the author of the collection.

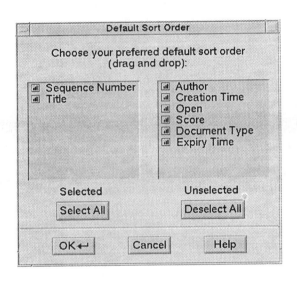

In the Default Sort Order dialog, individual sort criteria can be selected and deselected both by double-clicking and by dragging and dropping between the boxes. The order of selected sort criteria is significant. Each individual criterion can be applied in descending rather than ascending order by clicking on the ▦button which precedes it. In the example above, the members of collections for which no particular sort order has been defined will henceforth be listed first by ascending order of sequence number, then in ascending alphabetical order of title.

Other options include Scan Attributes and Global Viewers. Turning Scan Attribute on brings up Harmony's **Attribute window** and continually updates it to reflect the Hyper-G object currently beneath the mouse cursor. This allows quick scanning of objects in the collection browser and their associated attributes.

Turning Global Viewer off instructs the Session Manager principally to start a new document viewer every time a document is retrieved, resulting in multiple document viewers. Turning Global Viewer on instructs the Session Manager to reuse existing document viewers by displaying documents in an existing viewer of the same type (if one is already available).

15.9   System status and communication with other users

The **Harmony Status Browser**, depicted in Figure 15.39, displays the current system status of the Hyper-G server Harmony is connected to. Status information includes the server name, up time, a performance index and a list of users currently connected to the server. By default, the status information is updated every 60 seconds, but this period can be changed by the user. The user's own current session is marked in the list with an asterisk (for example, *728 kandrews(system) in the figure).

It is possible to send arbitrary messages to one or more current users via the Hyper-G server. Messages are displayed on the user's terminal by their own Hyper-G client. In Figure 15.40, three users are undertaking a three-way conference. Such conferences can involve any number of users logged on to the Hyper-G server from anywhere in the world. This powerful facility can be used by a server administrator to notify all connected users of a pending server shutdown, for example. It is also used to send certain system messages.

15.10   The Harmony Information Landscape

The **Harmony Information Landscape** is a three-dimensional representation of Hyper-G's collection structure. In Figure 15.41, the part of the IICM Information Server dealing with the

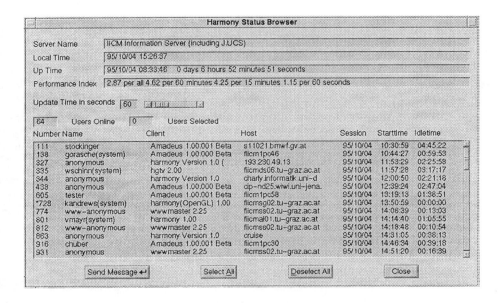

Figure 15.39   The Harmony Status Browser.

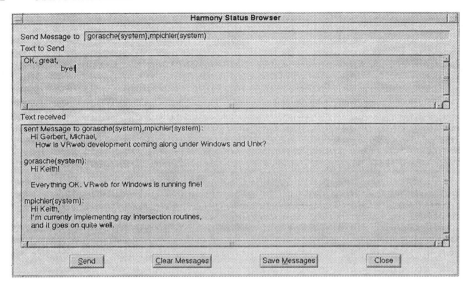

Figure 15.40   Sending messages between users in Harmony.

city of Graz is shown in the Information Landscape. This is essentially a three-dimensional alternative to the traditional two-dimensional collection browser view (see Figure 15.2). Flat blocks represent collections and clusters, taller blocks atop these represent individual documents. The height of the document blocks is proportional to the size of the document.

Users can fly over the landscape looking for salient features. The mouse buttons are used to control the speed and direction of motion. Movement is constrained, for example it is not possible to turn around and look back, so that drawing speed can be optimized (for the technically minded, movement is constrained so that the drawing order can be determined in advance and no Z-buffer is required, which results in substantial performance benefits on machines with no graphics hardware acceleration). A textured version of the landscape is also available for platforms with appropriate texture support.

Much of the functionality of the Session Manager is also available in the Information Landscape. Objects can be selected by single-left-clicking and activated by double-left-clicking. Attributes can be viewed by single-right-clicking, searches performed and so on. Location feedback in the landscape involves the user being taken by the hand and gently flown to the selected object. The Information Landscape and the collection browser are synchronized, so that changes in one are automatically reflected in the other.

Numerous settings can be configured interactively, including the color coding used for collections and documents, the logarithmic scaling factor applied to the height of the blocks and the relative sensitivity of the mouse. The landscape's **Overview Map**, shown in Figure 15.42, provides a sense of global context and orientation within the Information Landscape.

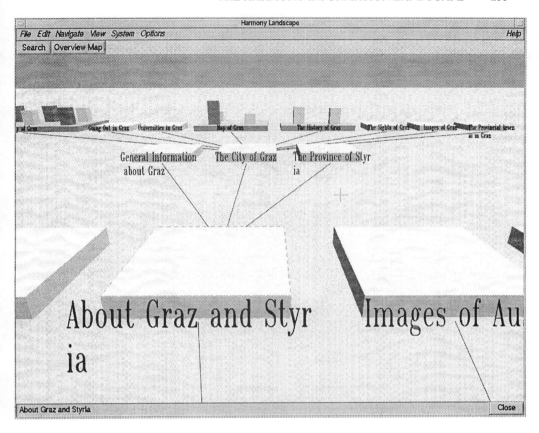

Figure 15.41   The Harmony Information Landscape.

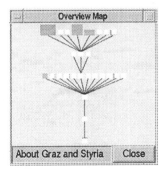

Figure 15.42   The Landscape Overview Map.

As with VRweb, Harmony's 3D viewer, the Information Landscape comes in two versions: a software-only Mesa version which runs on any UNIX platform and an OpenGL version which can take advantage of OpenGL hardware acceleration.

15.11 Further reading

The Harmony User Guide (Mayrhofer and Andrews, 1995), included in the Harmony distribution, is a practical how-to guide to Harmony. Published articles on Harmony include Andrews (1995) which looks at Harmony's information visualization features.

Good handbooks about HTML include Flynn (1995) and Graham (1995). An authoratative reference for image and video formats is Murray and van Ryper (1994). The standard reference for the PostScript language is Adobe Systems Inc. (1990).

The research paper by Pichler *et al.* (1995) describes the VRweb 3D viewer in more detail. Information on the Virtual Reality Modeling Language (VRML) is available at the VRML Repository (San Diego Supercomputer Center) or in Mark Pesce's book (Pesce, 1995). The OpenGL programming interface is covered in two books (Neider *et al.*, 1993; OpenGL Architecture Review Board, 1992).

16   Installing and configuring Harmony

Keith Andrews

This chapter provides technical and background information about the **Harmony client and authoring tool** for Hyper-G. Harmony runs on most major UNIX platforms under XWindows. The installation procedure is covered step by step and customization of Harmony's appearance and behavior is explained. Harmony's browsing and searching functionality is presented in detail in Chapter 15. Harmony's extensive authoring features are covered in Chapter 23.

16.1   The architecture of Harmony

Harmony is a **multi-process application**, as is illustrated in Figure 16.1. The Session Manager is the primary process; it communicates with the Hyper-G server, provides navigational facilities and coordinates all other activities. The Session Manager starts secondary processes, **document viewers**, of the appropriate type, to display documents as necessary. Native Harmony document viewers communicate using Harmony's own protocol, the **Harmony Document Viewer Protocol** (DVP), which defines various browsing, editing and link functions. There currently exist native document viewers for text, images, MPEG films, audio, 3D scenes and PostScript.

Harmony may be configured to run external programs in place of any native viewer and also for unsupported document types (the document is piped to standard input). However, since external programs do not "speak" Harmony's protocol, they are generally unable to support link activation and editing.

The Session Manager connects to the Hyper-G server on Hyper-G's assigned port number 418. This connection is kept open for the duration of the session and is the channel through which control information (all communication except actual documents) passes in both directions. Documents themselves are not sent from the server via the Session Manager to a document viewer, but directly from server to document viewer. In fact, the document cache in the Hyper-G server opens a connection back to the viewer, using a port dynamically assigned by the viewer. However, since certain network configurations (for example, machines behind a firewall or using an emulated SLIP connection) do not allow the server to

235

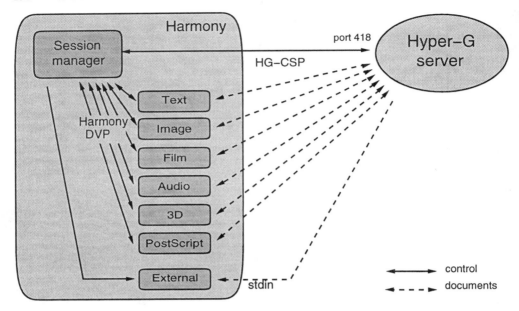

Figure 16.1   The architecture of Harmony.

connect back to the client on an arbitrary port, this connection procedure is (at the time of writing) being turned around so that the viewer connects to the server.

Harmony is written in C++ and uses a heavily modified version of the InterViews user interface toolkit.

16.2   Installing Harmony

16.2.1   Hardware and software requirements

Harmony is distributed free of charge in binary form for the following platforms: SGI IRIX, SunOs, Sun Solaris, HP-UX, DEC ULTRIX, DEC Alpha OSF/1 and Linux (list correct as of October 1995).

We recommend that you have at least 32 MB of RAM installed in your computer in order to run Harmony. Depending on the platform, Harmony requires up to about 30 MB of disk space; during the installation process you will need about twice this space.

Harmony is distributed in compressed form using GNU gzip. You will need to have gzip installed and in your path in order to install Harmony. The Harmony PostScript Viewer and the Harmony VRweb scene viewer also use gzip (and/or uncompress) to uncompress compressed PostScript documents and 3D models.

The Harmony PostScript Viewer uses `gs` (GhostScript), a freely available PostScript interpreter, to generate its page images. Make sure you have this tool installed and in your path if you plan to view PostScript documents (for example, for J.UCS). GhostScript is available from `ftp.cs.wisc.edu` in directory `/pub/ghost/aladdin` and many other FTP sites.

Harmony's 3D features (the Information Landscape of the Harmony Session Manager and the VRweb 3D scene viewer) run on all XWindows platforms when the software-only Mesa versions of `harmony` and `harscened` are used. The OpenGL versions of these programs only run on platforms where OpenGL is installed, but can utilize available graphics hardware.

16.2.2   Retrieving Harmony for your system

The first step in the Harmony installation procedure is to retrieve the appropriate file for your machine architecture by anonymous ftp from `ftp://ftp.iicm.tu-graz.ac.-at/pub/Hyper-G/Harmony` or from one of the mirror sites listed in Appendix A.

The distribution files for Harmony 1.1 are listed in Table 16.1. Of course, they may be named slightly differently for later releases.

Distribution files with an extra extension "-mesa" indicate support for Harmony's 3D features (VRweb and Information Landscape) using the Mesa software-only 3D graphics library. If there is more than one binary for one platform to support different kinds of 3D output devices, the library used is indicated in the name:

- ogl indicates a binary using OpenGL.

- mesa indicates a binary using the Mesa 3D library.

Binaries using the Mesa library can be used without any additional libraries installed on the system. OpenGL binaries can only be used if the required shared libraries are provided by the target system (we cannot provide them because of copyright restrictions). The only platform with built-in 3D support in the default binary is the SGI version using OpenGL.

Once you have the Harmony distribution, do the following:

Table 16.1   Harmony distribution files.

Platform	Operating system	Distribution file
HP 7xx	HP-UX-A.09.01	`harmony-1.1-HP-UX-A.09.01.tar.gz`
SGI	IRIX-5.3	`harmony-1.1-IRIX-5.3.tar.gz`
PCs	Linux-1.2.13	`harmony-1.1-Linux-1.2.13.tar.gz`
DEC Alpha	OSF1-V3.2	`harmony-1.1-OSF1-V3.2.tar.gz`
SunOs	SunOS-4.1.3	`harmony-1.1-SunOS-4.1.3.tar.gz`
Sun Solaris	SunOS-5.4	`harmony-1.1-SunOS-5.4.tar.gz`
DEC	ULTRIX-4.4	`harmony-1.1-ULTRIX-4.4.tar.gz`

(1) Put the distribution file in the directory where you want to install Harmony. If you are making a public installation, we recommend using the directory: `/usr/local/-Harmony`.

(2) Uncompress and untar the file. This can be done in one compound command, without having to physically store the uncompressed file, as shown below for the Linux version of Harmony:

```
gzip -cd harmony-1.1-Linux-1.2.13.tar.gz | tar xvf -
```

You will now have a directory `bin` for the Harmony binaries, and directories `icons`, `misc` and `3dfonts` for Harmony's data files. You may, if you wish, remove the compressed tar file now.

16.2.3 Setting up Harmony

Prior to running Harmony, you should perform the following steps:

(1) Set the environment variable `HARMONY_HOME` to the Harmony installation directory. For example, if you have installed Harmony in `/usr/users/test/harmony` and you are using the csh, type:

```
setenv HARMONY_HOME /usr/users/test/harmony
```

(2) Include `$HARMONY_HOME/bin` in your path.

Under UNIX, you must tell the command shell where to look for executable programs. For example, if you are using the csh, type something like:

```
set path=($HARMONY_HOME/bin $path)
```

(3) Make sure that Harmony's XWindows application defaults are active.

XWindows applications under UNIX often make use of so-called application defaults or resources. Harmony uses the Xresources in the file `$HARMONY_HOME/misc/Harmony`.

For Harmony to function properly, you must make sure that it finds its Xresources by doing at least *one* of the following:

  (a) Copy `$HARMONY_HOME/misc/Harmony` to the system app-defaults directory as `/usr/lib/X11/app-defaults/Harmony`. This sets Harmony's resources for all users on the system and can usually only be performed by the system administrator.

  (b) Set the environment variable `XAPPLRESDIR` to the directory containing the file Harmony, for example:

```
setenv XAPPLRESDIR $HARMONY_HOME/misc/
```

  (c) Copy `$HARMONY_HOME/misc/Harmony` into your home directory under the name `~/Harmony`.

(d) Include $HARMONY_HOME/misc/Harmony in your local ~/.Xdefaults file, which is typically automatically loaded into the X server when you log in.

(e) Explicitly load $HARMONY_HOME/misc/Harmony into the X server.

For example: xrdb -merge $HARMONY_HOME/misc/Harmony

Personal settings are best made in one's own ~/Harmony or ~/.Xdefaults file.

Other points which you should note are:

- The release notes in the misc directory describe any peculiarities of the current version (known bugs and limitations, and so on).

- Once Harmony is running, you will probably have to configure the fonts Harmony uses (see Harmony Xresource file) to match your screen resolution and the fonts available on your particular XWindows installation – the X font model does not allow us to specify a single set of fonts which look good and are available universally.

- The Harmony PostScript viewer has a hefty appetite for temporary disk space. The page images generated by GhostScript typically occupy about 1 MB per page. By default, the PostScript viewer uses a directory ~/.harpsd in the user's home directory for these temporary files, but this can be changed by setting the X resource Harmony.PostScript.tmpDir.

16.2.4   Running Harmony

To run Harmony, enter for example:
harmony or
harmony -hghost *name*
where *name* is the name of the desired Hyper-G server. A list of Harmony's command line options is displayed by: harmony -h.

You might like to point Harmony at some of the following Hyper-G servers:

- hyperg.iicm.tu-graz.ac.at

The IICM Information Server. Here you can find a description of the IICM, a Harmony Tutorial, online documentation on Hyper-G, the VRweb VRML viewer and J.UCS (*Journal of Universal Computer Science*), information about Graz and Austria, a collection of MPEG films, a collection of 3D models and much more besides.

- hyperg.tu-graz.ac.at

Graz University of Technology's Information System (TUGinfo) run by the university computer center. It contains a wealth of information about Graz University of Technology, personnel, courses, recent theses, pointers to other information servers in Austria and worldwide and fully searchable versions of the ACM SIGGRAPH Online Bibliography and the HCI Bibliography.

- `hyperg.hmu.auckland.ac.nz`

  The University of Auckland Hyper-G Server, run by the Department of Computer Science's HyperMedia Unit (HMU). Information about the HMU, the Department of Computer Science, the University of Auckland, New Zealand and so on. Take a look at the aerial views of Waitemata Harbour!

- `gds.esrin.esa.it`

  Earth Observation Guide and Directory Services (GDS) of the European Space Agency. Satellite images, mission reports and related information.

By default, Harmony connects to the server `hyperg.iicm.tu-graz.ac.at`.

16.2.5 Interoperability with WWW and Gopher

Harmony is essentially a Hyper-G authoring tool and not (directly) a WWW or Gopher client. Interoperability with these network tools is provided by the Hyper-G server – Harmony accesses WWW and Gopher sites via the Hyper-G server it is connected to! To use Harmony to browse the wider Web, it is advisable to use a Hyper-G server electronically near to your site or install your own local Hyper-G server as a proxy. You can then access Web sites with a command like:

```
harmony -hghost hyperg.local -goto http://www.somewhere.edu/
```

16.2.6 Feedback

Please direct any feedback (comments, suggestions, bug reports and so on) concerning Harmony by electronic mail to:

```
harmony@iicm.tu-graz.ac.at
```

We are very interested in your feedback, even though we may not be able to respond personally to every piece of mail.

16.3 Configuring Harmony

16.3.1 Customizing Harmony via Xresources

Harmony has an extensive set of Xresources which can be modified to customize its appearance and behavior. The file `$HARMONY_HOME/misc/Harmony` in the Harmony distribution describes the resources and contains examples of their use. Here, only a few selected Xresources will be discussed. To customize Harmony, copy the file `$HARMONY_HOME/misc/Harmony` to your home directory, or cut and paste the resources you need into your `~/.Xdefaults` file.

`Harmony.hghost` specifies the Hyper-G server to which Harmony connects by default. This is typically your local Hyper-G server, but can be set to any Hyper-G server, for example:

```
Harmony.hghost:   hyperg.iicm.tu-graz.ac.at
```

`Harmony.language` allows you to configure default language preferences. In the example below, the user has English as first preference and German as second:

```
Harmony.language:   english|german
```

`Harmony*double_buffered` controls double buffering in Harmony's windows. By default, double buffering is turned on to enable smooth scrolling. However, if your display platform has limited RAM, setting double buffering off substantially reduces Harmony's demands on X server resources, at the cost of a certain amount of flicker during scrolling operations.

```
Harmony*double_buffered:   off
```

`Harmony.Text.editcommand` specifies the editor to be used to edit text documents. The name of a temporary file containing the text is appended by the Harmony Text Viewer as a final parameter to the edit command. The editor must be started explicitly in the foreground, if this is not the default (for example, Jot on an SGI).

```
Harmony.Text.editcommand:   emacs -geometry 80x50+100+100
Harmony.Text.editcommand:   jot -f
Harmony.Text.editcommand:   asWedit
```

16.3.2   The user configurable tool menu

Harmony also has a user configurable tool menu, which is added to the Session Manager's File menu. Menu entries are specified using Xresources like:

```
Harmony.Session.Collection.tools:   haradmin|apanel
```

```
Harmony.Session.Collection.Tools.haradmin.menuentry:
HarAdmin
```

```
Harmony.Session.Collection.Tools.haradmin.commandline:
haradmin -hghost $host -hgport $port
```

```
Harmony.Session.Collection.Tools.apanel.menuentry:
Audio Panel
```

```
Harmony.Session.Collection.Tools.apanel.commandline:
apanel
```

Variables like $host and $port are substituted into the command before execution.

16.3.3   Configuring external viewers

External viewers can be configured both to replace native Harmony document viewers and for generic document types which have no native Harmony viewer. To configure Harmony to use an external viewer instead of the Harmony Film Player, for example, the Xresource `Harmony*ExternalViewer.film` can be set (there are equivalent resources corresponding to each native Harmony viewer):

```
Harmony*ExternalViewer.film:  mpeg_play -dither color
```

External viewers for generic documents are specified in a similar fashion. The Xresource `Harmony*ExternalViewer.Generic.xxx` specifies the viewer to be started for generic documents of subtype `xxx`. For example, to view DVI files which have been uploaded to the server as generic documents of subtype `dvi`:

```
Harmony*ExternalViewer.Generic.dvi:  passto xdvi -paper a4
```

As `xdvi` does not accept files on standard input, a simple shell script `passto` is used to write the document to a temporary file and then start `xdvi` with the temporary file as a parameter:

```
#!  /bin/sh
cat > $$.tmp
$* $$.tmp
rm $$.tmp
exit
```

16.4   Further reading

A good guide to UNIX is *UNIX in a Nutshell* (Gilly, 1992). Newcomers to XWindows should consult a guide such as *XWindow System User's Guide* (O'Reilly *et al.*, 1988).

17 Using the Amadeus client

Thomas Dietinger, Gerbert Orasche

Amadeus is the first Hyper-G PC client for Microsoft Windows. It is designed to make most of the features of Hyper-G available to a broad range of users. Because it should be seen not only as a **viewer**, but also as an **authoring tool** for those who are not computer science specialists, one of the key features is its user friendliness. Another important point is that it works on standard PCs and not just on high-end machines. Last but not least, it is implemented in very modular form to ease maintenance and extensions.

Some of the key features of Amadeus are:

- native 32-bit (Windows 95/Windows NT 3.51) application. It runs also under Windows 3.1x with the help of the Win32s extension;

- easy to use installation program;

- typical Windows-like features:

  - MDI (multiple document interface);
  - dockable toolbar with toolbar-tips;
  - context-sensitive pop-up menus;
  - extensive online help and so on.

- numerous built-in document viewers for several data formats:

  - text (HTML, generic SGML);
  - raster-images (GIF, JPEG, TIFF, PCX, BMP, XBM, ...);
  - movies (MPEG, AVI);
  - PostScript documents (PostScript 1 and 2, PDF in preparation);
  - 3D scenes (VRML and SDF).

- built-in converters from RTF (Rich Text Format) to HTML. With these you can use ordinary word processors (that are capable of saving text in RTF) to create new text documents for Hyper-G. For Microsoft Word, a separate document template is available which, in conjunction with another converter, makes it very easy to create professional text layouts.

This chapter gives a quick overview of how to use Amadeus. It will explain how to benefit from the hierarchical structure of Hyper-G, how to surf through the information space using links and how to find what you are interested in using the powerful search capabilities of Hyper-G. The second part of the chapter explains each of the several built-in viewers in detail.

Amadeus can be used freely by everyone. For commercial use (for example, resale after adoptions or changes) contact the Hyper-G Consortium; see Appendix C. You can find Amadeus on the CD-ROM that comes with this book (see Appendix B) or you may download the current version via anonymous FTP from our FTP server `iicm.tu-graz.ac.at` in the directory `/pub/Hyper-G/Amadeus`. This is also the place where you will find the PostScript version of the Amadeus manual.

17.1   Navigation and browsing

In this section we will give a basic introduction to the three possible ways to navigate with Amadeus. Choose the one which fits your needs best! For a detailed reference to all features, consult the Amadeus manual.

17.1.1   Hierarchical navigation using the Collection Browser

The Collection Browser is the most important tool to help prevent you from getting "lost in hyperspace." It displays the content of the Hyper-G database in a hierarchical way, so it is easy for you to find out where you are in relation to the other documents in the database. The collection browser consists of two parts:

- A hierarchical tree view for visualizing the structure; some branches are opened, but most are not, to help you keep an overview (in a huge database there would be thousands of branches!).

- A list browser that gives you detailed information about the content of a selected collection.

The hierarchical tree view

The hierarchical tree view looks quite similar to the folder view of Windows 95 Explorer. You can open a branch by pressing the `plus` key on the numeric keypad or by clicking on the `plus` sign. If you press the `minus` key on the numeric keypad it closes this branch and all its sub-branches.

Note 1: The hierarchical tree view is missing in some older implementations of Amadeus (for example, version 1.0)

Note 2: Because WWW and WAIS do not provide a hierarchical structure, the tree view does not apply to these two protocols. Currently the tree view is supported by the following protocols: Hyper-G, local database, Gopher, FTP, local file and Network News.

The List Browser

The list browser visualizes a collection of documents by displaying the most important attributes of them. This will help you to quickly identify the desired object which you want to browse or modify. Attributes shown are:

- The object's `Type`, visualized by a descriptive icon.

- The object's `Name`.

- The `Author` of the object (that is, the name of the person who loaded the document into the database).

- The `ModificationDate` of the object.

- The `Score` of an object gets assigned to after a full text query (only applicable when the list browser displays search results).

- The `Number` of objects a collection or cluster contains (only available with these two document types).

You may use the cursor keys or the left mouse button to mark an object. Once you have chosen a document, you can download it and display it on a viewer. This is done either by pressing the `Return` key, or double-clicking on it with the left mouse button. Another possibility is that you do not want to view the object but want to do something with it, such as move it to another location or change some of its properties. This can simply be done by selecting the correct Amadeus menu entry after you have marked the object you want the operation to perform on. You may also pop up a context-sensitive menu by clicking with the right mouse button on the desired object.

Note: Additional windows of the list browser (without the tree view) may also be used by Amadeus to display search results or status information.

Related commands

Two commands that are also important in this context should be mentioned. These are:

- The `children` command. Clusters are a special type of collection and automatically show their member objects, instead of displaying them in the list viewer. In some circumstances it might be handy to look at each of the documents separately, such as when you want to change properties of a document, or you want to delete one. This is exactly where you need the `children` command: it displays the contents of a cluster in the list viewer so that you can select each object in the cluster separately. For collections, this is done by default.

- The `parents` command. Normally you see the parent of a certain object directly in the tree view. However, an object can have more than one parent and you may want to display the other ones! This is when you need the `parents` command. The result is displayed in a new list browser in addition to the one assigned to the tree view.

Note: In earlier versions of Amadeus when the tree view was still missing, these two commands were particularly important for navigating through several levels of the collection hierarchy.

17.1.2   Surfing the Web using hyperlinks

The second way to navigate the Web has been made popular by standard WWW clients like Mosaic and Netscape: hyperlinks. You simply have to click on special marked areas of text to follow a link to a new document to display it. In Hyper-G this feature has been extended to all kinds of documents. This way you may also follow links in images, PostScript files, movies, 3D scenes and sound documents with Amadeus. The procedure is the same as with usual WWW clients: just click on special highlighted areas of a document to follow a link to related objects. To avoid getting lost, you can combine this with the location feedback the tree view provides.

Note: Links may also be accessed from the keyboard. Use Tab and Shift-Tab (Backtab) to select a link and press Return to follow it.

Related commands

There is currently no implementation of a "local map" as supported by Harmony. However, there are some commands that might help you in browsing and authoring in this context:

references This command displays a list of all documents that contain links that refer to the selected document (that is, all links coming into the document) in a new list browser.

links This command displays a list of all documents pointed to by links in the selected document (that is, all links going out of the document) in a new list browser.

annotations This command displays all documents that are annotations to the currently selected one in a new list browser.

17.1.3   Finding what you are looking for: Search capabilities

We now come to the third method of navigating through hyperspace. Powerful search capabilities are one of the most important functions in Hyper-G. Amadeus provides you with two ways of defining the search region (or "scope") within the database and three different search types.

The search region

You may search in the "whole home database" or restrict the search to "activated collections." A collection may be activated by selecting it first in the tree view or the List Browser and then using the "activate" command. Alternatively you may also drag a collection to the already opened "activated collections list" and drop it there.

The search types

The "Titles" search type   With this search type you may perform Boolean searches in the Hyper-G information network.

This is not a full text search. Rather, an object is found when the keywords entered appear in the title of the object or have been attached to it as additional keywords. When used on a WAIS source or Gopher index, the exact effect is determined by the remote database implementation, but in most cases it will default to a full text search. When using title search we distinguish between **ordinary search** and **prefix search**.

With *ordinary search*, when entering a keyword (such as "foo") you will find all objects (documents, collections, destination anchors) with the word specified in the title or as a keyword; upper and lower case are ignored. National character sets can be entered as 8-bit codes (ISO Latin-1) or in SGML notation. The output will be a list of matching objects, sorted by score.

When entering more than one word, they are ANDed (in other words, a blank is the AND operator). Hence, `foo bar` will match only objects that contain both "foo" and "bar." The OR operator is "|" and so `foo|bar` will match all objects containing either "foo" or "bar."

You may use the following operators (and combinations of them):

- ! or NOT;

- & or && or AND;

- | or || or OR;

- &! or ANDNOT.

The precedence of the operators is (in decreasing order): NOT, AND, OR. ANDNOT is used to reduce the amount of search results and is *not* the same as NOT and AND. If you make a full text search NOT finds all objects that are not the following word and after this the AND is performed. To reduce the amount of (temporary) hits and improve the search performance please use the ANDNOT operator.

If you want to look for a search query that is an operator, you have to put it in quotes: `mother 'and' father` would search for titles containing "mother" and "and" and "father."

Prefix searches allow you to locate words starting with a special initial segment by using the wild-card character *. For example, `foo*` would match everything containing a word that starts with "foo" (like foobar). You may combine this with AND and OR operators as above (like in "uni* california").

Note: due to a (deliberate) limitation in the server, you cannot use "*" to match all objects.

The "Attributes" search type   This search type offers the full functionality of the search type `Titles`. In addition, you may restrict the search to certain authors and objects inserted into the database after a certain date.

Note: Unlike the search titles command, this command cannot be used to search through remote databases (WAIS and Gopher indices).

As an example, to find all documents with author "foo" in the set of active collections that have been created after 1 April, 1993, you would enter:

Keyword: *(empty)* Author: foo   Date: 93/04/01

At most two out of the three fields can be left empty. As a special case, if the first two fields are left blank, the system will offer the current date as default. This is a convenient way to search for objects that have been created on the same day.

The "Full text" search type   This search type allows you to perform searches on the contents of text documents stored in the Hyper-G server. All text documents inserted into the server are automatically indexed for full text search.

Technically speaking, the Hyper-G full text engine can perform a combination of ranked, Boolean, weighted, fuzzy and nearest-neighbor searches on the documents as explained in the formal syntax description towards the end of this section. The following examples explain the meaning of the above terms in a more intuitive fashion.

Examples:

computer (primitive search)

When you enter only one word, you will receive a ranked list of the documents in the set of active collections that contain this word. The list will be truncated after 40 matches (this number can be changed with the Full Text Option command), and normalized such that the top-ranking document gets a score value of 100%. The ranking is computed based on the number of times the word appears in the document, where it appears (title, headings and subheadings count more), and the size of the document.

Since the Hyper-G full text engine employs a so-called **stemmer**, the above example would also match documents containing "computers," "computing," "compute" and the like. There are certain words (so-called **stop-words**) that usually appear very often (like "is" or "was") that you cannot search for, as they are not indexed. Whether you use upper case or lower case characters is irrelevant.

tell me about computer conferences (nearest-neighbor)

You may also enter a search string like this example. The first three words are stop-words and are ignored. The system will search for documents that contain most of the other (two) words, but usually will also deliver those that contain a high frequency of one of the words only.

computer & conference (Boolean search)

Sometimes you want to specify that the documents have to contain all the search terms, as in the example given. The & operator means AND (you may also use &&), while | means OR (you may also use ||), ! means NOT and &! means ANDNOT. You may of course combine these operators into more complex constructs, for example (personal & computer) | (ibm & pc) | macintosh | amiga to match a variety of personal computers. In this example, the brackets are not really necessary as the AND operator has precedence over OR.

Note: You may also use the keywords (OR, AND, NOT, ANDNOT) instead of the operators.

computer &[f] conferencing (fuzzy Boolean search)

The f makes the AND operator a fuzzy AND; in other words, it will also match documents that contain only one of "computer" and "conferencing," but with lower ranking.

`computer &[f] conferencing{3.5}` (weighted Boolean search)

Similar to the example above, but allows you to make "conferencing" 3.5 times more important than "computer" in the ranking.

Note: You may combine the above examples to construct arbitrarily complex queries.

Some of the features (for example, stemming and stop-lists) are language dependent. While, in principle, the Hyper-G indexer allows you to index words in any language that is based on the ISO Latin-1 alphabet, stop-lists and stemmers are currently available for English only.

Query syntax   This is a more formal description of the syntax of full text queries, where expressions in [ ] are optional, {} means 0 or more occurrences, and | means "or":

```
expr          ::= term {orop term}
term          ::= factor {andop factor}
factor        ::= node ['{'float'}']
node          ::= word {word} | '('expr')'

orop          ::= '||' | '|'
andop         ::= '&&' [optionlist] | '&'
                  [optionlist]

optionlist    ::= '[' option {',' option} ']'
option        ::= 'F' | 'f'
```

The `optionlist` is extendible. Proximity searches will be available in future versions.

Related commands   As mentioned before a search can be restricted to certain parts of the database in Hyper-G. This is supported by three commands:

`activate` This command adds the selected collection to the list of activated collections (that is, the collections to be examined in the next search). Alternatively you may drag a collection to the activated collections list browser.

`deactivate` This command removes the selected collection from the list of activated collections.

`show activated collections` This command will popup a new list browser displaying all currently activated collections.

17.2   Viewer and player descriptions

In this section we describe the different `viewers` Amadeus uses. Most of them are integrated into Amadeus. You can select the standard behavior when opening a multimedia document. Three initial window states are supported:

Minimized The new window is placed on the desktop as an icon. You have to activate it (mouse click) to bring it up to its normal size.

Normal The initial state of the viewer window is the one chosen by the Windows system. This is MS Windows' standard behavior.

Maximized In this mode the window is maximized when opened.

17.2.1   The Text Viewer

This part of Amadeus is similar to other Web browsers like Netscape or Mosaic. The **Text Viewer** displays text documents and it also supports images and hyperlinks. You can view all text documents on Hyper-G and first-generation WWW servers with this viewer.

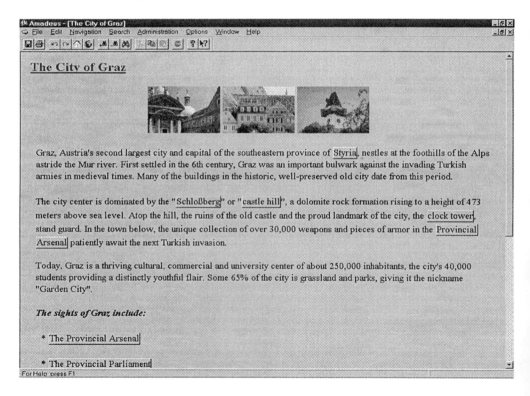

Figure 17.1   The Amadeus Text Viewer displaying a document.

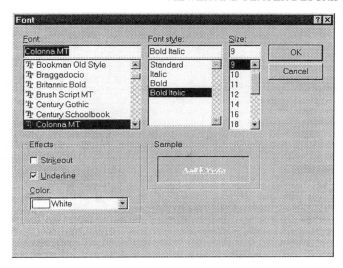

Figure 17.2   The Amadeus Font Selection Dialog.

To change the appearance of the text pages you can change the font type, height and special effects (for example, underline, strikeout). The text viewer has three classes of fonts:

Example font This is a fixed font (all letters have fixed size). This is useful for pre-formatted text (for example, source code listings and so on). This mode is activated by the HTML PRE and ADDRESS tags.

Headline font This font is used to display headings (H1 to H6 tags).

Default font This font displays normal text. You can choose the font you like most. All installed MS Windows fonts can be used.

In general it is possible to define light, medium, heavy and normal appearance of all font classes above. Font color and height can also be changed. See Figure 17.2 for a sample dialog.

Because of the limited bandwidth of wide area networks like the Internet it is sometimes useful to disable the automatic download of inline images. Just check the inline images on demand box in the viewer options menu. You can load the image by clicking on the standard icon Amadeus displays instead of the real image.

17.2.2   The Image Viewer

The **Amadeus Image Viewer** supports a wide variety of different graphic formats: JPEG, GIF, BMP, PCX, TIFF, EPS and XBM. You can set a number of options for the image viewer:

252 USING THE AMADEUS CLIENT

Figure 17.3   The Amadeus Image Viewer displaying Graz clocktower.

`Initial Size` If you have low screen resolution it is useful to define a fixed size for the image viewer window. You can enter width and height and the image will be stretched to this size. Otherwise it will be displayed using the size defined in the data coming from the server.

`Automatic Resize` If the `Auto Resize` option is enabled and the image viewer window is resized, then the image is stretched to the new size of the window. When the option is disabled, the image size does not change.

`Dithering` Dithering is needed when a true color (6.7 million colors) image is displayed using a lower number of colors (for example, 256). This needs quite a bit of computation time. Depending on your computer and graphics card you can select one of two different dithering modes. On slow machines you should select the `fast dithering` option. For high quality display of images use the `beautiful dithering` mode.

17.2.3   The PostScript Viewer

PostScript is one of the most widely used formats for high quality display of page-based documents. Although it is primarily known as a printer format, it is also used in electronic publishing, see also Chapter 28. The **Amadeus PostScript Viewer** interprets, displays and unpacks PostScript documents.

You can navigate through the document using the following features:

`page numbers` The number of the page to be displayed is entered in the text entry field enclosed in the toolbar.

`position related navigation` You can look at the previous, next, last or first page, by selecting the toolbar-buttons or menu items.

`hyperlinks` These are followed by activating (with a mouse click) a link displayed by a bounding box. If the destination of the link is inside a PostScript document the page is scrolled to display the destination area in the center of the window.

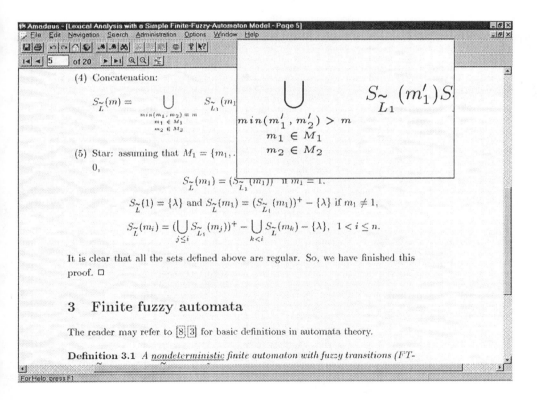

Figure 17.4   The Amadeus PostScript Viewer displaying a J.UCS article.

The resolution of most computer screens is low (about 75 to 100 dpi) and hence the document is initially displayed at a resolution of 100 dpi to get images of the size of a real printed page. Actually it is interpreted at a three times higher resolution (300 dpi) to enhance readability by using several shades of gray. To look at detailed structures the zoom rate can be increased in steps to 300 percent; to get a better overview of the contents of a page it can be decreased stepwise to 30 percent.

When zooming to minimum size, only headlines and big fonts can be read easily. To be able to read smaller text a magnifying glass is included; it is activated by pressing the right mouse button and moving the mouse. The magnifier doubles the size of the image. Its center corresponds to the position the mouse cursor pointed to before activation.

Another feature for reading multi-page documents is the possibility to lock the margin of the text. Consider reading an average text having a left margin of, say, one inch. On navigation to another page the viewport of the viewer is normally moved to the upper left corner. To read the text you have to scroll horizontally for one inch until you reach the text. Especially when reading longer papers (such as proceedings, scientific papers and so on) this is very annoying. After the selection of "lock margin," every new page is automatically scrolled to the proper horizontal position.

17.2.4   The Scene Viewer

With the **Amadeus 3D Scene Viewer** you can stroll through virtual worlds, look at models from different views and navigate through the Web by following hyperlinks. To achieve this, two different file formats are supported: the Hyper-G Scene Description Format (SDF) and the Virtual Reality Modeling Language (VRML). VRML seems to have become *the* new standard on the Web. It supports inline scenes, different levels of detail and much more.

Many applications can use 3D graphics to advantage: electronic shopping, virtual museums or new user interfaces for huge databases. See Chapters 28 and 29 for more details.

According to the scene you look at, you can make use of the viewer in one of the five **navigation modes** which best fits your needs:

Flip Object This mode is useful to look at one object from all sides (for instance, an airplane, engine or molecular model). You can zoom, rotate and translate it as if you had it in your own hand.

Walk In bigger scenes like a virtual museum or city this mode simulates walking on the ground, also allowing you to veer to the left or right, turn your head or move up and down as if you were in an elevator.

Fly In big scenes you should use this mode to get a bird's eye view. You can control speed by pressing the plus and minus keys and the flying direction by the position of the mouse cursor relative to the mid-point of the window. If you have ever used a flight simulator you will be familiar with this mode.

Fly to In this mode you can select a "point of interest" (POI), such as a particular house in a village, and fly to or from this point along the line between the virtual eye and the POI

Figure 17.5   The Amadeus 3D Scene Viewer displaying Lightscape's model of Jerusalem city hall. (Rendered with the Lightscape Visualization System (TM). Model courtesy of and ©1994 A.J. Diamond, Donald Schmitt & Co., Toronto, Canada.)

using the cursor up/down keys. Alternatively, you can fly a banking turn (pressing the control and shift keys simultaneously) and then directly move along a line perpendicular to the surface you are aiming at.

Heads up After selecting this mode you see four icons projected into sight using a head up display. The functionality of the icons is (from up to down): walking, panning, translating and switching to the fly-to mode. This mode is the most universally applicable one. It is also very easy to use and the best choice for beginners.

The Amadeus Scene Viewer also supports different **rendering modes**. Select one of them depending on your computer and the size of the scene. In wireframe mode, only the boundaries of the polygons are drawn. Due to its speed you should use this mode for big scenes or slow computers. In hidden line mode, lines covered by surfaces in front of them are removed. In flat shading mode, the polygons are filled with a uniform color. The speed of these two modes is nearly equal, so choose the one you like more. Smooth shading provides good rendering quality, but is slow. Colors are approximated along the surface to give a natural view of the scene. For best quality the Scene Viewer provides the texture mapping mode. Realistic images are mapped onto the surfaces of the scene. Depending on the number of textures and the complexity of the objects in the scene, this mode can be even slower than smooth shading.

The human eye perceives smooth motion at approximately ten frames per second and higher. Especially when using smooth shading, slow PCs are not able to produce this frame rate. To provide high frame rates for navigation in such situations you can configure the Scene Viewer to automatically switch back rendering quality to a faster mode. For instance, when your rendering mode is texture mapping, you can select flat shading as the interactive mode. When you walk through the scene, you see it flat shaded, but the moment you stop it is rendered using the textures. The advantage of this quality switch back compared to "level of detail acceleration methods" (for example, only rendering bounding boxes in motion) is that you see all objects in their normal size and shape when moving.

In some scenes, surfaces need only be seen from one side (for example, a cube you are looking at only from the outside), while in others they need to be seen from both sides (a house you are going into). For better performance, switch off the two-sided polygons option if you do not need to see both sides of the surfaces.

Sometimes it happens that the scene or object you are looking at disappears from view. Then you should reset the view to the initial camera position using the accelerator key or menu item. With the "level view" you can make your virtual eye look horizontally.

VRML is an object-oriented plain text format based on the Silicon Graphics Open Inventor format. It is editable with any text editor and parsed by VRweb when a new scene is opened. Especially when developing your own VRML scenes it is often useful to know about parser errors or the complexity of the scene. Select the parser output menu item for viewing messages from the parser and the polygon count of the scene.

To save bandwidth in the Web, dimensional scenes are usually sent in compressed form (the VRML scene compression ratio varies from 1:3 to 1:10). The Amadeus Scene Viewer unpacks compressed data automatically. If you see compressed versions on the server you are browsing, select them to save transmission time.

17.2.5   The Movie and Sound Player

The **Amadeus Movie Player** displays animations (MPEG movies). It was still under development at the time of writing. It will be enhanced to display other animation formats (for example, Quicktime and AVI). Link support is also not included yet. You can start and stop reproduction with either the menu items or the viewer toolbar. The Amadeus Sound Player is also under development. The Windows standard sound recorder is used instead as an external program. The Windows WAV and UNIX AU formats are supported. Both players will be ready when this book is out, including full Hyper-G link capabilities.

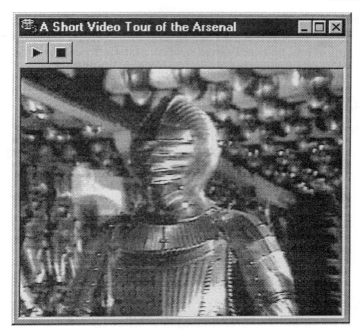

Figure 17.6   The Amadeus Movie Player displaying a film about the armory in the "Zeughaus".

17.3   Outlook

With the release of Windows 95, Microsoft entered a new era for user interaction. Many new controls, programs and styles were added. The double click became obsolete and a context-sensitive menu is displayed on a click with the right mouse button.

Future versions of Amadeus will be fully integrated into the new user interface. We are working on extending the collection browser to display the hierarchy of the Hyper-G database and plugging it into the Windows 95 Explorer as another extension of the network neighborhood. Moving and copying of collections is done by drag and drop. It is also planned to have more than one connection to either local or online databases simultaneously. This also simplifies the export of data from an online Hyper-G server to a local database (see also Section 13.7).

Integration of additional protocols is another part of Amadeus'future. It will be possible to use Mail, News, FTP and IRC directly while browsing. A local map will offer new navigational facilities similar to the Harmony local map (for details see Section 15.3).

Further development is being carried out to support additional communication features and a new status information window. The Hyper-G mail service is enhanced to enable conference sessions of two or more users. The conversation can be automatically imported into the database.

Finally, user and group management will be integrated into Amadeus. You will be able to fully administrate a Hyper-G server from your Windows desktop.

17.4   Further reading

For additional information and literature references please look at the end of Chapter 18.

18 Technical description of Amadeus

Thomas Dietinger, Gerbert Orasche

Now that you know how to use Amadeus we want to give you a more technical view of the basics. We first describe the **installation** of Amadeus, then we go deeper into the technical details by describing **command line options, configuration files** and **technical implementation**. At the end of the chapter you will be introduced to the standalone viewer that comes with Amadeus.

18.1 Installation of Amadeus

Amadeus comes either as a set of installation disks or as a collection of compressed files (pkzip format with the extension .zip) which you need to uncompress into a temporary directory. If you do not have enough disk space, you can extract each zip file onto one formatted plain disk to make your own set of installation disks.

Before you start the setup of Amadeus you have to determine what type of installation is required. Basically there are three setup modes:

- installation on local hard disk;

- installation of Amadeus binaries on a file server;

- client installation of Amadeus configuration file and icons on local hard disk (only if a file server installation already exists).

Each of them has several advantages and disadvantages. The following description will help you to choose the right one for your environment.

Note: Depending on your type of installation, you may not need to have all Amadeus disks. This might be useful if you have to download the Amadeus zip files over the network and want to save bandwidth. Look at the file `index.txt` which will reside in the same directory as the other Amadeus files. It describes the purpose of each file and whether you need it for your setup.

18.1.1   Local installation

All Amadeus binaries will be installed locally (directly on your PC), thus resulting in high performance (through quick hard disk access) but at the cost of quite a bit of disk space. To fine-tune Amadeus according to your needs there are three setup options:

Minimum installation This installs only those parts of Amadeus that are really required to start it. Of course some of the more specialized viewers (like PostScript or VRML) will not work in this case! You can choose this mode if you do not have enough free disk space or if you just want to take a quick look at Amadeus to test it out.

Maximum installation This option installs everything you have on the setup disks onto your system. Choose this if you have sufficient free disk space and want to make full use of all the features of Amadeus.

Custom installation This lets you individually decide which parts of Amadeus should be installed and which should be left out. After each (de)selection, a status message is updated that tells you how many bytes are free and how many are still required on the target disk.

Note (only for Windows 3.1x users): After you have finished your installation, Windows 3.1x will restart if the setup program has installed Win32s or WinG, a high speed graphics library. This will only be done if the current version is not already installed. If you start Amadeus for the very first time, a graphic speed test will be done (you will see a test pattern) to check which display method is best for your video driver. If you have difficulties during this step, read the file amadeus.faq, which comes with the Amadeus files.

Note: On the CD-ROM that comes with this book you will find a complete set of Amadeus installation files. Please refer to the CD-ROM documentation for detailed instructions.

18.1.2   File server installation

This kind of installation is a very good choice if you are going to install Amadeus on a number of PCs and have a file server which is accessible by the PCs. In this case all Amadeus binaries (except Win32s and WinG for Windows 3.1x systems) reside on the file server. Only the Amadeus configuration file amadeus.ini, which stores your personal settings, will be copied to the local PC. The great advantage of this is not only that you need very little hard disk space on the local PC, but that it is also very easy to update to a new Amadeus version by simply installing a new version on the file server. Then all Amadeus clients will run the new version without any change on the individual PCs!

One disadvantage is that starting Amadeus may take a bit longer. In addition, performance will not be as good if access to the network is slower than to the local hard disk. This clearly depends on the network architecture.

Note: If you choose this option all Amadeus disks will be required!

18.1.3   File server client installation

After you have copied the Amadeus installation files to your file server (with the file server option), you need to install Amadeus on the local PCs, using the Amadeus setup program on the file server. This should have been generated during the file server installation process. The install program will copy Win32s, WinG (only if necessary – thus only under Windows 3.1x) and amadeus.ini to the local disk and create an icon to access Amadeus.

Note 1: You only have to do this once, and not after every upgrade of the Amadeus file server binaries.

Note 2: On the CD-ROM you will find a prepared file server installation so that you can easily test Amadeus without having to install it locally (except Win32s, WinG, the configuration file and the subdirectory). Please refer to the CD-ROM documentation for detailed instructions.

18.2   Configuration files and command line parameters

These allow you to fine-tune Amadeus and adjust it according to your needs. Command line options (see Table 18.1) override the same settings in the configuration file. It is often useful to install several icons with command line options in the icon properties, each for different environments. Of course only the most important options are adjustable using the command line.

If you want to change the default behavior of Amadeus, you have to alter some settings in the amadeus.ini file. Hint: another way to provide different configurations would be to make a file server installation (even on the local PC) and install several client configurations. There is no waste of disk space, because you only need one additional amadeus.ini file and a subdirectory for each configuration.

18.2.1   Command line options

The hghost **command line option**

Typically you would specify a Hyper-G server here (either directly with the host name only or using a URL) but you may also define another protocol type if you do not have a Hyper-G server in place, or want to use Amadeus as a WWW or Gopher client.
Example for specifying a Hyper-G server directly (without a URL):

```
-hghost hgiicm.tu-graz.ac.at
```

Currently the following URLs are supported:

- **Hyper-G Protocol**

  ```
  hyperg://{<user>{:<password>}@}<host>{:<port>}/<collection>
  ```
  or

Table 18.1   The command line options.

Switch	Default	Note
-hghost <hghost>	hgiicm- .tu-graz.ac.at	specifies which Hyper-G database to connect to. For example, hyperg-.hmu.auckland.ac.nz (New Zealand), tracy.esrin.esa.it (Italy), email.tuwien.ac.at (Vienna, Austria), hyperg.edvz-.uni-linz.ac.at (Linz, Austria)
-hgport <hgport>	418	specifies a different port number
-lang <language>	english	specifies a different user language
-coll <startcoll>	anonymous	jumps directly to a specified collection at startup
-sort	#T	sets default sort order for collection browser

```
hyperg:<global object id>
```
Examples:
```
hyperg://hyperg.tu-graz.ac.at:418/~anonymous
hyperg:0x811b9908_0x00077da0
```

- **HTTP (WWW) Protocol**
```
http://<host>{:<port>}/<path>
```
Example:
```
http://www.tu-graz.ac.at/~anonymous
```

- **Gopher Protocol**
```
gopher://<host>{:<port>}/<path>
```
Example:
```
gopher://gopher.tu-graz.ac.at/1~anonymous
```

The lang command line option

This sets the preferred language when connected to a Hyper-G server. Currently the following languages are supported:

- English
- German

- French

- Spanish

- Italian

- Styrian

The `coll` command line option

This sets the starting collection when connected to a Hyper-G server and the user has not specified the Hyper-G server using a URL. It is mainly used for compatibility with other Hyper-G tools.
Example:

```
-hghost hgiicm.tu-graz.ac.at -coll hyperg
```

The `sort` command line option

This sets the default sort order for the collection browser. The sort order defines how objects are going to be sorted depending on their attributes. It is specified using a combination of the following characters:

- on 1st position: sort descending (default ascending)

\# Sequence number. Note: This attribute may be assigned to every Hyper-G object to affect the display order. If an object does not have a sequence number it is handled like an object with number 0. Negative sequence numbers are permitted.

A Author

C Creation time

E Expiry time

O Opening time

P Parent (after search only)

S Score (after full text search only)

T Title

t Type

For example, AT means sort by author first, and then (if authors are equal) by title.

The default sort order is \#T. This means that a sequence number overrides all other attributes if the sequence attribute has been specified, otherwise sorting by title in alphabetically ascending order is carried out. After a search, however, the default sort order is -SPT, that is, the documents are sorted by descending score value (after full text search or WAIS search), then by parent collection, then by title.

Note: The - (descending) flag works for all sort attributes. It is not possible to specify it for individual attributes.

18.2.2   The `amadeus.ini` file

Most of the `amadeus.ini` file settings are made by Amadeus itself or through menu commands and options. However, there are some settings that might be interesting for the advanced user.

The section Amadeus

Field	Default value	Meaning
`Port`	`418`	specifies default port number for communicating with the Hyper-G database (usually port 418)
`Server`	`hgiicm.-` `tu-graz.ac.at`	specifies the default Hyper-G database
`ShowLogo`	`1`	specifies whether the welcome logo is shown or not (1=yes, 0=no)
`Collection-` `Head`	`1`	specifies whether the opening text pages are shown automatically (1=yes, 0=no)
`LocalData-` `Path`		specifies the path to the control file for the local database. If this field is omitted Local-Amadeus will look in the Amadeus working directory (default).

The section Text

Field	Meaning
`Import#<nr>`	used to specify several text import filters
`Export#<nr>`	used to specify several text export filters
`Editor#<nr>`	used to specify (external) editors for modifying and creating new text documents (can be combined with import and export filters)

The `Import` Field

Syntax:
`Import#<nr>=<filter>,<description>,<filename extension>`
`<nr>` is a unique ascending number in the range 000–999, which identifies the import filter.
`<filter>` is an external filter application, or one of the following built-in internal filters:

- `internalRTF`, for converting RTF text to HTF;

- `internalHTF`, no conversion, just syntax checking;

- `internalTXT`, for converting ISO-text to HTF.

CONFIGURATION FILES AND COMMAND LINE PARAMETERS

Note: When using an external filter application, users may also use `$in` and `$out` as parameters for the in (foreign format) and out (HTF format) file!

`<description>` is a description of the import filter format. It will be displayed in the list of import filters.

`<filename extension>` is an extension that is added to the converted (temporary created) filename to ensure correct recognition of the file format by the editor application (if used in conjunction with the `Editor` field, see below).

The `Export` field

Syntax:
`Export#<nr>=<filter>,<description>,<filename extension>`

`<nr>` is a unique ascending number in the range 000–999, which identifies the import filter.
`<filter>` is an external filter application, or one of the following built-in internal filters:

- `internalTXT`, for converting HTF to formatted ISO-text;

- `internalHTF`, no conversion, pass through.

Note: When using an external filter application, you can also use `$in` and `$out` as parameters for the in (HTF format) and out (foreign format) file!

`<description>` is a description of the export filter format, which will be displayed in the list of export filters ("save as" dialog).

`<filename extension>` is an extension that is added to the converted (temporary created) filename.

The `Editor` field

Syntax:
`Editor#<nr>= <editor commandline>,<export filter nr>, <import filter nr>,<description>`

`<nr>` is a unique ascending number in the range 000–999, which identifies the import filter.
`<editor commandline>` is an external text editor application, or the built-in editor:

- `internalHTF`, very simple editor for HTF or ISO-text.

`<export filter nr>` specifies the unique number of the export filter, or −1 if none is required (conversion is carried out before the launch of the editor).

`<import filter nr>` specifies the unique number of the import filter, or −1 if none is required (conversion is carried out after saving the text in the editor).

`<description>` is a description of the import filter format, which will be displayed in the list of import filters.

Example:
`Editor#000=internalHTF,-1,-1,Built-in HTF Editor`

The section TextViewer

The `DefTabWidth` **field**

Field	Default value	Meaning
DefTabWidth	50	defines the multiplication factor for tab stops in pixels

This field sets the multiplication factor of the TAB stops. If you specify 100, say, tab stops are set at 100, 200, 300, 400, ...

The section Generic

This section is used to define the behavior of Amadeus if you want to display generic (user defined) Hyper-G objects like Excel spreadsheets or AutoCAD drawings (specified using the "subtype" attribute). Hyper-G clients are usually unable to display them and they have to be configured individually.
Syntax:
`<subtype>=<viewer> {$arg0} ...{$arg9}`
    Note the following rules for using user defined arguments:

- `$argn` (where n is a number in the range 0–9) are the arguments specified at `Arguments=` in the document.

- `$arg0` specifies the document file name, thus it should always be specified.

- You may change the order of the arguments (for example, `$arg2 $arg3 $arg4 $arg1`).

- You may mix the argument placeholders with other chars, but you have to separate the arguments with spaces or tabs! For example, `-a -b -c $arg1 $arg0`, but NOT `$arg2ab$arg3c $arg0`.

Hint: Look in the `amadeus.ini` file, where you find some comments on additional entries.

18.3   Technical implementation

18.3.1   Design concepts of Amadeus

The basic idea behind Amadeus was to implement a well-designed structure of independent module layers that could be easily extended, reused in other applications and substituted by completely new code without the need to understand the whole project. To support a broader range of platforms, it was desirable to use C++ as the primary programming language.
    Roughly speaking, Amadeus consists of three layers with numerous classes:

- The **protocol and Hyper-G object** layer provides the basic functionality for accessing and handling various data objects available with different Internet protocols (such as Hyper-G documents, FTP-directories, News groups and so on).

- The **command layer** is the control center of Amadeus and works as the connection between the user interface and the core functions.

- The **viewer layer** provides an application interface to independently develop and test a new document viewer without needing to understand or even possess the complete source code of Amadeus.

Note: In 1996, the Hyper-G Consortium will release a complete toolkit for implementing new clients for Hyper-G and other Internet services based on the classes and layers described in this section.

18.3.2 The protocol/object concept

Initially it was planned that Amadeus should only be a native Hyper-G client and every access to the Internet should go via a Hyper-G server, but soon the demand arose to access other Internet services that were not yet supported by the server. When it was decided to implement a local database engine in Amadeus, it was necessary to split the logical representation of database objects (like text, images, collections, anchors, ...) and the physical methods to access them. That led to two (C++) base classes with virtual functions, from which all other important classes are derived:

`HGObject` This class is for the logical representation of objects; the HG stands for Hyper-G for historical reasons, in spite of being the basis for all objects, not only Hyper-G objects;

`BaseProt` This class provides the access functions for all kinds of objects and protocols.

The `HGObject` classes

This and all derived classes should represent database objects from a logical point of view and should encapsulate physical differences (for example, for accessing document data). All objects are characterized by a certain set of properties and virtual member functions (like inserting, deleting, moving and so on). Every object knows its original protocol via a pointer to the `BaseProt` class (see next section) and thus how to physically perform operations on this object using the virtual member functions of `BaseProt`. This makes it possible to use the same types of documents (for example, images) based on different protocols (for example, Hyper-G and Gopher). This has the advantage that functions that are unique to this type of document need only be coded once. There is no need to provide a `HyperGImageDocument` and a `WWWImageDocument`, but instead just an `ImageDocument`. Furthermore, new protocols can easily be added without having to change the `HGObject` classes or other parts of the Amadeus source code.

Only one very basic function has to be extended, namely, the `makeObjectById` function. This takes a unique object identifier (for example, a URL or a global Hyper-G object ID) as the input parameter, evaluates it, creates the required protocol class (derived from `BaseProt`) and uses the protocol to get the object attributes. The result is an object derived

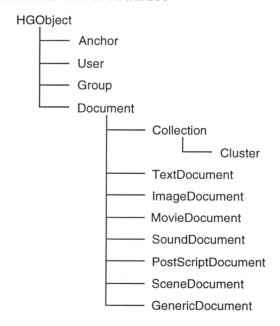

Figure 18.1   The HGObject class hierarchy.

from HGObject. Of course this function also considers the behavior of connection-oriented protocols like Hyper-G and FTP, where no new connections to the same host must be established (this is done by keeping a list of open connections) and some additional features like using Hyper-G as a proxy-server for WWW and Gopher.

Note: Future versions of this function will also support dynamic loading of protocol libraries (DLLs), so that it is guaranteed to keep hardware requirements low when only a few protocols are used.

Figure 18.1 gives an overview of currently supported object types.

HGObject contains many attributes like the title, the author, access rights and so on, describing the properties of an object and member functions used to perform actions on it. Additional attributes and functions are included in derived classes.

The BaseProt class philosophy

The main goal of this class is to define as completely as possible a set of functions that might be required to make full use of all features a certain protocol can provide. If only these functions are used for generating the logical representation of the database objects (DBOs), it is quite easy to implement a new protocol that immediately works within Amadeus.

As a basis, the following operations on DBOs are included:

- retrieving

- inserting

- deleting

- moving

- duplicating (physically copying, within the same protocol type)

- linking (making a new relation between two objects)

- unlinking (deleting a relation between two objects)

- locking

- unlocking.

Then there are some functions that deal with two different types of data:

- data stream

- list of DBOs.

To keep the class simple to implement and use this is done by only six different functions:

- opening with a special opening mode (specifying the type of operation)

- reading a data stream (getData)

- writing a data stream (putData)

- getting a list of objects (getList)

- putting a list of objects (putList)

- closing the stream or list.

Similar to ordinary file operations, we also use a special kind of file descriptor as a common element of control between these functions. This descriptor is internally implemented as a C++ class, called `BaseFD`, from which other classes may be derived.

Currently the following modes for open operation are implemented. The list can be expanded if required:

`getDataMode` for reading a data stream from a server;

`putDataMode` for writing a data stream to a server;

`getChildrenMode` for getting the children of an object (directory/collection/cluster);

`getParentsMode` for getting the parent(s) of an object (resulting object is a directory/-collection/cluster);

`getReferencesMode` returns a list of anchors pointing to this object;

`getLinksMode` returns a list of all anchor objects pointing *from* this object to others. In Hyper-G source anchors, as well as the corresponding destination anchors, are included;

`keyQueryMode` for making a key query by specifying what (attributes) and where to search for (whole or parts of database);

`fullTextQueryMode` for making a full text query by specifying what (string) and where to search for (whole or parts of database).

These are only the basic functions a new protocol might support. An `HGObject` derived class that deals with them has to be aware that some of them may also return "not implemented" as a result. This makes it possible to create new protocols that only include a subset of the above operations (for example, FTP which does not support links, or http which does not know anything about a hierarchy). Functions that are special features of a certain protocol may be included in a derived class, but must be type checked and casted in order to have access to them.

The design has also the advantage that Amadeus can easily be extended to support other non-Internet services like access to a local file system, to other databases (for example, via ODBC (Object DataBase Connectivity)) and so on.

18.3.3   The command stack and history list

Amadeus does not immediately execute a command when it is initiated by the user but collects it on a stack. This has the advantage that it may be executed asynchronously when the time is convenient and the operation is allowed.

All information required for performing the command is stored in this command object. This makes it easy to reuse the command at a later time and store it on a history stack in the meantime. Commands are also C++ classes derived from a base class (called `Command`).

Currently these classes are tied to the foundation classes and development environment Amadeus is based on (Visual C++ 2.2 and MFC 3.2) because many Windows dialogs are included in them. But an attempt will be made to divide these classes into Windows-specific and universal usable (C++) code when the toolkit mentioned is released.

18.3.4   The viewer concept

Amadeus can deal with external and built-in viewers. However, currently only viewers that are directly integrated into Amadeus can support link handling. To prevent successive growth of the code size, future versions will load internal viewers dynamically and thus make it possible to execute Amadeus even on a smaller machine.

External viewers are controlled via settings in the `amadeus.ini` file and magic numbers. Magic numbers are a special sequence of numbers or characters that are unique for a specific data format and are used to find out the document type (in Hyper-G Amadeus already knows the basic type, for example whether it is an image or a movie, but it does not know whether it is JPEG, GIF or some other format). As soon as Amadeus knows the exact format, it looks in its configuration file to find out which viewer is assigned to view it. If there is an entry it tries to launch an external application or to open an internal viewer window (after loading the required dynamic link libraries). This makes it possible to have different viewer applications for several data formats (such as AU and WAV) even if they are the same basic document types (in this case, sound).

Currently, internal viewers are based on the document-view architecture of the Microsoft Foundation Classes (MFC). This will change in the future so that other development environments will also be supported. To simplify development of new viewers, a collection of base classes and some dummy classes was designed that provides the same interface as the Amadeus classes, but does not include network functionality. These classes also contain simulation for link management to fully test new viewers in a standalone project (that is, without the real Amadeus sources).

The most important classes are:

`CApplication : public CWinApp class` Base class for all viewer applications (includes things like accessing the configuration file, providing several types of cursors and so on);

`CMDITemplate : public CMultiDocTemplate` Extended class for handling the MFC template macro (serving as the connection between documents, frames and views);

`CViewerDocument : public CDocument` Base class for all documents that want to access HGObjects and derived classes. Includes basic HGObject dummy classes and link emulation;

`GUIControls` Provides (platform independent!) functions for handling interruption of lengthy operations and displaying progress indicators (visualized by derived classes);

`CMDIMainFrame : public CMDIFrameWnd` Base class for frames in an MDI application (like Amadeus);

`CSDIMainFrame : public CFrameWnd` Base class for frames in an SDI application (like the Public Terminal Viewer "Easy").

18.4 Standalone viewers

The distribution of Amadeus contains two of the internal viewers in standalone form: the PostScript and VRML viewers. You can export documents and the related intra-document links to your local storage. When you look at the document locally, links are displayed and can be followed. Before you can access the latter feature you have to export the links.

The following is a brief outline of how to do it:

(1) `Start Amadeus` and navigate to a PostScript or VRML document.

(2) `Activate the viewer window` and select the `Save As` menu item.

(3) Enter the `path` and the `filename` to which the document should be saved.

(4) Activate the `Save Anchors` menu item and enter the same `path` and `filename` as in the previous step.

After this you will have produced one file containing the data (with the extension `.ps` for PostScript or `.wrl` for VRML) and another containing the links (`.hgl` for Hyper-G links).

18.4.1 The standalone PostScript Viewer

Especially for electronic journals (for examples see Chapter 28), it is useful to be able to distribute a single article together with links to the references. To read the document, the user needs only the PostScript viewer and the data. Amadeus or a network connection is not needed.

Inter-document links are not implemented yet. This could be easily done, but with the development of local Amadeus (for details see Chapter 13) it was no longer important.

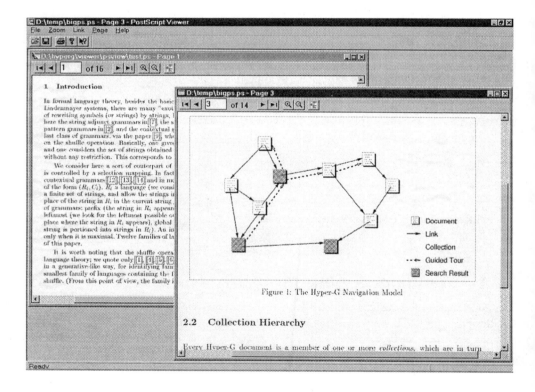

Figure 18.2   The standalone PostScript Viewer displaying files with hyperlinks.

In the following you see an example of a Hyper-G link file for a PostScript document:

```
ObjectID=0x000000a2
Type=Anchor
Title=en:
GOid=0x811b9908 0x0013f5db
Author=jucs
TimeCreated=95/05/01 15:07:53
TAnchor=Src
Position=1:1398,850,608,50
Dest=0x000000a7

ObjectID=0x000000a7
Type=Anchor
Title=en:
GOid=0x811b9908 0x0013f672
Author=jucs
TimeCreated=95/02/27 09:11:52
TAnchor=Dest
Position=14:543,2070,1467,132
```

The object ID is the key to finding source and destination anchors for the included links. The global ID (GOID) is an unambiguous number identifying this object in the whole Hyper-G world. It is not important for the standalone viewer. For links (in HGL files, only links are encoded) the `type` field is always `Anchor`. `TAnchor` stands for anchor type and has the value `Src` for a source and `Dest` for a destination anchor. This example shows an intra-PostScript link at page 1 pointing to a destination at page 14.

The source rectangle starts at the point (1398,850) and has a width of 608 and a height of 50 pixels. If the user clicks this area the viewer searches the list of links for the ID given in the `Dest` field. In the above case this is `0x000000a7`. The destination rectangle is coded analogously to the source rectangle (page:x,y,w,h). The page origin is in the upper left corner.

18.4.2   The standalone VRML Viewer

The standalone version of the Amadeus 3D viewer is also known as VRweb. VRweb is a joint project between IICM (Hyper-G team), NCSA (Mosaic team) and the University of Minnesota (Gopher team). It can be used with all WWW clients capable of starting an external viewer to display VRML scenes and models. For the Mosaic and Gopher clients, interfaces have been developed to enable the viewer to handle inline scenes and hyperlinks.

Unlike all other VRML viewers VRweb is available in source code under a special license. It is free of any fee for academic or research purposes and internal business use. No additional commercial libraries like OpenInventor are required to compile VRweb. The user interface is similar to the Amadeus scene viewer.

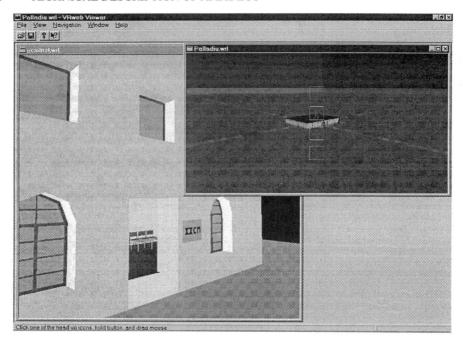

Figure 18.3   The standalone 3D Scene Viewer displaying some models.

VRweb will be enhanced to collaborate with Web browsers (for example, using Mosaic's client to client interface) to follow hyperlinks and fetch inline scenes.

18.5   Further reading

The standard book for Windows programmers containing nearly everything about the basics is the book by Petzold (1992). Further information about the Microsoft Foundation Classes and Visual C++ is given in Parker (1995) and a good textbook for programming is Kruglinkski (1993).

If you are interested in graphics formats consider the encyclopedia of graphics file formats (Murray and van Ryper, 1994). Gall (1991) explains the MPEG movie format. Adobe Systems Inc. (1990) is *the* reference manual of the PostScript Standard by Adobe Systems.

You can obtain more information about the VRweb project from Pichler *et al.* (1995). OpenGL Architecture Review Board (1992) contains a reference for Silicon Graphics' 3D programming library OpenGL, while Neider *et al.* (1993) is a programmer's guide. The Inventor Mentor (Wernecke, 1994) describes the Inventor format.

19 Other Hyper-G clients

Günter Nagler, Gerbert Orasche, Peter Sammer

In this chapter three further Hyper-G clients are discussed: the **Hyper-G Terminal Viewer** for slow network connections, the **Easy** viewer for Kiosk applications and presentations, and **Hyper-G clients for Macintosh** environments.

19.1 Hyper-G Terminal Viewer

If you access a Hyper-G server via a modem connection or work on a computer without any Web client, **HGTV** is the viewer for you. Since HGTV is line-oriented it is very fast, but at the price of not being able to display inline images. Multimedia objects can be downloaded and displayed locally. Many common protocols, including ZModem and Kermit, are supported.

To make your Hyper-G server accessible via Telnet connections you can define it to use HGTV instead of a login shell. This enables any type of computer with terminal emulation to connect to the server. It is also useful for implementing gateways to character-based services (for example, videotex systems).

19.1.1 Installation

For installation of HGTV, you need the Perl script `hginstclient`. Copy it to a temporary directory and change the access rights with `chmod u+x hginstclient`. Please note that you have to install Perl before executing the script! Now invoke the script with either of the following command line parameters:

`-home` makes a private installation of HGTV. The files will be stored in your home directory. Other users on your computer will not be able to use the viewer.

`-hyperg` installs the public version. Program files are copied to `/usr/local/Hyper-G`.

If the script asks you where to put files, just press the return key to accept the default settings. To get the newest version of HGTV rerun the install script or configure a **cron** job for it.

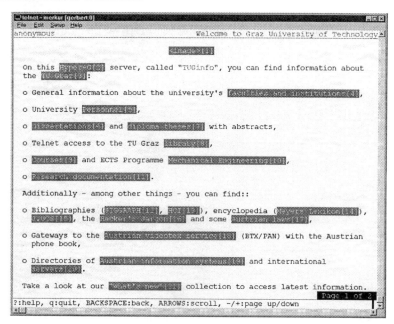

Figure 19.1   HGTV displaying the welcome page of the Graz University of Technology Hyper-G server.

19.1.2   Command line parameters

HGTV is invoked from the command line by entering `hgtv`. Do not forget to update the `PATH` environment variable to the appropriate value for your HGTV installation.

Command line options for HGTV are:

Help To get help on command line options, default values, supported languages and transfer protocols and paths to important files enter `hgtv -help` in the command line.

Host You can name a host to connect to by typing `hgtv -hghost <Hyper-G Server>`. You can also define a default host in the configuration file `hgtv.rc` for when a host is not entered in the command line.

Language Hyper-G can store documents in multi-language versions. For details see Section 22.4.2. You can specify your preferred language with `hgtv -L <language>`.

Sort order The sort order affects the display sequence of collections, search results and documents.

Transfer protocol When accessing non-textual documents binary data is sent. Depending on the connection to the server you should select the protocol. If you are using modem lines the ZModem protocol is a good choice.

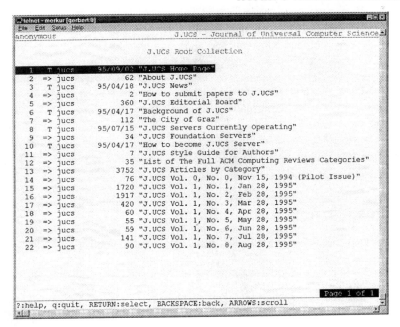

Figure 19.2   HGTV displaying the J.UCS root collection.

For explanation of further options please look at the manual pages or online help.

19.1.3   User interface

Basically, the terminal viewer is in one of two operating modes:

Text display (see Figure 19.1) A text is displayed on the terminal. The text formatting is done at run-time. This is useful when using terminals with different screen sizes.

List display (see Figure 19.2) Every line corresponds to an object in the Hyper-G database. In general a line consists of a line number, the type author, creation date, and title of the object. You can choose one by entering its number or pressing the enter key (actual selection).

You can get online help by pressing the ? key.

19.2   Easy: The public terminal viewer

Although the Hyper-G clients Amadeus and Harmony are ideal for many applications, they are mainly for computer literates. The Hyper-G team has also designed an alternate Hyper-G client called **Easy** which was provided to meet the needs of novice users and public terminal applications. Museums, tourism agencies and advertisement agencies have shown much interest in interactive multimedia presentations of their products. **Public terminals** located in popular places can reach a large number of consumers. Also, Easy is just that: it is easy to use and delivers pleasing results on the screen. It is thus likely to become a popular tool for presentations.

19.2.1   Public terminal applications

This special Hyper-G client is ideal for use in public terminal applications where many users consume information available on an increasing number of Hyper-G servers. Most people using public terminals are typically computer novices and so it is important that the user interface be as simple to use as possible. This is the reason why this viewer is called *Easy*. More complex interactive parts that are available in other clients (like editing) are missing. The Easy viewer concentrates more on presentation features than on functionality. It allows authors to define the appearance of a page in detail to make it as attractive as possible. Easy tries to guess a page design that will display good-looking pages automatically.

19.2.2   Easy surfing through the Net

An Easy user navigates through a potentially huge set of Hyper-G and Web pages by simple use of a pointing device. For single user computers this will be a mouse device; for public terminal applications touch screens or trackballs are more likely to be the preferred input devices. The interaction controls on the screen are larger than usual so that they can easily be touched by a person's finger. When a user hits an interactive rectangular area, called a **control**, the pointing device's cursor symbol changes from an arrow to a hand. After releasing the finger from the screen, or releasing the mouse button, the control starts an action that usually leads to another page. Quick jumping from one interesting page to another is called **surfing**. A keyboard is only needed if the information provider allows searching or if users are asked to fill out an electronic form. A special group of buttons, called the **toolbar**, provides additional ways to reach interesting pages. The available toolbar navigation buttons are:

Backward, Forward Backward performs a dynamic undo that leads to pages that were just in sight. Forward does a dynamic redo and is only available immediately after backward was used.

Previous, Next Navigate to "neighboring" pages in the same collection. These commands are used to visit a sequence of pages that are closely related in some way.

Up Navigate to the parent collection visited recently. This feature is not available when the current page was reached by following a hyperlink or by issuing a search command.

Parents Get all parents of the current page. If the current page has more than one parent, a list of all parents is displayed. Otherwise the command leads directly to the unique parent page.

History Get an overview of recently visited pages.

Home Go to the home page of a registered user or to the anonymous home page of the current server.

Root Navigate to the top-level page of the current server. From here we can obtain a list of other Hyper-G servers known to the current server by requesting the parents of the top-level page.

Language Set priorities of preferred languages. The captions for the controls and titles of documents and the multilingual documents themselves will be displayed in a language closest to the most preferred language. Since English is internationally spoken it is recommended that authors provide their information at least in English.

Search Offers a simple search dialog that requires a keyboard for entering words or phrases. These words will be searched either in document titles and keywords or in full text documents. The resulting titles of matching pages will be displayed and the users can choose one that looks interesting. The results of recently performed search commands are also shown by the history command.

Some of these controls may be disabled in an Easy installation.

19.2.3   Standard formats used by Easy

Easy does not expect that all document authors will provide details of their page design. Designing costs much time and requires experience. The average author of documents is not an artist and will be satisfied when information is displayed in an acceptably neat way. Nevertheless, there is sometimes a demand for a particular kind of presentation of material. Easy lets the authors choose how much they want to influence the layout of a page. Easy knows a set of basic configurable **page styles**. When Easy is installed, a system administrator can configure the basic page styles according to the wishes of information providers. Easy automatically chooses one of the configured styles to display documents that contain no layout hints. Document authors can suggest a preferred style for a document and can overrule some of the default attributes suggested by the style. Some document authors may want to create their own styles for their documents. In this case they have to write a style description text in Hyper-G.

A page style describes all controls that can be used on a page together with all available properties that can influence a control. Each property has pre-assigned standard attributes that are used if the author does not have a need to override them. Styles can be *derived* in the object-oriented sense from available basic styles. This means that style-editing authors can create a style with a new name based on an already available style by modifying all attributes for which the default values are not optimal. The functionality of a style is programmed in Easy and can only be influenced by attributes. For example, authors can prohibit searching on all pages displayed using a certain style, or allow a picture to be scrolled if it is too large for display without scaling it in the available space and so on. For authors that are also programming experts, the SyncPage style provides a time-dependent script language to describe complex dynamic layouts.

If the author does not assign a certain style to a document, Easy tries to select a style by itself. To do so Easy inspects all Hyper-G documents that have to be displayed on the current page and chooses a style that can handle those document types best. The following example demonstrates how Easy assigns a style to a single document that is to be viewed on the current page. Displaying a text document can be done very nicely by a TextBook style that displays the text lines in two columns and, with the help of a pleasing background image, looks like a book or note pad. The TextBook style lets users leaf through the book until they want to see new material or follow a link found inside the text (see Figure 19.5).

To display a group of documents (as found in a cluster), Easy arranges the documents inside screen areas that are permitted by the style: in particular, no document should hide something interesting on the page like a logo or a copyright notice. Each document type has certain needs with regard to screen area. If documents are scaled too small, only certain parts of them can be displayed and the others become visible only when the user selects a control (like a "more" button). Easy tries to distribute screen space in such a manner that those documents that potentially need a lot of space get it (like text, collection item list and so on), but makes sure that remaining documents get at least their minimal space requirement. Collections, clusters and text documents will be displayed first before other (usually bigger) documents are transferred over the network. Thus the page is already functional without the need to wait for the end of data transmission. Users have the ability to navigate to other pages if they do not want to wait until the transfer of time-consuming documents is finished.

19.2.4 How authors and administrators may influence Easy layout

Even if an excellent set of standard styles is available, authors will sometimes have special needs concerning page design. To prevent the author from having to use a complex programming language, Easy was designed so that authors cannot change the functionality of a style. However, authors can influence the layout of a page in a variety of other ways. Authors will find the definitions and attributes of styles in text files in the Easy program directory. Style definition files have the file extension .sty and are loaded at Easy startup. Easy administrators and authors can create a new style based on one of the already existing styles by the *derivation* method. A style usually has a name. The standard page style is called **DefaultPage**. A new style, for instance MusicBoxPage, can be derived from DefaultPage style as follows:

```
DefaultPage MusicBoxPage;
```

`MusicBoxPage` automatically now has the same attributes as `DefaultPage`. To change attributes of `MusicBoxPage` you could specify:

```
DefaultPage MusicBoxPage = {
' this is a comment.  A comment starts with a "'" character
' and finishes at the end of the line
backgr.filename =
"hyperg://hgiicm.tu-graz.ac.at/backgrounds?musicbox";
sound.start = 5; ' play sound after 5 seconds
}
```

This assigns a new background image to the style `MusicBoxPage` and initiates playing the sound five seconds after downloading it. The image must be accessible in a Hyper-G collection named `backgrounds` in the `hgiicm.tu-graz.ac.at` server and has the word `musicbox` in its title. Easy system administrators put the description of a new style definition into a text file named `musicbox.sty` and copy it into the Easy program directory and it will then be loaded when Easy is initiated. Document authors who create their own styles can place the style definition on their Hyper-G server in a generic Hyper-G object of subtype `Layout`. The access rights must be set so that Easy can load the style when referenced by a document.

When a new style has been designed, there are number of possible ways to use it with Easy. The easiest way is to add a layout hint to the document to be displayed in this fashion. Typically, this is a cluster or collection but it can also be a single document (like text, movie, sound) as well. Each Hyper-G document may have an attribute called `Layout`. A Hyper-G client like Amadeus or Harmony can set this field to:

```
Layout=MusicBoxPage()
in hyperg://hgiicm.tu-graz.ac.at/styles?musicbox
```

Between the parentheses additional attribute modifications can be applied that overrule the definitions of the style.

```
Layout=MusicBoxPage(title.visible = FALSE)
in hyperg://hgiicm.tu-graz.ac.at/styles?musicbox
```

This causes a certain Hyper-G document to be displayed according to the MusicBoxPage style but the page title will not be shown. The reference to a style definition object (in `hyperg://hgiicm.tu-graz.ac.at/styles?musicbox`) can be omitted when a standard style is used (like `TextBook`).

19.2.5   The `DefaultPage` style

This page style (see Figure 19.3) is used whenever authors have not chosen a specific style and none of the standard style guessing rules suggest a certain style. As a default, this style can handle all standard Hyper-G documents. The `DefaultPage` style is derived from a general style Page and therefore inherits some attributes and objects that are available for all pages, for example a background image (backgr), a page title (title), a toolbar (toolbar). For each document type supported, an object is available in the style definition that keeps all default values. The main task of the DefaultPage style is to arrange the documents on the screen automatically. The title of the document to be displayed is centered at the top of the page. When a group of documents (a cluster) is to be displayed, the title of each document is shown. An abbreviated definition of the standard DefaultPage style follows:

```
Page DefaultPage =
{
Collection collection;
Movie movie;
Sound sound;
Image image;
Text text;
' and other objects for support of other
' Hyper-G document types some of the default
' attributes that are assigned:
backgr.filename = "book1.i";
title.pos = "65/640 27/480 460/640 55/480";
area = "30/640 24/480 225/640 416/480";
toolbar.area = "560/640 0/480 80/640 480/480";
}
```

Single rectangular areas (pos) and multiple rectangular areas (area) are specified in resolution-independent coordinates. For example 65/640 means that at resolution 640×480 the x-coordinate would be 65 pixels away from the left side of the screen. At higher resolution the value will be automatically scaled relative to the new resolution. Filenames can be locally stored on a hard disk (path) or are Hyper-G URLs that are recognized by the prefix hyperg:. Easy will get Hyper-G data from the specified server and cache it on the local hard disk. When a Hyper-G URL is used again, Easy will take the cached data from the local disk.

19.2.6   The CADPage style

The CADPage style (see Figure 19.4) is a basic page style for those authors who prefer to construct their own personally designed page style. Document authors usually prefer to use styles derived from CADPage style rather than to assign the CADPage style to their documents directly. CADPage is also used as the basic style for some standard page styles such as the following:

MoviePage A movie is played within a television screen, optionally sound is played and one additional text or image is optionally shown in an area below the movie area.

MusicPage The page shows a radio set with switches to turn the sound on and off. An optional text or image will also be displayed by this style.

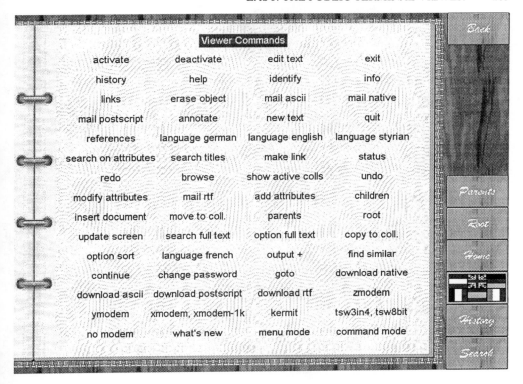

Figure 19.3   Hyper-G collection displayed using style DefaultPage.

`TextImagePage` This style handles pages that contain one image and one text. It displays the text below the image which is resized as large as possible without changing its aspect ratio.

Unlike the `DefaultPage` style, the `CADPage` style does not arrange documents on the screen; style editors or authors using this style must place the objects themselves by setting the attributes `pos` and `area`. The first image found in a cluster is named `image1`, the second `image2` and so on. Each of the objects can be assigned individual attributes.

Easy administrators and authors of styles derived from the `CADPage` style can add user-defined text labels and images to their pages. These can be used to place headers, logos and copyright notices in the pages. These objects must have a name beginning with the prefix `user`. The type of a user-defined object must be `Label` or `Image` or at least derived from one of these. For example, a copyright notice could be defined as follows:

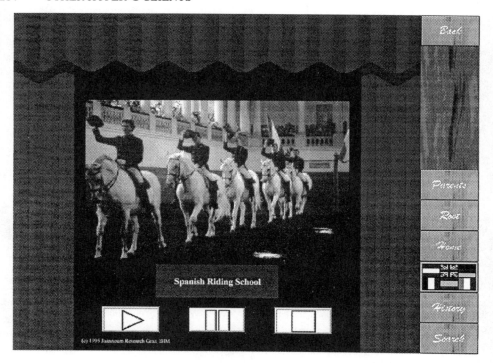

Figure 19.4   Video clip displayed using style `MoviePage` derived from the `CADPage` style.

```
Label IHM_Copyright = ' copyright notice of institute
' for hypermedia
{
pos = "10/640 465/480 200/640 10/480";
' near left bottom edge of page
alignment = LEFT;
fgcolor = 0xFFFFFF; ' rgb 255-255-255 is white
const caption = "(c) 1995 JOANNEUM RESEARCH Graz, IHM";
fontsize = 16; ' small font
transparent = TRUE; ' the background is visible
' between text characters
}
```

The writers of objects and styles may use the keyword `const` in front of a style attribute assignment. This increases the priority of the attribute when it is assigned to a document (in the field `Layout`) or when a new style is derived from this one.

   Such derived objects can easily be added to styles derived from `CADPage`:

```
CADPage IHMDesign =
{
   ' here the author of this style must set attributes of
   ' documents
   backgr.filename = "ihmlogo.tif";
   Image image1 =
   {
      pos = "0/640 0/480 560/640 240/480";
      mode = CENTER; ' image shown 1:1
      title.pos = BOTTOM; ' show title below the image
   }
   Text text1 =
   {
      pos = "0/640 240/480 560/640 480/480";
      fontsize = 24; ' large font
      title.visible = FALSE; ' title of text will be hidden
   }
   ' and by specifying the following line the
   ' object defined above is used:
   const IHM_Copyright user_copyright;
         ' use const so that nobody can overrule
         ' the default attributes of this object
}
```

A caption can also be specified in more than one language like the following copyright notice in English (language code en) and German (language code de):

```
caption = "en:(c) 1995 JOANNEUM RESEARCH Graz,
    IHM|de:(c) 1995 Forschungsgesellschaft
    JOANNEUM Graz, IHM";
```

All objects used in a page have their own set of attributes that influence their layout and behavior. To get a list of currently available objects, their attributes and standard styles, look in the Easy manual available on the IICM anonymous FTP server and on the CD-ROM. For demonstrating the variety of attributes of one typical object, the object Label is shown in this chapter. Such Label objects are used in various places:

- Document and page titles.

- Toolbox buttons are derived from them.

- Collections use labels to display list items.

- They are used to define user objects in CADPage style and other styles.

Some of Label's default attribute values are as follows:

```
Object Label = ' some attributes like visible are
' inherited from basic type Object
{
Boolean transparent = TRUE;
' background is visible through the caption
Color bgcolor = 0xFFFFFF;
' rgb color white that is used when not
' transparent
Color fgcolor = 0x000000;
' text color of caption is set to color black
String fontname = "Tms New Roman";
' choose a pleasing text font
Value fontsize = 24;
' caption is drawn with large characters
String caption;
' caption can be language dependent and is
' optional
Boolean fitcaption = TRUE;
' the object is automatically resized to size
' of caption
Boolean border3d = FALSE;
' draws 3D-type border often used by
' button controls
Boolean border = FALSE;
' draws a frame around the control
Boolean bullet = FALSE;
' draws a left-aligned bullet
Alignment alignment = CENTER;
' caption can be aligned LEFT, CENTER or RIGHT
File bgpicture;
' a background image can be used, this
' can also be a Hyper-G URL
Rect pos; ' resolution-independent coordinates of a
' rectangular area
Value fadein = 0;
' the object is displayed with fade effect
' 0 means no special effect (currently only this
' value is available)
Value fadeout = 0;
' the object disappears with fade effect
Value start = 0;
' the object will be displayed at specified time
' (seconds since page is displayed)
' by default the object will be displayed from
' beginning
```

```
Value end;
' the object will hide at specified time
' (seconds since page is displayed)
' default end is when the user leaves the page
' and other attributes
}
```

Most objects have the attributes start and end. Using these time attributes the authors can construct styles that have time-dependent changes without needing a programming language. For example, one could design a page style, based on the CADPage style, that changes images every five seconds and automatically leaves the page after a certain time. The users can interrupt the sequence at any time.

19.2.7   The TextBook **style**

The TextBook style (see Figure 19.5) is used to display text documents in two columns. The contents of the documents are divided into pages which are numbered. There are additional controls that users can use to leaf through the book.

The TextBook style has the following definition:

```
Page TextBook =
{
backgr.mode = ZOOM;
backgr.filename = "book2.i";
' background designed as a book with two pages
area = "65/640 27/480 460/480 418/480";
' the attributes of the following objects are not
' mentioned in detail
Label pagenumber_left;
Label pagenumber_right;
Label previouspage;
Label nextpage;
Text text;
}
```

19.2.8   The SyncPage **style**

The SyncPage style can be used to define more complex relations between different multimedia documents. Page layout changes over time can easily be specified using a special script language called **SyncScript**. In this way it is possible to synchronize actions, such as the displaying and hiding of several images and simultaneous playback of video and audio.

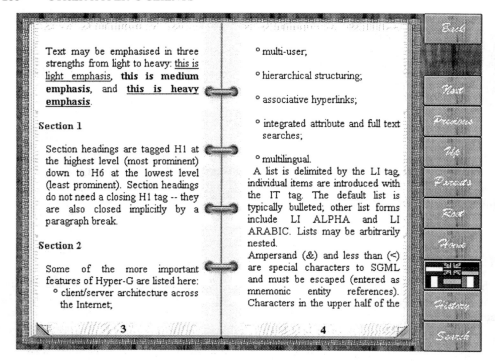

Figure 19.5   A text document displayed using style TextBook.

Generating a SyncScript

The author of a `SyncPage` document must first create a SyncScript file. This is a simple text file which can be edited with any text editor and consists of single command lines with a certain format. A number of commands are available (see Appendix G) to create or remove objects or change their attributes. By default, the style attributes of all objects have the values which were specified by an Easy administrator in the style definition file under the style named `SyncPage`. The SyncScript is stored on a Hyper-G server as a `generic` object with the subtype `sync`. All other resources, such as images, texts and videos, have to be imported into the server as usual.

Accessing a SyncScript

If a SyncScript object is accessed directly using Easy, the corresponding `SyncPage` will be started automatically. The same happens if a cluster containing a SyncScript is accessed. When a collection containing a SyncScript is opened, the `SyncPage` style is only interpreted by Easy if the author has used Amadeus or Harmony to set the collection attribute:

```
Layout = SyncPage()
```

Applications of SyncPage

Originally, the SyncPage style was developed as a tool to enable the synchronized display of music and graphics. The command scale and functionality of SyncPage have now been extended to the extent that it is possible to design dynamic start pages and cyclic presentations. This can be done because SyncPage also has commands to navigate to other Hyper-G pages, which can of course also be SyncPages. Moreover, it is possible to generate automated demonstrations, where at certain predefined moments, the user can decide how to continue. For instance, a document could be designed so that at certain points the user could decide whether to quit, continue the presentation, or skip to a particular section. In other words, SyncPage is ideal for creating interactive documents.

Examples

The first application to which the SyncPage style was applied was a piece of music where the score sheets are shown together with a marker following the music. The start of the *Jupiter Symphony* by W. A. Mozart was the chosen piece of music and Figure 19.6 shows the corresponding score sheet.

Figure 19.6   Synchronized presentation of music and score sheets displayed with Easy using the SyncPage style.

The following lines are part of the corresponding SyncScript. You can see that first all necessary objects (images, text, sound) are loaded:

```
// =================== JUPITER.SYN ==========================

0 Load IMG 1 "#1" "40/640 28/480 500/640 420/480"
0 Load IMG 2 "#2" "40/640 28/480 500/640 420/480"
0 Load IMG 3 "#3" "40/640 28/480 500/640 420/480"
0 Load IMG 4 "#4" "40/640 28/480 500/640 420/480"
0 Load IMG 5 "#5" "220/640 40/480 30/640 30/480"
0 Load LBL 0 "W. A. Mozart:  Jupiter Symphony"
"205/640 437/480 200/640 20/480"
0 Load SND 1 "#1"  ""
```

The next part shows the lines that control the situation in Figure 19.6:

```
17000 Hide IMG 2
17000 Show IMG 3
17000 MoveTo IMG 5 "160/640 40/480"
18000 MoveTo IMG 5 "240/640 40/480"
19000 MoveTo IMG 5 "310/640 40/480"
20000 MoveTo IMG 5 "380/640 40/480"
21000 MoveTo IMG 5 "450/640 40/480"
22000 Hide IMG 3
22000 Show IMG 4
22000 MoveTo IMG 5 "205/640 40/480"
```

IMG 2, which represents the second page of the score sheet, is hidden and IMG 3, the third page, is shown. IMG 5 represents the marker, which moves (through the bars in the score sheet) at intervals of 1000 milliseconds, the speed of the music. After this page is finished, IMG 3 is hidden and IMG 4 is displayed with the marker starting again on the left side.

Another application which shows screenshots from a dynamic presentation is illustrated in Figure 19.7. On a static background examples of images are presented, which change their position and display area during the presentation according to the statements in the Sync-Script.

The upper part of Figure 19.7 shows the screen shortly after the beginning of a presentation of the members of an institute. All images are already loaded and are being displayed. During the presentation these images are scrolled into the final position so that the full images are presented. The upper right image of the boss becomes hidden and a second one is shown at a different location. Sound is also played during the presentation. From the following parts of the script we see how this was achieved:

```
// ============ HOUSE.SYN ===============

0 Hide TBR
0 Change BGR "#1"
0 Load IMG 0 "#2" "294/640 22/480 75/640 96/480"
0 SetMode IMG 0 SCROLL
0 ScrollTo IMG 0 "57/640 8/480"
0 Load IMG 2 "#3" "24/640 235/480 77/640 110/480"
0 SetMode IMG 2 SCROLL
0 ScrollTo IMG 2 "95/640 10/480"
```

... and so on for each image. After loading, the images are displayed and scrolled:

```
6000  Show IMG 0
9000  Show IMG 2
9000  Show IMG 3
12000 Show IMG 4
12000 Show IMG 5
15000 Hide IMG 0
15000 Show IMG 1
18000 ScrollTo IMG 2 "52/640 10/480"
18000 ScrollTo IMG 3 "55/640 8/480"
18000 SetArea IMG 4 "384/640 239/480 77/640 110/480"
18000 SetArea IMG 5 "476/640 239/480 77/640 110/480"
```

19.2.9 Future extensions

The Hyper-G team will increase the variety of available styles and attributes. Some future styles are:

GeographicMapPage A large picture, which can be scrolled, containing a geographical map with icons placed upon it. The icon controls can be activated and will lead to a new page that contains information about this geographical place.

RandomPage A document is chosen randomly from a set of Hyper-G documents and displayed. After a specified time the document is replaced by another randomly chosen document.

PanoramaPage A picture containing a panorama (360 degree lookaround) of a geographical location is displayed. The picture can be scrolled horizontally. At certain positions additional links are enabled and visible sights are described.

Figure 19.7   Dynamic presentation of members of an institute (displayed with Easy using a `SyncPage` style).

19.3   Hyper-G and Macintosh

In this section we describe developments affecting Macintosh clients and how to access Hyper-G with existing tools.

19.3.1   Native Hyper-G clients for the Macintosh

Two native Hyper-G clients for Macintoshes are now under development and one is currently available:

Porting Amadeus Amadeus is based on Microsoft Visual C++ and Microsoft Foundation Classes (MFC). Since a cross-development toolkit for the Macintosh platforms (Motorola and PowerPC) is available, the Amadeus team plans to port the whole project. The client will have the same functionality and low-level architecture as the Windows version. Also, all future versions of Amadeus will then be available on the Macintosh simultaneously.

Enhancing Gopher The Gopher team at the University of Minnesota is modifying their Gopher client to make it capable of handling the Hyper-G protocol.

Hyper-G Terminal Viewer This browser was described at the beginning of this chapter (see Section 19.1). It can be used from any Macintosh capable of Telnet sessions. It is mainly used to administrate Hyper-G servers or to access slow network connections.

19.3.2   Using WWW clients

All Web clients for the Mac can be used to access Hyper-G servers using the WWW Gateway (for details see Chapter 20).

20 Hyper-G and WWW

Christian Derler, Gerald Mesaric

Imagine – although nobody has really been able to do so until now – that you have developed the ultimate information system. Even if you had, you would still have to remain backward compatible with other systems, or users would not be able to upgrade to your system without a lot of trouble. Among others, it was for this reason that **Hyper-G** was designed to be **fully compatible** with earlier common information systems like **Gopher** and **WWW**. However, Hyper-G is not a new exotic system, but just an extension of WWW, easing some problems that have emerged when using WWW for large amounts of data. Thus Hyper-G should be seen as a powerful WWW server, both for the user and the administrator.

Backward compatibility means, in practice, four things:

(1) implementing **client gateways**, so that you can go on using your favorite browsers to access Hyper-G servers;

(2) developing **server gateways**, so that you can browse WWW and Gopher servers by using Hyper-G viewers and so that you can create hyperlinks to this kind of first-generation information systems;

(3) providing **tools**, so that `users` and `administrators` can move their data from WWW and Gopher servers over to the Hyper-G database without much manual intervention;

(4) ensuring that WWW **editing tools** can be used to create Hyper-G pages.

In this chapter we will focus on the **interoperability** of Hyper-G and WWW, describing the **WWW gateway** to the clients (`wwwmaster`) as well as the server gateway provided by the Document Cache Server (`dcserver`). We will also present a tool to insert any net of HTML documents into a Hyper-G database and describe how HTML documents are stored within the server. If you are interested in the same questions concerning the Gopher information system, read Chapter 21, where Mark McCahill – the "father of Gopher" – explains the cooperation now going on between Gopher and Hyper-G.

20.1   Accessing Hyper-G servers with WWW clients

Because of the very high distribution of WWW client programs, it is obvious that Hyper-G access with WWW clients is a key issue. In order to offer Hyper-G functionality to an enormous number of users, a gateway program has been developed which is installed with every Hyper-G server. This gateway handles requests from WWW clients acting as a protocol converter and creates a WWW representation of Hyper-G "on the fly." In fact, the gateway program is in a sense a WWW server since it meets two requirements:

- It talks the client–server protocol used by WWW when communicating with clients.

- It can provide documents in formats used by WWW.

The difference from a usual WWW server is that the gateway does not retrieve resources from a simple file system, but has a Hyper-G server as its back-end database.

20.1.1   Providing connection-oriented access with a connection-less protocol

The implementation of the WWW gateway for Hyper-G was based on the idea of maintaining the connection between the gateway and the Hyper-G server during the processing of consecutive HTTP requests. The gateway can therefore be seen either as a *Hyper-G client* by the Hyper-G server, or as a *WWW server* by the WWW client that issues requests. Therefore, we can distinguish two interfaces to the gateway:

(1) The *WWW side* handles transactions between WWW clients and the gateway according to the HTTP protocol. In other words, for every new request a new connection between the WWW client and the gateway has to be established.

(2) The *Hyper-G side* maintains a session: a connection between the gateway and the Hyper-G server is established when the gateway receives the first request from a new user (that is, a user for whom no Hyper-G session is currently maintained). This connection is maintained during the processing of consecutive requests from the same user and is closed at the end of a session.

The main problem to deal with is to determine how a session ends. After all, a WWW client, using the connectionless protocol HTTP, does not know of the existence of a Hyper-G session. If the user of a WWW client does not request any more information, the gateway will simply receive no more requests from that particular client. This is the reason why the gateway has to wait a certain period of time for requests and then, when nothing is received from that client during this period, it will close the connection to the server, thereby ending the Hyper-G session. The default value used in this *time-out* approach has been determined by practical experience, but can be changed by the system administrator.

Apart from being necessary for maintaining Hyper-G sessions, this concept has the advantage that the gateway can store information about a client's requests and keep this information until the next request from the same client. The gateway is maintaining a **state**, although the client–gateway protocol HTTP is actually stateless. The stored information can be, for example, the object ID of the last retrieved object, the user name of identified users, parameters influencing the screen layout of collection lists and so on. If this information were not preserved between the processing of consecutive requests, the client would be forced to somehow transmit this information with every single request. The only way of making this possible using the HTTP protocol would be the generation of a long URL containing all of this information. This was not considered to be a practical solution.

It remains to be discussed what happens if the client sends a request after the session has timed out. The way the gateway handles this is by treating the request as the first request from a new user and starting a new Hyper-G session. Of course, state information will be reset to its default value in this case.

Since senders of requests arrive in an arbitrary sequence at the gateway, it is important to be able to distinguish them so that each is assigned to a particular Hyper-G session. Using the Internet address of the client host for user differentiation is definitely not sufficient since multiple client programs can run on the same host machine. The solution which is implemented in the gateway is to include some kind of identifier in the URLs used in requests to the gateway. As the path part of a URL is not actually understood by the client, a string, called the **session key** in the following, can be included in the URL. This allows the gateway to recognize the request as a further request from a client for which a Hyper-G session is maintained. Consequently, if the identifier is missing or if it is invalid (that is, it cannot be assigned to a current session, probably because it refers to a session that has been timed out), the gateway can assume that the request is the first request from a new user: it will therefore set up a new session.

20.1.2   The user's view of Hyper-G

This section describes how information is presented to the user of a WWW client when accessing resources via the gateway. Moreover, it explains how the user can interact with the WWW gateway (and consequently with the Hyper-G server) and how the gateway allows you to use certain features of the Hyper-G system, such as searching, identification and so on.

What is shown in the following can be seen as the "*user interface*" of the gateway, although the actual appearance of information received from the gateway is, of course, under the control of the client program. Despite the fact that the gateway is actually a server program from the user's point of view, it is responsible for generating the interface to the Hyper-G system. To fulfill this task, the gateway can use facilities provided by HTML, such as fill-out forms, inline images, "clickable" icons, and so forth. It is clear, however, that the design of the "user interface" is restricted to features offered by HTML.

It has to be kept in mind that the visual appearance of this interface obviously differs from one client program to another. This is why the following description can only be seen as a general guideline for the user. Please refer to online documentation for a more detailed and up-to-date description of the WWW access to Hyper-G.

All the following "screenshots" were obtained by sending requests to WWW gateways of particular Hyper-G servers using WWW clients like Mosaic or Netscape. The screenshots represent the "user interface" originally implemented for the WWW gateway, but they can only serve as examples because the files that are the source of these pages may be modified for customization (see Section 20.1.10). Hence, it is possible that these pages look different at other Hyper-G sites.

20.1.3   The menu line

At the top of most pages received from the gateway, a **menu line** is displayed. This menu line usually contains some icons and the name of the Hyper-G user for whom the current session is maintained. This can be seen at the top of Figure 20.1. The example icons have the following meanings:

- Identification

- Get Options Menu

- Get Search Form

- Get Online Help

- Go to your Home Collection.

20.1.4   Collection lists

The **collection list** displays members of the current level of Hyper-G collection, together with some optional additional attribute information. Each entry in this list represents one member of the collection and contains a "document type icon" and a link to that particular document (see Figures 20.1 and 20.2).

The amount of **attribute information** (author, date, size and so on) displayed for each member can be changed by modifying the display setting in the options menu. The default is to display no attributes.

The "info icon" at the beginning of each line in a collection list provides the user with all attributes for this particular Hyper-G object.

The user can also toggle the display of the *collection head*. When on, the collection head document (typically a description of the collection) is displayed before the actual collection list. When off, the collection head document appears in the collection list like any other document. In Figures 20.1 and 20.2 the same collection list is shown. The difference is that in Figure 20.1 the collection head is displayed, but no attribute information is given. In contrast, Figure 20.2 does not show the collection head, but attributes are displayed with every member of the collection.

Note that the number of members displayed can differ from the number of objects actually in the collection. This depends on the user's identification status since only those members are displayed for which the user has access rights.

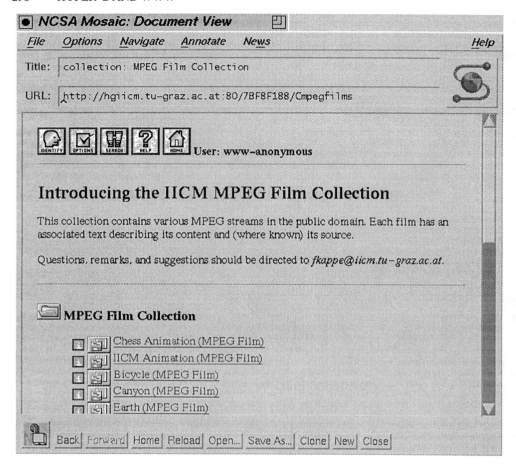

Figure 20.1   Collection list (displayed with Mosaic).

20.1.5   Documents

The way that **documents** are presented to the user depends, of course, on their type. Text documents, collection lists and clusters have a menu line displayed at the top and some attributes such as author, creation date and modification date displayed on the bottom, both separated by a horizontal rule from the actual document.

As **clusters** usually contain more than one document, they are treated in a special way. All documents contained in a cluster that are not text or image documents are listed with their title and type icon as in a collection list (actually a cluster is a special type of collection). This can be seen in Figure 20.3. They can be viewed (or heard, in case of an audio document) when the user follows the corresponding links. Image documents are shown as inline

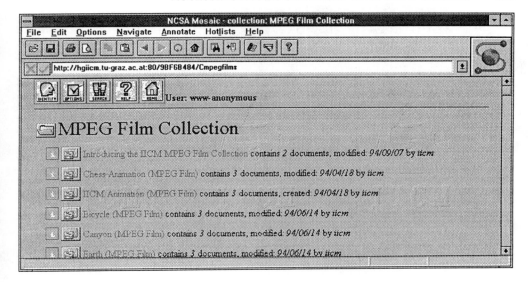

Figure 20.2   Collection list (displayed with WinMosaic).

images. Among text documents, however, the gateway tries to find one written in the preferred language of the user. Only this one is displayed. If there is no such text, some other text document contained in the cluster will be used. All other text documents are not displayed.

Documents of other types such as images, audio, films, 3D scenes, PostScript documents, compressed PostScript documents, HM-Card documents and other documents of "generic" types are sent to the WWW client preceded by a MIME header, indicating the content type. Depending on the capability for handling these documents, the client will either deal with them itself, or start another application to do the job.

20.1.6   Searching

The gateway uses HTML fill-out forms to provide a user interface for searches in Hyper-G databases. Both a **simple search form** and an **extended search form** (see Figure 20.4) are available. The simple form can be accessed from the icon in the menu line. A link to the extended search form is contained in the simple form. The following types of search are available:

- title and/or keyword search;

- content search (full text).

Both forms allow the user to specify a search query which is then submitted to the Hyper-G server. The search query consists of words separated by operators:

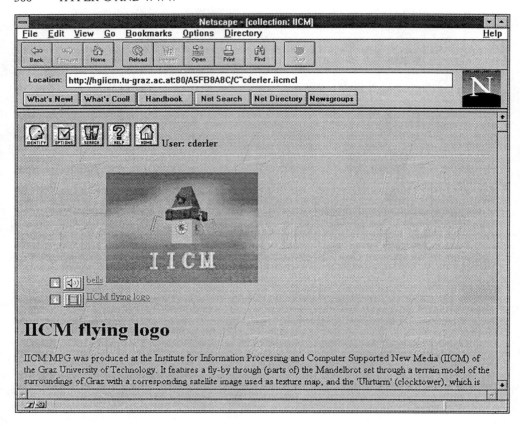

Figure 20.3   Cluster (displayed with WinNetscape).

- The OR operator may be specified as: |, or, oder (case-insensitive).

- The AND operator can be: &, and, und (case-insensitive).

- A space is interpreted as an AND operator.

- The ANDNOT operator may be specified by &!, andnot, or undnicht (case-insensitive).

Search terms may be truncated using an asterisk and brackets may be used to form the query:

- hyper*;

- (Graz) | (Styria).

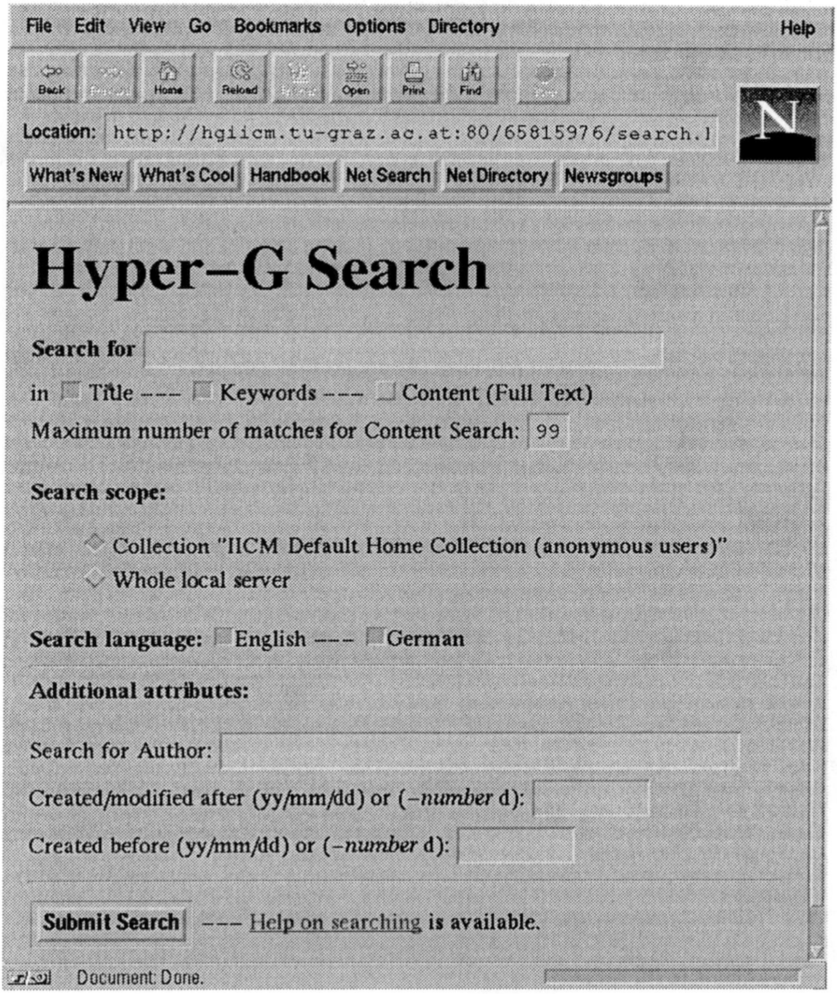

Figure 20.4   Extended search form (displayed with Netscape).

The **scope** of the search can be the whole server or may be focused on a particular collection (including its sub-collections), which does not have to reside on the same Hyper-G server. The collection to search in is normally the collection where the user has clicked on the search icon. Its name is displayed in the search form. However, the search form can also be modified by server administrators (see Section 20.1.10) so that users can choose the search scope from a predefined list of collections.

The extended search form provides the following additional features:

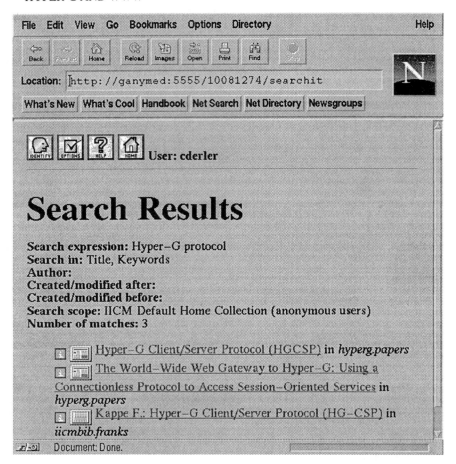

Figure 20.5   Result of a title/keyword search (displayed with Netscape).

- The number of matching objects returned by content search can be limited (the result list is ranked by score).

- Additional attributes such as "author" or "creation date" can be specified for all types of searches.

- The language(s) within which to search can be specified.

The **search result list** (Figure 20.5) displays the same attributes as for members of the collection list. In addition, the name of one of the parent collections of each object is displayed. Moreover, in case of content search, the "score" of each document is displayed.

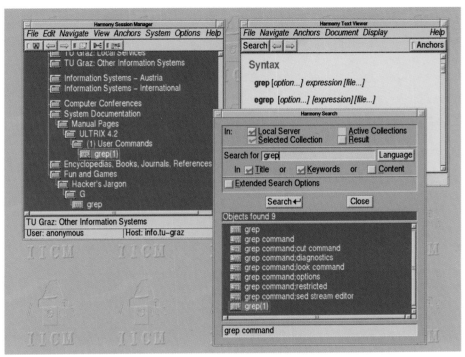

Color Plate 1   Location feedback in Harmony (see Section 15.3)

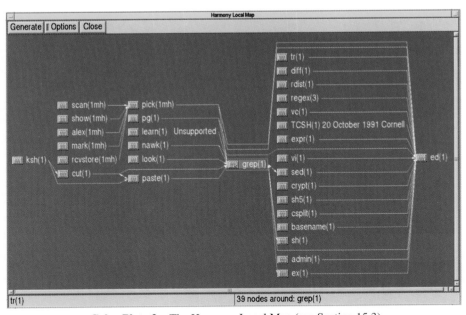

Color Plate 2   The Harmony Local Map (see Section 15.3)

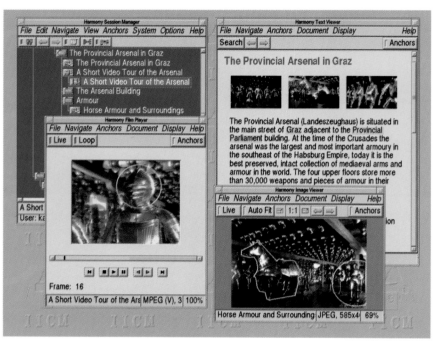

Color Plate 3   Film, image, and text viewers of Harmony (see Section 15.2)

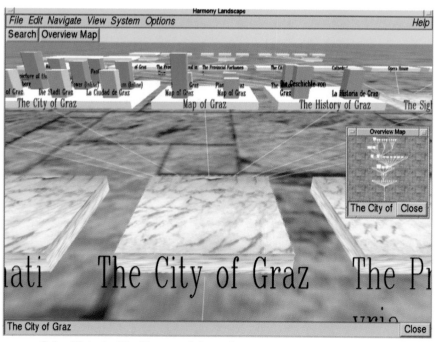

Color Plate 4   The Harmony Information Landscape (see Section 15.10)

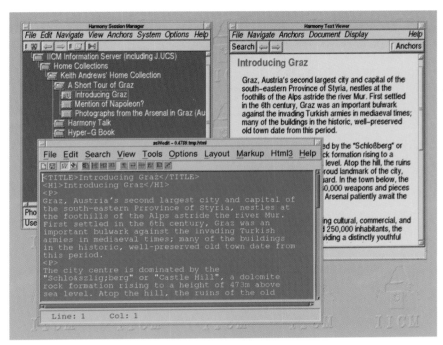

Color Plate 5 Editing text with AsWedit from the Harmony Text Viewer (see Section 23.2)

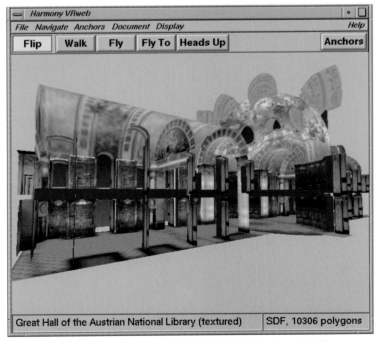

Color Plate 6 VRweb for Harmony (see Section 15.2.6)

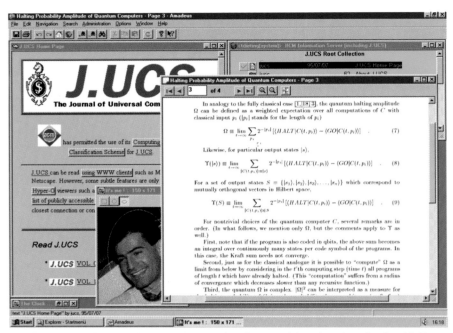

Color Plate 7 Text, image and Postscript viewers of Amadeus (see Section 17.2)

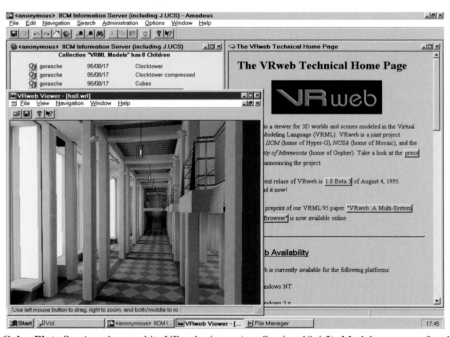

Color Plate 8 Amadeus and its VRweb viewer (see Section 18.4.2). Model courtesy of and copyright © 1994 A.J. Diamond, Donald Schmitt & Co., Toronto, Canada; rendered with the Lightscape Visualization System™.

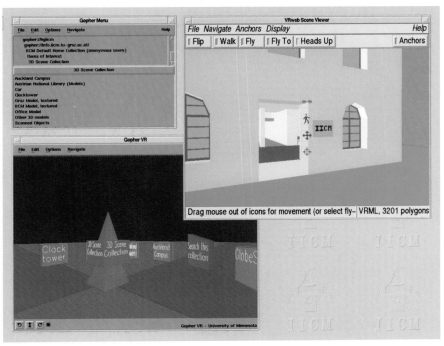

Color Plate 9 VRweb and GopherVR (see Section 6.9)

Color Plate 10 The Easy public terminal viewer (see Section 19.2)

Color Plate 11   Looking at a Hyper-G sequence with Netscape (see Section 9.2, Chapter 20)

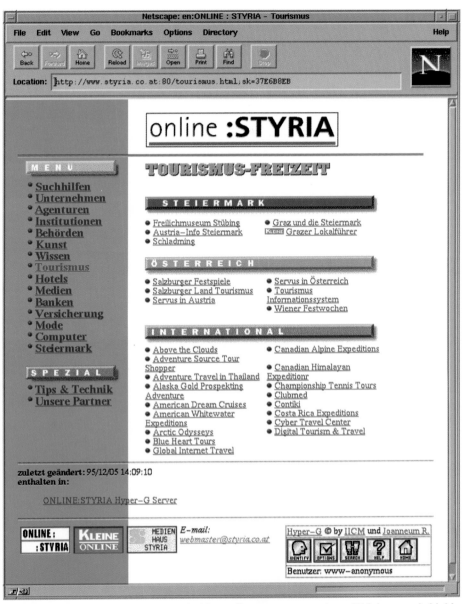

Color Plate 12 The user interface of a Hyper-G server as seen using a Web browser is highly configurable (see Chapter 20)

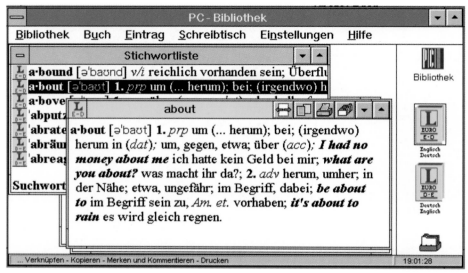

Color Plate 13   Searching a English-German dictionary in the PC Library (see Chapter 26)

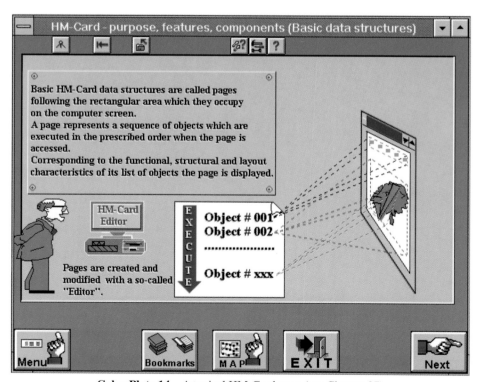

Color Plate 14   A typical HM-Card page (see Chapter 27)

20.1.7   The options menu

Status   By clicking on the Get Status button, a page containing statistics of the Hyper-G server to which the gateway is connected followed by a "who-is-online list" appears (Figure 20.6).

This list contains all currently active Hyper-G sessions for this particular server. Each line starts with a session number, followed by the user name, the name of the client host or the gateway host (as the WWW gateway is a Hyper-G client from the server's point of view), session start date/time, and idle time. Users with name www-anonymous in Figure 20.6 are anonymous users connected to the Hyper-G server via the WWW gateway.

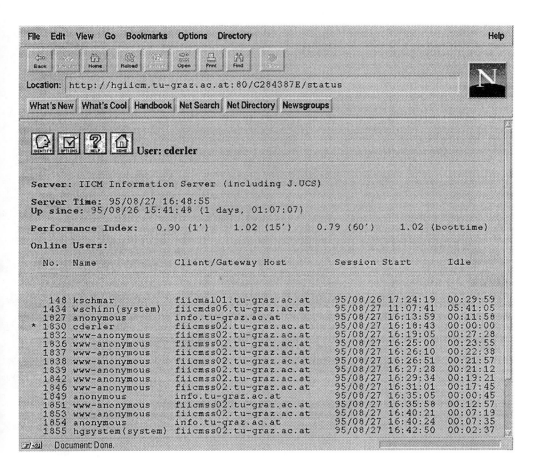

Figure 20.6   Status page (displayed with Netscape).

Preferred language To support the multilingual concept of Hyper-G, the gateway provides a form within the options menu which allows users to change their preferred language.

This has two effects:

(1) The Hyper-G server will try to fetch documents in the preferred language, if available in the database.

(2) The gateway presents its user interface (forms, menus, search results, messages, online help and so on) in the preferred language.

Changing the preferred language does not, of course, affect documents already loaded. Accessing such a document (or collection list) through the back feature of the client typically does not reload the document automatically.

Note that Hyper-G is inherently multilingual. In contrast, providing multilingual information using WWW is a very inelegant process. You have probably seen messages with a link which says something like: This is also available in language xxx.

Display settings The amount of attribute information displayed for each member of a collection list can be changed. Possible attributes are:

• for collections: number of sub-documents, author;

• for clusters: number of sub-documents, modification date (if present, otherwise creation date), author;

• for all other documents: size, modification date (if present, otherwise creation date), author (not for remote documents).

The options menu contains a form with three toggle buttons. With the first one, the display of the author's name can be switched on or off. The second one controls the displaying of creation/modification date and size/number of sub-documents.

The display of the "collection head" can also be toggled. When on, the collection head document, if there is one present in the collection, will be displayed before the actual collection list. When off, the collection head document will appear in the collection list like any other member of the collection.

User identification Users may identify themselves by clicking on the identification icon of the menu line. The WWW client, if capable of the WWW basic authentication scheme, will prompt the user for name and password. Assuming that a user has an account on the Hyper-G server the gateway is connected to, the user is then logged in as an identified Hyper-G user, which can be verified by looking at the "who-is-online list."

Identification extends the user's access rights. For example, searches often result in more matches, and more members are possibly shown in some of the collection lists. This is because, when a user is not authorized to access a collection, not even its name will be displayed. Note that this is to avoid frustrating users who otherwise might see names of all kinds of interesting collections that they cannot view!

Online help Help on using the WWW gateway to Hyper-G can be accessed through the help icon of the menu line. The help page displayed contains links to further pages which cover the topics: identification, searching, collection lists and language setting.

20.1.8   Annotations and references

For each document the user can get a list of all **references**, that is, documents that have links pointing to the current document. The same is possible with annotations of that document: in fact, annotational links in Hyper-G are special types of links.

It is even possible to make **annotations** to a Hyper-G document using a Web client. One way of doing this is by typing in some remarks into a fill-out form which is presented to the user. This annotation is then inserted into the Hyper-G server as a text document with an annotational link to the current document. The other way is to specify a URL or a name of a document. The gateway will then create an annotational link between these two documents.

20.1.9   Insertion of new collections and documents

The WWW gateway allows you to create new collections within the collection hierarchy of a Hyper-G server. The user can type in the name and title of a collection which will then be created as a member of the collection currently listed.

It is also possible to add a new document or a document cluster to a given collection. This can be done by specifying a URL or a name of a document which will then be inserted into the collection (either a reference or a duplicate).

20.1.10   Customizing the WWW gateway

The gateway provides the user of a WWW client with an interface to the Hyper-G system. Most of the elements which make up the user interface are kept in a number of *HTML files* provided with the gateway. This has the advantage that large parts of the user interface can be modified by simply editing text files. **Customizations** can be made, for example, by system administrators in order to adapt the user interface of the gateway to individual needs of different sites running a Hyper-G server.

Whenever the gateway needs a certain part of the user interface (for example, a form or a menu line with clickable icons), it reads the corresponding file and sends it to the client. However, the problem that arises is that some pieces of information can only be provided by the gateway program at run-time and therefore cannot already be contained in the file (for instance, the name of the current collection, the user name, the server name, attribute information about the current object). This is why a set of **placeholders** to be used within the HTML files have been specified. These placeholders are recognized by the gateway program when it reads the file. The gateway then replaces the placeholders with their current values and sends them to the client.

For a complete list of placeholders and file names see the manual page which is provided with the gateway. Some file names are directly known by the gateway, others appear only in anchors within other files or are "included" in other files using the `%%include:` placeholder.

This open concept allows an easy adaptation of the user interface. For instance, if somebody wants an entry field to specify a search query on the bottom of every document or collection list, this can easily be achieved by putting a fill-out form into the footer file. Another possibility for a modification would be to put an inline image anchor into the menu line file. This anchor would point, for example, to some kind of logo, which will then appear at the beginning of every page.

20.2   The server gateway

The other way around is to access WWW servers using Hyper-G clients, which is also possible of course. Unlike WWW clients, Hyper-G viewers use a Hyper-G server as a kind of gateway to access WWW hosts. You create so-called WWW remote objects, which reside on the server, to make a connection to a WWW site. Every time you want to create a hyperlink to this site you just have to link to this corresponding WWW remote object.

If you insert into the server HTML documents that contain URLs which point to a remote server, all the remote objects necessary for creating the hyperlinks will be inserted automatically; you do not have to do more work than you would do for any other HTTP/WWW server. If you want to link from collections to WWW documents residing on another server, you will have to insert the remote object by yourself. By using the second-generation authoring tools Harmony and Amadeus, this is a very easy task: see Chapters 23 and 24 on how to insert remote objects.

There are mainly two reasons why explicit remote objects for connecting to other information systems are used:

(1) Hyper-G provides link consistency. The remote objects help us to provide this consistency up to the point when you leave the Hyper-G server to go, say, to a WWW server.

(2) If WWW links resided within text documents, it would not be possible to have WWW remote links within other data types such as collections or multimedia documents.

Concerning link consistency, a destination anchor is associated with the remote object. Of course, it is not possible to guarantee that your link to a WWW server will not become outdated, but if you only put in one remote object for each URL, then it will be much easier for you to update outdated links. Just edit or remove the one remote object and all associated documents will be updated automatically. Another advantage is to be able to show WWW remote connections in advanced navigation tools such as the local map in Harmony.

The gateway to WWW (and also to most other remote systems) is provided through the document cache server (`dcserver`). The `dcserver` acts much like a proxy server and a cache. It talks HTTP protocol to the WWW server and hands the fetched WWW documents over to the Hyper-G client. One advantage of this approach is of course automatic server caching. Whenever you access WWW documents from a link out of a Hyper-G database, you will not really leave your home Hyper-G server. This is important, because it is thus possible to link remote objects to your Home Collection without leaving the WWW server. You do not have to go "back."

As you might have already guessed, the Hyper-G way of having "bookmarks" is to make a kind of bookmark collection in your home server. The advantage of having your bookmarks within the database is that you can connect from any computer (a PC, a Macintosh or a UNIX workstation) to your home server without having to convert all the bookmark files for the various systems and viewer applications just because you are not working on your usual machine.

All in all, the approach of making the server the connection to WWW makes the use of Hyper-G much more consistent. You create all local and remote objects the same way, just by putting them into collections. You can also make links to remote objects in the same way as to local documents. You can search for your entry points into WWW as usual by keyword or title search. You can even find recently created "bookmarks" by searching for creation date and time. Hyper-G tries to do everything to prevent you from getting lost in hyperspace.

20.3   Migration to Hyper-G

Hyper-G is – like Gopher – a hypermedia system that lets you structure your information. A directory dealing with file systems in FTP or Gopher is called a "collection" in Hyper-G. A collection is some kind of ordered list of entries. Because these entries are also allowed to be collections, you can create a real collection hierarchy. The second type in Hyper-G for structuring information is the "cluster." It lets you create multi-language documents, "cluster" several kinds of multimedia documents together (for example, a video clip and a textual description), or even hide documents like remote links or inline images inside. If you want to know more about structuring information using Hyper-G, refer to Chapter 22. For getting more information on collections and clusters in the sense of object types, refer to Chapters 9, 10 and 11.

Usually – because of the structuring possibilities provided by Hyper-G – a Hyper-G server contains information in a much more structured way than WWW servers do. Therefore, if you want to "roll over" from WWW to Hyper-G, you will have to structure your data in some way:

(1) The easiest way is just to put all your HTML documents into one collection and add the attribute `PresentationHints=FullCollectionHead` to your start document, contained within the collection. If users browse the collection, they will only see the start document. Even with a Hyper-G viewer they will not get to the underlying collections (if there are any), unless they explicitly open the collection (for example, by using the "c"-shortcut with Harmony). Treating WWW to Hyper-G conversion this way is easy, but you would then have decided that you do not want to use some of the most powerful features of Hyper-G.

(2) Another way to structure your information is to do it by hand. Of course this means that you have some work to do, but if you do it right, it will save you much work

in the future. If you want to know more about how one should structure information systems and what advantages this concept provides for both the user and the system administrator, see Chapter 22.

(3) The best way to start (if you do not want to invest a lot of time into thinking about what collections to create in which way) is maybe to use the loadwww utility. This tool was designed to insert a whole hyperweb of interlinked HTML and other multimedia data automatically into a Hyper-G server.

20.3.1 The loadwww tool

The loadwww utility uploads the directory structure and contents of an existing WWW server into a Hyper-G server. All HTML and multimedia documents are inserted in the Hyper-G database.

The directory structure is converted to a collection hierarchy, so that directory /path/dirname is mapped to a collection named path/dirname, which is a sub-collection of collection path. The root of the directory hierarchy is mapped to collection /, which must have been created before running loadwww. The same procedure applies to documents, which get also the name /path/filename.

The WWW gateway retrieves collection foo when accessed with URL /foo/ or /foo. Documents with URL /foo/bar are also handled correctly. This means that existing URLs (for example, stored in user's hotlists) remain valid when moving to a Hyper-G server, provided that the hostname remains the same.

Internal links (those pointing to the same server) are stored within the link database and consistency is maintained automatically. External links (pointing to other servers, and non-HTTP URLs) are also stored in the link database, but without guaranteed consistency, as is the case with any other WWW server.

The loadwww tool provides a number of command line arguments: refer to the online documentation or to the up-to-date manual pages for a detailed listing of all available options. A detailed description is not provided here as it would probably be soon outdated.

Notice that the loadwww utility does not structure your information in a new way: it just takes your WWW directory tree and converts it to a Hyper-G collection hierarchy. This basic structure is created automatically and in a very fast way, but in general it is not a very good hierarchy. Our suggestion is to use automatic conversion for testing if Hyper-G can handle information in a way you like: you may decide to create a well-designed collection tree by hand or modify the automatically created one later on as the need arises.

20.3.2 HTML in Hyper-G

Hyper-G supports HTML (HyperText Markup Language) as a native data type; you do not have to convert your WWW text documents to insert them into a Hyper-G server. Although nowadays HTML supports some features that HTF (Hyper-G Text Format) does not provide, you should not forget that there are one or two capabilities of HTF that are not available in HTML.

For example, in Hyper-G you can have nested anchors within HTML documents, but you will not be able to create overlapping links as they are available in HTF. The reason for this is that HTML anchors do not provide anchor IDs, so there is no way to decide how, or if, anchors overlap (because you cannot tell which part of one anchor belongs to a particular link).

20.3.3 Reusing your "old" WWW URLs

At the time you decide to roll over your server to Hyper-G a lot of bookmarks will point to various documents residing on your WWW site. To prevent your users from losing these bookmarks the Name=URL attribute was implemented, not only for collections but for all other document types as well. A Name is unique on one particular server.

When you move a document from your WWW server to Hyper-G, all you have to do is to add a Name attribute with the original path of the document on your WWW server. If the WWW gateway detects such a *normal* WWW URL, it will look up the real object ID of the document by querying the name index and return exactly the object the users expect to get.

To get the same effect for your former directories on the file system of your WWW server, you have just to specify the path of the directory as the Name of your collection. If you insert all documents that have been located in this particular directory into the collection, your brand new Hyper-G server will react the same way as your former WWW server did, but will provide a lot of valuable new features at the same time.

Notice that you are not allowed to use a Name that starts with 0x, because otherwise the WWWgateway would think that you are referring to an Object ID.

20.4   Hyper-G as a powerful WWW server

As mentioned in the introduction to this chapter, Hyper-G should really be seen as an extension of WWW. Hyper-G is a more sophisticated WWW tool for more professional users: it has been designed to manage big amounts of hypermedia data. Thus it would be a real "overkill" to set up a Hyper-G server just to store your own home page and the pictures of your last holidays on it. But if you are going to start a real information system (having to deal with about 100 or even up to millions of nodes) then you should really consider Hyper-G to be your Web server. One of the most important features of Hyper-G is that a growing number of people think that it is indeed the best WWW server for dealing with large amounts of data.

In the first part of this chapter we discussed the user's point of view on accessing a Hyper-G server using a WWW client like Mosaic or Netscape. In fact, the user has fewer advantages when using Hyper-G than the system administrator and all service providers. Although you might be able to set up a WWW server that mimics most features of a Hyper-G server, this would be lots of work! The system administrator would have to write scripts to check in and out links of HTML documents to maintain some kind of weak (only on the local server) link consistency. It would be necessary to install two search engines (title and full text) just to provide the two most frequently used search facilities of Hyper-G and a gateway to some kind of relational database to store attributes (name/value pairs) in a similar style to the way a Hyper-G server would. Also, among other things, structuring tools available in Hyper-G would have to be emulated in a tedious way.

Another advantage of using Hyper-G as a sophisticated WWW server is Hyper-G's own security system. For administrators this means that they can find out – because all accesses to the server are logged – what each person did to the database at a particular time. Of course, anonymous users are allowed in Hyper-G to avoid the big-brother syndrome. An important feature is also that the administrator can give write access to some parts of the collection hierarchy to some persons or groups: the information management itself can be decentralized in this fashion.

Identified users can restrict read access to those parts of the server they have write access to so that (parts of) the database are "for their eyes only." Hyper-G is more secure than WWW, because you can have usernames and passwords on Hyper-G which differ from those on your UNIX host. Thus it is not as easy to break into Hyper-G servers as with most WWW servers: if you want someone to access only parts of an ordinary WWW server, you have to use the UNIX security system, since WWW documents are stored directly using the UNIX file system.

The Hyper-G server concept has many advantages over ordinary HTTP/WWW servers that are not immediately obvious if you have not really worked with both systems. The main advantage of course is that you have an advanced Web server with data management facilities, search capabilities, link management including bidirectional hyperlinks, a UNIX-like security system and multi-language support without having to write a lot of software on your own. All this is provided with your Hyper-G server software.

20.5   Further reading

The World Wide Web Consortium (W3C) maintains a WWW server which is a valuable source of information on the HTTP protocol and on HTML: `http://www.w3.org/-pub/WWW/`. A rather good book on WWW is December and Randall (1994). The books *Managing Internet Information Services* (Liu *et al.*, 1994) and *The Whole Internet* (Krol, 1994) also provide substantial information about WWW and its relation to other Internet technologies.

21   Hyper-G and Gopher

Gerald Mesaric, Klaus Schmaranz

As a second-generation Web system, Hyper-G has been designed to be fully interoperable with **Gopher**; Hyper-G servers can be accessed by Gopher clients and vice versa.

To provide a **migration** path from Gopher to Hyper-G, a tool exists to insert any existing Gopher server into a Hyper-G server. Migrating a Gopher server to Hyper-G makes administration easier and adds all the functionality of Hyper-G to Gopher.

The first section of this chapter describes how Hyper-G can deal with existing Gopher servers. Following is a description of the existing Gopher gateway and of all extensions planned for the near future which should allow Hyper-G servers to be accessed as if they were standard Gopher servers. The remainder of this chapter is then dedicated to a migration tool that allows insertion of existing Gopher servers into a Hyper-G server.

21.1   Accessing Gopher servers with Hyper-G

As is the case with Hyper-G servers, **Gopher servers** also have a hierarchical data structure, so it is easy to integrate Gopher directories seamlessly into Hyper-G. Gopher directories are simply mapped to remote collections in Hyper-G and documents are members of those collections as can be seen in Figure 21.1.

At the moment remote Gopher directories and documents are accessed using the standard Gopher protocol rather than **Gopher$^+$**. As a result, additional features of Gopher$^+$ servers like abstracts and alternate views are not yet accessible through Hyper-G servers. This will change in the near future. Gopher access with Hyper-G will then support the full Gopher$^+$ protocol and additional document information will be handled by Hyper-G transparently.

As is done with all remote documents, Gopher directories and documents are also cached by the Hyper-G server, so simply using Hyper-G to access Gopher servers has the advantage that Hyper-G acts as a proxy.

A user's personal home collection in Hyper-G can also contain a hierarchically structured hotlist of Gopher documents which has significant advantages over simply storing bookmarks with a Gopher client. This collection is accessible by the user from all over the world, whereas local bookmarks are only available from the user's local account. Also, links from

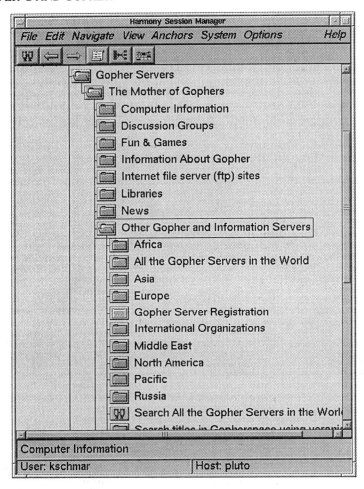

Figure 21.1   Seamlesss integration of Gopher directories in Hyper-G.

within other documents can point to Gopher directories and documents as if they were native Hyper-G documents.

21.2   Accessing Hyper-G servers with Gopher clients

Hyper-G servers can already be accessed with Gopher clients through the Hyper-G to **Gopher gateway**, though soon much more should be possible. At the time of writing, the Gopher gateway could only speak the standard Gopher protocol, but it will shortly be enhanced to

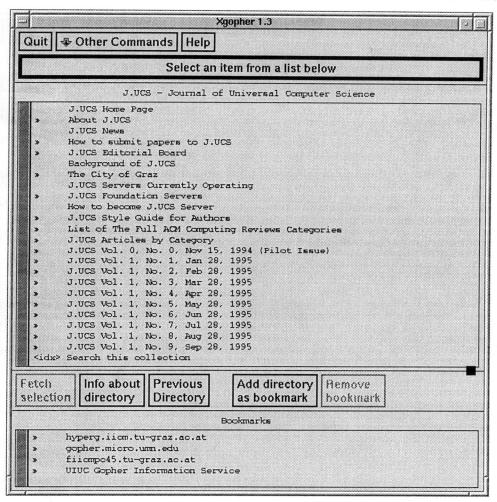

Figure 21.2   Accessing a Hyper-G server using XGopher.

provide all Gopher+ and also GopherVR features. Since implementation should be finished by the time this book appears, we describe here the features that will be supported in the new version of the gateway. Figures 21.2 and 21.3 show how a Hyper-G server presents itself to a Gopher client. Hyper-G collections are mapped to Gopher directories, documents naturally remain the same and the native Hyper-G search engines are represented by a Gopher search.

The enhanced Gopher+ gateway will be functionally very similar to Hyper-G's WWW gateway and provide the same features:

- multilingualism;

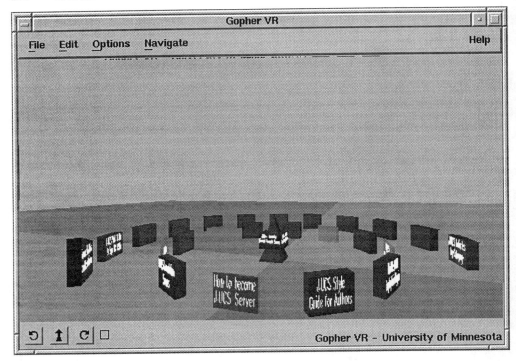

Figure 21.3   Accessing a Hyper-G server using GopherVR.

- user identification;

- customization, such as language settings, display settings, status information and so on;

- sophisticated search mechanisms.

In order to offer Hyper-G features to a large number of Gopher users it is obvious that most of the Hyper-G features have to be translated in the Gopher gateway on the fly. This includes search mechanisms as well as abstracts, hyperlinks and naturally all the user identification mechanisms, display and language settings and Hyper-G status information. User identification and session-dependent settings are done in the same way as in the WWW gateway.

The same is the case with search mechanisms: the gateway supports Gopher forms to let the reader choose between Boolean, title and full text searches and combinations thereof. Further, different views of a document are supported using Hyper-G's clustering mechanisms.

Hyper-G documents, as well as collections, can have abstracts and special descriptions using Hyper-G's clustering mechanisms which are given special attributes that are handled by the Gopher gateway. This allows Hyper-G to store the abstracts and 3D descriptions belonging to documents and collections.

21.3   Migration to Hyper-G

The Gopher information system is one of the "spiritual fathers" of Hyper-G. Gopher directories are very similar to Hyper-G collections. The hierarchical structure that Gopher provides makes it much easier to migrate from Gopher to Hyper-G than from any other common networked information system.

The original Gopher protocol was simple and easy to implement, but it had one major shortcoming: it did not support additional information about documents. The solution to this problem was the Gopher$^+$ protocol which added meta-information to the basic Gopher system. As with Hyper-G, meta-information is stored separately from the document data. Meta-information in Gopher$^+$ can be converted without loss into Hyper-G object attributes.

21.3.1   Gopher$^+$ meta-information

In Gopher, additional information about documents is stored in ASCII representation in a separate file. There are multiple sections that begin with a plus ("+") and the name of the section in capital letters: +INFO, +ADMIN, +VIEWS and +ABSTRACT. The data fields within these sections can be converted to Hyper-G attributes as follows:

+INFO   This section holds the Gopher item description (containing the selector string). The selector string is used as the name of the document in Hyper-G.

+ADMIN   This section provides fields for the full name and Email address of the administrator and the date and time of the last modification. The name is inserted into the DocAuthor field in Hyper-G and the first part of the Email address is used for specifying the Hyper-G author attribute. The modification date is simply converted into the TimeCreated field.

+VIEWS   Multiple views are also an important feature of the Gopher$^+$ protocol. Each line in the +VIEWS section represents one view, holding information about the mime type, the size and the language of the document. In Hyper-G alternate views are put together in a cluster.

+ABSTRACT   The abstract section holds (normally) only a few lines of ASCII text giving a short description of the contents of the document or directory. In Hyper-G the abstract information is inserted into the Description field.

Converting all the Gopher$^+$ meta-information to Hyper-G object attributes in the way described above makes it possible to perform a seamless migration to Hyper-G. Because of the Gopher$^+$ gateway, Gopher clients can still access the data as usual (even using the same URLs). On the other hand, you have updated your server to a next-generation hypermedia system and you can now use sophisticated authoring tools such as Harmony and Amadeus. Although this conversion could be done by hand it is strongly recommended that you use the loadgopher utility.

21.3.2   The `loadgopher` tool

The migration tool from Gopher to Hyper-G – `loadgopher` – is a network utility written entirely in Perl. You specify a complete Gopher start URL (`gopher://gopherhost/-gopherpath`) and the utility will contact the Gopher server, get the document and all related meta-information and then insert a Hyper-G object (data and attributes) into a specified collection and server.

A special option `-rec` (recursive) can be specified if you want to insert a whole subtree of Gopher directories into a Hyper-G server. You can even convert an entire Gopher[+] server to a Hyper-G system just by calling `loadgopher`, specifying your Gopher root (home) directory as the start URL. All Gopher directories are inserted as Hyper-G collections. All Gopher paths are converted to name attributes in Hyper-G so you can "reuse" your old URLs.

21.4   Further reading

A good introduction to the Gopher information system is *Internet Gopher User's Guide* (Lindner, 1994). The Gopher protocol is described in the RFC 1436: *The Internet Gopher Protocol* (Anklesaria *et al.*, 1993b). An unpublished source of information about the benefits of Gopher[+] is available via FTP (Anklesaria *et al.*, 1993a). Finally a very informative article co-authored by McCahill (the "father" of Gopher) presents the *Evolution of Internet Gopher* (McCahill and Anklesaria, 1995).

22 Structuring information using Hyper-G

Gerald Mesaric, Walter Schinnerl

In this chapter we describe the **general principles of structuring and providing information with Hyper-G**. Chapters 23, 24 and 25 explain in detail how to do this with Harmony, Amadeus and a set of special database manipulation tools.

When you first start a Hyper-G server it will be empty except for some demo material that comes with the installation. It will now be up to you to decide how to fill it with information. In general this requires thinking about two things:

(1) Who should be able to insert information? Who should be able to read it?

(2) Where should "authors" insert information and how should your server's contents be organized and presented to the user?

22.1 Users and user groups

Let us first describe the underlying concepts. Hyper-G supports a **hierarchical model of users and user groups**. Users can identify themselves using a username and password, though this is optional: if they do not identify themselves they are user anonymous.

A user may belong to a number of user groups, and every user group may belong to a number of other groups. For example, user hmaurer belongs to group iicm (his department) which in turn belongs to group tu-graz (the university).

On the other hand, every Hyper-G object "belongs" to a certain user, and may have access permissions attached to it, defining who may read, modify or delete this object (see Section 22.3). For example, a certain document may only be readable by all members of the group tu-graz. In this case, user hmaurer would be allowed to read it, because he is a member of group iicm which is a member of tu-graz. In addition, Hyper-G users may have an associated "home collection," where they can create their own view of the information space and store private objects (see Section 22.9).

The user hgsystem and the group system are created when the server is first installed. The group system is intended for Hyper-G system administrators: every member of this group has system privileges. With such privileges you may create Hyper-G users and user groups. The user `hgsystem` is automatically a member of the `system` group.

Creating and editing of Hyper-G user accounts and groups is done by using two tools that come with the server. The first tool is called `hgadmin` and is a terminal utility that is fully menu-driven. Although it is easy to work with this tool, there is also an XWindows version of the Hyper-G administration utility available. The GUI (Graphical User Interface) version is called `haradmin`. It lets you create new users and groups in a very simple and self-explanatory way; it also provides sophisticated browsing and editing capabilities. For a detailed description of `hgadmin` and `haradmin` see Section 14.8.

22.2   Collection hierarchies

Collection hierarchies as available in Hyper-G, although already provided in systems such as Gopher, are particularly powerful when access rights can be added. We have already discussed user accounts and groups in Section 22.1. The next logical step is to define a suitable collection hierarchy for your server. In doing so, you should keep in mind that the collection hierarchy serves roughly four main purposes:

- It lets the user navigate in a hierarchical fashion. Depending on the client, a hierarchy will be shown to the user in a graphical browser (Harmony) or as a sequence of menus (other clients). This will help to prevent users from getting "lost in hyperspace."

- It lets the user specify the scope of searches. Searches can be limited to certain parts of the hierarchy (that is, collections and their sub-collections, recursively). This helps users to retrieve only the information relevant to them.

- It lets you update collections (that is, inserting or deleting documents) without having to create or delete any links pointing to these documents.

- It lets you organize access permissions. You can specify that a certain user or group may write information only into specific parts of the hierarchy, or that a part of the hierarchy is only readable by certain users or user groups.

The first two points are more important for the user, the last two for authors and the system administrator. Collection hierarchies together with access rights allow you to organize your information management in a very decentralized way. Every department and even every user can keep their own documents up to date. The webmaster or infomaster should only be responsible for the uniformity and consistency of the style of how information is provided, of the layout and the structure of data. Even the popular "What's New" section of a server can be maintained decentrally. Designated persons within every department can be responsible for inserting all new information into this collection or page.

Figure 22.1 shows an information structuring proposal for mathematics departments that has been recommended to all departments that want to take part in the project "Distributed Information Systems for Mathematics" in Germany.

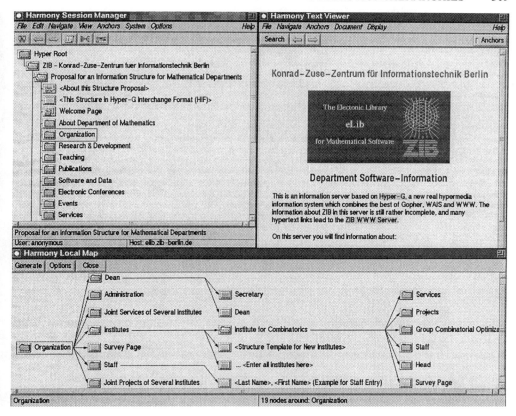

Figure 22.1   Collection hierarchy of a mathematics department.

Once you have created a collection hierarchy you can use the **move to collection** and **copy to collection** commands to rearrange the hierarchy by moving (copying) subtrees around. Copying in this context does not mean duplicating, but attaching a collection subtree to another collection.

For importing and exporting collection hierarchies to and from the Hyper-G server, the utilities `hifimport` (see Section 25.3.2) and `hifexport` (see Section 25.3.1) are available. For deleting or unlinking documents from collection hierarchies, the `hgerase` tool (see Section 25.2.8) tool can be used.

In addition, users may be allocated a personal "home collection": this is their default entry point; here they can also organize their own view of the information space and store private objects. In such a home collection it is often convenient to include the default home collection, that is, the entry point for anonymous users of the server at issue.

22.2.1 Structuring the top level

Technically speaking, the collection hierarchy on a Hyper-G server is not a tree (where every item – with the exception of the root – has exactly one parent), but a directed acyclic graph, or **DAG** for short, in which an item may be a member of more than one collection. Acyclic means that the collection hierarchy stored on a Hyper-G server cannot contain loops (otherwise certain algorithms that the server performs on the hierarchy would not work – especially recursive searching). The Hyper-G server is aware of this and will not let you create loops.

When the server is first installed, the so-called **root collection** (with the name `rootcollection`) is automatically created. Within this collection you should classify the public and private area. You can do this by creating a publicly accessible collection (see Section 22.2.4) that will be the entry point of anonymous users (we suggest using ˜anonymous as its name), and another collection, only accessible to the group of users with home collections. This one (for example, with name ˜home) will be the root of all home collections.

Under ˜anonymous you then create the "public menu" of your server, containing all that should be visible to anonymous users. It is a good idea to place an item "Welcome to . . . " (or similar) as the first item. Other items could be "About this server" and entry points for each department of your company or university. Within the departments you can designate collections for its members which are their "Welcome Pages" (very often also called "Home Pages").

Under the ˜home collection you could then insert the private home collections of the departments, with read access restricted to the group of all department members. Under the department home collection you could create the personal home collections of the department members (see Section 22.9.1). We suggest using ˜hmaurer as the name for the home collection of user hmaurer and hmaurer as the name of his public "Welcome Page." The above setup allows ˜anonymous and the "Welcome Page" also to be sub-collections of ˜hmaurer (see Figure 22.2), without generating a loop.

22.2.2 Choosing names and titles

For referential purposes, every collection has to be given a **unique name**. For clusters and all other document types the name is optional. The name is different from the title which is displayed to the user. The title can be arbitrarily long and need not be unique. The name should be short and must be unique so that this collection or document can be referenced from the outside using the name. You should try to choose readable names (since some clients display the name of parent collections for query results). You should keep in mind that the name is not changed, even if the collection or document is moved within the hierarchy. The server will not let you create a collection or document with a name that already exists. The name of your collection or document will also be part of the URL pointing to it. Therefore everyone should be able to get some useful information about the content of your collection or document from its name.

It is often helpful to provide some kind of context hierarchy in a similar manner to that found in a thesaurus. We suggest the use of dots "." to separate levels within such a context hierarchy and to use an underscore character "_" where you would normally put

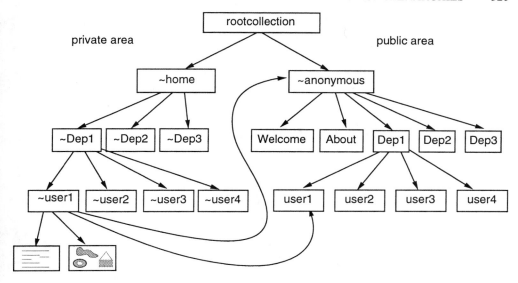

Figure 22.2   Example for structuring the top level.

a whitespace character. Remember that even today there are many UNIX and PC terminal emulations supporting only seven-bit shells. Therefore we further recommend using only the ASCII seven-bit subset of your character table: all users should be able to enter the name of an object on their keyboard!

The **title** of a Hyper-G object is something entirely different. It is displayed in the collection browser and is indeed the title of the document and not header information which is stored within the document. Titles should be as self-explanatory as possible, since documents can easily be copied out of context to another location. For example, do not choose "General Information" as the title for a general-purpose description of some person, but instead choose something like "Hermann Maurer: General Information." In this way, even if you copy several such documents containing information about different people into a single collection, you will still be able to tell which is which.

22.2.3   Keywords

Every object in Hyper-G should have a title, as otherwise it is invisible to the collection browser. But not every object needs a **keyword**.

Keywords have the usual meaning: you can add keywords to a document to describe its content in a very compact way and using Hyper-G it is possible to search for those keywords. Searching for title and keywords is the default search option in most clients, so if you have used uncommon terms in your documents and you want users to find them, attach some (but not too many) keywords to the object.

This feature is particularly interesting for non-text documents. Images, movies, audio files, 3D scenes and remote objects typically have no text information associated with them, so if you want people to find these documents, you should add descriptive terms that are not covered in the title as keywords. Again, do not use common words as keywords or too many keywords, as otherwise keyword searches will tend to find too many documents and users may become discouraged from using this facility.

22.2.4   Creating collections

Creating collections is usually done in one of two ways. If you just intend to create a few individual collections you should use Hyper-G clients such as Harmony or Amadeus (see Chapters 23 or 24). On the other hand, mass-insertion of collections is performed by calling the `hginscoll` command which is part of both the server and the tools software. Usually this command is called by data insertion or manipulation scripts; see Section 25.2.1 for details.

If you insert a new collection without specifying any additional attributes, all values will be set to their defaults. The default sort order of items is first by sequence number (an attribute you may supply to any Hyper-G object) and second by title. You may override this for any collection with the `SortOrder` attribute (see Section E.1). The default author is the user that is inserting the collection. The default creation date and time are set to the current date and time.

A very special and also rather important attribute not for collections but for documents within a collection is the `PresentationHints=CollectionHead`. If a client gets such a document when opening a collection, it is displayed together with the collection. How `CollectionHead` documents are displayed depends on the client, but as a rule of thumb, Hyper-G viewers will normally show the document in another window and WWW browsers will normally append the `CollectionHead` document on top of their HTML collection page.

`CollectionHead` documents are used to describe the contents of a collection or just to give it a better or more interesting design and layout. Good `CollectionHead` documents can help users when it is up to them to decide if they wish to browse the collection tree further. You should use `CollectionHead` documents as often as possible, especially if you can give users more information about what kind of data they can find within this collection tree.

Although any kind of document can be used as a `CollectionHead` in Hyper-G, we suggest using a text document with maybe a few (small in byte-size) colored inline images so that people browsing your server with WWW clients will also have no problems viewing the information. You should keep in mind that WWW clients will place your `CollectionHead` documents as the initial part of your collection page and so it is important not to create documents which are too long.

In most cases you will want your `CollectionHead` document to be displayed as the first item within the collection list. One easy way to do this is to use either the default sort order or any other sort order which sorts first according to sequence numbers (see Section 22.2.5) for your collection. Then put your document into a cluster and assign a *negative* sequence number to the cluster. When you insert the cluster into any collection that contains otherwise only documents with non-negative sequence numbers, you can be sure that your CollectionHead document will always be displayed in first place.

Another attribute mainly intended for access with WWW clients is the `Presenta-tionHints=FullCollectionHead`. If a WWW client gets a document with this attribute while opening a collection, *only* this document is displayed; all other members of the collection are not listed. In this case the author of the collection is responsible for providing links in the `FullCollectionHead` document to all documents and sub-collections which should be accessible to the user.

Attributes in Hyper-G are not static. If you want to modify or add attributes, you can do this by using the `modify attributes` and `add attributes` commands. These commands are again either available in a rather interactive, user-driven environment (using Hyper-G clients such as Harmony and Amadeus) or by calling `hgmodify` if you intend to modify many attributes at once (see Section 25.2.9 for a description).

22.2.5   Sequence numbers

Another attribute in the Hyper-G information space is `Sequence`. The sequence number should be numerical and may be positive or negative. A newly inserted document – if not otherwise specified – has the default sequence number 0. Sequence numbers are mainly used for two purposes:

(1) if you want to create a special sort order for the items in a collection list (for example, for defining some kind of ranking);

(2) if it is useful for you to sort things on title or creation date, but you need one or two documents (maybe an introduction to the content) on top or at the bottom of the list. As mentioned earlier, to ensure that items appear at the top of a list, it is possible to specify negative sequence numbers.

It is recommended that you use step in intervals of, say, 10 or 100 so that later you can insert new documents between old documents.

22.3   Access permissions

Access permissions form the last piece in the puzzle of decentralized information management. Even if you have already set up all your users and groups and created a proper collection hierarchy, you still need to specify the appropriate access rights for each collection. If you do not specify any access rights, default values are supplied: read access for everyone, write permission only for the author. For a detailed description of the `Rights` attribute see Section 11.2.

22.3.1 Opening and expiry time

In addition to the `Rights` attribute, access is controlled by the `TimeOpen` and `TimeExpire` attributes. If the document has "expired" it becomes invisible to everyone but the users with write access to the document (the object is not physically removed from the database, however). Expiry dates are not checked for users with system rights. Similarly, an object is invisible before the date specified by `TimeOpen` to everyone but the users with write access to the object and group `system`.

The `TimeExpire` attribute is very valuable if you hold information on your server that is only valid until a prespecified date or time. A common example of the use of expiry times is a calendar of upcoming events. The events are announced a long time before they take place and the expiry time of each event is given as `TimeExpire`. If the sort order of an `Upcoming Events` collection is set to "sort by `TimeExpire`" you will automatically get a chronological order of the events with the next on the top. Another example of the use of expiry times is an online registration form which is only valid until a certain date. Using other Web systems the system administrator would be responsible for removing the announced events or the registration form from the server. In Hyper-G the database will handle such things automatically.

Indeed, by adding a small script running automatically every day much more is possible. The tool `hgmvexp` moves all expired documents and collections from a given source collection to a specified destination collection and optionally sets a new `TimeExpire`.

As an example, you can use this tool for the administration of your calendar of events. Suppose you have the collections `Upcoming Events` and `Events of the last four weeks`. You could automatically move expired events from the `Upcoming` to the `Last four weeks` collection and set the new `TimeExpire` to `+28` days by starting `hgmvexp` periodically. Additionally you could have a private `Events Archives` collection and simultaneously move the expired documents from the `Last four weeks` to your `Archives` collection, changing the `TimeExpire` back to the original (`-28` days). Now you could use this archive for the annual report of all events of the year; after having completed the report you might move the old events with the tool `hgmvcp` to collection `Archives.Erase` (see Section 25.2.7 for an example) and then delete them by starting the tool `hgerase` (see Section 25.2.8).

22.3.2 License and price

Sometimes there is a need to restrict access to data not only to a specific group of users but in a more general way for all anonymous and identified users. You can manage this by using the `License` which allows only a specified number of users simultaneous access to the documents.

To illustrate the basic idea of this license, imagine a library which has three copies of a certain book. If a reader borrows one copy of this book there are only two copies remaining for somebody else; only three readers can borrow such a book simultaneously. Sometimes there is a maximum number of books which can be borrowed by one reader at one time and also a maximum time the reader can hold the book.

The situation is similar with licensed documents. You can decide how many "copies" are available, how long it can take to read one of these documents and how many of these documents are available in total for one user. The only difference is that the time is counted per document and not for all documents together.

This makes it possible for a Hyper-G service provider to buy a license for an encyclopedia, for example, and to ensure that only a certain number of users can read articles simultaneously. In this case every document belonging to the encyclopedia should have the license field L: in the Rights attribute (see Section 11.3). This entry contains the name of the collection which holds the license definition as an attribute. The license definition consists of three parts and defines the maximum number of users at the same time, the maximum number of documents per user and the timeout (in seconds).

With Hyper-G charging identified users for documents is also possible: for charging and accounting purposes you can give each document a Price and users a certain amount of virtual "money" which allows them to "buy" the documents at some cost.

A document can have more than one price; with the same document you can associate a different price for certain users or user groups. When users try to access a document with a certain cost, their "account" is checked. If their account is greater than the cost, the account is reduced by the cost and the document is transmitted; otherwise access to the document is denied. Only the authors of documents with costs and users with system rights can access those documents without checking and reducing their accounts. Of course, only users with system rights are allowed to manipulate users' account field.

22.3.3   Hiding documents

In some cases you may want to *hide* documents on your server. In other words, you may want users to access them (for example, by following links), without seeing the documents in the collection hierarchy. This may be either to prevent user confusion when browsing through your information, or it may be a design or layout decision.

One way to hide images and allow users still to access the data via hyperlinks works *only* for inline links: you specify read access author only (R:a) for the collection containing your images. No other users can now see this collection, but they are still allowed to follow inline links to images contained within this collection. Be sure to allow read access to the images themselves!

However, a better way to hide documents is to use the PresentationHints=-Hidden attribute. A document that resides within a cluster or collection and has this attribute set will not be displayed when you select the cluster or collection in the collection browser or follow a link to it. You will only be able to see such documents by either getting the children of the cluster or collection explicitly (for example, by using the c shortcut with Harmony) or by creating a hyperlink that points to them. The main purpose of this attribute is to hide remote objects and inline image collections within clusters or collections: you can keep the associated objects "near" the referencing document without the users seeing them.

22.4 Clusters

While a collection is displayed as some kind of menu and lets the user choose one of its members, a cluster is displayed by viewing all or most of its members simultaneously.

A cluster pools together many single media items and presents them as a single complex "multimedia document." This makes it possible, for example, to show text and images at the same time while also playing an audio track.

However, the cluster concept is also used by clients to choose one of a number of documents which only differ in their language. This allows you to define explicitly a sub-group of documents to be displayed for certain language conditions. In this case a cluster is used as a "multilingual document."

The exact rule for displaying a cluster is:

(1) All *language-independent* members of the cluster are displayed. Language-independent objects have *more than one* `Title` attribute (in different languages).

(2) From the remaining *language-dependent* members, one of each document type (that is, one text document, one picture and so on) is chosen based on the user's language preferences and displayed. Language-dependent objects have *exactly one* `Title` attribute.

In some (rare) hypermedia applications it may be necessary to display a number of language-dependent documents of the same document type in one cluster (for example, two images, each in two languages). To achieve this effect, the author can group related documents of different languages in language-independent sub-clusters.

Individual clusters are very easily created interactively using a Hyper-G client such as Harmony or Amadeus. Once created, you can insert documents as if the new cluster were a collection. Mass-insertion of clusters can be performed using the `hginscoll` command with option `-cluster` (see Section 25.2.1).

22.4.1 Multimedia documents

One of the reasons that clusters have been implemented is to manage **multimedia documents**. An example for this might be presenting information about a person. Suppose that a cluster contains a picture, some text about the person, and perhaps a recorded message. If this cluster is accessed all the single media items will be displayed or played together at the same time. In such a case, you would first create a cluster and then insert the image, text and audio document into it.

If we take the example above and extend it to include two or more pictures of the person, we first insert the additional images into this cluster. After this we have to make all the images within this cluster language-independent by giving them a second title with a different language prefix. This guarantees that more than one document of the same document type (in our case "image") is displayed.

You can also do special "tricks" using clusters. Suppose you have a video stream without any audio track, but you have an audio file that you want to play while the movie is shown. The easiest way of playing the video and the audio file at the same time is to put them together into one cluster. If users open the cluster, they will be able to watch the movie while listening to the audio file.

22.4.2   Multilingual documents

A **multilingual document** consists of a cluster and more than one language-dependent document of the same document type. Multilingualism is a very important feature, expecially for European countries and also for parts of Canada and South East Asia. In short, multilingual documents are necessary wherever more than one language is common within a small region. This feature is also very interesting in countries where the inhabitants are not native English speakers: it allows the same information to be presented in the national native language and in the international English language.

A text which you want to present in different languages (for example, English and German) is the most common example of a multilingual document. In this case, you would first create a cluster with an English and a German title and then insert into this cluster the English text with an English title and the German text with a German title. Because the title attributes are not being stored within the document, multilingualism is not restricted to textual documents. You can use this powerful feature for every kind of media.

You can also (mis)use the multilingualism feature if you want to provide information in the same language but in different variants. For example, you could define a "lay language" for non-specialists and an "expert language" for specialists and let the users choose what language they want. This technique has been applied successfully in museum applications such as MONZ, see Chapter 29.

Any document that has two or more titles is regarded as a language-independent document (no document may have two titles with the same language prefix). All other documents (with just one title) are considered language-dependent. In most cases when you make use of multilingualism only your text documents will be language-dependent, but there are also examples of multilingualism in images and audio documents.

Suppose you have some kind of logo, and some words are written within. If you want to present it on the Web, you have to provide these words in English, so that nearly everyone can read it. But if you are also interested in presenting something in Germany, France or Italy, for example, it would be better to publish a version of this logo in the corresponding native language as well. You have the same problem with digitized speech. Thus genuine multimedia documents like movies or audio documents can also be language-dependent. Observe that even 3D scenes may sometimes contain a few written words (for example, names of shops in a virtual shopping center).

22.5   Documents

After you have decided on a collection hierarchy and inserted a few collections, you may want to insert information (that is, **documents**) into the empty skeleton. Again you may either do this interactively using a Hyper-G client or use the tools provided with your server installation to insert documents from the command line or from scripts. Hyper-G is a so-called genuine hypermedia system which means that you can

- insert every kind of media into the server and

- create hyperlinks in nearly any kind of document (including movies, PostScript and 3D scenes).

By the way, a recent investigation on the "Yahoo!" Web server (a very well-known Web directory service) showed that 80% of the survey respondents are male, with an average age of 35, an average salary of US$35 000, and – what is rather important in this case – with a 14.4 kbit modem. Remember that loading video and audio streams as well as big images and rich textured VRML scenes is a very time-consuming task with a 14.4 modem!

Therefore we suggest only using relatively small well-compressed images on your "Welcome Pages" to give the user the chance to get some basic information out of your site without having to wait for a long time. Here "small" does not mean the size of the image on the display, but the size in bytes.

Video and audio streams are usually the biggest, so make sure that the user knows that a link is pointing to such a large file. If possible, add the size of the file to the hyperlink text. If you use Acrobat/PDF or PostScript files, try – if it is not too much work – to provide also an HTML text version for those who do not have fast Web access. Don't forget that, especially in Europe, telephone fees are rather high and modem connections can be very expensive.

With all these considerations for slow access, observe that Hyper-G is also useful in fast LANs where such restrictions may not apply.

22.5.1   Hyperdocument authoring guidelines

The **construction of hyperdocuments** requires somewhat different precepts to the writing of traditional linear reports and essays. Here are seven rules of thumb for creating good hyperdocuments:

(1) **Perceivable structure**. Design hyperdocuments to have a firm, perceivable structure, so that readers can form a reliable mental map of the hyperdocument.

(2) **Self-contained nodes**. Individual nodes should be as self-contained as possible, since few assumptions can be made about where readers have jumped in from. This applies both to the content and to the title of a node.

(3) **Manageable chunks**. Individual pieces of text should be no longer than the equivalent of a few printed pages, and typically only a few paragraphs. Longer texts become unmanageable and require excessive scrolling, unless linking within the text is used.

(4) **Reuse existing resources**. Overlapping hyperdocuments, for example a reference manual and a tutorial, can often share some of the same underlying chunks of material.

(5) **Cite rather than copy**. References to other hyperdocuments are generally preferable to copies, since copies can become outdated.

(6) **Avoid the "here" syndrome**. Texts should be readable despite any hyperlinks.

> *The* **Harmony Tutorial** *is now available.*

is infinitely preferable to:

> *The Harmony Tutorial is now available by clicking* **here**.

particularly when the link display has been turned off, when reading a printed hard-copy version of the document, or for users accessing the document with a nongraphical, terminal-style client with no mouse. Furthermore, as Hyper-G provides automatic link management, the link itself is removed automatically when its destination is deleted, but the underlying text is not.

(7) **Sign your work**. In a multi-author environment, the author's signature (a link to a personal hyperdocument) adds a friendly touch.

22.5.2 Text documents

Usually, **text documents** in Hyper-G are inserted in the well-known HyperText Markup Language (HTML). HTML is defined in terms of the ISO Standard Generalized Markup Language (SGML). HTML markups capture the *logical* structure of a text; formatting and layout is done later by the viewing application. If you really need to have a special layout for your information, or layout is a very important property of your application, we suggest using either PostScript or PDF instead of HTML.

In SGML, so-called **tags** are used to specify headings, indentation, emphasis, itemized lists, paragraph breaks, and so on. For links within the text documents, anchor tags are used. Start tags are delimited by $<$ and $>$ and end tags by $</$ and $>$.

Ampersand ($\&$) and less than ($<$) are special characters in SGML and must be escaped (entered as mnemonic entity references) as `&amp;` ($\&$) and `&lt;` ($<$). Characters in the upper half of the ISO Latin-1 character set may be entered either as entity references: `&auml;`, `&szlig;`, `&copy;` (for example, by seven-bit editors) or directly.

Before you actually insert the text file into a Hyper-G database, the command `hgparse` can be used to verify that the text document is correct and to check the visual appearance of the text. This utility will check the SGML syntax of your text document and tell you if there are errors. Although Hyper-G does not insist on displaying only correct HTML, error-free documents will increase performance and platform independence.

22.5.3 Inline images

To display an image inside a text document (**inline image**), it has to reside somewhere in the Hyper-G database as an image document. A special tag is used to define an inline image within the text document. The image is inserted at the tag position and aligned with the current text line. The following graphic formats are supported: GIF (Graphics Interchange

Format), TIFF (Tag Image File Format), JPEG (Joint Photographic Experts Group) and XBM (X BitMap).

Inline images can be referenced directly within the text documents in the form of an HTML (<IMG...>) inline anchor. You normally do this either by uploading existing HTML documents or by inserting mass data into your server. A much more convenient method of inserting inline images provided by Hyper-G is to reference the images by "pointing and clicking" with the mouse using interactive authoring tools such as Harmony or Amadeus.

22.5.4   Image, movie, audio and scene documents

The "traditional" multimedia types are **images**, **movies**, **audio documents** and **3D scenes**. If you want to insert these kinds of documents you should first consider grouping them together with a descriptive text in a cluster (to give the user some information about the multimedia data). Generally, these documents are large in data volume and you should inform the user of this fact.

You should never put uncompressed images on your host: they take too long to download and use up too much disk space on your server. Try to compress your images using JPEG for photo-like images or paintings and GIF or (compressed) TIFF for drawings and charts. When using video, you should insert MPEG files rather than any other proprietary format. The same is true for audio files: use AU (SUN Audio) or WAV format. The use of common document types will increase platform independence: most WWW and Hyper-G clients will be able to view your documents.

Although you could insert any kind of 3D scene into your server, Hyper-G supports currently only two common file formats: Wavefront and the popular VRML (Virtual Reality Modeling Language). VRML will probably be (or maybe already is) the standard format for 3D scenes, therefore you should use this format rather than any other.

In Hyper-G you can insert links not only into text documents, but also into all multimedia types covered in this section. In images the links are displayed as geometric shapes. Movies represent "dynamic" data that changes its appearance over time. In order to have a hyperlink *follow* the pictures, you have to create several anchor shapes so that the link can be interpolated between the various frames (tracking motion). In 3D scenes you specify a number of polygons to serve as a link.

Image, movie, audio (sound) documents and 3D scenes can be inserted either by using Hyper-G clients such as Harmony and Amadeus or by using the Hyper-G command hginsdoc. Harmony and Amadeus also provide sophisticated tools to create, edit and delete hyperlinks in multimedia documents. For a description of the hginsdoc utility, see Section 25.2.3; for information on hypermedia authoring using Hyper-G clients see Chapter 23 for Harmony and Chapter 24 for Amadeus.

22.5.5   PostScript and PDF documents

If layout is important for your hypermedia application you should use either **PostScript** or **Acrobat/PDF** for your textual information. In Hyper-G you can also have hyperlinks in

PostScript documents, therefore you are not forced to convert to PDF if you want to make use of interlinked printable WYSIWYG documents.

Keep in mind that PostScript was designed as a printer language and therefore it has some shortcomings concerning output on display devices. PDF was designed by Adobe to reduce these shortcomings and to provide a device-independent and portable document format. PDF is often referred to as the "Acrobat" format. This is not quite correct: PDF is the "Portable Document Format" and Acrobat is the name of Adobe's PDF software family (Adobe's PDF viewer is called Acrobat Reader).

To insert a PostScript or PDF file into Hyper-G use the insert dialog of Harmony or Amadeus. You can also use the `hginsdoc` command on the command line or in scripts.

22.5.6 Generic documents

If you want to insert special data types which are not directly supported by Hyper-G such as HM-Card (see Chapter 27), Excel spreadsheets or MIDI (Musical Instrument Digital Interface) files you should import them as **generic documents**.

Each generic document has to be associated with an application. This is done by specifying the `SubType` field of a generic document. It is also possible to pass arguments to the application. This is done by using the `Arguments` field.

You should keep in mind that users will want to use the associated application on their own machine and may have to be informed how to load a generic document. One way to do this might be to insert a descriptive `CollectionHead` document into the collection containing the generic documents.

If generic documents are accessed with Harmony the user should specify the appropriate application by defining `Harmony*ExternalViewer.Generic.SubType` in the Xresource file. Generic documents are piped by Harmony into standard input.

If Amadeus is used for accessing generic documents the association between subtype and application has to be defined, too.

For WWW clients the corresponding MIME (Multipurpose Internet Mail Extensions) type will be `application/x-SubType`. You have to define this MIME type and associate it with so-called **helper applications**. Using either a Macintosh or Microsoft Windows you will have to define everything in the preferences of your WWW client. Using the UNIX operating system, you will have to place a file called `.mailcap` into your home directory that holds the MIME types and the filenames and command line parameters of the associated helper applications.

For very special document formats it is possible to add a `MimeType` attribute to the generic object. The gateway to the WWW will hand this information as is through to Web browsers such as Netscape and Mosaic. This facility makes it very easy to handle even exotic data formats within Hyper-G.

22.6   CGI objects and programs

The **Common Gateway Interface**, or **CGI**, is a standard for interfacing external applications with information servers, such as Hyper-G or other Web servers. A **CGI program** is executed on the server in real time, so that it can process some input and generate dynamic information for output. A detailed description and documentation for the Common Gateway Interface can be found at the "Hoohoo" server run by the NCSA HTTPd Development Team under URL `http://hoohoo.ncsa.uiuc.edu/cgi/`.

22.6.1   CGI objects

In the Hyper-G database, CGI programs are referenced by `CGI objects` which contain the name of the CGI program within the `Path` attribute. In general the `Path` attribute of a CGI object starts with `cgi-bin/` and is followed by the name of the corresponding CGI program (for example, `Path=cgi-bin/prog-cgi` for the program with name `prog-cgi`). Optionally the program name is followed by extra path information `/extra-path` and/or a query string `?query`.

Each time a client requests a CGI object the server will execute the corresponding CGI program in real time. The output of the program will go more or less directly to the client.

CGI objects are created interactively using authoring tools such as Harmony or Amadeus with the `insert` command. The `hginsdoc` tool allows you to insert such objects as well.

22.6.2   CGI programs

In Hyper-G the **CGI programs** need to reside outside the database in the special server directory `/usr/local/Hyper-G/dcserver/cgi/cgi-bin`. This directory is normally under direct control of the Hyper-G server administrator (usually the UNIX user `hg-system`), prohibiting normal users, who have no write access to this directory, from creating CGI programs. A CGI program can be written in any language that allows it to be executed on the server system. For example, you can use a scripting language like Perl or any UNIX shell or a programming language such as *C* or *C++*. We recommend that you write CGI scripts instead of programs since they are easier to modify and maintain than a typical compiled program.

In order to pass data about the information request from the server to the program, the server uses environment variables which are set when the server executes the CGI program. The following environment variables are set:

`SERVER_SOFTWARE` The name and version of the server software.

`SERVER_NAME` The server's hostname, DNS alias, or IP address.

`GATEWAY_INTERFACE` The revision of the CGI specification (for example, `CGI/1.1`).

`SERVER_PROTOCOL` The name and revision of the server protocol.

SERVER_PORT The port number to which the request was sent.

REQUEST_METHOD The method with which the request was made.

PATH_INFO The extra path information, as given by the CGI object.

SCRIPT_NAME A virtual path to the program being executed.

QUERY_STRING The information which follows the ? in the "Path" Attribute of the CGI Object or query information (for example, form input).

REMOTE_HOST The hostname making the request.

REMOTE_ADDR The IP address of the remote host making the request.

AUTH_TYPE The protocol-specific authentication method used (for example, Hyper-G).

REMOTE_USER The Hyper-G username retrieved from the server.

REMOTE_IDENT The remote username retrieved from the server.

CONTENT_TYPE The content type of the data.

CONTENT_LENGTH The length of the said content as given by the client.

HTTP_ACCEPT The MIME types which the client will accept.

HTTP_USER_AGENT The browser the client is using to send the request.

HTTP_REFERER The URL which referenced this program.

CGI programs send their output to standard output (stdout) and can return different document types. They can send back an HTML text, an image or perhaps even an audio document. In order for the client to know this, the CGI program must tell the server what type of document it is returning. CGI requires you to place a short standard MIME header on the output. This header consists of text lines terminated by a blank line. For example, to send back HTML to the client, the output should read:

```
Content-type:    text/html
<HTML><HEAD>
<TITLE>.....
```

When you write CGI programs, make sure any files are accessed by absolute path, that is, beginning from the root of the file system!

22.6.3 Decoding FORMs with CGI

CGI programs may be used to process the contents of fill-out forms which are specified by the FORM tag within an HTML document:

```
<FORM ACTION="url"> ...   </FORM>
```

The ACTION attribute is the URL of the CGI object which represents the corresponding program to which the form contents will be submitted. There are two methods which can be used to submit the contents of forms. These methods are GET and POST. If the form has no METHOD attribute or METHOD="GET" in its FORM tag, the CGI program will receive the form input in the environment variable QUERY_STRING. If the form has METHOD="POST", the CGI program will receive the form input on standard input (stdin). The server will not send an EOF on the end of the data; instead the environment variable CONTENT_LENGTH should be used to determine how much data should be read from stdin. It is a general recommendation to use the POST method with fill-out forms.

For example, to receive the form input on stdin in the CGI script prog-cgi, the form should specified with:

```
<FORM METHOD="POST" ACTION="/cgi-bin/prog-cgi"> ...</FORM>
```

22.7 Remote objects

On Hyper-G servers, all links are stored in an object-oriented database to provide link consistency. This consistency is extended over the whole Web of Hyper-G hosts as far as possible. Observe that some inconsistencies, such as when one server is temporarily down, cannot be resolved satisfactorily.

Links are consistent to the point when you leave the Hyper-G network, that is, when you access a so-called **remote object**. Remote objects are pointers to documents stored on other information systems that are directly supported by Hyper-G (WWW, Gopher, FTP and so on).

If you do not want to "see" your remote objects within the collection hierarchy, we suggest that you create a cluster and insert both the document that has a link to the remote object and the remote object itself into this cluster. Having done this specify the attribute PresentationHints=Hidden for the remote object and it will not be displayed when a user selects the cluster: it will only be seen within the collection browser if you open the cluster manually like a collection by using the children command in either Harmony or Amadeus.

22.7.1 Links to other Hyper-G servers

You may notice that above your root collection there is a (virtual) collection called hyper root. The children of this collection are the other Hyper-G servers your server knows about. In fact, your server should have information about all other servers located outside firewalls and should be "interested" in being known by other servers (there is a special server-to-server protocol that ensures that). Note that it may take some time after you first start your server before your server shows up!

Using a Hyper-G client you may navigate through the collection hierarchies of other Hyper-G servers either from the `hyper root` or by using a Hyper-G URL in the `Go to` command. When you find a useful collection or document somewhere, you may use the `copy to collection` command to create a pointer to that information in your local collection hierarchy. You just need to enter the name of the collection where this copy should be put.

22.7.2   Links to FTP, Gopher, WWW and WAIS servers

Pointers to FTP, Gopher, WWW and WAIS servers, as well as Telnet sessions, can be created interactively using the `insert` command. Choose the appropriate (remote) document type. Depending on the protocol, supply your additional information. The `hginsdoc` tool allows such remote objects to be inserted as well. For a concise description of `hginsdoc`, see Section 25.2.3.

When making links to other information systems it is clearly not possible to have any real link consistency. All Hyper-G can do is to provide a special type `remote object` that lets you know when you leave the Hyper-G environment. Hyper-G implements remote objects as a special document type for mainly three reasons:

- link consistency up to the point of remote links;

- representation of outside-hyperlinks in navigation tools like the collection browser or the local map;

- being able to search for remote links (using title and keyword search).

If you refer to remote documents in HTML texts and you insert these texts into Hyper-G, then the system will create all remote objects for you. The fact that you do not have to create remote objects yourself does not mean that they are not there. They still keep up as much consistency as possible and help you to navigate through hyperspace.

22.8   Hyperlinks

In Hyper-G all links are stored in an object-oriented database. A hyperlink consists of a *source anchor*, the visible representation of the link, and a *destination anchor* which can be used to specify a document or only a part of it as the destination of the link. Anchors may appear anywhere in any kind of document and they may be arbitrarily nested and overlapping.

If the target document does not exist (yet), an "open" link is inserted into the database. Open links are not shown when accessing the source document. Every time a new document is inserted, it is matched against the open links for the corresponding collection subtree. If a matching link is found, the link is closed (that is, it is now visible and you can follow it from the source to the destination). This feature allows us to insert a number of documents with circular references in any order easily. Also, when a document is deleted the links pointing to it are marked as open and can no longer be selected by the source documents. However, when a document with the same title is inserted into the same collection, the links are restored again.

A destination anchor may specify an area of a document. The default destination anchors for text, image, movie and audio are the entire document, for PostScript the first page and for a 3D scene (VRML) the default camera position. You can give a title to destination anchors so that you can search for them, put them into collections or clusters and attach links to them.

In text documents, hyperlinks can be created, as is common in HTML, by using an HREF reference to a URL. Of course, you can also use Hyper-G authoring tools such as Harmony and Amadeus to create your links interactively by point-and-click methods. With these applications it is very easy to make source and destination anchors even in multimedia documents such as videos, PostScript and VRML documents. See Chapters 23 and 24 for details.

Hyper-G provides a *connection-oriented* protocol, therefore it is not a performance problem to fetch many small parts of a document rather than one large document. Especially if you insert long text documents, you should think about splitting the documents into smaller pieces and providing some kind of simple navigation within the text pieces (previous – contents – next). It is much easier for users to handle small interlinked pieces of information than to read big documents.

If you create a link to a collection that contains a `CollectionHead` document, following the link will result in displaying both the collection list and the document.

22.9   Home collections

The home collection of one user is not the same as the popular "home page." Ordinary home pages are more like a public "welcome page" than a home page.

In Hyper-G we can separate the one from the other. In a home collection only the owner is allowed to read and write (by default) and therefore it can be used as a kind of personal Web organizer. Hyper-G also provides public "welcome pages" that are accessible to all users on the Web.

22.9.1   Creating home collections

If you are a user with system privileges (for example, the Hyper-G Server Administrator) you should first insert a new collection with a title, for example "First_Name Family_Name's Home Collection" into the department's home collection. You should give this collection the name ~username (for example, ~hmaurer for the user hmaurer) and the rights attribute R:u username;W:u username. Only the user is allowed to read and write in this collection.

If you want to allow the user to change the attributes (Title, Rights, SortOrder, ...) of the home collection itself you should change the author of this collection to `username`.

The second step is to associate the home collection name with the username. This is done with the `haradmin` or `hgadmin` tool by editing the user and adding the name of the home collection to the username. Now the home collection is created and the user can use it for private purposes.

22.9.2   Using home collections

If Hyper-G users are auto-identified (see Section 14.8) when starting a Hyper-G client, the associated home collection is their default entry point.

Identified Hyper-G users address their home collection by selecting `Home` in the navigate menu of the Hyper-G clients or the appropriate icon at the beginning of each document if they are using a WWW client. The "Home" for anonymous users is usually the server entry point!

Thus your home collection can be used as your personal Web organizer: you can store your Email addresses, your hotlist and bookmarks, your favorite FTP server addresses and even an archive of Emails in there. All this resides on the server side and therefore is independent of the clients you use.

You can structure your "Home" nicely by using collection hierarchies and you can create and edit even those documents that are intended to be placed on your welcome page within your home collection. When you have done the editing you only have to "move" the document to your welcome page to make it publicly accessible.

Adding an interesting document found on any Hyper-G, WWW or Gopher server as a bookmark (or to the hotlist) is performed by copying this document into the personal home collection. Removing such a bookmark is done by unlinking this document from the home collection. All Hyper-G clients support the `copy to collection` and `unlink from collection` function!

22.10   Advanced structuring

Hyper-G is one of the first second-generation hypermedia systems, providing **genuine hypermedia and sophisticated information management and structuring facilities**. Structuring means providing data in such a way that people can:

- find the information they are searching for very quickly,

- navigate through the information space without getting lost, and

- provide and maintain their own data on the Web in a very easy way (multiple users and groups on one server).

The Hyper-G way of doing this is to have multiple applications created by multiple users on the same host. This approach is possible because Hyper-G provides advanced structuring facilities and its own security system. The advantage of managing information this way is that if people who have the same interests work together on one server, finding information about specific topics is much easier and faster.

22.10.1 Multi-collection hierarchies

One way to structure information so that it is easy to access and to define search scopes is to provide **multi-collection hierarchies**. This means that one document is a member of more than one collection. This approach can be rather useful if you have data that can be structured in multiple ways.

Let us consider an example: a staff directory of a big company or university would usually be divided into a number of sub-collections of reasonable size. However, rather than imposing one structuring regime (for example, by department) Hyper-G offers many structuring (and hence access) criteria without physically retaining more than one copy of the basic documents.

Thus, you can structure the directory either alphabetically (collections for A, B, C ...), by department, by position, by building, by room or you can use multi-collection hierarchies. Just put each personnel record initially into your A to Z collections and then link it to the collection of the corresponding department, position and so on. The data of the personnel

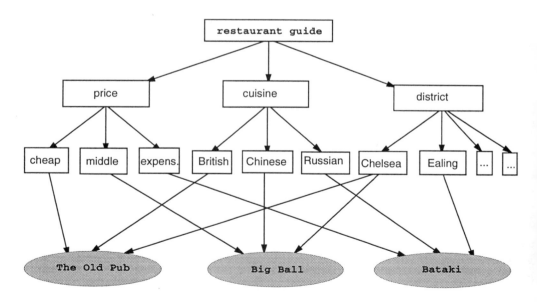

Figure 22.3   Multi-collection hierarchy used for a restaurant guide.

Figure 22.4   Apple's eWorld on the Web.

record itself is only stored once in the server, hence you have no problems editing its contents, but users can now choose how they want to navigate and search through your database.

Figure 22.3 shows another example of a multi-collection hierarchy: a restaurant guide where each restaurant can be accessed by price (cheap, middle, expensive), by cuisine (British, Chinese, Russian) or by district (Chelsea, Ealing, ...). Each restaurant is assigned the appropriate categories (for example, "The Old Pub," cheap, British, Chelsea).

The fact that the collection size (here the number of restaurants) can automatically be shown can help the user in choosing a place to dine.

22.10.2   Image maps

Another way to structure information is by providing either two- or three-dimensional **information spaces**. The easiest way to do so is to provide an "image map" which is just a map of a building or set of buildings. You can then add hyperlinks to this image that point to the different departments, rooms, shops and so on.

Of course, image maps do not have to be maps of buildings: they are also used for providing **context maps**. Context maps are images which represent the main topics of a hypermedia application. A popular example is Apple's eWorld online service (see Figure 22.4 and URL http://www.eworld.com/webcity/). You get an image map of a small village, where each building represents some kind of service. Diagrams of position hierarchies or technical figures are also common examples for context maps.

You should use colors in your image maps to make it easier to use. Do not use uncompressed image documents for image maps. An image that is big in byte-size can take a long time to download. Since not all viewers can display image maps, you should also provide alternatives such as a collection tree or a text representation. For example, Lynx is a pure text viewer: it was created as a WWW client for remote login and it is not capable of displaying images.

22.10.3   Virtual reality

The last approach for advanced data structuring we want to mention here is to provide three-dimensional information spaces using VRML scenes. In fact it is the same process as is used for image maps, the only difference being that the scenes shown are 3D: Hypermedia turning into **VR** (**virtual reality**), one might say.

Although this way of structuring information is already possible with VRweb, Hyper-G's VRML viewer, we want to suggest this as a future method unless Hyper-G servers are used in wide bandwidth LANs. The average bandwidth on the Web is still too small for VR applications; 3D hardware is still too expensive.

22.11   Examples of hypermedia applications

In the last section of this chapter we want to present a few examples of hypermedia applications that make use of advanced structuring facilities. Not all of them have been created using Hyper-G. However, we believe that structuring information using sophisticated authoring tools such as Harmony or Amadeus and a database that assures link consistency makes a system administrator's life a lot easier.

22.11.1   J.UCS – the *Journal of Universal Computer Science*

The *Journal of Universal Computer Science* (J.UCS) is an electronic journal published by Springer Publishing Co. Encouraged by Cris Calude from Auckland and Arto Salomaa from Turku the editor of this book started a new kind of online journal which tries to solve some problems observed in earlier attempts:

- All data has to be transmitted over very long distances.

- Special file formats are used for hypertext documents that authors normally are not aware of.

To overcome the first problem, the **replica option** of Hyper-G has been used. This option allows you to insert data into a Hyper-G server while letting the database know that this data is only a mirror, not the original source of the information. J.UCS is mirrored on a number of servers all over the world.

The solution to the second shortcoming was to use PostScript for submission and editing. Because of Hyper-G's ability also to have hyperlinks in PostScript documents it is relatively easy to link annotations to the original papers: to point to other contributions and so on, without modifying the original contributions.

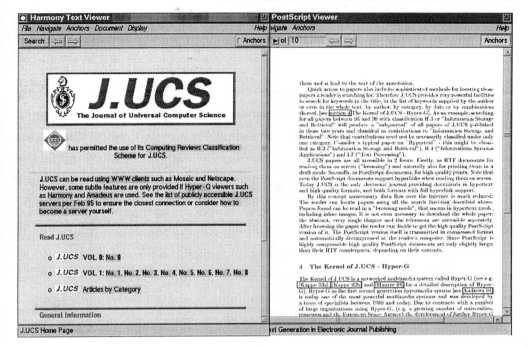

Figure 22.5   J.UCS – The Journal of Universal Computer Science.

Using OCR software J.UCS also offers a hypertext version, giving readers the choice of whether they want to read a paper in PostScript or in HTML format (see Figure 22.5 and URL `http://hyperg.iicm.tu-graz.ac.at/jucs`).

22.11.2   TUGinfo – Graz University of Technology information system

One of the main goals of the Hyper-G project is to provide a networked hypermedia system that can manage large amounts of data. The **TUGinfo** information server of the Graz University of Technology is a good example of such an information system (see Figure 22.6 and URL `http://hyperg.tu-graz.ac.at`). The database of the TUGinfo server holds about 85 000 documents of every kind of media (including PostScript, images and movies).

The data stored on the system includes university personnel records, bibliographic references for diploma theses and dissertations, lecture notes, information on courses, popular bibliographies such as SIGGRAPH and HCI and much more. The server is intended to be a valuable source of information for students, personnel and anonymous users from outside the university. Therefore multi-collection hierarchies are used to represent different views for

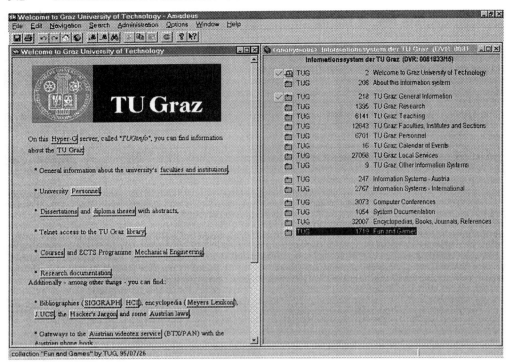

Figure 22.6   Graz University of Technology Information System.

different users and groups. The server will also be extended more and more in the direction of providing a digital library.

Much of the information provided is maintained in a very decentralized way. For example, the research documentation – which is also publicly available on this server – is created and maintained by the institutes themselves using their own Hyper-G accounts. A printed version of the research documentation can be obtained by exporting the respective collection from the Hyper-G server into a PostScript file.

This is exactly the way we propose to work: editing in a decentralized way over a network with all parties editing those parts of the information that they know best and then – if the need arises – converting the data on the server into printable format. There is a script provided by Hyper-G that lets you do this in a very easy way.

22.11.3   Earth Observation Guide and Directory Service – GDS

One of the best known Hyper-G information providers is the European Space Agency (ESA). The **GDS service** contains information about earth observation data, systems and applications and contains more than 50 000 documents which are maintained professionally. It carries details about ESA's and international remote sensing programs and satellite missions, and provides multimedia material to those working with the data products. GDS also carries information for newcomers who are interested in the science and exploitation of Earth observation.

See Figures 5.3 and 5.4 for example pages of the GDS service.

22.11.4   Musée des Arts et Métiers in Paris

Although our last example of a hypermedia application was not created using Hyper-G, the **Museé des Arts et Métiers** is one of the most beautiful and informative information servers on the Web. Although they do not seem to use any special server tools or search engines, they did the logical structuring of their information very well. The guide to this museum is a good example of a well-designed image map.

Their so-called "Visite guidée' is an image map which presents a detailed map of the building (see Figure 22.7; http://web.cnam.fr/museum/data/Visite_guidee.-html). The plan is a kind of abstract pseudo three-dimensional colored drawing that is projected into two-dimensional space. Although the image is rather big, its size in bytes is very

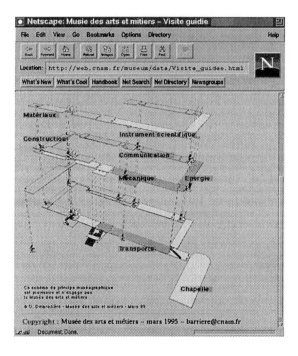

Figure 22.7   Museum of Arts and Crafts in Paris – Guided tour.

small. We think that the Conservatoire National des Arts et Métiers in Paris represents one of the few information providers on the Web that did a good job in providing a clickable image map for advanced navigation. By mentioning this explicitly we pay tribute to them.

22.12 Further reading

A good choice for those who want to know more about Authoring for the Web and also other types of Web services is *Managing Internet Information Services* by Liu *et al.* (1994). It also includes documentation on HTML. In *The World Wide Web Unleashed* (December and Randall, 1994) the section "Weaving a Web" covers provider issues in detail. For information provider materials the URL: `http://www.w3.org/hypertext/WWW/Provider/-Overview.html` ("Putting Information onto the Web") is a good starting point. The "Style Guide for Online Hypertext" from Tim Berners-Lee can also be found there.

23 Authoring with Harmony

Keith Andrews

This chapter explains how to use **Harmony's extensive authoring facilities** to structure and manage information on a Hyper-G server. Harmony has facilities to insert new objects into a Hyper-G server, edit or delete existing ones and create or remove links between documents. The collection structure can be manipulated and objects moved between collections or reused in multiple collections. Harmony also supports annotations and structured discussions. In contrast to browsing, where a user can access the server anonymously, authoring usually requires that the user be identified and have the appropriate access rights; the Harmony dialogs for identification and changing passwords are described in Section 15.7.

23.1 Object and document creation

For the purposes of the following explanation, let us assume that a hypermedia collection containing a short tour of the city of Graz is to be created. A Hyper-G user `kandrews` has been created and this user has a home collection and full access rights to it. It is common practice to work on draft versions of hyperdocuments in one's home collection, possibly protected from outside access, and later move or hook them into an appropriate location in the collection structure and make them visible. Figure 23.1 shows Keith Andrews' home collection just prior to starting work on this task.

23.1.1 Creating collections and clusters

The **Harmony Insert Dialog** is used both to create completely new Hyper-G objects and to upload files accessible on the UNIX file system onto the server. Figure 23.2 shows the Insert Dialog being used to create a collection for the tour of Graz. The collection is called `A Short Tour of Graz` in English and `Eine kurze Reise durch Graz` in German. The author (or owner) of the collection is `kandrews`, and the collection is protected so that only members of the group `iicm` can read it initially. A reasonably intuitive name, `graztour`, has been assigned to the collection, because this name will later appear in URLs referencing the collection.

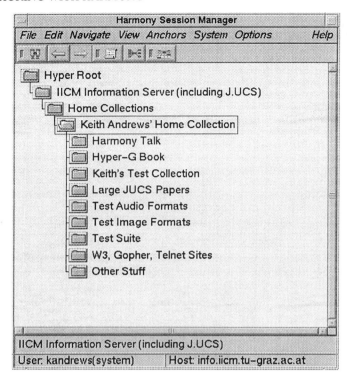

Figure 23.1   Home collection where objects will be inserted.

By default, objects are inserted into the current collection at the time the dialog was activated. A different collection can be specified by selecting the desired collection and pressing the Insert Dialog's `Current` button. Keywords and a description could also be associated with the collection, but these have been left empty for the time being. When the `Insert` button is pressed, this new empty collection is inserted as a sub-collection of `Keith Andrews' Home Collection`:

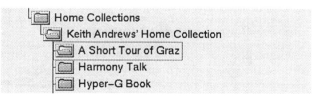

Creating clusters is equally straightforward. In Figure 23.3 a cluster is being inserted into the previously created collection. The cluster has been given both English and German titles and has inherited the same access rights as its parent collection (by default, the Insert Dialog initializes the Rights attribute to the same value as the new object's parent collection).

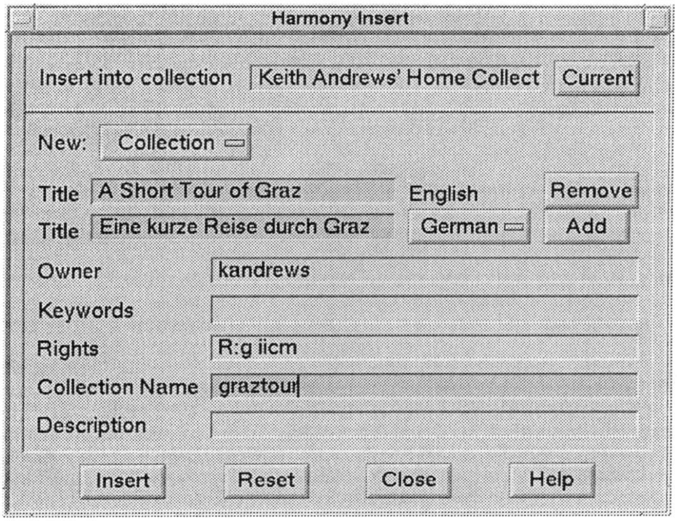

Figure 23.2   Inserting a collection with the Harmony Insert Dialog.

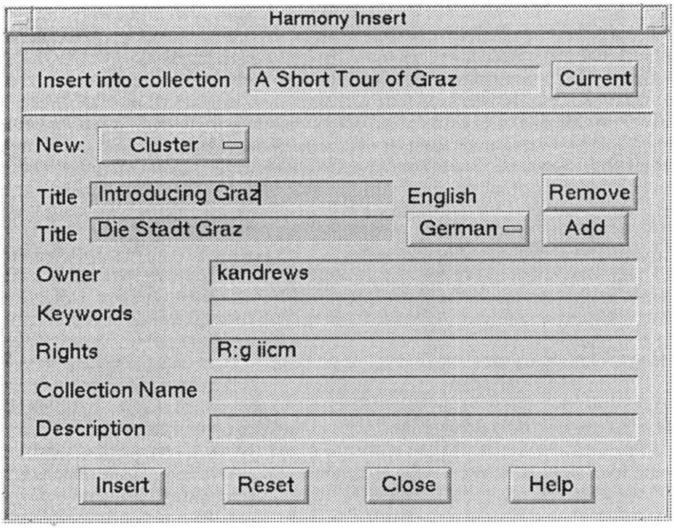

Figure 23.3   Inserting a cluster.

Titles in additional languages could be assigned using the Add button. The cluster is created and inserted into the collection A Short Tour of Graz:

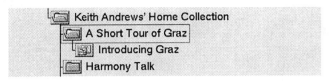

Of course, at this point the newly created cluster is still empty – it is time to learn how to upload documents onto the server.

23.1.2   Inserting documents

By choosing New: Text in the Insert Dialog's selector, text documents can be inserted into the Hyper-G server. The text can either be uploaded from an existing file or created from scratch in an editor. Figure 23.4 shows the text document graz-en.html being uploaded

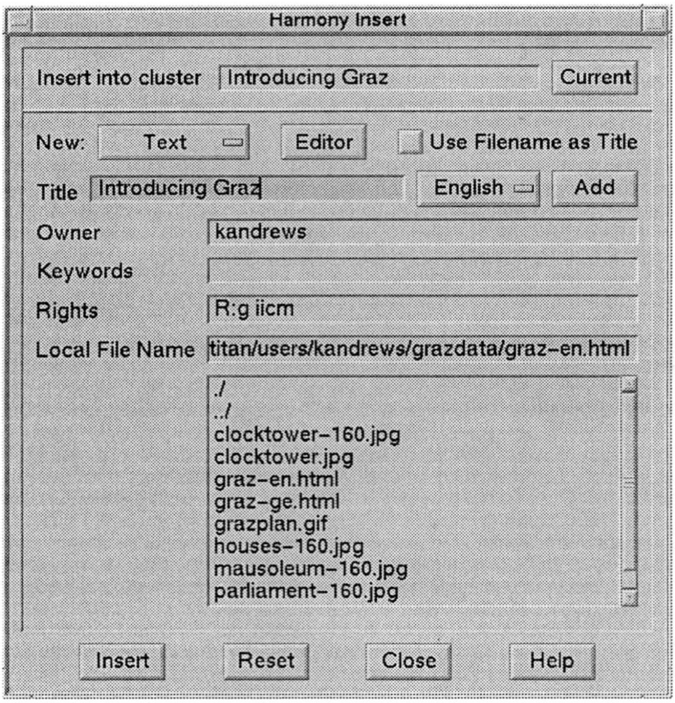

Figure 23.4   Uploading a text document.

from the user's UNIX home directory into the previously created cluster. Text documents are generally written in HTML, although Hyper-G's original text format HTF is still supported. In the near future, support will be available for arbitrary SGML documents with appropriate DTDs and style sheets. Clicking on the `Editor` button rather than specifying a filename would cause Harmony to start an empty editor for the new document, rather than uploading it from a file.

Since this particular text is written in English, only an English title has been assigned. After repeating the same Insert procedure for the equivalent German text `graz-ge.html`, the cluster now contains two member text documents:

These documents can be displayed in the **Harmony Text Viewer** like any other text documents by simply double-clicking their icons. Figure 23.5 shows the first two paragraphs of the English text.

Let us continue the example collection about Graz. Three small JPEG images will now be uploaded into the previously created cluster `Introducing Graz` to be used later as inline images. The Insert Dialog for uploading an image looks like the one in Figure 23.6. Since these images are independent of language, they are given titles in both English and German. The word `Inline` in the titles is purely for the author's information, it is not interpreted by the system in any special way. After uploading all three JPEG images, the cluster now has five member documents:

At this point, each image can be inspected in the **Harmony Image Viewer**, as illustrated in Figure 23.7 for the Clock Tower image. Note that the user has turned the AutoFit feature off, so as not to distort the small inline image by overly enlarging it.

The Insert Dialog can, in fact, be used to insert any kind of document or collection. The new object's type is simply chosen from among the choices in the New selector. The **Harmony Session Manager** performs a rudimentary magic number check on documents prior to uploading them, so as to detect when a document would be uploaded as the wrong type, for example an image declared as a text document. In such cases a warning dialog appears.

PostScript documents and 3D models, which may be very large in uncompressed form but usually respond well to compression, are generally compressed (GNU gzip or UNIX compress) externally by the user before inserting them into the Hyper-G server. Transparently to the end user, clients retrieve the compressed files across the Net, hence saving bandwidth, and decompress them locally.

23.1.3   Creating remote objects

Remote objects include documents and directories on WWW, Gopher and FTP servers, and Telnet sessions to remote sites. Access to such remote objects from within a Hyper-G context is achieved by creating a Hyper-G **remote object** to represent the remote entity and specifying its attributes (such as Host and Port) accordingly.

To continue with our example, Bert Bos of the University of Groningen in Holland has, on his WWW server, a nice set of photographs of the Arsenal in Graz, which he took during

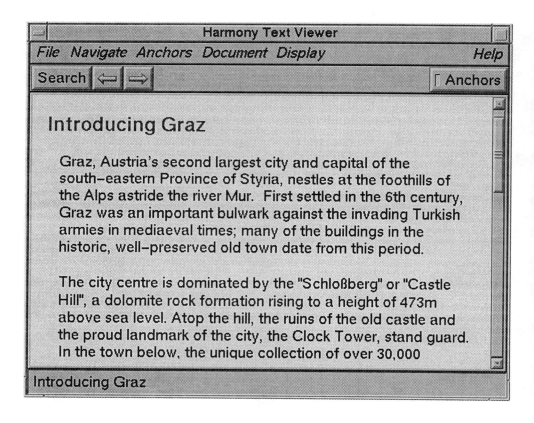

Figure 23.5   The newly uploaded text document.

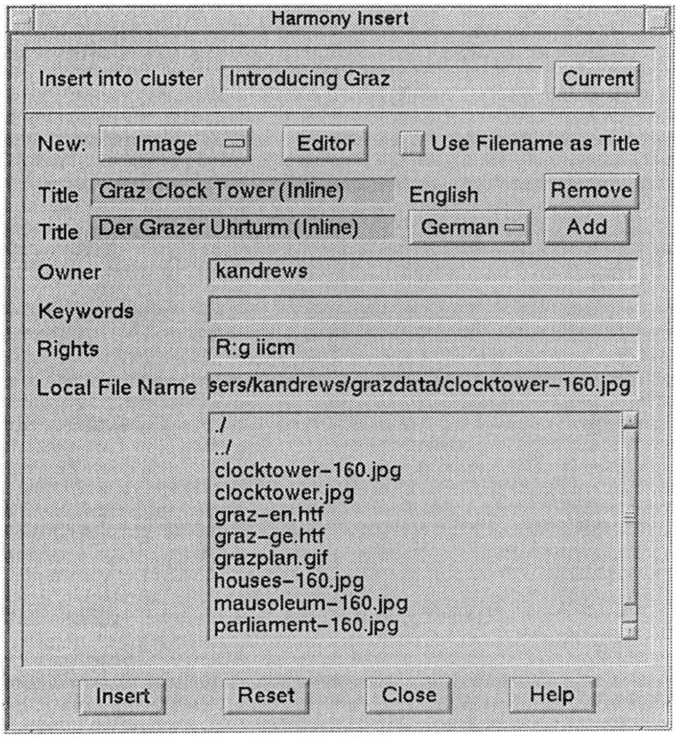

Figure 23.6   Inserting an image document.

his 1993 visit. Figure 23.8 shows the Insert dialog being used to create a reference to the remote WWW page introducing this set of photographs. The object appears in the collection structure as a new text document:

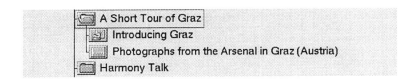

The object can now be accessed with Harmony or any other Web browser, as shown in Figure 23.9 using Netscape.

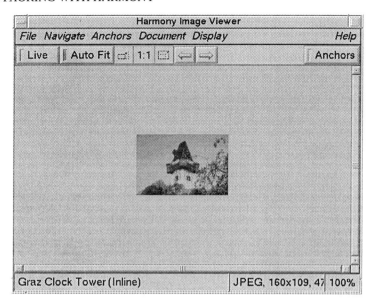

Figure 23.7   Inspecting the new image document.

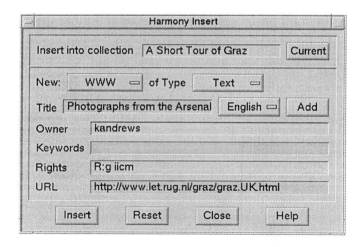

Figure 23.8   Inserting a remote WWW document.

23.2   Document editing

As well as facilities for uploading documents prepared in advance, Harmony provides for **interactively editing documents** already located on a Hyper-G server. Whereas interactive

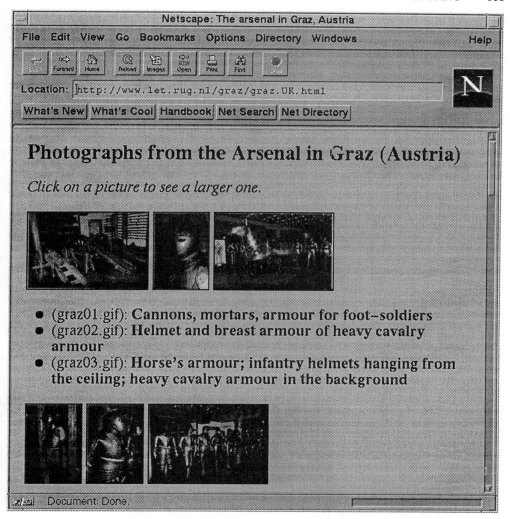

Figure 23.9   Viewing the remote WWW object just inserted.

link editing is possible in all supported document types (see Section 23.4), interactive content editing is currently implemented only for text and image documents, but will be extended to other document types in due course.

The general mechanism used by Harmony for document editing can be described informally as follows. When the Edit function is activated, the document viewer writes a temporary copy of the document it is displaying to a file and starts an external editor to edit the temporary file. Modifications to the temporary file (after saving to disk) can be optionally

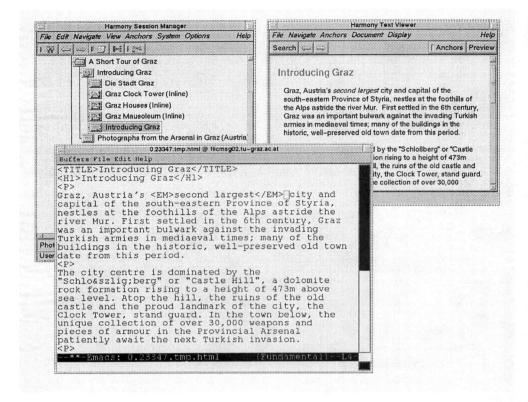

Figure 23.10   Editing a text with Emacs from the Harmony Text Viewer.

previewed in the document viewer. When the external editor is exited, the document viewer presents a dialog box asking the user whether or not the modified version of the document should be uploaded back to the Hyper-G server, replacing the original.

23.2.1 Editing text documents

The Harmony Text Viewer's **Edit** function starts the Emacs editor by default. Figure 23.10 shows Emacs being used to edit the English text about Graz. Having corrected a spelling mistake and emphasized the words *second largest*, the user has saved the file to disk (without exiting Emacs) and is previewing the modified document in the Text Viewer.

Harmony can, of course, be configured to use any editor for text documents, for example a dedicated HTML authoring tool such as AsWedit (as shown in Figure 23.11) or Symposia. To specify the desired editing tool, use the Text Viewer's editcommand Xresource:

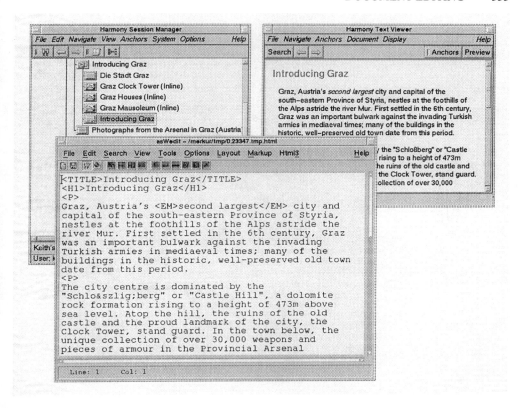

Figure 23.11   Editing a text with AsWedit from the Harmony Text Viewer.

```
Harmony.Text.editcommand:          asWedit
```

The name of the temporary file is appended to the command automatically.

When editing is finished and the external editor has been exited, the Harmony Text Viewer presents a dialog box asking the user whether or not to insert the modified version of the text document.

Hyperlinks in Hyper-G are not stored embedded in documents but externally in a separate link database. Anchor regions in a text document are defined by character offsets. To ensure that link anchors in a text remain associated with the same text region (word, phrase and so on) when a file is edited, they are merged into the temporary text file prior to editing. Hence, link anchors slide around with their associated regions as the text is edited. When editing is finished, the links are extracted and re-inserted into the Hyper-G link database, and the document per se is inserted back into the Hyper-G document server.

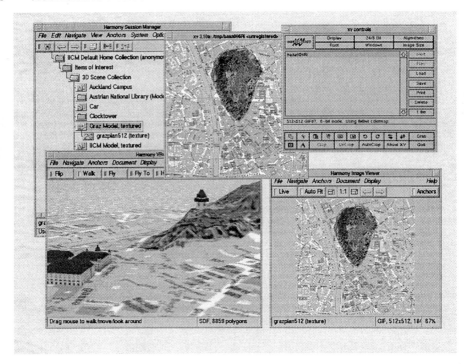

Figure 23.12   Editing an image with XV.

23.2.2   Editing image documents

Interactive **editing of images** is analogous to text editing. The image is written to a temporary file by the Harmony Image Viewer and an external editor is started. Figure 23.12 shows an image used as a texture in a 3D cityscape of Graz being edited with XV. When the editor is exited, the Image Viewer asks whether or not to upload the new image in place of the original version.

Hyperlinks in image documents are defined in terms of a virtual coordinate space, where (0,0) is the lower left corner of the image and (1,1) the upper right. Operations which do not change the aspect ratio of the image, such as making it brighter or saving in a different format, are perfectly safe. However, cropping or otherwise changing the aspect ratio of the image will cause link anchors in the image to slide, since the Image Viewer does not attempt to remap the positions of link anchors. In such cases, it is necessary to manually check and, if necessary, reposition any anchors in the image.

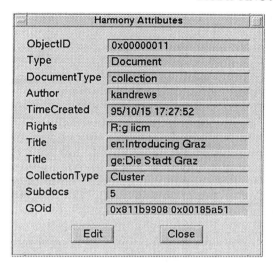

Figure 23.13   Harmony Attribute Window.

23.3   Modifying attributes

The attributes of a collection, cluster or document can be displayed in Harmony's **Attribute window** by right-clicking the corresponding object in the collection browser or alternatively via Session Manager or document viewer menus. Staying with our Graz example, the attributes for the cluster Introducing Graz are shown in Figure 23.13. This is the cluster we created previously as an introduction to our collection A Short Tour of Graz:

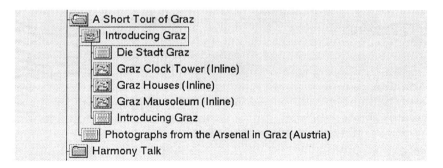

Clicking the Edit button puts the Attribute window into edit mode, as can be seen in Figure 23.14. The attributes are rearranged automatically, so that those which may be modified are at the bottom of the list. In the figure, the cluster is being specified as the collection head for the collection to which it belongs. This is achieved for any collection by setting the PresentationHints attribute CollectionHead for one member of the

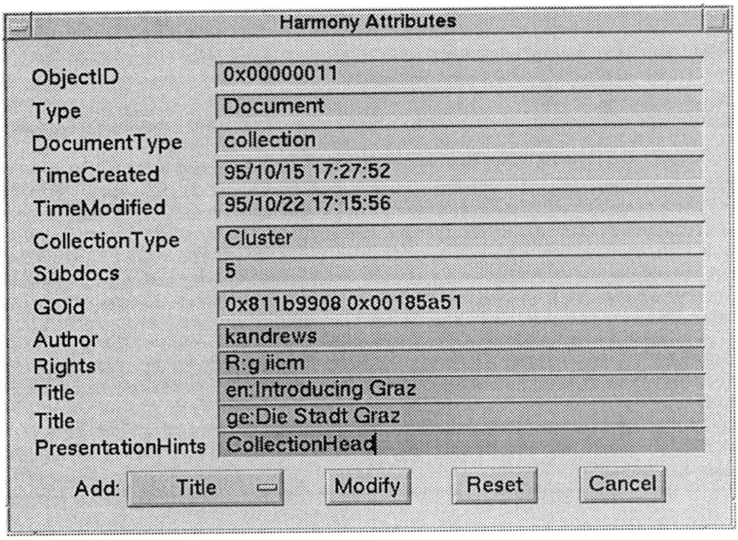

Harmony Attributes	
ObjectID	0x00000011
Type	Document
DocumentType	collection
TimeCreated	95/10/15 17:27:52
TimeModified	95/10/22 17:15:56
CollectionType	Cluster
Subdocs	5
GOid	0x811b9908 0x00185a51
Author	kandrews
Rights	R:g iicm
Title	en:Introducing Graz
Title	ge:Die Stadt Graz
PresentationHints	CollectionHead

Add: Title   Modify   Reset   Cancel

Figure 23.14   Editing attributes in the Attribute Window.

collection. From now on, when the collection A Short Tour of Graz is opened, the introductory cluster Introducing Graz will automatically be displayed.

A common structuring technique is to place small images being used as inline images inside the cluster where they are used, as was done in Section 23.1.2. However, when the cluster is accessed, the default presentation rules of a cluster would interpret each inline image as a separate image for display purposes, starting an Image Viewer for each one. This default behavior can be overridden by assigning the inline images the Hidden characteristic in the PresentationHints field. Henceforth, the inline images will only be displayed inline in the text and not also as images in their own right.

Other Hyper-G attributes, such as Title and Rights, are assigned and modified analogously. A detailed description of all Hyper-G object attributes is given in Appendix E.

23.4   Interactive link editing

Harmony has extensive features for the **interactive creation of hyperlinks**. Links in Hyper-G emanate from a source anchor (sensitive region) in a document and may point to a collection, a cluster, a whole document or a specific destination anchor in a document. The Harmony document viewers generally represent source anchors in pink and destination anchors in blue by default.

Anchors are Hyper-G objects in their own right and may possess attributes such as Title, Author and Rights. The position of an anchor is specified in the Position

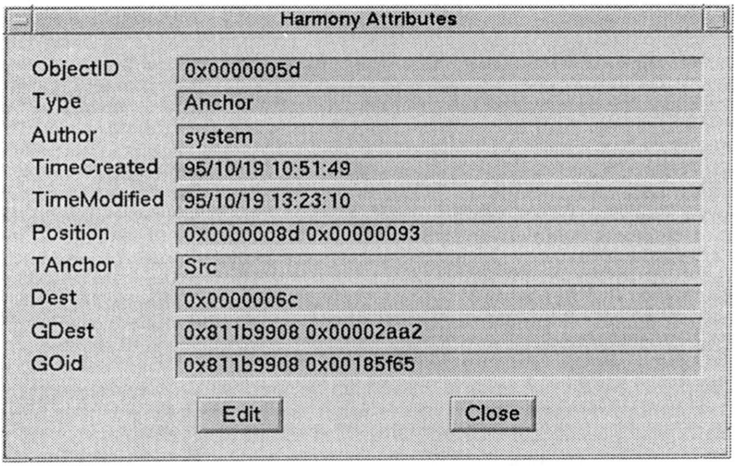

Figure 23.15   Attributes of an anchor object.

attribute of the anchor object. The format of entries in this field depends upon the type of document containing the anchor. An example of the attributes for a source anchor in a text document is shown in Figure 23.15.

The link creation process comprises four steps: defining a source anchor for the link, defining a destination anchor, assigning any link attributes, and then completing the link.

23.4.1   Creating links in text documents

Anchor regions in text documents are defined in terms of character offsets. In the example in Figure 23.15, the source anchor extends from character 141 to character 147 in the text (8d and 93 in hex respectively). Link anchors are defined interactively in the Harmony Text Viewer by selecting a region of text (for example, by dragging the mouse with the left or right button depressed) and defining the region as a source, destination, or inline source anchor. This is illustrated in Figure 23.16, where a source anchor is being specified from the word "Schloßberg" in the text. Activating the function **Define as Source** brings up **Harmony's Link Creator**, depicted in Figure 23.17. The source of the link has been entered in the corresponding **Source Anchor** box. The user has also defined the destination of the link to be a cluster called "The Castle Hill." Clicking the button `Create Link` completes the link and it can be followed immediately thereafter.

An appropriate destination was found in this case by searching the Hyper-G server, as can be seen in Figure 23.18 which illustrates the entire course of this sample link creation process. The actual definition of a destination anchor proceeds in a manner similar to defining a source anchor, with the special case that, by default, a destination anchor in a text document covers the whole document.

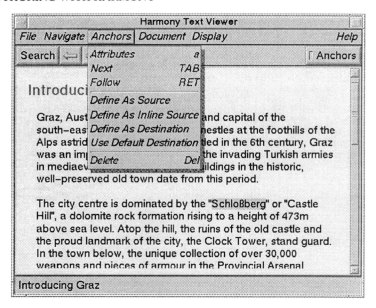

Figure 23.16   Creating a source anchor in a text.

23.4.2   Placing inline images in text documents

Hyper-G implements **inline images** in text documents simply as a special link of type `inline`. The procedure for placing inline images is identical to that for creating links. A region of the text is marked, immediately preceding which the image will be placed. In Figure 23.19, the word `Graz` has been selected and the image will be inserted directly before it. From the **Text Viewer menu**, this selection is then defined to be an inline source anchor, bringing up the Harmony Link Creator shown in Figure 23.20.

The destination of the inline link (that is, the image to be inlined) is now specified, and the inline link is created. The resulting text with inlined image is shown in Figure 23.21. The inline image can be centered by editing the text document and adding the appropriate tag.

Assuming that the user creates inline links to all three small images previously uploaded, the finished introductory document looks something like that shown in Figure 23.22.

23.4.3   Creating links in image documents

Anchor regions in image documents are defined in terms of a virtual coordinate space, where (0,0) is the lower left corner of the image and (1,1) the upper right. The image shown in Figure 23.23 has two source anchors (links) defined, a circle and a polygon, whose positions are defined in the `Position` attribute as follows:

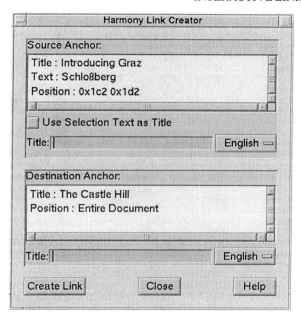

Figure 23.17   The Harmony Link Creator.

```
Circle 0.921321 0.283395 0.177331
Polygon 0.0734733 0.642748, 0.0734733 0.642748, ...
```

Link anchors are defined interactively by selecting an anchor shape (in the Anchors menu) and using the right mouse button to define the region. For rectangular, circular and elliptical anchor shapes, it is sufficient to drag and release the right mouse button to define the anchor region. For polygonal regions, each right mouse click defines a vertex of the polygon and a middle-click completes the polygon. Any freshly marked anchor region can be repositioned by Control-right-dragging the shape.

Once the anchor region is satisfactory, the region is defined as a source or destination anchor, and the Link Creator dialog appears. The procedure now continues in the same way as explained for text anchors.

A destination anchor in an image will cause the image to be panned so that the region of the image containing the anchor is in view. This is illustrated in Figure 23.24, where a link to a particular region of a large map of Graz has been followed.

23.4.4   Creating links in film documents

Anchors in film clips are created by specifying the position and size of an anchor region for a set of key frames; linear or spline interpolation is used to determine the position of an anchor

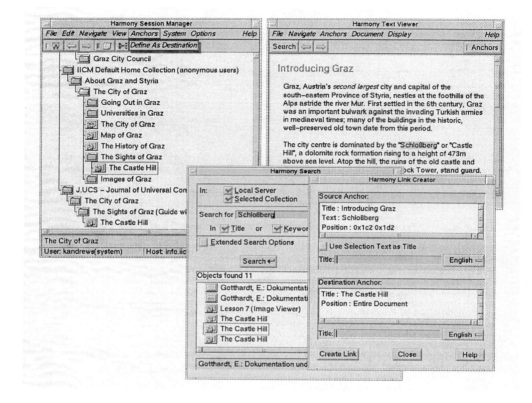

Figure 23.18   Typical link creation procedure in Harmony.

in between key frames. Anchors may be rectangular, circular or elliptical in shape. The sequence of screen shots in Figure 23.25 shows a circular link anchor being created to track the helmet of a piece of cavalry armor. The anchor's size and position are first specified for frame 1 of the film, then for frames 15, 30 and 45. The marked anchor region can be played back to check its effect and how it is interpolated between key frames. When a satisfactory result has been achieved, the marked region can be defined as either a source or destination anchor using the Anchor menu. In this particular example, an anchor was created with the following Position attribute:

```
Circle Linear 4:    1   0.45      0.675781   0.204084,
                   15   0.60625   0.667969   0.201556,
                   30   0.7875    0.695312   0.208885,
                   45   0.99375   0.703125   0.234791
```

A simplified form of anchor, namely a range of frames, can be specified for a destination anchor. Figure 23.26 shows frames 196 to 370 of the Arsenal film clip being defined as the destination of a link. The frame range can be marked approximately by right-dragging across

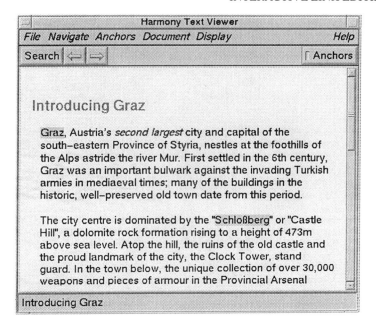

Figure 23.19   Placing an inline image.

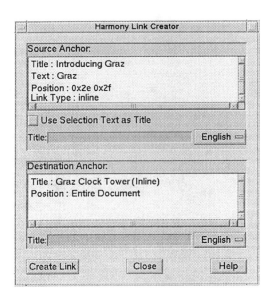

Figure 23.20   The Link Creator for an inline image.

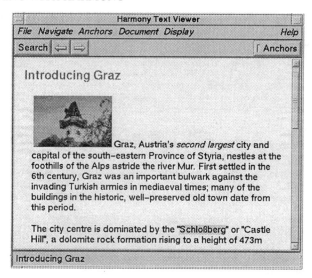

Figure 23.21   The inserted inline image.

the play bar, or exactly by entering the precise frames in the **Settings panel**.

23.4.5   Creating links in audio documents

An **anchor region in an audio document** is defined by a starting and ending position (time) in the audio stream. Currently, only destination anchors are supported, that is, links can be made to particular regions of an audio document. Figure 23.27 shows the **Harmony Audio Player** after a link has been followed to the latter part of the document.

The Audio Player must be set up to use NAS (the Network Audio System) in order to be able to process link anchors. When the Audio Player is configured to use a native audio play command (which is currently the default due to the lack of a widely installed audio server such as NAS), the audio stream is simply passed on to this external program and not examined further.

23.4.6   Creating links in PostScript documents

An anchor region in a PostScript document is a rectangular region defined in terms of PostScript page coordinates. A new region is marked by right-dragging the mouse. Figure 23.28 shows a destination anchor being defined in the Harmony PostScript Viewer to cover Figure 1.c of the paper. Source anchors are typically highlighted by colored frames, destination anchors by "downlighting" the rest of the current page. Anchors in a PostScript

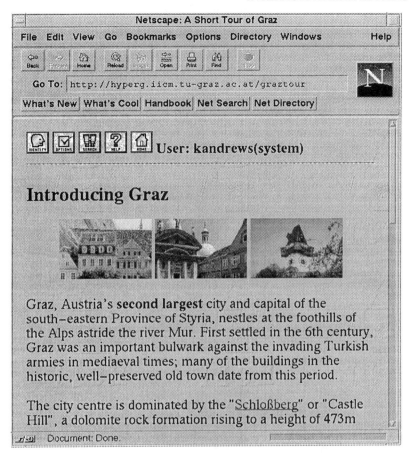

Figure 23.22   The finished introductory page with three inline images.

document may be repositioned and resized by Control-right-dragging the mouse. Dragging a corner or an edge of an anchor resizes it, dragging the interior repositions it. The repositioned link anchors can then be saved back into the server through the Anchors menu.

23.4.7   Creating links in 3D documents

In a **3D model**, source and destination anchors are conceptually distinct. A source anchor can be attached to an arbitrary part of a 3D model. In the Graz model shown in Figure 23.29, a source anchor is being created from the Clock Tower object in the model to more detailed information about the tower. The currently marked object is highlighted by drawing its bound-

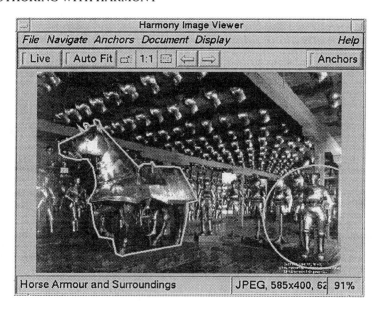

Figure 23.23   Source anchors in an image document.

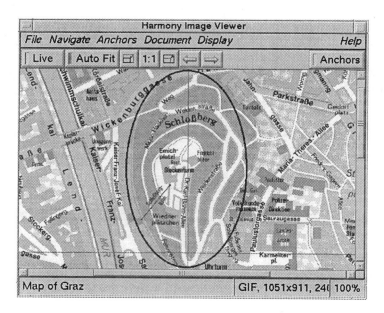

Figure 23.24   Elliptical destination anchor in an image document.

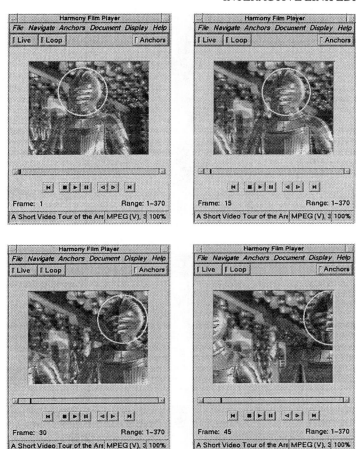

Figure 23.25   Creating an anchor in a film clip.

ing box.

A destination anchor, on the other hand, is not attached to part of a model, but instead indicates a specific camera position and orientation, that is, a specific view of the model. Destination anchors are defined by navigating to the desired viewing position and defining the current position as a destination anchor.

23.4.8   Link attribute modification

Since link anchors in Hyper-G are objects in their own right, they may possess attributes such as Title, Author and Rights. Selecting an anchor in a Harmony document viewer (by left-clicking) and choosing to display its attributes via the Anchors menu brings up Harmony's

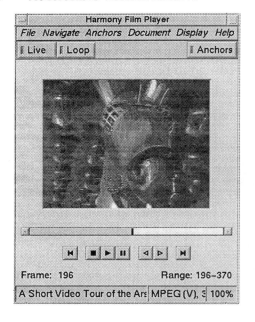
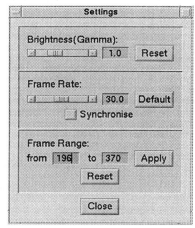

Figure 23.26   Frame range as a destination anchor.

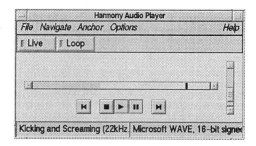

Figure 23.27   Destination anchor in an audio document.

standard Attributes window (see Section 23.3). The attributes shown in Figure 23.30 are those of the source anchor from the word Schloßberg which was created in Section 23.4.1. The default access rights allow the author of an anchor write access, and all other users read access. In our example, the author of the anchor is kandrews, and hence the anchor object's attributes may be edited, as shown in Figure 23.31, where a title has been added to the anchor.

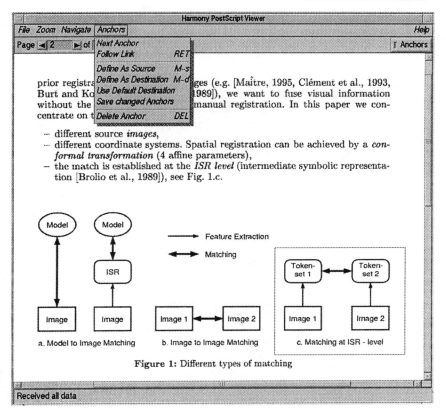

Figure 23.28   Creating a destination anchor in a PostScript document.

23.4.9   Link deletion

A link is **deleted** interactively by selecting its source anchor in the appropriate document viewer (left-clicking) and choosing the Delete item from the Anchors menu. In the Harmony Text Viewer, multiple anchors can be selected and then deleted in one operation by shift-left-clicking the anchors. Before actually performing the deletion, Harmony presents the confirmation box shown in Figure 23.32.

23.5   Structure editing

A prime characteristic of Hyper-G is its ability to structure information into collections and sub-collections in a manner orthogonal to referential hyperlinks. This helps alleviate disorientation by presenting a firm, perceivable structure to users. Harmony's facilities for creating

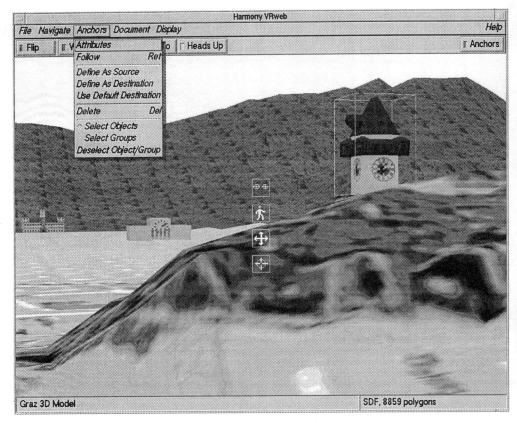

Figure 23.29 Creating a source anchor in a 3D model.

new collections were described in Section 23.1.1. Naturally, Harmony also has facilities for moving existing documents and collections between collections and for making documents and collections members of multiple parent collections.

23.5.1 Moving objects

Assuming that the A Short Tour of Graz collection has been completed and is now in a presentable form, the author may want to move it from his home collection into a publicly accessible collection. This is achieved with the Move command from the Edit menu, as shown in Figure 23.33. After the move operation, the collection has been removed from the home collection and made a member the collection named graz. This would also be the right time to adjust any access rights on the collection and its members so that anonymous users can

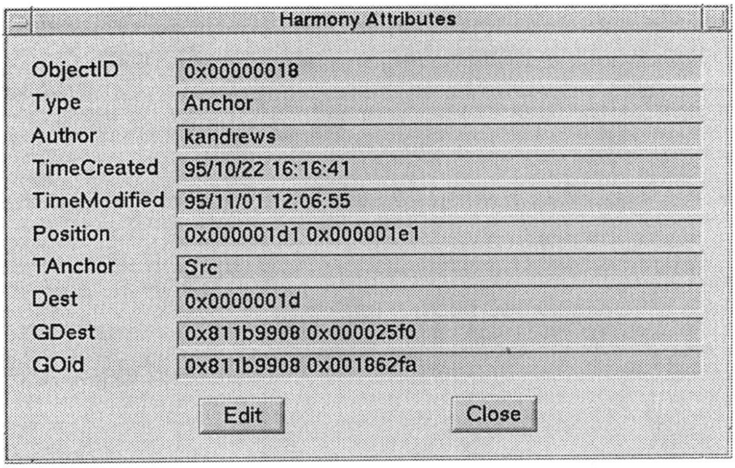

Harmony Attributes

ObjectID	0x00000018
Type	Anchor
Author	kandrews
TimeCreated	95/10/22 16:16:41
TimeModified	95/11/01 12:06:55
Position	0x000001d1 0x000001e1
TAnchor	Src
Dest	0x0000001d
GDest	0x811b9908 0x000025f0
GOid	0x811b9908 0x001862fa

Edit   Close

Figure 23.30   Attributes of the Schloßberg anchor object.

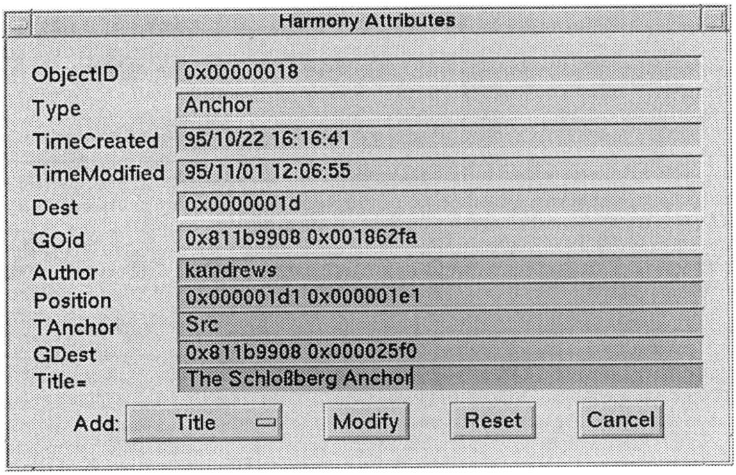

Harmony Attributes

ObjectID	0x00000018
Type	Anchor
TimeCreated	95/10/22 16:16:41
TimeModified	95/11/01 12:06:55
Dest	0x0000001d
GOid	0x811b9908 0x001862fa
Author	kandrews
Position	0x000001d1 0x000001e1
TAnchor	Src
GDest	0x811b9908 0x000025f0
Title=	The Schloßberg Anchor

Add: Title   Modify   Reset   Cancel

Figure 23.31   Editing the anchor's attributes.

read its contents.

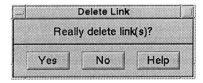

Figure 23.32   Link deletion confirmation box.

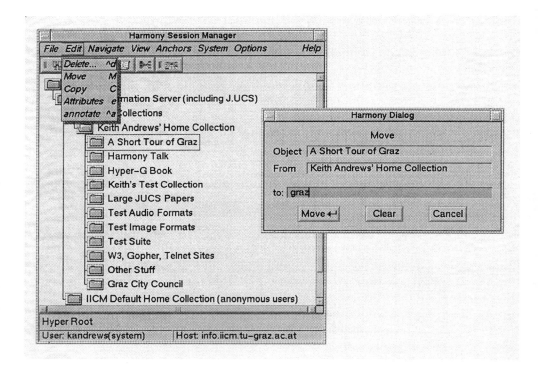

Figure 23.33   Moving a document or collection.

23.5.2   Copying objects

The alternative to moving an object is to **"copy"** it into an additional collection. The object then belongs both to the original collection and to the additional collection, and appears in both locations in the collection hierarchy. The term "copy" is somewhat misleading, because the object is not physically copied, it simply becomes a member of both collections (the same operation in HGTV is called "link"). Perhaps "join" or "insert" would be better names. The dialog box for the Copy operation is shown in Figure 23.34.

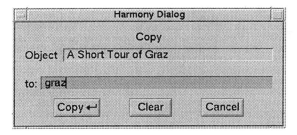

Figure 23.34   "Copying" a document or collection.

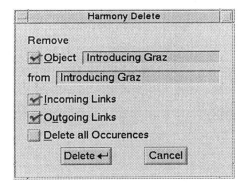

Figure 23.35   Deleting a document or collection.

23.6   Deleting objects

An object can be **deleted** interactively by selecting it and then activating the Delete function from the Edit menu. The **Harmony Delete window** shown in Figure 23.35 is presented. If the object belongs only to one collection, then it is physically deleted, and by default so are any incoming and outgoing links associated with it. If the object is a member of multiple parent collections, then deleting it simply removes it from the specified collection and has no further consequences. Specifying deletion of all occurrences forces the object's removal from all parent collections and its physical deletion. Currently, collections can be physically deleted only if they are empty, that is, their members must be deleted first.

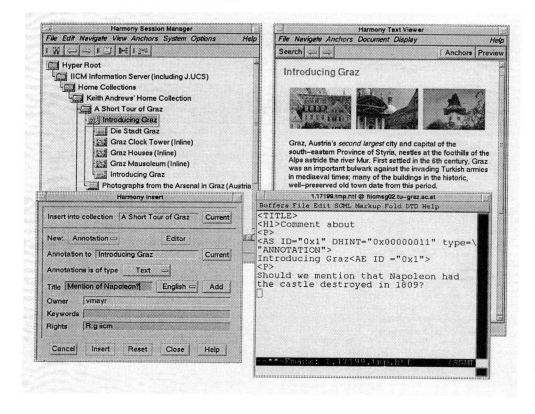

Figure 23.36   Creating an annotation to the `Introducing Graz` cluster.

23.7   Annotations

Conceptually, an **annotation** in Hyper-G is really just a special kind of link. Annotations are not restricted to being pieces of text, but can be documents of any type: they are associated with the collection, cluster or document upon which they comment by a link of type `Annotation`.

Annotations are created using a variant of the Harmony Insert dialog which was discussed in Section 23.1. To annotate an object, the object is selected and the `Annotate` function in the Harmony Session Manager's Edit menu is activated. Harmony presents the user with an Insert dialog pre-configured for inserting an annotation. The annotation may either be uploaded from disk or created afresh with an editor. In the example shown in Figure 23.36, a colleague (Vanessa Mayrhofer, `vmayr`) is editing a new annotation about the introductory cluster `Introducing Graz`.

In the case of a textual annotation, a link back to the document being annotated is pre-inserted into the template text document, as can be seen in Figure 23.37. When the comment

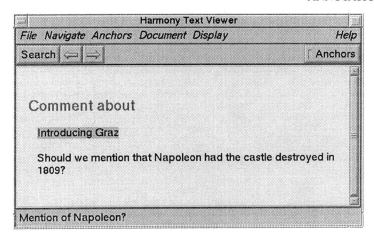

Figure 23.37   The finished annotation.

or remark is finished, the editor is exited, and a dialog box asks for confirmation that the annotation should be inserted into the server. By default, annotations are inserted into the collection to which the annotated object itself belongs, but this can be changed in the Insert dialog. In the example, a new text document Mention of Napoleon? (the annotation) has been inserted into the collection A Short Tour of Graz to which the cluster Introducing Graz belongs:

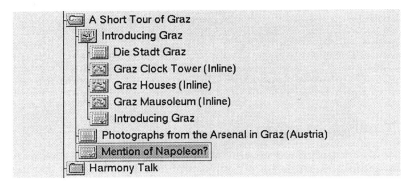

Since annotations are a kind of link type, annotation relationships can be comfortably viewed in **Harmony's Local Map**. Figure 23.38 shows the Local Map for the annotation in our example. By annotating annotations, a structured discussion can evolve. A good example of this is Hermann Maurer's "Social Aspects of Telematics" course at Graz University of Technology, in which students and professors discuss a series of short essays online using pseudonyms. Figure 23.39 shows two levels of the discussion about an essay concerning the dynamics of information.

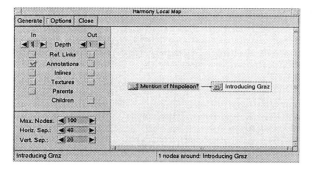

Figure 23.38   The annotation relationship in the Local Map.

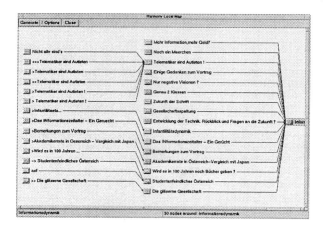

Figure 23.39   Structured discussion using annotations.

23.8   Further reading

A number of HTML authoring tools are now freely available for UNIX platforms, including asWedit (Stochniol) and Symposia (INRIA/GRIF). The most popular image manipulation tools for UNIX are XV (Bradley) and the PBMPLUS utility suite (Poskanzer). The best resource for MPEG is Luigi Filippini's online Web site (Filippini). The mpegUtil utility (Lougher) allows MPEG clips to be extracted and concatenated. A good printed source of information on image and video formats is *Graphics File Formats* by Murray and van Ryper (1994). The Network Audio System is described in Fulton and Renda (1994). The Audio page of the WWW Virtual Library (available at http://cnidr.org/talks/whyzdist.-html) has numerous links to audio software and samples. The VRML Repository (San Diego Supercomputer Center) maintains a list of modeling tools and conversion utilities for VRML.

24 Authoring with Amadeus

Thomas Dietinger, Christian Huber, Gerbert Orasche

In this chapter we explain how to manage information in the Hyper-G server using **Amadeus**. The first section describes how to insert, copy, move, unlink and delete documents and collections. The following section shows how to use the Winword template to create text documents. Finally, we describe creation of hyperlinks and modifying Hyper-G attributes.

24.1 Collection and document handling

In this section we describe how to **insert, edit and delete documents, collections and clusters** with Amadeus. In what follows, documents, collections and clusters will also be referred to as objects.

24.1.1 Inserting objects

The **New** command in the File menu allows you to insert different objects into the Hyper-G database. Before you choose this command, you have to select where (in which cluster or collection) you want to insert the new document (using the collection browser). Then you can click on **New** and a pull-down menu will open allowing you to select which kind of document you want to insert:

- a new collection
- a new cluster
- text
- image
- movie
- sound
- 3D scene

- PostScript

- generic

- a remote connection

- an annotation.

When you select one of these options, a dialog box will appear. There are effectively only four different cases here since the options Image, Movie, Sound, Scene, PostScript and Generic all show the same dialog box with different titles: see Figure 24.1. In each case you must specify a title for your document and you may provide it with access rights.

On the right-hand side of this dialog box you will find a small file selector. Use it to select the document you want to insert into the database. On the left-hand side you enter some information about the document. Author, creation time and language will be taken from the present settings but can be changed. In the first input line you insert the title of the document. If you want to specify access rights, use the Rights edit field.

Inserting collections or clusters

The dialog boxes that appear when you insert a new collection (see Figure 24.2) or cluster are almost the same. Title, language, author, creation time and access rights are required in both dialog boxes. The New Collection command additionally prompts you for a description and a unique name. You can find more information about creation of unique names in Section 22.2.

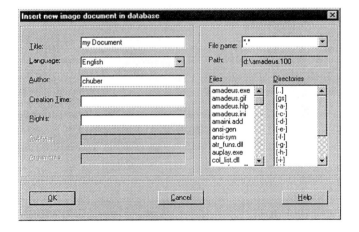

Figure 24.1   The "Insert new image document in database" dialog.

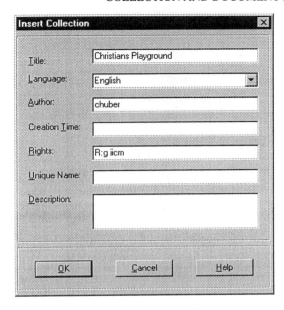

Figure 24.2   The "Insert collection" dialog.

Inserting text documents

If you select the Text command, a dialog box will open (see Figure 24.3). Here you enter the collection name and the title of the document. You also choose which document to insert, using the file selector, and set the correct language and the type of object (RTF, HTF or TXT). You may also set an expiry date, which specifies when a document should no longer be visible in the database. Use this option whenever possible. It is one of the simplest yet most powerful mechanisms of Hyper-G to avoid the well-known problem of obsolete information on the Web.

Hint: After selecting a collection or cluster to be the current object (for example, by positioning the cursor on the parent collection in list mode), the name of this collection is taken to be the default. Please specify the correct language, as this is very important for the display of the title and for searching!

Inserting remote objects

With this command (see Figure 24.4) you can insert a special document which provides links to other remote databases (Host field). Valid types are (currently): Telnet, Gopher, http (WWW), FTP and WAIS. You can also specify a port number and a startup directory (Gopher, http), a path (FTP), a user (Telnet) or the database name (WAIS). Of course, you can also specify the usual Hyper-G document attributes like Title (this should always be

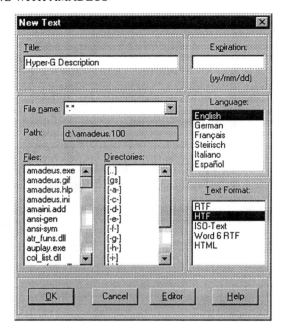

Figure 24.3   The "New text" dialog.

added), `TitleLanguage`, `Author`, `CreationTime` (set to server time if left empty) and access rights.

Inserting annotations

This command allows you to enter a (possibly public) **annotation**. The document to be an-notated must first be selected as the current document (by reading it in or positioning the cursor on it in the collection browser). After entering the command, a dialog box similar to the New Text command will appear. Here you are prompted to enter the name of the parent collection of the new text and the title of the annotation. If only one parent exists, this is the default parent collection. Next you enter the language, the default being the language of the document. You can then either click on the Edit button to enter a few lines with the simple built-in editor or select a prepared file with the file selector. Be sure to specify the correct text format: RTF, if you want to insert an RTF document, TXT for plain ISO text (for example, from Email, or if you use the built-in editor because you do not know anything about the HTF or HTML formats!). When you open the text editor it will contain a few lines that were gen-erated automatically, including a link specification pointing to the document to be annotated. Do not edit these lines!

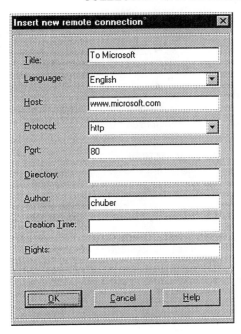

Figure 24.4   The "Insert new remote connection" dialog.

24.1.2   Modifying documents

You will use this function mainly for editing text documents. When Amadeus is installed, three editors are predefined:

Built-in text editor This is a very simple edit field showing you the source code of the document. You can edit in exactly the same way as you do in Windows.

Windows Notepad The Notepad application is started and the document source code is preloaded. When you are finished, just close Notepad and press yes after being requested to save.

Word 6.0 When you select this option, Microsoft Word for Windows is started. Ensure that you have installed the Hyper-G template properly, as described in Section 24.2.

In addition you can define your own text editors, such as your favorite HTML editor. For details refer to Section 18.2.2.

You can also edit documents which are not just plain text. This is a feature which is very useful for generic documents like Excel charts or any other file format you may have configured a viewer for. How to install additional viewers is described in Section 18.2.2.

24.1.3   Copying objects

With the `Copy` command you can copy the current object to another collection or cluster (a Hyper-G object may be a member of more than one collection). A collection itself can also be copied.

To copy do the following: select the desired object in the collection browser and invoke the copy command, either by selecting it in the File menu or by opening the context-sensitive menu. A dialog box now asks for the source object (initially the currently active object) and the destination collection. Use the collection browser again to select the destination of the copy. Press the `Destination` button to fix your selection. Alternatively, you can enter the name of a collection or the object ID of a cluster.

Note: You must have write access for the destination collection or cluster.

The only restriction for copying is that you are not allowed to create cycles in the collection hierarchy. In other words, you cannot have, say, collection A being a member of B and B being a member of A.

When you copy an object it is not physically copied (this would require additional space in the document server): only a new link (not a hyperlink, but a UNIX style symbolic link!) from the specified collection/cluster to the object is generated. You can use this function to generate your own personal "bookmarks" in your home collection. Having bookmarks on the server is a big advantage because you can access them with any client, using any computer in the network.

24.1.4   Moving objects

If you want to move the selected object to a different collection use the `Move` command. After the command has been entered, the viewer prompts you with a dialog box for the target collection (similar to the `Copy Object` command, see Figure 24.5). This can be specified either by directly entering the collection name, the collection's object ID (which can be found with the `Edit/Attributes` command) or by selecting the target collection with the collection browser.

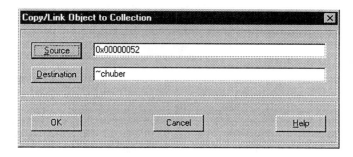

Figure 24.5   The "Copy/link object to collection" dialog.

You must have write permissions for both the target collection and the collection which contains the object you are moving, otherwise the message *** Error: Access denied *** will appear. The message Database modified is displayed if the command completed successfully. The message *** found nothing *** indicates that the target collection was incorrectly specified.

24.1.5   Unlinking objects

Using the Unlink command you can unlink a selected object from a collection. It is not physically deleted if there is more than one parent referring to it; only the link between the parent collection and the object is removed. (Thus you may still find the object using a search, or following a link to this object from a different collection). If there is more than one parent collection, you will get a dialog box (see Figure 24.6) which asks you to select a particular collection to unlink from.

Note: If the object is going to be physically deleted, you will get a warning message. You cannot undo this operation.

24.1.6   Deleting objects

The Delete command can be used to physically delete the selected object (the active text document or the highlighted object in the collection browser, if one is active) from the Hyper-G database. You can only delete objects if you have write permission for the object. Naturally, you will have to identify yourself before you issue this command.

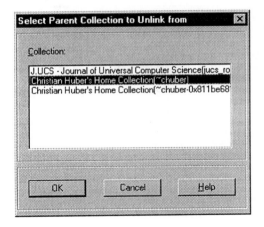

Figure 24.6   The "select parent collection" dialog.

Note: This command erases the current object from all of its parent collections. In order to remove it only from specific parent collections use the `Unlink from collection` command – this is much safer!

24.1.7   Saving documents

With the `Save As` command you can save the selected document to disk (see Figure 24.7). This is useful when you want to look at it later or simply want to have it in an archive. You can specify a path and filename directly in the edit box or select the path using the controls. Depending on the type of the document, some additional options appear in the dialog:

text document   You can select the file format here. The possibilities are: HTML, ISO text, RTF, Word 6 RTF and HTF. If you want to process the document with Microsoft Word 6.0, select the Word 6 RTF format.

image   Select one of the supported image file formats: BMP, GIF, JPEG or TIFF.

3D scenes   Select either the VRML or the SDF format.

sound   Select either the AU or the WAV sound format.

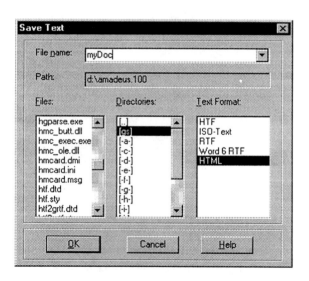

Figure 24.7   The "Save text" dialog box.

24.1.8 Saving Hyper-G anchors

The Save Anchors command is primarily for internal use and saves all attached anchors as well as the document. If you use a standalone Hyper-G viewer, you can also follow internal links with this viewer. An example is the standalone PostScript viewer. For details see Section 18.4.

24.2 Editing text documents with the HTF word template

Hyper-G can store several different text formats, but the most preferred ones are HTML and HTF. There are presently many editors and word processors with HTML capabilities available and so we will not describe how to produce HTML scripts here. Instead we will show how you can easily create and edit HTF documents with Microsoft Word 6.0 using a special template.

It is very important to know that HTF is a format that describes not the appearance but the structure of the text. You can specify, for instance, that a certain part of text is a "heading" (a logical markup) but not that it should be displayed with "Times New Roman, 20pt, bold" (a layout markup). Word supports this with several styles which can be assigned to a paragraph. It is a very good habit to use these styles in every document you write, because then it is quite easy to reformat a whole document – if you want to change all headings from Times New Roman to Helvetica, for instance. Word preserves this information when you store the text in RTF format, so Amadeus can convert it successfully to HTF format. If you do not use the styles, but modify font attributes directly, it will be quite hard to extract the structure information (Amadeus has to guess) and the result will not be so good. If you modify an RTF text which does not contain structure information, its appearance may change after each conversion.

Word supports several sets of styles, called templates. In the following we describe the hyperg.dot template.

24.2.1 Installation

The hyperg.dot template will be copied into your Amadeus directory during the installation of Amadeus. To derive full benefit from the file, it would best to move it to the MS-Word template directory.

After you have done this, if you do not have Word in the search path, you have to specify Word's exact path at the fields Import, Export and Editor in the section Text of your amadeus.ini configuration file. Future versions of Amadeus may have a special dialog box for this purpose.

24.2.2 Usage

A style can only be assigned to a whole paragraph. If you want to change parts of a paragraph, you have to divide it into several pieces beforehand. You can use the toolbar to change the current style. If you do not see the HTF format toolbar, you can activate it by checking the dialog box entry ViewToolbar→Formatting. The following is an explanation of each HTF style you can use with the template.

The "Normal" style

This style is used to specify parts of text which do not require further structuring. It corresponds to ordinary text paragraphs. Line breaks may be entered with Shift-Return and are not treated as the end of the paragraph.

The "HR" style

The HR style has the same characteristics as the normal style but includes a horizontal rule before the first line of the paragraph.

Header 1 ... Header 6

Headers are used to structure a document into parts that belong together. The number specifies the hierarchical order of the header, where 1 means most important (resulting in a big heading) and 6 least important (resulting in a small heading). There are some important things to notice:

- Every document must begin with Header 1.

- You should not skip a header level while going down the hierarchy. Thus, after Header 2 you must have Header 3 and not Header 4.

- You can skip several levels when going up the header hierarchy. Thus, Header 2 can follow Header 4.

    Note: You may specify the title of the document in the dialog box File→Summary Info→Title.

The "Preformatted" style

You can use this style if it is important that the formatting of the paragraph looks exactly the way you specified. To achieve this you can rely on the following:

- A monospaced font will be used to display the paragraph.

- Automatic line breaks will only happen at the end of the paragraph.

The "Block Quote" style

This style can be used for quotations and strong emphasis. Most clients display this style by moving the text a bit to the right, or making it a bit smaller, thus indenting left and right.

The "Listing" styles

The HTF template supports several types of listing style. The main difference between them is their use of numbering symbols:

list-number displays ascending Arabic numbers at the beginning of each paragraph;

list-alpha displays ascending Latin letters;

list-bullet displays bullets;

list-plain does not display any numbering symbol.

The "Glos Term" and "Glos Def" styles

If you want to use a new term and define it afterwards, you should use the style "Glos Term" for the new term immediately followed by the style "Glos Def" for the definition.

Tables

Although there is no HTF style for tables, they may be used in the Word document. Amadeus converts each table line to perforated text. Unfortunately Word cannot convert these lines back into tables when it loads the text again for editing! There are also some important restrictions to observe when working with tables:

- Tables must not contain manual line breaks (automatic line breaks are allowed).

- You cannot use additional character styles within tables.

Character styles

Although HTF contains a small set of allowed character styles they should be used with care because there is no guarantee that they will be displayed in the same way by the client. These are:

- **Bold**

- *Italic*

- <u>Underline</u>

    Note: Do not use combinations of these styles as this is not supported by all clients.

24.3   Creating links

Link creation is one of the most powerful features of Amadeus. Try it and you will see how easy it is! With a few clicks you can define hyperlinks in images, PostScript, text and so on, without knowing anything about language definitions, data formats and server–client protocols.

24.3.1   The link creation dialog

In Figure 24.8 you see the dialog for creating links. It is the same for all types of document. The top part of the window refers to the source, the bottom part to the destination anchor of the link (for link details see Chapters 8 and 9). A description of the definition of anchors in the specific viewers follows in the next few paragraphs. After defining the anchors, press the OK button and the link will be created. Always check your access rights and do not forget to identify yourself.

24.3.2   Links in hypertext

Links in text documents are well known from other hypertext systems like the World Wide Web. A wide variety of authoring tools is available to generate HTML documents. They all require that links be entered by providing a URL. Amadeus has a more user-friendly way: links can be generated with a few clicks, without needing to enter any addresses from the keyboard.

Here's how you do it! Open a text document and mark the desired text you want to define as the source anchor. Open the context-sensitive menu (right mouse click) and select the `create link` option. You will see a dialog similar to Figure 24.8.

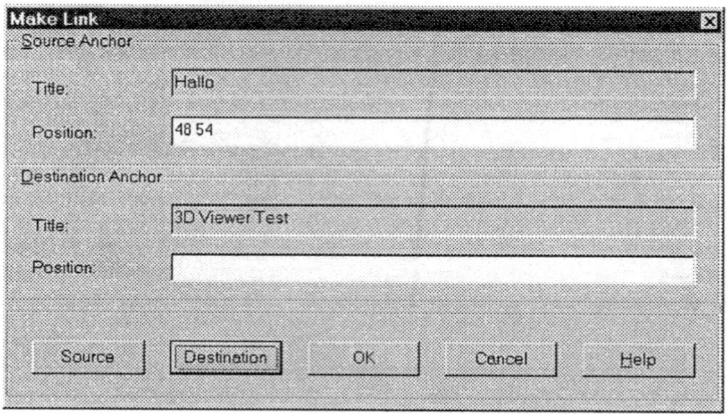

Figure 24.8   The "Amadeus link creation" dialog.

The entries for the source anchor are filled automatically. Now navigate to the object you want the link to point to (this can be an image, a movie, a collection and so on). Once you have found the destination, select the `Destination` button of the link creation dialog. Now press the `OK` button. That's all there is to it!

If you want to define an incoming link (destination anchor), you mark the area you want it to point to and select the link `destination` option. When the link is followed the text is scrolled to this position. To delete links click with the right mouse button.

24.3.3   Links in images

The **Amadeus Image Viewer** supports links in images having the following shapes: circles, ellipses, boxes or polygons. Before anchor definition select the appropriate link shape by clicking the buttons in the toolbar. Then you can define the anchor by pressing the left mouse button and dragging the mouse. To create the link, proceed as described for the text viewer.

24.3.4   Links in PostScript

The **Amadeus PostScript Viewer** is capable of defining rectangular anchor areas. As in the Image Viewer's box mode, anchors are defined by clicking the left mouse button and dragging the mouse until the box is the appropriate size.

24.3.5   Links in 3D scenes

Anchor definition and display in the **Amadeus Scene Viewer** is very similar to the Harmony scene viewer. Because the standalone 3D viewer, VRweb, is not yet integrated into Amadeus, you will not see links using the version on the CD-ROM included with this book.

24.4   Deleting links

This section is quite a short one, because **deleting links** with Amadeus is very easy. You can do it by simply selecting the desired link with one click of the left mouse button. The link is then deleted by invoking the `Delete Link` command either by directly accessing it in the menu or by opening the context-sensitive menu with the right mouse button.

Note: This function cannot be undone!

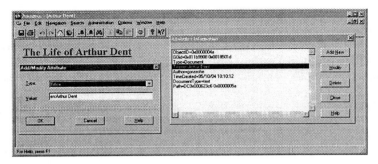

Figure 24.9   The "Amadeus attribute" dialog.

24.5   Managing Hyper-G attributes

Attributes are additional information stored logically for each object in the Hyper-G database. You can change some, but not all of them. For instance, the unique name of a collection cannot be changed, but its title can. Please see Chapter 11 and Appendix E.1.

Whenever you want to view, change or add attributes to a Hyper-G object, just select the `Properties` menu item or the context-sensitive menu activated with the right mouse button. Then you see a dialog similar to Figure 24.9. To modify an attribute, mark it with a single mouse click and press the `Modify` button. If you want to add a new attribute, press the `Add New` button. Another dialog appears: the `Add/Modify Attribute` dialog, see Figure 24.9. Select the type of the attribute and enter a value in the appropriate field. The deletion of an attribute works analogously.

Normally you will use presentation hints, sequence numbers and access rights quite frequently. Hint: Do not forget to identify yourself to gain access rights for any changes!

24.5.1   Defining a collection head

Here is an example showing how to add the `CollectionHead` attribute for the selected document:

(1) Navigate to the document you want to open automatically when the collection is entered.

(2) Press the right mouse button in the text viewer window or in the session manager on the desired document and select `Properties`.

(3) Select the `Add New` function.

(4) Enter `PresentationHints` in the type field or select it using the combo box.

(5) Type `CollectionHead` in the value field.

(6) Press the `OK` button.

24.5.2   Defining access rights

This next example shows how to define access rights for a document. We want to give un-link access to the user adent, write access to the group iicm, and read access to the user anonymous:

(1) Navigate to the document for which the access rights are to be changed.

(2) Press the right mouse button in the viewer window or in the session manager on the desired document and select properties.

(3) Select the Add New function.

(4) Enter Rights in the type field or select it using the combo box.

(5) Type U:u adent; W:g iicm; R:u anonymous in the value field.

(6) Press the OK button.

For details about definition of Hyper-G access rights see Appendix E.1. Note: The system administrator always has write access rights!

24.5.3   Language independence

If you want to make a multimedia document *language-independent*, you should put the different versions into a cluster. For example, assume we have a cluster containing two text documents, one in German and one in English. With the title attribute you can specify more than one title for the cluster. The user will automatically see the appropriate title according to Amadeus' actual language setting:

(1) Navigate to the cluster you want to make language-independent.

(2) Press the right mouse button on the cluster and select the Properties command.

(3) Press the Add New button.

(4) Enter Title in the type field or select it using the combo box.

(5) Type en:English Title for the English title or ge:Deutscher Titel for the German title into the value field.

(6) Press the OK button.

For a list of currently supported language short cuts see Appendix E.1.

25 Database manipulation tools

Gerald Mesaric, Walter Schinnerl, Klaus Schmaranz

Automated hypermedia authoring and offline database manipulation tools are the main topics covered in this chapter. **Data conversion tools and scripting** are described and a practical example is given of an insertion script written in Perl. For mirroring and backup purposes the HIF tools are useful. These utilities and the `replicate` feature are explained in detail in the last section of this chapter.

25.1 Automated hypermedia authoring

Although much of the work of setting up and maintaining a hypermedia application has to be done by hand, there are several tasks that can be **automated**. Whether this automation is an easy task or not depends both on the **application** and primarily on the **formats** of your raw data. We use the plural "formats" on purpose: when creating multimedia applications you usually have to deal with many different document formats.

When you decide to create a new hypermedia application on a specific topic, the raw data to be used in your database will probably already exist in some fashion. You will either:

- have the data in printed form;

- reuse non-interlinked files in electronic form;

- extract the data from a database.

If you have the data only in printed form, creating the hypermedia application is likely to be a tedious task. You will have to scan images and probably also text and maybe convert audio and video clips into a digital representation. The conversion process from a printed form to a digital representation – such as files on a hard disk – will involve a lot of manual work.

The second case, in which you already have your data in electronic form, but in which the documents are not interlinked, will also pose a difficult problem in automating the conversion, though here you will more readily succeed. Using some kind of fuzzy string matching and cross-reference databases makes it possible to guess when and where a hyperlink should be inserted into a document and to where it should point.   You can also perform some automatic structuring this way, trying to find out what documents are closely related to one another and putting them automatically together into one collection. Of course, these approaches are not complete solutions, but they can save a lot of work and time by giving you an interlinked database to start with.

The third and best alternative is if you have the information in some kind of (traditional) database. You will then usually be able not only to extract the data itself, but also some kind of relationship. These relations between data sets allow you to write quite good automatic scripting utilities which do most of the work for you. It should be possible to do automatic hyperlink creation as well as automated structuring. How much work will still have to be done by hand depends mostly on the data formats used and the consistency of your documents.

Well-documented and easy to parse data formats are the main key to scripting applications. It is particularly "easy" to parse a document when the format is in seven-bit ASCII representation. If you are reusing a database, the best way to parse such information is to extract the data in ASCII format, a feature available in nearly every database program. Most ASCII export filters let you either put one data set per line (with fixed-length fields) or print out each field on a separate line (name/value pairs) with a blank line to separate the data sets.

Using the ASCII export feature of the database rather than parsing the original format has mainly two advantages:

- Database formats are often very cryptic and difficult to parse; they also contain much redundant information that is not very useful for creating a hypermedia application (for example, index information).

- Parsing ASCII format is portable in two ways. You can easily use the same scripting application on different platforms and hence reuse your code for parsing other data sets: you do not have to reinvent the wheel each time you need such a tool.

However, you should never forget that writing a scripting utility is also work. Just how much work will depend on what you want it to do and, as previously mentioned, on the format of your raw data. If you only intend to make a demo collection with a small number of documents, using scripts is probably more work than doing everything manually. However, in cases where an automatic conversion tool is not already available and you have to insert or modify large amounts of information, then it is likely that you will save time and effort by writing one yourself.

25.1.1   Existing tools for common data formats

If the data you intend to insert into your Hyper-G server is available in some kind of standard document format, you should first look in the tools directory of the IICM FTP server or a Hyper-G mirror site. The developers of Hyper-G have implemented a number of conversion utilities for common data formats that are frequently used either in UNIX environments or on the Web, such as BibTeX files, interlinked WWW documents and Gopher hierarchies.

Another place to search for such tools is the contrib directory, where you can find third-party tools that are also available for free over the Web. The contrib directory should be accessible by all Hyper-G FTP servers. If you do not find anything useful in there, you can try a distributed search over the Hyper-G network or even try to find a WWW utility that fits your needs. In most cases it is very easy to modify the script to work with Hyper-G, or you can just use the script as is and then call the `loadwww` utility to insert the resulting material into your server.

In this section we will describe a few useful utilities developed at the IICM. In a sense all tools work the same way – you specify some kind of input files and the scripts generate two types of output data:

- several files that hold the converted data itself, and

- a script that is generated by the tool that inserts the files automatically into the Hyper-G database.

The utilities are all written in **Perl** (Practical Extraction and Report Language). Perl is available on nearly every platform. It provides sophisticated facilities for processing textual data involving string matching using regular expressions. The generated data insertion scripts just consist of a sequence of Hyper-G commands and should work with every type of UNIX shell. To get these utilities to work you must have Perl and either the Hyper-G tool distribution or the server installed on your machine.

This chapter only describes the basic functionality of the tools mentioned. For complete documentation of options and specific usage, please refer either to the Hyper-G online documentation or to the manual pages that come with the tools. Due to continually emerging new software, this information is unfortunately not available in the form of a book as it would become quickly outdated.

BibTeX bibliographies (`bibtex2hyperg`)

In UNIX environments (but also on many other platforms) LaTeX and its bibliographic index format BibTeX are very frequently used. One reason for this is that LaTeX provides a professional way of writing scientific papers, with sophisticated context and layout capabilities and support for formulae and tables. A further reason is that both the LaTeX text processing format and the BibTeX reference format are well documented and all software is available under the GNU Public License.

Originally developed for inserting the SIGGRAPH bibliography into the Graz University of Technology Hyper-G server, the Hyper-G development team decided to enhance the `bibtex2hyperg` utility and make it available to the public. The `bibtex2hyperg` tool takes as arguments a number of BibTeX files from which it generates HTML texts. A data insertion script is also created which inserts a collection hierarchy (there is an option for this) and the HTML text documents into a Hyper-G server.

Inserting a "web" (`loadwww`)

A tool which at its beta stage was known as `html2hyperg` was developed to insert a whole web of interlinked HTML and multimedia documents into a Hyper-G server. The abbreviation

HTML in its name indicated its capability to convert HTML to HTF. Nowadays Hyper-G supports HTML as a native text format and therefore this feature is no longer needed.

The `loadwww` tool can either be used to insert one directory of HTML documents including its associated multimedia data and remote hyperlinks, or to insert a whole hierarchy of interlinked WWW data. You can find a more detailed description of this utility and also information about when you should use it in Section 20.3.

Reusing Gopher hierarchies (`loadgopher`)

The Gopher information system, which was "invented" by Mark P. McCahill at the University of Minnesota, is one of the spiritual parents of the Hyper-G project. Gopher was the first system to provide a hierarchical structuring facility for a distributed scalable information system. In fact, Gopher directories are very similar to Hyper-G collections and can be quite easily "reused" when migration to Hyper-G is desired.

The `loadgopher` utility is a network tool. You have to specify a Gopher URL (protocol, hostname, type and path) which points to your desired start document and a Hyper-G server and collection to insert into. You can then either just fetch this document and insert it into the database or get the whole directory subtree of the Gopher server and convert it to Hyper-G. A more detailed description of this utility is given in Section 21.3.

25.1.2 Scripting with Perl

Perl (Practical Extraction and Report Language) is one of the most commonly used scripting languages and it is available on many platforms including the UNIX, Microsoft DOS and Macintosh operating systems. Perl provides sophisticated string matching and text file processing facilities which make it the perfect Hyper-G and WWW scripting language. In fact, most CGI scripts are written in Perl today.

Another advantage of Perl is that its syntax is very similar to C and therefore easy to learn for anyone familiar with C, C++ or Objective C. This section is not intended to be a Perl reference or programming tutorial. We will only present some basic concepts, so that you will be able to read the sample Perl script below.

All conditional and loop statements can be used in much the same way as in C (`if`, `else`, `while` and so on). The main procedure starts at the beginning of the file and subroutines are called by `&subroutine ()` and defined by `sub subroutine () {...}`. Comments are indicated by a preceding #.

Variable names are case-sensitive and have special character prefixes, depending on the type of the variable: $ for numbers and strings and % for arrays.

There are some special operators in Perl for string manipulation and matching you should know about:

- The . operator concatenates two strings.

- The / operator is used for string matching. A $^$ denotes the beginning of a line, a $ marks the end of a line. You can match using regular expressions.

- A second / operator behind a regular string matching expression forces Perl to substitute it by the string behind the second / operator.

25.1.3 An example

In general, all text-based conversion scripts work the same way: they read one line of text and parse it according to certain *tags*. String matching is used to do this in Perl. Scripts manage to get information out of these tags by comparing them to values stored within the script. Finally, they end up with one or more new lines of text that hold the data in a different format. You normally loop over the file until an end of file (EOF) occurs.

We now present an elementary but very typical example of a Perl script which we shall call bib2html.pl. The script takes a very simple input file of bibliographic data and converts all entries into HTML files. Then it inserts each file into a previously specified collection.

In the input file, blank lines are used to separate data sets. It is important that there is at least one blank line at the end of the file, because the script also uses blank lines to insert previously parsed information. Here is our demo input file:

```
TITLE = "Hyper-G: The Next Generation Web Solution"
EDITOR = "Hermann Maurer"
AUTHOR = "Frank Kappe, Klaus Schamaranz, Gerald \
       Pani, Keith Andrews, et al."
PUBLISHER = "Addison-Wesley Publishing Company"
YEAR = "1996"

TITLE = "The Annotated C++ Reference Manual"
AUTHOR = "Margaret A. Ellis, Bjarne Stroustrup"
PUBLISHER = "Addison-Wesley Publishing Company"
YEAR = "1992"
ISBN = "0-201-51459-1"

TITLE = "Being digital"
AUTHOR = "Nicholas Negroponte"
PUBLISHER = "Hodder & Stoughton"
YEAR = "1995"
ISBN = "0-7336-0135-9 HB"
```

Now we present the actual listing of the bib2html.pl Perl sample script:

```
#!/usr/local/bin/perl
$bibFile = $ARGV[0]; # Get the first command line argument

if (($bibFile eq "") || ($bibFile =~^^--?he?l?p?/)) {
   print "Usage:  bib2html [bibfile] [collection]\n\n";
   exit (1);
}
```

```perl
$collection = $ARGV[1]; # Get second argument

if ($collection eq "") {
   print "Error:  no collection specified.\n";
   print "Usage:  bib2html [bibfile] [collection]\n\n";
   exit (1);
}

# Initialize variables
$title = ""; $editor = ""; $author = "";
$publisher = ""; $year = ""; $isbn ="";

open (bibFile) || die "ERROR: File $bibFile does not exist.\n\n";

while (<bibFile>) {

   # Blank lines separate the data sets
   if (/^\s*$/) {
      if ($title ne "") {
         # Insert the data if the title is set

         $layout = "<HTML>\n";
         $layout .= "<HEAD>\n";
         $layout .= "<TITLE>$title</TITLE>\n";
         $layout .= "</HEAD>\n";
         $layout .= "<BODY>\n";
         $layout .= "<H1>$title</H1>\n";
         $layout .= "<DL>\n";
         $layout .= "<DT>Title<DD>$title\n";
         if ($editor ne "")
         {$layout .= "<DT>Editor<DD>$editor\n";}
         if ($author ne "")
         {$layout .= "<DT>Author<DD>$author\n";}
         if ($publisher ne "")
         {$layout .= "<DT>Publisher<DD>$publisher\n";}
         if ($year ne "") {$layout .= "<DT>Year<DD>$year\n";}
         if ($isbn ne "") {$layout .= "<DT>ISBN<DD>$isbn\n";}
         $layout .= "</DL>\n";
         $layout .= "</BODY>\n";
         $layout .= "</HTML>\n\n";
      }

      $title = ""; $editor = ""; $author = "";
      $publisher = ""; $year = ""; $isbn ="";

      # Create temporary HTML file and write test to file
      $htmlName = "bib_html.tmp";
      $htmlFile = ">".$htmlName;
      open (htmlFile);
```

```
            print htmlFile $layout;
            close (htmlFile);

            # Insert temporary file into the Hyper-G server
            system
            ("hginstext -pname '$collection' -html -file $htmlName\n");

            # Delete temporary file
            system ("rm -f $htmlName");

    }

    # Match the different fields in the input file
    if (/^TITLE\s*=\s*\"([^\"]*)\"/) {$title = $1;}
    if (/^EDITOR\s*=\s*\"([^\"]*)\"/) {$editor = $1;}
    if (/^AUTHOR\s*=\s*\"([^\"]*)\"/) {$author = $1;}
    if (/^PUBLISHER\s*=\s*\"([^\"]*)\"/) {$publisher = $1;}
    if (/^YEAR\s*=\s*\"([^\"]*)\"/) {$year = $1;}
    if (/^ISBN\s*=\s*\"([^\"]*)\"/) {$isbn = $1;}
}

close (bibFile);
```

The bib2html.pl script is really a very basic example. In a "real" application you would probably cut off all leading and trailing spaces from the data fields. You might also reformat the authors field and put the authors in the title of the HTML documents. However, the sample script will give you a good start for creating your own data conversion and insertion scripts, perhaps even for advanced automatic data manipulation facilities such as updating or automatic link generation.

25.1.4 Advanced automatic data manipulation

Data updating tools

One way to save time when inserting information into a Hyper-G server is to *update* only those parts of the data that have changed. The biggest problem that you normally run into when writing update scripts is to find out which information is new, which is outdated and which has changed.

In general there are two approaches for finding out what has changed:

(1) holding a *local* copy (that is, on your hard disk) of the information you inserted last time, or

(2) using the information stored on the Hyper-G server directly.

All you have to do now is to compare the new data with either the data on your local files or in the Hyper-G server. It depends on the application which approach is the better one.

In general, the first way is easier. You can either use ASCII database files which are easy to parse and modify, or write your HTML texts and object records directly to some kind of local Hyper-G database file. To query the Hyper-G server itself about object records and data stored on the server, you can use the low-level Hyper-G data manipulation tools described in detail in Section 25.2.

To decide which information is not up to date any more, it is best to follow three steps:

(1) When you come to an entry within the new information that is not available in the old data, create it.

(2) If there is an old entry in the database and the information is not up-to-date, update it and delete the old entry. If there is an old entry and nothing is to change for the data, mark it as deleted.

(3) All old entries that have *not been deleted* so far are outdated. Delete them in the server.

A good way to manage the old entries in Perl is to read the entire old database files into memory before you start to parse the new input files. You can use "associative arrays" to hold the data. This makes it possible to use your actual object IDs or whatever you use as a key to separate the entries as an *index* value. Trying to access an entry with such an index value using just an associative array returns either the record itself or an empty string. If you get an empty string, you know that this object did not exist in the old data and is therefore a new object you have to create.

On the other hand you can use a kind of `foreach` statement to loop through all entries that are still in the array when you have finished parsing: in this case you must have deleted every old entry after processing it. Each entry you get within the loop has to be deleted physically on the server since it is outdated.

Half-automated and automated hyperlink generation

If you have already managed to set up a hypermedia application, you know that it can be a lot of work to create all the links between corresponding documents by hand. However, in some cases it is possible to automate the process of hyperlink generation. Although in general you will also have to do some work by hand, it is possible to save a lot of time by writing scripts that provide either half-automated or fully automated link creation. By half-automated link generation we mean that the user is always asked before a link is created.

The problem with automated link generation is not the making of the link itself, but deciding which parts of a document should become a link and where this link should point to. There are two possible situations:

(1) You have some files you want to interlink, but you have no information about what to link where.

(2) You have some additional input files that describe some of the relationships between your pieces of information.

To solve the first problem for every situation is nearly impossible. All you can do is to parse through the files, extract keywords or full text information and add all the words you find to a cross-reference table (containing information about which words are contained in multiple files, statistical information and so on). Then you can tell if files are in some way *similar* to one another by comparing the percentage of equal words, for example. You should not forget about so-called "stop-words" (very common words), that is, do not put words like "the," "is" or "and" into your cross-reference tables. If you find a word in one document that is not very common and that occurs in the title of another document, your script could decide to insert a link from the first to the second document.

Another situation you could have to deal with is that you already have references within your documents in the form of "see section...," "refer to..." and so on. It is the same process as described before, but using this approach it is much easier to find the source anchor of a link. Even now you could run into some problems, because sometimes it is hard to decide where a particular source anchor ends.

Managing the second situation is in general a much easier task. You have additional information on where to insert hyperlinks and where they should point to. However, even in this context it is sometimes not easy to match the source against the destination (especially if you are dealing with strings rather than numbers). For example, you might have a cross-reference table of publishers that you want to link to your journal database. If the cross-reference table holds only the names of the publishers you could have some problems matching them to the names contained in the text.

The most frequent problems you run into are possibly abbreviations, typing errors and the likelihood that some extensions are missing (for example, Addison-Wesley Publications = Addison-Wesley = A.W. Publications = A.W.). Of course you can match in a very *fuzzy* way, but the problem is that if you are matching too "fuzzily," you will probably create bad links.

Thus, automatic link creation is not an easy topic. You will have to do a lot of "trial and error" to make your scripts work. Whether it is worth the effort of creating such a script really depends on your particular situation and on the amount of data you are going to process.

"Guessing" structure from context

By applying the algorithms (or similar ones) described in the last section you can not only automate link generation, but also try to structure the data in some way. Of course, you will run into the same problems that you had when creating links automatically and it is up to you to decide if it is easier to do the structuring by hand or to write a script.

One way to structure data is to try to create cross-reference tables from your input data. You can compare each file to each other and on the percentage of similarity (that is, percentage of equal words) you can decide whether you want to cluster files together. For multimedia data you may want to put several different media types that refer to the same context into one Hyper-G cluster. To make it easier to access data of one media type, you can try to put similar documents into the same collection.

Again, having some additional information to start with makes the task of automated structuring a lot easier, for example if you already have a pre-created collection hierarchy that represents a kind of thesaurus. Probably you would have a relation (in a file somewhere) that describes what keywords a document must contain to be put into a particular collection. Again, typing errors and abbreviations can be a problem.

However, the same rules apply to the task of automated structuring of information as apply to most things that should be *automated*. You – the author of the hypermedia application – have to decide if it is worth the effort of writing a script to automate this process. You should not forget that a lot of problems can be solved by developing and using such utilities, but in some cases you will still be faster doing everything manually.

25.2   Offline Hyper-G database tools

In this section we describe the basic functionality and use of the most important Hyper-G **database tools** which are intended to be called by scripts for mass-manipulation of documents and can also be used as shell commands.

A full description of options and specific usage of these tools can be found on the enclosed CD-ROM or in the Hyper-G online documentation, available over the Web. Each of these tools also has a corresponding manual page in the /usr/local/Hyper-G/man directory of the Hyper-G server. If you want to use these manual pages you should add this directory to the environment variable MANPATH.

All of these tools come with the server distribution, but you can also get them (independent of your server platform) from the tools distribution (tools directory of the Hyper-G FTP servers). The tools are available for all Hyper-G server platforms and can usually be found in the /usr/local/Hyper-G/bin/$CPU directory of the Hyper-G server.

Options

All of these tools support the option

- -help or -h

which displays a short description of options and default values. Figure 25.1 shows what is displayed if you enter hginfo -h at the command line.

The options (command line parameters), environment variables and default values shown in Table 25.1 are the same for most of the tools.

The first three options are the same for all tools, the others for all tools for inserting objects. The sequence of evaluation of the parameters is: firstly the default values, secondly the environment variables and finally the options are evaluated. Thus options have the highest priority.

In the following examples we want to focus on the most essential options of each tool. This is why for the -hghost and -hgport options the default values are assumed.

Identification

All of the above tools have a built-in auto-identify feature (see Section 14.8). Using auto-identification there is no need to supply username and password in the command line. Before

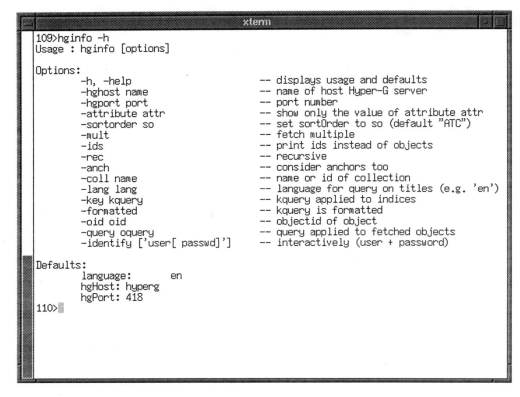

```
109>hginfo -h
Usage : hginfo [options]

Options:
      -h, -help                        -- displays usage and defaults
      -hghost name                     -- name of host Hyper-G server
      -hgport port                     -- port number
      -attribute attr                  -- show only the value of attribute attr
      -sortorder so                    -- set sortOrder to so (default "ATC")
      -mult                            -- fetch multiple
      -ids                             -- print ids instead of objects
      -rec                             -- recursive
      -anch                            -- consider anchors too
      -coll name                       -- name or id of collection
      -lang lang                       -- language for query on titles (e.g. 'en')
      -key kquery                      -- kquery applied to indices
      -formatted                       -- kquery is formatted
      -oid oid                         -- objectid of object
      -query oquery                    -- query applied to fetched objects
      -identify ['user[ passwd]']      -- interactively (user + password)

Defaults:
      language:        en
      hgHost: hyperg
      hgPort: 418
110>
```

Figure 25.1   Output of the command `hginfo -h`.

Table 25.1   Options, environment variables and default values.

Option (long/short)	Environment variable	Default value	Short description
-hghost/-hgho	HGHOST	hyperg	name of the server
-hgport/-hgpo	HGPORT	418	port number of the server
-language/-lang	HGLANGUAGE	en	language of the title
-cdate/-cdat	HGCDATE	actual time	creation time
-edate/-edat	HGEDATE		expiry time
-odate/-odat	HGODATE		opening time
-rights/-righ	HGRIGHTS		access rights
-pname/-pnam	HGPNAME		parent collection name
-user/-user	HGUSER		identify as user

you use these tools you should find out if auto-identification from your actual account and host is possible.

If auto-identification is not possible (for example, because your machine has a shadow password file) you have to identify "manually" with the -iden[tify] option. In this case you either have to supply the Hyper-G username and password as parameters or enter the unspecified parameters (username, password) interactively.

Users with system rights, that is, members of the group system, are allowed to change their identity to another user without supplying the password of this user. This can be performed with option -user and allows the insertion of documents where the Author attribute is set to another user.

Return codes

Each of the above tools delivers a *return code* which should be interpreted, particularly when you use it in scripts. If the return code is zero, everything is okay and you can continue with the execution of further commands which depend on the previous one. If the return code is greater than zero, a server error occurred; if it is less than zero, something is wrong which is specific to the tool and its options. The return code has to be interpreted as a signed byte value; note that this is not done correctly on all platforms or shells. To be sure you should check if the value of the return code is greater than 127 and in this case subtract 256 from it to make it negative. In *Perl* the value of the variable $? must first be divided by 256 (or shifted right 8 times) to get the actual return code. Then it has to be interpreted as a signed byte value: this can be done by packing and unpacking it as a signed character. The following Perl function is called by &exit_value($?) and gives back the correct return code:

```
sub exit_value {
    local($status) = @_;
    $status = $status >> 8; # divide by 256
    $status = unpack('c', pack('c', $status));
        # declare as signed char
    return $status; }
```

25.2.1   Inserting collections and clusters

The insertion of collections and clusters can be performed using the hginscoll tool. Because every object in Hyper-G has to be a member of at least one collection, the creation of such collections is very fundamental.

Example

We want to insert eleven sub-collections with titles Publications of 1985, Publications of 1986,..., Publications of 1995 and with names publ_85, publ_86, ... , publ_95 into an already existing collection with name publ. We can perform this with the following shell script or by directly entering the following commands:

```
#! /bin/csh
foreach i (85 86 87 88 89 90 91 92 93 94 95)
hginscoll -pname publ -name publ_$i \
      -title "Publications of 19$i"
end
```

Example

We want to insert a multilingual cluster with two titles (in English and German). For this we use the `-form[atted]` option in combination with the `-title` option: this allows you to give an object extra attributes that cannot be specified as separate options. The attributes have to be separated by \ and typically consist of `attributename=value`, for example, `Sequence=20`.

Although it is not necessary, we give this cluster a name which makes it easier to reference it later:

```
hginscoll -cluster -pname '~anonymous' \
   -name IICM.Welcome -form \
   -title 'Title=en:Welcome to the IICM \
      Title=ge:Willkommen am IICM'
```

25.2.2   Inserting text documents

The `hginstext` tool allows you to insert text documents. If no file is specified, `hginstext` reads from standard input. Any given file (and standard input too) may contain more than one text (each TITLE tag marks the beginning of a new text). With option `-html` you specify HTML format and with option `-base` the default base address for HTML documents can be specified.

Before you really insert an existing text file into the Hyper-G database, the command `hgparse` should be used to verify that the HTML document is correct and to check the visual appearance of the text. If the document does not contain valid HTML, self-explanatory error messages are produced.

Mass-insertion of text documents and insertion of text extracted from forms can be performed by using the `hginstext` command called by scripts.

Example

Suppose we have the following text file `example.html`:
```
<HTML>

<HEAD>
<TITLE>An Example Text Document in HTML</TITLE>
</HEAD>
```

```
<BODY>
<H1>An Example Text Document in HTML</H1>
The TITLE tag specifies the document title in the database.
The H1 tag introduces a level-one heading in the text and is
typically used for the actual text heading.
<P>
Paragraphs are delimited by the P tag.<BR>
The BR tag forces a line break.  Text may be emphasized in
two strengths:  <EM> light emphasis </EM> and <STRONG> strong
emphasis </STRONG>.
<P>
A source anchor definition (hypertext link) looks like this:
<A HREF="/examples/destination.html">anchor text</A>
where 'examples/destination.html' is the name of the
destination document.
</BODY>

</HTML>
```

If we want to insert the file example.html into a collection with name test and manually identify as the Hyper-G user hguser we would perform the following command:

```
hginstext -identify hguser -pname test \
        -base 'http://localhost/test/' example.html
```

After entering the correct password for hguser and if this user is allowed to write in the collection test, the text document is inserted with the name test/example.html.

25.2.3   Inserting non-text documents, CGI or remote objects

The hginsdoc tool is used to insert image, movie, audio, scene, PostScript or generic documents, CGI objects or remote objects with HTTP, Gopher, WAIS, FTP or Telnet protocols.

The option -type determines the type: I (Image), M (Movie), S (Audio), 3D (Scene), G (Generic), P (PostScript), C (CGI) or R (Remote).

For the insertion of documents the option -path is mandatory and specifies the name of the file to be inserted. For the insertion of remote objects it is optional and can be used for the path. The protocol of remote objects is specified with the -prot option. CGI objects are inserted by specifying the relative URL of the CGI program (residing in the server's CGI-directory) with option -relurl.

If you want to replace an existing image, movie, audio, scene, PostScript or generic document you can use the options -oid and -path. The -oid option specifies the object identifier of the document you want to change and -path the name of the file which holds the new data.

Example

We want to insert the URL of the HTML 3.0 Specification `http://www.w3.org/-hypertext/WWW/MarkUp/html3/Contents.html` into a collection with name `~hguser.hotlist`. The remote object should only be readable for its creator (author):

```
hginsdoc -pname '~hguser.hotlist'
    -title 'HTML 3.0 Specification' -rights 'R:a' \
    -type R -prot http -host www.w3.org \
    -path '/hypertext/WWW/MarkUp/html3/Contents.html'
```

25.2.4   General selection method

The general method for selecting objects follows three steps:

(1) Preselect an initial set of object(s) by using a key query (`-key`), by the name of their parent collection (`-coll`) or by a given object identifier (`-oid`).

(2) Optionally select all descendants (`-rec`) and/or anchors (`-anch`) of the preselected items.

(3) Optionally filter the selected objects by using an object query (`-query`).

Preselection of objects

With the option `-key` you can search for indexed attributes. This results in a very fast handling of the query. The result of a `-key` query always consists of one or more object identifiers (IDs).

- `-key string` returns the IDs of all objects containing `string` as a *keyword* or *name* or in the *title*. Only titles in the default language (English) are searched.

- `-lang lg -key string` returns the IDs of all objects containing `string` as a *keyword* or *name* or in the *title* of the given language (`lg`).

- `-formatted -key keyquery` returns the IDs of all objects which match the `keyquery`. This allows you to search for all indexed attributes (for example, `Name`, `Keyword`, `Title`, `TimeCreated` and `Author`), to check them for equality or range and to combine these queries with logical "or," "and" or "and not." For a detailed description of `keyquery` see the manual page `keyquery.1`.

The combination of the options `-key` and `-coll` works as follows. Option `-key kquery` (without `-coll`) searches the whole database, option `-key kquery -coll collection` searches only in the descendants of the `collection` and option `-coll collection` (without `-key`) selects only objects which are children of `collection`.

Selection of descendants and anchors

In the second step you can optionally decide about descendants and anchors of the preselected objects. The option -rec selects all descendants, that is, recursively children of selected collections. With the option -anch the anchors of selected documents are additionally selected.

Filtering the selected objects

The last step is to optionally filter the selected objects by using an object query. This is performed by using the option -query which allows searching for any attribute (for example, Title, DocumentType), and by using the operators "<" (less than), ">" (greater than), "=" (equal) or "~" (regular expressions) for matching the attribute fields. It is also possible to combine these queries with logical "or," "and" or "not." For a detailed description of objquery see the manual page objquery.1.

The -mult option allows you to get multiple objects without producing an error. This option should be used if more than one object is expected as a result of the query and the options -rec or -anch (which imply the -mult option!) are not specified.

25.2.5   Getting object information

The hginfo tool may be used to search in the Hyper-G database and to get information about objects. It allows you to search for any attribute (for example, Author, TimeCreated, DocumentType, Rights, Title, Keyword) and to get all attributes or only one attribute (option -attr) or only the object ID (option -ids) of the matching objects.

Example: Searching for keywords, names and titles

hginfo -key Amadeus -mult
This will give us all attributes of all objects in the database which contain Amadeus as keyword or name or in the title. Because there is no language specified only titles in the default language (usually English) are searched.

Example: Searching for titles

hginfo -form -key 'Title=ge:Amadeus' -ids
In this case we get a space-separated list of object IDs from all objects in the server which contain Amadeus in the German title.

Example: Searching for an author recursively under a collection

hginfo -form -key 'Author=hmaurer' -coll '~anonymous' -anch
All descendants of collection ~anonymous are searched for author hmaurer. In addition to all documents which match the query, all anchors of the selected documents are listed.

Example: Listing all children of a collection

```
hginfo -coll '~anonymous' -mult -sort '#T' -attr Title
```
In this case we get the titles of all children of collection ~anonymous in the default sort order.

Example: Listing all sub-collections (recursively) of a collection

```
hginfo -coll 'stamps' -rec -attr Name \
    -query '(DocumentType=collection) \
    &&(\!CollectionType=Cluster)'
```
The names of all sub-collections of collection "stamps" are listed. Note that we have to escape ! (the "not" operator) at the shell by \!.

25.2.6   Extracting documents

The hggetdata tool is used to extract one or more text, image, movie, audio, scene, PostScript or generic documents and to write them to standard output or store them in separate files.

The filenames are composed of an optional prefix (given by the option -fpfx), the object ID and the type of the document (<fpfx><oid>.<doctype>).

Text documents can be extracted together with their anchors: this is specified with option -anch.

The option -type restricts the extraction to a given document type: T (Text), I (Image), M (Movie), S (Audio), 3D (Scene), G (Generic) or P (PostScript).

Example

```
hggetdata -coll tutorial -rec -fpfx 'tutorial.'
```
The above command will extract all documents of collection tutorial and prefix the filenames with tutorial..

25.2.7   Moving, copying and unlinking objects

The hgmvcp tool can be used to

- *move* (option -move from to)
- *copy* (option -copy to)
- *unlink* (option -unlink from)

collections and documents in the Hyper-G database.

The general selection method (without options `recursive` and/or `anchors`) can be used to select a set of objects which are subsequently moved or copied from one collection to another or unlinked from a collection.

The option `-list` only prints a list of objects found and can be used to control the selected objects before really manipulating them.

Example

The following command moves all documents in collection `Archives` which expired before 1 January, 1996 to collection `Archives.Erase`:

```
hgmvcp -coll Archives -mult \
       -query 'TimeExpire<96/01/01' \
       -move Archives Archives.Erase
```

Note: Moving an object from collection `source` to collection `destination` can also be performed by copying it to collection `destination` and subsequently unlinking it from collection `source`.

If we want to copy all accessible documents in the server which contain `vrweb` in the English title, as keyword or name of the collection `~hguser.vrweb`, we perform the following command:

```
hgmvcp -key vrweb -mult -copy '~hguser.vrweb'
```

Of course, the selected documents are not duplicated but appended to the collection `~hguser.vrweb`. Normally if you do not have write access to these documents you are not allowed to delete them, but you can unlink all documents from your collection `~hguser.vrweb` with the following command:

```
hgmvcp -coll '~hguser.vrweb' -mult \
       -unlink '~hguser.vrweb'
```

25.2.8   Deleting objects

Two commands are available for the deletion of objects. The `hgdelobj` command is used when you want to delete individual objects, children of a given collection, or any object which matches a given query; the `hgerase` command is used when you want to recursively remove a collection hierarchy.

hgdelobj: Deleting objects by selection

Again the general selection method except for the option "recursive" can be used to select a set of objects which are subsequently deleted with all their anchors. The option `-confirm` can be used to confirm the selected objects before really deleting them.

Note: Collections and clusters are only deleted if they are "empty," that is, if there are no children within them.

Example

We want to delete all Hyper-G user accounts which are members of the user group `lecture1`. Before really deleting a user account we want to be asked for confirmation. This can be done with the command:

```
hgdelobj -form -key 'Group=lecture1' -mult \
    -query 'TType=User' -confirm
```

hgerase: Erasing or Clearing Collection Hierarchies

With the tool `hgerase` it is possible to erase or clear a collection hierarchy. The collection from which to erase or clear recursively downwards is specified in the command line.

Erasing (option `-erase`) means unlinking or deleting all documents, clusters and sub-collections within the given collection. *Clearing* means only unlinking or deleting all documents: clusters and collections themselves are not erased.

Unlinking or *deleting* is specified with option `-delete`. With `-delete` all selected objects are deleted. More precisely, if the objects are also members of any other collections or clusters, they will be deleted there as well, even if these are not descendants of the specified collection. If option `-delete` is not specified, all selected objects are unlinked recursively from the collections and clusters within the given collection hierarchy, but only deleted if they are not members of at least one other collection outside the given collection hierarchy.

Example

We want to delete the collection `Archives.Erase` including all sub-collections and clusters. We use the command:

```
hgerase -erase -delete Archives.Erases
```

By specifying the `-delete` option we also delete objects which are members of other collections or clusters, in other words, all occurrences of the selected objects are deleted.

25.2.9   Modifying objects

The `hgmodify` tool can be used to change attributes (for example, title, author, rights, name) of objects. The general selection method (see Section 25.2.4) is used to select a set of objects which are subsequently modified according to the modification command.

The structure of the modification command specified with the option `-comm` is as follows:

- `rem attr=val`: remove the attribute `attr` with the value `val`;

- `add attr=val`: add the attribute `attr` with value `val`.

If more than one command is to be executed the commands have to be separated by a backslash (\) character. For example, `-comm 'rem attr=val1\add attr=val2'`.

The option `-list` only prints a list of matching objects and can be used to control the selected objects before really modifying them.

Example

We want to change the access rights of all objects and anchors under collection iicm.internal recursively from R:a (readable only for the author) to R:g iicm (read access for group iicm). For this we can use the following command:

```
hgmodify -coll iicm.internal -rec -anch \
        -comm 'rem Rights=R:a\add Rights=R:g iicm'
```

Example

In the following example the name of a collection is changed from xyz to abc. In this case we "add" a new unique name to the collection which automatically removes the old name:

```
hgmodify -form -key 'Name=xyz' -comm 'add Name=abc'
```

25.3   `hifimport` and `hifexport`

For exporting data from and importing data to a Hyper-G server, the special data format **HIF** (Hyper-G Interchange Format) has been defined. HIF is a human-readable format defining object descriptions, collection hierarchy, anchors and either uuencoded data (documents) or external document data files.

The tools hifexport and hifimport also accept some additional parameters to control the way data is exported from and imported to Hyper-G servers.

According to the design of the HIF format, hifexport and hifimport can be used to mirror data between servers. Also, HIF files can be machine generated from other sources like databases and then used to insert the data into a Hyper-G server (see Appendix E for details on HIF). Machine generation of HIF files from existing databases and then inserting the documents in a Hyper-G server is an easy way to use existing data stored in a local database with all the hyperlink, structure and search possibilities added to it.

25.3.1   Exporting documents using hifexport

Exporting data with hifexport is useful for doing small personal backups and especially for mirroring data to other Hyper-G servers.

In the simplest case hifexport takes a single parameter, the collection name (or several collection names). It exports all data contained in the collections specified recursively and writes it to the standard output.

The default server and port number that hifexport connects to is controlled by the environment variables HGHOST and HGPORT. By default, hifexport tries to automatically identify the user (see Section 14.8.1 for details). If automatic identification is unsuccessful hifexport operates as an anonymous user.

If a user named wonko wants to export the personal home collection wonko_home and automatic identification applies for the login, the command

```
hifexport wonko_home > wonko_home.hif
```

produces the HIF file wonko_home.hif with the contents of the user's home collection.

To control the server and port hifexport connects to and to identify interactively the following command line parameters are relevant:

-hghost <hostname> defines the Hyper-G server hifexport connects to;

-hgport <portnumber> defines the port hifexport connects to (default: 418);

-identify allows interactive user identification.

For a list of all command line parameters, see the hifexport manual page located in ~hgsystem/man/man1.

If you are not sure about which default host and port number hifexport will be using, type hifexport -h and you will be shown the details. If the default values are not the desired ones, use the parameters -hghost and -hgport described above to override the defaults.

If you are not sure whether you will be automatically identified from the user account under which you are starting hifexport, use the parameter -identify. You are then prompted for username and password. As an example, if you want to export the whole contents of your personal home collection it is probably necessary to be identified, since normally not all documents in your personal home collection can be read anonymously.

Since the Hyper-G database is a distributed network database with seamless server structure, there can be arbitrary references to remote collections in the collection hierarchy that is exported by hifexport. In this case hifexport also exports the remote collections and documents from remote servers transparently. This behavior is not always desirable: imagine there is a reference to a collection with a huge literature database that is physically on another server somewhere on the other side of the world. Firstly, it should not be necessary to export the collection and secondly, data transfer of many megabytes from the other side of the world can be painfully slow (and expensive).

For this reason hifexport accepts the -local parameter which causes it to export only data physically residing on the local Hyper-G server together with references to the remote documents instead of the remote documents themselves.

If you have a collection hierarchy with many huge multimedia documents it is very often interesting to export simply the text and then export the multimedia documents separately. To export only the text, hifexport supports the -textonly switch which causes it to skip all non-text documents.

If you plan to export a collection hierarchy where all collection names have a certain prefix, the parameter -stripprefix <prefix> allows you to strip away this prefix if required. This feature is especially needed for collections where several physical copies exist on the same server. Collection names on a server have to be unique. In this case physical copy 1 could get the name prefix one_, this prefix can be stripped when exporting this collection by using -stripprefix one_ from all collection names and another prefix, for example two_, is then given to the second copy when inserting it and so on.

In many cases it is not even desirable to export the whole collection hierarchy lying under the collection(s) that are exported. For this purpose Hyper-G's powerful query mechanisms are very useful to define arbitrarily complicated sets of data for export. Hyper-G queries are supported by `hifexport` using the `-query` parameter. For a detailed description of possible Hyper-G attributes that can be used in an object query, refer to Appendix E. Here are a few examples of queries that are often very useful:

- *Export only documents that were created by author wonko*
  `'Author=wonko'`

- *Export the collection hierarchy only, without exporting documents*
  `'DocumentType=collection'`

- *Export documents that were inserted or modified after 1 December, 1995*
  `'TimeCreated>95/12/01 || TimeModified>95/12/01 || \`
  `DocumentType=collection'`
  In this case it is necessary to add the third part of the query `DocumentType=collection` to export the documents recursively. If the third part of the query were omitted, only documents in the top-level collection would be exported; collections would not be considered because they would not match the query.

- *Export only PostScript documents*
  `'DocumentType=PostScript||DocumentType=collection'`
  Again it is necessary to include the `DocumentType=collection` part to the query to search recursively.

- *Export documents with keywords that start with info*
  `'keyword~info.*||DocumentType=collection'`
  In this case we use the *regexp match* operator ~ instead of the = sign with a regular expression in the query. Again, `DocumentType=collection` is included in the query to search recursively.

Queries can be arbitrarily complicated. As an example, *'export all of user wonko's PostScript and text documents that are readable only by the usergroup staff and have been modified (not created) after 95/09/05, from the collection* `documents` *to the file* `complicated.hif'` can be accomplished using the following command:

```
hifexport -hghost <your host> -identify -query \
  '(DocumentType=collection||\
  DocumentType=PostScript||\
  DocumentType=text)&&\
  author=wonko&&Rights=R:g staff&&TimeModified>95/09/05' \
  documents > complicated.hif
```

Up to now all exported data has been written to a single large file including the documents in uuencoded format. Sometimes it is very useful to have a meta-information file that does not contain documents and to have all documents in single files in a subdirectory of their own. This is especially important when the document files have to be manipulated and then inserted back into the server.

A useful application would be offline conversion of images to another image format, such as the conversion of all GIF files in a collection to JPEG.

For this purpose use the switch -splitdoc to write separate meta-information and document files. The path where the document files are stored is set by the parameter -path. The command hifexport -splitdoc -path doc my_collection > my_collection.hif exports all collections and documents in my_collection, writes the document meta-information to the file my_collection.hif and stores the documents themselves in the subdirectory doc. Using -splitdoc also causes the documents to be written in raw format instead of uuencoded format as is normally the case when writing everything to a single large HIF file.

Normally anchors in documents are stored separately in the HIF file; this is also true for text documents. Sometimes it is desirable to have all anchors included in the text documents instead of stored separately, especially for editing the exported text documents and reinserting them again without scrambling the hyperlinks. To achieve this hifexport supports the switch -tagmode which causes hifexport to merge all the anchors into the text documents.

When using hifexport with the -splitdoc option to edit hifexported documents be careful not to create undefined hyperlinks. As an example, suppose links in an image are stored as relative coordinates. Converting images to other data formats or resizing images does not change relative coordinates and so nothing bad can happen. But if parts of the original images are cut out, then the positions of anchors in those images are no longer valid since they describe the previous positions.

There may be some special collections on the server that should not be mirrored and instead only a reference to the remote collection on the master server should be inserted. Normally this is used for collections that are changing very rapidly and would thus have to be mirrored too often. For such special collections hifexport supports the option -referenceonly <coll_names>. Here coll_names is a list of collection names separated by commas. Do not forget to place single quotes around the list, otherwise the shell will try to interpret the list which would lead to an error. The collections that are marked to be only references get a special tag in the *HIF* file which is evaluated by hifimport when mirroring the data.

25.3.2   Importing documents using hifimport

So far you have read how to export data from a Hyper-G server using hifexport and also how to export data in a such a way that you can manipulate it offline. The complementary tool to hifexport which enables you to insert data back into the Hyper-G server is hifimport. This program takes a HIF file and inserts the whole collection hierarchy, including documents, into a Hyper-G server and can even update or replace certain documents in the server itself.

In the simplest case you have exported some documents from one server to a HIF file and want to insert those documents into another server, for example for mirroring.

Suppose you have not used the -splitdoc option with hifexport and all the data is therefore stored in one single HIF file. You can simply use the command

```
hifimport -hghost hostname parent_collection HIFfile
```

to insert the documents in `HIFfile` to `parent_collection` on the Hyper-G server `hostname`. Now `hifimport` will prompt for your username and password on the server you want to import the documents into. The collections and documents that were exported with `hifexport` are then inserted there as children of `parent_collection`. If the environment variable `HYPERG_HOST` is set to the proper host the `-hghost` option can be omitted. As is the case with `hifexport`, `hifimport` also supports the `-hgport` option to connect to a nonstandard port.

Be careful when importing documents to a Hyper-G server using `hifimport`. Collection names (only names, not titles!) have to be unique on a Hyper-G server. If the documents in the HIF file contain one or more collections that happen to have the same name as a collection already on the Hyper-G server you are importing into, then the collection cannot be created on this server. Instead, all documents that were in this collection on the original server are inserted into the already existing collection on the destination server. Naturally, this insertion will only occur if you have the access rights to insert the documents there. Whether documents are added or replaced in the collection on the destination server depends on the value of the `-overwrite` option `hifimport` was given (see below).

As an example, consider a master server and a slave server as shown in Figures 25.2 and 25.3.

The collection `uni_info` on the master server is exported using `hifexport` and

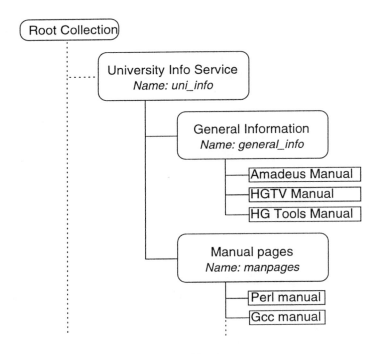

Figure 25.2   Master server.

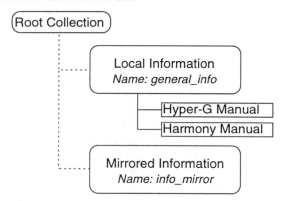

Figure 25.3   Slave server.

imported into the slave server using hifimport with parent info_mirror and without the -prefix option. A name clash occurs for the collection with the name general_info. The collection cannot be created twice on the slave server, so all of its contents are inserted into the existing collection named general_info on the slave server, as shown in Figure 25.4. Very often this is intentional, but if not you have to use a prefix when importing the documents as shown in Figure 25.5.

Names given to documents must also be unique. If a name clash occurs for documents they cannot be created on the destination server and, in this case, are either skipped or replaced depending on the -overwrite option hifimport was given (see below).

If name clashes occur that you want to avoid, use the -prefix <prefix> option with hifimport. In this case hifimport generates new collection and document names by preceding the old names with your given prefix. Note that collection names are used to directly reference collections. Therefore if you give collections a prefix, make sure it is easy to remember.

Of course, there are also cases where the insertion of documents into existing collections instead of creating new ones is desired, such as when incrementally updating existing collection hierarchies on mirror sites.

After this short excursion concerning the behavior and dangers of hifimport, let us turn our attention back to the other command line options and the way they influence data import.

If you have a HIF file that was generated by hifexport with option -splitdoc, the option -path with the pathname where your document files are stored is used to tell hifimport the path to the document files.

Another very important option that can be used with hifimport is -replicate. This option causes hifimport to insert all documents as replicas of the original documents. See Chapter 10 for an explanation of the replica mechanism.

Documents that are inserted as replicas of the original documents get a special replica ID on the mirror server. If you are hifimporting documents that contain links pointing to

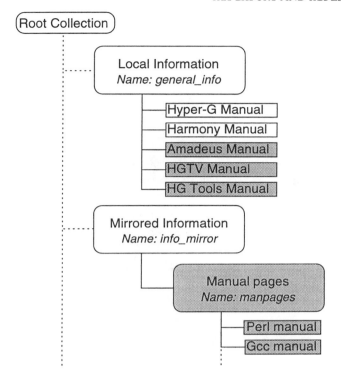

Figure 25.4   Import to slave server with a name clash.

documents that are not included in the HIF file, hifimport first searches for an existing replica of the destination document on the server. If such a replica is found the hyperlink now points to the replica, if not, a link to the remote document is created. But creating a link to the remote document does not mean that the remote document must always be downloaded from the remote server! If at a later time a replica of the remote document is inserted into the server the replica is taken instead of downloading the remote document.

Data insertion with hifimport is also controlled by another very important option: -overwrite <what>. This option controls the way documents are inserted if other versions of those documents already exist on the destination server. <what> can be one of the following:

never If a document already exists on the destination server, skip this document in the HIF file.

old If the document already exists on the destination server and this document is older than the document in the HIF file, overwrite it; if the document in the destination server is newer, then skip the document in the HIF file.

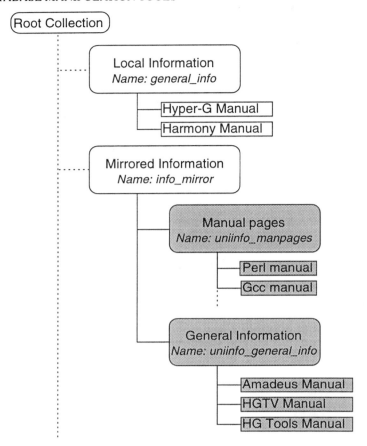

Figure 25.5   Import to slave server using the prefix `uniinfo_` to avoid a name clash.

replace Always replace existing documents with the documents in the HIF file.

insert Always insert all documents in the HIF file. If a document already exists in the destination server it is duplicated.

The `-overwrite` option not only affects documents themselves but also anchors. As an example, if you change the destination of an anchor in a document but do not change the document itself, the changed anchor is updated in the destination server according to the `-overwrite` parameter given.

The replace option is very useful for changing image formats. The images can be exported using `hifexport` with the `-splitdoc` option. Then the format of the exported images can be changed and everything can be inserted again using `hifimport` with the `-overwrite replace` option.

Normally, when inserting documents with hifimport, the Author attribute of the document is set to the author you are identified as. You can override this if you are identified as user hgsystem or in user group system (and only users of the system group are allowed to do this!) with the option -author <name>, where name can be either an account name on the destination server or the keyword HIF. If you use the keyword HIF then the author of the documents is set to be same as that stored in the HIF file.

If you want to use hifimport to transmit data over very slow and unreliable network connections there is also the option -timeout <seconds>. This option generates a timeout after the specified time of inactivity and tries to resend a document from the start after a timeout occurs. After five unsuccessful retries, the document is skipped and import continues with the next document in the HIF file.

25.3.3   Setting up mirror servers and replicating information with HIF

To avoid being too theoretical, here is a small example of how the HIF tools can be used in a real-life application.

Suppose you have a travel agency and you want to publish tourist information on the Web. You would also like to replicate the information on other sites to speed up data transmission, but to prevent having to mirror too often, you want last-minute information that changes very quickly to be kept centrally on your main server (like cheap spare seats in planes).

The collection hierarchy on your master Hyper-G server in this example could look like the one shown in Figure 25.6.

Assuming that the collection hierarchy contains many images, videos and other multimedia information, it is very useful not to export the full collection hierarchy to a single HIF file, but to have several smaller files. If hifimport fails due to a broken network connection, or for some other reason, it is only necessary to start hifimport with the remaining HIF files instead of letting hifimport check all documents on the remote server again. If you use the -overwrite old option, hifimport does not insert all documents again, but in this case, it still has to check whether the documents already exist on the remote server: with slow network connections, even this can be very time-consuming.

The collection Last Minute Information contains rapidly changing information and therefore should not be mirrored to the remote servers. For this reason the -referenceonly option is used with hifexport.

The collection Other Services contains remote links to other Hyper-G servers and only the remote links should be mirrored, not the contents. To achieve this use the option -local with hifexport.

Now we export all the collections to different HIF files (the server that contains the master copy has the hostname master in the following example):

```
hifexport -hghost master -identify -local \
    -referenceonly 'last_minute_info' \
    tourist_guide_general last_minute_info other_services > \
    general_documents.hif
```

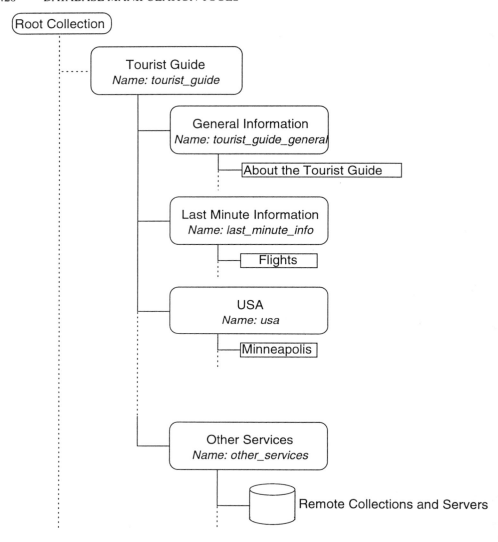

Figure 25.6   Example collection hierarchy for a tourist guide.

This exports the three collections tourist_guide_general, last_minute_info and other_services, making last_minute_info only a reference to the collection on the master server and making only remote links to the collections in other_services instead of exporting the remote data. When prompted for identification, identify as user guide_adm.

```
hifexport -hghost master -identify usa > usa.hif
hifexport -hghost master -identify austria > austria.hif
hifexport -hghost master -identify new_zealand > \
new_zealand.hif
...
```

Again identify as guide_adm when prompted by hifexport.

After having exported all the data, but before having mirrored the documents the first time, a user account has to be set up on the remote server. For example, this account may also be named guide_adm as on the master server and the main collection named tourist_guide.

Having prepared the remote server, the documents are uploaded (the mirror site has the hostname slave in the following example).

```
hifimport -hghost slave -overwrite old \
    -replicate -timeout 180 \
    tourist_guide general_documents.hif
hifimport -hghost slave -overwrite old \
    -replicate -timeout 180 \
    tourist_guide usa.hif
hifimport -hghost slave -overwrite old \
    -replicate -timeout 180 \
    tourist_guide austria.hif
hifimport -hghost slave -overwrite old \
    -replicate -timeout 180 \
    tourist_guide new_zealand.hif
...
```

When you are prompted for identification, identify yourself as guide_adm. The option -overwrite old is not necessary for importing documents the first time, but is necessary for later updates and also if hifimport is not able to finish the import of a HIF file and has to be started again. The value for -timeout is set to three minutes which should be long enough even for very slow network connections.

After having imported all the HIF files to the mirror site, you should be prepared to perform an incremental update of the mirror site if documents on the master change.

Changed documents can be exported by a simple query for documents that have been added or changed since the last mirror update. See Appendix E.2 for details on objects and object queries in Hyper-G. As an example, if the last mirror update was 1 February, 1996, the hifexport of all new documents in our example would be:

```
hifexport -hghost master -identify -local\
    -referenceonly 'last_minute_info' \
    -query 'TimeCreated>96/02/01||TimeModified>95/02/01||\
    DocumentType=collection' \
    tourist_guide > AfterFeb01.hif
```

Since the number of documents that changed is not too large, it is no longer necessary to split the documents across several HIF files. The mirror site is then updated with the command:

```
hifimport -hghost slave -overwrite old \
    -replicate -timeout 180 \
    tourist_guide AfterFeb01.hif
```

25.4   Further reading

For an up-to-date description of all offline Hyper-G database manipulation tools please refer to the online documentation: `http://hyperg.iicm.tu-graz.ac.at/hyperg` or to the manual pages that come with the server distribution. Information on general aspects of hypermedia authoring can be found in *Hypertext/Hypermedia Handbook* (Berk and Devlin, 1991). *Learning Perl* (Schwartz, 1993) is a good introduction to the Perl scripting language. Larry Wall – the "father" of Perl – was co-author of *Programming Perl* (Wall and Schwartz, 1991). Information about BibTeX can be found in *Making TeX Work* (Walsh, 1994).

26 Hyper-G and the PC-Library

Helmut Mülner

In this chapter we discuss the **PC-Library**, a tool to create powerful standalone hypermedia applications that can be (and have been) sold as such. However, the hypermedia databases created can also be imported into Hyper-G. The PC-Library is thus a powerful way of creating information for the Web in cases where preparation for the Web only would not be commercially feasible.

26.1 General

The PC-Library (the German name PC-Bibliothek is trademarked) has been developed in parallel with Hyper-G. It is based on the same general concept but focuses on different issues.

It is intended as a tool to market electronic reference material on floppies and CD-ROMs at a time when such marketing on the Web is still difficult. The goal is, however, also to publish the material on the Web, while not relying entirely on such Web publishing for revenues. One main difference from other sources of information on the Net is that this data comes from publishers whose only asset is this material. Not only must adequate tools to view this material be developed, but publishers must also be convinced that they are not giving away the source of their income. They must believe that they can earn money by publishing on the Web without risking "data piracy."

The PC-Library is an MS-Windows application for working with electronic books and encyclopedias. So far there is only a German version of the program. A test version in English has also been implemented.

The basic idea of the PC-Library is in its name: it just works like a real library, where you keep books you have bought in a book shop. If you want to look up something in a book, you take it out of your library (shelf) and put it on your desktop, together with other books and other items you work with. The PC-Library uses the same metaphor: you can buy single titles in a book shop and you put them in your library by installing them on your computer. As a side effect, the PC-Library software can be updated automatically. With a mouse click or two you can take a book out of your library and put it in your working area or vice versa.

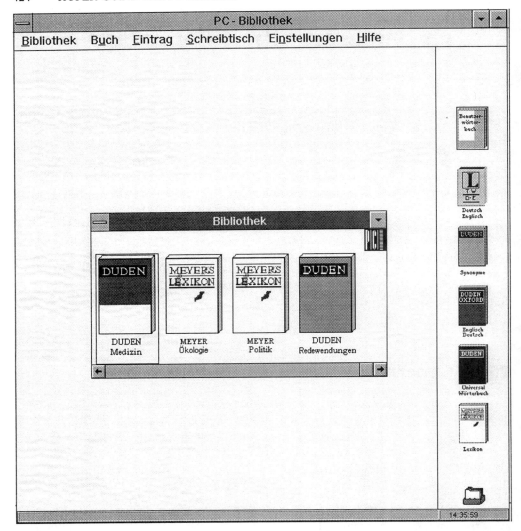

Figure 26.1   The Library in the center and the desktop at the right-hand side.

26.1.1   Features

The PC-Library offers a number of desirable features that cannot be found in similar applications:

- Every word is clickable, making every word into a hyperlink to its definition or its occurrences.

- Fast retrieval of information for keywords and full text.

- Users can select arbitrary font style and size.

- Fault-tolerant searching allows language-specific mismatches so that typical spelling errors can be compensated.

- The "user book" is an empty book where users can insert their own information. Otherwise this book is treated the same as all other books, that is, you can perform keyword searches and full text searches.

- Annotations and additional keywords to every article provide the users with the means to "work" with the books.

- Physical book mode is an option that corresponds to the layout of the "original" book. It allows you to view the surroundings of the retrieved information.

- Network versions allow the installation of books on a networked drive (the standard editions can only be installed on a local drive). They use the same mechanism as Hyper-G: five licenses for a book mean that five users can use this book concurrently. The licensing mechanism works in combination with any PC-based network system. It can even recover from the sudden death of PCs that are just using some material from the PC-Library. This is an event that occurs surprisingly often in the world of personal computers using certain "operating systems."

26.1.2 Published titles

The currently existing corpus of information consists of the following books. We have listed the original German titles. Translation to English is left as an exercise for the reader (or you can skip to the end of this chapter).

Langenscheidt Taschenwörterbuch Englisch mit Tonausgabe (CD-ROM)
Langenscheidt Taschenwörterbuch Englisch (Floppies, CD-ROM)
Langenscheidt Taschenwörterbuch Französisch (Floppies, CD-ROM)
Langenscheidt Eurowörterbuch Englisch (Floppies, CD-ROM)
Langenscheidt Eurowörterbuch Französisch (Floppies, CD-ROM)
Langenscheidt Eurowörterbuch Italienisch (Floppies, CD-ROM)
Langenscheidt Eurowörterbuch Spanisch (Floppies, CD-ROM)
Langenscheidt Eurowörterbücher Englisch, Französisch, Italienisch und Spanisch (CD-ROM)
Duden 1 – Rechtschreibung(CD-ROM)
Duden 5 – Fremdwörter (Floppies)
Duden 7 – Herkunft (Floppies)
Duden 8 – Synonyme (Floppies)
Duden 10 – Bedeutungswörterbuch (Floppies)
Duden 11 – Redewendungen (Floppies)
Duden 12 – Zitate und Aussprüche (Floppies)
Duden Oxford (Deutsch/Englisch) und Duden Universalwörterbuch (CD-ROM)

Duden Medizin (Floppies)
Duden Informatik (Floppies)
Meyer Lexikon (Floppies)
Schülerduden Ökologie (Floppies)
Schülerduden Politik (Floppies)
Langenscheidt Musterbriefe Englisch für Export und Import (Floppies)
Langenscheidt Russisch (Floppies)

For the near future the following titles are planned:

Langenscheidt Musterbriefe Französisch für Export und Import (Floppies)
Dubbel, Springer (CD-ROM)
LaBoe, Springer (CD-ROM)
Duden 1 – Rechtschreibung alt/neu (CD-ROM)
Duden 2 – Stilwörterbuch (Floppies)
Neuauflage mit Erweiterungen Meyer Lexikon
Neuauflage mit Erweiterungen Duden 5 (CD-ROM)
Neuauflage Duden Oxford und Duden Universalwörterbuch (CD-ROM)
Bildwörterbuch (CD-ROM)
English–Maori Dictionary

26.2   The PC-Library as part of a general electronic library

The PC-Library is a project that we believe will support the realization of the dream of every scientist at a scientific workplace: to have immediate access to all information needed. An electronic library should provide fast and easy access to reference material which can be held either on CD-ROM locally, on a CD-ROM server or a Hyper-G server in the local net, or in some database somewhere in the world.

26.3   Integration with other programs

An electronic library makes work and life easier for scientists and writers. However, it is not just that access should be easier than in books, it should be possible to actively use material found. One such facility is provided by the PC-Library.

If you want to have an explanation of some term you are reading or typing with your word processor, just press some magic key combination (which is configurable) – the PC-Library is activated and searches for the term in its active volumes, that is, those volumes that you have specified at some earlier stage to be of interest to you. You select the correct definition. Once again the same magic key-press and you are back in your word processor with the explanation ready to be inserted in your text, complete with copyright notice and perhaps some other attribution.

26.4   The PC-Library and Hyper-G

PC-Library data can be converted to Hyper-G by a suitable converter. This converter is at the moment only available for internal use. The PC-Library does not use SGML to store its data, but an internal format that is a kind of "compiled" and reduced SGML which also includes compression. For the publisher, this has the advantage that the data in the books cannot be (mis)used directly. From this format, a suitable SGML representation (or other formats, such as RTF) can be re-created.

Important differences from Hyper-G are:

- The PC-Library uses a "flat" format, that is, one book is a continuous file of data, and the substructure is defined by separate index files.

- The PC-Library utilizes a large subset of Unicode (using UTF encoding) because books often contain characters from the IPA (International Phonetic Alphabet) lexicographic symbols ("born," "died," "airport" and so on), Greek and Cyrillic characters, and others.

To demonstrate the possibility of using PC-Library data in Hyper-G, the MEYER encyclopedia has been converted and is available in Hyper-G (see Figures 26.2 and 26.3). Further books will be made available in Hyper-G as part of the LIBERATION project.

Converting Web data to PC-Library format is straightforward: the SGML encoding is just compiled into the internal format. Many of the titles produced so far (and most of the planned titles) come from the publishers in SGML encoded format, confirming that this process has been used successfully a number of times.

26.5   PC-Library Version 2

A new version of the PC-Library will be available in 1996. By the time you read this book, this should already have happened.

This new version includes:

- A new data model for internal storage allows you to keep more information about SGML originated data and includes management of hierarchical collections like in Hyper-G.

- An improved retrieval engine that allows for arbitrary wild-cards, regular expression searches, a second kind of approximate matching, and restricting searches to collections or parts of the data defined by SGML tags.

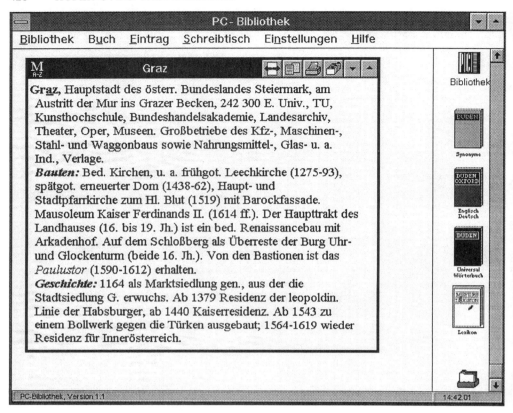

Figure 26.2   Entry Graz in Meyer's Encyclopedia (PC-Library).

- A new user interface combines the power of the Multi Document Interface (MDI) with the simplicity of a Single Document Interface (SDI) with dockable floating windows. Every kind of window in the new PC-Library can be converted from an MDI window to a dockable floating window and vice versa, and every kind of window can be restricted to a certain number of occurrences. Thus, users can configure as many document windows as they want. Configurations can be stored, and at installation time users can decide between two configurations: a basic SDI configuration with most windows docked (for "dummies"), and a typical MDI configuration (for "sophisticated" users that can handle more than one window).

An important kind of window will be a tree view of the hierarchical collections including not only the books and their parts, but also the desktop, a history, keywords, user-defined keywords, bookmarks, color marks, annotations and search results.

Figure 26.3   Entry Graz in Meyer's Encyclopedia (Hyper-G version).

26.6   Further reading

For more details of specific points concerning the PC-Library see Mülner (1989), Mülner (1991) and Maurer *et al.* (1994c).

The LIBERATION project mentioned is part of the Telematics Application Library sector within the Fourth Framework Program of the European Community (1995–1998). LIBERATION stands for **LIB**raries: **E**lectronic **R**emote **A**ccess **T**o **I**nformation **O**ver **N**etworks. Two journals (J.UCS by Springer and J.NCA by Academic Press) and some 40 books, plus some courseware, will be made available on Hyper-G servers as part of this project.

For readers without a German–English dictionary from the PC-Library, the translations of the book titles listed earlier are as follows:

Langenscheidt Pocket Dictionary German–English with sound (CD-ROM)
Langenscheidt Pocket Dictionary German–English (Floppies, CD-ROM)
Langenscheidt Pocket Dictionary German–French (Floppies, CD-ROM)
Langenscheidt Euro Dictionary German–English (Floppies, CD-ROM)
Langenscheidt Euro Dictionary German–French (Floppies, CD-ROM)
Langenscheidt Euro Dictionary German–Italian (Floppies, CD-ROM)
Langenscheidt Euro Dictionary German–Spanish (Floppies, CD-ROM)
Langenscheidt Euro Dictionaries English, French, Italian and Spanish (CD-ROM)
Duden 1 – General Wordbook (CD-ROM)
Duden 5 – Foreign Words (Floppies)
Duden 7 – Etymology (Floppies)
Duden 8 – Synonyms (Floppies)
Duden 10 – Word Definitions (Floppies)
Duden 11 – Phrases (Floppies)
Duden 12 – Citations and Proverbs (Floppies)
Duden Oxford (German/English) and Duden Universal German Dictionary (CD-ROM)
Duden Medicine (Floppies)
Duden Informatics (Floppies)
Meyer Encyclopedia (Floppies)
Pupil's Duden Ecology (Floppies)
Pupil's Duden Politics (Floppies)
Langenscheidt Example Letters in English for Export and Import (Floppies)
Langenscheidt Russian (Floppies)

For the near future the following further titles are planned:

Langenscheidt Example Letters in French for Export and Import (Floppies)
Dubbel, Springer (CD-ROM)
LaBoe, Springer (CD-ROM)
Duden 1 – Grammar old/new (CD-ROM)
Duden 2 – Handbook of Style (Floppies)
New Edition Meyer Encyclopedia
New Edition Duden 5 (Floppies)
New Edition Duden Oxford and Duden Universal Dictionary (CD-ROM)
Picture Dictionary (CD-ROM)

27 Hyper-G and HM-Card

Srinivasan Parthasarthy

This chapter deals with **HM-Card**, a new **multimedia authoring tool for presentational and instructional purposes**. HM-Card is of particular interest for Hyper-G users, since material created by HM-Card can not only be used in standalone mode but can be embedded into Hyper-G for worldwide distribution on the Web.

In this chapter we only give a rough survey of HM-Card. We refer the interested reader to the new book on HM-Card (Maurer and Scherbakov, 1995).

27.1 What is HM-Card?

HM-Card is a PC-based hypermedia and multimedia authoring system. In fact, it consists of three main software components which empower authors to create interactive multimedia applications that can be used for a variety of purposes. Multimedia applications may range from simple interactive kiosk-type presentations to complex Computer Aided Instruction (CAI) material with vector graphics and answer-judging facilities. Currently, HM-Card runs under Microsoft Windows 3.xx, Windows NT and Windows 95, but migration to other operating sytems, in particular UNIX and Macintosh, is planned in the near future.

The presentations created by HM-Card can be browsed in standalone mode or they can be integrated into Hyper-G or WWW and disseminated over the Web. Multimedia material prepared with HM-Card is stored in a hypermedia database which is based on the so-called **HM Data Model** (see below) which facilitates modularity, reusability and automatic hyperlink maintenance.

27.2 HM-Card: An introduction

HM-Card enables users to create, in a program-free fashion, multimedia applications that contain complex hyperlinks. The three main components of HM-Card are the **Editor**, **Linker** and **Viewer**.

The *editor* is basically used for creating so-called HM-Card **pages**. An HM-Card page can be understood from the conventional point of view as a set of linearly ordered multimedia objects (text, image, movie, sound and other media objects) that is displayed as a unit. Obviously, this does not mean that all objects are displayed simultaneously or in some fixed order. As will be explained later, the display order of the objects can be manipulated by the author to a great extent. Apart from conventional hypermedia objects like text and images of various formats, movies and sound, HM-Card offers a rich variety of vector graphic objects, input objects (buttons, edit fields, password fields, check buttons, clickable area), mailboxes, answer-judging facilities, complex animation facilities and more.

HM-Card pages are combined into so-called **S-collections** with the help of the *linker*. S-collections can be considered modular units with a well-defined navigational paradigm: roughly speaking, the particular navigational strategy is reflected in how navigational links are available during browsing and in a consistent set of operations. The HM-Card database consists essentially of such S-collections. An S-collection can contain both HM-Card pages and other S-collections. S-collections are the basic operational unit in HM-Card. For a brief discussion of the properties of S-collections, refer to Section 27.3.1 and for a detailed discussion, see some of the papers and the book mentioned in Section 27.6.

The third component of HM-Card is the *viewer*. The viewer is used for navigating (or displaying) the databases created using the editor and linker. The viewer allows the user to modify several presentational aspects during navigation. This includes changes in the presentation metaphor and modifying the properties of buttons that represent hyperlinks. Additionally, the viewer supports keyword search, rich annotational features and "recording" and "playback" of macros. If you are interested in developing multimedia applications using HM-Card, you can refer to Section 27.4 for a more detailed description. However, for understanding the terminology, you should first read Section 27.3.1.

27.3   HM-Card: Terminology and functionality

This section presents a brief overview of the HM Data Model in order to define the terminology and concepts which are both discussed in this chapter. For more details refer to Section 27.6 which contains information on articles and online tutorials.

27.3.1   HM Data Model

The HM Data Model has been developed by the IICM at the Graz University of Technology over the past three years. Readers familiar with the trends in hypermedia data modeling techniques should be aware of the fact that in recent years there has been a considerable amount of critique of the basic "node-link" paradigm (see also Chapters 3, 4 and 8). Recent years also witnessed a variety of proposals for efficiently combatting the problems inherent in the node-link model. In a way, this whole book is a major contribution.

In the HM Data Model, external hyperlinks (often called "cut-across" links) are suppressed. The hypermedia database is perceived as a set of well-defined modular units of information. Those modular units will be called S-collections in the sequel. S-collections encompass the links and further augment the navigational facilities by encapsulating a navigational paradigm.

Every S-collection has a unique identifier, a name used by other S-collections for addressing, and generally an associated page which will be called content or label, henceforth. An S-collection encapsulates a particular internal structure. The internal structure is a set of pages and/or other S-collections (called members henceforth) related by a number of computer-navigable links. One of the members of the S-collection must be designated as the head of the S-collection. An S-collection without the internal structure of links is called a void S-collection or just an HM-Card page. The various types of S-collections are discussed below.

Note also that links are encapsulated within a particular S-collection: they may only be defined between members of the same S-collection.

The major benefits resulting from such a modeling technique is:

Modularity The database consists of well-defined components, enabling modular evolution of the database which is essential for collaborative database design.

Reusability S-collections can be quite easily reused and perused in comparison with hypermedia documents in conventional hypermedia data models, since links pointing out of S-collections and leading into them simply do not exist.

Customization The modular approach enables the navigational paradigm of every S-collection to be tuned according to the user's wishes.

Manageability The fact that the database is perceived as a set of well-defined modules simplifies the task of management. In comparison, it is a formidable task to administer hundreds of HTML documents which are linked to each other unless support facilities as available in Hyper-G can be used.

Automatic link maintenance The HM Data Model assures link consistency automatically. Links are maintained locally in every individual S-collection. The object orientation of the model simplifies the task of creating and removing links when a new S-collection is added into the database or inserted into another S-collection.

The HM Data Model provides a number of predefined subclasses of S-collections that define a particular "topology" of encapsulated links.

Basically HM-Card provides seven subclasses of S-collections: envelope, folder, menu, freelinks, grid, external and information page.

Envelope All members of an envelope are fully linked; each member is linked to every other.

Folder An ordered list of members, each member having links to the "next" and "previous" member within the ordered list.

Menu A simple hierarchical structure; the head of a menu S-collection includes links to all other members, and each member is provided with a link back to the head.

Freelinks Members of a freelinks S-collection may be arbitrarily connected together.

Grid Members of a grid S-collection can be sequentially scanned using different sorting criteria. In other words, a grid can be considered as a "multi-sorted folder." For instance, employees of a company can be scanned in order of corresponding attributes (age, salary and other such attributes) or in alphabetical order. Also, some attributes attached to the head of an S-collection can be dynamically calculated using other attributes attached to members of the same S-collection, as parameters. For instance, the average and total salary of all employees of a company can be dynamically calculated and displayed as a part of the information on the company. A description of attributes which are used for such purposes is called a *form*. Forms can be specified as parameters of S-collections of any type by means of the forms button. This is a required parameter for S-collections of type Grid.

External S-collections of this type are not only provided with a content (they have no members), but with a special external procedure which is executed as a result of the Zoom_In operation applied to this S-collection. S-collections of this type are normally used to provide access to information resources used by other systems like, for example, a database management system. The name of an external S-collection becomes an important attribute, as the name defines a command line which is used to launch the corresponding external procedure. Note that content is a mandatory parameter for S-collections of this type.

Information page A primitive chunk of multimedia information called an information page. The HM-Card editor is used for creating an information page.

27.3.2   Navigation in the HM Data Model

Let us now take a look at how navigation is achieved in the HM Data Model despite the absence of "cut-across everything" links. When an HM-Card database is opened, all S-collections within the database are activated. In other words, they are entitled to respond to operations that are generated as a result of either user interactions or the internal system messages. An S-collection can be addressed using the method **access**. All subsequent messages are redirected to the most recently accessed S-collection. In the HM Data Model, the user can be situated either outside the premises of the S-collection or "within" it. When the user is situated outside (as a result of the method access) only the head of the S-collection is displayed. The links to other S-collections are not available to the user and hence are not displayed on the screen.

In order to enable access to the links, the user has to perform a so-called zoom_In operation. On receiving the zoom_In message, the S-collection switches itself to a state called *current container*. Now the links to other member S-collections are available and hence displayed to the user. Note that only the current container is eligible to receive messages from the system. Following a particular link triggers an access message which is rerouted by the current container to the target S-collection. As a result of a zoom_In operation on a member collection, the status of *current container* is delegated to it by the system.

There exists a complementary method to `zoom_in` which is called `zoom_out`. As a result of this message, the "zoomed out" S-collection loses the current container status and the system delegates the status back to the S-collection which previously possessed it. The S-collection can be attributed with so-called `automatic zoom_in` and `automatic zoom_out` properties.

27.3.3   Working with the database

New S-collection instances are created with the operation `create`, whereby the name, content and head are assigned to it. Once an S-collection has been created, new members can be inserted and existing members removed by means of the operations `insert_member` and `remove_member`. All links within S-collections belonging to the classes menu, envelope and folder are maintained automatically in accordance with their associated link structure.

Of course, the regularly structured subclasses do not restrict you from using S-collections having arbitrarily connected members. Users can create an S-collection of class freelinks and explicitly define its link structure using the messages `insert_link` and `remove_link`.

At any point, an S-collection can be deleted with the `delete` operation. In this case, its content and all links encapsulated within it cease to exist. If a deleted S-collection has been included as a member in other S-collections, then a `remove_member` operation on these S-collections is performed before the S-collection is physically deleted.

27.4   Creating multimedia applications

Several commercial packages offer tools for creating multimedia applications (see Section 27.6). Some are capable of producing excellent slide-show presentations, some support rich navigational paradigms, some are programming-free like HM-Card, others require scripting. However, only very few commercial packages provide rich question–answer facilities coupled with complex answer-judging facilities, not to speak of animation. HM-Card is the only software package that satisfies the following:

- ability to produce interactive kiosk-applications, multimedia presentations, manuals, courseware material;

- graphical interface for editing, defining and creating hyperlinks, vector graphics, complex animation, answer-judging, response evaluation, import of images (different formats), OLE and so on;

- modular design of courseware material, supporting effective reuse and administration of the hypermedia database;

- standalone presentation of the material;

- distribution of material with networked information systems like Hyper-G;

- complex navigational strategies with a high degree of customization.

27.4.1   Editor, linker and viewer: Tools for designing multimedia applications

The process of creating a multimedia presentation involves creating HM-Card pages, structuring the pages, linking structured collections of HM-Card pages and finally defining the navigational metaphor (or customizing the navigational buttons). The HM-Card software consists of three main components: editor, linker and viewer. This section provides only an outline of these components.

27.4.2   Editor

The editor is used for creating and modifying HM-Card pages. It provides a wide range of conventional editing facilities for operating with media objects in a WYSIWYG fashion. The media objects range from common text, graphics, movies and sound to complex answer-judging, analysis and branch objects, mailboxes and so on. The editor allows easy integration of material which already exists in some electronic form by providing adequate support for several well-known data representation formats and their conversion. Media objects can be imported in their native format by Windows' OLE method. Thus, one HM-Card page can be edited as a compound document that consists of objects created by various applications that support Windows OLE. Whenever the user wishes to edit such an object, the corresponding application associated with the object will be launched; when the user terminates the session, the results are updated accordingly in the HM-Card page. Creation of HM-Card pages can be considered as the first stage of the design process.

HM-Card objects

HM-Card objects can be classified into two main categories: *internal objects* – HM-Card provides a built-in support for both the creation and the display and manipulation of these objects; *imported objects* – such objects are usually created with other applications. HM-Card can display some of the imported objects (like image files), while for others an external viewer is required (see below).

Internal objects

Vector graphics HM-Card provides a powerful set of vector graphics capabilities, such as line, rectangle, ellipses and so on. The author can manipulate their style and color as in several other commercial packages.

Text object Various fonts including different styles and sizes are supported by HM-Card in order to integrate textual information into an HM-Card page.

Message object The message object is used for displaying any kind of intermediate information on the screen; this can be used for short notification messages in response to user inputs.

Mailboxes This object is used for storing values (integer, Boolean, string and so on). The mailbox cannot be displayed. The value of the mailbox can be used for controlling the execution sequence of objects.

Input objects The input object is generally used for accepting user inputs. It consists of a number of fields or buttons.

Edit field The input object allows the user to type a string into the edit field. The input objects provide format conversions to integer, real, upper case and lower case. The input objects allow authors to create so-called password fields.

Button Conventional Windows buttons like ok/cancel buttons, Bitmap buttons, radio buttons, checkboxes and so on can be created using HM-Card.

Analysis and branch objects The execution order of objects can be manipulated with the help of the analysis and branch objects. The analysis objects allow the user to create well-formed formulae (WFF) in which the values from mailboxes and input objects can be used. The branch object is analogous to the GOTO command of conventional programming languages. These objects cannot be displayed.

Snapshot The user can capture a portion of the screen and store it in the clipboard for redisplay at a later stage.

Fill This object is used for filling a region with a particular color or pattern.

Pause The pause object is used for temporarily halting the execution. The pause object can be a simple timer which halts the execution for the defined amount of time and restarts the execution automatically or waits for a key hit or mouse click.

Beep and flash These objects can be used by the author to capture the attention of the user.

Gadgetry The gadgetry object is used for special visual effects which are especially useful in kiosk applications.

Animation HM-Card provides powerful animation facilities. Linear animation, arbitrary trajectories, scaling, timed sequences and so on can be implemented on displayable objects.

Group HM-Card allows a certain set of objects to be combined into one single so-called group object. A complete HM-Card page or an animation object can be aggregated into a group object. Group objects simplify reuse.

Navigational object Basic navigational operations of the HM Data Model (that is, zoom_in, zoom_out, next, prior and keyword search) can be incorporated into information pages in the form of objects.

Import objects

Text object HM-Card provides a built-in editor for text creation and manipulation of text with various fonts, styles and sizes. It operates only with the fonts that are installed in Windows. Text can also be imported into an HM-Card page. The text object can viewed in a separate window or integrated into the page.

Image object Image files of conventional formats (Windows Bitmap, CompuServe GIF, JPEG, TIFF and so on) can be imported into an HM-Card page.

Movie object Movie files in MPG or AVI format can be imported into HM-Card. Currently, HM-Card does not provide a built-in viewer for these formats, but any external viewer can be used to display them.

OLE object An OLE object can be embedded into an HM-Card page.

DLL object This allows the application designers to enhance the functionality of HM-Card by writing their own Dynamic Link Library. HM-Card provides an API for reading and writing data from or into the HM-Card internal objects (such as input objects and mailboxes), and passes on the display context of the window to the external user-defined DLL.

Executable object This object is useful for launching external applications from within an HM-Card page and passing on arguments to it. It works as if the program had been executed from the command line.

27.4.3   Linker

The linker is used for providing the logical, contextual or semantic relationships between HM-Card pages. The linker generates complex link structures in the form of S-collections. An S-collection may have links to HM-Card pages and to other S-collections. The aggregation of such S-collections constitutes a hypermedia application. Every hypermedia presentation is physically stored in a separate hypermedia database. As described in Section 27.3.1, each S-collection provides an inherent link structure. The link representation can be subjected to a high degree of customization. In other words, the author can impose various kinds of metaphors on the links to suit the domain.

The linker provides a rather simple interface for creating S-collections and editing the links between them. The linker operates with the current S-collection (all the operations are applied to the current S-collection). When an S-collection is created (operation `create`) it automatically becomes the current S-collection. The user has to define the attributes for the S-collection (the head, label, type, navigational buttons and so on). A head and type must be assigned to every S-collection. Every S-collection within a hypermedia database must be supplied with a unique name.

An S-collection can be made a member S-collection of the *current S-collection* with the operation `insert`. Note that the link structure between member S-collections are defined by the type of S-collection and are maintained automatically by the linker. Obviously, a member

S-collection can be removed from the current S-collection by the `remove` operation. In this case, the author does not have to bother about link maintenance. The current S-collection can be physically deleted from the hypermedia database as a result of the operation `delete`.

As mentioned earlier, complex navigational strategies can be synthesized as a result of manipulating the execution sequence of the media objects within the scope of HM-Card pages and by defining any kind of desirable link topology among S-collections. The linker provides adequate freedom in defining the user interface (especially the link representation for so-called customizable navigational buttons) thereby enabling authors to develop purpose-built hypermedia applications and fine-tune them to any subject domain.

27.4.4   Viewer

The viewer is a standalone program for browsing hypermedia applications created with the editor and the linker. The viewer enables the user to control various parameters (such as the form of link representation), apply keyword search and create annotations. The linker additionally enables the user to record the keyboard and mouse inputs of a session which can be played back. This feature is especially useful for creating hypermedia tours. The HM-Card viewer supports three levels of annotation: administrator, expert and user. These are very useful in the case of courseware for supporting collaborative work, evaluation of student response and self-evaluation.

27.5   Organizing a courseware library with the help of Hyper-G

The previous sections of this chapter mainly focused on designing multimedia applications using HM-Card. Applications may range from simple slide-shows and interactive presentations to complex interactive courseware material. This section describes the possibility of creating a worldwide network of large courseware repositories using HM-Card modules.

The Web has revealed tremendous potential for transporting information. However, complex animations or user-input analysis are difficult to implement using current formats of representing information. This complicates the straightforward production and dissemination of high-quality courseware material.

The powerful design strategies and the rich set of objects allow HM-Card to produce powerful and compact courseware material.

27.5.1   Courseware libraries

HTML is extremely useful for representing textual information with embedded graphics, but is not powerful enough for creating high-quality courseware material. The main goals of a courseware library are:

- To provide simple access to users. Users should be able to browse the courseware both online and offline. Online browsing demands that the user is connected to the network. For users without any connection to the network (or for low-bandwidth connections) probably offline browsing is more suitable. The courseware is distributed via floppies or CD-ROMs or downloaded via FTP and then browsed using the viewer.

- To allow adequate reuse of the courseware material. Reuse is not achieved by simply creating a link to the necessary material. This would produce the same effect as "spaghetti-links" in hypermedia. Authors should be able to determine the level of granularity when allowing their material to be reused, or when reusing courseware material from other authors. Courseware generally consists of lessons, chapters, sections, subsections and so on. For instance, consider the case when the author of a course on "hypermedia" wants to allow other authors to reuse the chapter on "Human–Computer Interaction" free of charge and other chapters commercially. The monitoring system of the courseware repository is responsible for managing the links: links to the chapters that are commercially distributed should be billed. Additionally, the author can allow a group of authors to use the chapters free of charge. In this case, the system administering the courseware repository should be able to support UNIX-like multi-level user account management.

- To allow collaborative authoring of courseware. Several authors should be able to work on the same courseware simultaneously.

- To support versioning control. The courseware library should allow authors to maintain several versions of the courseware. In case of reuse, by default the latest version should be used. However, the author should be able to define a particular version for reuse.

- Copyright protection. The courseware library should be protected from copyright and license violations, illegal amendments, reuse and usage.

Powerful Web-based systems like Hyper-G provide comprehensive built-in facilities for creating such repositories and enable users to view and retrieve information from these repositories in an organized fashion. Furthermore, associative browsing of information can be easily achieved by establishing hyperlinks of a semantic, referential or contextual nature between such units.

Hyper-G servers offer efficient security mechanisms, multi-level user accounts and billing mechanisms; see Chapter 10 and Section 11.3.

Courseware units (HM-Card modules) can refer to other courseware units stored in the same or in some other repository. The Structured Interchange Format based on the Document Linking and Embedding principle discussed in Section 27.5.2 solves this problem quite satisfactorily.

The Institute for Information Processing and Computer Supported New Media (IICM) and Addison-Wesley have decided to establish a courseware market based on conventional Web formats like HTML and HM-Card interactive modules.

27.5.2   Structured Interchange Format

Hypermedia applications developed by means of HM-Card consist of a number of hypermedia database files and supplementary files (text files, image files, sound files and so on) imported into the HM-Card pages. Generally, for the sake of convenience and for easy administration, all files belonging to a certain courseware package or presentation are kept in one directory. HM-Card has an option to combine all the files belonging to a certain presentation into one single file which will be called a **module** in the sequel.

A module can be considered as an independent unit. When a module is executed by the viewer, the files are extracted into a temporary directory and the presentation is started from a predefined S-collection, specified during the creation of the project. Additional options such as viewing the presentation in a separate window, adjusting to the current Windows resolution and so on, are also set during creation.

Thus, a module is a document which can be viewed with an HM-Card viewer. The HM-Card viewer can be started from the command line with this module as an argument. This will result in the execution of the presentation. This functionality is used in incorporating HM-Card presentation modules into network-based information systems like Hyper-G or WWW. The module can be transported over the Net: any Web browser can run the HM-Card viewer and pass on the module as an argument.

When two different information systems contain references to each other, a so-called interchange format is usually employed. Such a format defines how the navigation paradigm is switched at run-time when the user follows a link from one information system into the other. Let us first consider how this is realized between Hyper-G and HM-Card.

A module is stored in a Hyper-G database as a generic document. HM-Card modules are assigned the subtype hmcpage. When a generic document of subtype hmcpage is accessed, the Web browsers must execute the HM-Card viewer and pass on the generic document as an argument. The viewer unpacks the module and starts the execution of the application. The user can then start to navigate through its contents. On completion, the user closes the viewer and can continue browsing the Hyper-G database. It must be noted that the HM-Card software package currently runs only under Windows 3.xx, Windows 95 and Windows NT, so this process of executing the module is only possible with Windows Web clients.

Similarly, it is possible to access Hyper-G or WWW pages from HM-Card. The HM-Card pages can contain an object (an external S-collection) that refers to a URL. When such an object is executed, the appropriate viewer is executed and the address of the URL is passed as argument. The user can start browsing from the URL within Hyper-G or WWW. On completion, the Web client must be closed in order to continue the navigation within HM-Card from the point of interruption. In the near future, a Dynamic Data Exchange (DDE) protocol will be implemented in HM-Card which will enable synchronous data exchange between Web clients and the HM-Card viewer. Thus, the user can follow a URL from an HM-Card package (the corresponding Web client will be executed) and, without closing the Web client, continue the navigation within the viewer. On the other hand, when the HM-Card module is executed as a result of following a link pointing to it from Web clients, the user need not close the viewer application in order to invoke the HM-Card viewer again when another link to a module file is activated. The viewer application can run in the background, receive the contents via the DDE protocol and unpack the current module and display it.

How to contribute to the courseware market

In order to contribute to the effort, interested authors should upload courseware prepared with HM-Card and a short description in HTML format to the FTP server `ftp://ihm-iicm.-tu-graz.ac.at/pub/marketincoming`. The material submitted to the courseware market will be superficially examined for technical correctness and legal acceptability in accordance with Austrian laws. A complete course consisting of several lessons can also be submitted to the repository. If the author wishes to distribute the material commercially, the material will be refereed by Addison-Wesley. Then, if the material is accepted for commercial distribution, the author can negotiate royalties. In this case, a short description and the introductory chapter would be made available on the Web free of charge and the complete HM-Card courseware would be commercially available on floppy disks, CD-ROMs or over the Web from Addison-Wesley. For complete details regarding the marketing details, please consult `http://ihm-iicm.tu-graz.ac.at/market`.

27.5.3 An illustrative example of creating an HM-Card application

The first stage in creating a presentation is the creation of an HM-Card page using an editor, see Figure 27.1. First of all, define a unique name for the page. If a page with the same name already exists in the database, you can either modify the page or redesign it, in which case the previous contents will be deleted.

By default, the background color for the page is black and the foreground color is white. The objects (see Section 27.4.2) can be selected from the toolbar displayed under the menubar. By default, a new object is inserted after the current object (the most recently edited object). You can duplicate the object, move it, modify the properties or delete it. For proper alignment, you can switch on the option for displaying a grid. You can preview the page in order to see how the page is displayed to the user during a session.

When you have finished creating pages, you can combine them into complex S-collections. These are created with the help of the linker. You should assign a unique identifier, choose a type and assign a "head." Additionally, you can attribute several other parameters to the complex S-collection which influences the user interface and offer customized navigational features. These features include:

automatic zoom_in A `zoom_in` operation is automatically performed when the user accesses the S-collection.

automatic zoom_out A `zoom_out` operation is performed when the user accesses the head of the S-collection for the second time.

link visualization For S-collections of type freelink or menu the links can be visualized in the form of scrollable lists, pushbuttons, clickable areas or hot-words.

predefined layout You can define a predefined screen layout for S-collections. This layout is displayed for every member S-collection. It is especially useful when you want to

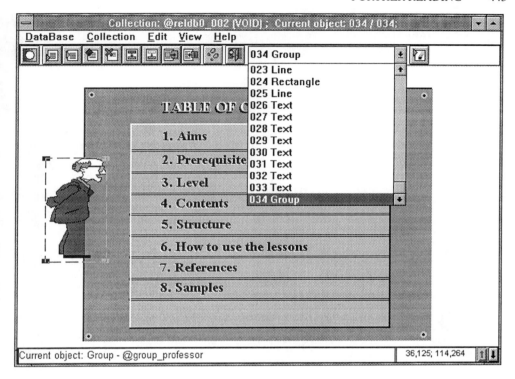

Figure 27.1   Creating a page with HM-Card.

display information (for example, a help button) in the context of a particular S-collection for all its members.

Analogous to the editor, you can preview a complex S-collection to see how it is visualized. Figure 27.2 shows the the dialog box for inserting member S-collections into the current S-collection.

You can view the presentation using the viewer. If you feel that a page has to be re-defined or amended then you can directly invoke the editor from the executor and make the necessary corrections. Section 27.6 contains references to information sources for more details on authoring with HM-Card. Figure 27.3 shows the S-collection displayed when the user navigates using the viewer.

27.6   Further reading

The article by Maurer *et al.* (1995) is a good starting point for learning more about HM-Card and its authoring elements.

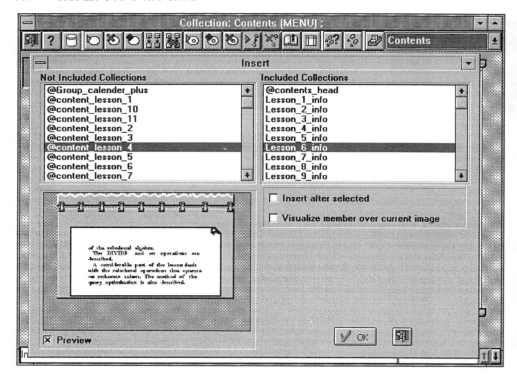

Figure 27.2   Designing a complex S-collection.

The book *Multimedia Authoring for Presentation and Education: The Official Guide to HM-Card* (Maurer and Scherbakov, 1995) contains a comprehensive description of HM-Card. The book contains an elaborate explanation of the authoring process, for creating online and offline multimedia presentations.

The articles by Maurer *et al.* (1993a), Maurer *et al.* (1994d) and Maurer *et al.* (1994e) provide further details on the theoretical aspects of the HM Data Model. The article by Maurer *et al.* (1993b) discusses the user interface issues and the navigational aids. The article by Maurer *et al.* (1994b) contains a comprehensive description of concepts involved in embedding HM-Card applications into Hyper-G.

The URL http://www.iicm.tu-graz.ac.at/hmcard contains a lot of online information about HM-Card, HM Data Model, courseware created with HM-Card and so on.

For more details on the courseware market consult the URL http://ihm-iicm.-tu-graz.ac.at/market. You can download several courses from the FTP site iicm.-tu-graz.ac.at/pub/hmcard/dbcourse.zip or they can be browsed online at the URL http://info.iicm.tu-graz.ac.at. Web browsers should be adjusted in order to view the HM-Card modules online; the URL http://www.iicm.tu-graz.ac.at describes how this can be done.

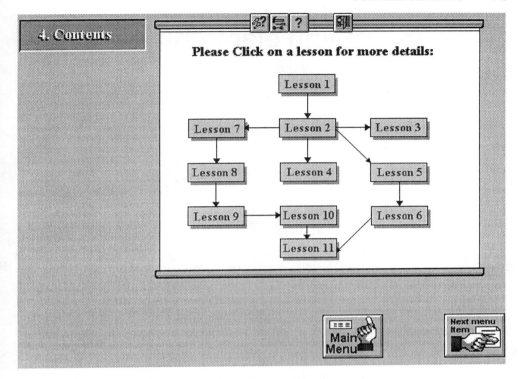

Figure 27.3   Navigation in S-collections.

For information on how to adjust Web browsers like Netscape, Amadeus or Mosaic to run HM-Card refer to `http://www.iicm.tu-graz.ac.at/hmcard`.

28 Hyper-G and electronic publishing

Klaus Schmaranz

Electronic publishing is booming on the Web these days. In this chapter we give an overview of how Hyper-G can be and already is used for professional electronic publishing **on the Web and on CD-ROM**.

Hyper-G is designed to meet all requirements of professional electronic publishing by providing stable bidirectional links in all supported document types. It allows you to search for titles, keywords and the contents of documents, or a combination of all three, with user-definable scope. The scope of searches can range from one collection on a single server to all collections on all servers worldwide. The highly sophisticated replication mechanism (see Chapter 10 for details) makes mirroring of documents to other servers easy, helping to keep access and transmission times low for readers. User access control and billing mechanisms are also supported by Hyper-G, features which should appeal to publishing companies who wish to get involved in electronic publishing.

Since not everybody has Internet access yet, it is also important to be able to provide a CD-ROM version of your data and for archival purposes, a printed paper version. Hyper-G supports preparation of multimedia CD-ROMs by using the local Hyper-G database as well as the handling of existing type-setting information used for paper publications. Therefore Hyper-G supports hybrid Web/CD-ROM/paper publications to the maximum extent possible.

28.1 Types of literature

Before considering technical aspects of electronic publishing it is necessary to distinguish between different kinds of literature having different requirements and different focuses.

28.1.1 Traditional literature

Traditional literature is here considered to be books and journals as they have been published on paper over centuries. Electronically distributed traditional literature should also meet the requirements of paper-based literature:

- Publications have to be stable. Printed publications cannot be modified at a later stage. It is also important that electronic literature is never modified once it has been published, even though it is easy to manipulate electronic documents. In many areas of publishing, especially in scientific publishing, authors frequently quote other publications. Changing a paper that has been quoted is clearly unacceptable.

- Publications have to be quotable. It is certainly not enough that hyperlinks can point to them. After printing out electronic publications or when referring to electronic publications in standard paper-based articles, there are no hyperlink facilities. It is thus absolutely necessary to be able to quote electronic papers in a page-oriented manner, as is the case with paper-based articles.

- Publications must also be accessible in non-electronic form. Since not all readers have the necessary equipment to read electronic publications, either on the Web or on CD-ROM, it is important to provide a printed version for those readers.

- All published material has to be kept in archives for a long time. In the case of electronic publications this not only means that electronic documents must be stored reliably, but also that rapidly changing hardware and software environments must be taken into account. To ensure that archived material is useful over a long period of time, it is necessary to store printed versions in addition to the electronic versions and to be able to convert electronic material to new data formats if necessary.

Hyper-G makes it easy to fulfill the above requirements and make traditional publications more valuable by publishing them electronically:

- Classification of documents is easy due to Hyper-G's structured collection hierarchy.

- Hyper-G's highly sophisticated search mechanisms make location of interesting documents easy.

- Hyper-G supports PostScript with hyperlinks and in the near future also PDF. These formats are both page-based and therefore fulfill the requirements to publish traditionally quotable material. They can also be used for high-quality printouts on the reader's desktop and for archival purposes.

- Hyper-G supports the publishing process to the maximum possible extent, from submission to a referee, right up to the final publication (see also Section 28.3).

28.1.2   Multimedia literature

Multimedia literature also includes non-printable material such as sound, video or 3D scenes. This can be in the form of traditional literature with multimedia add-ons for explanatory purposes, but it can also be a completely different kind of literature that is no longer based on readable text.

Examples of traditional media with multimedia add-ons are journals, books or encyclopedias in which the verbal description of a complex process is enhanced by a model or a simulation to make it easier to understand. In these cases, the requirements that were pointed out in the previous section apply to the printable part. Additionally, care must be taken to maintain an electronic archive for the multimedia material. Archiving electronically does not just mean copying the data to a tape, but that the complete environment must be preserved and, if necessary, reformatted at a later stage when new systems can no longer deal with old archive material. Since the lifetime of storage media such as magnetic tapes and CD-ROMs is short compared with that of paper, it means that archived material should be copied from time to time before the lifetime of the storage media expires.

Beyond traditional media with add-ons, multimedia publishing also covers completely new forms of electronic literature that is no longer based on written text. This literature can be highly interactive and is likely to change very rapidly over time. As an example, a 3D globe model could contain hyperlinks to information on countries in the form of images, video and sound documents. Additionally, Earth observation data could be provided, such as images of the weather, radar, temperature maps and much more.

Hyper-G supports the traditional approach with add-ons as well as the modern multimedia-only approach to the maximum extent possible by allowing hyperlinks in arbitrary document types, even in 3D scenes, movies and sound. Due to the database that is the kernel of the Hyper-G server, it is easy to manage rapidly changing information. This makes highly interactive pure multimedia publishing possible.

28.1.3   HTML literature

We consider HTML literature in this context to be a kind of literature of its own, due to the fact that lots of electronic publications have been written in HTML for the Web. HTML literature is characterized by the fact that text is formatted to fit into a given window and reformatted every time the window is resized. Therefore HTML literature is literature where layout must not matter too much.

Typical examples of HTML publications are personal home pages, descriptions of companies and products, manuals, catalogs and directories. A lot of advertising is also done in HTML, but since advertising is mostly layout dependent, most HTML advertisements consist of many inline images and only small reformattable text parts.

28.1.4   Interactive literature

Hypertext and hypermedia need not follow the well-known page-based book paradigm for literature. Instead, readers can have much more freedom to navigate by browsing collection hierarchies and following hyperlinks. Multimedia add-ons like 3D models can serve as the central point of a document from which other documents can be accessed by appropriate pointers. The reading order of a web of interlinked documents is no longer sequential, as it is with paper-based literature, but is instead defined by the reader.

Hyper-G supports another form of interaction beyond interactively choosing the reading order – publications can be annotated by identified readers without changing the documents themselves, due to bidirectional links in Hyper-G. By using annotations, documents can be extended, leading to two levels of interaction: readers of annotated documents have interactive documents in the sense that they can choose the reading order and also in the sense that they can interactively influence those documents if they are identified users.

A possible scenario for such interactive literature could be a Web-based interactive novel. Suppose that a novel is written by an author and published electronically on the Web. The novel is about several people but the author has written from the point of view of a single person only. Readers of the novel can themselves be authors and present other points of view for the same scenario. The result is a novel where readers can choose which person's episodes they are interested in and jump between different episodes, compare them, and if they wish, write another part to extend the novel.

28.2   Document formats for electronic publishing

After this short introduction to some of the different types of literature, let us now return to some technical details of electronic publishing.

One of the major decisions for electronic publishing is which document format to use for the distribution of publications.

The document format for the electronic publication of traditional literature is widely dictated by the requirements stated earlier, especially in the scientific area. Another point to take into consideration here is that not all readers of traditional publications really want to read on screen. Very often the online version is used for locating interesting documents that are then printed for further reading.

For multimedia publications a CD-ROM version is often desirable. One reason is to be able to provide for readers without Web access and another is that CD-ROM publishing can differ slightly from Web publishing due to different transmission speeds. In fast local networks the Web version can contain documents that need higher bandwidths than can presently be adequately handled by CD-ROM drives, for example high-quality videos. On the other hand, CD-ROMs can contain documents that need more bandwidth than the Web can provide for long-distance data transfers.

28.2.1   HTML

HTML is probably the most obvious candidate document format for electronic publishing on the Web (see Figure 28.1). It provides hypertext features and HTML viewers are available for most hardware and operating system platforms. Additionally, SGML-based formats like HTML have the advantage that they preserve the document semantics instead of the format and therefore are easily convertable to other document formats if required. In the past year, a large number of user-friendly HTML editors have become available for many different platforms, making it easy for authors to write HTML texts.

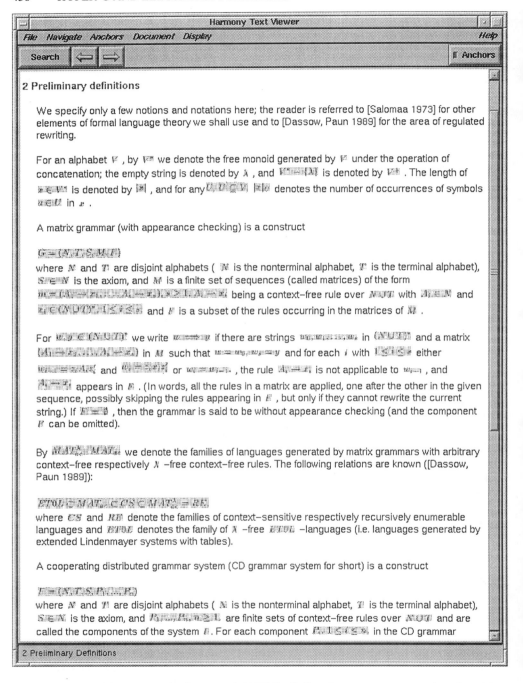

Figure 28.1 A Mathematical paper in HTML (inline images representing formulae are marked gray).

But there is also the other side of the coin. Because HTML was defined to preserve the semantic structure of a document instead of its layout, the rendering of the document is now the responsibility of the reader. As a result, readers of a paper format it as they want to see it, and this need not necessarily be the layout the author had in mind. More than that, the layout of a paper is often used by authors to express relations in a particular context; if the layout is redefined by the reader, the context can get lost.

HTML is a document-based instead of a page-based format that meets the requirements of hypertext. Bearing in mind the different types of publishing discussed at the start of this chapter, HTML is only conditionally useful for traditional publishing. It is not page oriented and high-quality printouts cannot be made due to the lack of layout information and symbol character sets. Papers dealing with very special knowledge areas, for example mathematics, physics, chemistry, just to mention a few, need to be able to display such things as formulae, figures and drawings, charts and atomic structures. Special characters are needed for this purpose, and up to HTML 2.0 all special characters had to be embedded as inline images, a chore for authors and publishers, with the added disadvantage that the amount of data transmitted over the Network can be enormous.

HTML 3.0 overcomes many problems with special characters, but at the moment there are few viewers that can fully render HTML 3.0 documents, nor does HTML 3.0 support vector graphics. For many areas of scientific publishing where figures are important, vector graphics have to be converted to a pixel-based format. This is again a lot of work for authors and publishers and again results in much larger files.

From our point of view, HTML is a good format for the text part of multimedia literature and interactive literature but not for traditional scientific literature. It does not fulfill the requirements for quotable and high-quality printable documents to the extent demanded and it is not suitable for scientific publishing in certain areas because of the poor support for symbol character sets and vector graphics.

28.2.2   SGML with special DTDs

As pointed out above, the HTML DTD is not really suitable for traditional publishing. On the other hand, many publishing houses and other companies are using highly specialized SGML DTDs for internal use. SGML documents are rendered by special programs and used for high-quality printing. So far this sounds like the solution we are all looking for.

Hyper-G can store arbitrary SGML documents together with the special DTDs that are necessary. The problem is that except for the two native Hyper-G clients Harmony and Amadeus, there are virtually no clients available that can handle generic SGML. Depending on the features that are implemented in the special DTD, even those two clients can have difficulties rendering the documents. In the worst case, all readers are forced to install additional software which will certainly limit the readership. The same is the case if readers want to make printouts; they need specialized software to get acceptable quality.

Another drawback of special SGML DTDs is that a specialist is needed to define a complicated DTD, and this process is very time-consuming and expensive. For these reasons, the SGML approach is well suited to in-house use or for a special readership, but problems arise when documents are to be published for a wider audience.

Again, an advantage of SGML is that the semantic structure of a document is preserved and not the layout, but as mentioned before this can also be a disadvantage. Depending on the complexity of the DTD, the borders between layout and semantic structure of a document will tend to float and semantic structures can be misused for defining layout. Depending on the needs of the publisher, it is worth considering whether it would be better to adopt a layout-based format like PostScript or PDF and add semantic information to the document, for example, in the form of comments in the PostScript or PDF document.

SGML with special DTDs is very interesting for internal use and for archival purposes. According to the area of publishing, DTDs can be extended where appropriate. To reach a broad readership, SGML documents can be kept inside the publishing company as working documents and for archival purposes but could be reformatted to other formats when making them accessible to the public on the Web.

One aspect where SGML with special DTDs is useful, also for a broad readership, is CD-ROM publishing with Hyper-G. A CD-ROM containing the local Hyper-G database also contains all the necessary software, Harmony and Amadeus, to view the documents. In this case no installation of new software is necessary because everything runs directly from the CD-ROM. This overcomes incompatibility and acceptance problems.

28.2.3 PostScript

Using SGML-based hypertext formats for electronic publishing provides readers with many of the advantages they would expect from electronic publications, such as hyperlink facilities and search mechanisms. The drawbacks of SGML-based formats are missing page layout mechanisms and missing page structure, both essential requirements for professional electronic publishing of traditional material.

Another important point to consider when talking about electronic publishing is the question of old archive material. Publishing companies' archive material is very likely to be either in PostScript or in some page description language used for printing machines. Normally, page descriptions for printing machines are convertible to PostScript and therefore PostScript can be seen as the common denominator. This makes publishing of archive material easy.

Using PostScript for electronic publishing overcomes all problems of general layout. Additionally, PostScript is page-based instead of document-based and useful for high-quality printouts. From this point of view, it is the ideal format for publishing traditional material, fulfilling all the requirements pointed out at the beginning of this chapter.

A drawback of PostScript compared to the SGML-based approach is that normally PostScript documents do not contain semantic structure unless they were produced by specialized software that left special marks or comments in the PostScript file.

Although there is no practical way to get the semantic structure back from a standard PostScript file itself, the structure can be seen when rendering the document. A typical page is built from headings, paragraphs, graphics and other structural elements. Hyper-G includes tools that perform document reverse engineering to identify semantic structure as well as text extraction on a PostScript document.

A feature that is important for electronic publishing and is not included in the definition of PostScript itself is hyperlinks. Using PostScript with Hyper-G adds all the hyperlink facilities to PostScript (see Figure 28.2). The same is the case with full text search – PostScript documents that have been analyzed with the special Hyper-G tools mentioned above get a full text index in the Hyper-G database, allowing searching in the contents of PostScript documents.

Since hyperlinks as well as the full text index for PostScript documents are stored in separate parts of the Hyper-G database, those features are added to PostScript documents without changing the document itself. For this reason no compatibility problems can arise.

Last but not least, PostScript is an author-friendly format: nearly all word processors today can produce PostScript output, either directly or using the printer interface and writing the output to a file.

PostScript with hyperlinks and a full text index in Hyper-G is nearly the ideal format for publication of traditional literature. There is only one point that causes some problems: dependencies between pages are allowed. This means that a font can be set on one page and used on the next, or that variables and subprograms can be defined with arbitrary contents that are used somewhere later in the document. Although there are structuring conventions defined by Adobe, those conventions are not mandatory. This results in the necessity to render PostScript documents sequentially from beginning to end to make sure that the outcome is correct. Sometimes this can be very time-consuming.

28.2.4 PDF

As was pointed out in the previous section, PostScript fulfills the requirements of high-quality printouts, flexibility and publication on a per page basis. At the time it was developed, nobody knew about hypermedia systems, so the additional functionality to make PostScript behave like hypertext was added in Hyper-G's implementation. The problem remaining is that pages in PostScript documents are not necessarily independent. The result is that jumping to a page somewhere inside the document can be time-consuming since all pages preceding it have to be rendered too.

To fulfill the needs of electronic publishing Adobe has defined a new format, PDF (Portable Document Format), which is based on PostScript. PDF supports hyperlinks, and in combination with Adobe's Acrobat software, full text searching is possible.

PDF has all the advantages of PostScript, as described in the previous section, and supports all features that were added to PostScript in Hyper-G. Additionally, single pages in PDF files are independent and are directly addressable without parsing or even rendering the whole document. The only problem with PDF is that Adobe's Acrobat software is presently the only viewer that supports all features of PDF and Acrobat is not yet ported to all main hardware and operating system platforms.

Due to PDF's roots, PostScript files can be converted to PDF using Acrobat Distiller. Thus authors can write PDF documents without using new unknown software by simply producing PostScript files and distilling them.

PDF as a native Hyper-G document format including stable hyperlinks, as is the case with all links in Hyper-G, will be available by the middle of 1996. By this time, the native

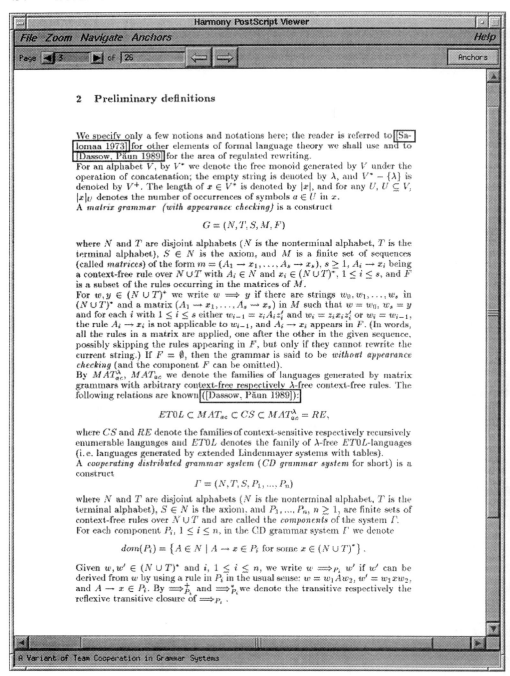

Figure 28.2   A PostScript document with hyperlinks in Hyper-G.

Hyper-G clients Harmony and Amadeus will also fully support PDF as an internal format. As well, a standalone version of the PDF viewer for use with other clients will be available.

28.3   Submissions and electronic refereeing

The document format used for submissions to electronic journals should not be a specialized hypertext format (such as HTML) as this would force authors to leave their well-known environments and deal with new word processors and styles of writing. Even when papers are published in HTML, conversion should be done by the publisher, if necessary, to make electronic publishing as user-friendly as possible.

The most common document format with regard to flexibility and compatibility is PostScript. Nearly every word processor today can produce PostScript output either directly or using the printer interface and redirecting output to a file. To produce PostScript output, authors can simply use their favorite word processor and need not deal with new software. Using Hyper-G's special conversion tools it is possible to convert PostScript to other formats like HTML if needed.

Electronic publishing not only changes the way papers are distributed, it also opens completely new aspects of refereeing when using Hyper-G. The main reason is that Hyper-G provides user access rights which make it more than just a read-only database.

Submitted papers are inserted in the Hyper-G database and are only readable by the referees and the author. The referees for a certain paper get a user account on the Hyper-G server. If required, the referees' Hyper-G user accounts can easily be set up so that the referees remain unknown to the author.

Referees' comments are inserted directly into the Hyper-G server, annotating the refereed paper. They are only visible to the particular referee who wrote them and, if the referee wishes, also to the author. The author can see the progress and can even get in contact with the referees by annotating the referees' comments. It is the referees' decision whether to discuss comments with further annotations.

28.4   Preparing material for electronic publishing

Let us suppose that you want to publish material electronically on the Web, additionally make a CD-ROM version and, as a publisher, you also need a printed version of the electronic journal for archival purposes.

Preparing different documents in different formats for the Internet, CD-ROM and printed paper versions is normally very time-consuming and expensive. Hyper-G fully supports distribution of hyperlinked PostScript documents that can be used for the printed version as well and Hyper-G also supports preparation of CD-ROMs from a collection hierarchy. There are nearly no additional costs for the publisher even though publications are distributed in three different ways.

Preparation of electronic or hybrid publication material is always done in the Hyper-G server. Depending on whether you want a CD-ROM version and/or a paper version too, you can make a snapshot of the collection hierarchy and also print the documents for the paper version.

28.4.1 Preparing the Web version

The first question is which data format to use. This highly depends on the kind of literature that will be published as well as on the distribution medium, as has been pointed out in the above sections.

Let us suppose that you want to publish traditional material on the Web, on CD-ROM and also on paper. It is very useful to start with a page-based format such as PostScript and, depending on the contents of the articles, you could also provide a parallel HTML version of the material for quick browsing. This is especially useful for readers who only use the electronic version for locating interesting articles and then, if the article is interesting, download the high-quality PostScript version to print it out. For this reason, the HTML version should be split into an abstract and single chapters, making browsing of parts of this version easy and quick.

The first step in preparing electronic publications is to find a meaningful and functional collection hierarchy, to ease navigation and retrieval of interesting papers. For this purpose, it makes sense to create one collection hierarchy structured by volumes and issues and one or more collection hierarchies structured by categories. Hyper-G makes preparation of such parallel hierarchies easy, due to the copy and move facilities. In this case, copy does not mean a physical copy, but only another reference to an article in another collection.

All electronic papers in the Hyper-G server should also have keywords supporting the search for papers belonging to certain thematic areas. Of course, a full text search can also lead to good results, but the keywords given by the author are usually more specific than searching in the text of the papers.

Depending on the journal's distribution philosophy, whether it is free of charge or not, or whether it should be only accessible to certain usergroups, collections as well as documents must be given the correct user access rights. See Section 11.2 for details of user access rights and Section 11.3 for details of billing mechanisms in Hyper-G.

One interesting point when preparing the collection hierarchy is that of inline images. It is normally not desirable for readers to find too many inline images in the collection hierarchy in addition to the relevant documents. To hide them from readers, there is a simple trick: insert all inline images into one or more collections and give the collections the access rights R:a (only the collections, not the images!). The effect is that only the author can see the collection itself: it is not accessible to other users, but the images are "world-readable" and can therefore be used as inline images in documents.

28.4.2 Making a CD-ROM

Having prepared the Web version of the electronically published material, it is easy to make a snapshot of the collection hierarchy and produce a CD-ROM. For this purpose, export the collection hierarchy using `hifexport` (see Section 25.3 for further details of this program).

The resulting HIF (Hyper-G Interchange Format) file is then used to make the local database as described in Chapter 13. This database together with all local database viewers is then used to burn the CD-ROM master.

28.4.3 Bidirectional links and annotations

Since all links in Hyper-G are bidirectional, it is easy for identified users to annotate papers without changing the contents. An identified user can insert a document into a collection where write access is allowed with a hyperlink pointing to the annotated paper.

Annotations are very useful for letting the reader know about new results, additional material and naturally also for discussions about the paper. Since annotations themselves can be annotated this is an ideal way to hold a discussion forum. From this perspective, electronic publishing with Hyper-G actually enhances traditional paper-based publications.

If annotations are to be made by readers, it makes sense to create a separate collection for annotations with write access permission for all readers of the journal. This would be especially useful if it were planned to replicate the collection hierarchy to other servers too. Annotations are then automatically exported to all mirror sites when replicating the contents. For further details on replication and mirroring see Section 25.3.

28.5   Journals and books published with Hyper-G

At the moment there are several electronic journals, books and conference proceedings published with Hyper-G that have appeared on the Web as well as on CD-ROM and paper:

J.UCS – the *Journal of Universal Computer Science* by Springer,

J.NCA – the *Journal for Network and Computer Applications*, formerly J.MCA – the *Journal for Micro Computer Applications* by Academic Press,

Few Body Systems – a reputational physics journal by Springer,

Telematics by the Telematics Engineers Society, Austria,

ED-MEDIA 95 conference proceedings by the American Association for the Advancement of Computers in Education,

Datenstrukturen (Ottmann T., Widmayer P.) – one of the most important German books on data structures,

Die Elberfelder Bibel – a hypertext version of the Bible,

Meyers Lexikon – one of the most widespread encyclopedias in German-speaking countries,

The PC-Library – several encyclopedias and dictionaries,

Others – some 30 additional books by Addison-Wesley.

just to mention the most important ones. The first journal published with Hyper-G was J.UCS – *Journal of Universal Computer Science* (see Figure 28.3). The pilot issue of J.UCS appeared in November 1994 and regular service started in January 1995. J.UCS is free for a trial period of two years until the end of 1996, after which access to J.UCS will be available on a subscription basis. Since J.UCS was the prototype for a new generation of electronic publishing and is at present also the most technologically sophisticated journal of the above mentioned, we will give a short overview of what is now known as J.UCS technology.

Philosophically, J.UCS is a high-quality refereed monthly electronic journal published on the Web as well as on CD-ROM and paper. The CD-ROM and paper versions appear yearly for archival purposes. Annotations are allowed in J.UCS. Due to the fact that J.UCS is a high-quality journal, annotations are also refereed to avoid their use for personal disputes.

Another aspect of high quality in J.UCS is the way that the Web version is distributed: papers in J.UCS, except for those which are too mathematical, are available in hyperlinked PostScript and hypertext format. This makes browsing easy. Readers can also choose to print out the PostScript version yielding the same quality as the version used by Springer for printing.

High quality also means that quick access to interesting papers must be possible, otherwise the journal would lose much of its worth for readers. For this purpose, J.UCS is replicated on a number of servers around the world and readers can choose the server geographically convenient for them.

Publications in J.UCS are structured into pages that are numbered consecutively so that papers can be quoted exactly as they are in conventional journals with name(s) of author(s), title, name of the journal, volume number, issue number and page number(s).

With the permission of ACM, papers appearing in J.UCS are categorized following the ACM Computing Reviews categories. A complete overview of the possible categories is given in every January edition of ACM Computing Reviews as well as in J.UCS itself.

The main submission format is PostScript. After the trial period of two years, subscribers will be able to choose between two methods: subscription on a library basis, or private subscription.

Subscription on a library basis means that the subscriber, in this case very likely a library or computing center, operates a Hyper-G server with a replica of J.UCS on it. Depending on the number of subscriptions, the journal is accessible by that number of users simultaneously. After accessing the journal the issue will be locked for a certain amount of time. This is comparable to borrowing an issue of a printed journal from a library. Naturally, the server operator is not forced to make J.UCS publicly accessible but can define user access rights to limit the user group. In the case of a university, this would typically be the university members and students and eventually one extra subscription that is publicly accessible.

Private subscription does not mean that subscribers must operate their own Hyper-G servers. Instead each private subscriber is provided with a Hyper-G account on a geographically convenient J.UCS mirror site, allowing J.UCS to be read from this server. In this case only the subscribers themselves have access to their particular J.UCS subscriptions and their

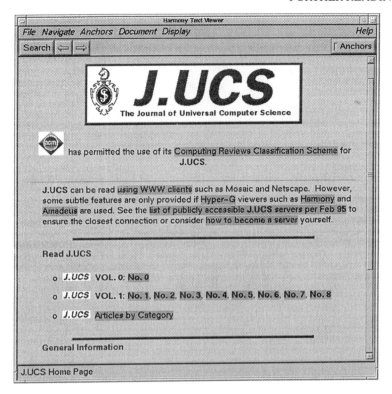

Figure 28.3   The home page of J.UCS – the *Journal of Universal Computer Science*.

user accounts and passwords are independent of the number of library subscriptions on the server.

28.6 Further reading

Electronic publishing covers a wide range of knowledge in different areas. If you want to know more about data formats, further interesting literature is ISO (1986) and Berners-Lee and Conolly (1993) about SGML and HTML and Adobe Systems Inc. (1990) and Adobe Systems Inc. (1993) about PostScript and PDF respectively. Nielsen (1995) gives a good survey of multimedia and hypertext and a description of the PC-Library can be found in Maurer *et al.* (1994c). Other aspects of digital libraries are covered by Maurer and Lennon (1995) and Marchionini and Maurer (1995). Last but not least, journals and books published with Hyper-G, including J.UCS, can be found in the IICM Electronic Library (http://-hyperg.iicm.tu-graz.ac.at).

29   Some Web applications based on Hyper-G

Hermann Maurer, Robert Stubenrauch

In this chapter we discuss some application areas (**training, conference support, virtual communities, general information systems, entertainment and gambling**) that seem particularly appropriate to be supported by modern second-generation hypermedia systems such as Hyper-G. For each area we give a short introduction and a motivation for using hypermedia solutions. We report actual instances of concrete Hyper-G realizations and discuss some of the specific issues regarding design and implementation inherent to the domains.

29.1   Hyper-G for teaching, training and support

The saga of trying to use computers for educational purposes goes back well over 30 years. It is a saga of many attempts, few successes and many failures. Before we give a brief review, we want to clarify some terminology used in this book: educational software is called *courseware* throughout. We understand this term as embracing approaches such as CAI (Computer Assisted Instruction), CBL (Computer Based Learning), CML (Computer Managed Learning), CSL (Computer Supported Learning), TS and ITS (Tutoring Systems and Intelligent Tutoring Systems) and so on, without wanting to go into the sometimes lengthy debates concerning where a particular piece of courseware fits into the maze of acronyms and classifications.

29.1.1   History and what we should learn from it

The first serious attempts to use computers for educational purposes date back to the early sixties. Despite expensive and unsophisticated hardware (text-only terminals with just keyboard input) some packages like Plato, although not successful on a grand scale, continued to be used by some institutions for more than 20 years. The main reason for the comparative success of Plato was its sophisticated record-keeping system (useful for both student guidance and quality control), supported by the then popular arrangement of dumb terminals attached

460

to a central computer system. Three main reasons are usually quoted to explain why Plato (and similar systems) did not do better than they did:

(a1) bad price/performance ratio on the equipment side;

(a2) lack of (color) graphics and animation to better visualize processes;

(a3) high effort to produce good quality courseware.

   With the advent of personal computers points (a1) and (a2) changed dramatically and (a3) got a bit better due to so-called What You See Is What You Get (WYSIWYG) editors. This resulted in a new wave of enthusiasm culminating in efforts such as COSTOC and first versions of Authorware.

   To the surprise of many specialists, the new systems did not achieve the breakthrough expected, either. Careful analysis yielded the following reasons:

(b1) Decentralization, due to personal computers and standalone configurations, annihilated one of the crucial success factors of earlier systems, the careful record-keeping of how students used what material.

(b2) The cost of authoring systems (compared to, say, graphics editors) was unjustifiably high.

(b3) Production costs for good quality material remained high (typically 100 hours effort for one hour of instructional material).

(b4) Lack of sophisticated interactivity and insensitivity towards individual student needs: most courseware was still of the "page turning variety," students working in a "tunnel" from which they could not escape.

   From 1985 onward, much effort was invested into point (b4) by investigating "intelligent tutoring systems," "student modeling," extensive use of "simulations" and so on. Success was limited, due to the very high costs involved in creating good courseware this way. Attempts to reduce the "tunnel" syndrome by introducing new navigational paradigms were partially successful, yet points (b1)–(b4) in totality remained sufficiently unresolved to prevent much success.

   The most crucial change occurred in the late eighties with the emergence of true multimedia and the notion of "hyperlinks," allowing fairly free navigation within a certain instructional domain. Tribute has to be paid to HyperCard and its clones. Suddenly, inexpensive or even free authoring packages became available; difficult to prepare vector graphics could be replaced by easily scanned images; and the "hyperlink" paradigm seemed to eliminate the feared "tunnel" syndrome. As a consequence, tens of thousands of educational modules using HyperCard and similar tools, or more recently Web tools, have been created.

   It is instructive to realize why this new approach stimulated computer-based education, but still did not create the final breakthrough. Recent studies list the following reasons:

(c1) Since scanned images are so much easier to use than carefully prepared vector graphics (diagrams), they are often used even if vector graphics would be more appropriate for the instructional aim at issue.

(c2) Replacing the "tunnel effect" and "page turning" by arbitrarily free navigation leads to "getting lost in hyperspace" and disorientation.

(c3) The use of images, video and audio clips increases data volume to an extent that network-based or floppy-based distribution becomes infeasible.

(c4) Preparation of small packages is easy; indeed so easy that everyone, even those who have never considered pedagogical or design issues, suddenly believes they are an expert courseware designer.

(c5) It is not enough to prepare small courseware packages; large databases of modules, of reusable, easily maintainable and customizable modules are necessary.

(c6) Courseware should be available both in standalone and in networked mode.

Novel authoring systems such as HM-Card discussed in Chapter 27 eliminate most of the problems mentioned. Since HM-Card integrates well with Web systems such as Hyper-G, it is a good solution for many courseware applications.

As backup and reference, an electronic library of books, journals, transparencies and other materials as described in Chapter 28 is required.

Thus, courseware (for example, based on HM-Card or glitzy Web pages) should always be seen as part of and in connection with electronic libraries ("digital libraries").

Indeed, having electronic libraries available makes what is called "authoring on the fly" and integrated networked multimedia educational environments more and more realistic.

29.1.2   Authoring on the fly

Authoring on the fly, a term coined by Maurer in 1994, refers to the possibility of preparing a substantial piece of courseware during the process of actually delivering a lecture.

The basic idea is simple enough: a lecture is delivered by extracting prepared multimedia material from a Hyper-G server and projecting it with a videobeam or LCD panel. The prepared multimedia material may just look like ordinary color transparencies, but might also include animation, movie clips, sound effects, simulation and other educational material. Thus, Hyper-G and the material prepared is just used for presentation purposes, so far.

Now comes the twist: as the lecture is delivered, the voice, face (or the whole body for gestures) and actions of the lecturer such as pointing to or highlighting certain material shown are recorded, digitized and stored in Hyper-G together with the original presentation material. Thus, after the lecture is finished it is available as a Hyper-G document that can be reused at leisure at any later time: authoring of a one-hour piece of courseware complete with everything takes just one hour! Of course, the effort to produce the material to present or – more realistically – to select from the, hopefully, comprehensive electronic library has also to be taken into account.

If the above sounds too good to be true ... well, it is not quite as simple in reality as it sounds. First, if the lecturer's video is digitized continuously, it will create large amounts of data; and experiments have shown that the continuous video of a lecturer is actually more distracting than helpful. A few still pictures of the lecturer or some key scenes are much more effective. This requires either some post-editing, or careful preparation on the part of the lecturer, involving decisions such as "now a still picture of myself," "now a video clip," "now nothing" and so on. Ingenious ideas and tricks are currently being tried out to automate this: nobody is claiming to have found the ultimate solution but good results are now possible.

The audio track is another matter: when listening to a speaker live, a few pauses, mistakes, coughs and so on are quite OK, but they do not feel right in connection with a piece of canned courseware. Thus, post-editing of the soundtrack is necessary if a certain quality is desired.

There is also the problem of how to "index" such a piece of courseware to jump to any segment desired directly, how to deal with questions students might want to ask, and so on. We will come back to this in Section 29.1.3 but we will discuss some concrete authoring on the fly experiments first.

Note, however, that lecturing in the way described does not restrict students to a particular location, as long as the material can be "broadcast" (digitally) to them. Thus, authoring on the fly incorporates teleteaching in a very natural way.

29.1.3 Authoring on the fly experiments

The Freiburg experiment

In Freiburg, Germany, a group led by Ottmann has developed tools for creating multimedia documents "on the fly" when presenting a lecture. The lecture is also broadcast via the so-called MBone-net (Multicast Backbone network) to several hosts all over the world. The multimedia documents created are embedded into Hyper-G.

The main goal is to capture as much as possible of the advantages of the traditional forms of preparation of college teaching material and to combine them with the advantages of multimedia computer systems.

To prepare a presentation, the instructor first decides on the topic and prepares colored slides in PostScript format. This can be done by using standard tools like Showcase on Silicon Graphics machines, or Framemaker or LaTeX. As one example, Ottmann uses the area of algorithms and data structures, among them backtracking and the Towers-of-Hanoi problem. A Silicon Graphics workstation (Indy) is used as the hardware platform.

The lecture is then delivered by making use of the MBone **wb** (Whiteboard). The wb offers functions such as loading PostScript files, drawing, writing and marking objects and also their deletion. Thus, after loading the slides into the wb, they are orally commented by the instructor, marked and illustrated with online drawings, making use of functions the wb offers. Several other people at distant hosts may "attend" the lecture via the MBone. They use the MBone tools **sd** (session directory), **nv** (net video), **vat** (visual audio tool) and wb to get the video (about three frames per second), audio and also the explanation of the slides on the wb.

Students can follow the lectures both locally in Freiburg on student workstations and on remote hosts at different universities in Germany. The audience can also ask questions.

The transmission rate and the synchronization of the different data streams (audio, video and whiteboard actions, in particular slide changes) is quite good, even on the remote sites.

Feedback from the audience reveals that the video of the lecturer is not as important as the sound and the action on the wb. Thus, even a still picture of the lecturer, combined with sound and wb movements, would be acceptable.

From a technical point of view, the wb output is recorded with **MCASTREC**, a novel program to record a whiteboard session, and is then converted into a format which is readable by an external Hyper-G viewer, SYNCVIEW. A text file with the paths of the PostScript slides and titles also has to be edited.

The result is a multimedia document consisting of the sound and video of the lecturer's talk, and also the demonstrations on the wb. This multimedia document is embedded into the Hyper-G database by making use of a number of specialized tools.

GENHYPDOC creates several shellscripts corresponding to the title file of the multimedia document and also creates a hypertext file with links to the scripts. **INSHYP** generates a Hyper-G collection containing the multimedia document. The external Hyper-G viewer SYNCVIEW presents this document by synchronizing the wb actions with video and sound. It is also possible to scroll backwards and forwards in the document by using a slider.

By making use of Hyper-G's feature of destination anchors, an author can place links to specify positions inside the document. For instance, in a text file of the contents of the lecture, links from text passages to the corresponding section within the hypermedia document can be added.

Figure 29.1 shows a screenshot of a typical session. In the upper left corner, the face of the lecturer is shown and there are a few simple control buttons in the lower left corner. The main window shows a graphic presentation of the "Tower of Hanoi" problem: the parts labelled "Start" and "Goal" are contained in a "transparency" that was prepared; the bottom part is being drawn dynamically by the lecturer. A slidebar separating the left strip from the main window allows you to move backwards and forwards within the lecture at will.

Other experiments and the future

A group under Jennifer Lennon at the University of Auckland is currently implementing an ambitious Hyper-G-based Interactive Lecturing System (HILS) that will work without MBone tools and integrate a number of novel features.

An experiment based on substantial digital libraries is carried out at Virginia Tech under the supervision of Professor Ed Fox. In particular, the RISKS Internet Digest studied in "Computer Professionalism" is based on Hyper-G because of its ready support for searching and structural browsing.

At the same time, the Freiburg group is improving the whiteboard tools available and is moving towards more general platforms. Within an EU project, LIBERATION (an acronym for LIBraries: Electronic Remote Access To Information Over Networks), a substantial Hyper-G-based digital library of books, journals and courseware is being created in cooperation with three major international publishers.

All these experiments are decisive steps towards an integrated networked multimedia educational environment.

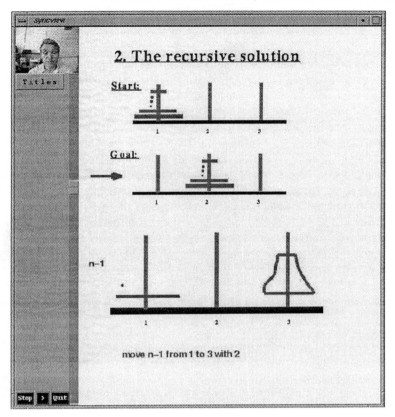

Figure 29.1   Authoring on the fly: A typical session.

The Integrated Networked Multimedia Educational Environment

An Integrated Networked Multimedia Educational Environment (INME) consists of:

(1) a substantial electronic library containing books, journals, transparencies, courseware modules, pictures and other types of multimedia material;

(2) an authoring on the fly setup as described in Section 29.1.2, including a network to distribute lectures both live and as "canned" course modules to remote sites ("teleteaching");

(3) a mechanism to deal with questions asked by students, even in remote locations and "asynchronously."

Such an INME combines modern lecturing techniques, an electronic library, tools for fast preparation and dissemination of courseware, teleteaching and all aspects courseware ever wanted to deal with.

Current INME systems as described in this chapter are the first prototypes of powerful systems that will be built based on modern hypermedia systems such as Hyper-G.

We have not yet discussed point (3) – mechanisms for dealing with student questions – in this chapter, although a number of interesting proposals have been discussed in the literature. In addition to clever question–answer dialogs, using systems such as Authorware or HM-Card, or using some of the techniques applied in intelligent authoring systems, there are a number of approaches that seem particularly promising. We mention just a few as examples and refer to the literature for more details.

Suppose a student has a question concerning a particular formula or statement on the screen. The student moves a "question-mark icon" to the material at issue and drops it there. If an explanation for this "question" is available in the Hyper-G database, it is shown: such explanations enter the database because an instructor has anticipated potential problems, or because another student has asked the same question (by dropping a question mark) before and the question has been answered in the meantime. If no answer to a question asked this way is available yet, an Email message is sent to the (potentially remote) instructor. If the instructor is online (for example, because the student is using the material during a period where the instructor has "electronic office hours") the answer will come back immediately, or otherwise at some later stage by Email. In both cases the answer is added to the database.

Of course, many questions cannot be asked just by dropping a question mark in some spot. In these cases students must type a question. The answer comes back either immediately or else at some later stage via the network and is stored in Hyper-G together with the question. When students retrieve information for which textual questions have been asked and answered at some earlier stage by someone else, then an icon is shown indicating "questions have been asked concerning this material before." Clicking on the icon displays the first lines of all questions asked before. The user now decides whether a question similar to one currently of concern has been asked before, or whether a new question has to be formulated.

In both above approaches, it is assumed that, after a certain period of time, most relevant questions will have been asked and hence will have been integrated. This decreases the need for an online tutor or instructor, or allows a single tutor to handle many students at the same time, since only a few new questions emerge.

Observe that students can use the "background" electronic library to look up any topics they are interested in or need help with, thus changing the whole way courseware is being used.

In earlier attempts, courseware would have to be worked through more or less sequentially, or at the other extreme, was offered as a web of information with no guidance. What we have described – and no fully working system doing all we have explained exists at the time of writing – is a combination of both approaches: the courseware provides a basic "route" and necessary guidance; a set of questions that is generated as needed (not as "guessed" by the author as in earlier systems) is available and a rich corpus of background material in the electronic library can be used to complement whatever may be missing in the courseware because of the particular level of knowledge of a student.

It seems conceivable that such integrated networked multimedia educational environments will finally provide the answers for computer supported teaching and teleteaching that many of us have been waiting for.

29.2   Hyper-G in museums and exhibitions

Museums and exhibitions are places where information in the form of objects of various types is presented to an audience. In the past, the objects had to be *real* objects (works of art, objects of natural history, technical objects and so on) or information presented by conventional media such as posters or videos. However, the desire to present real exhibits to as large an audience as possible is often hampered by conservation and security considerations, physical constraints and financial limitations.

29.2.1   Virtual exhibits and virtual museums

Today, modern hypermedia can provide the technical infrastructure to host **virtual museums** and **virtual exhibitions**. In such environments, the exhibits presented to the visitor are either computer assisted presentations of real objects, or synthetically generated objects that might either resemble (simulate) real objects or be representations without any counterparts in reality.

In many cases, it is undesirable to expose valuable items to the general public, because environmental factors (light, humidity, vibration and so on) may cause permanent damage to them. Under such circumstances, the only way to present the objects might be through computer simulations based on 3D models. Modern virtual reality research already provides such solutions in many areas. Hyper-G, for instance, comes with an integrated VRML-based 3D viewer which allows you to comfortably inspect and "walk through" complex 3D objects. In combination with devices such as head mounted displays and data gloves or suits, users can actually "enter" such virtual environments and experience them very realistically. Natural applications of such systems would include virtual walks through archaeological sites that are otherwise inaccessible to the general public and inspecting environments that are otherwise inaccessible to human beings for physical reasons, such as traveling through the planetary system, entering a volcano cone or joining a blood cell on its journey through the human body.

Another interpretation of the term "virtual museum" is that in addition to the exhibits it presents, the museum itself is virtual. In other words, visitors no longer physically enter a particular museum building, but remotely access the presentations through a computer-based medium such as the Web. Of course, many museums will offer a mix of both possibilities in the future: there will be a real museum building hosting a number of interesting real objects as well as a collection of virtual exhibits which, in turn, might be available in a virtual museum when accessed via the Web.

29.2.2   Supporting museum administration

Whether objects are real or virtual and how these objects are presented to the visitor is just one cluster of issues when considering hypermedia systems in museum and exhibition settings. Other, less spectacular aspects of which visitors are usually more or less unaware –

but which are nevertheless essential – concern the **organization** and **administration** of museums. Large museums may well house millions of items. Organizing, structuring, categorizing, maintaining and exhibiting at least parts of such collections is a tremendous challenge which obviously calls for computer assistance. Again, second-generation hypermedia systems offer solutions. Whether through gateways to external databases (which, unfortunately, rarely offer multimedia solutions) or as part of the system, they allow you to structure very large amounts of multimedia data in a convenient way. Hyper-G, for instance, with its hierarchic structure of collections, is flexible enough to cope with different data models as they are used in museums to categorize and administer various types of items.

If the objects of the museum collections are documented appropriately, including representations as images, video and audio clips and perhaps even 3D models, they can (partially) be made available to the general public at **kiosks** or via the Web more or less as a "by-product." Similarly, the production of museum related publications such as catalogs can be supported to a large extent. This might even result in offering regular visitors the opportunity to produce their own "personal catalogs" on CD-ROMs that can be ordered and taken home shortly after. The order takes place at one of the hypermedia kiosks (info booths) where visitors select the contents according to their personal interests in a simple interactive procedure.

Such kiosks are already in use in many places, for example to help visitors to find their way to preferred exhibitions. However, they can offer more than just the usual floorplan of the museum. They should for instance allow you to interactively search for specific items. The result of such queries should be detailed instructions on how to find the exhibits or, if they are (currently) not available to the public, the presentation of virtual substitutes as explained above. In future museums, personal portable hypermedia assistants are conceivable that have wireless access to the central museum database. These assistants – multimedia versions of the simple walkman voice assistant we sometimes encounter nowadays – give detailed explanations of objects automatically whenever the visitor approaches a new object. The level of detail of explanations could possibly be adjusted to individual preferences.

29.2.3   Example: AEIOU – A presentation of Austria based on Hyper-G

In the year 996, Austria was mentioned in a written document for the first time. This is reason enough to celebrate the nation's millennium in 1996. On this occasion, various projects have been launched, one of which is a substantial hypermedia documentation and – most importantly – presentation of the country. Hyper-G was chosen as the technical platform – after all it has mainly been developed in Austria. The project was named **AEIOU** after a cryptic acronym the Habsburgs used to paraphrase the greatness of their nation.

The overall aims of AEIOU concerning the Austrian audience are education and to establish a certain awareness of new media in the general public. Users from all over the world who access the system via the Web will be presented with a favorable impression of the nation and can take advantage of specific information, be it of a touristic nature, official contact addresses or the like.

The data kernel of AEIOU is an "Encyclopedia of Austria" which is also issued as a conventional book – clearly without any multimedia extensions. With this encyclopedia in the background, a universal source of information on the nation is available with a rich link structure comprising all parts of AEIOU. Among the other sections are the "Handbook of Austrian Music" (with numerous audio clips), about 2500 images from all over the country with descriptions in five major European languages (Hyper-G's elegant way of handling multilingual documents comes into play!) and a large collection of videos available in MPEG format.

AEIOU comes in the following three environments, where all versions basically rely on the same body of multimedia data but are "packaged" differently:

A series of CD-ROMs Hyper-G allows easy data exchange between data provided by networked Hyper-G servers and standalone CD-ROM versions. The AEIOU CD-ROMs will thus contain material of the general Web version with emphasis on ease of usability. However, deep functionality can also be offered, since users can be expected to invest a minimum of time to explore extended features in a relaxed private atmosphere. In contrast to the Web, the CD-ROM format on the one hand allows you to offer large individual documents fast, but on the other hand, limits the total available storage. The CD-ROMs mainly aim at private households and educational settings.

Public kiosk version Served by Hyper-G servers (either on the Web or local), the main characteristics of the kiosk version is its extremely simple user interface. This is necessary because this AEIOU version aims at a general public audience in environments such as fairs, exhibitions, or simply crowded public places such as railway stations. The kiosks therefore are physically robust devices with touch screens. Due to the simple interface and the general impatience of occasional users with sophisticated interfaces, the functionality is confined to basic features.

Web version The Web version is clearly the most comprehensive and challenging one. After all, it will grow in the future and regular updates will keep the contents up to date. For a full worldwide information set, all essential data must be provided in English. Due to bandwidth restrictions, offering large documents on the Web is problematic. Thus, a certain discipline on the information provider's side is necessary, in particular regarding multimedia data such as audio and video. The Web version of AEIOU is best accessed via native Hyper-G clients that offer full Hyper-G functionality, but other Web browsers can be used as well.

29.2.4   Example: MONZ – A museum supported by Hyper-G

MONZ – the Museum of New Zealand – is New Zealand's largest museum. A beautiful new museum building set in a park-like landscape at Wellington's waterfront is currently under construction. A wide range of multimedia exhibits is planned for the opening in 1998. The first pilot was already shown in early 1995: it and much of the networked multimedia infrastructure are based on Hyper-G and HM-Card.

Hyper-G is used for internal applications by curators, for "kiosk" applications to the general public and to offer some general information on the Web. The kiosk applications are based on HM-Card (see Chapter 27 on Hyper-G using the public terminal viewer Easy

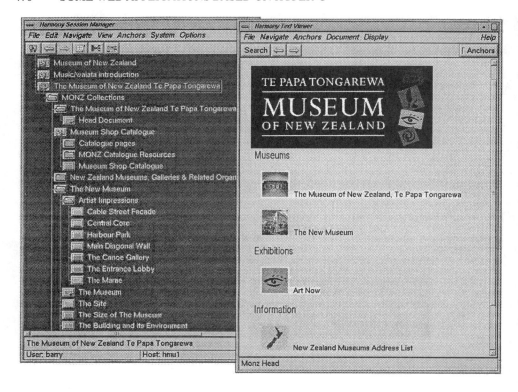

Figure 29.2   MONZ: A large museum application of Hyper-G.

(see Section 19.2) and the combination of Hyper-G with a standalone version thereof (see Chapter 13): this approach provides rapid access with virtually no delays and also makes it particularly easy to produce CD-ROMs from material prepared on Hyper-G servers for internal or Web purposes. Figure 29.2 shows a typical Hyper-G screen, with a nice graphic presentation of some main items on the right and information where this document is located in the collection hierarchy on the left. Figure 29.3 shows how Hyper-G can be used for implementing arts collections on the Web. Observe that small iconized pictures are used as inline images but can be expanded (and then manipulated in many ways) if desired.

One of the challenges in connection with MONZ was the integration of Hyper-G with a Smalltalk-based museum administration system called Tekahui. Tekahui contains technical data on tens of thousands of objects of the museum and Hyper-G multimedia data (pictures, 3D models, audio and video clips) relating to them. Curators accessing Tekahui can display textual data from Tekahui together with multimedia material transferred from Hyper-G on the same screen. Conversely, information accessed in Hyper-G fetches selected data from Tekahui to complement the multimedia material shown.

It is worth mentioning that the multilingual capability of Hyper-G is used in the

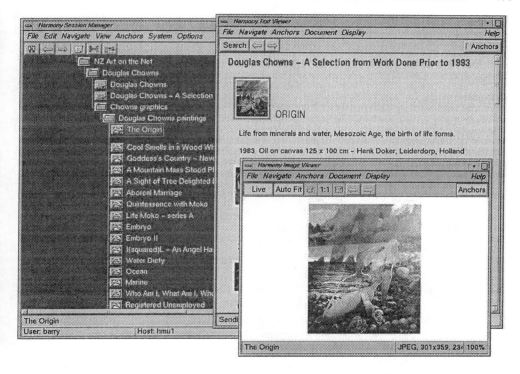

Figure 29.3   MONZ: Hyper-G used as a virtual gallery of pictures.

museum context, not only to permit information display in one of a number of languages (for example, English or Maori) but also in "technical" or "lay" English. Observe further that an English–Maori dictionary, currently in the planning phase, will allow "point-and-click" translation of individual words, a huge asset in a multicultural and multilingual country such as New Zealand.

29.2.5   Planning hypermedia support for museums

Large museums host collections that consist of hundreds of thousands of items. Thus, an essential issue is storage capacity, in particular if the objects are to be digitized at high quality (images, audio, 3D objects). Also, museum collections are traditionally categorized in many different ways, due to the needs of the various scientific domains. The classification schemes of various departments of a museum will hardly be compatible with each other; this is a challenge in database design on its own.

Other crucial aspects of hypermedia support for museums concern user access to data. On the one hand, very specific tools must be provided for scientists to allow thorough investigation of the material. On the other hand, lay visitors call for much simpler ways of interacting which may be applied more or less intuitively. Furthermore, it might be desired to present (parts of) the museum on the Web. This introduces yet another platform and an associated audience which requires a specific interface.

29.3 Hyper-G for conference support

Conferences are typical events that involve heavy "n to m communication" processes. A large number of people – hundreds and sometimes thousands – meet to share and exchange their knowledge and experiences. Usually they do so in a very concentrated way, both in terms of place and of time. Typically, conferences take place at locations close enough to allow participants to meet physically (the "conference center") and participants need to come to those locations to be there all at the same time. While traveling to conferences might provide scientists with highlights and indispensable direct personal contacts, it is certainly an expensive way to communicate with colleagues. It is even more expensive if we consider the major drawbacks of the traditional type of conference, in which most people are confronted with too many people in too little time and are just overwhelmed by the sheer amount of information as reflected in heavy-weight printed proceedings.

Today's means of computer mediated communication can assist us to cope with some of the issues raised above and have the potential to give us many more benefits that go beyond them. Modern hypermedia systems can serve as supporting platforms accompanying the conference through all its stages, from the planning to the post-conference phase. Both conference participants and administrators may take advantage of this support.

29.3.1 Purposes of a universal conference support system

The following list is an overview of possible purposes that might be covered by a universal conference support system (an E in brackets indicates coverage by the ED-MEDIA 95 support system described below).

Prior to the conference:

(1) Distribute invitation and call for contributions (E)

(2) Download electronic styleguides for paper submission (E)

(3) Electronic paper submission and distribution to referees (E)

(4) Register interactively

(5) Support hotel booking (by automatic fax or Email)

(6) Learn about locations (conference center, city map...) (E)

(7) Plan off-conference activities (tourist information) (E)

(8) Identify talks you want to attend by studying the online proceedings (E)

(9) Comment papers, possibly influencing the presentation at the conference (E)

(10) Get a flavor of the look-and-feel of the venue (E)

(11) Pre-record talks that otherwise would have to be cancelled

(12) Provide information on persons involved (including participants) and support establishing contacts (yet respect privacy) (E)

(13) Document the current state of organization.

During the conference:

(14) Inform about last-minute changes and latest schedule

(15) Supply a bulletin board system for discussions and personal messages

(16) Provide general Web access

(17) Provide a uniform infrastructure for presentations and/or virtual exhibitions

(18) Play back pre-recorded talks

(19) Record talks for later publication.

After the conference:

(20) Read/print out papers (E)

(21) Provide access to (parts of) recorded talks

(22) Provide written transcripts of talks

(23) Stay in contact with conference series by links to future activities (E)

(24) Support activities as a result of the conference (new interest groups etc.) (E)

(25) Electronic continuation of panel discussions.

While discussing proceedings, it is clear that the electronic kind of proceedings which we mean in the context of a conference support system can potentially go far beyond the traditional role of printed paper-bound proceedings. They may include truly interactive sections. In fact, a good part of presentations given today at conferences are computer supported: speakers use computer programs at least to present a linear sequence of "slides," but sometimes such presentations also include animated and dynamic parts which could not be done without computer support at all. Furthermore, at conferences dealing with computers as such, many of the presentations are demonstrations of computer programs. It would be natural to include such programs in the electronic proceedings and let readers use them actively instead of just passively following the presentation. However, many of the pre-release demos that can only be handled by their developers could be a problem; compatibility issues between various platforms is of course another.

Altogether, a hypermedia system supporting a conference should allow for general comprehensive documentation of the event. The first two phases of a conference (prior to, during) can best be handled dynamically in an online hyperdocument, whereas the final phase (after) can also be well presented on long-term media such as CD-ROMs. It is clear that at the moment no single system is powerful enough to cover all the issues raised above. However, as we will see in the example we give below, existing systems such as Hyper-G are already capable of serving quite a number of them.

29.3.2   Virtual conferences

If we go a few steps beyond what we have outlined so far, we may think of completely dispensing with direct physical contact between conference participants. Instead, we could develop our conference support system into a platform for a *virtual conference* which would be nothing but a computer mediated meeting-place, allowing the sharing of experiences and knowledge, from person-to-person style up to large communities. In fact, the first concrete steps in that direction have already been taken in the form of CSCW (Computer Supported Collaborative Work) and video conferencing systems. In particular, the MBone technology (multicast backbone, a virtual network on top of the Internet) allows – among other things – distribution of live audio, video and presentations on the Net. There are a number of examples of actual "virtual conferences" on the Web; they do not quite fulfill their promises yet. Part of their problem is that synchronous communication (be it textual, oral or visual) turns out to be problematic in the context of virtual conferences due to the large number of participants and simply because of time-zone reasons. And after all – as we all have learnt from the intrusive nature of the telephone – in many situations it is undesirable, distracting and often simply unnecessary to communicate synchronously. Even more so, if alternatives such as computer mediated forms of asynchronous multidirectional communication are being offered. In general, since hypermedia systems allow you to be in contact with colleagues and latest information on a global and permanent basis, traditional conferences might be considered obsolete at some point in the future. In fact, for the scientific world, the Web already *is* a sort of a global ongoing virtual conference which colleagues may join at any time they want. However, *real* personal contacts are indispensable and nobody wants to miss them. Thus, future conferences will focus on bringing *people* together temporarily, while *information* will be permanently shared on the basis of global hypermedia systems.

29.3.3   Example: ED-MEDIA 95 online support

ED-MEDIA 95 – the World Conference on Educational Multimedia and Hypermedia – took place in Graz, Austria, 17–21 June, 1995. The conference was accompanied by an effort to provide growing online support. This was started about half a year before the conference actually took place and was intended to result in a final documentation in the form of a CD-ROM.

Hyper-G was chosen as the platform for the database to be created. The ED-MEDIA 95 conference support system met many of the possible purposes of a universal conference support system, as indicated by (E) in the list on page 472. In addition, it certainly served as a promotional vehicle for Hyper-G which was almost an unavoidable by-product : -). Note that the system was not intended to be used *during* the event, though it certainly could have served most of the purposes listed above, for example, 15 to 17 and partly 18.

The heart of the ED-MEDIA 95 database is the papers of the electronic proceedings, available in PostScript format in order to provide authentic online presentation and high-quality printouts. Prior to the conference they were only accessible to registered participants who received a Hyper-G account/password sent by letter mail. To keep participants from revealing their password to all their friends, access per user was limited to three times per paper. Further material going beyond the printed proceedings was:

- abstracts of invited and keynote lectures;

- personal information about invited speakers, keynote speakers and some committee members, including pictures and links to their Web home pages;

- hypertext schedule;

- city map and pictures of the conference center;

- list of registered participants, including pictures and links to their Web home pages (if provided);

- rich set of multimedia material, including 3D-scenes and "virtual walk-throughs" of the conference city and venue.

Figure 29.4 is a screen shot that depicts the ED-MEDIA 95 home page with the main entries, a document of the social event section and a paper in the background. Figure 29.5 shows a part of the tourist section, with a clickable map of the province and information on one of the sites. Participants were asked to provide their pictures (by FTP or Email) and/or URLs of personal home pages. This information was linked to their entries in the list of registered participants in order to allow getting in contact prior to, at, or after the conference. The ED-MEDIA 95 database comprises a total of about 1000 documents. Roughly, one half of this is genuine conference material, particularly the PostScript papers. The second half is mainly tourist material and information about institutions involved and their projects.

The complete ED-MEDIA 95 Hyper-G collection remains online as documentation of a conference computer support. It is also available in a CD-ROM edition which includes the complete set of Hyper-G viewers for all platforms available at that time (see Chapter 13 for information about local Hyper-G versions). The ED-MEDIA 95 CD-ROM was handed to every registered conference participant in addition to the printed proceedings.

29.3.4   Planning hypermedia support for conferences

Planning a conference support system involves the same steps as planning any other kind of hyperdocument. These are basically: gather audience information, define purpose and objective, gather domain information, specify and design the hyperdocument and finally, implement

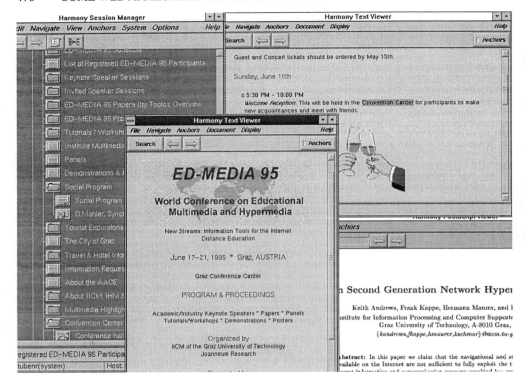

Figure 29.4   ED-MEDIA 95: Home page, social events and a paper.

the hyperdocument. Note that different requirements for different (yet intersecting) groups of persons have to be met. These include:

Authors Electronic publishing issues

Presenters Inform about infrastructure, schedule and so on.

General audience and participants Registration, tourist info and so on.

All Documentation, information, reference, (temporal) virtual community.

It cannot be over-emphasized that hyperdocument implementation for conference support includes setting up appropriate communication channels for delivering the large amounts of information involved. This includes submission of preliminary papers, distributing them among referees, submitting final papers and personal information, including images! Common methods of information delivery include FTP, floppy and Email either sent by individuals or automatically delivered as a result of form filling. For the convenience of the participants,

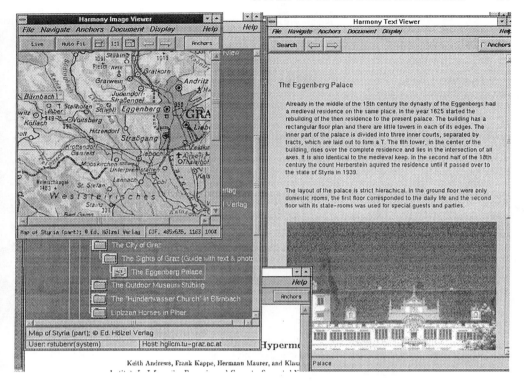

Figure 29.5   ED-MEDIA 95: Tourist info.

as many as possible of these channels should be supported. For the convenience of the hyperdocument developer, automatic processing of the incoming material should be supported as much as possible. Hyperdocument developers should expect that with hundreds of contributions from different individuals, serious problems will arise from the large number of different and inconsistent formats and different methods of delivery. These are typical problems of electronic publishing (see Chapter 28), but may be particularly critical in the context of conferences, due to the large number of contributions on the one hand and extreme time limitations on the other.

Scripting is also necessary to allow interactive online registration, including automatically updating the publicly accessible list of registered participants. Also, it might be desired – as was the case with ED-MEDIA 95 – that only registered users have the advantage of accessing certain areas of the hyperdocument. In case of ED-MEDIA 95, this was done with the online proceedings, prior to the conference. If so, user accounts and passwords must be created automatically and delivered to the user. This might be done by Email, or by sending snail mail if preferred for security reasons. In order to keep users from spreading their password among colleagues it might be desirable to limit the accesses per user and document. Hyper-G provides the necessary functionality.

If it is planned to issue the online material on offline media such as CD-ROM (without connection to the Web), it has to be taken into account that the material must be self-contained, so that no links will be pointing outside (which would at worst result in confusion and at best just in loss of information). Also, some information will probably be obsolete at the time the conference actually takes place. Typically, this includes registration/reservation, calls for support and similar information. It has to be decided which data must be revised before being pressed on CD-ROM. Technically speaking, however, it is very easy to take a Hyper-G collection, export it and put it on a CD-ROM together with a local Hyper-G version without any changes to the contents.

29.4   Hyper-G as a platform for virtual communities

A **virtual community** is a distributed community which relies heavily on computer supported communication; so much so, that people do not necessarily ever meet physically. However, it is often the case that people do want to meet eventually. All kinds of emotions and social phenomena can occur in virtual communities, as they do in traditional "real" communities.

Communities can be virtual to varying degrees. A traditional sports club, for example, might run a Web page for promotional purposes. However, nobody would call the club "virtual" only for this reason. On the other hand, the online presence of a chess club might shift within years from an information platform that supports activities *in real life* (IRL) to a truly virtual community, where members no longer meet physically on a regular basis, but play "virtual chess" via the Web.

There are many possible types of virtual communities. Some that actually are already around on the Web include:

- Virtual communities of customers of virtual shops (cybermalls)

- Virtual companies (teleworking)

- Virtual citizens of virtual cities or worlds (so-called MUDs, Multi-user Dungeons).

29.4.1   Technical requirements for virtual communities

As with all communities, communication is vital for virtual communities, be it one-to-one, one-to-many or many-to-many style. Thus, an essential feature of any technical platform for virtual communities must be to support communication to the best possible extent. Confining ourselves to textual communication, the Web already offers good basic means. For synchronous worldwide communication, there are thousands of channels based on IRC (Internet Relay Chat). Asynchronous communication is carried out by private Email and public forums (the USENET newsgroups). Hyper-G offers a wealth of possibilities to support communication, such as fill-in forms, annotations to existing documents and links to remote documents.

Drawing analogies to the real world, individual members of communities may want to adopt a fake *identity* or even remain anonymous in certain situations, such as games and gambling (which are of course sensible issues!). Individuals want to rule their *private areas* where they can restrict access as they want (Home Pages!). Virtual communities will want to maintain some set of data which is important to them, be it sales records, game scores, discussion archives or whatever. Structuring and maintaining this data and making it accessible to a distributed virtual community is a challenge on its own.

Most of the above aspects can be integrated into second-generation hypermedia systems today. With some possibly necessary extension to standard solutions, the Web and second-generation hypermedia systems such as Hyper-G are a good choice as technical platforms for virtual communities.

29.4.2 Example: The Web Society server

The Web Society is an international non-profit organization that has been founded out of a concern that the Internet is growing at a rate that requires accompanying measures to be addressed. This includes issues concerning the contents (quality), juristic ("freedom of speech," security, privacy) and social aspects and technical ones (for example, standardization). See Appendix D for further details about the aims of the Web Society. Since the Web Society is an association of Web users who naturally communicate through the Net in the first place, it can legitimately be considered a fully virtual community.

In order to attract a large number of Web users, in addition to offering a number of "offline benefits," the Web Society appropriately decided to run a substantial Web site as a service for its members and for the general public. The server

- distributes information about and promotes the Web Society;

- allows interactive online registration;

- provides a platform for moderated discussions;

- provides original Web related information;

- provides links to Web resources that relate to the aims of the Web Society;

- provides personal Web space for members (home pages);

- provides a contact address for human support in various Web related kinds of problems;

- allows easy submission of (member) contributions.

The Web Society decided to use Hyper-G as the technical basis for its server. Some of the above services should be restricted to members, whereas others would be open to the general public. When registering with the appropriate online form (see Figure 29.6), a new member is automatically included in the member collection and receives a Hyper-G account/password which allows access to the internal sections of the server. In order to keep the member from passing on this data to third persons, access is restricted to a certain number

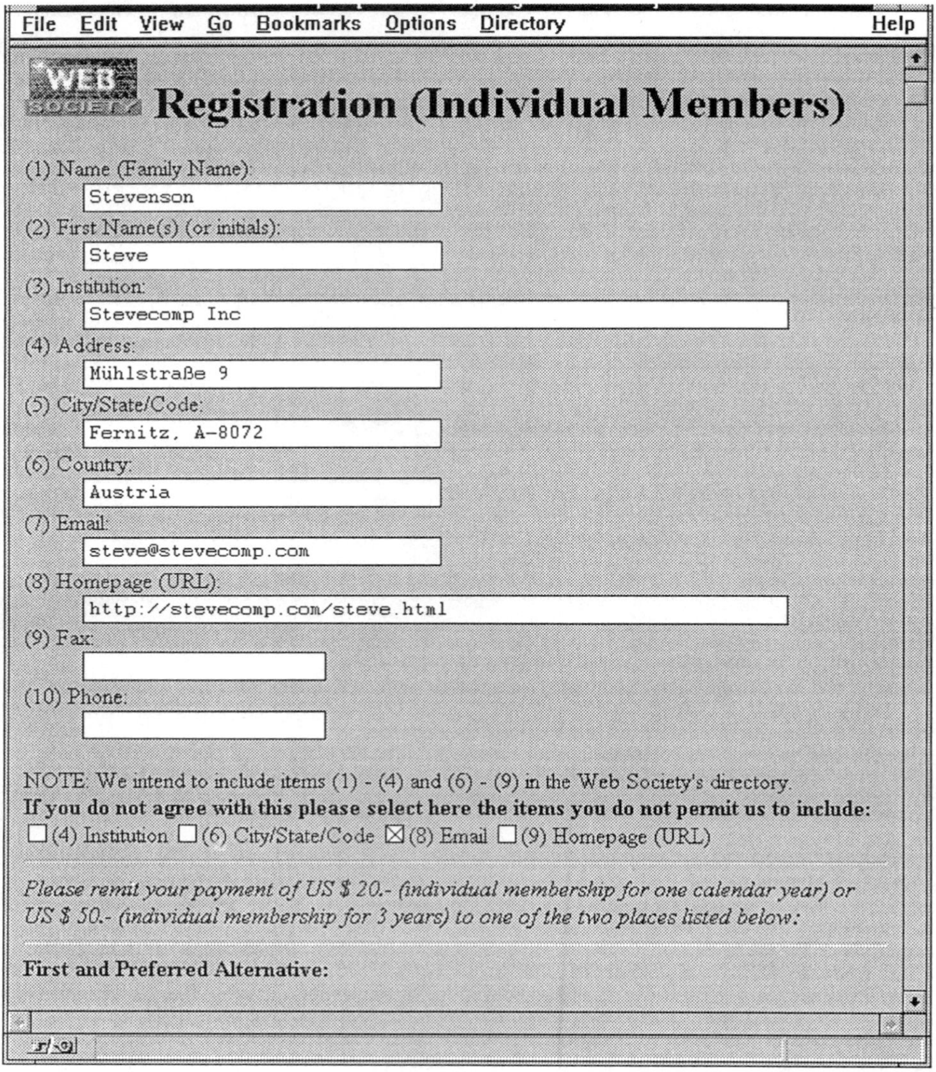

File	Edit	View	Go	Bookmarks	Options	Directory		Help

WEB SOCIETY # Registration (Individual Members)

(1) Name (Family Name):

    Stevenson

(2) First Name(s) (or initials):

    Steve

(3) Institution:

    Stevecomp Inc

(4) Address:

    Mühlstraße 9

(5) City/State/Code:

    Fernitz, A-8072

(6) Country:

    Austria

(7) Email:

    steve@stevecomp.com

(8) Homepage (URL):

    http://stevecomp.com/steve.html

(9) Fax:

(10) Phone:

NOTE: We intend to include items (1) - (4) and (6) - (9) in the Web Society's directory.
If you do not agree with this please select here the items you do not permit us to include:
☐ (4) Institution ☐ (6) City/State/Code ☒ (8) Email ☐ (9) Homepage (URL)

*Please remit your payment of US $ 20.- (individual membership for one calendar year) or
US $ 50.- (individual membership for 3 years) to one of the two places listed below:*

First and Preferred Alternative:

Figure 29.6   Web Society registration form.

of times per document. Each member also gets assigned a certain amount of private "Web
space," that is, a Hyper-G collection is created to which only the member at issue has write
permission. This generous (but still limited) amount of space allows members to build personal home pages and, among other things, build their own views of the Web Society server
by copying parts of the material into their private collections.

One principle of the server is to offer interaction and submission of contributions whenever possible. The idea is that the contents of the server reflect the interests and expertise of its members. Permanent contributions can be made to the *interesting sites* section and to the *columns*. Temporary contributions (that may well be archived) can be made in moderated *discussion forums* on various topics. All of these communication and submission processes are moderated to ensure high quality. Technically speaking, the user fills in HTML forms whose associated scripts in turn send Email to mail daemons for automatic processing or to human moderators who forward material approved for automatic insertion.

Figure 29.7 is a screen shot of the Web Society's home page with parts of the column section in the background. The original Web Society server will be mirrored by other sites worldwide as this becomes necessary.

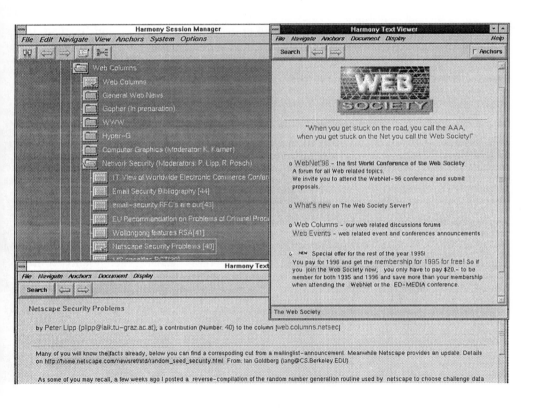

Figure 29.7   Web Society home page.

29.4.3 Planning hypermedia support for virtual communities

In the case of a platform for a virtual community, the Web database which is to be designed has only a kernel of more or less static information. This kernel is surrounded by a flow of communication which may lead to permanent documents. For the communication processes involved, convenient support has to be established. In particular, Email and group discussions must be seamlessly integrated into the system.

Healthy communities have a dynamically changing membership. This must be taken into account from the very beginning of planning a virtual community platform. (Semi-) automatic restructuring should be provided in order to maintain growing data sets. For instance, an ever-growing collection tree of members might be automatically restructured whenever more than a certain number of members exist in one collection. Archives of discussion forums can be treated similarly, structuring according to the age of the contributions and introducing new levels of collections when necessary. Such automatic restructuring can be executed with particular ease in Hyper-G due to its link concept discussed earlier.

Some manual adjustments will be unavoidable, though. For instance, new discussion forums and categories of "site collections" will probably be introduced manually. Thus it is important that the hyperdocument is structured in a way that allows easy updates and modifications. In particular, (text) documents that contain explicit lists of links to other individual documents should be avoided; they are likely to be erased, renamed or extended. Hyper-G can completely manage without such documents because structured Web databases are implicitly supported by the notion of collections. Hyper-G also provides excellent tools for maintaining the collection structure, both built into its clients (move and copy features) and as an extra set of tools.

29.5 Hyper-G as a general information system

Our time is often called the "information era." After the industrial revolution, human society is currently undergoing the next radical change, one result of which is that information is generally considered as one of its most valuable goods. Second-generation hypermedia systems such as Hyper-G allow wide access to huge data collections to the general public through worldwide information networks such as the Web. With today's user interfaces, such infrastructures are no longer restricted to experts but open to the general interested public.

It is impossible to give a comprehensive list of hypermedia applications. However, some main domains of applications can be identified; these include public authorities, business, entertainment, education and training and science. In this chapter we focus on campus information systems as already maintained by many universities all over the world.

29.5.1 Example: TUGinfo – A campus information system

The Graz University of Technology, Austria, runs an information system on the Web based on Hyper-G (which is no surprise; after all, Hyper-G was developed at the IICM, an institute of this university). Two features of Hyper-G seem particularly valuable for such an application. Firstly, the hierarchical collection structure which allows the same data to be offered easily in different contexts. For instance, the same information about an institute can be offered in a project related collection as well as in the collections of the persons involved without requiring a physical copy. Secondly, Hyper-G's search facilities are essential to provide fast and easy access to specific information.

In order to give an impression of this service, we briefly describe the sections as they appear at the server's home page. Each entry represents a Hyper-G collection (see also Figure 22.6).

Welcome and About The aims of the server; what's new; usage statistics; Hyper-G documentation.

General information A brief history of the university; valuable information for (potential) students: how to enroll; the accommodation situation in Graz; cost of living; list of lecture halls; list of faculties and studies.

Research For each faculty, all institutes are introduced, together with current projects and recent publications.

Teaching Offers a complete list of courses; furthermore, abstracts of diploma and doctoral theses since 1990.

Faculties, Institutes and Sections A hierarchical directory of all faculties, institutes and sections with all necessary information.

Personnel The official directory contains all staff members of the university in alphabetical order with contact information (some with photos).

Calendar of Events Information about local lectures, talks and conferences.

Local Services A number of specific services, most importantly the online access to the university libraries; others include directories of streets and ZIP codes and a campus-wide mailbox service.

Other Information Systems at the TUG Links to individual Web pages of institutes at the TUG.

Information Systems – Austria Links to selected Austrian Web services, ordered by domain; this includes a link to PAN, Austria's public videotex service with, for example, the online phone book of all of Austria.

Information Systems – International Links to selected international Web Services, including a complete list of all Hyper-G servers in the world that are reachable on the Web.

Computer Conferences Campus-internal discussion forums that are also used to support various lectures and exercises.

System Documentation Hyper-G documentation, UNIX manual pages and others.

Encyclopedias, Books, Journals, References Large list of electronic publications, partly links to off-site material; includes a general German encyclopedia and the journals J.UCS (*Journal of Universal Computer Science*), FBS (*Few Body Systems*) and J.NCA (*Journal of Network and Computer Applications*).

Fun and Games

29.6 Hyper-G in entertainment and gambling casino settings

Hypermedia systems with much truly multimedia material are handicapped in wide area networks such as the Internet by insufficient bandwidth. Thus, on the Web, it is not practical to offer extensive high-quality video footage or hi-fi audio material, let alone complex 3D models or scenes, because of the time (and potential cost) involved in transferring large volumes of data.

For this reason, systems like Hyper-G can be used in fairly novel ways when embedded in fast local area networks. It is thus no coincidence that three of the very largest Hyper-G servers are not on the Web but only work in local environments!

A particularly unusual application was addressed in a study to use Hyper-G in a hotel complex housing a gambling casino. In such a context each room would be equipped with a powerful workstation with a built-in video camera. Each such "private communication center" (PCC) would act as (video) telephone, information system, education system (if learning how to play Roulette or Black Jack can be called education!), video-on-demand, teleshopping and multi-person interactive game center, where users would "slip into" new personalities (John Doe into the role of "Superman" and Doris Milner into "Catwoman") and roam virtual 3D landscapes to experience all kinds of adventures together. Putting this together with telegambling provides a powerful mix, bound to intrigue a certain clientele! See Section 29.7 for further reference.

29.7 Further reading

For some information on Plato and COSTOC mentioned in Section 29.1 see Huber *et al.* (1989). For HM-Card consult the new book by Maurer and Scherbakov (1995). The idea of "authoring on the fly" is first mentioned by Maurer (1994b) and expanded by Ottmann and Bacher (1995). The latter paper also describes the "Freiburg Experiment" explained in Subsection 29.1.3. The work in Auckland is carried out by Jennifer Lennon in conjunction with Jeff Adie and others. A short introduction to Ed Fox's work can be found in Fox (1995a), a longer exposition is Fox (1995b). For information on digital libraries consult the special issue of the *Communications of the ACM* (1995). For using digital libraries for education see Maurer and Lennon (1995) and Marchionini and Maurer (1995). For a first proposal for an integrated networked multimedia educational environment see Lennon and Maurer (1994b).

For some information on MBone consult, for example, Macedonia and Brutzman (1994) or Erikson (1994).

Some of the ideas possible in a multimedia-based museum are already described in Maurer and Williams (1991). More recent sources are, for example, Maurer and Schneider (1995) and Jayasinha *et al.* (1995). Note that a number of conferences dealing with multimedia in museums are now offered each year. For a detailed description of hypermedia in a gambling casino setting we refer to Maurer (1995).

Howard Rheingold gives a fascinating sociologic insight into early (pre-Web) virtual communities (Rheingold, 1993). The AEIOU project is described in detail in Maurer (1994a).

URLs

- ED-MEDIA 95 collection (conference support):
  `http://hyperg.iicm.tu-graz.ac.at/edmedia`

- Web Society (virtual community):
  `http://www.websoc.org`

- Graz University of Technology (campus information system):
  `http://info.tu-graz.ac.at`

30 Hyper-G and security

Peter Lipp, Reinhard Posch

The almost daily presence of the Web in the media has resulted in a tremendous increase of interest and a corresponding increase in network activities. Few new users (and amazingly few of the old ones as well) are aware of the risks and dangers awaiting them. To users, a network often looks like a black box where data goes in and magically pops out somewhere else without being accessible to someone else on its way through. Unfortunately, that's wrong. Currently, almost all traffic is still transported unencrypted over the network (since the networks themselves do not yet provide such service automatically) and is thus accessible to many requiring only a minimum amount of skill and technical knowledge.

This section identifies threats, covers the basics necessary to understand solutions available and introduces examples of how problems can be avoided in practice.

30.1 Introduction

The Web Security FAQ starts off with the question: "What's to worry about?" And right away it becomes clear that there is a lot to worry about. As soon as you install any software that communicates with other software using the Internet as a service, you add a number of potential risks to your system. Nearly all of the former network services, be it sendmail, the UNIX mail-transport program, or TFTP, a trivial FTP service, had, and maybe still have, properties or bugs that proved to be dangerous to the systems. Therefore it is very important to think about what can happen in the Web and be prepared. Web servers of any kind are big software packages and there are a numerous ways that they can fail and create problems. This is true for any big system.

However, there are additional types of threat inherent in the Web:

- Private and confidential information stored on a server or in transit to a browser may fall into the hands of unauthorized persons.

- Private and confidential information sent from a browser to a server might be intercepted by others (typical examples are address and credit card information).

- Information might have been changed on the way from the server to the browser.

There are cryptographic solutions available that can solve all these types of problems:

- Data exchanged between a server and a browser has to be encrypted, if confidentiality is desired.

- A **Message Integrity Check** can be calculated and sent with the message. This only helps against benign modifications, as an attacker would be able to change the MIC as well.

- Digital signatures can be used to make sure that there is no undetected change in the information sent (see Further reading for details).

This is valid for all kinds of messages going over a network. For the Web in general, two different approaches to implementing security features have been presented. They differ in the layer of the ISO/OSI model they implement security at and in the flexibility offered to the application.

One group provides security just above the transport layer by adding security to the socket services (**SSL, PCT**). This allows their use by other applications, like FTP or Telnet, as well. This does require the client to attempt to access the server and be denied before the security mechanism is employed.

The other approach (**S-HTTP, SHEN**) puts security into the application layer. Security can be brought to the user interface, by introducing new elements into the HTML specification. These elements contain information that is necessary for clients to know that they have to initiate a secure transaction. By providing the application with as much security-relevant information as possible, this also puts more emphasis on visibility of security, a very important aspect. One of the main goals to be achieved with the support of the software, especially in the browser, is to make the user aware that security functions are employed, that security is important for the user and that the software can be trusted. Without the user's trust, all security functionality is of academic value.

Time and market forces will show which of the proposed solutions will be dominant. In any case, good security needs a clearly structured Web server, so that a security layer can be embedded smoothly. Hyper-G has such a clear structure: security can therefore be easily integrated in a consistent way. Such features are currently under implementation.

30.2 S-HTTP, SHEN, SSL, PCT

Many of the Web applications require confidential data transfer between mutually authenticated clients and servers. Examples are warehouse-type ordering systems or information distribution on a subscription basis. Currently neither Hyper-G nor other HTTP-based software has more than rudimentary support for security. Four approaches to enhance the security of the Web have been discussed: the Secure HyperText Transfer Protocol (S-HTTP), SHEN, a Security Scheme for the World Wide Web, the Secure Socket Layer (SSL) and PCT, a very new proposal by Microsoft. SSL and PCT provide for a protocol-independent means to exchange information securely between two applications. This means that any application can use protocols like Telnet, FTP or HTTP in a secure way but more or less transparent to the application.

S-HTTP provides for secure communication mechanisms between an HTTP client–server pair in order to enable spontaneous commercial transactions for a wide range of applications, drawing on the approaches and philosophies of the **PEM** and **MIME** efforts (PEM and MIME will be explained later in this chapter). The design intent is to provide a flexible protocol that supports multiple operation modes, key management mechanisms, trust models, cryptographic algorithms and encapsulation formats. SSL, PCT and S-HTTP are currently defined in draft documents; there is a good chance that some of them will become Internet standards soon. SLL, PCT and S-HTTP are in development in the USA and, if at all, only crippled versions will be made available to Europe because of the ITAR regulations. This makes a serious development effort in Europe particularly urgent.

30.2.1   S-HTTP

Most Web browsers support several Internet application protocols, like Gopher, WAIS, FTP, HTTP or Hyper-G. The primary protocol used between Web clients and servers, though, is the HyperText Transfer Protocol (HTTP). The original HTTP specification contained nearly no support for any cryptographic mechanism appropriate for such transactions.

This is why secure HTTP (S-HTTP) was introduced. In the defining document of S-HTTP we find:

S-HTTP provides secure communication mechanisms between an HTTP client–server pair in order to enable spontaneous commercial transactions for a wide range of applications. Our design intent is to provide a flexible protocol that supports multiple orthogonal operation modes, key management mechanisms, trust models, cryptographic algorithms and encapsulation formats through option negotiation between parties for each transaction.

S-HTTP provides several security mechanisms for clients and servers which are intended to provide a wide range of security options suitable for the many possible uses of the Web. It uses MIME formats for the wrapping of Web pages.

S-HTTP intentionally restricts itself to standardizing message format (and protocol), independent of policy and implementation details. This allows its use in a broad variety of contexts. As a protocol, S-HTTP supports a wide variety of cryptographic algorithms and operation modes. Clients and servers can negotiate on the message digest, digital signature, and asymmetric and symmetric encryption algorithms.

30.2.2   SHEN

The concept of Shen, A Security Scheme for the World Wide Web, by Phillip Hallam-Baker from CERN, is closely related to the S-HTTP concept. The guiding philosophy behind his proposal has been to build as far as is possible upon existing protocols and specifications, in particular PEM, to enable the implementation of integrated mail, news and Web systems. Shen is not a competitor to S-HTTP. On the contrary, the plans are that a common consensus for an interworking standard will result from the work on S-HTTP and Shen.

30.2.3   The Secure Socket Layer

The Secure Socket Layer Protocol is designed to provide privacy between two communicating applications, for example a client and a server. The protocol is also designed to authenticate the server, and optionally the client. SSL requires a reliable transport protocol (such as TCP) for data transmission and reception.

The advantage of the SSL Protocol is that it is application protocol independent. A "higher level" application protocol (such as HTTP, FTP or Telnet) can layer on top of the SSL Protocol transparently. The SSL Protocol can negotiate an encryption algorithm and session key, as well as authenticate a server, before the application protocol transmits or receives its first byte of data. All of the application protocol data is transmitted encrypted, ensuring privacy.

The SSL protocol provides *channel security* with three basic properties:

Privacy After setting up a secret key in an initial handshake phase, this key is then used to encrypt all messages transferred between the browser and the server. Symmetric cryptography is used for data encryption (DES, RC4 and so on).

Authentication The server is always authenticated; the client can optionally be authenticated. Asymmetric cryptography is used for authentication (for example, public-key cryptography), and a certificate is needed for each party to be authenticated.

Reliability The message transport includes a message integrity check using a Message Authentication Code (MAC) which ensures that the information received is the same as the data that was sent. This property is normally called *Integrity*. Secure hash functions (for example, MD2, MD5) are used for MAC computations.

The SSL protocol is actually composed of two protocols. At the lowest level, layered on top of some reliable transport protocol like TCP/IP, is the SSL Record Protocol. The SSL Record Protocol is used for encapsulation of all data transmitted and received, including the SSL Handshake Protocol which is used to establish security parameters.

30.2.4   Private Communication Technology Protocol

Microsoft defines PCT as follows:

Like SSL, the protocol is intended to prevent eavesdropping on communications in client–server applications, with servers always being authenticated and clients being authenticated at the server's option. However, this protocol corrects or improves on several weaknesses of SSL. The PCT protocol's record format is compatible with that of SSL. Servers implementing both protocols can distinguish between PCT and SSL clients because the version number field occurs in the same position in the first handshake message in both protocols.

We suspect that there must have been some non-technical reason for giving this proposal a totally new name, since it really is only a slightly improved version of SSL!

30.3   PGP and PEM/MOSS

PGP and PEM/MOSS have been designed as solutions for security problems for electronic mail. This chapter describes their principles and sets them in relation to Hyper-G. It also discusses the problem of public-key certification and how a system of certification authorities can help solve that problem.

30.3.1   PGP

PGP (an abbreviation for Pretty Good Privacy) is a general-purpose encryption program based on public key cryptography. It has been written by Philip Zimmermann. PGP is the most widespread encryption software in the world and is a *de facto* standard for privacy enhancement of electronic mail. Why should you use PGP? Phil Zimmermann says:

> *It's personal. It's private. And it's no one's business but yours. You may be planning a political campaign, discussing your taxes, or having an illicit affair. Or you may be doing something that you feel should not be illegal, but is. Whatever it is, you do not want your private electronic mail (Email) or confidential documents read by anyone else. There's nothing wrong with asserting your privacy. Privacy is as apple-pie as the Constitution.*

You can read the whole background information simply by acquiring a copy of PGP and reading the file PGPDOC1.DOC. Or you can browse the Web and find the text at, for example, http://www.netresponse.com/zldf/why_PGP.html.

PGP is available for many platforms, including UNIX, VMS, MS-DOS, OS/2, Macintosh, Amiga, Atari and Archimedes. The latest freeware versions of PGP are 2.6.2 (USA only) and 2.6.2i (international version). Important: Due to export restrictions and the license situation, US citizens have to use the US Version, international users are not allowed to use the US Version but have to use the international version. There is no drawback in this, as the two versions offer the same services and the international version does not contain crippled cryptography. The real reason for this is that in the USA one has to use RSAREF, a free software library by RSA Inc., that implements the RSA algorithm. In addition to these two versions, there are many other versions of PGP, including a commercial variant from ViaCrypt.

A question that often arises is whether the use of PGP is legal. The answer is **yes**, if you do not live in a country where encryption is illegal (France, China and others). You also can use PGP2.6.2i for commercial purposes, if you are outside the USA. In Europe there is a patent on the IDEA algorithm held by Ascom-Tech AG, Switzerland. They have granted permission for the freeware version of PGP to use the IDEA cipher for non-commercial use everywhere. Commercial or government users from the USA and Canada must obtain a licensed version from ViaCrypt, who have a license from Ascom-Tech for the IDEA cipher. Ascom-Tech AG also currently allows commercial users of PGP outside the USA or Canada to use IDEA in PGP without paying royalties to Ascom-Tech, because there is no commercial version of PGP available outside the USA or Canada. If you want to use it commercially, make sure that this is still true and contact Ascom-Tech AG for details.

30.3.2   PEM and MOSS

PEM, an acronym for Privacy Enhanced Mail, defines message encryption and message authentication procedures for text-based electronic mail messages using a certificate-based key management mechanism. The specification is limited by specifying the application of security services to text messages only. The PEM specification can be found in RFCs 1421–4. While being a good concept, the use of PEM is not very widespread, primarily because its implementation and integration into user interfaces is not yet good enough.

MIME, an acronym for Multipurpose Internet Mail Extensions, is a specification for a format of Internet mail messages. It allows for a mixture of textual and non-textual message body-parts. Following MIME, an electronic mail message consists of two parts: the headers and the body. The headers are standard headers as defined in RFC 822. MIME is not concerned with the headers but with the structure of the body. There are no security considerations in MIME whatsoever.

MOSS, an acronym for MIME Object Security Services, combines PEM and MIME in the sense that MOSS deals with MIME messages while being based on the PEM protocol. Many of PEM's features and most of its protocol specification are included in MOSS.

30.3.3   Common features of PGP and MOSS

In order to make use of the PGP or MOSS services, a user is required to have at least one public/private key pair. The public key must be made available somehow to other users with whom secure communication is desired. The private key must not be disclosed to any other user.

The private key of the sender is used to digitally sign the message. The recipient can then use the public key of the sender to verify the signature and thus the authenticity of the message.

If senders want the message to be confidential and only recipients should be able to read it, they encrypt the message using the public key of the recipient. Thus they can make sure that only the owner of the private key, the recipient, will be able to read the message.

The main problem of all this is that the public key must be made available somehow to other users with whom secure communication is desired. PGP and PEM/MOSS use different approaches to a solution. PEM uses certificates, which bind a distinguished name to a public key and are issued by a certification authority. This results in a hierarchical structure of certification authorities. MOSS has relaxed this quite a lot and, while still understanding certificates, is quite close to the PGP approach, which uses mutual key exchange and verification using fingerprints. As this is quite cumbersome, users can mutually sign keys and thus establish chains of trust. Key distribution centers, which do not sign keys, but only store them, have also been established.

SSL and S-HTTP also support certificates. SSL requires them for the server and S-HTTP allows secure transactions without using certificates.

Anarchical systems are fine for an anarchical Web, but if you want to do business using public-key encryption, a certification scheme might still be of importance. For certain areas, security features like digital signatures and public-key encryption require public-key certification services. Even if these security services are implemented in application tools, they cannot be used unless they are connected to an interworking certification infrastructure. For Europe, the ICE-TEL project (sponsored by the EU) will develop security tools and services and provide a general-purpose security infrastructure to all users in the open networks who want to apply such security services based on public-key encryption schemes. They will be in line with the general security concept currently being developed for the Internet.

30.3.4 Relation to Hyper-G?

The principles described above do not apply to Email only. There is no principal difference between a MIME Email message and a Web or Hyper-G page. Both can contain text and other data, like images or sound. Thus PGP, PEM and MOSS could all be used in Hyper-G to secure data transfer.

30.4   Electronic commerce

The foundation of all economic commerce is the exchange of value. The problem with commerce on the Web is that it uses "virtual transactions." The parties involved cannot exchange conventional cash. They can use credit cards instead, but this is not without risks.

Credit card information is not yet secure in cyberspace. There is a lot of work currently in progress that will change that soon, but for today this still holds. Even if there have not been many reports of credit card misuse originating from the Web, it is still relatively easy to intercept your credit card information and use it repeatedly. Others think this risk is no worse than leaving your credit card information at the gas station, and then they even have a copy of your signature. While this is quite true, one cannot excuse one weakness with the existence of another.

Not only because of this, but also because there is much money potentially involved, there is a wealth of new systems for electronic commerce, from special credit-card-based online-payment systems and electronic checks to electronic cash. This chapter will introduce many of them, and evaluate their relevance for Hyper-G.

30.4.1 First Virtual (FV)

FIRST VIRTUAL Holdings Inc. claim to be the world's first electronic merchant banker – a financial services company created specifically to enable virtually anyone with Internet access to buy and sell information worldwide using the Internet (http://www.fv.com). The philosophy behind FV is that secure Internet commerce should be

- broadly available;
- easy to participate in;

- compatible with the ways of using the Internet that people already know, like ordinary Email.

FV considers other schemes too complicated to understand, too difficult to use, or too limited in their scope.

FV mainly aims at merchants, selling information the shareware way. Selling "hard goods" is possible, but not the standard. Customers have to apply for an FV-Account, send their credit card information to FV and choose an account name. If customers want to buy something, they tell the merchant the account name and are sent the information or software or whatever else they were interested in. Customers now have time to review what they want to buy, following the shareware principle. Later on, FV sends an Email message to the customer, asking for confirmation of the transaction. If the customer accepts, the amount is charged to the credit card, otherwise the merchant is informed that the customer does not want to buy the item.

FV does not use encryption, because, in their words:

Encryption is almost always cumbersome and difficult. And it always adds an additional step, and something else to worry about. After all, even banks and armored cars are subject to robbery attempts, and sometimes those attempts succeed.

Rather than build encryption into our system, we decided to design a system in which no sensitive information like checking account numbers would ever have to travel over the Internet in the first place. The result is First Virtual.

30.4.2   Ecash

Most commerce over the Internet is done using credit cards. This has the drawback that no anonymity is possible, compared to when you do "real" shopping and pay by cash. This is what ecash from *DigiCash* aims at:

Ecash is designed for secure payments from any personal computer to any other work-station, over Email or Internet. Ecash has the privacy of paper cash, while achieving the high security required for electronic network environments exclusively through innovations in public-key cryptography.

With ecash, customers can draw digital money from electronic banks to their electronic wallet which is typically stored on their computer (see Figure 30.1 for an example view of the ecash application). There are several shops that currently accept ecash in the worldwide trial currently ongoing. When a customer wants to buy something, the shop tries to set up an online connection to the wallet on the user's PC (Figure 30.2 shows a request by the EBS Lottery Shop) and to withdraw the price of the goods in ecash. If the wallet owner accepts the withdrawal, the cash is transferred to the shop and the goods can be delivered.

Ecash provides the highest security possible by applying public-key digital signature techniques and by protecting ecash withdrawals from the user's account with a password that is only known to the user.

Ecash software works on all major platforms and can easily be integrated into Hyper-G to sell information stored in the system.

Figure 30.1   The ecash application window.

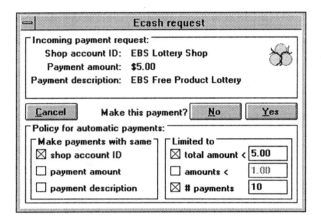

Figure 30.2   An ecash request by the EBS Lottery Shop.

30.4.3   CyberCash

CyberCash offers secure credit card services and will soon offer money payments services on the Internet. Consumers with a personal computer, an Internet browser and a network connection are ready to shop and pay safely and conveniently.

30.4.4   NetCash

This is another product closely resembling ecash. It is claimed that:

NetCash is the first fully functional form of virtual currency. It works very much like physical cash but without the physical symbols. Rather than a wallet filled with bills, you have a virtual wallet (a file in your computer) filled with virtual bills. These are nothing more than information, specifically a serial number identifying each bill and the monetary value it represents.

30.4.5 NetBill

NetBill offers an electronic payment scheme for buying goods and services securely over the Internet. The NetBill transaction protocol is especially designed to handle low cost items; for example, journal articles at 10 cents a page. The protocol also ensures that both the consumer and merchant are protected: the consumer is guaranteed the certified delivery of goods before payment is processed, and the merchant is guaranteed that the consumer cannot access the goods until payment has been received.

30.4.6 Globe ID

Globe ID aims to provide users and merchants with a secure, efficient and user-friendly mechanism for commercial transactions on the Internet (http://globeid.gctech.-fr). Globe ID uses the existing traditional banking and credit card infrastructure. Users and merchants both open an account at a GlobeID bank. Only payment transactions between a **user's wallet** and a **merchant's wallet** are allowed. The wallets are administrated by Globe ID. Information is physically stored on a secure and fault-tolerant information management system. The system is administrated and maintained by a certified financial institution.

The Globe ID electronic wallet concept is fairly close to the well-known everyday wallet equivalent. For small transactions, an agreed amount of money is debited from the client's wallet and credited to the merchant's wallet. When an individual wallet is empty, the client can refill it using a credit card. For large transactions, the client can choose to use a credit card directly and leave the wallet contents unchanged. For small payments, only debiting the wallet contents is allowed.

The following activities are performed during a GlobeID transaction:

- When a client wants to buy a product and tells the merchant, the merchant creates a "payment request ticket" and sends it to the GlobeID payment server.

- The payment server then asks the client for authentication using a secret key.

- If the authentication was successful, GlobeID debits the user account, credits the merchant account and issues a "receipt."

- On reception of this receipt, the merchant server will deliver the final product.

All sensitive data (such as credit card numbers) is transferred using strong encryption methods. Receipts and payment tickets are protected using electronic signatures.

30.4.7 Secure Electronic Payment Protocol specification (SEPP)

IBM, Netscape, GTE, CyberCash and MasterCard have cooperatively developed a draft document defining a **Secure Electronic Payment Protocol** (SEPP) – an open, vendor-neutral, non-proprietary, license-free specification for securing online transactions. This has been made available for review and comment recently.

30.5 Summary

While it is true that there are a lot of security risks on the Web, we have seen that there are at least as many solutions available. Furthermore, people seem to become much more aware of that situation. This will hopefully result in a high demand for good and secure implementations. Currently one can observe increasing development of new ideas and technology in the area of security and the Web which will enable us to provide those implementations to users. Hyper-G will provide state of the art security technology soon which will be compatible with Web standards or practices.

30.6 Further reading

As you have seen, there are many different aspects of computer security, even when only considering Web applications. This explains why there is such a lot of interesting literature on the subject to recommend.

If you want to get a thorough general overview on cryptography, to be able to understand the advanced topics, read Schneier (1995). Frequently Asked Questions on Web security are answered in (Stein) and in chapters from Stein, Cheswick and Bellovin (1994) and Liu *et al.* (1994).

There is a working group in the Internet Engineering Task Force that deals with Web Transaction Security (WTS). The first output of this group is a requirements document that can be found in Bossert *et al.* (1995). Other Internet drafts and Requests For Comment (RFCs) can be found on the following sites:

- Africa: `ftp.is.co.za` (196.4.160.8)

- Europe: `nic.nordu.net` (192.36.148.17)

- Pacific Rim: `munnari.oz.au` (128.250.1.21)

- US East Coast: `ds.internic.net` (198.49.45.10)

- US West Coast: `ftp.isi.edu` (128.9.0.32)

You can find the S-HTTP proposal (Rescorla and Schiffman, 1995) on these sites as well as all the documents on MIME, PEM and MOSS (Linn, 1993; Kent, 1993; Balenson, 1993; Kaliski, 1993; Borenstein and Freed, 1993; Crocker *et al.*, 1995; Galvin *et al.*, 1995 and many others). More info on SSL can be found in Hickman and Elgamal (1995) and the PCT-Protocol is specified in Benaloh *et al.* (1995). For the Secure Electronic Payment Protocol specifications, see Secure Electronic Payment Protocol Draft. Version 1.1 (1995).

A technical discussion of electronic cash by David Chaum can be found in Chaum (1991, 1989), the software is available at `http://www.ecash.com`. All the other electronic commerce systems can of course be found online too, like First Virtual at `http://www.fv.com`, DigiCash at `http://www.digicash.com`, Netcash at `http://www.netbank.com` and Netbill in Cox *et al.* (1995).

31 The future

Frank Kappe, Hermann Maurer, Klaus Schmaranz

This chapter describes some of the **future developments** concerning Hyper-G. This includes developments that are well advanced but are not released at the time of writing as well as features and applications available in, or through using, Hyper-G that have been specified but for which no completion date can be announced yet. Last but not least, we mention a list of features under consideration or under development elsewhere over which the Graz Hyper-G team has no direct control.

31.1 More document formats

As we have already seen in Chapter 28 PDF is a very interesting format for professional electronic publishing and is becoming more and more widespread. For this reason PDF will be included in Hyper-G as one of the native document formats. All hyperlinks in PDF documents will be extracted by the Hyper-G server and stored in Hyper-G's separate link database to achieve stable hyperlinks with user access rights, as is the case with all hyperlinks in Hyper-G. The viewers for PDF will also be available as standalone viewers and therefore work with the native Hyper-G clients Harmony and Amadeus, as well as with all other Web clients like Mosaic, Netscape or Arena.

Another format that will be integrated in Hyper-G in the near future is Quicktime. The first step will be to integrate Quicktime movies and sound since this is widely used by professional film studios for small video clips such as previews for new movies.

Another data format has become more and more popular: Quicktime VR. In Quicktime VR it is easy to make a panoramic shot of a real scene consisting of several pictures with very cheap electronic cameras. This panoramic shot is then converted to a Quicktime VR scene and the result is a photo-realistic 3D scene of the real world. In comparison to a real 3D model, this method allows you to capture a scene in a few minutes whereas a 3D model takes an enormous amount of time and computing power to create. Naturally the scene then only looks like a 3D scene, which it is not really, but very often this is enough. Additionally, a Quicktime VR scene does not need much computing power to be rendered, whereas real 3D models can require much more, depending on the complexity of the scene.

31.2   Gateways

On the server side, the gateways for WWW and Gopher access of a Hyper-G server will be enhanced. At the moment the WWW gateway already provides many more features than first-generation Web servers, such as user identification, customizable settings for language and attributes and advanced search facilities. But Hyper-G allows much more sophisticated features that one can only see when accessing a Hyper-G server with a native client. These sophisticated features include local link maps with visualization of incoming and outgoing hyperlinks and, even more interesting, write access to the Hyper-G database. HTTP can also support the use of forms generated on the fly, with Java applets inserted into the HTML pages. We are also considering a separate VRML gateway that will generate VRML scenes instead of HTML documents to represent the collection structure. For example, a collection may be rendered as a room, with doors leading to other rooms (collections), and different items representing documents (for example, pictures on the wall, TV sets, text document on a table).

Similarly, future enhancements of the Gopher gateway will implement full Gopher+ support including features like abstracts and GopherVR scene descriptions, to offer Gopher server administrators a migration path to Hyper-G.

In order to better support bibliographic databases, the Z39.50 gateway will be implemented in both directions. This will allow access to a Hyper-G server with a Z39.50 client, and access to a Z39.50 server with Hyper-G and Web clients through the Hyper-G server.

31.3   Hyper-G as a documentation management system

The Institute for Hypermedia Systems (HMS) of JOANNEUM RESEARCH is currently engaged in a project for the European Space Agency (ESA) that will bring the functionality of a full documentation management system to Hyper-G.

This includes automatic classification of documents based on keyword extraction, (semi-)automatic generation of hyperlinks, version management, and the ability to make use of a variety of text formats, including generic SGML.

Semi-automatic link generation will be supported for **vocative hyperlinks** and **glossary links**. Vocative hyperlinks are phrases appearing in the text like "see Section 3.5," "Wonko describes in [Wonko 95] how ..." and so on. The hyperlink generation process will parse a document, try to match typical phrases and, if such phrases are found, try to find destinations for such vocative hyperlinks. Phrases to match as well as the destinations to these source anchors are defined in a so-called VLCL (Vocative Link Creation Language).

Glossaries are Hyper-G collections containing several documents that serve as destinations for links. Those documents have several keywords that are matched against the contents of a given document and, if a keyword is found in the running text, a hyperlink is created from the keyword found to the destination document. As a special case, an encyclopedia is a glossary collection with both link endpoints in the same collection (that is, pointing from the encyclopedia to the encyclopedia).

Version control mechanisms will be implemented in Hyper-G, allowing you to keep old versions of documents in parallel with the new documents. Especially for documentation purposes it is very often necessary to retain the old version of a document when a new version is inserted. Also hyperlinks that have been created in and to old documents are transferred to the newer version automatically.

31.4   Communication and collaboration

Hyper-G, with its structured information management, is also an ideal tool for Email and news. On the one hand, structuring of newsgroups can be done using the collection hierarchy, on the other, hyperlinks will be used for follow-ups in both directions. The local map and different link types give an overview of discussion threads.

In general Hyper-G will support many more interactive components in the future, including cooperative work to the maximum extent possible. One of the interactive features of Hyper-G is the messaging mechanism that is already implemented. At the moment it is possible to send messages to users that are currently connected to a Hyper-G server. Since a message can be sent to more than one user simultaneously this feature can be used for conferencing. The next extension to the messaging mechanism will be a facility not only to send messages directly to logged in users but also to be able to post a message to users not currently on the system. Another extension to the messaging system will be to automatically insert messages sent to a user in a collection hierarchy, as will be done with Email and news. The messaging feature can also be used to support shared workspaces and whiteboards.

When mail and news are integrated in Hyper-G, it will be possible to "subscribe" to arbitrary collections, which transform Hyper-G from a passive information system, where the user has to look for information, to an active communication and information system, where the system informs users of new material matching their interests (see "Further reading").

By the end of 1996, a computer conferencing system for asynchronous, multiperson, structured discussion built on top of Hyper-G will be available for network supported cooperation, discussion and project management. It will include version control and a graphical representation of the flow of arguments akin to what was available in gIBIS.

31.5   Electronic libraries and teaching support

Hyper-G will be used increasingly for the implementation of electronic libraries, often also called digital libraries. As part of the EU project LIBERATION (standing for LIBraries: Electronic Remote Access To Information Over Networks) three scientific journals, some 50 books, over 20 one-hour units of courseware and other material including a number of special-purpose encyclopedias will become available. Hyper-G's search facilities and customization features will be particularly important in this application area which is expected to be one of the major uses of Hyper-G. This will be combined with modern versions of the "authoring on the fly" concept mentioned in Section 29.1, the computer conferencing features from Section 29.3 and HM-Card explained in Chapter 27 to yield the most powerful computer-based teaching and learning environment ever.

31.6   Security and billing

While Hyper-G has a powerful scheme of access rights, it does not currently make use of encryption for secure transfer of data between client and server. This is going to change in the near future (see also Chapter 30). While Hyper-G supports price tags for documents (see Section 11.3), the actual transfer of real money (billing) is currently outside the scope of the system. It is likely to be augmented by a cash transfer mechanism such as *ecash* proposed by *DigiCash* (see Section 30.4.2) in the future, so that Hyper-G server operators may charge for information easily.

31.7   Miscellaneous improvements

Since hyperlinks also have attributes like access rights, author, creation and modification dates, it is easy to implement user-defined link filters. Those filters could be, say, "show only hyperlinks created by author wonko after 23 February, 1995." This helps a lot in cooperative work since everybody can place their own hyperlinks in a document visible only to the owner rather than making them world-readable which would lead to a completely link-overloaded and therefore difficult to read document.

One of the basic concepts of Hyper-G is the connection-oriented protocol that allows automatic caching, user identification, customized sessions, message mechanisms and much more. However, there are some very special cases where it would be useful to let the client connect to another server instead of letting the server do this job. As an example, consider an interesting journal found on the Web which is mirrored to other servers. Suppose one of them is geographically more convenient for the reader. In this case the reader will want to reconnect to the new server without restarting the client and manually connecting to this server. A special hyperlink with a "reconnect" attribute would do this job.

At the moment mirroring of data in Hyper-G is done with FTP sites, as has been the case for many years. Documents are exported from the master server and imported to the slave server. A much smarter technology would be the concept of **super-caching**. This means that documents get special attributes to tell them what happens when they are transmitted to another server. If this server is a mirror site then the document is inserted in the database on the remote server instead of simply being stored in the cache. If it is a normal server the document behaves as usual. Another attribute attached to the document is used to tell the server to mirror this document to another server immediately without a user first downloading it. In combination with another attribute, the idle time of a document, mirror sites can also decide how long a document remains on the mirror site without any user accessing it. After this period of time the document is automatically deleted, but it is mirrored again the next time a user accesses it on the remote server. Using this technique it is easy to control mirroring, especially on small servers that do not have enough disk space. The caching attributes can also be used for exactly the opposite – they may not allow caching for certain documents. It is useless to cache documents that change very rapidly because they normally only consume cache memory but have to be downloaded every time because they have changed.

Hyper-G's database can not only store documents in one of its native document formats but also store documents of arbitrary generic formats. For this reason a Hyper-G server could act as a main information server for an institution including all of today's services like WWW, Hyper-G, Gopher, Email, News, FTP, Archie and others. The benefit of letting a single Hyper-G server act as a server for all services is that only the Hyper-G database needs administration, which is easy, instead of administering all the different systems that would otherwise be needed. All the specialties of Hyper-G like search, user access rights, expiry date and more then apply to all services.

The Hyper-G server as well as the clients will in the future provide an API to allow programmers to write very specialized server or client modules easily, for example a revision control system for source code or documentation similar to RCS but with a database as a kernel. The benefits of such a system would be a seamless integration of different versions of source code and documentation with additional hyperlink, structuring and searching mechanisms.

31.8 Global search

Data on a Hyper-G server is routinely indexed by Web search engines such as Lycos, InfoSeek or WebCrawler. However, these search engines all have the same scalability problems (they try to index an exponentially growing Web in one place), are always outdated, know only about a small part of the Web (because indexing cannot keep up with the growth) and do not allow you to narrow the search scope.

Hyper-G can in theory do much better, because it already has a distributed database. In fact, you may issue a global search by broadcasting it to all known Hyper-G servers. However, this is a costly operation.

Using Hyper-G's distributed database and p-flood for implementation of a distributed search index would allow fast global searches, while still allowing the search scope to be limited.

It should be pointed out that we do not expect to implement all the features described above ourselves (although we have started working on some). Rather, we hope that via the Hyper-G Consortium other partners with specific interests will implement specific features (see Appendix C). In this respect, this chapter defines the research agenda for the forthcoming years.

31.9 Migration to future systems

One last, but very important argument for putting your data into a Hyper-G server is this:

The Web is evolving very fast. It is likely that in a few years both first-generation and second-generation Web systems will have been superseded by a third generation. While we do not know what it will look like (maybe a new version of Hyper-G, maybe not), we argue that it will be easier to move your data to this third-generation system if you already have it in a second-generation system such as Hyper-G. Some reasons for this are as follows:

(1) Your Hyper-G data is structured in collections, clusters and sequences. It will be easier to automatically map this onto the structure of the future system – whatever that will be – than the flat, node-link model hypertext of first-generation Web systems.

(2) Your Hyper-G data has meta-information attached (such as author, title, keywords, access rights, size, type, creation and modification time, copyright and so on; see Appendix E for the full list), so the conversion process knows more about the data to convert. Also, it is likely that future systems will support meta-information for documents.

(3) Your Hyper-G links are kept in a link database, with links also having meta-data (link type, creation time, author, access rights and so on). The information in the link database creates additional meta-information for the document (such as number of incoming links, or document version). Again, the system knows more about the documents and the links involved.

(4) Your Hyper-G data is cleanly separated from the user interface (unless you tried really hard to circumvent this). From our previous experience with videotex systems, we can say that combining content and presentation is the biggest stumbling block in converting information to new systems. When the user interface is built right into the content, the content is only browsable using the interface it was designed for. A page designed for point-and-click interfaces relying heavily on graphics is difficult to convert to text for transmission over slow lines, or for reading to a blind user. Likewise, it will not be suitable for, say, tomorrow's 3D user interfaces (see also Section 8.2.6 for a discussion of this topic).

In conclusion, we contend that documents embedded in a Hyper-G collection hierarchy are likely to be convertible to next-generation systems quite easily. Conversion will be eased by the fact that such documents have meta-data already attached and user interface elements are generated on the fly, instead of being contained within the contents. On the other hand, a simple, unstructured set of Web pages is tomorrow's legacy data.

31.10 Further reading

An article on QuickTime VR is found in the proceedings of SIGGRAPH '95 (Chen, 1995). The notion of *vocative links* is defined in DeRose (1989); Chang (1993) describes the automatic generation of hyperlinks. The *Active Communication/Information System* was described in Kappe and Maurer (1994). For information on gIBIS see Conklin and Begeman (1988). The three electronic journals mentioned are the *Journal of Universal Computer Science*, *Few Body Systems* (both published by Springer) and the *Journal for Network and Computer Applications* (J.NCA) by Academic Press.

A   Online resources

Frank Kappe

This appendix describes where to find further information about Hyper-G on the Web. **On-line resources** are particularly valuable, since – unlike a book – they often contain the latest updates. There are Internet information services containing additional and up-to-date documentation on various aspects of Hyper-G. Other sites distribute the software itself (updates of what you find on the CD-ROM). And there are mailing lists for discussion among users and developers, as well as mail addresses for reporting problems.

A.1   Documentation

Most of this book was written around October 1995. Even though the authors tried to anticipate features of a target date of around January 1996, it is likely that some aspects will already have changed when you read this book. The Web is evolving fast.

For this reason, updates and errata will be provided on IICM's server at:

`http://hyperg.iicm.tu-graz.ac.at/hgbook/updates`

An online version of this book will be available at:

`http://hyperg.iicm.tu-graz.ac.at/hgbook`

Lots of background information on Hyper-G, including press releases, research papers, technical documentation, frequently asked questions, lists of servers and so on, can be found on IICM's server under:

`http://hyperg.iicm.tu-graz.ac.at/hyperg`

as well as on the server of the Hyper-G Consortium (see Appendix C):

`http://hyperg.hgc.org`

A.2   Software

The Hyper-G software (server, clients, utilities) can be downloaded by anonymous FTP from:

`ftp://ftp.iicm.tu-graz.ac.at/pub/Hyper-G`

503

This is the primary server in Graz, Austria. FTP mirror servers are available at the following sites:

- Australia:
  `ftp://ftp.cinemedia.com.au/pub/Hyper-G`

- Austria:
  `ftp://ftp.tu-graz.ac.at/pub/Hyper-G`

- Czech Republic:
  `ftp://sunsite.mff.cuni.cz/Net/Infosystems/Hyper-G`

- Germany:
  `ftp://elib.zib-berlin.de/pub/InfoSystems/Hyper-G`
  `ftp://ftp.ask.uni-karlsruhe.de/pub/infosystems/Hyper-G`

- Italy;
  `ftp://ftp.esrin.esa.it/pub/Hyper-G`

- New Zealand:
  `ftp://ftp.cs.auckland.ac.nz/pub/HMU/Hyper-G`

- Portugal:
  `ftp://ftp.ua.pt/pub/infosystems/www/Hyper-G`

- Spain:
  `ftp://ftp.etsimo.uniovi.es/pub/Hyper-G`

- Sweden:
  `ftp://ftp.sunet.se/pub/Networked.Information.Retrieval/-Hyper-G`

- UK:
  `ftp://unix.hensa.ac.uk/mirrors/Hyper-G`

- USA:
  `ftp://ftp.ncsa.uiuc.edu/Hyper-G`
  `ftp://ftp.utdallas.edu/pub/Hyper-G`

Of course, you should try to access your "nearest" server in terms of bandwidth. Within the above directories, you will find the following subdirectories:

Server	Hyper-G Server Installation Script and Instructions
Harmony	Harmony binaries
Amadeus	Amadeus binaries
Easy	Easy binaries
VRweb	VRweb binaries and source
UnixClient	HGTV installation script
papers	research papers on Hyper-G
talk	slides and images used for Hyper-G talks.

A.3   Communication

A number of mail addresses are available for user support. Bug reports to the developers of Harmony and Amadeus should be sent to:

`harmony@iicm.tu-graz.ac.at`

and

`amadeus@iicm.tu-graz.ac.at`

respectively. VRweb bugs should go to:

`vrweb-bugs@iicm.tu-graz.ac.at`

All other problems (for example, server problems) should be reported to:

`hgsupport@iicm.tu-graz.ac.at`

Mail sent to these addresses go to the developers. Please discuss trivial problems and things of interest to a wider community in the USENET newsgroup

`comp.infosystem.hyperg`

Alternatively, you may join the mailing list (mirrored from and to the newsgroup):

`hyper-g@iicm.tu-graz.ac.at`

by sending mail to

`listproc@iicm.tu-graz.ac.at`

with the following message body:

`subscribe hyper-g <Your Name>`

This is recommended if you run a Hyper-G server, since notes about new versions, known bugs and similar things are usually broadcast to this mailing list. The mailing list is archived by Achim Bohnet (`ach@rosat.mpe-garching.mpg.de`) at `http://www.rosat.mpe-garching.mpg.de/mail-lists/Hyper-G`

A special mailing list (`vrweb@iicm.tu-graz.ac.at`) is for VRweb-related issues; subscribe by sending mail to `listproc@iicm.tu-graz.ac.at` with the message body:

`subscribe vrweb <Your Name>`

It is good practice to read the FAQ (frequently asked questions) on IICM's server (`http://hyperg.iicm.tu-graz.ac.at/hyperg-faq`) before posting trivial questions to newsgroups or mailing lists.

B   About the CD-ROM

Klaus Schmaranz

B.1   Contents of the CD-ROM

On the CD-ROM that comes with this book you will find everything needed for a quick start with Hyper-G as well as manual pages and lots of online documentation. This includes:

- The Hyper-G server for all platforms supported.

- Tools to be used with the Hyper-G server for all platforms supported.

- Harmony, the native UNIX Hyper-G client.

- Amadeus, the native MS-Windows Hyper-G client.

- VRWeb, the standalone VRML viewer for all supported platforms.

- A non-commercial version of HM-Card, an authoring and presentation tool for MS-Windows.

- A local database with documentation and demo documents to be used with the local Harmony and Amadeus versions as well as a snapshot of J.UCS – the *Journal of Universal Computer Science*.

- Manual pages for all Hyper-G tools.

- Online documentation on tools, data formats and Hyper-G object attributes as well as format descriptions of HTML, HTF and HIF.

- Several HIF files with documentation, demo documents and multimedia documents such as video clips, audio clips and 3D scenes that are useful if you are operating your own Hyper-G server.

506

B.2 Structure of the CD-ROM

On the CD-ROM you will find several subdirectories with a README file in each subdirectory describing how to install these parts. If binaries exist that can be started directly from the CD-ROM the README file also explains how to start them.

You will also find a README file in the root directory of the CD-ROM containing last-minute information. Please read the contents of this file first before running or installing anything from the CD-ROM.

Sometimes you will find two README files, README.DOS and README.UX, if the subdirectory contains information for both MS-DOS and UNIX. In this case please read the appropriate file for your current operating system.

Under UNIX, all subdirectory names and filenames will be in either all lower case or all upper case letters depending on how your CD-ROM driver deals with the ISO-9660 file system. In the following list of subdirectories on the CD-ROM the subdirectory names are all listed in lower case.

`server` Hyper-G server binaries and installation utilities.

`tools` Offline tools to be used with the Hyper-G server or the Hyper-G local database. This subdirectory is itself divided into two application-oriented subdirectories:

> `hgtools` Tools for Hyper-G server administration and offline database manipulation.
>
> `ldbtools` Tools for preparation of a local Hyper-G database from a HIF file.

`harmony` Harmony, the native Hyper-G UNIX client.

`amadeus` Amadeus, the native Hyper-G MS-Windows client.

`vrweb` VRWeb, the standalone VRML viewer for UNIX and MS-Windows.

`hmcard` HM-Card, an authoring and presentation tool for MS-Windows.

`localdb` A collection of documentation and demo documents in a local database. It is used by the local database variants of Harmony and Amadeus.

`data` HIF files of manual pages, documentation and demo data to be inserted in a Hyper-G server.

`man` UNIX manual pages on Hyper-G and all tools that belong to Hyper-G.

`doc` Technical documentation on Hyper-G.

C The Hyper-G Consortium

Hermann Maurer

The currently most popular Internet tool, WWW, was designed at a time when the explosive growth of the Internet could not yet be predicted. WWW is now reaching and exceeding its limits with a growing number of very large applications.

A team based in Graz, Austria, has recognized this trend sufficiently early and – with the help of specialists from all over the world – has developed the "second-generation" WWW system Hyper-G. Growing enthusiasm and acceptance of Hyper-G has made it necessary to tighten the cooperation and coordination of the large number of groups both in Europe and elsewhere that work with Hyper-G. For this reason the foundation of an international **Hyper-G consortium** was announced on the occasion of the meeting "Multimedia Content for the Information Society" sponsored by the EU Commission on 25–26 September 1995 in Linz, Austria.

The Director of the Hyper-G Consortium is the internationally recognized computer scientist Professor Bruno Buchberger from RISC (Research Institute for Symbolic Computation) at the University of Linz, Austria.

The Hyper-G Consortium is proud once more to offer leading-edge technology developed in Europe to the whole world. It is expected that European organizations on all levels will profit from and support these developments substantially.

Prof. Bruno Buchberger and Prof. Hermann Maurer
Linz and Graz, Austria, 25 September 1995

C.1 Background

Hyper-G is the first "second-generation" Web system. It supports all the usual features of WWW but goes beyond it in a number of ways. A few of the key features are:

- For information and service providers it supports a range of data management tasks and the structuring paradigms vital for the maintenance of large hypermedia databases (for instance, hierarchical information structuring, guaranteed link consistency and a hierarchical access control scheme).

- For users it provides powerful search and navigational features essential to locate and work with information in a substantial information space (for example, information visualization tools).

- For both it allows customization, personalization and annotations; and it supports structured discussions and cooperation, thus going much beyond the information system functions provided by standard WWW systems.

- It comes with powerful viewers that are WWW compatible but offer much additional functionality, particularly for navigation and editing of Hyper-G Web databases.

- It allows a variety of additional data types beyond HTML (such as PostScript, VRML and MPEG) all with full hyperlink capabilities.

C.2   History

Hyper-G was developed by a team from the Graz University of Technology and JOANNEUM RESEARCH in Austria with partial funding from the Austrian Federal Ministry of Science and Research, and with the support of colleagues from all over the world. It is based on the analysis of the early ideas of Ted Nelson, the work carried out at the Massachusetts Institute of Technology and Brown University, inputs from Ben Shneiderman, the Gopher team at the University of Minnesota, and the WWW group at CERN, and on ideas and inputs from Ivan Tomek and many others.

Since about 1994, when the first versions of Hyper-G were released, the number of organizations and persons interested in using Hyper-G and developing systems on the basis of Hyper-G has increased steadily to an extent that it is now impossible to list all important contributions. However, the work carried out at the University of Auckland, by Ed Fox at Virginia Tech, the inputs received from the first very big user, the European Space Agency and their software partners (particularly Intecs and Siemens PSE), Dieter Fellner in Bonn, Thomas Ottmann in Freiburg, MONZ, the largest museum in New Zealand, and publishing companies such as Addison-Wesley and Springer, to name just a few, have been increasingly instrumental in determining the direction in which Hyper-G is moving. Valuable user feedback has also been obtained from over a hundred Hyper-G installations, some publicly accessible, others used in local area networks behind firewalls.

It is this growing number of organizations and persons involved in further developing Hyper-G that has made better and institutionalized coordination of Hyper-G efforts essential. This is the aim of the Hyper-G Consortium.

C.3   How the Hyper-G Consortium (HGC) works

The main aim of the Hyper-G Consortium is to coordinate efforts around the further development of Hyper-G and software based on Hyper-G. Any organization seriously interested in the further development of Hyper-G or of software using or based on Hyper-G is cordially invited and advised to join the HGC.

The HGC is administered by Professor Bruno Buchberger from RISC, the Research Institute for Symbolic Computation of the University of Linz, Austria. The HGC has members and sponsors.

Sponsors of the HGC support the idea of the HGC both in a material and philosophical way; sponsorship of the HGC is negotiated between prospective sponsors and the HGC on a case by case basis. Sponsors are listed as such wherever applicable and receive a report on the HGC twice a year.

Members represent those organizations interested in future developments of Hyper-G or in using Hyper-G as the basis of other software developments. Members pay an annual membership fee starting in 1996. For non-profit organizations the fee is US$ 500 per year, for other organizations US$ 5000. Members enjoy a number of benefits:

- They influence and prioritize future features and directions of Hyper-G by both electronic discussions and by being able to attend the two annual meetings of the HGC without registration fee.

- They have access to the software (source code and documentation) that is administered by the HGC. Software can be submitted for this purpose to the HGC: it is then evaluated and, if approved, added to the corpus of HGC software.

- Access to HGC software includes the right to use it for the purposes of the member institution at no charge, and to work with it and modify it as is deemed necessary. All HGC software must be marked as such; however, whenever HGC software is used for commercial purposes as a whole or in part all rights for its usage have to be negotiated with the originator of the software, that is, one or more HGC members, or with the HGC itself if the software is owned by HGC (for example, because it was developed under an HGC grant, see below).

- Note that members contributing to HGC software profit from the visibility and quality control of the HGC ; the initial HGC software consists of the software for the Hyper-G server and its clients Amadeus (Windows) and Harmony (XWindows), and the 3D scene viewer VRweb based on VRML.

- At the HGC Consortium meetings (two per year, one usually in Europe, the other elsewhere) all consortium members are informed about forthcoming developments of members relating to Hyper-G both in the immediate and mid-term future; they will have the opportunity to contribute and help to define priorities.

- After each meeting, members will receive comprehensive documentation of activities that have taken place since the last meeting and those planned for the future.

- The HGC will organize at least one Hyper-G workshop each year; HGC members will pay no registration for these workshops.

- HGC members can apply to HGC for research and development grants in connection with Hyper-G: all HGC income (through sponsorship and membership fees) is used for such grants, except that needed for HGC administration.

C.4   Contact addresses and events

Hyper-G Consortium
RISC University of Linz
Professor Dr. Bruno Buchberger
HGC Secretary: Dr. Tudor Jebelean
HGC@risc.uni-linz.ac.at
Fax: 0043 - 7236 - 3231 30

C.5   List of current members and sponsors

Members

California State University at Long Beach (USA)
Glass Wings (Australia)
Graz University of Technology (Austria)
Intecs (Italy)
Konrad-Zuse-Centre for Information Technology, Berlin (Germany)
Sapporo Hyperlab (Japan)
Technical University of Prague (Czech Republik)
University of California, Los Angeles (USA)
UNIMAS (Malaysia)
University of Auckland (New Zealand)
University of Bonn (Germany)
University of Dortmund (Germany)
University of Freiburg (Germany)
University of Hagen (Germany)
University of Linz (Austria)
University of Minnesota (USA)
University of Paderborn (Germany)

Sponsors

Academic Press (UK)
Addison-Wesley (Germany)
Boeing (USA)
Daimler-Benz (Germany)
dpunkt Pub. Co. (Germany)
Media House Styria (Austria)
Project Xanadu (Japan)
SONY (Austria)
Springer Pub.Co. (Germany)
WIFI-IIC (Austria)
Xanadu Australia (Australia)

D The Web Society

Hermann Maurer

The **Web Society**, an international non-profit organization, has been founded according to Austrian law and initially has two offices in Graz, Austria, and Charlottesville, USA.

D.1 Motivation for the foundation of the Web Society

The Web Society was founded out of a concern that the worldwide computer network, the Internet (called the "Web" in what follows), is growing at a rate that requires accompanying measures to be addressed.

- Despite the emergence of powerful Web tools such as Gopher, WWW and Hyper-G, and despite the plethora of directory services, information can still be hard to find.

- The level of quality, consistency and suitability of information is often hard to determine and difficult to control.

- Information should be generally available, yet techniques for providing, for example, youth protection where desired, or protection against personal attacks, should be available. In particular, techniques for limiting access to specific servers or authors, or excluding such specific sources, should be able to be used at the discretion of the owner of a server or client.

- The need for standardized and open systems must be impressed on all organizations providing information, applications and tools for the Web.

D.2 Executive council and other officers

The Web Society's first general assembly was held in Graz, Austria, on 15 May 1995.

An executive council of four persons and a number of other officers were elected as follows:

512

President Hermann Maurer, Austria (Graz University of Technology)

Vice President (Standards) J.-F. Abramatic, France (INRIA)

Vice President (Public Matters) Robert Cailliau, Switzerland (CERN)

Vice President (Finances) Mark McCahill, USA (University of Minnesota)

One further position on the executive council remains open for a potential future representative of one other non-profit organization heavily involved in Web activities.

Decisions of the executive council are carried out by the President after approval of a majority of the executive council.

Secretary Frank Kappe, Graz University of Technology, Austria

Arbitration Ivan Tomek, Acadia University, Canada; Arnoud De Kemp, Springer Publishing Co., Germany

Controllers Walter Schinagl, University of Graz, Austria; Gerhard Pail, Graz University of Technology, Austria

Administration Gary Marks, AACE, USA; Gabriele Leitner, Graz University of Technology, Austria

D.3 Aims of the Web Society

(1) The Web Society will support general, widely accessible and disciplined use of the Web and other wide area or metropolitan networks.

(2) The Web Society will support all activities to make the use of the Web easier and more efficient by advocating the development of standards and open systems.

(3) The Web Society will support the activities of W3C with respect to the standardization of WWW protocols, and activities aimed at integrating various Web services such as Gopher, WWW, Hyper-G, FTP, Newsgroups and full text servers.

(4) The Web Society will support the provision of index services, Web guides and other tools for the navigation and use of the Internet.

(5) The Web Society will represent all Web users who are interested in keeping the Web open to the extent permissible by local laws.

(6) The Web Society will debate necessary sets of mechanisms and rules for the use of the Web (see Note 1 below).

(7) The Web Society is not concerned with the hardware and protocol infrastructure for the Web, but with information, services, tools and applications of the Web.

(8) The Web Society will support all moves to protect persons against invasion of privacy, yet is opposed to material that is openly accessible where authors cannot be identified, even if they violate local laws.

(9) The Web Society will discuss to what extent servers should obey local laws; and to what extent some servers should permit pseudonyms (with or without true identity escrow) as per local law; some servers or clients may filter information provided by such servers or pseudonyms at the discretion of the owner of the servers or clients.

(10) The Web Society will support the notion that common carriers should convey traffic regardless of source or destination; filtering, if any, is a responsibility of the client (or local server).

(11) The Web Society will have an ongoing discussion of its aims and will decide on changes or expansions of its aims at the annual general assembly.

Note 1 (as exemplification of point 6 above)

The fact that the Web at this point allows unlimited access to all kinds of information has both negative and societal implications. It is this aspect that is addressed here. To be specific, here are two examples:

- Some organizations may want to permit access only to certain designated sites to avoid prohibitive network costs.

- In places were laws do not permit access to certain types of information (for example, youth protection laws), control of access to such information should be possible.

This is done not because the Web Society believes in censorship (and indeed it does not intend to take a strong position in such a debate) but for purely pragmatic reasons: unless local laws are observed by the Web, the Web has no chance of becoming as ubiquitous as seems desirable.

D.4   Concrete actions of the Web Society

(1) The Web Society will operate a substantial Web server with a growing archive of news, relevant literature, structured discussion corners and many other items on

`http://info.websoc.org/`

and on mirror sites to be set up as the Web Society grows. Some of this will only be available for Web Society members.

(2) The Web Society will organize an annual WebNet conference; the first such event takes place in San Francisco, USA 16-19 October 1996, and is sponsored by AACE. See

`http://info.websoc.org/`

for details.

(3) The Web Society will prepare, with the help of members, reports and statements for local, regional or national governments to provide the basis for legislative actions where this is necessary.

(4) The Web Society will cooperate with other societies, and become a member of other umbrella organizations to foster its aims.

(5) The Web Society will contribute to appropriate publications, newsgroups and mailing lists.

(6) The Web Society will operate structured Web-based discussions on various topics of interest.

(7) The Web Society will offer all members space on the Web Society's servers for self-presentation at the discretion of the Society.

(8) The Web Society will provide listings of open/desired positions and other professional information for members free of charge.

D.5 Member services and member dues

(1) The Web Society has individual and corporate members with an annual membership fee of US\$ 20 (three years US\$ 50) and US\$ 200, respectively. Issues raised by corporate members have to be dealt with at the next meeting of the executive council and within six weeks at the latest. Issues brought forward by individual members are dealt with at the discretion of the executive council but have to be dealt with before the next general assembly.

(2) Members of the Web Society have access to all information on the Web Society's server; they have reduced registration fees at a variety of conferences, including the annual WebNet, ED-MEDIA and others.

(3) Members of the Web Society have access to the AACE member periodical, *Educational Technology Review*, free of charge. They have a discount on all journals of the Association of Advancement of Computers in Education (AACE). Similar agreements are being negotiated with other conferences and societies.

(4) Members of the Web Society receive technical help to as large an extent as possible.

(5) Members of the Web Society can subscribe to a "News Profile." They are automatically informed of news items on the Society's server that are of particular interest to them.

(6) Members of the Web Society can make information available about themselves.

(7) Members of the Web Society will have their own private "home collections" (only accessible to them) on the Web Society's server. This server will be mirrored when the load and geographical distribution makes it necessary.

D.6   From the credo of Web Society members

Unless ordinary Web users have a strong representation they will not be heard, and tariff and legal decisions will be taken without heeding their interests.

This is what the Web Society intends to be:

A strong representation of Web users and non-profit Web developers, much like an AAA of the Web (for non-US citizens: the AAA is the club representing many US motorists). When you get stuck on the road you contact the AAA; when you have problems with the Web you contact the Web Society.

E Object attributes and the Hyper-G Interchange Format

Frank Kappe

E.1 Object attributes

This section contains descriptions of all attributes of the various Hyper-G objects, in alphabetical order. The description of the object class hierarchy is contained in Section 11.1.2. The following table gives an overview of all attributes available. "Object Class" gives the "highest" object class in the class hierarchy of Section 11.1.2 where this attribute is applicable. "Editable" describes who may set this attribute: the value "user" means the attribute can be set by users with write access (see Section 11.2); "system" means the attribute can be set by the system user only; "server" means the attribute is generated and stored by the server itself; "synthetic" means that the attribute is not directly stored but set by the server on the fly. The "Indexed" field specifies whether or not the attribute is indexed (that is, can be searched for real fast), while "Multiple" specifies whether the attribute may appear more than once in a single object record.

Attribute	Object class	Editable	Indexed	Multiple
Account	User	system/server	no	no
Arguments	GenericDocument	user	no	no
Author	HGObject	system	yes	no
CollectionType	Collection	user	no	no
Cost	Document	synthetic	no	no
Database	SQLDocument	user	no	no
Dead	Server	server	no	no
Descr	Group,User	system	no	no
Description	Collection	user	no	no
Dest	Anchor	synthetic	no	no
DHint	Anchor	user/server	yes	no
DocCount	Server	server	no	no
DocumentType	Document	no	no	no

517

Attribute	Object class	Editable	Indexed	Multiple
GDest	Anchor	synthetic	no	no
GOID	HGObject	synthetic	no	no
GopherType	GopherDocument	user/synthetic	no	no
Group	User	system	no	yes
Home	User	system	no	no
Host	RemoteDocument	user	no	no
Host	User	system	no	yes
Keyword	HGObject	user	yes	yes
Layout	HGObject	user	no	no
License	Collection	user	no	no
LinkType	Anchor	user	no	no
MimeType	Document	user/synthetic	no	no
Modified	Server	server	no	no
Name	Collection	no	yes	no
Name	Document	user	yes	yes
ObjectID	HGObject	server	yes	no
OHName	Server	server	no	no
Parents	HGObject	synthetic	no	no
Passwd	User	user	no	yes
Path	Document	server	no	no
Path	RemoteDocument	user	no	no
Port	RemoteDocument	user	no	no
Position	Anchor	user	no	no
PresentationHints	Document	user	no	no
Price	Document	user	no	no
Protocol	RemoteDocument	user	no	no
Pwd	SQLDocument	user	no	no
Repl	HGObject	server	yes	no
Rights	HGObject	user	no	no
Score	HGObject	synthetic	no	no
Sequence	HGObject	user	no	no
Serv	HGObject	synthetic	no	no
Size	WAISDocument	synthetic	no	no
SortOrder	Collection	user	no	no
SQLStmt	SQLDocument	user/synthetic	no	yes
SString	Server	server	no	no
SubType	GenericDocument	user	no	no
Subdocs	Collection	synthetic	no	no
TAnchor	Anchor	no	no	no
TimeCreated	HGObject	user	yes	no

Attribute	Object class	Editable	Indexed	Multiple
TimeExpire	HGObject	user	no	no
TimeModified	HGObject	server	yes	no
TimeOpen	HGObject	user	no	no
Title	HGObject	user	yes	yes
Type	HGObject	no	no	no
UGroup	Group	system	yes	no
Uid	SQLDocument	user	no	no
UName	User	system	yes	no
UserAttr	HGObject	user	no	yes
UServer	Server	server	no	no
WaisDocID	WAISDocument	synthetic	no	no
WaisType	WAISDocument	user/synthetic	no	no

We now give more detailed descriptions of every attribute, in alphabetical order.

E.1.1 Account

This attribute is part of the User object. It holds a non-negative 32-bit integer in hexadecimal notation (of course, clients may convert it to decimal for presentation). Its value can only be set by system users, and by the server itself. The purpose of the Account attribute is to store the balance of the current user's account in "virtual money," which may or may not be related to real money in some currency.

System users may set the Account to a certain value (for example, as a result of a user's payment). The server decrements this value whenever the user accesses a priced document, until the value would become negative. In this case, the document is not transferred and the server sends an error code (INSUFF_FUNDS). Nothing is deducted, however, when accessing an object's meta-data. Thus, searching and collection listings are free, only looking at documents themselves may cost. Of course, anonymous users cannot access priced documents. Also, clients are expected to inform users of the document's price before attempting to load it, unless the user has chosen to accept documents priced below a certain threshold. More information on accounting and billing is to be found in Section 11.3.

Example The user has 1000 units of "virtual money" left.

    Account=0x000003E8

See also Attributes Price and Cost, and Sections 11.3 and 14.8.1.

E.1.2 Arguments

The Arguments attribute of generic documents allows up to 10 additional arguments to be passed to the helper application that gets started by the client. By convention, the first argument specifies a preferred filename for the document, the others have arbitrary meaning, depending on the type of document.

In general, it is the user's responsibility to configure the client to make use of generic documents and start the correct helper application with correct arguments.

Example
```
MimeType=application/x-excel
Arguments=excel.xls 25
```
See also Attribute `MimeType`, Section 22.5.6 and client configuration files.

E.1.3 Author

The author (or more precisely: the owner) of the document or anchor. This attribute is used to determine access rights (together with the `Rights` attribute; see Section 11.2 in this book). It can only be modified by system users and is searchable. Its contents should correspond to an existing Hyper-G user, that is, there should be a `User` object with the same contents in its `UName` attribute.

Example
```
Author=fkappe
```
See also Attributes `Rights` and `UName`, and Section 11.2.

E.1.4 CollectionType

The `CollectionType` attribute is applicable for collections only, and can have the following values:

CollectionType	Description
(default)	a collection
Cluster	a cluster
Sequence	a sequence

While a collection usually results in some sort of menu presented to the user, the elements of a cluster are shown together, and the elements of a sequence are visualized in the order defined by the collection's `SortOrder` (a detailed description is contained in Section 9.2). Do not confuse the sequence collection type with the `Sequence` attribute. The `CollectionType` attribute may be set and modified by any user with write permission for the collection object.

Example
```
CollectionType=Cluster
```
See also Attributes `Layout`, `PresentationHints`, `Sequence` and `SortOrder`, and Section 9.2.

E.1.5 Cost

When a user accesses a document with a `Price` attribute, the server uses the information in the `Price` attribute to dynamically generate a `Cost` attribute, taking the user's identity and group memberships into account (offering the smallest possible price, of course). The attribute value is a non-negative 32-bit integer in hexadecimal notation. This amount is then deducted from the user's Account, if possible (otherwise, access is denied).

Since anonymous users have no Hyper-G account the document is inaccessible to them. No Cost attribute is generated for the Author (owner) of the document, users with write permission, and system users (members of user group system). They can access the document for free, even without having a Hyper-G account.

Example The document costs 100 units of "virtual money" for this user.

    Cost=0x00000064

See also Attributes Account and Price, and Section 11.3.

E.1.6 Database

The Database attribute is applicable to SQLDocument objects only. It contains information specific to the type of database the object is linked to. First, the kind of database is specified (currently, oracle: is the only type supported), followed by database-specific fields. For Oracle databases, t: indicates that the so-called "tnsnames" mechanism for mapping symbolic database names to databases should be used. Finally, the symbolic database name follows. Other information needed to access the database is contained in the attributes Host, Port, Uid, Pwd and SQLStmt.

Example

    Database=oracle:t:db1

See also Attributes Host, Port, Uid, Pwd and SQLStmt, and Chapter 12.

E.1.7 Dead

This attribute is available only for Server objects. Its value is a time stamp (seconds since 1 January 1970), which is set by the server when the server described by that object could not be reached.

Example

    Dead=0x307cd8f6

See also Attribute Modified and Section 10.6.1.

E.1.8 Descr

This attribute of User and Group contains a human-readable description of a user or user group. Since the contents of the user record are never revealed to others, its primary purpose is to let the system administrator remember the real identity or meaning of a user or group name.

Example In a User object:

    UName=fkappe
    Descr=Frank Kappe (fkappe@iicm.tu-graz.ac.at)

In a `Group` object:
```
UGroup=iicm
Descr=Members of the IICM
```
See also Attributes `UName`, `UGroup` and Section 9.5.

E.1.9   Description

This attribute of `Collection` objects contains a short description of the collection's contents, or how they are organized. It is shown together with the title of the collection in the HGTV browser and the WWW gateway. However, because both the length of the description (it should be less than two lines) and its functionality (no formatting instructions, inline images, links and so on) is limited, use of `Description` has been superseded to a large extent by the `PresentationHints=CollectionHead` construct. It is still useful, however, when only a short description is needed. Like the `Title`, a collection may have a number of descriptions in different languages (that is, they start with a language code like `en:`).

Example
```
Title=en:My List of Publications
Description=en:Entries are in reverse chronological order
```
See also Attribute `PresentationHints`.

E.1.10   Dest

This synthetic attribute is calculated for source anchors by the Hyper-G server. It specifies the `ObjectID` of the destination anchor or destination document or collection, unless the link is flagged as open. The client may use this ID directly to fetch the destination object.

Example
```
TAnchor=Src
Dest=0x0000003D
```
See also Attributes `GDest`, `DHint`, `TAnchor` and Section 11.1.

E.1.11   DHint

This attribute is applicable only for source anchors of open links (see Section 11.1 for a description of the "open link" concept). If the link points to a not-yet-existing collection, the value of `DHint` is simply the collection name. If the link points to a not-yet-inserted document or destination anchor, the value of `DHint` is the collection name under which the destination is supposed to appear (recursively, that is, including sub-collections), plus a unique portion of the title or keyword of the destination object. As soon as a matching object is inserted into the Hyper-G database, the link is closed.

This attribute can either be set by the client inserting the source anchor (if the destination is not yet available in the database), or by the server when the destination is deleted.

Example
```
TAnchor=Src
DHint=mycollection en:Test Document
```
See also Attributes Dest, GDest, TAnchor and Sections 11.1 and 25.2.2.

E.1.12   DocCount

This attribute of Server objects contains the document count of a remote server (in hexadecimal).
Example
```
DocCount=0x000103D4
```
See also Attribute Subdocs.

E.1.13   DocumentType

This (mandatory) attribute of Document objects specifies the type of the uocument and determines which of the derived classes is created (see Section 11.1.2). The value is set when the document is first created and cannot be changed afterwards. Currently, the following values are defined:

DocumentType	Description
CGI	a CGI script
collection	a collection (including cluster and sequence)
Generic	a generic document
Image	a raster image
Movie	a movie (digital video)
PostScript	a PostScript document
Program	an executable program (for example, a Java applet)
Remote	a remote document (for example, Gopher, HTTP, SQL, Telnet)
Scene	a 3D scene description in VRML or SDF format
Sound	an audio document
text	a text document

In general, clients are expected to understand and recognize the most common formats for the various document types. The optional MimeType attribute can give additional encoding information, however.
See also Attributes CollectionType, Arguments, MimeType, Protocol and SubType.

E.1.14   GDest

Like the Dest attribute, GDest is calculated for source anchors by the Hyper-G server. It specifies the GOID of the destination anchor or destination document or collection, unless the link is flagged as open. It can be used to generate a permanent reference to the destination (for example, to generate a URL).

Example
```
TAnchor=Src
GDest=0x811be681 0x00009f43
```
See also Attributes Dest, DHint, GOID, TAnchor and Sections 11.1 and 10.1.

E.1.15   GOID

The Global Object ID of the object. This is a 64-bit entity, composed of a 32-bit birthplace ID (the Server ID of the server the object was created at) plus a 32-bit local Object ID that is unique within that server. The GOID is therefore a globally unique identifier for the object (like a URN) that does not change over time. It can be used for reference from the outside (for example, in composing URNs or URLs, saving browser hotlists and histories and so on).

A Hyper-G client would not directly use the GOID to access an object. Rather, a GOID can be converted to a 32-bit (virtual) ObjectID by the HG_MAPID command of the Client/Server Protocol (Appendix F). Objects are always accessed using their 32-bit ObjectID.

Example
```
ObjectID=0x00000024
GOID=0x811be681 0x0002af43
```
See also Attributes GDest, ObjectID and Repl, and Sections 8.3.1 and 10.1.

E.1.16   GopherType

This attribute of GopherDocument objects specifies the document type (see Table E.1.16), according to the Gopher protocol specification (Anklesaria *et al.*, 1993b).

Example
```
DocumentType=Remote
Protocol=gopher
GopherType=1
Host=boombox.micro.umn.edu
Path=/
```
See also Attribute Protocol and Internet RFC 1436 (Anklesaria *et al.*, 1993b).

E.1.17   Group

This attribute of User and Group objects specifies the name of a "parent group" the user or group belongs to. Since users and groups may be members of a number of groups, the attribute may appear any number of times. It may also be missing, in which case the user or

Table E.1   Gopher document types.

GopherType	Description
0	item is a text file
1	item is a directory
2	item is a CSO phone-book server
3	Error
4	item is a BinHexed Macintosh file
5	item is DOS binary archive of some sort
6	item is a UNIX uuencoded file
7	item is an Index-Search server
8	item points to a text-based Telnet session
9	item is a binary file
+	item is a redundant server
g	item is a GIF format graphics file
I or :	item is some kind of image file
S or <	item is some kind of sound file
T	item points to a text-based tn3270 session

group does not belong to any group. Of course, it can be set only by system users (that is, users that are members of the user group named `system`).

Example

```
UName=fkappe
Group=iicm
Group=hms
```

See also Attributes UName, UGroup and Section 22.1.

E.1.18   Home

This optional attribute of `User` objects specifies the name of the user's home collection. A home collection is a private space where users can construct their own view of the information space and store information (for example, annotations, bookmarks, mail). The home collection should not be confused with the "home page" of the WWW, which is an access point for the general public.

Although the name of the home collection is arbitrary, we suggest using ˜foo for user name foo. The access rights of this collection should be set so that only the user may read or write into this collection.

Example The user record:

```
UName=fkappe
Home=˜fkappe
```

The corresponding home collection should contain:

```
Name=˜fkappe
```

```
Author=fkappe
Rights=R:a
```
See also Attributes `Author`, `Name`, `Rights` and `UName`, and Section 22.9.

E.1.19 Host

This attribute is used in two different objects for different purposes:

(1) In `RemoteDocument` objects the `Host` attribute contains the host name of the host to contact in order to retrieve the remote document (which may in fact be a collection of remote documents, for example generated by a query). The host name may also be an IP address, but a fully qualified domain name is preferable.

Example a `RemoteDocument`:
```
Protocol=http
Host=www.w3.org
Path=/hypertext/WWW/Provider/Overview.html
```
See also Attributes `Path`, `Port`, `Protocol` and `UName`.

(2) In `User` objects the `Host` attribute contains a trusted host together with a user on that host, in the form "user@host", where the host is specified by its IP address. If a client connection to the server is made from the IP address, and the client sends the user's username and encrypted password (for example, under UNIX this is normally found in the `/etc/passwd` file) in an IDENTIFY command (see Appendix F), and they match the user name specified in the `Host` and `Passwd` fields of the user record, the user is "auto-identified." Auto-identification is most useful for running tools that insert information automatically without manual intervention (see Chapter 25).

The `Host` attribute may appear a number of times in the same user record, like the `Passwd` attribute, meaning that a number of users at different hosts with different passwords can be treated as a single Hyper-G user in auto-identification mode.

Example a `User` object:
```
UName=wonko
Passwd=2eCD46Fa231A5
Passwd=Zdaxh7A9/EBxM
Host=mpm@193.123.5.1
Host=wonko@129.27.153.10
```
See also Attribute `Passwd` and Section 14.8.

E.1.20 Keyword

This attribute can be used to specify keywords for this object. It can appear any number of times. Its use is to specify additional, searchable keywords that do not appear in the `Title` of the object. Unlike the `Title` attribute, the contents of `Keyword` are treated as language-independent.

A typical use is to attach a unique keyword to a document or destination anchor, so that hyperlinks pointing to it can easily be generated using the DHint mechanism.

Example

```
Keyword=ID1234
Keyword=hypertext hypermedia Hyper-G
```

See also Attributes DHint and Title, and Section 25.2.2.

E.1.21   Layout

The Layout attribute can be attached to Document objects (which includes Collection, Cluster and Sequence). The Layout attribute may be interpreted by a client (currently, only by Easy) to choose how to lay out the document, or the contents of the collection, cluster or sequence. Layouts may be either predefined or defined by the author (see Section 19.2). In the latter case the Layout attribute contains a URL pointing to the layout specification. Certain layouts define the spatial relationships of documents, while others allow synchronization of documents over time (for example, the SyncPage layout).

Example Specify the predefined MoviePage layout for this cluster (which should contain a movie, of course), without showing the title:

```
Layout=MoviePage(title.visible=FALSE)
```

To use an author-defined layout:

```
Layout=MyMoviePage() in hyperg://www.tu-graz.ac.at/styles
?mymovie
```

See also Section 19.2.

E.1.22   License

The License attribute is applicable to collections. Together with the L: field of the Rights attribute it allows a whole collection to be treated as one logical unit, and restricts simultaneous access to this unit to a certain number of users (see Sections 11.3 and 22.3.2). When a user retrieves a document from the licensed collection for the first time, one license is assigned to that user, and thus locked for others. The user may continue reading other documents from that collection. If the user does not retrieve any documents during a certain timeout period the license is unlocked.

The value of License consists of three hexadecimal numbers: the timeout period in seconds, the number of simultaneous users, and the number of documents a user may retrieve in a single "grab" of the license.

Example The collection containing Meyer's 10-Volume Encyclopedia on IICM's Hyper-G server has the following attributes:

```
Name=ref.m10
License=0x0000012C 0x00000003 0x00000014
```

Every document of the encyclopedia must contain a reference to the collection it belongs to in the L: field of the Rights attribute:

`Rights=L:ref.m10`
See also Attributes `Cost`, `Price`, `Rights` and Sections 11.3 and 22.3.2.

E.1.23 LinkType

This attribute of source anchors specifies the type of the link. The client will interpret (some of) the link types and behave differently for certain types. The value should be interpreted in a case-insensitive fashion. Currently, the following values are defined:

LinkType	Description
annotation	pointing from annotation to annotated document
applet	pointing from text to a piece of code
background	pointing from text to background image
inline	pointing from text to inline image
intag	a catch-all for various references within HTML tags
reference	the default (a clickable link)
texture	pointing from 3D scene to texture image

Example
    `LinkType=Annotation`
See also Attribute `Position`.

E.1.24 MimeType

Although clients are expected to automatically recognize and handle a variety of encodings themselves, `MimeType` may be used to specify a certain encoding explicitly. In particular, it is used to distinguish between different SGML DTDs, and to define types of `GenericDocument`. The possible values are defined in the MIME (Multipurpose Internet Mail Extensions) Internet standard.
Example
    `MimeType=text/html`
See also Attribute `Arguments` and Internet RFC 1341 (Borenstein and Freed, 1992).
Notes: This attribute was called `SubType` in earlier implementations. There may still be a number of documents with `SubType` around. When accessing a Hyper-G server using a WWW client, the WWW gateway will produce an HTTP MimeType header element automatically, even if the `MimeType` attribute is not present.

E.1.25 Modified

This attribute is available only for `Server` objects. Its value is a time stamp (seconds since 1 January 1970), which is set by the server when the server description was last updated (for example, because the number of documents on the server has changed by more than a certain threshold).

Example

```
Modified=0x307cd8f6
```

See also Attributes Dead, Subdocs and Section 10.6.1.

E.1.26   Name

The Name attribute is used to attach a name to a document or collection. The Name serves as an external reference to the object (for example, it can be converted to a URL). Therefore, it needs to be unique within a server (which is enforced by the server). It should be short and human-readable, and may contain slashes ("/") but no spaces. Other features are slightly different for collections and documents:

- For Collections, the Name attribute is mandatory.

- For other Documents, the Name attribute is optional.

Example for a document:

```
Name=fkappe.home Name=~fkappe/home.html
```

See also Attributes DHint, GOID and Title.

Note: You should be careful when changing the Name of a collection or document. It means that URLs saved in hotlists of WWW clients become dangling references. It is thus advisable to provide an additional name.

E.1.27   ObjectID

A unique identifier for the object (a 32-bit hexadecimal number). The ID is used to uniquely refer to a Hyper-G object, either stored in the local server, or stored in a remote server, or generated on the fly, for later access. It cannot be set by users.

Warning: In general, the ObjectID of the same object may be different on a different server connection. The client should not make any assumptions based on the ObjectID or store it for reuse in a future session. It is only guaranteed to be unique within a single session. The GOID attribute contains a persistent ID of the object, if available.

Example

```
ObjectID=0x0001F3EC
```

See also Attribute GOID and Section 10.1.

E.1.28   OHName

This attribute of a Server object contains the server's official host name, that is, its primary name as a fully qualified domain name. It is used to access the server when retrieving remote objects, and to have a short but human-readable name to show to the user (see the `Serv` attribute).

Example
```
UServer=129.110.16.2 OHName=infoserv.utdallas.edu
SString=The University of Texas at Dallas
```
See also Attributes `Serv`, `SString` and `UServer`.

E.1.29   Parents

This synthetic attribute specifies the name of (one of) the parent collections of the object. It cannot be set by the user, but is calculated by the server on client request (a flag set in the OBJECTBYIDQUERY command of HG-CSP, see Appendix F).

This is typically done after a search operation. The `Parents` attribute holds the `Name` of the object's parent collection. If the object is a member of more than one collection, a + is appended to the arbitrarily chosen collection name. The purpose is to offer the user immediate location feedback on where the object was found, on clients that do not support location feedback by a collection hierarchy browser, like HGTV.

Example The document is in user `fkappe`'s home collection, plus some others.
```
Parents=~fkappe+
```
See also Attribute `Name`.

E.1.30   Passwd

The `Passwd` attribute of the `User` object stores a user's password in encrypted form. The encryption algorithm used is the same modified DES as in the UNIX `/etc/passwd` file, which is necessary for auto-identification (see the `Host` attribute). It encrypts the first eight characters of the password into a 13-byte string, where the first two characters are the "salt" used to initialize the encryption. The `Passwd` attribute may be set/changed only by the user itself and members of user group `system`. A user may have a number of passwords assigned.

Example The is an encryption of "passwd1":
```
Passwd=VZea.s7fd5NmE
```
See also Attributes `Host` and `UName`.

E.1.31   Path

The `Path` attribute serves two purposes:

- For Hyper-G documents, it contains a reference necessary to access the document (see Figure 10.2). The value `Path` is generated and maintained by the `dcserver`, and cannot be modified by the user. It consists of two parts: the first is a reference understood by `dcserver`, the second is the size of the object in hexadecimal notation.

Example The document size is 9184 bytes.
`Path=DC0x000103C4 0x000023E0`

- For `RemoteDocument` objects, the `Path` attribute contains information that should be sent to the specified `Host` using the specified `Protocol` and `Port`, in order to fetch the desired information. In this case, the `Path` can be changed by users with write permission. For `RemoteDocuments` with `Protocol=telnet`, the `Path` optionally specifies a user name to use for login.

  Example This is a WWW document:
  ```
  Protocol=http
  Host=www.w3.org
  Path=/hypertext/WWW/Provider/Overview.html
  ```

See also Attributes `Host`, `Port`, `Protocol` and Section 10.1.

E.1.32 Port

The `Port` attribute of `RemoteDocument` objects defines the port number to use when opening a connection to the specified `Host` using the specified `Protocol`. The default value of `Port` depends on the value of `Protocol` as follows:

Protocol	Default port
FTP	20
Telnet	23
Gopher	70
http	80
WAIS	210

Example
```
Protocol=http
Host=cache.tu-graz.ac.at
Port=75
```
See also Attributes `Host` and `Protocol`.

E.1.33 Position

The `Position` attribute of (source and destination) anchors specifies the position of the anchor within the document the anchor belongs to (see Section 11.1). While the `Position` is always one line of human-readable ASCII, its format depends on the document type. The following Hyper-G document types may have anchors attached:

- **DocumentType=Text**
  The format is `Position=start end`, where `start` and `end` are (inclusive) integer byte offsets in the text, in decimal or hexadecimal notation.

Examples:
```
Position=123 127
Position=0x5b 0x19c
```
The default destination anchor is the whole text, scrolled to the top.

- **DocumentType=Image**
  The following formats are defined:
  ```
  Position=Rect x0 y0 x1 y1
  Position=Circle x y r
  Position=Ellipse x0 y0 x1 y1
  Position=Polygon x0 y0, x1 y1, ..., xn yn
  ```
  For Rect, (x_0, y_0) specify the lower left corner and (x_1, y_1) the upper right corner of the rectangle.

  For Circle, (x, y) specify the center of the circle and r specifies its radius (in terms of extent along the x axis).

  For Ellipse, (x_0, y_0) specify the lower left corner and (x_1, y_1) the upper right corner of the bounding rectangle of the ellipse (whose conjugate diameters are assumed to be aligned horizontally and vertically).

  For Polygon, (x_i, y_i) are the vertices of a (general) polygon.

  Coordinates are real numbers in a normalized coordinate space from the lower left corner of the image (0,0), to the upper right corner of the image (1,1).

  Examples:
  ```
  Position=Rect 0.16666 0.40877 0.77567 0.78966
  Position=Circle 0.4 0.4 0.321
  Position=Ellipse 0.16666 0.40877 0.77567 0.78966
  Position=Polygon 0.13 0.877, 0.94 0.96, 0.979 0.48,
  0.83 0.83
  ```
  The default destination anchor is the whole image.

- **DocumentType=Movie**
  The following formats are defined:
  ```
  Position=Rect interp n :   f1 x0 y0 x1 y1, ...,
  fn x0 y0 x1 y1
  Position=Circle interp n :   f1 x y r, f2 x y r, ...,
  fn x y r
  Position=Ellipse interp n :   f1 x0 y0 x1 y1, ...,
  fn x0 y0 x1 y1
  ```
  where interp is either Linear or Spline and specifies the kind of anchor interpolation used between key-frames, $n(\geq 1)$ is an integer specifying the number of key-frames, and f_i defines the frame number of key-frame i.

  For Rect, $(x_0, y_0), (x_1, y_1)$ specify the position of a rectangular anchor at key-frame i.

  For Circle, $(x, y), r$ specify the position of a circular anchor at key-frame i.

For `Ellipse`, $(x_0, y_0), (x_1, y_1)$ specify the bounding rectangle of the ellipse (whose conjugate diameters are assumed to be aligned horizontally and vertically) at key-frame i.

Coordinates are real numbers in a normalized coordinate space from the lower left corner of the image (0,0), to the upper right corner of the image (1,1).

Example: (this is one line)
```
Position=Rect Linear 3 :
          125 0.16666 0.40877 0.77567 0.78966,
          150 0.10000 0.40000 0.70000 0.70000,
          166 0.16666 0.40877 0.77567 0.78966
```

The default destination anchor is the whole document.

- **DocumentType=Sound**
  The format is `Position=start end`, where `start` and `end` are real number offsets in seconds from the start of the audio stream.

  Examples:
  ```
  Position=0 1.5
  Position=31.05 31.55
  ```

  The default destination anchor is the whole audio stream.

- **DocumentType=Scene**
  For 3D scenes, source and destination anchors are different. Source anchors are objects within the scene, while destination anchors are camera positions (points to jump to).

  - **Source anchors**
    The syntax is:

    ```
    Position=object
    Position=object/group
    ```

    where `object` refers to a named object in the scene description file (VRML or SDF). Objects without a name may be referenced by "Object N", where N is the object's number in the scene description file. `group` refers to a named part of an object, that is, a group of polygons. If no group is given, the anchor affects the whole object.

    Examples:
    ```
    Position=Object 27
    Position=globe/africa
    ```

  - **Destination anchors**
    The syntax is:

    ```
    Position=(px, py, pz) (lx, ly, lz)
    ```

    where (p_x, p_y, p_z) define the camera position, and (l_x, l_y, l_z) define the "lookat point" in the scene.

Example

```
Position=(0.1, 0.2, 0.3) (4.0, 5.0, 6.0)
```
The default destination anchor is the default camera position.

- **DocumentType=PostScript**
  The syntax is:

```
Position=version@page:x,y,w,h
```

where `version` is the version identifier of the anchor format (currently V20), `page` is the page number (≥ 1), (x, y) is the upper left, and (w, h) are the width and height of a rectangle on the page, based on a specific page calculated at 300 dpi. As is typical for PostScript, the coordinates system has its origin at the bottom left of the page.

Example

```
Position=V20@7:294,1351,1305,93
```

The default destination anchor is the first page.

See also Section 11.1.

E.1.34   PresentationHints

The `PresentationHints` attribute of `Document` objects is used to define rendering aspects of a document or cluster within its parent collections or clusters. The following values are defined:

PresentationHints	Description
CollectionHead	This document (or cluster) is visualized whenever the collection is visualized (for example by following a link pointing to the collection), in addition to the collection listing.
FullCollectionHead	Like CollectionHead, but without listing the collection. It is the author's responsibility to ensure that links to all members have been made, or else some of them will not be reachable other than by searching (unless this is a desired feature).
Hidden	When accessing the parent cluster(s) of this document, it is not opened. This is most useful for placing background, inline and texture images within a cluster together with the document that references them (and also referenced remote documents). They can only be accessed directly by opening the cluster with a browser's "children" command.

Example

```
PresentationHints=Hidden
```
See also Attribute `Description`, Section 22.2.4.

E.1.35 Price

The `Price` attribute allows a price to be attached to a Hyper-G document. When users retrieve the document, the price is deducted from their `Account`, unless it would become negative. As in real life, the price of an object may depend on who wants to buy it. It is always accessible for free for users with write permission (including its author and system users). It is possible to define different prices for members of specific user groups or specific users. The price itself is specified as a currency-independent, integral number (relationships to real currencies, if any, have to be defined by the server administrator). Negative prices are not possible, and the balance of user accounts is always positive (or zero).

The syntax is as follows: an unsigned 32-bit integer (the price), optionally followed by a colon and a specification of users and user groups (like in the `Rights` attribute). This may be repeated a number of times (different prices for different user groups) separated by semicolons.

Example The document should be worth 100 units (64 in hexadecimal), but members of user group websoc and user wonko get a rebate of 20% and pay only 80 units (50 in hexadecimal), while user fkappe pays nothing.

```
Price = 0x00000064; 0x00000050:  g websoc, \
    u wonko; 0x00000000:  u fkappe
Cost = 0x00000050
```

In the above example, the document was accessed by user wonko, so the server generated a `Cost` attribute of 80. Note that nothing is deducted until the user actually retrieves the document.

See also Attributes `Account` and `Cost`, and Sections 11.3 and 14.8.1.

E.1.36 Protocol

The `Protocol` attribute of `RemoteDocument` objects specifies which protocol to use in accessing the remote object. The following protocols are defined:

Protocol	Description
ftp	a file or directory on an FTP server
gopher	a Gopher object (see GopherType)
http	a WWW document (MimeType may specify the type)
sql	an SQL database object (see Chapter 12)
Telnet	a Telnet session
wais	a WAIS object

Note that documents on remote Hyper-G servers are not treated as `RemoteDocument` objects, but look like ordinary objects, with the exception that the `Serv` attribute is set.

Example A Telnet session (using "info" to log in):

```
DocumentType=Remote
Protocol=telnet
Host=info.tu-graz.ac.at
Path=info
```

See also Attributes Host, MimeType, Path and Port. For SQL objects, the attributes Database, Pwd, SQLStmt and Uid are also relevant.

E.1.37 Pwd

This attribute specifies the password to use in order to access an SQL database. See attribute SQLStmt for a complete example.

E.1.38 Repl

The Repl attribute is set in replicas, that is, objects that are exact copies of other objects. It contains the GOID of the remote object the object is a copy of. The Repl attribute is indexed, so that the dbserver can decide very fast whether a local instance of a remote object (referred to by its GOID) exists. The idea is that users access remote documents through their local server (see Section 9.6). When the user tries to access a remote object, the local server first checks whether there is a local replica available. If this is the case, the user is given the local object instead of the remote object, and no interaction with the remote server is required.

Example

```
Repl=0x811be681 0x0002af43
```

See also Attribute GOID and Sections 11.4 and 9.6.

E.1.39 Rights

Access rights are specified in the Rights attribute of a Hyper-G object (that includes documents, collections, and anchors). The attribute value is composed of read (R:), write (W:) and unlink (U:) permission fields, separated by semicolons. For each field, the value a means that the Author of the object has access, u users means that the specified users (user names separated by blanks) have access, and g groups means that the members of the specified user groups (group names separated by blanks) have access. While each field may appear only once, colons may be used to combine field values (for example, R:a,u users,g groups).

Access restrictions are also imposed by the TimeExpire and TimeOpen attributes. See Section 11.2 for an in-depth description of the rather complex evaluation of access rights, including default values, examples, and the meaning of the I: and L: fields.

Example Members of user group abcd and user xyz have read permission, only the author of the object has write and unlink permissions (the write field is not present and thus the defaults are used):

```
Rights=R:g abcd,u xyz
```

See also Attributes License, TimeExpire and TimeOpen, and Sections 11.2 and 11.3.

E.1.40   Score

This synthetic attribute specifies the score value of this object. It cannot be set by the user, but is calculated by the Hyper-G full text server (ftserver) during full text search operations (the commands GETOBJBYFTQUERY and GETOBJBYFTQUERYCOLL; see Appendix F). Consequently, it is only present when the object has been found before using a full text search, and is only valid with respect to that search.

The Score is usually normalized by the client so that the highest-ranking match is assigned a score of 1000. The user sees the normalized integer values.

Example
```
Score=675
```
See also Section 10.5.2.

E.1.41   Sequence

The value of this attribute is a number that can be used to manually define a specific sort order on Hyper-G objects within a collection or sequence (see the SortOrder attribute). Do not confuse the Sequence attribute with the sequence collection type. It is not necessary to use Sequence for standard sort orders (for example, alphabetic by title, by creation time, by author).

By default (that is, no Sequence attribute is present), the value used is 0. Negative Sequence values make the object appear near the top of the list (the beginning of the sequence), before the defaults; positive numbers let it appear near the end (the higher the number, the further down the list). It is good practice to reserve numbers between items, so that additional items can be squeezed in later; for example number items as: 100, 200, 300, ...

Example
```
Sequence=-100
```
See also Attributes CollectionType and SortOrder, Section 9.2.

E.1.42   Serv

This synthetic attribute is generated by the server for objects from remote Hyper-G servers. It presence indicates that the object is not a local object. Its value is the official host name OHName of the birthplace server part of the GOID. Its purpose is to give clients a means of indicating to the user that this object is a remote object and where it is supposed to come from.

Example
```
Serv=infoserv.utdallas.edu
```
See also Attributes GOID and OHName.

E.1.43   Size

This attribute is applicable only for a WAIS document, and specifies its size in bytes.
Example
```
Size=2513
```
See also Attributes WAISDocID and WAISType.

E.1.44   SortOrder

This attribute defines the order in which the collection's children (that is, the sub-documents and sub-collections) should be displayed. For collections of type Sequence the sort order defines the sequence in which the sub-documents are visualized.

Objects are sorted by sorting on the object's attributes. The value of SortOrder is a string composed of the following characters:

- sort next attribute descending (default ascending)

\# sort by Sequence attribute

A sort by Author attribute

C sort by TimeCreated attribute

E sort by TimeExpire attribute

O sort by TimeOpen attribute

P sort by Parent attribute

S sort by Score attribute

T sort by Title attribute

t sort by DocumentType attribute

All attributes with the exception of Sequence are sorted in alphabetic order. Sequence is sorted in numerical order. The default (no Sequence attribute given) is zero; objects with negative Sequence values appear before the defaults, then the defaults, then the objects with positive Sequence values (unless -# is specified in the SortOrder).
Examples: The default sort order is:
```
SortOrder=#T
```
which means look at a sequence number first, else (if no Sequence attribute is present or they are equal for two objects) use the title. The following setting may be useful in an electronic discussion collection:
```
SortOrder=-CAT
```
See also Attributes Author, DocumentType, Parent, Sequence, TimeCreated, TimeExpire, TimeOpen, Title.

E.1.45 SQLStmt

The SQLStmt attribute of SQLDocument is used to select items from an SQL database. Its value is an SQL "select" statement, which controls what columns and rows should be extracted from a relational database, and their mapping to either a text document or a "virtual collection." There may be multiple SQLStmt attributes in a single object, in which case they are evaluated in order to map the relations to a collection hierarchy (see examples below).
Examples: In the simplest case, there is just one SQLstmt:

```
Type=Document
DocumentType=Remote
Protocol=SQL
Uid=scott
Pwd=tiger
Host=fstghp37.tu-graz.ac.at
Port=1470
Database=oracle:t:edvz
SQLStmt=select name,salary from employees
MimeType=text/html
```

When the user selects this object, the columns name and salary are extracted from table employees, and formatted as one HTML text. If MimeType=text/html were missing, a "virtual collection" would be created, with an individual text document for each employee. Let us look at a more complex example (everything but SQLstmt omitted):

```
SQLStmt=1=select distinct instno,institute from ects;2
SQLStmt=2=select courseno,title from ects where instno=\
!instno;1;2
SQLStmt=3=select courseno,title,teacher,sem from ects \
      where courseno=!courseno
```

These three SQLstmts effectively map this object to a virtual three-level collection hierarchy when the user accesses the object. We assume that in our SQL database there is a table named ects with descriptions of university courses. Every course description consists of a course number (courseno), a title, a teacher, a semester (sem) and the number (instno) and name (institute) of the institute the teacher is associated with.

The first SQL statement (starting with 1=) is evaluated first. It finds the distinct institutes (instno and institute) contained in the table ects. For each institute, a new SQLDocument is created on the fly. The ;2 at the end of the first statement tells the server to use the second column specified (institute; the institute name) as the title of these objects. The dynamically generated objects contain the following SQLStmts:

```
SQLStmt=1=select courseno,title from ects where instno=\
5060;1;2
SQLStmt=2=select courseno,title,teacher,sem from ects \
      where courseno=!courseno
```

The SQLstmts have been shifted up (2= becomes 1=), and placeholders like !instno have been replaced by their values (for example, 5060), as they were found by the previous SQLStmt. They are presented to the user as a collection of SQLdocuments. Let us assume the user selects such an object. A new "virtual collection" of objects like this is created:

```
Title=506026 Networking Protocols
SQLStmt=1=select courseno,title,teacher,sem from ects \
     where courseno=506026
MimeType=text/html
```

According to the specification in the previous SQLStmt (;1;2), the course number and title are used together as the title of the object. Since it is the last object in the hierarchy (only one SQL statement), activating it will lead to an HTML-formatted document, which contains the columns courseno, title, teacher and sem. The layout of the HTML document is controlled by a server-side configuration file.

Of course, it would be easy to map the table ects to a completely different collection hierarchy (for example, first by institute, then by teacher; or first by semester, then by institute) onto the same data. The important aspect here is that the end user can be offered multiple views (looking like collection hierarchies) of a relational database without knowing anything about its structure or column names. The author has to know about the column names and their meaning, but can construct such views in a programming-free environment.

See also Attributes Database, Host, Port, Uid and Pwd, and Chapter 12.

E.1.46   SString

The SString attribute of Server objects contains a readable description of the server. Its purpose is to show it to the user, instead of the less intuitive OHName or UServer attributes.
Example
```
UServer=129.27.2.5
OHName=info.tu-graz.ac.at
SString=Info System of Graz University of Technology
```
See also Attributes OHName and UServer.

E.1.47   SubType

This attribute of GenericDocument has been replaced by the MimeType attribute, although there are still documents with SubType around. New documents should be created using MimeType.
See also Attribute MimeType.

E.1.48   Subdocs

This synthetic attribute of collections gives the number of sub-documents of the collection (recursively). Only "real" documents are counted (not collections).

Example

        Subdocs=76450

See also Attribute DocCount.

Note: There is a little bug in the way a document belonging to two collections is counted. In fact, it is counted in both collections, which is desired, but the super-collection that contains the two collections (recursively) counts the same document twice. Whole collections which are members of more than one collection are handled correctly, though.

E.1.49   TAnchor

The TAnchor attribute of Anchor objects defines whether the anchor is a source or destination anchor (the Hyper-G data model disallows use of the same anchor for both purposes). Only two values are possible:

TAnchor	Description
Dest	a destination anchor
Src	a source anchor

Example

        TAnchor=Dest

See also Attributes Dest, DHint, GDest and Position, and Section 11.1.

E.1.50   TimeCreated

The time this object was created. It is usually set by the server when the object is first inserted into the database. However, it may be overridden by a client specifying a different time. For example, in a bibliographic database TimeCreated could be set to the time the article or book was published, rather than the time it was inserted into the database. This would allow users to restrict searches to items within a specific time frame (the TimeCreated attribute is indexed). However, this "feature" is likely to disappear in the future and be replaced by a new attribute for the document's "real" creation date.

All times in Hyper-G are specified in universal time (=GMT)!

Example

        TimeCreated=94/07/15 10:12:30

See also Attribute TimeCreated.

E.1.51   TimeExpire

After the date specified the object becomes invisible to users other than those with write access to the object (which includes the owner and system users; see Section 11.2). The object is not physically removed from the database, however. Users with write access may therefore extend the object's lifetime, move it to a different collection (see Section 22.3.1) or simply delete it.

Example

        TimeExpire=96/02/28 23:59:59

See also Attribute `TimeOpen`, Sections 11.2 and 22.3.1.

E.1.52   TimeModified

The time of the last modification of this object, that is, document modification or attribute modification. This attribute is not under control of the user, but is automatically maintained by the server. It is indexed together with `TimeCreated`, so a query for objects modified in a certain time frame will also match objects that were created in this time frame and never modified since.

Example

        TimeModified=95/04/15 18:30:17

See also Attribute `TimeCreated`.

E.1.53   TimeOpen

The opposite of `TimeExpire`. An object is invisible before the specified date to users other than those with write permissions.

Example

        TimeOpen=96/01/01 00:00:00

See also Attribute `TimeExpire`, Sections 11.2 and 22.3.1.

E.1.54   Title

Specifies the title of the object, that is, something that should be displayed when showing a list of objects (for example, a collection listing or search result), and can be searched for. An object may have a number of titles in different languages, so this attribute may appear more than once (however, only one title per language is allowed). The first two characters specify the language, followed by a colon (:) followed by the title itself. Languages are defined according to the ISO 639 standard, but not all are supported by all Hyper-G clients (yet). Current clients and servers accept the following languages:

en	English
de	German (ge is also OK)
fr	French
it	Italian
sp	Spanish

Example
```
Title=en:An English Title
Title=de:Ein deutscher Titel
```
See also Attributes Keyword and Name.

E.1.55 Type

The Type attribute specifies the (first-level) type of the object at hand (sub-type of HGObject; see the hierarchy definition in Section 11.1.2). The following values are defined:

Type	Description
Anchor	an anchor (TAnchor defines source or destination)
Document	a document (DocumentType defines sub-type)
Group	a group object
Server	a server object
User	a user object

While the Type of an object is defined by the user creating it, it cannot be changed (even by system users) afterwards.

Note For historical reasons, this attribute is stored as TType in the object server, and converted to Type in Document and Anchor objects when sent to the client. For other objects, the name TType remains.

See also Attributes DocumentType and TAnchor, and Section 11.1.2.

E.1.56 UGroup

The UName attribute is the "name" of a Hyper-G user group, and the key to the corresponding group record. The "name" is a short name, while the Descr attribute may contain a more exhaustive description of the user group's purpose. The Group attributes contain groups this group is a member of.

Example
```
UGroup=iicm
Group=tu-graz
Descr=Members of the IICM
```
See also Attributes Descr, Group and Section 14.8.2.

E.1.57 Uid

This attribute specifies the username to use in order to access an SQL database. See attribute SQLStmt for a complete example.

E.1.58   UName

The UName attribute is the "name" of a Hyper-G user, and the key to the corresponding user record. The "name" is a short login name, which may also be a pseudonym (see Section 9.5). Of course, it must be unique within a server. In addition, the user record may contain the user's real name, password(s), user groups the user is a member of, trusted hosts, home collection and account balance.

The server never reveals the user record to users other than the user in UName and system users. When the server is first started, a user named hgsystem, a member of user group system, with auto-login from the local host's server account is created.

Example a fairly complete user record:

```
UName=wonko
Descr=Wonko the Sane
Passwd=2eCD46Fa231A5
Host=wonko@129.27.153.10
Group=iicm
Group=jucs_admin
Home=~wonko
Account=1100
```

See also Attributes Account, Descr, Group, Home, Host, Passwd and Section 14.8.1.

E.1.59   UserAttr

In principle it is possible to store any attribute in addition to those described in this section. If the attribute name has no special meaning to the server, it is stored and retrieved together with the object, but otherwise ignored. However, inventing and storing arbitrary attributes may lead to problems when the set of attributes with meaning to the servers or clients is extended later, and attribute name conflicts may arise.

For this reason, the UserAttr attribute is defined to store user-defined auxiliary data. It may appear any number of times in an object. It is good practice to store a "sub-attribute" name within the UserAttr value field. The UserAttr attribute is not indexed. The Keyword attribute may be used to store indexed user attributes.

Example

```
UserAttr=Copyright=1995, The Hyper-G Consortium
UserAttr=Filename=fvw35.jpg
```

See also Attribute Keyword.

E.1.60   UServer

The UServer attribute stores the 32-bit Server ID of a remote server, and is the key to its server record. For historic reasons, this server ID is not stored as a 32-bit hexadecimal number as in the GOID attribute, but looks like an IP address, and in fact by default is the IP address of the server, until it is first moved to a different machine. The OHName attribute stores the server's official host name which is used for accessing the server, and the `SString` stores a human-readable description of the server.

Example

```
UServer=193.170.33.112
OHName=sun.risc.uni-linz.ac.at
SString=Research Institute for Symbolic Computation
(RISC-Linz)
DocCount=6412
Modified=0x308a60a2
```

See also Attributes `Dead`, `DocCount`, `GOID`, `Modified`, `OHName` and `SString`.

E.1.61   WaisDocID

This synthetic attribute is set only in temporary objects resembling a WAIS search result. It stores a value that is needed and understood only by the corresponding WAIS server in order to retrieve the document.

E.1.62   WaisType

The `WaisType` attribute defines the type of a WAIS document or server description. Currently, the following values are possible:

CollectionType	Description
GIF	an image in GIF format
PICT	an image in PICT format
TEXT	a text document (default)
TIFF	an image in TIFF format
WSRC	a WAIS source (server)

See also Attribute `Size`.

E.2   The Hyper-G Interchange Format

E.2.1   Introduction

The Hyper-G Interchange Format (HIF) is used to archive, transport and import/export parts of a Hyper-G collection structure between Hyper-G compatible applications. A common use is to export Hyper-G collections, and import them into a standalone version of Hyper-G (see Chapter 13) or into other servers (see Section 25.3).

HIF therefore describes all aspects of a Hyper-G collection tree, including the collection relations and links between documents, in a location-independent fashion. It also includes links to documents outside the hierarchy (but not the documents).

HIF is in principle a "clear text" format, which means it is human-readable, can be edited using any text processor, and can be sent by electronic mail. It is possible to store all documents together with the structure information in one (large) file, or in a number of files. In the latter case, the individual files contain the documents in their native format, that is, usually not human-readable.

The HIF format closely resembles the Hyper-G data model, with a class hierarchy of documents, collections, clusters, anchors and attributes thereof as defined in Sections 11.1 and E.1.

E.2.2 Writing a HIF File

The collection hierarchy in HIF is maintained by Parent attributes which are contained within the object description of documents. Note that a document (including collection and cluster) may have multiple parents.

The Parent attribute for the top-level objects is left empty, so that the HIF contents may be attached anywhere in the target system.

The documents themselves may either be contained within a single HIF file, or written to individual files. In the latter case, the HIF file contains references to filenames in the Filename attribute. The hifexport command can be used to export collection hierarchies to a HIF file.

E.2.3 Reading a HIF File

HIF is defined in such a way that the reader may safely ignore objects or attributes that are unknown or not supported, and should skip them in the interpretation process.

When importing a HIF into an existing Hyper-G structure care has to be taken to maintain the uniqueness of the collection names. The top-level objects have to be attached to some (user-specified) parent collection, and already existing collections (more precisely: collection names) found during the importing have to be made unique or skipped, either by user interaction or automatically. The hifimport command imports a collection hierarchy contained in a HIF file into a Hyper-G server.

E.2.4 Abstract Syntax Notation

```
<hiffile> ::= <header>
          <document>+
<header> ::= 'HIF ' <version> <nl>
          (<comment> | <headerline>)*
<version> ::= '1.0'
<nl> ::= ['\r'] '\n'
<comment> ::= ('#' <line>) | <ws> <nl>
```

```
<ws> ::= (' ' | '⌒')*
<line> ::= <(ISO Latin-1 character)>* <nl>
<headerline> ::= (<ws> 'Author=' <line>) |
         (<ws> 'User=' <line>) |
         (<ws> 'Program=' <line>) |
         (<ws> 'TimeCreated=' <timestamp>) |
         (<ws> 'Server=' <line>)
<timestamp> ::= <date> ' ' <time> <nl>
<date> ::= <year>'/'<month>'/'<day>
<year> ::= <digit><digit>
<month> ::= <digit><digit>
<day> ::= <digit><digit>
<time> ::= <digit><digit>':'<digit><digit>':'<digit><digit>
<digit> ::= '0' .. '9'
<document> ::= <comment>*
      <ws> 'BEGIN ' <doctype> <nl>
      (<comment> | <docattr>)*
      <data>
      <anchors>
      <ws> 'END ' <doctype> <nl>
<doctype> ::= 'Collection' | 'Cluster' | 'Sequence' |
      'Text' | 'Image' | 'Movie' | 'Sound' | 'PostScript' |
      'Scene' | 'Generic'
<docattr> ::= (<ws> 'Arguments=' <line> |
      (<ws> 'Author=' <line>) |
      (<ws> 'CollectionType=' <line>) |
      (<ws> 'Database=' <line>) |
      (<ws> 'Description=' <language> ':'  <line>) |
      (<ws> 'DocumentType=' <line>) |
      (<ws> 'GOID=' <line>) |
      (<ws> 'GopherType=' <line>) |
      (<ws> 'Host=' <line>) |
      (<ws> 'Keyword=' <line>) |
      (<ws> 'Layout=' <line>) |
      (<ws> 'License=' <line>) |
      (<ws> 'MimeType=' <line>) |
      (<ws> 'Name=' <line>) |
      (<ws> 'ObjectID=' <line>) |
      (<ws> 'Parent=' <line>) |
      (<ws> 'Path=' <line>) |
      (<ws> 'Port=' <line>) |
      (<ws> 'PresentationHints=' <line>) |
      (<ws> 'Protocol=' <line>) |
      (<ws> 'Pwd=' <line>) |
      (<ws> 'Repl=' <line>) |
```

```
          (<ws> 'Rights=' <line>) |
          (<ws> 'Sequence=' <line>) |
          (<ws> 'Serv=' <line>) |
          (<ws> 'SQLStmt=' <line>) |
          (<ws> 'Size=' <line>) |
          (<ws> 'SortOrder=' <line>) |
          (<ws> 'SubType=' <line>) |
          (<ws> 'TimeCreated=' <timestamp>) |
          (<ws> 'TimeOpen=' <timestamp>) |
          (<ws> 'TimeExpire=' <timestamp>) |
          (<ws> 'TimeModified=' <timestamp>) |
          (<ws> 'Title=' <language> ':' <line>) |
          (<ws> 'Type=' <language> ':' <line>) |
          (<ws> 'Uid=' <line>) |
          (<ws> 'UserAttr=' <line>) |
          (<ws> 'WaisDocID=' <line>) |
          (<ws> 'WaisType=' <line>)
<language> ::= 'en' | 'de' | 'ge' | 'sp' | 'it' | 'fr'
<data> ::= <fileref> | <plaindata> | <uuencoded>
<fileref> ::= [<ws> 'Path=' <line>]
          <ws> 'Filename=' <line>
<plaindata> ::= <ws> 'BEGIN DATA' <nl>
          <line>*
          <ws> 'END DATA' <nl>
<uuencode> ::= <ws> 'BEGIN UUENCODE' <nl>
          <(uuencoded-data-line)>*
          <ws> 'END UUENCODE' <nl>
<anchors> ::= <anchor>*
<anchor> ::= <comment>*
          <ws> 'BEGIN ANCHOR'<nl>
          (<comment> | <anchattr>)*
          <ws> 'END ANCHOR' <nl>
<anchattr> ::= (<ws> 'Author=' <line>) |
          (<ws> 'Dest=' <line>) |
          (<ws> 'DHint=' <line>) |
          (<ws> 'GDest=' <line>) |
          (<ws> 'GOID=' <line>) |
          (<ws> 'Keyword=' <line>) |
          (<ws> 'ObjectID=' <line>) |
          (<ws> 'Position=' <line>) |
          (<ws> 'Rights=' <line>) |
          (<ws> 'Serv=' <line>) |
          (<ws> 'TAnchor=' ('S' | 'D') <nl> |
          (<ws> 'TimeCreated=' <timestamp>) |
          (<ws> 'TimeOpen=' <timestamp>) |
```

```
(<ws> 'TimeExpire=' <timestamp>) |
(<ws> 'TimeModified=' <timestamp>) |
(<ws> 'Title=' <language> ':'  <line>)
```

E.3 Further reading

The encoding of languages is defined in the ISO 639 standard.

F   Hyper-G Client–Server Protocol (HG-CSP)

Frank Kappe, Gerald Pani

F.1   Introduction

This specification describes the **protocol** between a **Hyper-G client** and the **Hyper-G server** (more specifically, the `hgserver` process of the Hyper-G server). The protocol is described on a low level (the socket level), as this documentation is supposed to be used to create new Hyper-G clients (including gateways to other protocols) on arbitrary platforms and with arbitrary programming languages. It should be explicitly noted that the standard Hyper-G components (which are written in C++) usually do not bother about individual bytes sent over the network, but use a C++ class `HgStub` which passes objects between clients and server. This explains why the protocol is not designed to be human-readable. It is, however, compatible with the dispatch library of the InterViews toolkit.

In addition to the Hyper-G client–server Protocol there is a server–server protocol (used to maintain information base consistency across server boundaries) and a client–client protocol (allows Hyper-G clients to pass messages and events to each other using the server), as well as protocols used for communication between the individual parts of the Hyper-G server (`hgserver`, `dbserver`, `ftserver`, `dcserver`; for an overview the reader is referred to Chapter 10). These protocols are beyond the scope of this document.

F.1.1   Status of this appendix

This appendix describes the Hyper-G client–server Protocol version 7.05. An up-to-date version is available in hypertext form on the Hyper-G server of Graz University of Technology. If you prefer reading linear text on paper, a PostScript version is available by anonymous FTP from `ftp.iicm.tu-graz.ac.at` in the file `/pub/Hyper-G/papers/Protocol.ps`.

F.1.2 Glossary

This section defines a number of frequently used words.

anchor An anchor denotes a section of a document (possibly the entire document). For example, an anchor may be a word or phrase in a text document, or a small area in a large picture. It is either the source or the destination of a link.

attribute Attributes are pieces of information attached to objects (author, creation time, title, keywords, expiry time, type of object and so on). Some of them can be used to search the database for documents with certain attributes.

author In the Hyper-G system, the word "author" refers to the user who entered a piece of information into the database – not necessarily the person who originally created the information. For example, in the case of a picture of the "Mona Lisa," the author would be the person who inserted that picture into the system, rather than Leonardo da Vinci.

client The part of Hyper-G that displays documents and realizes the user interface.

cluster A specialized collection object (see below). Documents that are members of clusters should be visualized together (this is how multimedia objects are realized in Hyper-G).

collection A group of items, which may be either documents or collections. Can be compared to a "directory" in a file system. This definition yields a "collection hierarchy," which looks like a tree, but with any number of "roots" and with the property that a collection may be a sub-collection of several collections (directed acyclic graph). For example, a biochemistry collection might be a sub-collection of both a biology collection and a chemistry collection.

document A type of object that is intended to be displayed by the client. A document must be a member of at least one "parent collection" and may have a number of source and/or destination anchors attached. Hyper-G supports a number of document types. One of these types (text) is handled specially by the server: that is, the contents of text documents are searchable, which is why there are specialized functions that deal with text documents in the protocol.

object Generic term for an entity stored in the Hyper-G database. Documents, links, anchors and collections are examples of objects. An object has a set of attributes, each of which has one or more values. In particular, every object is assigned a unique object identifier.

link The essence of hypertext. A user may click on one endpoint of a link (the "source anchor") and jump to the other endpoint (the "destination anchor").

search Any object that has been inserted into the Hyper-G database can automatically be searched for. The protocol basically supports two kinds of searches: Boolean searches based on attributes of objects, and full text searches that are defined for text documents.

server The part of Hyper-G that stores the documents, links and so on.

F.2   An overview of the protocol

The protocol is based on TCP/IP, connection-oriented, asynchronous and (almost) stateless. The client sends messages to the server that initiate server transactions, and the server returns messages with the results of transactions and/or error codes.

Connection-oriented means that the TCP connection is not closed and re-opened between transactions, but rather stays open for the duration of a session.

Asynchronous means that, although usually the client will send a message to the server and wait for the return message giving the results of the requested transaction, this need not always be the case. A client may choose to issue a number of commands in succession, and look at the results later. Likewise, some commands do not require waiting for a response at all. Also, the server may choose to send an unsolicited message to the client at any time.

The protocol is almost stateless in the following sense: after some initial negotiation during the initialization of the connection, the available transaction commands may be issued in any sequence. The server does not maintain any state information (other than the Hyper-G database itself) or reuse (intermediate) results of previous transactions.

F.2.1   Opening and closing the connection

Opening a connection to the Hyper-G server is started by the client (of course) by opening a TCP connection to the server's well-known port number 418.

The server then initiates a negotiation on the data format that is to be used for this connection. The Hyper-G servers understand both formatted (that is, clear text) and binary transfer modes. By default, the server will offer to do a binary connection by sending a T (binary=true) character in response to the connection request. The client may also send a T for binary or refuse to do so by sending an F (for false). The client does not need to wait until it receives something from the server before sending this character.

When both have sent and received a T, binary mode is enabled. Client and server now need to agree on a certain byte order. Both send a B if they would prefer big-endian byte order and 1 if they would prefer little-endian byte order. If client and server receive the opposite of what they have sent, they will both perform byte swapping on their outgoing messages (incoming messages are always left unchanged).

After this negotiation is completed (and the message format to be used is thus defined) the server will send an initial READY message containing the server's identification parameters (see Section F.3.17), or an error message if the connection is refused for some reason. The client should also send a READY message to indicate it is willing to accept messages, and to agree on the protocol version, compression mode and distribution mode to be used (see section on message format below). Following this, messages may be sent in arbitrary order.

No special action is necessary to shut down the connection. The client may just close the TCP connection. The Hyper-G server may also drop the connection, typically after 12 hours of inactivity (that is, no messages have been received from the client for 12 hours). On some servers (for example, those that offer licensed material) this period may be significantly shorter (a few minutes).

F.2.2   Message format

Once the initialization procedure is completed, the client and server can communicate with each other by exchanging messages. The semantics of these messages are similar to remote procedure calls. The client sends a message containing a server command and, except for a few functions that do not require a response, the server then sends a message containing the response. Commands and responses are identified by a message identifier.

There are actually two exceptions to this: the server may send a READY response even when no READY command has been sent (see Section F.3.17), and the client may send an HG_BREAK command while waiting for a response, in order to prematurely terminate the request pending.

A message is composed of the following elements:

(1) LENGTH: An integer containing the length in characters of the message (*including* this integer). If the format has been set to BINARY (see Section F.2.1), this is a 32-bit unsigned integer. If the format is FORMATTED, it is sent as 10 characters containing a right-justified string representation of a decimal number, that is, spaces followed by a series of digits. This lets the receiver of the message know how much information to expect, allocate appropriate buffers and so on.

(2) VERSION/MESSAGE-ID: An integer normally used for a unique MESSAGE-ID except in the case of a READY message, where it is used for VERSION negotiating.

If the format has been set to BINARY, the VERSION/MESSAGE-ID identifier is transmitted as a 32-bit integer. Otherwise (that is, the format is FORMATTED) it is separated from the preceding LENGTH with a blank, and sent as a variable-length string representation of the decimal value (terminated by a blank).

(a) VERSION: The VERSION identifier is a 32-bit integer composed of three subfields:

31 30	29 ... 14	13 ... 00
flags	reserved	version

The version field specifies the actual protocol version. The current version is 7.05. It will be incremented on major protocol releases (only those that require changes in the existing command structure; this is not necessary for minor bug fixes or new, additional commands), so that messages from old clients (servers) will be recognized and can be dealt with appropriately by the server (client). The protocol version of the connection is defined as the minimum of the client and server version numbers, and is usually determined during the initial exchange of READY messages (see Section F.2.1).

The flags field contains individual bits that switch certain functionalities on and off. Currently, only the two most significant bits are defined (the DISTRIBUTED bit (31) and the COMPRESSED bit (30). If the distributed bit is set, the server should provide access to remote data (that is, data that resides on different Hyper-G servers) as well. Otherwise, only data on this server can be accessed. Setting this bit has an important effect on the ObjectIDs that are passed to the client. If DISTRIBUTED is not set, these are the physical Hyper-G ObjectIDs on this server, and they remain constant over sessions. If DISTRIBUTED is set, however, these are virtual ObjectIDs generated on the fly by the server and cannot be reused in future sessions. In any case, ObjectIDs are 32-bit unsigned integers. If the compressed bit is set, this means that the server should send text and objects in compressed form.

The other flag bits and the reserved field are reserved for future use.

(b) MESSAGE-ID: The client should use this to determine which response belongs to which command. The response to a command always has the same MESSAGE-ID as the corresponding command. The client could use increasing numbers to do this job.

(3) MESSAGE-TYPE: Each message (that is, command and response) is assigned a type. This lets the receiver of the message know which kind of message is being received, and therefore what kind of information to expect. The number for a given command is the same as the number for its response. These numbers are given in the next section.

(4) MESSAGE-DATA: The parameters of the command (if this message is sent by the client) or the return values of the command (if sent by the server) follow. The data is composed of a sequence of strings and numbers, depending on the type of the message (command or response). Currently, only three different data types are used:

- Integer: Sent as a 32-bit integer, if in BINARY transmission mode. In FORMATTED mode it is sent as an optional minus sign (-), followed by a series of decimal digits terminated by a space. ObjectIDs, enumerates (for example, error codes) and Boolean values are also sent as integers.

- String: In both transmission modes, a string is sent as a sequence of characters, terminated by a zero byte. Consequently, a zero byte cannot be passed directly in a string.

- IntArray: An array of integers may be sent by first sending an integer indicating the length of the array, and then the elements of the array, in order.

F.3   Description of messages

This section contains a short description of each kind of message that may be sent, in the order of their message identifiers. The order of message identifiers assigned to messages is based on historic evolution of the protocol and is of no further relevance. Some message identifiers are not assigned. These typically have been used by some previous version of the protocol and are either obsolete commands or have been replaced by a new command with another message identifier.

For each message, we provide the message identifier together with a symbolic name, the parameters sent and return values received (from the client viewpoint), a short description of what the procedure does, and possible error codes returned. Section F.4 contains an overview of all error codes.

The notation `int` indicates that an integer is sent, `string` indicates that a string is sent and `int foo[]` indicates that an array of integers is sent, with the number of integers sent equal to the integer sent immediately before, except when noted otherwise. The notation `optional` indicates that the argument may not be sent (for example, if it is null). The notation `remainder` indicates that the argument fills up the rest of the message. The other notation should be obvious.

F.3.1   Command 2: GETDOCBYANCHOR

Send `int anchID`

Recv `int error, int docID`

Description This command returns the document ID (`docID`) of the document to which the given anchor (`anchID`) is attached. If `anchID` is not an anchor but a document, `docID` is set to `anchID`, otherwise it is set to 0.

Errors If `error` is not zero, an error has occurred, for example:

RSERV_NRESP Remote server not responding

See Section F.4 for a list of all possible error codes.

F.3.2   Command 3: GETCHILDCOLL

Send `int parentID`

Recv `int error, int count, int childIDs[]`

Description Retrieves the children (sub-collections only) of the given parent collection (`count` items). Use the GETCHILDDOCCOLL command to get the documents of the parent collection (for performance reasons, the server uses two different relations for sub-collections and sub-documents). Use the GETCHILDREN command to get both collections and documents.

Errors If the `parentID` is not the object ID of a collection, or it contains no sub-collections, a count of 0 is returned. If `error` is not zero, an error has occurred, for example:

RSERV_NRESP Remote server not responding

See Section F.4 for a list of all possible error codes.

F.3.3 Command 4: GETPARENT

Send `int childID`

Recv `int error, int count, int parentIDs[]`

Description Retrieves the parents of the given `childID`.

Errors If the child has no parents (that is, it is a root collection), a count of 0 is returned. If `error` is not zero, an error has occurred, for example:

RSERV_NRESP Remote server not responding

See Section F.4 for a list of all possible error codes.

F.3.4 Command 5: GETCHILDDOCCOLL

Send `int parentID`

Recv `int error, int count, int childIDs[]`

Description Retrieves the children (document only) of the given parent collection (`count` items). Use the GETCHILDCOLL command to get the sub-collections of the parent collection. Use the GETCHILDREN command to get both collections and documents.

Errors If `parentID` is not the object ID of a collection, or it contains no sub-documents, a count of 0 is returned. If `error` is not zero, an error has occurred, for example:

RSERV_NRESP Remote server not responding

See Section F.4 for a list of all possible error codes.

F.3.5 Command 7: GETOBJECT

Send `int objectID`

Recv `int error, optional remainder objRecord`

Description Use this command to retrieve the full object record of a given `objectID`. The object record (`objRecord`) is a string of lines that contain the object's attributes. It is sent only if `error` is 0 (OK), and fills the remainder of the message (the length can be determined by examination of the LENGTH element (see section MessageFormat).

Errors If `error` is not zero, an error has occurred, for example:

RSERV_NRESP Remote server not responding

NOTFOUND The object could not be found (for example, because `objectID` was not a valid ID)

NOACCESS No read permission for the object, or it has expired or is otherwise unavailable

See also the security note for the OBJECTBYIDQUERY command.

F.3.6   Command 8: GETANCHORS

Send `int docID`

Recv `int error, int count, int anchIDs[]`

Description Returns a list of anchors that are attached to the given document (`docID`). There is no distinction between source and destination anchors. You need to fetch the anchor object to determine whether a given anchor is a source or destination anchor (`TAnchor=Src` or `TAnchor=Dest`).

Errors If the given docID is not the object ID of a document, or no anchors are attached, a count of 0 is returned. If `error` is not zero, an error has occurred, for example:

RSERV_NRESP Remote server not responding

See Section F.4 for a list of all possible error codes.

F.3.7   Command 9: GETOBJBYQUERY

Send `string indexQuery`

Recv `int error, int count, int matchIDs[]`

Description This command is used to perform searches on the set of attributes of Hyper-G objects. It can only be applied to indexed attributes. Use the `OBJECTBYIDQUERY` command to match a set of objects returned by this command against other, non-indexed, attributes. The search is performed over the whole database of the server the client is connected to. Use the `GETOBJBYQUERYCOLL` to restrict the search to parts of the collection hierarchy, and to perform distributed searches on other servers. The command returns the IDs of the matching objects, with one exception: if the object is a document that is a member of a cluster, the cluster's ID is returned instead. Currently, the indexed attributes of Hyper-G objects are:

Attribute	valid for objects of type
Author	documents, anchors, collections
Group	user profiles
Hint	source anchors
Host	user profiles
Keywords	documents, collections
Name	collections
Repl	documents, anchors, collections
TimeCreated	documents, anchors, collections
TimeModified	documents, anchors, collections
Title	documents, destination anchors, collections
UName	user profiles
UGroup	user profiles
UServer	server objects

The syntax of `indexQuery` is as follows:

```
<EXPR> ::= "(" <EXPR> ")" |
   <EXPR> "||" <EXPR> | /* OR */
   <EXPR> "&&" <EXPR> | /* AND */
   <EXPR> "&!" <EXPR> | /* AND NOT */
   <INDEXFIELD> "=" <VALUES> |
   <INDEXFIELD> ">" <SIMPLEVALUE>
         "<" <SIMPLEVALUE> /* BETWEEN */

<INDEXFIELD> ::= "Title" | "Keyword" | "TimeCreated" |
   "TimeModified" | "Author" | "Name" | "Hint" |
   "UName" | "UGroup" | "Host" | "Host" | "Group" |
   "UServer"

<VALUES> ::= <VALUE> |
   <VALUE> <VALUES> /* value AND values must be true */

<VALUE> ::= <SIMPLEVALUE> /* ordinary word */
   <SIMPLEVALUE>"*" /* words with prefix simplevalue */
   <SIMPLEVALUE>"^" /* words >= simplevalue */
```

Status The list of indexed attributes can be extended in future versions.

Errors If nothing is found no object IDs are returned (`count` is 0). If `error` is not zero, an error has occurred, for example:

CMD_SYNTAX Query is invalid

Q_OVERFLOW Too many intermediate results

Note When too many objects are found (that is, more than a certain threshold value set in the server), not all possible matches will be returned (Q_OVERFLOW). This also applies to intermediate results: for example, the query `Title=atom && TimeCreated=93/01/01^` will probably not be able to retrieve all documents created after 1 January 1993 that contain the word `atom` in their title, even if there are only five, when the rest of the database contains 100 000 documents created after 1 January 1993. While this limitation will disappear when the link server is supplied with a query optimizer, you may meanwhile circumvent this problem by first issuing this command with only the `Title=atom` query and then reducing the matches using the `OBJECTBYIDQUERY` command (which is a bit slower, however).

F.3.8 Command 10: GETOBJBYQUERYCOLL

Send int collCount, int colls[], string indexQuery

Recv int error, int count, int matchIDs[]

Description This command works like the GETOBJBYQUERY command. However, the search is not performed on the whole database of the server the client is connected to. Rather, it is limited to the set of collections supplied (collCount, colls) and their sub-collections (recursively).

If the connection is a distributed one (that is, the DISTRIBUTED flag has been set, see Section F.2.2), the command will also search remote collections (that is, collections that physically reside on some other Hyper-G server) if they are explicitly supplied in the colls array. This feature can be used to perform the same query over a number of Hyper-G servers in parallel. Remote collections are not searched automatically when they only appear as some sub-collection of one of the local collections specified.

Errors If nothing is found, no object IDs are returned (count is 0). If error is not zero, an error has occurred, for example:

RSERV_NRESP Remote server not responding

CMD_SYNTAX Query is invalid

Q_OVERFLOW Too many intermediate results

Note The limitations mentioned for the GETOBJBYQUERY command apply, with the additional problem that (partial) queries that match a large number of objects cannot be performed, even if applied only on a small subset of the collection hierarchy, until the query optimizer appears. Of course, in such a case one may first retrieve the IDs of this small subset, and then apply the OBJECTBYIDQUERY command.

F.3.9   Command 11: OBJECTBYIDQUERY

Send int fillParent, int objCount, int objIDs[],
optional string query

Recv int error, int matchCount, int matchIDs[], int offsets[],
remainder records

Description Like GETOBJECT, this command is used to retrieve the object records (with the object's attributes) from object IDs. This command is more powerful in that it lets you retrieve a number of object records with one command. In addition, a query may be performed on the object records to narrow down the set of objects retrieved. The query is not limited to the indexed attributes, and is more powerful than the index query of the GETOBJBYQUERY[COLL] commands, but slower as it is performed directly on the attribute values.

If fillParents is non-zero, the objects will have an additional attribute Parents (created on the fly), which holds the Name attribute of the object's parent collection. If the object is a member of more than one collection, a + is appended to the arbitrarily chosen collection name.

objCount and objIDs[] specify the object IDs for which the object records should be returned. The syntax of query is as follows:

```
<EXPR> ::= "(" <EXPR> ")" |
    "!" <EXPR> | /* NOT */
    <EXPR> "||" <EXPR> | /* OR */
    <EXPR> "&&" <EXPR> | /* AND */
    <ATTRIBUTE> <OPERATOR> <VALUE>

<ATTRIBUTE> ::= /* any attribute name (Author, DocumentType ...)   */

<OPERATOR> ::= "=" | /* equal */
    "<" | /* LESS THAN (STRING COMPARE) */
    ">" | /* greater than (string compare) */
    " " /* regular expression matching */
```

The `matchCount` and `matchIDs[]` parameters return the IDs of the objects that are actually returned (see security note below), `records` contains a large string holding all object records, and `offsets[]` is an array of `matchCount` elements that holds the byte offsets of the individual object records in `records`.

Security note It is here (and in the simple GETOBJECT command) that Hyper-G's read access rights are checked. This is because access rights to objects are contained within the `Rights` attribute, so that the object record has to be fetched from the low-level database in order to determine whether a user is allowed to access it. This is why it is normal for this call to return fewer object records than have been requested. The commands that return object IDs (for example, GETCHILDCOLLS) always return all object IDs, even if the user is not supposed to access them. The client should be aware of this and not assume that because GETCHILDCOLLS returned a number of object IDs, they can actually be retrieved with this command.

Errors It is normal for this call to return zero object records (see note above).

F.3.10 Command 12: GETTEXT

Send `string objRecord`

Recv `int error, optional remainder text`

Description Use this command to retrieve the actual text document associated with the object record `objRecord`, which has been previously retrieved using the GETOBJECT or OBJECTBYIDQUERY command. The text will be in HTF format, but will contain no anchors. Alternatively, you may use the PIPEDOCUMENT command to receive a (text) document asynchronously on a second connection.

Errors If the text could not be retrieved, `error` is set, in which case the text is not transmitted.

F.3.11   Command 14: INSDOC

Send int parentCollID, string objRecord, optional remainder doc

Recv int error, optional int docID

Description This command allows a new document to be inserted into the Hyper-G database. The parentCollID specifies the parent collection in which the document is to be inserted; objRecord is a sequence of attribute-name, attribute-value pairs, like:

```
Type=Document
DocumentType=Image
Title="en:This is an English title"
Author=fkappe
TimeCreated=93/11/26 12:35:17
Rights=W:g tu-graz
```

This command can be used to insert new text documents (use the EDITTEXT command to change existing texts), in which case doc contains the text. The text must be in HTF format HTF, without anchors.

On successful return (error is 0), docID is the new object ID that has been assigned for this object. For documents other than text (that is, doc is empty), this command only creates a Hyper-G object for the document. The document itself has to be inserted subsequently using the PUTDOCUMENT command.

Errors If error is not zero, an error has occurred, for example:

FATHERDEL Parent collection specified does not exist (any more)

FATHNOCOLL Parent collection specified is not a collection

NODOC Object record passed is not a document

NOLANGUAGE No or unknown language specified in Title attribute

See Section F.4 for a list of all possible error codes.

F.3.12   Command 17: INSCOLL

Send int parentCollID, remainder objRecord

Recv int error, optional int collID

Description This command allows a new collection to be inserted into the Hyper-G database. The parentCollID specifies the parent collection in which the collection is to be inserted; objRecord is a sequence of attribute-name, attribute-value pairs, like:

```
Type=Document
DocumentType=collection
Title="en:This is an English title"
Title="ge:Das ist ein deutscher Titel"
Author=fkappe
TimeCreated=93/11/26 12:35:17
```

On successful return (`error` is 0), `collID` is the new object ID assigned to this collection.

Status As the same effect can be accomplished using the `INSERTOBJECT` command, this command exists only for reasons of backward compatibility and is likely to disappear in future protocol versions. New implementations should use the `INSERTOBJECT` command.

Errors If `error` is not zero, an error has occurred, for example:

FATHERDEL Parent collection specified does not exist (any more)

FATHNOCOLL Parent collection specified is not a collection

NOLANGUAGE No or unknown language specified in `Title` attribute

See Section F.4 for a list of all possible error codes.

F.3.13   Command 19: GETSRCSBYDEST

Send `int dest`

Recv `int error, int count, int srcs[]`

Description This command can be used to find the source anchor ids (`srcs`) of a given destination anchor id, or destination document id, when the destination is a whole document (`dest`).

Errors If `error` is not zero, an error has occurred, for example:

RSERV_NRESP Remote server not responding

USR_BREAK Break by user

See Section F.4 for a list of all possible error codes.

F.3.14   Command 22: MVCPDOCSCOLL

Send `int move, int fromID, int toID, int count, int docs[]`

Recv `int error`

Description This command allows a number of documents to be moved or copied from one collection to another, or to be unlinked from a collection.

In "move" mode, move is set to true, fromID specifies the collection the documents should be moved away from, and toID specifies their new parent collection. The document IDs are supplied in docs[] (count of them).

In "copy" mode, move is set to false, and toID specifies the collection the documents should be "copied" to, that is, they are linked under this new collection as well as the old one. fromID is irrelevant in copy mode and should be set to 0. This command allows a number of parent collections to be attached to a document.

If toID is set to 0 in move mode, the collections are "unlinked" from the collection given in fromID, but not moved anywhere. If fromID was the only parent collection of a given document, it is deleted from the database.

Errors If error is not zero, an error has occurred, for example:

FATHNOCOLL Source collection specified is not a collection

DESTNOCOLL Destination is not a collection

SRCEQDEST Source and destination collection are identical

NODOCS No documents supplied

See Section F.4 for a list of all possible error codes.

F.3.15   Command 23: MVCPCOLLSCOLL

Send int move, int fromID, int toID, int count, int colls[]

Recv int error

Description Behaves like MVCPDOCSCOLL, but moves/copies/unlinks collections instead of documents. However, if in "unlink" mode fromID was the only parent collection of a given collection, it is deleted only if it is empty.

Errors See MVCPDOCSCOLL. In addition, the error code NOTEMPTY may occur.

F.3.16   Command 24: IDENTIFY

Send int encrypt, string name, string passwd, optional string clientInfo

Recv string userData

Description This command is used to identify the user to the Hyper-G database. This command must be used before any of the commands that modify the database can be used (otherwise, the NOACCESS error will occur when such a command is used). By default, the user is identified as anonymous.

The name specifies the Hyper-G user name, while passwd is the password. If encrypt is set to true, the client supplies passwd in encrypted form (according to modified DES, same as UNIX passwords), otherwise it is passed in clear text. The clientInfo is used to transmit the type of client (for statistics). The server will return the object id of the users UserObject and the name of the user itself (for example, 0x0000000 anonymous, if the identification failed).

Errors None.

F.3.17   Command 25: READY

Send (nothing)

Recv optional remainder message

Description The READY command is rather special. It is sent by the client after the initialization sequence (see Section F.2.1) to tell the server that the client is ready to receive messages, to agree on the protocol version to be used and to pass additional information concerning the protocol (see Section F.2.2). The client should *not* wait for a response.

An important difference from the other commands is that the server may send a READY response at any time (that is, without the client sending a READY command first). This feature is used to distribute asynchronous messages to the client.

Immediately after the initialization process (see Section F.2.1) the server sends a message containing the string $ServerString$serverstring where serverstring is replaced by a string identifying the server (this string can be set by the server provider to identify the server, and is intended to be human-readable, for example "University of Some City CWIS"). This is currently the only message format defined. See also the COMMAND command.

Status It is very likely that the set of defined message formats will be extended in the future. In particular, there will be messages that inform the client that certain objects in the database have been updated, and messages that can be used to pass clear-text information to users (for example, "Server shutdown in 5 minutes").

Errors None.

F.3.18   Command 26: COMMAND

Send int respond, string command

Recv `optional remainder message`

Description This (meta-)command is used to send commands to the Hyper-G server that are not directly related to manipulating objects. Rather, the (sub-)commands modify the server's state or retrieve administrative information from the server. Most of the commands do not require waiting for a response. In this case, `respond` should be set to false if asynchronous behavior is wanted. The following commands are defined (in alphabetical order):

- `contwrite` Enable write operations on the Hyper-G database (after a `stopwrite` command). Can only be issued by a user with system privileges. No response is returned.

- `kill [id]` Kill (disconnect) connection with ID `id` (a number obtained using the `who` command). Can only be issued by a user with system privileges. No response is returned.

- `message [id] [string]` Send an arbitrary message (contained in `string`) to connection `id`, which is either a user number obtained using the `who` command, or the string `ALL` in which case the message is broadcast to all users connected. Can only be issued by an identified user. No response is returned.

- `stat` Return server statistics. Currently, the local server time, server start time, uptime in seconds, and the number of object records retrieved in the last minute, 15 minutes, 60 minutes, and since server start are returned.

- `ftstat` Return full text server statistics. Currently, the server start time, uptime in seconds, and the number of queries in the last minute, 15 minutes, 60 minutes, and since server start are returned.

- `dcstat` Return document server statistics. Currently, the server start time, uptime in seconds, and the number of text, image and other documents retrieved in the last minute, 15 minutes, 60 minutes, and since server start are returned.

- `stopserver` Shut down the server. Can only be issued by a user with system privileges. No response is returned.

- `stopwrite` Disable write operations on the database, for example during a backup. Users performing such operations will get a WRITESTOPPED error (see Section F.4). Use `contwrite` to enable write access afterwards. Can only be issued by a user with system privileges. No response is returned.

- `who` Return a list of users currently connected to the server. For every user, a line with user number, user name, client host, login time, and time since the last transaction is returned. The line associated with this connection has an asterisk in the first column.

Errors None

F.3.19   Command 27: CHANGEOBJECT

Send int objectID, remainder commands

Recv int error

Description This command allows individual attributes of an object record to be removed, added or modified. The object is specified by objectID; commands adhere to the following syntax:

```
<COMMAND> ::= <REMCMD> |
    <ADDCMD> |
    <REMCMD> "<ADDCMD>

<REMCMD> ::= "rem " <ATTRIBUTE> "=" <VALUE>

<ADDCMD> ::= "add " <ATTRIBUTE> "=" <VALUE>
```

Note that in order to delete or remove an attribute its old value has to be supplied (some attributes are allowed more than once). A command like

```
rem attr=value\add attr=value
```

allows you to modify attributes in one operation.

Errors If error is not zero, an error has occurred, for example:

NOACCESS No permission to modify object

CMDSYNTAX Error in command syntax

CHANGEBASEFLD Change of base attribute (that is, attributes that cannot be changed, like ObjectID or Type)

NOTREMOVED Attribute not removed (for example, because the value was wrong)

FLDEXISTS Attribute already exists and may exist only once

NOLANGUAGE No or unknown language supplied (Title attribute)

See Section F.4 for a list of all possible error codes.

F.3.20   Command 28: EDITTEXT

Send int docID, string oldPath, string author, remainder text

Recv int error

Description Use this command to replace an old HTF text with a new one. The text must be in HTF format, without anchors. The docID parameter specifies the ID of the document, which must already exist. The oldPath parameter specifies the old path variable of the document (this is verified against what is specified within the object record to ensure that nobody else has updated the document in the meantime). The `author` parameter is obsolete.

Status The `author` parameter may be removed in future protocol versions.

Errors If `error` is not zero, an error has occurred, for example:

NOACCESS No permission to modify object

NOTFOUND The `docID` was not found

EXIST The `Path` attribute of the text object and `oldPath` are not equal

LOCKED The document is locked by somebody else

FTINDEX The full text indexer failed in indexing the document

F.3.21   Command 29: GETANDLOCK

Send `int objID`

Recv `int error, optional remainder objRecord`

Description Similar to GETOBJECT: returns object record from object ID (provided that access permissions are OK). However, the object is also marked as "locked" in the database, which means that another user trying to use GETANDLOCK on the same object would fail (see "Errors") until the object has been unlocked again (with the UNLOCK command), or until the connection of the user that locked the object is closed.

Clients must use this mechanism to implement write-locks, to ensure that no two users can modify the same object at the same time. Specifically, the CHANGEOBJECT and NEWTEXT commands have to be surrounded by GETANDLOCK and UNLOCK. Unlike GETOBJECT, GETANDLOCK guarantees that the attributes returned are the current state of the object and cannot be modified by somebody else between operations.

Errors If `error` is not zero, an error has occurred, for example:

NOACCESS No permission to access object

LOCKED Object is locked by another user; try again later

See Section F.4 for a list of all possible error codes.

F.3.22   Command 30: UNLOCK

Send `int objID`

Recv `(nothing)`

Description Removes the lock flag from object `objID` after a previous GETANDLOCK operation on that object. The lock flag is also removed when the connection that locked the object is closed. Note that this command does not return a response.

Errors None.

F.3.23 Command 31: INCOLLECTIONS

Send int retColls, int oidCount, int oids[], int collCount, int colls[]

Recv int error, int count, int returnIDs[]

Description A client may issue this command to check whether a set of objects (documents or collections) specified by oids[] is part of the collection hierarchy defined by colls[]. When retColls is false, the subset of oids[] that is part of the collection hierarchy (that is, the documents or collections that are children of one or more collections of colls[] or their sub-collections, recursively) is returned in returnIDs[]. When retColls is true, however, the set of collections that have one or more objects of this subset as children are returned in returnIDs. For example, this option allows a client to highlight the part of the collection hierarchy containing the matches of a previous query in a graphical overview.

Errors It is normal for returnIDs[] to be empty.

F.3.24 Command 32: INSERTOBJECT

Send string objRecord, string params

Recv int error, optional int objID

Description Allows to inserted an arbitrary object into the Hyper-G database. objRecord is the object record to insert, while params allows parameters that are not part of the object record to be specified, for example the parent collection, if applicable.

The format of params depends on the type of object that is to be inserted. For anchors, a Doc=0x12345678 value (with 0x12345678 replaced by the hexadecimal representation of the document ID of the document the anchor should be attached to) is required. For documents or collections, Parent=0x12345678 denotes the object's parent collection. For link objects, Src=0x12345678 specifies the source anchor, while an optional Dest=0x12345678 denotes the destination (if not present the link is left open).

On successful return objID is the new object ID that has been assigned for this object.

Status The params for links are likely to be rendered obsolete in new protocol versions, as the information currently stored in the link object will be stored directly in the source anchor in the future.

Errors If error is not zero, an error has occurred, for example:

FATHERDEL Parent collection specified does not exist (any more)

FATHNOCOLL Parent collection specified is not a collection

NOLANGUAGE No or unknown language specified in Title attribute

See Section F.4 for a list of all possible error codes.

F.3.25   Command 33: INCOLLSCLUSTER

Send `int oidCount, int oids[], int collCount, int colls[]`

Recv `int error, int count, int returnIDs[]`

Description This command works similar to `INCOLLECTIONS` with the `retColls` parameter set to false (see section InCollections), but with some exceptions. Let `oid` be an element of `oids`:

- If there is a parent of `oid` which is not a cluster and `INCOLLECTIONS` is true for this parent, add `oid` to `returnIDs`.
- For each parent `par` of `oid` which is a cluster, add `par` to `returnIDs`, if `INCOLLECTIONS` is true for **par**.

Errors It is normal for `returnIDs[]` to be empty.

F.3.26   Command 34: GETOBJBYFTQUERY

Send `string query`

Recv `int error, int count, int oids[], float weights[]`

Description This command is used to perform searches on the contents of text documents stored in the Hyper-G server. Text documents inserted into the Hyper-G database are automatically indexed and ready for searching.

The search is performed over the whole database of the server the client is connected to. Use the `GETOBJBYFTQUERYCOLL` to restrict the search to parts of the collection hierarchy, and to perform distributed searches on other servers. The command returns the IDs of the matching text document, as well as a set of weights that can be used for ranking.

The syntax of `query` is as follows (expressions in [ ] are optional, {} means 0 or more occurrences), | means "or":

```
<EXPR>       ::= <TERM>   <OROP> <TERM>
<TERM>       ::= <FACTOR>   <ANDOP> <FACTOR>
<FACTOR>     ::= <NODE> [ "" <FLOAT> "" ]
<NODE>       ::= <WORD> | "(" <EXPR> ")"
<OROP>       ::= "||" | "|"
<ANDOP>      ::= "&&" [ <OPTIONLIST> ] | "&" [ <OPTIONLIST> ]
<OPTIONLIST> ::= "[" <OPTION>   "," <OPTION>   "]"
<OPTION>     ::= "F" | "f"
```

The option list is extensible, to foresee proximity searches in the future.

Errors When no objects are found, `count` is set to 0 and no objects or weights are returned.

F.3.27 Command 35: GETOBJBYFTQUERYCOLL

Send `int collCount, int colls[], string query`

Recv `int error, int count, int oids[], float weights[]`

Description This command works like the GETOBJBYFTQUERY command. However, the search is not performed on the whole database of the server the client is connected to. Rather, it is limited to the set of collections supplied (`collCount, colls`) and their sub-collections (recursively).

If the connection is a distributed one (that is, the DISTRIBUTED flag has been set, see Section F.2.2), the command will also search remote collections (that is, collections that physically reside on some other Hyper-G server) if they are explicitly supplied in the `colls` array. This feature can be used to perform the same query over a number of Hyper-G servers in parallel. Remote collections are not searched automatically when they only appear as a sub-collection of one of the local collections specified.

Errors If nothing is found, no object IDs are returned (`count` is 0).

F.3.28 Command 36: PIPEDOCUMENT

Send `int docID, int port, string host, optional string special`

Recv `int error`

Description This command is used to actually retrieve a document from the Hyper-G server. In order not to block the command connection (that is, the connection these commands are sent over) by sending large chunks of data (for example, images) and to allow parallel receiving of a number of documents (for example, movie and sound), the document is sent over a separate connection.

Establishing a connection: As in FTP, the connection is opened actively by the document server. The client must previously have opened an IP port and be listening on it. The parameters `host` and `port` are used to pass that destination address to the server. `host` is a string parameter that contains the IP address of the client in numbers-and-dots format (the document server will refuse to do a name server lookup).

Retrieving the Document: Once the connection is established, the document is sent, optionally preceded by a header. The connection is closed once the whole document has been sent. The only way to determine if the entire document was sent is to have it preceded by a header (containing the document size). To accomplish this, the string parameter `special` is interpreted by the server and searched for the line `Refno=0x12345678`, which has to be passed by the client. A header is sent if the number (a hex value of 8 characters) is greater than zero.

Header Format: The header is a null-terminated ASCII string. It looks like:

```
HGHDR\n
sz=1234\n
```

`ref=2345\n`

The first line is to provide a (most probably) unique prefix to determine if the stream's head is a header. This is for two reasons. The first is that in earlier times there were servers that were not able to send a header, so if a client requested one it could not be guaranteed that one was actually sent. Nowadays all servers can send headers so this reason is purely historical. Second, when inserting documents via PUTDOCUMENT, the same header structure may be used (actually, clients are encouraged to do so). The first line's tag allows the server to determine the presence of a header.

The remaining lines may appear in any order or may be omitted. `sz=` is the size of the document (decimal), excluding the header itself. `ref=` is the same number the client passed in `special` (decimal). This is extremely useful since this is sometimes the only way for the client to associate the pending PIPEDOCUMENT requests with the arriving documents. Consider a client retrieving several documents simultaneously, such as text and image from within a cluster. It will issue two requests and (hopefully) get positive replies, but may not yet have been notified of the connections by the underlying TCP module. In particular, TCP cannot guarantee that the client will be notified of the connections in the same order they arrived. Therefore, the presence of a header with appropriate reference numbers is essential to the client.

Note While text documents may be retrieved using this command, it is also possible to retrieve them over the command connection using the GETTEXT command, avoiding the overhead of establishing a connection for short documents (as texts usually are).

Note Take the basics of this description as a substitute for all the other commands that deal with a separate connection, namely PUTDOCUMENT and PIPEREMOTE. The header format is the same in both directions (to the server or from the server). Further changes to connection management (such as clients opening the connection actively) will be stated here; the descriptions of the other two commands simply refer to this command.

Errors If `error` is not zero, an error has occurred. Errors may come either from the database (greater than 0 and less than 512) or from the document server (greater than 1024). Possible database errors are:

NOTFOUND The `docID` does not exist

WRGTYPE Either the document is not a local Hyper-G document (for example, a remote Gopher document), or its path variable is empty

Possible document cache server errors are:

NOCONNECTION The connection to the document server is broken

CONNECTCLIENT The document server could not connect to the client

SERVERTIMEOUT The document server did not respond for a certain amount of time

OPENSTORE_READ The given document was not found in the internal store

OPENFILE The given document was supposed to come from an external file which could not be opened

F.3.29 Command 37: DELETEOBJECT

Send `int objID`

Recv `int error`

Description Deletes the object associated with `objID`. Depending on the type of the object, other objects may be deleted as well (for example, anchors attached to a document). If the object is a document, the preferred way is to use the `MVCPDOCCOLLS` command to remove it from a specific collection, because `DELETEOBJECT` removes it from all collections (even those that you do not have permission to see, for example another user's bookmark collection), provided that you have write permission for the object.

Errors If `error` is not zero, an error has occurred, for example:

NOACCESS No permission to delete the object

NOTEMPTY Attempt to delete non-empty collection

See Section F.4 for a list of all possible error codes.

F.3.30 Command 38: PUTDOCUMENT

Send `int docID, int port, string host, string path,`
`optional string special`

Recv `int error`

Description This command is used to insert documents using a secondary data connection. The command works like the `PIPEDOCUMENT` command in that the document is transmitted over a different connection from the one that the commands are sent over.

See `PIPEDOCUMENT` for a complete description of the connection management (the meaning of the parameters `host` and `port`) and the format of a header to precede the document. Clients are encouraged to send a header since otherwise there is no way for the document server to detect incomplete data.

Before using this command, a client must have inserted the corresponding object record.

Note While this command may be used to insert text documents as well as documents of all other supported types, the `EDITTEXT` or `INSDOC` command should be used for this to avoid the overhead of establishing a connection for small amounts of data (as text is in general).

Status The `path` parameter will disappear in future protocol versions. It is unused here.

Errors If `error` is not zero, an error has occurred. Errors may come either from the database (greater than 0 and less than 512) or from the document server (greater than 1024). Possible database errors are:

NOTFOUND The `docID` does not exist

WRGTYPE Either the document is not a local Hyper-G document (for example, a remote Gopher document), or its path variable is empty

Possible document cache server errors are:

NOCONNECTION The connection to the document server is broken

CONNECTCLIENT The document server could not connect to the client

INVALIDADDRESS The Internet address was not in numbers-and-dots format

OPENSTORE_WRITE The server could not get resources to write the document to

CLOSESTORE The server was unable to insert the document

F.3.31   Command 39: GETREMOTE

Send `string object`

Recv `int error, remainder text`

Description This command is used to retrieve documents originating from a non-native (that is, not Hyper-G) server. The document is identified by the object record in the Hyper-G object syntax. Currently supported protocols are http and Gopher.

A sample remote object:

```
ObjectID=0x00000000
Type=Document
Title=??:Libraries of the University of
        Minnesota Integrated Network Access
Sequence=20
DocumentType=Remote
Protocol=gopher
Host=pubinfo.ais.umn.edu
Port=0
GopherType=T
```

where only the attributes `Type`, `DocumentType`, `Protocol`, `Host` and `Port` are required.

Errors If `error` is not zero, an error has occurred. Errors can come only from the document cache server inside the Hyper-G server complex, and have numbers larger than 1024.

NOCONNECTION (1026) The connection to the document server is broken

SERVERTIMEOUT (1049) The document server did not respond for a certain amount of time

INVALIDOBJECT (1052) Error in the object

CONNECTREMOTE (1063) The document server could not connect to the non-native server

F.3.32   **Command 40:** GETREMOTECHILDREN

Send string object, optional string query

Recv int error, int count, int offsets[], remainder records

Description This command is used to retrieve "children" of documents originating from a non-native (that is, not Hyper-G) server. It works like the GETREMOTE command and accepts an additional query string. The resulting documents (for example, a Gopher directory listing) are transformed into Hyper-G objects and returned.

Errors If error is not zero, an error has occurred. Errors can only come from the document cache server inside the Hyper-G server complex, and have numbers larger than 1024.

NOCONNECTION (1026) The connection to the document server is broken

SERVERTIMEOUT (1049) The document server did not respond for a certain amount of time

INVALIDOBJECT (1052) Error in the object

CONNECTREMOTE (1063) The document server could not connect to the non-native server

F.3.33   **Command 41:** PIPEREMOTE

Send string host, int port, string object, int refno

Recv int error

Description This command is used to retrieve documents originating from a non-native (that is, not Hyper-G) server. The document is identified by the object record in the Hyper-G object syntax. Currently supported protocols are http and Gopher.

The command works like the PIPEDOCUMENT command in that the document is transmitted over a different connection from the one that the commands are sent over.

See PIPEDOCUMENT for a complete description of the connection management (the meaning of the parameters host and port) and the format of an optional header to precede the document. Unlike PIPEDOCUMENT, the header is issued by a separate integer parameter refno. However, its meaning is as described in PIPEDOCUMENT.

The object contains an object as described in GETREMOTE.

Errors If error is not zero, an error has occurred. Errors can only come from the document cache server inside the Hyper-G server complex, and have numbers larger than 1024.

NOCONNECTION (1026) The connection to the document server is broken

CONNECTCLIENT (1041) The document server could not connect to the client

SERVERTIMEOUT (1049) The document server did not respond for a certain amount of time

INVALIDOBJECT (1052) Error in the object

CONNECTREMOTE (1063) The document server could not connect to the non-native server

F.3.34   Command 42: HG_BREAK

Send (nothing)

Recv (nothing)

Description This command is used to abort the currently active command. This command will return with error USR_BREAK set.

F.3.35   Command 43: HG_MAPID

Send int servId, int oId

Recv int error, int virtOId

Description This command is used to create a virtual object id from a global object id (given by servId and oid).

F.3.36   Command 44: GETCHILDREN

Send int parentId

Recv int error, int count, int children[ ]

Description Retrieves the children (collections and documents) of the given parent collection (count items).

Errors If parentID is not the object ID of a collection, or if it contains no children, a count of 0 is returned. If error is not zero, an error has occurred, for example:

RSERV_NRESP Remote server not responding

See Section F.4 for a list of all possible error codes.

F.4   Error codes

The error codes returned by the Hyper-G Server are divided into three groups, corresponding to the server module that generated the error:

(1) Error codes between 1 and 511 are link server errors.

(2) Error codes between 512 and 1023 are full text server errors.

(3) Error codes between 1024 and 2047 are document cache server errors.

An error code of 0 means that no error occurred.

The following table shows the link server error codes with their associated mnemonic names and a short (human-readable) description that could be output on a terminal, for example.

Attribute Indexed	Object class Multiple	Editable
1	NOACCESS	Access denied
2	NODOCS	No documents
3	NONAME	No collection name
4	NODOC	Object is not a document
5	NOOBJ	No object received
6	NOCOLLS	No collections received
7	DBSTUBNG	Connection to low-level database failed
8	NOTFOUND	Object not found
9	EXIST	Collection already exists
10	FATHERDEL	Parent collection disappeared
11	FATHNOCOLL	Parent collection not a collection
12	NOTEMPTY	Collection not empty
13	DESTNOCOLL	Destination not a collection
14	SRCEQDEST	Source equals destination
15	REQPEND	Request pending
16	TIMEOUT	Timeout
17	NAMENOTUNIQUE	Name not unique
18	WRITESTOPPED	Database now read-only; try again later
19	LOCKED	Object locked; try again later
20	CHANGEBASEFLD	Change of base-attribute
21	NOTREMOVED	Attribute not removed
22	FLDEXISTS	Attribute exists
23	CMDSYNTAX	Syntax error in command
24	NOLANGUAGE	No or unknown language specified
25	WRGTYPE	Wrong type in object
26	WRGVERSION	Client version too old
27	CONNECTION	No connection to other server
28	SYNC	Synchronization error
29	NOPATH	No path entry

Code	Mnemonic	Description
30	WRGPATH	Wrong path entry
31	PASSWD	Wrong password (server-to-server server authentication)
32	LC_NO_MORE_USERS	No more users for license
33	LC_NO_MORE_DOCS	No more documents for this session and license
34	RSERV_NRESP	Remote server not responding
35	Q_OVERFLOW	Query overflow
36	USR_BREAK	Break by user
37	N_IMPL	Not implemented

The following table shows the full text server error codes with their associated mnemonic names and a short (human-readable) description that could be output on a terminal, for example.

Attribute	Object class	Editable
Indexed	Multiple	
513	FTCONNECT	No connection to full text server
514	FTTIMEOUT	Connection timed out
515	FTINDEX	Something wrong with full text index
516	FTSYNTAX	Query syntax error

The following table shows the document cache server error codes with their associated mnemonic names and a short (human-readable) description that could be output on a terminal, for example. Where necessary, a more specific description (which is not part of the error string) is given in C++ comments.

Attribute	Object class	Editable
Indexed	Multiple	

The following error codes concern the connection internal to the Hyper-G servers

1025	REQUESTPENDING	Request pending
1026	NOCONNECTION	No connection to document server
1027	WRONGVERSION	Wrong protocol version
1028	NOTINITIALIZED	Not initialized
1029	BADREQUEST	Bad request

The remaining error codes are of a more general nature

1030	BADLRN	Bad document number

Code	Mnemonic	Description
1031	OPENSTORE_WRITE	Cannot write to local store
1032	OPENSTORE_READ	Cannot read from local store
1033	READSTORE	Store read error
1034	WRITESTORE	Write error; an internal failure (for example, disk full)
1035	CLOSESTORE	Close error; the update of internal data structures after inserting user data failed
1036	BADPATH	Bad path
1037	NOPATH	No path
1038	OPENFILE	Cannot open file; mainly occurs when attempting to read the "old" documents (that is, those where the path is a file name with offset/length)
1039	READFILE	Cannot read from file; same
1040	WRITEFILE	Cannot write to file
1041	CONNECTCLIENT	Could not connect to client
1042	ACCEPT	Could not accept connection
1043	READSOCKET	Could not read from socket
1044	WRITESOCKET	Could not write to socket
1045	(unused)	
1046	TOOMUCHDATA	Received too much data; the client wrote more than was specified in the header
1047	TOOFEWDATA	Received too little data
1048	(unused)	
1049	NOTIMPLEMENTED	Not implemented
1050	USERBREAK	User break; a job was terminated by the user's exit (usually the user will not see this error because (s)he exited)
1051	INTERNAL	Internal error; a trash can for system errors (for example, could not set non-blocking IO ...)
1052	INVALIDOBJECT	Invalid object; object syntax error (mainly occurs when retrieving non-Hyper-G data)
1053	JOBTIMEOUT	Job timed out; the client did not read/write for a certain amount of time (which is configurable at the server's side)
1054	OPENPORT	Cannot open port; ... for several reasons

Code	Mnemonic	Description
1055	NODATA	Received no data; the client did not send any data
1056	NOPORT	No port to handle this request; a request to receive a document from a remote HG server was timed out
1057	NOTCACHED	Document not cached
1058	BADCACHETYPE	Bad cache type; … an error with a more internal nature
1059	OPENCACHE_WRITE	Cannot write to cache; as with the store errors above
1060	OPENCACHE_READ	Cannot read from cache; same
1061	NOSOURCE	Do not know what to read; same as BADCACHETYPE
1062	CLOSECACHE	Could not insert into cache; same as OPENCACHE_WRITE
1063	CONNECTREMOTE	Could not connect to remote server
1064	LOCKREFUSED	Lock refused; could not lock the stores

F.5   An example C client

This section contains a simple C program that opens a connection to a Hyper-G server, performs a command who command, and prints the result (that is, the list of users currently connected to the server). It uses a library of low-level C functions that encapsulate most of the client–server communication. See documents hg_comm.h, hg_comm.c and hg_who.c below.

F.5.1   hg_comm.c

```
****************************************************
* hg_comm.c
*        a simple C interface to Hyper-G that lets
*        you send and receive commands.
****************************************************

#include <stdio.h>
#include <string.h>
#include <sys/types.h>
#include <sys/socket.h>
#include <netinet/in.h>
#include <netdb.h>
```

```
#include <fcntl.h>
#include <unistd.h>
#include <sys/param.h>
#include <errno.h>
#include <malloc.h>
#include <stdlib.h>
#include "hg_comm.h"

static int set_nonblocking(int fd);
static int set_blocking(int fd);
static int hg_read_exact(int sockfd, char *buf, int size);
static int hg_read(int sockfd, char *buf, int size);
static int hg_write(int sockfd, char *buf, int size);
static int send_hg_msg(int sockfd, hg_msg *msg, int length);
static void build_msg_header(hg_msg *msg, int length,
int version_msgid, int msg_type);
static char *build_msg_int(char *buf, int val);
static char *build_msg_str(char *buf, char *str);
static int swap(int val);
int version = VERSION;
/* int version = VERSION | F_DISTRIBUTED | F_COMPRESSED; */
static int msgid = 0;
static int sock_flags = -1;
static int non_blocking = 0;
static int do_swap = 0;

int open_hg_connection(char *server_name, int port)
{
   int sockfd;
   struct sockaddr_in server_addr;
   struct hostent *hp;
   char server_host[MAXHOSTNAMELEN];

   if ((hp = gethostbyname(server_name)) == NULL) {
      perror("gethostbyname");
      return(-1);
   }
   bzero((char *)&server_addr, sizeof(server_addr));
   server_addr.sin_family = AF_INET;
   if (port != 0)
      server_addr.sin_port = htons(port);
   else
      server_addr.sin_port = htons(HG_SERVER_PORT);
   bcopy(hp->h_addr, (char *) &server_addr.sin_addr, hp->h_length);
   if ((sockfd = socket(AF_INET, SOCK_STREAM, 0)) < 0) {
      perror("socket");
      return(-1);
   }
   if (connect(sockfd, (struct sockaddr *) &server_addr,
```

```
            sizeof(server_addr)) < 0) {
        perror("connect");
        close(sockfd);
        return(-1);
    }
    if ((sock_flags = fcntl(sockfd, F_GETFL, 0)) == -1)
        perror("open_hg_connection:  F_GETFL");
    if (set_nonblocking(sockfd) == -1) {
        fprintf(stderr, "open_hg_connection:  set_nonblocking");
        return(-1);
    }

    return(sockfd);
}

hg_msg *initialize_hg_connection(int sockfd)
{
    char buf, c;
    hg_msg *ready_msg;
    int i = 0x01;
    int len;

    buf = 'T';
    if (hg_write(sockfd, &buf, 1) == -1) {
        fprintf(stderr,
            "initialize_hg_connection:  hg_write (1) returned -1\n");
        return(NULL);
    }
    if (hg_read_exact(sockfd, &buf, 1) == -1) {
        fprintf(stderr,
            "initialize_hg_connection:  hg_read (1) returned -1\n");
        return(NULL);
    }
    if (buf == 'F') {
        fprintf(stderr,
            "initialize_hg_connection:  got >>F<< from server\n");
        return(NULL);
    }
    if (buf != 'T') {
        fprintf(stderr,
            "initialize_hg_connection:  neither >>F<< nor >>T<< from server\n");
        return(NULL);
    }

    buf = c = (*(char *)&i) ?  'l' :  'B';
    if (hg_write(sockfd, &buf, 1) == -1) {
        fprintf(stderr,
            "initialize_hg_connection:  hg_write (2) returned -1\n");
        return(NULL);
```

```
    }
    if (hg_read_exact(sockfd, &buf, 1) == -1) {
        fprintf(stderr,
            "initialize_hg_connection:  hg_read (2) returned -1\n");
        return(NULL);
    }
    if (c != buf) {
        fprintf(stderr,
            "initialize_hg_connection:  swapping necessary\n");
        do_swap = 1;
    }

    if ((ready_msg = recv_ready(sockfd)) == NULL) {
        fprintf(stderr,
            "initialize_hg_connection:  recv_ready returned NULL\n");
        return(NULL);
    }

    return(ready_msg);
}

static int set_nonblocking(int fd)
{
    if (sock_flags == -1)
        sock_flags = fcntl(fd, F_GETFL, 0);
    if (fcntl(fd, F_SETFL, O_NONBLOCK) == -1)
        return(-1);
    non_blocking = 1;
    return(0);
}

static int set_blocking(int fd)
{
    if (fcntl(fd, F_SETFL, sock_flags) == -1)
        return(-1);
    return(0);
}

static int hg_read_exact(int sockfd, char *buf, int size)
{
    int try = 0;
    int len = 0;

    if (!non_blocking)
        set_nonblocking(sockfd);
    while (size > 0) {
        len = recv(sockfd, (void *) buf, size, 0);
        if (len == -1) {
            if ((errno == EAGAIN) || (errno == EWOULDBLOCK)) {
```

```
            if (++try > 5)
                return(-1);
            sleep(3);
        }
        else return(-1);
    }
    else {
        size -= len;
        buf += len;
        try = 0;
    }
}

    return(0);
}

static int hg_read(int sockfd, char *buf, int size)
{
    int try = 0;
    int len = 0;

    if (!non_blocking)
        set_nonblocking(sockfd);
    while (len == 0) {
        len = recv(sockfd, (void *) buf, size, 0);
        if (len == -1) {
            if ((errno == EAGAIN) || (errno == EWOULDBLOCK)) {
                if (++try > 5)
                    return(-1);
                sleep(3);
            }
            else return(-1);
        }
    }
    return(len);
}

static int hg_write(int sockfd, char *buf, int size)
{
    int try = 0;
    int len = 0;

    if (!non_blocking)
        set_nonblocking(sockfd);
    while (size > 0) {
        len = send(sockfd, (void *) buf, size, 0);
        if (len == -1) {
            if ((errno == EAGAIN) || (errno == EWOULDBLOCK)) {
                if (++try > 5)
```

```
                  return(-1);
               sleep(3);
            }
            else return(-1);
      }
      else {
         size -= len;
         buf += len;
         try = 0;
      }
   }
   return(0);
}


hg_msg *recv_hg_msg(int sockfd)
{
   hg_msg *msg;

   if ((msg=(hg_msg *)malloc(sizeof(hg_msg)))==NULL) {
   perror("recv_hg_msg");
   return(NULL);
   }
   if (hg_read_exact(sockfd,(char *)&(msg->length),4)==-1) {
      fprintf(stderr,"recv_hg_msg:  hg_read (1) returned -1\n");
      free(msg);
      return(NULL);
   }
   if (hg_read_exact(sockfd,(char *)&(msg->version_msgid),4)==-1) {
      fprintf(stderr,"recv_hg_msg:  hg_read (2) returned -1\n");
      free(msg);
      return(NULL);
   }
   if (hg_read_exact(sockfd,(char *)&(msg->msg_type),4)==-1) {
      fprintf(stderr,"recv_hg_msg:  hg_read (3) returned -1\n");
      free(msg);
      return(NULL);
   }
   if (msg->length > HEADER_LENGTH) {
      if ((msg->buf=(char *)malloc(msg->length-HEADER_LENGTH))==NULL) {
         perror("recv_hg_msg");
         free(msg);
         return(NULL);
      }
      if (hg_read_exact(sockfd,msg->buf,msg->length-HEADER_LENGTH)==-1) {
         fprintf(stderr,"recv_hg_msg:  hg_read (4) returned -1\n");
         free(msg->buf);
         free(msg);
         return(NULL);
      }
   }
```

```
    }
    else
        msg->buf = NULL;

    return(msg);
}

hg_msg *recv_ready(int sockfd)
{
    hg_msg *ready_msg;

    if ((ready_msg = recv_hg_msg(sockfd)) == NULL) {
        fprintf(stderr, "recv_ready:  recv_hg_msg returned NULL\n");
        return(NULL);
    }
    if (ready_msg->msg_type != READY_MESSAGE) {
        fprintf(stderr, "recv_ready:  recv_hg_msg returned wrong message\n");
        return(NULL);
    }

    return(ready_msg);
}

hg_msg *recv_command(int sockfd)
{
    hg_msg *comm_msg;

    if ((comm_msg = recv_hg_msg(sockfd)) == NULL) {
        fprintf(stderr, "recv_command:  recv_hg_msg returned NULL\n");
        return(NULL);
    }
    if (comm_msg->msg_type != COMMAND_MESSAGE) {
        fprintf(stderr, "recv_command:  recv_hg_msg returned wrong message\n"
        return(NULL);
    }

    return(comm_msg);
}

static int send_hg_msg(int sockfd, hg_msg *msg, int length)
{
    char *buf, *tmp;

    if (length < HEADER_LENGTH) {
        fprintf(stderr, "send_hg_msg:  bad msg\n");
        return(-1);
    }
    if ((tmp = buf = (char *)malloc(length)) == NULL) {
        perror("send_hg_msg");
```

```
            return(-1);
        }
        memcpy(tmp, (char *) &(msg->length), 4);
        tmp += 4;
        memcpy(tmp, (char *) &(msg->version_msgid), 4);
        tmp += 4;
        memcpy(tmp, (char *) &(msg->msg_type), 4);
        if (msg->length > HEADER_LENGTH) {
            tmp += 4;
            memcpy(tmp, msg->buf, length-HEADER_LENGTH);
        }
        if (hg_write(sockfd, buf, length) == -1) {
            fprintf(stderr, "send_hg_msg:  hg_write returned -1\n");
            free(buf);
            return(-1);
        }

        free(buf);
        return(0);
    }

    int send_ready(int sockfd)
    {
        hg_msg ready_msg;

        build_msg_header(&ready_msg, HEADER_LENGTH, version, READY_MESSAGE);
        ready_msg.buf = NULL;
        if (send_hg_msg(sockfd, &ready_msg, HEADER_LENGTH) == -1) {
            fprintf(stderr, "send_ready:  send_hg_msg returned -1\n");
            return(-1);
        }

        return(0);
    }

    int send_command(int sockfd, int command)
    {
        hg_msg comm_msg;
        char *comm_str, *tmp;
        int respond = 1;
        int length;

        if (command == STAT_COMMAND)
            comm_str = STAT_COMMAND_STR;
        else
            comm_str = WHO_COMMAND_STR;
        length = HEADER_LENGTH + sizeof(respond) + strlen(comm_str) + 1;
        build_msg_header(&comm_msg, length, msgid, COMMAND_MESSAGE);
        if ((comm_msg.buf = (char *)malloc(length-HEADER_LENGTH)) == NULL)
```

```
        perror("send_command");
        return(-1);
    }
    tmp = build_msg_int(comm_msg.buf, respond);
    tmp = build_msg_str(tmp, comm_str);
    if (send_hg_msg(sockfd, &comm_msg, length) == -1) {
        fprintf(stderr, "send_ready:  send_hg_msg returned -1\n");
        free(comm_msg.buf);
        return(-1);
    }

    free(comm_msg.buf);
    return(0);
}

static void build_msg_header(hg_msg *msg, int length,
          int version_msgid, int msg_type)
{
    if (do_swap) {
        msg->length = swap(length);
        msg->version_msgid = swap(version_msgid);
        msg->msg_type = swap(msg_type);
    }
    else {
        msg->length = length;
        msg->version_msgid = version_msgid;
        msg->msg_type = msg_type;
    }
}

static char *build_msg_int(char *buf, int val)
{
    int tmp;

    tmp = do_swap ?  swap(val) :  val;
    memcpy(buf, (char *)&tmp, 4);

    return(buf+4);
}

static char *build_msg_str(char *buf, char *str)
{
    int len = strlen(str)+1;

    memcpy(buf, str, len);

    return(buf+len);
}
```

```
static int swap(int val)
{
    int tmp;

    ((char*)&tmp)[0] = ((char*)&val)[3];
    ((char*)&tmp)[1] = ((char*)&val)[2];
    ((char*)&tmp)[2] = ((char*)&val)[1];
    ((char*)&tmp)[3] = ((char*)&val)[0];

    return(tmp);
}

void close_hg_connection(int sockfd)
{
    shutdown(sockfd, 2);
    close(sockfd);
}
```

F.5.2   hg_comm.h

```
*****************************************************
 * hg_comm.h
 *       a simple C interface to Hyper-G that lets
 *       you send and receive commands.
 *
 *****************************************************

#ifndef hg_comm_h
#define hg_comm_h

#define HG_SERVER_PORT 418

#define READY_MESSAGE 25
#define COMMAND_MESSAGE 26

#define F_DISTRIBUTED 0x80000000
#define F_COMPRESSED 0x40000000
#define F_VERSION 0x00003fff
#define VERSION 705L /* 7.05 */

#define HEADER_LENGTH 12

#define STAT_COMMAND_STR "stat"
#define WHO_COMMAND_STR "who"
#define STAT_COMMAND 1
#define WHO_COMMAND 2
```

```
typedef struct {
    int length;
    int version_msgid;
    int msg_type;
    char *buf;
} hg_msg;

extern int open_hg_connection(char *server_name, int port);
extern void close_hg_connection(int sockfd);
extern hg_msg *initialize_hg_connection(int sockfd);

extern int send_ready(int sockfd);
extern int send_command(int sockfd, int command);

extern hg_msg *recv_hg_msg(int sockfd);
extern hg_msg *recv_ready(int sockfd);
extern hg_msg *recv_command(int sockfd);

#endif
```

F.5.3   hg_who.c

```
**************************************************
* hg_who.c
*        print who is logged into the Hyper-G
*        server right now.
* Usage:   hg_who [server] [port]
**************************************************

#include <stdio.h>
#include <sys/param.h>

#include "hg_comm.h"

#define SERVER_STRING "$ServerString$"

extern int version;
char server_string[256];

int port = 0;

extern void print_msg(hg_msg *msg, char *str, int txt);

main(int argc, char *argv[])
{
```

```
int sockfd;
char server_host[MAXHOSTNAMELEN];
hg_msg *msg;
int len;

if (argc >= 2)
   strcpy(server_host, argv[1]);
else
   gethostname(server_host, sizeof(server_host));
if (argc == 3)
   port = atoi(argv[2]);
if ((sockfd = open_hg_connection(server_host, port)) < 0) {
   fprintf(stderr, "open_hg_connection returned -1\n");
   return(-1);
}
version = VERSION;
/* version = VERSION | F_DISTRIBUTED | F_COMPRESSED; */
if ((msg = initialize_hg_connection(sockfd)) == NULL) {
   fprintf(stderr, "initialize_hg_connection returned NULL\n");
   close(sockfd);
   return(-1);
}
if (msg->version_msgid & F_VERSION < VERSION) {
   fprintf(stderr, "Warning:  used version %d less than %d\n",
      msg->version_msgid & F_VERSION, VERSION);
}
version = msg->version_msgid;
len = strlen(SERVER_STRING);
strncpy(server_string, (msg->buf)+len, 255);
server_string[255] = '
0';

free(msg->buf);
free(msg);

fprintf(stdout, "\n%s\n", server_string);

if (send_command(sockfd, WHO_COMMAND) == -1)
   fprintf(stderr, "send_command (who) returned -1\n");
else
   msg = recv_command(sockfd);
if (msg != NULL) {
   print_msg(msg, "WHO_COMMAND", 1);
   free(msg->buf);
   free(msg);
}
else
   fprintf(stderr, "recv_command (who) returned NULL\n");
```

```
    close_hg_connection(sockfd);

    exit(0);
}

void print_msg(hg_msg *msg, char *str, int txt)
{
    char *ptr;
    int i;

    fprintf(stdout, "\nprint_msg:  >>%s<<\n", str);
    fprintf(stdout, "print_msg:  length = %d\n", msg->length);
    fprintf(stdout, "print_msg:  msgid = %d\n", msg->version_msgid);
    fprintf(stdout, "print_msg:  msg_type = %d\n", msg->msg_type);
    if (msg->length > HEADER_LENGTH) {
        ptr = msg->buf;
        for (i = 0; i < msg->length-HEADER_LENGTH; i++) {
            if (*ptr == '\n')
                fprintf(stdout, "%c", *ptr++);
            else if (iscntrl(*ptr))
                fprintf(stdout, ".", *ptr++);
            else
                fprintf(stdout, "%c", *ptr++);
        }
    }
    fprintf(stdout, "\n\n");
}
```

G   SyncScript commands

Günter Nagler, Peter Sammer

This section describes the commands available to write **SyncScripts**. SyncScripts are needed to display SyncPages. These are pages in Hyper-G where time-dependent behavior of different objects and their layout on the screen can be defined (see Section 19.2.8).

A SyncScript is a simple text file, where each command line has a certain format. It begins with a number that represents the time (in milliseconds) at which the following command should be executed. Then follows the command and optionally an object type, an object number, and parameters. Line comments are opened with //, while block comments are opened with /* and closed with */ as usual in C and C++.

G.1   Object types

Currently the following object types are available:

BGR	Background
TBR	Toolbar
IMG	Image
TXT	Text
LBL	Label
SND	Sound
VID	Video

G.2   Description of commands for all object types

G.2.1   Load

Synopsis `Load ObjTyp number "Location" "Rectangle"`

Description Downloads an object from a network or a local storage device and assigns it to the indicated display area. The object is not displayed yet.

Exceptions Not valid for BGR and TBR objects. LBL objects have to specify a `"Caption"` instead of a `"Location"`.

Parameters `"Location"` is a Hyper-G URL or reference (for example, `"#2"` gives access to the second image in the cluster where the SyncScript is located) or a path on a local storage device.

`"Rectangle"` specifies the upper left corner as well as the width and height of a rectangular display area of an object (independent of resolution).

`"Caption"` labels a LBL object with text.

Example `Load IMG 1 "10/640 120/480 150/640 100/480"`

For explanation of the coordinates see Section 19.2.5.

G.2.2   Show

Synopsis `Show ObjTyp number`

Description Displays an object on the screen.

Example `Show IMG 1`

G.2.3   Hide

Synopsis `Hide ObjTyp number`

Description Removes an object from the screen.

Example `Hide IMG 1`

G.2.4   MoveTo

Synopsis `MoveTo ObjTyp number Parameter`

Description Moves the upper left corner of the rectangular display area of an object to the specified point.

Parameter `"RectPoint"` specifies the upper left corner of a rectangular display area of an object (independent of resolution).

Example `MoveTo IMG 1 "10/640 120/480"`

G.2.5   Resize

Synopsis `Resize ObjTyp number Parameter`

Description Redefines the width and height of the rectangular display area of an object.

Parameter `"RectSize"` specifies the width and height of a rectangular display area of an object (independent of resolution).

Example `Resize IMG 1 "10/640 120/480"`

G.2.6   SetArea

Synopsis `SetArea ObjTyp number Parameter`

Description Redefines the rectangular display area of an object.

Parameter `"Rectangle"` specifies the upper left corner as well as the width and height of a rectangular display area of an object (independent of resolution).

Example `SetArea IMG 1 "10/640 120/480 150/640 100/480"`

G.2.7   Change

Synopsis `Change ObjTyp number Parameter`

Description Removes an old object and displays the new one, whereas the display area remains the same.

Exceptions Not valid for `LBL` and `TBR` objects.

Parameter `"Location"` is a Hyper-G URL or reference (for example, `"#2"` gives access to the second image in the cluster where the SyncScript is located) or a path on a local storage device.

Example `Change IMG 1 "#3"`

G.2.8   MakeTop

Synopsis `MakeTop ObjTyp number`

Description Brings an object to the front of the display.

Exceptions Not valid for `VID` objects.

Example `MakeTop IMG 2`

G.2.9 MakeBottom

Synopsis `MakeBottom ObjTyp number`

Description Puts an object to the back of the display.

Exceptions Not valid for `VID` objects.

Example `MakeBottom IMG 1`

G.2.10 Remove

Synopsis `Remove ObjTyp number`

Description Unloads an object from a SyncPage.

Exceptions Not valid for `BGR` and `TBR` objects.

Example `Remove IMG 1`

G.3 Description of commands for IMG and BGR objects

G.3.1 SetMode

Synopsis `SetMode ObjTyp number Parameter`

Description Defines the display mode of images.

Parameters `ASPECTRATIO, CENTER, TILE, SCROLL, ZOOM`

Example `SetMode IMG 2 SCROLL`

G.3.2 ScrollTo

Synopsis `ScrollTo ObjTyp number Parameter`

Description Defines the specified point as the new upper left corner of the display area (makes sense if the image is larger than the display area).

Parameter `"RectPoint"` specifies the upper left corner of a rectangular display area of an object (independent of resolution).

Example `ScrollTo IMG 2 "10/640 120/480"`

G.4 Description of commands for SND and VID objects

G.4.1 Play

Synopsis `Play ObjTyp number`

Description Starts the playback of the specified sound or video.

Example `Play SND 1`

G.4.2 Pause

Synopsis `Pause ObjTyp number`

Description Halts the playback of the specified sound or video (a new play command continues the playback).

Example `Pause SND 1`

G.4.3 Stop

Synopsis `Stop ObjTyp number`

Description Stops the playback of the specified sound or video.

Example `Stop SND 1`

G.5 Description of commands for LBL objects

G.5.1 SetCaption

Synopsis `SetCaption LBL number Parameter`

Description Assigns new text to a label.

Parameter `"Caption"` labels an `LBL` object with text.

Example `SetCaption LBL 1 "Presentation"`

G.5.2 SetFgColor

Synopsis `SetFgColor LBL number Color`

Description Defines the foreground color of text of a label.

Parameters `Color` allows RGB color definition as a hexadecimal number.

Example SetFgColor LBL 1 0x00FF00

G.5.3 SetBgColor

Synopsis `SetBgColor LBL number Color`

Description Defines the background color of a label.

Parameter `Color` allows RGB color definition as a hexadecimal number.

Example `SetBgColor LBL 1 0xFF0000`

G.5.4 SetImage

Synopsis `SetImage LBL number Parameter`

Description Defines a picture as the background of a label.

Parameter `"Location"` is a Hyper-G URL or reference (for example, `"#2"` gives access to the second image in the cluster where the SyncScript is located) or a path on a local storage device.

Example `SetImage LBL 1 "#3"`

G.5.5 SetMode

Synopsis `SetMode LBL number Parameter`

Description Defines the display mode of a background image of a label.

Parameters ASPECTRATIO, CENTER, TILE, SCROLL, ZOOM

Example `SetMode LBL 1 ZOOM`

G.5.6   SetFontSize

Synopsis `SetFontSize LBL number FontSize`

Description Defines the size of a font.

Parameters `"FontSize"` specifies the size of a font independent of resolution.

Example `SetFontSize LBL 1 "24/480"`

G.5.7   SetFontName

Synopsis `SetFontName LBL number Parameter`

Description Defines a font for a label.

Parameter `"FontName"` defines a font by specifying the corresponding Windows font-name.

Example `SetFontName LBL 1 "Arial"`

G.5.8   SetStyle

Synopsis `SetStyle LBL number Parameter`

Description Defines a style for a label.

Parameters `NOBORDER, 3DBORDER, BORDER, ALIGNCENTER, ALIGNLEFT, ALIGNRIGHT, TRANSPARENT, BULLET, ARROW, FITCAPTION`

Example `SetStyle LBL 1 ALIGNLEFT`

G.5.9   SetGoto

Synopsis `SetGoto LBL number Parameter`

Description Works as a button following a hyperlink after selection.

Parameters `"Hyper-G URL", "Collection name"`

Example `SetGoto LBL 1 "aeiou"`

G.6   Description of commands without object

G.6.1   TimerInterval

Synopsis `TimerInterval Parameter`

Description Defines minimal time intervals in which commands can be executed.

Parameter `milliseconds`

Default 100 milliseconds

Example `TimerInterval 50`

G.6.2   ResetTime

Synopsis `ResetTime`

Description Sets the time counter back to 0. All following time statements always refer back to the last executed ResetTime command.

G.6.3   ShowCursor

Synopsis `ShowCursor`

Description Displays the mouse cursor.

G.6.4   HideCursor

Synopsis `HideCursor`

Description Hides the mouse cursor.

G.7   Further commands

The following commands are also supported:

```
Forward
Previous
Next
Root
Home
Up
```

```
Parents
History
HyperRoot
Search Parameter
    Parameter:   "keyword", "title"
Goto Parameter
    Parameter:   "Hyper-G URL", "Collection name"
Language Parameter
    Parameter:   "language code"
```

A description of these commands can be found in Section 19.2.2.

H The authors

Frank Kappe

This appendix contains a few lines about the 21 authors of this book, in alphabetical order. The following abbreviations are used:

HMS is the Institute for Hypermedia Systems of JOANNEUM RESEARCH, Graz, Austria.

IAIK is the Institute for Applied Information Processing and Communications of the Graz University of Technology, Austria.

IICM is the Institute for Information Processing and Computer Supported New Media of the Graz University of Technology, Austria.

IIS is the Institute for Information Systems of JOANNEUM RESEARCH, Graz, Austria.

UMN is the University of Minnesota at Minneapolis, USA.

Keith Andrews is the author of Chapters 2, 3, 15, 16 and 23.

Keith (kandrews@iicm.tu-graz.ac.at; http://hyperg.iicm.tu-graz.ac.at/keith) works for the IICM. He coordinated the development of Harmony from its beginnings in 1991 until the summer of 1995 and now coordinates the VRweb project and work on information visualization. His research interests include hypermedia, human–computer interaction, and 3D computer graphics.

Christian Derler is co-author of Chapter 20.

Christian (cderler@iis.joanneum.ac.at) is a member of the IIS. He developed version 2.xx of the Hyper-G WWW gateway for his master's thesis.

Thomas Dietinger is co-author of Chapters 17, 18 and 24.

Thomas (tdieting@iicm.tu-graz.ac.at) is a member of the IICM. He coordinates the Amadeus and Easy development and has programmed large parts of Amadeus.

Christian Huber is the author of Chapter 7 and co-author of Chapter 24.

Christian (chuber@iicm.tu-graz.ac.at) is a member of the IICM. He is developing the Amadeus text viewer for his master's thesis.

Frank Kappe is the author of Chapters 5, 8, 9, 10 and 11, Appendices A, E, and H and co-author of Chapter 31 and Appendix F.

Frank (fkappe@iicm.tu-graz.ac.at; http://hyperg.iicm.tu-graz.ac.at/fkappe) is a member of the IICM. He coordinates the Hyper-G software development and programmed the first client (HGTV). His research interests include distributed hypermedia systems, scalable systems and information visualization.

Peter Lipp is co-author of Chapter 30.

Peter (plipp@iaik.tu-graz.ac.at) is a member of the IAIK. His research interests include network security and secure payment systems.

Hermann Maurer is the author of Chapters 1 and 4, Appendices C and D and co-author of Chapters 29 and 31.

Hermann (hmaurer@www.tu-graz.ac.at, http://hyperg.iicm.tu-graz.ac.at/maurer) is the head of the HMS and IICM. As such, he is responsible for the general direction of research and development efforts, international cooperation, funding and public relations of HMS and IICM. His main research interests include multimedia and networked multimedia systems and their applications to electronic publishing, multimedia presentation, computer supported communication and education.

Mark McCahill is the author of Chapter 6.

Mark (mpm@boombox.micro.umn.edu) is a member of the UMN, where he and his colleagues have developed the Gopher system. They are currently working on the Macintosh Hyper-G client and the Macintosh version of VRweb.

Gerald Mesaric is co-author of Chapters 20, 21, 22 and 25.

Gerald (gmesaric@iicm.tu-graz.ac.at) is a member of the IICM. He maintains the IICM Hyper-G server (among others) and works on a generic PDF viewer.

Steven Mitter is the author of Chapter 13.

Steven (smitter@hms.joanneum.ac.at) is a member of the HMS. He is the programmer of the PC library and other PC-based projects. He also developed the standalone Hyper-G database.

Helmut Mülner is the author of Chapter 26.

Helmut (hmuelner@hms.joanneum.ac.at) is a member of the HMS. He is project leader of a number of PC-based projects, including the PC library. He is also an expert on SGML, LaTeX, Perl, C, C++, LISP, Emacs and computer games.

Günter Nagler is co-author of Chapter 19 and Appendix G.

Günter (gnagler@hms.joanneum.ac.at) is a member of the HMS and implements *Easy*. He has also developed a number of PC-based standalone hypermedia systems for exhibitions.

Gerbert Orasche is co-author of Chapters 17, 18, 19 and 24.

Gerbert (gorasche@iicm.tu-graz.ac.at) is a member of the IICM. He developed Post-Script and VRML viewers for Amadeus and maintains the Windows version of VRweb.

Gerald Pani is co-author of Chapter 14 and Appendix F.

Gerald (gpani@hms.joanneum.ac.at) is a member of the HMS. He coordinates development of the Hyper-G server and has coded large portions of it himself.

Srinivasan Parthasarathy is the author of Chapters 12 and 27.

Srinivasan (psrini@iicm.tu-graz.ac.at) is a member of the IICM. He is the programmer of a number of PC-based projects and implemented parts of the SQL interface. His research interests include hypermedia data modeling and information retrieval.

Reinhard Posch is co-author of Chapter 30.

Reinhard (rposch@iaik.tu-graz.ac.at) is the head of the IAIK. His research interests include networking in general, computer security and VLSI design.

Peter Sammer is co-author of Chapter 19 and Appendix G.

Peter (psammer@hms.joanneum.ac.at) is a member of the HMS. He has been directing the development of several multimedia and hypermedia projects for different clients, world expositions, local fairs and other presentations.

Walter Schinnerl is co-author of Chapters 22 and 25.

Walter (wschinn@hms.joanneum.ac.at) is a member of the HMS. He maintains the server of the Graz University of Technology (among others) and writes scripts for mass insertion of information.

Klaus Schmaranz is the author of Chapters 28 and Appendix B and co-author of Chapters 14, 21, 25 and 31.

Klaus (kschmar@iicm.tu-graz.ac.at) is a member of the IICM. He developed the Harmony PostScript viewer, coordinates development of a PDF viewer and maintains the J.UCS collection. His research interests include electronic publishing and new document formats.

Achim Schneider prepared the index and polished this book.

Achim (aschneid@iicm.tu-graz.ac.at) was an early fan and promoter of Hyper-G while working on his Ph.D at the University of Auckland in New Zealand and roaming other parts of the world.

Robert Stubenrauch is co-author of Chapter 29 and prepared the glossary.

Robert (rstubenr@hms.joanneum.ac.at, http://hyperg.iicm.tu-graz.ac.at/ rstubenr) is a member of the HMS. He creates Web applications based on Hyper-G. His main professional interests are information design and electronic publishing over computer networks.

References

ACM SIGLINK Home Page. Available at `http://acm.org/siglink/`.

Adobe Systems Inc. (1990). *PostScript Language Reference Manual*, 2nd edition. Addison-Wesley, Reading, Mass.

Adobe Systems Inc. (1993). *Portable Document Format Reference Manual*. Addison-Wesley, Reading, Mass.

Akscyn, R., McCracken, D. and Yoder, E. (1987). KMS: A distributed hypermedia system for managing knowledge in organizations. In *Proc. ACM Hypertext '87*, pages 1–20.

Andrews, K. (1995). Visualising cyberspace: Information visualisation in the Harmony internet browser. In *Proc. of IEEE Symposium on Information Visualization (InfoVis 95)*, pages 97–104, Atlanta, Georgia.

Andrews, K. and Kappe, F. (1993). Strait-jacketing authors: User interface consistency in large-scale hypermedia systems. In H. P. Frei and P. Schäuble, editors, *Hypermedia '93, Zürich, Switzerland*, pages 130–137, Berlin. Springer.

Andrews, K., Kappe, F., Maurer, H. and Schmaranz, K. (1994). On second generation hypermedia systems. *Journal of Universal Computer Science (Pilot Issue)*, **0**(0), 127–135. Available at `http://hyperg.iicm.tu-graz.ac.at/jucs`.

Anklesaria, F., Lindner, P., McCahill, M., Torrey, D., Johnson, D. and Alberti, B. (1993a). Gopher+: Upward compatible enhancements to the Internet Gopher protocol. Available at `ftp://boombox.micro.umn.edu/pub/gopher/-gopher_protocol/Gopher+/Gopher+.txt`.

Anklesaria, F., McCahill, M., Lindner, P., Johnson, D., Torrey, D. and Alberti, B. (1993b). RFC 1436: The Internet Gopher protocol. Available at `ftp://ds.internic.-net/rfc/rfc1436.txt`.

Balenson, D. Privacy enhancement for internet electronic mail Part III: Algorithms, modes, and identifiers. Available at `ftp://ds1.internic.net/rfc/-rfc1423.txt`.

Barron, B., Ellsworth, J. and Savetz, K., editors (1995). 2nd edition. Sams.net Publishing.

Benaloh, J., Lampson, B., Simon, D., Spies, T. and Yee, B. Private communication technology protocol. Available at `http://www.microsoft.com:80/windows/-ie/pct.htm`.

Berk, E. and Devlin, J., editors (1991). *Hypertext/Hypermedia Handbook*. Software Engineering Series. McGraw-Hill, New York.

Berners-Lee, T. and Conolly, D. (1993). HyperText Markup Language (HTML). Available at `http://www.w3.org/pub/WWW/Markup/Markup.html`.

Berners-Lee, T., Cailliau, R., Groff, J.-F. and Pollermann, B. (1992). World-Wide Web: The information universe. *Electronic Networking: Research, Applications and Policy*, **2**(1), 52–58.

Berners-Lee, T., Cailliau, R., Luotonen, A., Nielsen, H. F. and Secret, A. (1994). The World-Wide Web. *Communications of the ACM*, **37**(8), 76–82.

Bernstein, M. (1991). The navigation problem reconsidered. In E. Berk and J. Devlin, editors, *Hypertext/Hypermedia Handbook*, Software Engineering Series, pages 285–297. McGraw-Hill, New York.

Blunden, B. and Blunden, M., editors (1994). *The Electronic Publishing Business and its Market*. IEPRC/Pira International, Leatherhead, Surrey, UK.

Borenstein, N. and Freed, N. (1992). MIME (Multipurpose Internet Mail Extensions), Internet RFC 1341. Available at `ftp://nic.ddn.mil/rfc/rfc1341.txt`.

Borenstein, N. and Freed, N. MIME (Multipurpose Internet Mail Extension) Part One: Mechanisms for Specifying and Describing the Format of Internet Message Bodies. Available at `ftp://ds1.internic.net/rfc/rfc1521.txt`.

Bossert, G., Cooper, S. and Drummond, W. Requirements for Web transaction security. Available at `ftp://ds1.internic.net/internet-drafts/-draft-ietf-wts-requirements-00.txt`.

Botafogo, R. A. (1993). Cluster analysis for hypertext systems. In *Proc. SIGIR'93*, pages 116–125, Pittsburgh, PA. ACM Press.

Botafogo, R. A., Rivlin, E. and Shneiderman, B. (1992). Structural analysis of hypertexts: Identifying hierarchies and useful metrics. *ACM Transactions on Information Systems*, 10(2), 142–180.

Bourne, S. R. (1982). *The UNIX System*. Addison-Wesley, Reading, Massachusetts.

Bradley, J. XV. Available at `ftp://ftp.cis.upenn.edu/pub/xv/`.

Buddine, L. and Young, E. (1987). *The Brady Guide to CD-ROM*. Prentice-Hall Press, New York, USA.

Buford-Koegel, J., editor (1994). *Multimedia Systems*. ACM Press.

Bush, V. (1986). As we may think. In S. Lambert and S. Ropiequet, editors, *CD-ROM — The New Papyrus*, pages 3–20. Microsoft Press, Redmond, Washington. Reprinted from *The Atlantic Monthly*, 171(1), July, 1945.

Case, J. D., Fedor, M. S., Schoffstall, M. L. and Davin, J. R. (1990). A Simple Network Management Protocol; Internet RFC 1157. Available at `ftp://nic.ddn.mil/-rfc/rfc1157.txt`.

Chang, D. T. (1993). HieNet: A user-centered approach for automatic link generation. In *Proc. ACM Hypertext '93*, pages 145–158.

Chaum, D. (1989). Online cash checks. In Quisquater and Vandewalle, editors, *Advances in Cryptology EUROCRYPT '89*, pages 288–293. Springer Verlag.

Chaum, D., editor (1991). *Numbers Can Be a Better Form of Cash than Paper*. Smart Card 2000, North Holland.

Chen, S. E. (1995). Quicktime vr — an image-based approach to virtual environment navigation. In *ACM Computer Graphics (Proc. SIGGRAPH '95)*, pages 29–38.

Cheswick, W. and Bellovin, S. (1994). *Firewalls and Internet Security: Repelling the Wily Hacker*. Addison-Wesley.

Communications of the ACM (1995). **38**(4). Special Issue on Digital Libraries.

Conklin, J. (1987). Hypertext: An introduction and survey. *IEEE Computer*, **20**(9), 17–41.

Conklin, J. and Begeman, M. L. (1988). gIBIS: A hypertext tool for exploratory policy discussion. *ACM Transactions on Office Information Systems*, 6(4), 303–331.

Coulouris, G. F. and Dollimore, J. (1988). *Distributed Systems: Concepts and Design*. Addison-Wesley.

Cox, B., Tygar, J. and Sirbu, M. (1995). Netbill security and transaction protocol. In *Proc. of the First USENIX Workshop on Electronic Commerce.*

Crocker, S., Freed, N., Galvin, J. and Murphy, S. MIME object security services. Available at `ftp://ds1.internic.net/rfc/rfc1848.txt`.

Crowston, K. and Malone, T. W. (1988). Intelligent software agents — using AI techniques in groupware has the potential to dramatically alter the way we organize our work. *Byte*, **13**(13), 267–272.

Dalitz, W. and Heyer, G. (1995). *Hyper-G — Das Internet-Informationssystem der 2. Generation.* dpunkt, Heidelberg. In German.

Danzig, P., DeLucia, D. and Obraczka, K. (1994). Massively replicating services in autonomously managed wide-area internetworks. Technical report, Computer Science Department, University of Southern California. Available at `ftp://catarina.-usc.edu/pub/kobraczk/ToN.ps.Z`.

Date, C. J. (1989). *A User's Guide to the Standard Relational Language SQL*, 2nd edition. Addison-Wesley.

December, J. Internet Tools Summary. Available at `http://www.rpi.edu/Internet/Guides/decemj/itools/internet-tools.html`.

December, J. and Randall, N. (1994). *The World Wide Web Unleashed.* Sams Publishing, Indianapolis, USA. Available at `http://www.rpt.edu/ decemj/works/-wwwu.html`.

Derler, C. (1995). *The World-Wide Web Gateway to Hyper-G: Using a Connectionless Protocol to Access Session-Oriented Services.* Master's thesis, Graz University of Technology, Austria. Available at `ftp://iicm.tu-graz.ac.at/pub/-Hyper-G/doc/derler.ps`.

DeRose, S. J. (1989). Expanding the notion of links. In *Proc. ACM Hypertext '89*, pages 249–257.

Dewan, P. (1993). A survey of applications of CSCW including some in educational settings. In *Proc. ED-MEDIA 93, Orlando, Florida*, pages 147–152, Charlottesville, VA. AACE.

DeYoung, L. (1990). Linking considered harmful. In A. Rizk, N. Streitz, and J. André, editors, *Hypertext: Concepts, Systems and Applications; Proc. ECHT'90*, pages 238–249. Cambridge University Press.

Engelbart, D. C. (1963). A conceptual framework for the augmentation of man's intellect. In P. D. Howerton and D. C. Weeks, editors, *Vistas in Information Handling, Vol. 1*, pages 1–29. Spartan Books, Washington D.C.

Erikson, H. (1994). MBONE: The Multicast Backbone. *Communications of the ACM*, **37**(8), 54–60.

Etzioni, O. and Weld, D. (1994). A softbot-based interface to the Internet. *Communications of the ACM*, **37**(7), 72–76.

Faschingbauer, J. (1993). *Volltextsuche in Großen Hypermediasystemen.* Master's thesis, Graz University of Technology, Austria. In German.

Feiner, S. (1988). Seeing the forest for the trees: Hierarchical display of hypertext structure. In *Proc. OIS'88*, pages 205–212, Palo Alto, CA. ACM Press.

Filippini, L. Moving picture expert group MPEG home page. Available at `http://-www.crs4.it/HTML/LUIGI/MPEG/`.

Flohr, U. (1995). Hyper-G organizes the Web. *BYTE*, **20**(11), 59 – 64.

Flynn, P. (1995). *The World Wide Web Handbook*. International Thomson Computer Press, London.

Foss, C. (1988). Effective browsing in hypertext systems. In *Proc. RIAO'88*, pages 82–98, Cambridge, MA. MIT.

Fox, E. (1995a). Hypermedia support for a digital library in computer science. *ACM SIGLINK Newsletter*, **4**(2), 11.

Fox, E. (1995b). Progress in interactive learning with a digital library in computer science. In *Proc. ED-MEDIA 95, Graz*, pages 7–12. AACE.

Fulton, J. and Renda, G. The network audio system. Available at `ftp://ftp.x.org/-contrib/audio/nas/xcon94paper.ps.gz`.

Gall, D. L. (1991). MPEG: A video compression standard for multimedia applications. *Communications of the ACM*, **34**(4), 46–63.

Galvin, J., Murphy, S., Crocker, S. and Freed, N. Security multiparts for MIME: Multipart/signed and multipart/encrypted. Available at `ftp://ds1.internic.-net/rfc/rfc1847.txt`.

Gay, G. and Mazur, J. (1991). Navigating in hypermedia. In E. Berk and J. Devlin, editors, *Hypertext/Hypermedia Handbook*, Software Engineering Series. McGraw-Hill, New York.

Gilly, D. (1992). *UNIX in a Nutshell*. O'Reilly & Associates, Inc., Sebastopol, California.

Graham, I. (1995). *The HTML Sourcebook*. Wiley, New York.

Haan, B. J., Kahn, P., Riley, V. A., Coombs, J. H. and Meyrowitz, N. K. (1992). IRIS hypermedia services. *Communications of the ACM*, **35**(1), 36–51.

Halasz, F. G. (1988). Reflections on NoteCards: Seven issues for the next generation of hypermedia systems. *Communications of the ACM*, **31**(7), 836–852.

Hickman, K. and Elgamal, T. The Secure Socket Layer. Available at `http://home.-netscape.com/newsref/std/SSL.html`.

Huber, F., Makedon, F. and Maurer, H. (1989). Hyper-COSTOC: A comprehensive computer-based teaching support system. *Journal of Microcomputer Applications*, **12**(4), 293–317.

INRIA/GRIF. Symposia. Available at `http://symposia.inria.fr/`.

Internet Guide. Available from Electronic Frontier Foundation at `http://www.eff.-org` or `http://hgiicm.tu-graz.ac.at/internet_guide`.

Internet Society Home Page. See `http://info.isoc.org/`.

ISO (1986). *Information Processing Systems — Text and Office Systems — Standard Generalized Markup Language (SGML), ISO IS 8879*. ISO.

ISO (1987a). *Information Processing Systems — Open Systems Interconnection — Specification of Abstract Syntax Notation One (ASN.1), ISO IS 8824*. ISO.

ISO (1987b). *Information Processing Systems — Open Systems Interconnection — Specification of basic encoding rules for Abstract Syntax Notation One (ASN.1), ISO IS 8825*. ISO.

ISO (1989). *ISO 9660*. International Organization for Standardization.

Jayasinha, C., Lennon, J. and Maurer, H. (1995). Interactive and annotated movies. In H. Maurer, editor, *Proceedings of ED-MEDIA'95*, pages 366–371. AACE.

Kaliski, B. Privacy enhancement for internet electronic mail Part IV: Key certification and related services. Available at `ftp://ds1.internic.net/rfc/-rfc1424.txt`.

Kantor, D. and Lapsley, P. (1986). Network News Transfer Protocol — A proposed standard for the stream-based transmission of news. Internet RFC 977. Available at `ftp://nic.ddn.mil/rfc/rfc977.txt`.

Kappe, F. (1991). *Aspects of a Modern Multi-Media Information System*. Ph.D. thesis, Graz University of Technology, Austria. Also available as IIG Report 308; IIG, Graz University of Technology (June 1991), and at `ftp://iicm.tu-graz.ac.at/-pub/Hyper-G/papers`.

Kappe, F. (1995a). Maintaining link consistency in distributed hyperwebs. In K. Chon, editor, *Proc. INET '95, Honolulu, Hawaii*, pages 15–24. Internet Society.

Kappe, F. (1995b). A scalable architecture for maintaining referential integrity in distributed information systems. *Journal of Universal Computer Science*, **1**(2), 84–104. Available at `http://hyperg.iicm.tu-graz.ac.at/a_scalable_architecture_for_maintaining`.

Kappe, F. and Maurer, H. (1994). From hypertext to active communication/information systems. *Journal of Microcomputer Applications*, **17**(4), 333–344.

Kent, S. Privacy enhancement for internet electronic mail Part II: Certificate-based key management. Available at `ftp://ds1.internic.net/rfc/rfc1422.txt`.

Krol, E. (1994). *The Whole Internet: User's Guide and Catalog*, second edition. O'Reilly & Associates.

Kruglinkski, D. J. (1993). *Inside Visual C++*. Microsoft Press, Washington, USA.

Lennon, J. and Maurer, H. (1994a). Applications and impact of hypermedia systems: An overview. *J.UCS*, **0**(0), 54–108. Available under `http://www.iicm.-tu-graz.ac.at/jucs`.

Lennon, J. and Maurer, H. (1994b). Lecturing technology: A future with hypermedia. *Educational Technology*, **34**(4), 5–14.

Lindner, P. Internet Gopher user's guide. University of Minnesota. Available at `ftp://boombox.micro.umn.edu/pub/gopher/docs/Gopher-Guide_Jan12-94.A4.ps`.

Linn, J. Privacy enhancement for internet electronic mail Part I: Message encryption and authentication procedures. Available at `ftp://ds1.internic.net/rfc/-rfc1421.txt`.

Liu, C., Peek, J., Jones, R., Buus, B. and Nye, A. (1994). *Managing Internet Information Services: World Wide Web, Gopher, FTP and more*. O'Reilly & Associates, Sebastopol, USA.

Lougher, P. mpegUtil. Available at `http://www.comp.lancs.ac.uk/computing/users/phillip/mpegUtil.html`.

Macedonia, M. and Brutzman, D. (1994). Mbone provides audio and video across the Internet. *IEEE Computer*, **27**(4), 30–36.

Maes, P. (1994). Agents that reduce work and information overload. *Communications of the ACM*, **37**(7), 31–40, 146.

Marchionini, G. and Maurer, H. (1995). The role of digital libraries in teaching and learning. *Communications of the ACM*, **38**(4), 67–75.

Maurer, H. (1994a). The A.E.I.O.U. hypermedia project. In *Proc. Computer Animation*

'94, pages 192–196. IEEE Computer Society Press.

Maurer, H. (1994b). Lecturing in the future: Bringing it all together. In *Proc. ED-MEDIA 94, Vancouver*, page 46. AACE.

Maurer, H. (1995). Hypermedia in a gambling casino setting. In R. Kuhlen and M. Rittberger, editors, *Hypermedia — Information Retrieval — Multimedia (Proc. HIM '95)*, Schriften zur Informationswissenschaft, pages 233–241. Hochschulverband für Informationswissenschaft (HI) e.V. Konstanz.

Maurer, H. and Lennon, J. (1995). Digital libraries as learning and teaching support. In *Proceedings of ICCE 95 — International Conference on Computers in Education*. AACE.

Maurer, H. and Scherbakov, N. (1995). *Multimedia Authoring for Presentation and Education. The Official Guide to HM-Card*. Addison-Wesley, Germany.

Maurer, H. and Schneider, A. (1995). Conferencing — Doing it the hypermedia way. In *Proc. ED-MEDIA 95, Graz*, pages 436 – 441. AACE.

Maurer, H. and Williams, M. (1991). Hypermedia systems and other computer support as infrastructure for museums. *Journal of Microcomputer Applications*, **14**(2), 117–137.

Maurer, H., Scherbakov, N. and Parthasarathy, S. (1993a). A new hypermedia data model. In V. Marek, editor, *Proc. DEXA'93, Prague, Czech Republic*, LNCS 720, pages 685–696. Springer.

Maurer, H., Kappe, F., Scherbakov, N. and Parthasarathy, S. (1993b). Structured browsing of hypermedia databases. In T. Grechenig and M. Tscheligi, editors, *Proc. VCHCI '93, Vienna, Austria*, LNCS 733, pages 51–62. Springer.

Maurer, H., Kappe, F. and Scherbakov, N. (1994a). Authoring a large distributed hypermedia system: Document Linking and Embedding (DLE) concept. In W. Herzner and F. Kappe, editors, *Multimedia/Hypermedia in Open Distributed Environments*, pages 230–243. Springer.

Maurer, H., Kappe, F., Scherbakov, N. and Parthasarathy, S. (1994b). Conceptual modeling in hypermedia: Authoring of large hypermedia databases. In *Proc. Hypermedia in Vaasa '94, Vaasa, Finland*, pages 294–304. Vaasa Institute of Technology.

Maurer, H., Mülner, H. and Schneider, A. (1994c). An Electronic Library and Its Ramifications. In *Proc. Symposium Didaktik der Mathematik, Schriftenreihe Didaktik der Mathematik, Klagenfurt*.

Maurer, H., Philpott, A. and Scherbakov, N. (1994d). Hypermedia Systems without Links. *Journal of Microcomputer Applications*, **17**(4), 321 – 332.

Maurer, H., Scherbakov, N., Andrews, K. and Parthasarathy, S. (1994e). Object-oriented modelling of hyperstructure: overcoming the static link deficiency. *Information and Software Technology*, **36**(6), 315–322.

Maurer, H., Scherbakov, N. and Schneider, A. (1995). Hm-card: A new hypermedia authoring system. *Journal for Multimedia Tools and Applications*, **1**(4), 305–326.

Maxwell, C. and Grycz, C. J. (1994). *Internet Yellow Pages*. News Riders Publishing.

Mayrhofer, V. and Andrews, K. (1995). Harmony user guide: Version 1.2. Technical report, IICM, Graz University of Technology. Available at `ftp://ftp.iicm.-tu-graz.ac.at/pub/Hyper-G/papers/hug.ps.gz`.

McCahill, M. P. and Anklesaria, F. X. (1995). Evolution of Internet Gopher. *Journal of*

Universal Computer Science, **1**(4), 235–246. Selected Proceedings of the Workshop on Distributed Multimedia Systems, Graz, Austria, Nov. 1994. Available at `http://info.iicm.tu-graz.ac.at/jucs`.

McCahill, M. P. and Erickson, T. (1995). Design for a 3D spatial user interface for Internet Gopher. In *Proc. of ED-MEDIA 95*, pages 39–44, Graz, Austria. AACE.

McCloghrie, K. and Rose, M. T. (1991). Management Information Base for network management of TCP/IP-based Internets: MIB-II; Internet RFC 1213. Available at `ftp://nic.ddn.mil/rfc/rfc1213.txt`.

Mecklermedia Internet World. See `http://www.iw.com/`.

Mülner, H. (1989). A System of Interactive Encyclopedias. In *Proc. Man & Machine, 4th Austrian-Hungarian Informatics Conference, Budapest*, pages 181 – 190. John v. Neumann Society for Computing Sciences.

Mülner, H. (1991). Hypermedia-Enzyklopädien. In *Analyzing and Modeling Data and Knowledge, Proc. Jahrestagung der Gesellschaft für Klassifikation, Salzburg*, pages 299 – 304. Springer. In German.

Murray, J. D. and van Ryper, W. (1994). *Encyclopedia of Graphics File Formats*. O'Reilly and Associates, Inc.

Neider, J., Davis, T. and Woo, M. (1993). *OpenGL Programming Guide*. Addison-Wesley.

Nelson, T. H. (1987). *Computer Lib/Dream Machines*, revised edition. Tempus/Microsoft Press.

Nelson, T. H. (1993). *Literary Machines*, 93.1 edition. Mindful Press, 3020 Bridgeway Suite 295, Sausalito CA 94965. Available from `http://www.eastgate.com/products/at_Books.html`.

Network Wizards. Internet Domain Survey. Available at `http://www.nw.com/zone/WWW/top.html`.

Nielsen, J. (1995). *Multimedia and Hypertext: The Internet and Beyond*. Academic Press, San Diego, CA.

Noik, E. G. (1993). Exploring large hyperdocuments: Fish-eye views of nested networks. In *Proc. Hypertext'93*, pages 107–121, Seattle, WA. ACM Press.

OpenGL Architecture Review Board (1992). *OpenGL Reference Manual*. Addison-Wesley.

O'Reilly, T., Quercia, V. and Lamb, L. (1988). *X Window System User's Guide*. O'Reilly & Associates, Inc., Sebastopol, California.

Ottmann, T. and Bacher, C. (1995). Authoring on the Fly. Report, Institute for Informatics, University of Freiburg, Germany.

Parker, R. O. (1995). *Easy object programming for Windows using Visual C++*. Prentice-Hall, Englewood Cliffs, NJ.

Pesce, M. (1995). *VRML: Browsing and Building Cyberspace*. New Riders/Macmillan.

Petzold, C. (1992). *Programming Windows*. Microsoft Press, Washington, USA.

Pichler, M., Orasche, G., Andrews, K., Grossman, E. and McCahill, M. (1995). VRweb: A multi-system VRML viewer. In *Proc. First Annual Symposium on the Virtual Reality Modeling Language (VRML 95)*, San Diego, California.

Posch, R. (1995). Information security in educational networks. In H. Maurer, editor, *Proceedings ED-MEDIA '95*, pages 45–50, Graz, Austria. AACE.

Poskanzer, J. PBMPLUS: Portable bitmap utilities. Available at `ftp://ftp.x.org/`.

Rearick, T. C. (1991). Automating the conversion of text into hypertext. In E. Berk and J. Devlin, editors, *Hypertext/Hypermedia Handbook*, Software Engineering Series, pages 113–140. McGraw-Hill, New York.

Rescorla, E. and Schiffman, A. The Secure HyperText Transfer Protocol. Available at `ftp://ds1.internic.net/internet-drafts/draft-ietf-wts--S-HTTP-00.txt`.

Rheingold, H. (1993). *The Virtual Community*. Addison-Wesley.

Ropiequet, S. (1986). *CD ROM 2: Optical Publishing*. Microsoft Press, Redmond, Washington, USA.

San Diego Supercomputer Center. VRML Repository. Available at `http://www.sdsc.edu/vrml/`.

Sarkar, M. and Brown, M. H. (1994). Graphical fish-eye views. *Communications of the ACM*, **37**(12), 73–84.

Savetz, K. The Unofficial Internet Book List. Available at `http://www.northcoast.com/savetz/blist.html`.

Sayles, J. (1989). *SQL — Structured Query Language*. QED Information Sciences.

Schneier, B. (1995). *Applied Cryptography — Protocols — Algorithms & Sourcecode in C*, 2nd edition. Wiley & Sons.

Schwartz, R. L. (1993). *Learning Perl*. O'Reilly & Associates, Inc., Sebastopol, California.

Secure Electronic Payment Protocol Draft. Version 1.1. Secure Electronic Payment Protocol Draft. Version 1.1. Available at `http://www.mastercard.com/Sepp/-sepptoc.htm`.

Spero, S. E. Progress on HTTP-NG. Available at `http://www.w3.org/pub/WWW/-Protocols/HTTP-NG/http-ng-status.html`.

Stein, L. How to set up and maintain a World Wide Web site: The guide for information providers. Available at `http://www-genome.wi.mit.edu/WWW/`.

Stein, L. The Web-Security FAQ. Available at `http://www-genome.wi.mit.-edu/Web/faqs/www-security-faq.html`.

Stochniol, A. asWedit. Available at `ftp://sunsite.doc.ic.ac.uk/pack-ages/www/asWedit/`.

Stubenrauch, R., Kappe, F. and Andrews, K. (1993). Large hypermedia systems: The end of the authoring era. In *Proc. ED-MEDIA '93, Orlando, Florida*, pages 495–502, Charlottesville, VA. AACE.

Tomek, I., Khan, S., Muldner, T., Nassar, M., Novak, G. and Proszynski, P. (1991). Hypermedia — Introduction and Survey. *Journal of Microcomputer Applications*, **14**(2), 63–100.

Utting, K. and Yankelovich, N. (1989). Context and orientation in hypermedia networks. *ACM Transactions on Information Systems*, **7**(1), 58–84.

Van der Lans, R. (1988). *Introduction to SQL*. Addison-Wesley.

Wall, L. and Schwartz, R. L. (1991). *Programming Perl*. O'Reilly & Associates, Inc., Sebastopol, California.

Wallace, G. K. (1991). The JPEG still picture compression standard. *Communications of the ACM*, **34**(4), 30–44.

Walsh, N. (1994). *Making TEX Work*. O'Reilly & Associates, Inc., Sebastopol, California.

Wernecke, J. (1994). *The Inventor Mentor*. Addison-Wesley.

Wired Ventures. *Wired Magazine.* See http://www.hotwired.com/.

Witten, I. H., Moffat, A. and Bell, T. C. (1994). *Managing Gigabytes: Compressing and Indexing Documents and Images.* Van Nostrand Reinhold, New York, NY, USA.

Glossary

Robert Stubenrauch

This glossary explains at a low technical level terms that are frequently used in this book and other sources. It should provide the reader with a more or less intuitive understanding of these concepts. More detailed explanations can generally be found in the main body of the text and can be accessed through the index.

In brackets we resolve acronyms. If a term has synonyms, these will be separated by commas. Terms in *italics* are cross-references to other entries in the glossary.

account A user account allows a user to use a specific computer (network) or a specific application. Accounts usually restrict access to certain areas and may totally prohibit the user from changing data.

anchor Hyper-G terminology: part of a *document* serving as the source ("source anchor") or the destination ("destination anchor") of a *link*. Anchors usually are highlighted when displayed by a *viewer*.

BBS (Bulletin Board System) A computer supported discussion forum that allows users to contribute to and read contributions on computer networks such as the *Internet*.

bookmark Allows you to save your current position on the *Web* (in a *hyperdocument*) so that you can easily find it again.

browser A program that allows you to navigate through a *hyperdocument* and display individual *documents*. *Viewers* are components of browsers.

CAI (Computer Assisted Instruction) A special instance of *courseware*.

CBL (Computer Based Learning) A special instance of *courseware*.

CGI (Common Gateway Interface) Standard interface to launch specific programs (*scripts*) on a *WWW server*, to transmit data to these programs and return results to the viewer. Interactive *forms* are a common application.

client Program that gives access to data provided by a *server*. Client and server must be based on the same communication *protocol*.

613

cluster Hyper-G terminology: a specific type of *Hyper-G* object used to treat strongly related *documents* such as text/image pairs or multilingual texts.

collection Hyper-G terminology: strictly technically speaking, a collection is a particular type of *Hyper-G* object that "contains" other Hyper-G objects, including other collections. More imprecisely, a Hyper-G collection is just any set of Hyper-G data in a particular context.

courseware A generic term for all kinds of educational software.

cyber... Overused prefix to denote something "virtual and interlinked," for instance "cyberspace."

daemon (Disk And Execution MONitor) A computer program that waits for specific events (such as *Email* or a request) and processes the incoming messages accordingly.

digital library A repository of digital *multimedia* information including books, journals, *courseware* and so on.

digital signature A kind of checksum that can only be generated by the signatory; uses *public-key cryptography*.

document Hyper-G terminology: data elements that may not be split into further components from the point of *navigation* (they are "atomic"). Each type of *document* has a specific *viewer*. In *Hyper-G* there are currently text, image, sound, video, PostScript, 3D and generic documents.

domain The *Internet* space is divided into several domains of various levels. Each computer and network on the Internet is assigned to such a (sub)domain.

dpi (Dots Per Inch) Unit to define the resolution of printed documents.

DTD (Document Type Definition) DTDs define sets of similar documents in terms of the *SGML* format.

electronic library see digital library

Email (Electronic mail) System to send personal messages through computer networks, in particular on the *Internet*.

FAQ (Frequently Asked Questions) Files or *hyperdocuments* on the *Internet* that answer common questions regarding specific topics.

form A *Web page* that allows you to interactively fill in data and send it to a *server*. Technically, forms are implemented using *CGI scripts* for processing the results.

FTP (File Transfer Protocol) A specific *Internet protocol*; by using FTP clients (which can be integrated in *Web clients*), files can be downloaded from (or uploaded to) remote *sites* that run FTP *servers*. FTP (or similar) is also the name of the respective client program. Sometimes the term is used as a verb, such as "FTP this file from . . . ."

gateway Computer program that translates one communications *protocol* into another "on the fly," thus allowing access across various platforms.

GIF (Graphics Interchange Format) Popular storage format for bitmap graphics, now being superseded by *PNG* due to patent restrictions.

Gopher A specific *Internet protocol* that gives access to hierarchically structured data. By using Gopher *clients* (which can be integrated in *Web* clients), Gopher databases on remote Gopher *servers* can be browsed. Gopher (or similar) is also the name of the respective client program. Sometimes the term is used as a verb, such as "Gopher to ...."

history In a *hypermedia* context, history is the automatically recorded track of the *navigation* activities of a particular user.

host Generic term for a computer in a network environment that provides some service, such as remote log in or running a *WWW server*.

HTF (HyperText Format) *Hyper-G's* proprietary SGML-conforming format for text *documents*. While still supported, Hyper-G's main text format is now *HTML*.

HTML (HyperText Markup Language) An *SGML*-based format that describes the structure of a *Web* text *document*, including embedded *links* to other documents.

HTTP (HyperText Transfer Protocol) Communications *protocol* of the *WWW* that allows *Web clients* to fetch particular *documents* from Web *servers*.

hyper... Overused prefix usually used to denote something "interlinked."

hyperdocument Quite vague term which may mean any network ("web") of information, that is, sets of basic documents interrelated by *hyperlinks* or "references." The set of data may but need not be structured. In *Hyper-G*, all *hyperdocuments* are implicitly structured by its superimposed *collection* hierarchy; in *WWW* there is no such structure support (unless you count the directory tree that holds the documents).

Hyper-G Hyper-G (the G stands for Graz, the "home town" of Hyper-G) is a second-generation distributed *hypermedia* system, interoperable with the *WWW*. This whole book is about Hyper-G!

hypermedia Extension of *hypertext* into the *multimedia* field. The term refers to pieces of *documents* of various types with interactive *links* between (parts of) them.

hypertext Pieces of text with interactive *links* between (parts of) them. The term was coined by Ted Nelson in the early 1960s.

inline image An image statically embedded in a text *document*, with a fixed position and size.

Internet, Net The global network of computer networks that is based on the *TCP/IP* communications *protocol*.

JPEG (Joint Photographic Experts Group) A storage format for bitmap graphics which allows very good data compression.

link, hyperlink A reference from a part of a *document* to (a part of) the same or another document that can be followed interactively, for instance by clicking on the source *anchor*.

map In a *hypermedia* context, a map is a graphical representation of a *hyperdocument's* structure that supports *navigation*.

MBone (Multicast Backbone) A set of tools to allow fairly broadband multimedia live "broadcasts" ("multicasting") via the *Internet*.

MIME (Multipurpose Internet Mail Extension) Convention that allows you to send *multimedia* documents via *Email*.

MPEG (Motion Pictures Expert Group) A storage format for digital movies which allows very good data compression.

multimedia Combination of various media: text, image, video, sound, interactive 3D models and so on.

navigation In a *hypermedia* context, navigation refers to finding one's way through a *hyperdocument*. *Web* systems may provide various types of support such as search, *history*, organizational *links* and so on.

Net see *Internet*

netiquette Commonly accepted unwritten rules of how to behave on the *Internet*.

news Usually refers to USENET news, a popular *BBS* network on the *Internet* and other computer networks.

newsgroup *News* forum dedicated to a specific topic.

page In the context of the *Web*, page means a particular *HTML document* ("home page, "web page"). Often used in the plural, the term is sometimes used synonymously with *hyperdocument*.

PDF (Portable Document Format) A *PostScript*-based page-oriented format that describes the layout of documents on-screen and for printouts. It includes *navigation* support within the *document* and *links* to other *documents* on the *Web*.

PGP (Pretty Good Privacy) Popular encryption software on the *Internet*.

PNG (Portable Network Graphics) Storage format for bitmap graphics, designed to replace the *GIF* format.

PostScript A page description language to specify the rendering of *documents* on high quality printouts.

protocol Technical specification of how two particular computer programs, possibly running on different computers, communicate and exchange data.

public-key cryptography Cryptographic method that uses two keys, one public and one private. One is used for encryption of a message and the other for decryption.

RFC (Request For Comments) Numbered set of documents describing various *Internet*-related standards and proposals.

server A computer program that provides data to *clients* based on a particular communications *protocol*. The term is also used for the computer on which such programs run. Client–server systems run on all sorts of networks, one of which is the *Internet*.

script A computer program written in a scripting language (UNIX shell scripts, Perl and so on). Regarding the *Web*, scripts are used to implement interactive features such as *forms*.

SGML (Standard Generalized Markup Language) A standard for describing semantically structured documents.

S-HTTP (Secure HyperText Transfer Protocol) An extension of *HTTP* that allows secure data transfer.

site The term "site" usually denotes a *server* on the *Internet* that provides a service in a particular context.

SSL (Secure Socket Layer) A special kind of *socket* that allows secure data transfer.

socket Interface software that allows interprocess communication. Originally only available with UNIX, sockets are now available on all systems.

TCP/IP (Transmission Control Protocol / Internet Protocol) The fundamental communications *protocol* of the *Internet* on which all application protocols (*FTP, Gopher, HTTP* and so on) are based.

teleteaching Teaching people in different physical locations using live broadcasts (digital or analog) and/or "canned" *courseware*, but at least with *Email* feedback.

Telnet A specific *Internet protocol* that allows you to log in and run programs on a remote UNIX *host* computer. Telnet is also the name of the respective *client* program.

TIFF (Tagged Image File Format) A storage format for bitmap graphics.

URL (Uniform Resource Locator) Standard "*Web* address" used to uniquely describe the type and location of a *document* on the Internet and to pass parameters from Web *clients* to *servers*. It is part of *HTTP*.

viewer A computer program to present a specific type of *document*. It may be seamlessly integrated into a *browser* so that the user is not aware of separate viewers. In a general sense this term is sometimes used synonymously with browser.

VR (Virtual Reality) Computer generated interactive "environment" providing a more or less perfect illusion of reality.

VRML (Virtual Reality Modeling Language) A human-readable standard format to describe 3D objects. Has recently gained some popularity on the *Web*.

WAIS (Wide Area Information Servers) System that allows full text search on the *Web*.

World Wide Web, WWW, Web, W3 A global *hypermedia* information system based on the *Internet*. Its technical basis is *HTTP* and *HTML*.

WYSIWYG ("What You See Is What You Get") A paradigm for editing data with computer programs.

Index

Achim Schneider

For purposes of alphabetization, the begin quote character ' and the dt character . is ignored at the start of an entry. Otherwise, the ordering is by the ASCII sequence.

Bold page numbers indicate the place where the command or concept is introduced, explained or defined. Italic page numbers refer to entries in the appendices.

The keyword index is set up with main entries and two levels of sub-entries. If a keyword cannot be found as a main entry, one should try to find it as a sub-entry to some more general term.